W9-CDF-525

READING IN SERIES

READING IN SERIES

A SELECTION GUIDE TO BOOKS FOR CHILDREN

EDITOR **Catherine Barr**

CONTRIBUTING EDITOR **Rebecca L. Thomas**

FOREWORD BY **Barbara Barstow**

R. R. BOWKER®

NEW PROVIDENCE, NEW JERSEY

Published by R. R. Bowker,
A unit of Cahners Business Information
Copyright © 1999 by Reed Elsevier Inc.
All rights reserved
Printed and bound in the United States of America

Reading in series : a selection guide to books for children / edited by
        Catherine Barr.

        p. cm.
        Includes indexes.
        ISBN 0-8352-4011-8

        1. Children's stories, American—Bibliography. 2. Children's litera-
ture in series—Bibliography. 3. Children's libraries—Book selection.
I. Barr, Catherine, 1951– .
Z1037.R36 1999
[PS374.C454]
016.813008'09282—dc21   98-49681
                                                                  CIP

ISBN 0 - 8352 - 4011 - 8

9 780835 240116

CONTENTS

FOREWORD

BARBARA BARSTOW

When I was a child in the fifties I read constantly, broadly, and totally without guidance. I look back now at the books I missed and wonder what difference reading them might have made in my life. I read no Beverly Cleary or Little House books but instead all the Nancy Drew and Betsy-Tacy books. I slavishly read Freddy the Pig, Mrs. Piggle-Wiggle, and Miss Pickerell but missed E. Nesbit. I devoured many fantasies but knew nothing of C. S. Lewis. Along with my friends, I loved ghost stories: hearing them, reading them, and telling them. We read Poe and the scary stories in Bennett Cerf's collections. Looking back, I know that if Goosebumps had been available, I would have been first in line.

During my first years as a children's librarian, I was taught to scorn Nancy Drew for the predictable plots, one-dimensional characters, and lack of real authorship (to say nothing of the racism and classism endemic to early editions of that series and its contemporaries). My early work experiences were distant and formal. I rarely knew my co-workers' first names. I learned to keep secret my childhood passion for Nancy, her independent lifestyle, and her loyal chums. Since those early years, there have been many changes in libraries; the place of series books, notably the paperback variety, is one of the more obvious ones.

Glitzy covers; clever titles; plots that address current concerns and appeal to vast numbers of children within an age group—these are just some of the components of today's popular series. Even more evident than in the early days of the Stratemeyer syndicate (which created Nancy Drew, the Hardy Boys, and many other series) is the mind of today's marketing guru. Today we have series targeted to just about every interest. We have books that are purposeful, didactic in their approach to plot and character development, alongside the classic series of C. S. Lewis and Madeleine L'Engle; we have books that are totally focused on a particular sport and a team while having none of the character development of single-volume titles from Knudsen, Dygard, or Slote; and we have series such as Animorphs that show children as empowered and overcoming adult evil. Even the old standards, Nancy Drew and the Hardy Boys, have cleaned up their act to some degree (obvious racism is now out though classism still remains strong) and created sub-series to attract older and younger readers and their spending power. A positive development in this generation of series books is their inclusiveness and the occasional series featuring people of color.

Why should you turn to *Reading in Series*? On a day-to-day basis, if you work with children in a public or school library or in a bookstore, you hear questions like these: "Is there a book that comes after this one?" "Do you have any more books about Ramona (or Clifford or Julian or the Baby-sitters Little Sisters)?" We all know that once a child (or adult) meets Beverly Cleary's Ramona, he or she has to read the sequels and follow Ramona through the next few years. The same is true for those who begin *The White Mountains* (Tripods series) by John Christopher, All-of-a-Kind Family by Sidney Taylor, Anastasia Krupnik by Lois Lowry, the Prydain Chronicles by Lloyd Alexander, or even series such as Curious George.

Yet knowing the name of the sequel or the order in which sequels appear can often be daunting to a librarian if the library does not own all of the titles or if he or she hasn't read them. *Reading in Series*, with its great breadth of series titles for K–8 readers, should be a tremendous time-saver and a great tool for excellence in customer service. Given the vast number of series that have been published in the last decade, it is probably impossible for any one person to have the time to be familiar with all series, both hardbound and paperback originals.

What is it about these books that brings children back to them again and again?

Successful authors create characters or groups of characters with whom a child can identify. Sometimes the connection is a familiar family situation, sometimes escape to a safer environment or heroes and hope. Young readers enjoy the reassurance that things will go well even if there are hurdles to be overcome.

The best books and sequels allow children to connect, to learn, and to grow—as does all good literature. While market-driven paperback series such as Goosebumps, Animorphs, Sweet Valley Twins, and the Boxcar Children provide young readers with superficial connections to adventure, suspense, and community, they still give readers a needed escape and a sense of accomplishment and belonging.

Well-written series will hold a child's interest for longer, inspiring curiosity about new plots and the fates of characters. Indeed, the success of a series lies mainly in the characterization. *Anastasia Krupnik* and its sequels describe growth and change in the principal character; the Baby-sitters Club entertains its audience with the predictability of the characters, their roles, their strengths, the situations they encounter, and the outcomes.

Though series books have been staples of children's reading since the nineteenth century, the last part of the twentieth century has seen a real burgeoning in their popularity among children and publishers (both fiction and nonfiction). Two major factors contributing to this growth have been a generally flourishing economy and a national concern for literacy that has prompted teachers and parents to put new focus on encouraging children to read.

Parents and adult caregivers, friends, and relatives are more aware of the important part they can play in fostering literate children. Their willingness to accept some responsibility for children's literacy has meant increased support for the sale of books through school book fairs and book clubs for children, as well as at the bookstore. School and public libraries have seen an increase in the use of their materials and in the demand for books in series, especially paperbacks. This is frequently encouraged by parents determined to foster any form of reading by children who are less than avid fans of books.

In Ohio, where library funding is relatively solid, many libraries place paperback series on standing order plans so that new titles will be available immediately to meet the demands of eager fans. This also allows librarians to put their energies into the selection and marketing of other materials. Of course, some of these standing orders are short-lived because series reading can be faddish and new series will supplant those waning in popularity.

The great and growing number of series and sequels guarantees that today's children can find books to meet their interests and developmental needs from an early age. A young child's first encounter with a series may be picture books like Curious George, Clifford, Arthur, Peter of *The Snowy Day*, and Madeline. They love the comfort of the familiar characters, the usually rhythmic or at least carefully understated and often lyrical language, and carefully crafted and very appealing art. A special bonus for parents or caregivers is that they can alternate the reading of several books about a favorite character rather than reading the same one repeatedly.

In many of the books popular with young children there is the same kind of imaginative escapism that readers of all ages seek. Think about how children respond to the antics of George, a curious and very mischievous monkey. No matter what the little monkey has done, the Man in the Yellow Hat is always loving and forgiving, presenting an ideal for both children and parents. Children love Clifford for the gentleness and friendship he offers despite his impossibly huge and totally unpredictable size. They enjoy the rhythmic language of Bemelmans's text, the unfamiliar lifestyle of Madeline, and of course the charming art. For the lucky child, there may even be a parent familiar enough with Madeline to be able to recite the text.

Today, if a book is successful, produces many sequels, and has a huge following of children, good marketing often pushes it to television and the toy market. Marc Brown's Arthur—available in books, on television, in read-alongs, and as a plush toy—is the perfect example of a very successful children's book character.

Primer series such as Sally, Dick, and Jane took a lot of imagination to make into sustaining reading for children of the forties and fifties. But since the arrival of Dr. Seuss's *Cat in the Hat* and Minarik's *Little Bear* in 1958, series books for children beginning to read have been flourishing. Well-written series accompanied by appealing art and design such as James Marshall's Fox, Jean Van Leeuwen's Oliver and Amanda Pig, and Newbery-winning Cynthia Rylant's Henry and Mudge, Mr. Putter and Tabby, and Poppleton give the beginning reader a wonderful taste of fine writing. They are carefully crafted to provide inviting language, good plots, and characters who are well enough developed to sustain a child's interest.

They also pay attention to a beginning reader's need for episodic stories and are frequently imaginative enough to transform the simplest language into good literature.

The Frog and Toad series by Arnold Lobel is one of the best examples. The stories contained in each volume are perfect for reading aloud, can be used in storytelling, and have themes that validate the child and his experiences. What child doesn't laugh uproariously at the antics of Peggy Parish's Amelia Bedelia? In book after book a young reader can feel superior to the well-intentioned maid who takes her instructions far too literally. Then as an introduction to mystery series there is Nate the Great by Marjorie Sharmat. The deadpan first-person delivery reminds adults of Joe Friday in Dragnet while it amuses children who love discovering their own ability to solve the mystery before Nate.

Children with a desire for purposeful reading can immerse themselves in The Magic School Bus series. They are never overwhelmed by the text; they can stay with the story or decide to read just the sidebars of additional facts. For the child who has little patience for narrative, the balloons of conversation will keep their eyes searching for new things while alleviating boredom. Lest librarians believe that children beginning to read have been exempt from the onslaught of numbered paperback series, they have only to remember Patricia Reilly Giff's very popular Kids of the Polk Street School, Bill Cosby's Little Bill, or Barbara Park's Junie B. Jones. Giff is an especially gifted humorist with an understanding of children and their concerns. Cosby provides children everywhere with positive stories featuring African American children. Park's Junie is a kindergartner with an outrageous take on the world and an uncontrollable desire to say what she thinks that is sure to inspire laughs from beginning readers.

Perhaps the greatest number of series books can be found in those targeted to upper elementary and middle school children. Though they may not be able to tell a child the order in which books appear in the series, most adults are familiar with the books of Wilder (Little House), Lewis (The Lion, the Witch, and the Wardrobe), and Lovelace (Betsy-Tacy). Some will be familiar with series by Belton (Ernestine and Amanda), Haas (Beware horse stories), Waugh (The Mennyms), L'Engle (Time Fantasy series), Taylor (Roll of Thunder, Hear My Cry) or even Bellairs (Johnny Dixon). Parents in particular may not be aware of the great number of books that have grown to fit particular niches. In many cases these are books for children of particular religious groups or books created by Christian publishing houses that use series to impart lessons on moral values while offering what they hope will be good stories. Some of these would be the Jewish Baker's Dozen series by Libby Lazewnik and others and Christian series such as McGee and Me. There are also popular, and sometimes short-lived, series that respond to interests in animals, sports, mysteries, or any number of other topics. During the last decade Pleasant Company's American Girl series (with its accompanying dolls) has become standard fare in libraries, bookstores, and schools. Rival series such as Dear America and American Diaries have now become equally if not more popular with readers.

With *Reading in Series* these and many other series will become known to librarians, teachers, parents, and children. The annotations will guide you to just the right books for each child. If budgets will allow, many of them may become parts of collections but even more will become available through interlibrary loan.

In the thirty years since I began work in public libraries, the changes have been tremendous. We no longer wear hats and gloves and are relaxed enough to be on first-name terms. We have also moved from stigmatizing "popular" series books to recognizing that they naturally fit into the lives of children, that the Stratemeyer syndicate titles can exist and be read alongside the very best of today's children's literature. It is no longer a case of "either/or" but "both"; a recognition of a child's need, as well as an adult's, to have a great variety of literature in his or her life. May this book help children to have access to both the best and the popular, the sustaining and the diverting, as they make their way toward adulthood.

Barbara Barstow is Children's Services Manager at Cuyahoga County Public Library in Cleveland, Ohio. She is the 1999 Randolph Caldecott Award Committee Chair. She is a past president of the Association for Library Service to Children and of the U.S. Board on Books for Young People.

PREFACE

Librarians and teachers frequently call children's fiction series a mixed blessing. Series are wonderful in that they encourage children to read, but keeping up with the growing number of titles being published is an ongoing struggle. Librarians not only must keep tabs on new titles in existing series, but also must evaluate each new series (and each re-packaging and re-presentation of an old series) and decide whether to purchase it. Teachers work to find series books that meet the needs of the variety of readers in their classrooms. Librarians frequently hear questions such as "Do you know any mystery books like the Boxcar Children but for a less-able reader?" and "What fantasy books do you recommend for middle-grade students?"

As we discussed these issues and more at conferences, in schools, and in libraries, *Reading in Series* was born.

RESEARCH AND SELECTION

One of the first considerations was how to identify the children's series. To create our initial listing, we used *The Whole Story: 3000 Years of Sequels and Sequences* (D. W. Thorpe, 1996). The author, John E. Simkin, has collected series and book titles for a large number of adult and juvenile series. Additional sources included *The Young Reader's Companion* (R. R. Bowker, 1993), *A to Zoo*, 5th edition (R. R. Bowker, 1998), and *Children's Catalog*, 17th edition (Wilson, 1996). Current reviewing sources such as *School Library Journal* and *Booklist* were examined for newer series and new books being added to existing series. In addition, we made use of online sources including publisher and author Web sites and amazon.com.

Using these resources, a master list was compiled and our contributors began to look for the books themselves. As we searched libraries and bookstores, the following criteria were applied:

1. The series we selected would be content-based, groupings of books with a consistent theme, setting, or group of characters. Series grouped by other criteria—for instance, grade level—are not included. Thus, Goosebumps—which includes monsters, creatures, and weird encounters—is here. The HarperCollins I Can Read series—which includes books by many different authors and featuring different characters—is not. Series such as Frog and Toad, Little Bear, and Arthur the Monkey, however, which are part of the I Can Read series but which feature several books with the same characters, are included.

2. To be considered for inclusion, a series needed three or more books.

3. The grade range of the books we selected is from kindergarten through grade 8. Board books, manipulative books, bathtime books, etc., are not included. Our contributors made the decision about grade level based on their knowledge of the audience, examination of the books, consultation with professional resources, and their experience as youth librarians. Thus, the Ghosts of Fear Street series, which has elements of horror and suspense for middle school and junior high readers, is included, but the Fear Street series, which includes more graphic details suitable for an older audience of teens, is not.

4. As we annotated each series, every effort was made to examine at least three books, hoping to offer better insight to librarians making purchasing decisions or recommending these books to readers.

5. A priority was given to new series: the books that readers were asking about. We scoured libraries, bookstores, publishers' catalogs, and Web sites looking for new series and the newest titles in existing series.

6. Older series were included, too, especially those that our contributors considered to be "classics." The Chronicles of Narnia, the Oz books, Avonlea, and the Little House books had to be included, of course. But other well-known series, such as Betsy-Tacy, Eddie Wilson, Mrs. Piggle-Wiggle, and Miss Pickerell, are here too. However, many popular teen series from past decades are not readily available in libraries and bookstores and many picture books from our own childhoods are not being read today. In selecting the "older" series to include, we relied on the judgment of our contributors and their ability to find copies of several titles in libraries and bookstores. Readers may want to consult Philip H. Young's *Children's Fiction Series: A Bibliography, 1850–1950* (McFarland & Co., 1997) for information on earlier series.

7. Our selection focused on including series books with some of the titles still in print. This was a problem, especially for many paperback series. Some very popular books that were published only a few years ago are no longer available, but we decided to include these series because they are still available in many libraries. Librarians and teachers who want to update their collections can use the Genre/Subject Index to find newer, similar books.

ANATOMY OF AN ENTRY

Each entry in *Reading in Series* provides the following information:
Series title: Cross-referenced as needed

Author: If individual books have different authors, they are listed with the books.

Publisher: Many series have had several publishers over the years. The publisher shown is the most recent publisher. In some cases both hardback and paperback publishers are listed.

Grade level: The series included are for grades K–8. Toddler and board books are not included. Young adult series are not included.

Genres: These are broad thematic areas that will help link similar series. The genres included are: Adventure, Animal Fantasy, Family Life, Fantasy, Historical, Horror, Humor, Mystery, Real Life, Recreation, Science Fiction, and Values.

Annotation: This descriptive examination of the series provides information about important characters, plots, themes, and issues in the series. Often, specific books are described in detail. There is information about related materials such as dolls, accessories, and toys.

List of titles in the series: This list was compiled using the books themselves and the selection sources mentioned above, as well as *Books in Print* (R. R. Bowker), barnesandnoble.com, and the CLEVNET database (which serves a large number of member libraries in northeast Ohio, including the Cleveland Public Library). Often, these resources (along with the publisher catalogs and Web sites) provided conflicting information about exact titles and copyright dates so there may be some inconsistencies; however, every effort has been made to be as complete and accurate as possible. Book titles are shown in chronological order by year of publication. Numbered series are shown in number order, which is usually also chronological. Where series include prequels or alternative reading orders, this is mentioned in the annotation.

Book covers have been included for many series. The cover shown may not be from the company listed as the current publisher of the series.

INDEXES AND APPENDIXES

Author and Title indexes will help the user who is searching for new series or titles or who knows only one title in a series. The Genre/Subject Index gives access by genre and by more specific topics. Thus, the fan of horror books can easily find more series in that genre; and young readers can quickly identify series about horses.

In addition, there are lists of series of special interest to boys or girls, for reluctant readers, and for students of English as a second language. These are not comprehensive lists; series were selected for their current appeal to readers. The books for boys often feature as the main characters a boy or group of boys who are involved in mysteries, sports, school problems, friendship, and the supernatural. The books for girls often feature one or more girls involved in mysteries, sports (horseback riding and skating, in particular), school problems, friendship, and growing up. The books for reluctant readers were chosen for their popular appeal and feature media tie-ins, monsters and creatures, and well-known characters such as Amber Brown, Arthur, and the Plant that Ate Dirty Socks. Some of the books for reluctant readers are included for their direct plots and simple text, and these have been marked with an asterisk (*) as being suitable for ESL students, too.

There will be many ways for librarians and teachers to use *Reading in Series*. The Genre/Subject Index will point the way to series on topics of interest. Do your students like the books about Ramona? Look at the genre Family Life to find similar books, including stories about Russell, Elisa, Julian and Huey, and Sam Krupnik. For readers who want legends of King Arthur and Merlin, consult the subject Arthurian Legends to find Jane Yolen's Young Merlin books and T. A. Barron's Merlin as well as the classic series from T. H. White.

Reading in Series is also a selection guide. Librarians may want to add new series or update titles in series that have already been purchased. If your students like mysteries, look at the new A to Z Mysteries. For hockey, there is Wolfbay Wings. For adventure, there is Survival! Add the newer titles to existing series or fill in titles you may have missed. Reading the annotations, you can compare series and make decisions about which will best fit your needs.

Compilation of this book involved the efforts of many librarians and teachers who are well qualified in fiction for children. Our principal annotators were:

Connie Parker   Cuyahoga County (Ohio) Public Library
Rebecca L. Thomas Shaker Heights (Ohio) City Schools
Deanna McDaniel   Westerville (Ohio) City Schools

We also received contributions from:
Jacqueline Albers   Cuyahoga County (Ohio) Public Library
Karen Breen   Program Officer, New Visions for Public Schools, New York, NY
Doris Gebel   Northport (NY) Public Library
Debbie Gold   Program Officer, Library Power, New York, NY

Additional annotations were provided by Teresa Gibbons of Hackettstown, N.J., and by Rock Hill Press staff Megan Lynch and Susan C. Olmstead.

We would like to thank Nan Hudes of R. R. Bowker for her support of this project, Nancy Bucenec of Bowker for her help in many areas, and the staff of Rock Hill Press for their contributions to the extensive research and production involved in this book, in particular Managing Editor Susan C. Olmstead, Database Manager Julie Miller, and Design and Project Manager Christine Weisel McNaull.

SERIES A–Z

A TO Z MYSTERIES

Roy, Ron

RANDOM HOUSE

GRADES K–3

MYSTERY

Ji Roy

Dink, Josh, and Ruth Rose are friends in Green Lawn, an average American town. Together, they solve mysteries beginning with every letter of the alphabet. The mysteries are simple enough that readers can collect clues and solve them along with the characters.

1. The Absent Author ◆ 1997
2. The Bald Bandit ◆ 1997
3. The Canary Caper ◆ 1998
4. The Deadly Dungeon ◆ 1998
5. The Empty Envelope ◆ 1998
6. The Falcon's Feathers ◆ 1998

ABALOC (APPLE LOCK)

Curry, Jane Louise

ATHENEUM

GRADES 3–6

FANTASY | MYSTERY

Small-town life is anything but dull in the Midwestern hamlet of Apple Lock. The school age children keep themselves occupied by delving into ancient mysteries and making fascinating discoveries. The plots are suspenseful, and the characters are well drawn. The books in this series are also fairly independent of each other, so children don't have to worry about reading them in order.

1. Beneath the Hill ◆ 1967
2. The Change-Child ◆ 1969
3. The Daybreakers ◆ 1970
4. Over the Sea's Edge ◆ 1971
5. The Watchers ◆ 1975
6. Birdstones ◆ 1977
7. The Wolves of Aam ◆ 1981
8. Shadow Dancers ◆ 1983

ABBY JONES, JUNIOR DETECTIVE

Giff, Patricia Reilly

DELACORTE; DELL YEARLING

GRADES 3–6

MYSTERY

Irrepressible girl detective Abby Jones keeps a memo book full of notes, just like her hero, police officer Garcia. She and her shy friend Potsie (Patricia Olivia Torres) are always on the lookout for crime in their city neighborhood. They work out several fast-paced contemporary mysteries, including strange noises in their neighbor's apartment, a stray purple-and-orange wallet Abby thinks might belong to a murderer, missing persons, and a scary Halloween escapade.

1. Have You Seen Hyacinth Macaw? ◆ 1981
2. Loretta P. Sweeney, Where Are You? ◆ 1983
3. Tootsie Tanner, Why Don't You Talk? ◆ 1987

THE ADAM JOSHUA CAPERS

Smith, Janice Lee

HARPERCOLLINS

GRADES 1–4

REAL LIFE

Elementary-schooler Adam Joshua and his classmates comically confront all kinds of everyday situations in this humorous series. Adam Joshua is fairly level-headed, while his best friend, Nelson, is always coming up with crazy ideas. Together, they enter a science fair, adopt "egg babies" for a class assignment, and celebrate holidays from Thanksgiving to Valentine's Day. Young readers are likely to recognize someone like themselves among the diverse personalities that make up Adam Joshua's class. This series has been reformatted in paperback with some renamed titles, different sequencing of stories, and attractive covers. The original hardbacks are still available, too. Both sets of books are listed here.

1. The Monster in the Third Dresser Drawer, and Other Stories About Adam Joshua ◆ 1981
2. The Kid Next Door, and Other Headaches: Stories About Adam Joshua ◆ 1984
3. The Show-and-Tell War, and Other Stories About Adam Joshua ◆ 1988
4. It's Not Easy Being George ◆ 1989

5. The Turkey's Side of It ◆ 1990
6. There's a Ghost in the Coatroom ◆ 1991
7. Nelson in Love: An Adam Joshua Valentine's Day Story ◆ 1992
8. Serious Science: An Adam Joshua Story ◆ 1993
9. The Baby Blues: An Adam Joshua Story ◆ 1994

THE ADAM JOSHUA CAPERS PAPERBACK SERIES (HARPERTROPHY)

1. The Monster in the Third Dresser Drawer ◆ 1995
2. The Kid Next Door ◆ 1995
3. Superkid! ◆ 1995
4. The Show-and-Tell War ◆ 1995
5. The Halloween Monster ◆ 1995
6. George Takes a Bow (-Wow): Stories About Adam Joshua (And His Dog) ◆ 1995
7. Turkey Trouble: Adam Joshua's Thanksgiving ◆ 1995
8. The Christmas Ghost: Adam Joshua's Christmas ◆ 1995
9. Nelson in Love ◆ 1996
10. Serious Science ◆ 1996

ADAM MOUSE *see* Cucumbers Trilogy

ADDIE

Lawlor, Laurie
WHITMAN; POCKET BOOKS
GRADES 4–6
HISTORICAL | REAL LIFE

Addie's father takes the family west from Sabula, Iowa, to the Dakota Territory to homestead 100 acres. Addie is unhappy about leaving her friends and slowly adjusts to the hard life of prairie homesteaders. She shows courage in the face of difficult situations of various kinds and learns to make new friends. Through the course of these stories, Addie comes of age, prepares to leave her family to attend high school, and meets a young man. *George on His Own* (Whitman, 1993) describes the efforts of Addie's brother to manage the family while Addie is away at school. *Addie's Forever Friend* is a prequel to *Addie Across the Prairie*.

1. Addie Across the Prairie ◆ 1986
2. Addie's Dakota Winter ◆ 1989
3. Addie's Long Summer ◆ 1992
4. George on His Own ◆ 1993
5. Addie's Forever Friend ◆ 1997

ADDIE

Robins, Joan
HARPERCOLLINS
GRADES K–3
FAMILY LIFE | HUMOR

These are delightful beginning readers. Making friends, having bad days, and running away are all simple adventures that any child learning to read will enjoy and be able to master.

1. Addie Meets Max ◆ 1985
2. Addie Runs Away ◆ 1989
3. Addie's Bad Day ◆ 1993

ADDIE

Rock, Gail
KNOPF
GRADES 3–5
FAMILY LIFE | HISTORICAL

First introduced as CBS TV specials, these four holiday stories set in the 1940s demonstrate something of the real meaning of the celebrations. Ten-year-old Addie can't understand why her father will not allow her to have a Christmas tree. Her kind and wise grandmother helps her come to understand why it is so difficult for her widowed father to have a Christmas tree. Other holidays provide opportunities to learn about friendship.

1. The House Without a Christmas Tree ◆ 1974
2. The Thanksgiving Treasure ◆ 1974
3. A Dream for Addie ◆ 1975
4. Addie and the King of Hearts ◆ 1976

ADDY *see* American Girls: Addy

ADRIAN MOLE

Townsend, Sue
GROVE PRESS
GRADES 7–8
HUMOR | REAL LIFE

Adrian recounts the often painful memories of his adolescent years, beginning with the tumultuous year he was 13. He does not get along with his new stepfather and tension builds in their small flat. Adrian's terse, candid observations cut to the heart of adolescence: fighting against change while longing for it. The reader will be torn between tears and laughter.

1. The Secret Diary of Adrian Mole, Aged 13 3/4 ◆ 1982
2. The Growing Pains of Adrian Mole ◆ 1984
3. Adrian Mole: The Lost Years ◆ 1994

ADVENTURES OF BENNY AND WATCH *see*

Boxcar Children: Adventures of Benny and Watch

ADVENTURES OF JENNA V. *see* Jenna V.

THE ADVENTURES OF MARY-KATE AND ASHLEY

Ji Mar

Various authors

SCHOLASTIC

GRADES 1–3

FAMILY LIFE | MYSTERY

The Olsen twins, Mary-Kate and Ashley, have achieved great popularity on TV and in movies. Three series (The Adventures of Mary-Kate and Ashley, The New Adventures of Mary-Kate and Ashley, and You're Invited to Mary-Kate and Ashley's) showcase the two girls as spunky, energetic sleuths running the Olsen and Olsen Mystery Agency. Their motto is "Will solve any crime by dinner time." In The Adventures of Mary-Kate and Ashley and The New Adventures of Mary-Kate and Ashley, the girls have adventures at Sea World, the U.S. Space Camp, on a cruise, and at a haunted camp. The You're Invited to Mary-Kate and Ashley's books focus on the party fun of a camping trip or a sleepover, for example. Included is a fan club membership form. This series capitalizes on the popularity of these appealing twins.

1. The Case of the Christmas Caper (Waricha, Jean) ◆ 1996
2. The Case of the Mystery Cruise (Thompson, Carol) ◆ 1996
3. The Case of the Fun House Mystery (Scholastic Inc.) ◆ 1996
4. The Case of the U.S. Space Camp Mission (Scholastic Staff, and Bonnie Bader) ◆ 1997
5. The Case of the Sea World Adventure (Dubowski, Cathy East) ◆ 1996
6. The Case of the Shark Encounter (Krulik, Nancy E.) ◆ 1997
7. The Case of the Hotel Who-Done-It (O'Neil, Laura) ◆ 1997
8. The Case of the Volcano Mystery (Thompson, Carol) ◆ 1997
9. The Case of the U.S. Navy Adventure (Perlberg, Deborah) ◆ 1997
10. The Case of Thorn Mansion (Alexander, Nina) ◆ 1997

THE NEW ADVENTURES OF MARY-KATE & ASHLEY

1. The Case of the Ballet Bandit (O'Neil, Laura) ◆ 1998
2. The Case of the 202 Clues (Alexander, Nina) ◆ 1998
3. The Case of the Blue Ribbon Horse (Swobud, I. K.) ◆ 1998
4. The Case of the Wild Wolf River (Katschke, Judy) ◆ 1998
5. The Case of the Rock and Roll Mystery (Eisenberg, Lisa) ◆ 1998
6. The Case of the Haunted Camp (Alexander, Nina) ◆ 1998

THE ADVENTURES OF THE BAILEY SCHOOL KIDS

Ji Dad

Dadey, Debbie, and Marcia Thornton Jones

SCHOLASTIC

GRADES 2–4

FANTASY | HUMOR

Bailey City is a weird place. The students in Mrs. Jeepers's third-grade class find mysterious adventures around every corner. There are even strange things happening at the library, where King Arthur's wizard, Merlin, has brought his magic! And there may be a dragon cooking the pizzas. After Mrs. Jeepers takes Howie, Eddie, Liza, Melody, and the rest of the class to Jewel's Pizza Castle for a party, Howie confronts the unusual owner of the place. Each book has unusual characters—vampires, genies, aliens, zombies, Martians, angels, and skeletons. There is lots of action, with plot twists that leave the reader guessing. The length of the books and the fast-paced plots will appeal to many readers.

1. Vampires Don't Wear Polka Dots ◆ 1990
2. Werewolves Don't Go to Summer Camp ◆ 1991
3. Santa Claus Doesn't Mop Floors ◆ 1991
4. Leprechauns Don't Play Basketball ◆ 1992
5. Ghosts Don't Eat Potato Chips ◆ 1992
6. Frankenstein Doesn't Plant Petunias ◆ 1993
7. Aliens Don't Wear Braces ◆ 1993
8. Genies Don't Ride Bicycles ◆ 1994
9. Pirates Don't Wear Pink Sunglasses ◆ 1994
10. Witches Don't Do Backflips ◆ 1994
11. Skeletons Don't Play Tubas ◆ 1994
12. Cupid Doesn't Flip Hamburgers ◆ 1995
13. Gremlins Don't Chew Bubble Gum ◆ 1995
14. Monsters Don't Scuba Dive ◆ 1995
15. Zombies Don't Play Soccer ◆ 1995
16. Dracula Doesn't Drink Lemonade ◆ 1995
17. Elves Don't Wear Hard Hats ◆ 1995
18. Martians Don't Take Temperatures ◆ 1996
19. Gargoyles Don't Drive School Buses ◆ 1996
20. Wizards Don't Need Computers ◆ 1996
21. Mummies Don't Coach Softball ◆ 1996

22. Cyclops Doesn't Roller Skate ◆ 1996
23. Angels Don't Know Karate ◆ 1996
24. Dragons Don't Cook Pizza ◆ 1997
25. Bigfoot Doesn't Square Dance ◆ 1997
26. Mermaids Don't Run Track ◆ 1997
27. Bogeymen Don't Play Football ◆ 1997
28. Unicorns Don't Give Sleigh Rides ◆ 1997
29. Knights Don't Teach Piano ◆ 1998
30. Hercules Doesn't Pull Teeth ◆ 1998
31. Ghouls Don't Scoop Ice Cream ◆ 1998
32. Phantoms Don't Drive Sports Cars ◆ 1998
33. Giants Don't Go Snowboarding ◆ 1998

THE ADVENTURES OF WISHBONE *see*
Wishbone Adventures

AERIEL TRILOGY

Pierce, Meredith Ann
LITTLE, BROWN
GRADES 5–8
FANTASY

Aeriel sets out on a quest to destroy the vampire Irrylath. She cannot resist the fatal allure of this creature and chooses to love him rather than destroy him. Though mortal again, Irrylath is still tormented by the witch through the pull of dreams, and once again Aeriel must fight the dark forces by gathering the gargoyles to do battle with the witch. It is with the aid of a shimmering pearl that Aeriel is able to wage the last battle with the powerful witch and break the spell cast on her husband.

1. The Darkangel ◆ 1982
2. A Gathering of the Gargoyles ◆ 1984
3. The Pearl of the Soul of the World ◆ 1990

AGE OF MAGIC TRILOGY

McGowen, Tom
LODESTAR/DUTTON
GRADES 4–6
FANTASY

The troll wizard Gwolchmig foresees the destruction of the Earth when creatures from beyond the sky will invade it within the year. He puts aside lifelong animosities to unite the five races of the Earth: trolls, humans, little people, Alfar (elves), and dragons. Twelve-year-old Lithim faces fierce opposition from the Atlan domain and devises a plan that will save Earth from destruction.

1. The Magical Fellowship ◆ 1991
2. A Trial of Magic ◆ 1992
3. A Question of Magic ◆ 1993

AIKEN FAMILY

Thompson, Mary Wolfe
DAVID McKAY
GRADES 2–5
ADVENTURE | HISTORICAL

Twelve-year-old Tabby and her brother Zeke journey with their father from Connecticut to Vermont in the 1770s to stake a claim for 100 acres of land. After building a small log cabin, Father leaves them alone while he returns to fetch Mother and three younger children. Tabby and Zeke survive many dangers before their family's return six weeks later. Two other books relate their efforts to survive winter, befriending other settlers and Indians. The series concludes when Tabby marries neighbor Nathan Armstrong and their first child is born.

1. Two in the Wilderness ◆ 1967
2. Wilderness Winter ◆ 1968
3. Wilderness Wedding ◆ 1970

AL (ALEXANDRA)

Greene, Constance C.
VIKING; PUFFIN
GRADES 5–8
REAL LIFE

Al is the new kid, "a little on the fat side," with glasses and pigtails, and a self-proclaimed nonconformist. She becomes the best friend of the unnamed seventh-grade narrator. Their friendship grows and helps them deal with the problems they face: Al's mother, divorced for several years, begins to date; her father visits for the first time in years; and Al sacrifices a summer visit at her father's farm to take care of her sick mother. Together, the friends face life's ups and downs with humor.

1. A Girl Called Al ◆ 1969

2. I Know You, Al ◆ 1975
3. Your Old Pal, Al ◆ 1979
4. Alexandra the Great ◆ 1982
5. Just Plain Al ◆ 1986
6. Al's Blind Date ◆ 1989

ALBERT

Tryon, Leslie

ATHENEUM

GRADES K–2

ANIMAL FANTASY

Albert is the most industrious duck in Pleasant Valley. He creates an unusual playground for the schoolchildren (with everything in alphabetical order). He patiently assists the P.T.A. president in preparing a Thanksgiving feast. In the spring, he organizes a baseball team. One of the newer books features Albert as a detective who solves a mystery involving pumpkins that are missing from Miss Patsy Pig's pumpkin patch. There is minimal text in these books. The detailed illustrations advance the story and provide enjoyment for readers, who often know more of what is going on than the characters do.

1. Albert's Alphabet ◆ 1991
2. Albert's Play ◆ 1992
3. Albert's Field Trip ◆ 1993
4. Albert's Thanksgiving ◆ 1994
5. Albert's Ballgame ◆ 1996
6. Albert's Christmas ◆ 1997
7. Albert's Halloween: The Case of the Stolen Pumpkins ◆ 1998

ALBERT THE DRAGON

Weir, Rosemary

ABELARD-SCHUMAN

GRADES 4–6

FANTASY

Albert is a friendly, vegetarian dragon who lives in a cave near a Cornish fishing village and has many adventures with his young friend Tony and his cousin Mary Ann. He pretends to let a knight defeat him in battle as a favor for a friend. When his young friends become too busy to play, he takes in a lost baby centaur. He learns a lot about parenting, which stands him in good stead when he later finds two dragon eggs and at last has a family of his own.

1. Albert the Dragon ◆ 1961
2. Further Adventures of Albert the Dragon ◆ 1964
3. Albert the Dragon and the Centaur ◆ 1968
4. Albert and the Dragonettes ◆ 1977
5. Albert's World Tour ◆ 1978

ALBRIGHT FAMILY *see* Sterling Family

ALDEN ALL STARS

Hallowell, Tommy, and David Halecroft
VIKING
GRADES 3–5
REAL LIFE | RECREATION

Soccer, baseball, basketball, and football are all featured in this sports series. Three seventh- and eighth-grade boys star in separate books. Nick is the wise guy and Dennis is the captain of the basketball team. Justin's sport is soccer; but Alden Junior High doesn't have a team, so he goes to soccer camp and stands out there. All of the books are loaded with sports details, but some points are also made about relationships and the importance of studying. Fans of Matt Christopher's books will enjoy this series.

1. Duel on the Diamond ◆ 1990
2. Jester in the Back Court ◆ 1990
3. Shot from Midfield ◆ 1990
4. Last Chance Quarterback ◆ 1991

ALDO SOSSI

Hurwitz, Johanna
MORROW
GRADES 2–4
HUMOR | REAL LIFE

Eight-year-old Aldo is interested in everything, especially animals. The first book, set in New York City, introduces the Sossi family, including his older sisters, Karen, age 11, and Elaine, age 13. Aldo's love of animals creates a conflict for him when a class project introduces chameleons to the cricket tank. Aldo becomes a vegetarian, and we get a glimpse of the strength of his loving, supportive parents. As he graduates into fourth grade, his family moves from city to suburbs, and Aldo deals with the difficulties of moving and making new friends. He tries an ice-cream-making business, but finds more success helping his mother do volunteer work for senior citizens. Companion volumes include *Tough Luck Karen* (1982) and *Hurricane Elaine* (1986).

1. Much Ado About Aldo ◆ 1978
2. Aldo Applesauce ◆ 1979
3. Aldo Ice Cream ◆ 1981
4. Aldo Peanut Butter ◆ 1990

ALEX

Levene, Nancy Simpson
CHARIOT BOOKS
GRADES 2–4
REAL LIFE | VALUES

Alex Brackenbury faces a variety of problems in this series, including a clumsy friend who struggles to participate in soccer, stuck-up girls who won't be her friends, and a neighborhood bully. Mother reminds her of the importance of being kind and asking for God's guidance. Dad helps her to accept the weaknesses of others and honor God. Each book in this series focuses on a specific value. For example, *Cherry Cola Champions* deals with compassion, and *Peanut Butter and Jelly Secrets* is about obedience. Each book cover states, "Readers will learn from Alex's mistakes and understand that they have the same sources of help that she turns to: A God who loves them and parents who understand." The books are listed here in the sequence given by the publisher.

1. Shoelaces and Brussels Sprouts ◆ 1987
2. French Fry Forgiveness ◆ 1987
3. Hot Chocolate Friendship ◆ 1987
4. Peanut Butter and Jelly Secrets ◆ 1987
5. Mint Cookie Miracles ◆ 1988
6. Cherry Cola Champions ◆ 1988
7. Peach Pit Popularity ◆ 1989
8. Salty Scarecrow Solution ◆ 1989
9. T-Bone Trouble ◆ 1990
10. Grapefruit Basket Upset ◆ 1991
11. Apple Turnover Treasure ◆ 1992
12. Crocodile Meatloaf ◆ 1993
13. Chocolate Chips and Trumpet Tricks ◆ 1994

ALEX AND THE CAT

Griffith, Helen V.

GREENWILLOW

GRADES K–2

ANIMAL FANTASY | HUMOR

Alex the dog lives happily with Robbie and his friend the cat. Sometimes he gets restless and has little adventures, which the cat wryly observes. One day when Robbie is teaching him tricks, Alex decides he would rather be a cat. He does nothing for a day, decides that is boring and happily goes back to being a dog. In November, he tells the cat how much he hates winter, and she suggests that he hibernate or migrate south. Alex considers these ideas until it starts to snow. He loves to play in the snow and decides to stay around. Different illustrators provide a very different look to the books in the series, and there is some variation in the lengths of the texts. All of the stories about Alex and the cat have been assembled into one new volume, also called *Alex and the Cat* (1997).

1. Alex and the Cat ◆ 1982
2. More Alex and the Cat ◆ 1983
3. Alex Remembers ◆ 1983

ALEX MACK *see* The Secret World of Alex Mack

ALEXANDER

Viorst, Judith

ATHENEUM; SCHOLASTIC

GRADES K–3

FAMILY LIFE | HUMOR

Judith Viorst does a wonderful job of exploring the everyday frustrations of children through the eyes of a little boy named Alexander. He tries to save money, has bad days, and struggles with his two older brothers and his mother. Ray Cruz's illustrations are delightful. These are books meant to be shared and enjoyed together.

1. I'll Fix Anthony ◆ 1969
2. Alexander and the Terrible, Horrible, No Good, Very Bad Day ◆ 1972
3. Alexander, Who Used to Be Rich Last Sunday ◆ 1978
4. Alexander, Who's Not (Do You Hear Me? I Mean It!) Going to Move ◆ 1995
5. Absolutely Positively Alexander: The Complete Stories ◆ 1997

ALFIE ROSE

Hughes, Shirley

LOTHROP, LEE & SHEPARD; CANDLEWICK

GRADES K–2

FAMILY LIFE | REAL LIFE

Alfie accidentally locks his mother and baby sister Annie Rose outside and can't reach the latch to let them in. Readers are introduced to the whole neighborhood as they get involved in the rescue. Double-page spreads illustrate both sides of the door. Delightful vignettes portray daily life for the children and their loving family. Companion volumes include *The Big Alfie and Annie Rose Story Book* and *The Big Alfie Out of Doors Story Book*. Four of the stories about Alfie have been gathered into a collection *All About Alfie*.

1. Alfie Gets in First ◆ 1982
2. Alfie's Feet ◆ 1983
3. Alfie Gives a Hand ◆ 1984
4. An Evening at Alfie's ◆ 1984
5. Rhymes for Annie Rose ◆ 1995
6. Alfie and the Birthday Surprise ◆ 1998
7. Alfie's ABC ◆ 1998

ALFRED HITCHCOCK AND THE THREE INVESTIGATORS *see* Three Investigators

ALI BABA BERNSTEIN

Hurwitz, Johanna

MORROW

GRADES 2–4

HUMOR | REAL LIFE

David, age eight, is tired of being one of four Davids in his class and is determined to set himself apart with his new name, Ali Baba. He celebrates an exciting ninth birthday when he invites all the David Bernsteins in the phone book to his party. Ali Baba, always intrigued by mysteries, thinks about becoming a detective and getting a dog.

1. The Adventures of Ali Baba Bernstein ◆ 1985
2. Hurray for Ali Baba Bernstein ◆ 1989
3. Ali Baba Bernstein, Lost and Found ◆ 1992

ALICE

Naylor, Phyllis Reynolds
ATHENEUM; DELL
GRADES 5–8
FAMILY LIFE | HUMOR

Affectionate and humorous, these stories feature Alice getting into all kinds of funny scrapes, mostly because of her good intentions. Putting up with the boys at school, getting her first boyfriend, making and keeping friends, and dealing with her father and older brother Lester are all part of the fun.

1. The Agony of Alice ◆ 1985
2. Alice in Rapture, Sort of ◆ 1989
3. Reluctantly Alice ◆ 1991
4. All But Alice ◆ 1992
5. Alice in April ◆ 1993
6. Alice In-Between ◆ 1994
7. Alice the Brave ◆ 1995
8. Alice in Lace ◆ 1996
9. Outrageously Alice ◆ 1997
10. Achingly Alice ◆ 1998

ALIEN ADVENTURES

Coville, Bruce
POCKET BOOKS
GRADES 4–7
HUMOR | SCIENCE FICTION

Rod Allbright's science project has just been invaded! Tiny aliens have landed there and they want Rod's help. First, they need to capture an interstellar criminal, then Rod is taken to another dimension. His troubles continue when Rod and the aliens go through space to the home of the Mental Masters. But the worst is yet to come when Rod's body is stolen by a fiend and his personality must share space with Seymour, a blue alien. Like Coville's My Teacher books, this series is a combination of science fiction and humor as Rod and the aliens stumble their way through intergalactic adventures.

1. Aliens Ate My Homework ◆ 1993
2. I Left My Sneakers in Dimension X ◆ 1994
3. The Search for Snout ◆ 1995
4. Aliens Stole My Body ◆ 1998

ALIENS

Various authors

RANDOM HOUSE

GRADES 2–4

HUMOR I SCIENCE FICTION

Aric is a space creature from Planet Ganoob who ends up on Earth in the home of Richard Bickerstaff. (Richard's mother opened a free sample of cereal that contained Aric.) Aric is on a mission to stop aliens from taking over Earth. In one book, an alien is disguised as a member of Richard's class. In another, aliens are planning to steal all of the desserts on Earth. In still another book, the aliens are bringing their toxic waste to Earth. Aric is a fast-talking extraterrestrial who makes wisecracks to Richard and his friend Henry Ball while he involves them in these funny adventures.

1. Aliens for Breakfast (Etra, Jonathan, and Stephanie Spinner) ◆ 1988
2. Aliens for Lunch (Etra, Jonathan, and Stephanie Spinner) ◆ 1991
3. Aliens for Dinner (Spinner, Stephanie) ◆ 1994

ALISTAIR

Sadler, Marilyn

SIMON & SCHUSTER

GRADES K–2

FANTASY I HUMOR

Alistair is an unusual boy in more ways than one. He is always polite and wears neatly pressed clothes. Every day he thanks his teacher for giving him homework. Also, he builds a spaceship and keeps an elephant for a pet, all without missing any school. In search of more pond life for his collection, he builds a small submarine, discovers some frog people, and saves them from a sea monster, all in time for supper. When captured by aliens, his main concern is some library books that are due; and when more aliens invade Earth, he is delighted when they present him with an unusual plant that he can use for a school project. Illustrations show the neatly dressed and unflappable Alistair in each bizarre situation.

1. Alistair's Elephant ◆ 1983
2. Alistair in Outer Space ◆ 1984
3. Alistair's Time Machine ◆ 1986
4. Alistair Underwater ◆ 1990
5. Alistair and the Alien Invasion ◆ 1994

ALL-OF-A-KIND FAMILY

Taylor, Sydney

BANTAM DOUBLEDAY DELL

GRADES 4–6

FAMILY LIFE | HISTORICAL

Five little girls live with their parents in a four-room flat on New York's Lower East Side before World War I. They don't have much money, but they have lots of companionship, books, outings, games, and friends. Frightening things happen to the family, too: Sarah and Ella come down with scarlet fever, and Henny gets lost at Coney Island. A new brother doesn't change the closeness of this all-of-a-kind family. Summers at Rockaway Beach, the celebration of Jewish holidays, and the victory parade at the end of World War I are some of the events chronicled in these warm stories of family life.

1. All-of-a-Kind Family ◆ 1951
2. More All-of-a-Kind Family ◆ 1954
3. All-of-a-Kind Family Uptown ◆ 1958
4. All-of-a-Kind Family Downtown ◆ 1972
5. Ella of All-of-a-Kind Family ◆ 1978

ALL-STAR MEATBALLS

Mooser, Stephen

BANTAM DOUBLEDAY DELL

GRADES 3–5

HUMOR | RECREATION

A group of misfit kids bands together to form the Meatballs Club—their name comes from the main weapon in a food fight. Homer King, Molly James, Darryl Pumpwater, Kate Barnett, Nicole Martin, and Luiz Cruzon join together to stand up to a rival gang, the Jokers. Their first adventure involves a home-run-hitting contest and a mix-up involving a new boy whose real name is Homer King. In a somewhat contrived plot twist, Homer King does win the contest and is, literally, the homer king! Many of the antics of the Meatballs revolve around sports—including baseball, wrestling, skating, football, and skiing—making these attractive to readers who like sports and humor.

1. Babe Ruth and the Home Run Derby ◆ 1992
2. The Terrible Tickler ◆ 1992
3. Scary Scraped-Up Skaters ◆ 1992
4. The Headless Snowman ◆ 1992
5. The Snow Bowl ◆ 1992

6. Muscle Mania ◆ 1993
7. Amazing Stories ◆ 1993
8. April Fools ◆ 1993

ALTERNATE ENGLAND *see* Wolves Chronicles

ALWAYS FRIENDS

Meyers, Susan
TROLL
GRADES 2–4
REAL LIFE

Meg, Cricket, Amy, and Brittany become the Always Friends Club as they enjoy parties, class activities, and neighborhood fun. Each girl is featured in two books in this series, which focuses on ordinary experiences like sleep-overs and pets but also includes special events like auditioning for a TV show and a haunted-house contest. In *Meg & the Secret Scrapbook*, Meg and Cricket find a scrapbook in the attic and find out that their mothers were best friends and even had a special club.

1. Amy's Haunted House ◆ 1995
2. Beautiful Brittany ◆ 1995
3. Cricket Goes to the Dogs ◆ 1995
4. Hello, Jenny ◆ 1995
5. Meg & the Secret Scrapbook ◆ 1995
6. Amy Onstage ◆ 1997
7. Brittany's New Friend ◆ 1997
8. Cricket's Pet Project ◆ 1997

AMANDA PIG *see* Oliver and Amanda Pig

AMBER BROWN

Danziger, Paula
PUTNAM
GRADES 2–4
FAMILY LIFE | HUMOR

Ji Dan

Amber Brown begins this series in third grade. Through the series, Amber faces with humor the trials of growing up, her parents' divorce, and her mother's friendship and marriage to Max. These short novels, written in the first person with plenty of witty dialog, have a ring of authenticity.

1. Amber Brown Is Not a Crayon ◆ 1995
2. You Can't Eat Your Chicken Pox, Amber Brown ◆ 1996
3. Amber Brown Goes Fourth ◆ 1996
4. Amber Brown Wants Extra Credit ◆ 1997
5. Forever Amber Brown ◆ 1997
6. Amber Brown Sees Red ◆ 1998
7. Amber Brown Is Feeling Blue ◆ 1998

AMELIA

Moss, Marissa

TRICYCLE PRESS (A DIVISION OF TEN SPEED PRESS)   Ji Mos

GRADES 3–6

REAL LIFE

Amelia's notebooks (the covers of these books look like actual composition books) are actually top-secret journals chronicling the ups and downs of this nine-year-old's life. The scrapbook-like design is a large part of the appeal of these books. *My Notebook (With Help from Amelia)* (1997) invites kids to begin their own journal-keeping.

1. Amelia's Notebook (With Help from Amelia) ◆ 1995
2. Amelia Writes Again ◆ 1996
3. Amelia Hits the Road ◆ 1997
4. Amelia Takes Command ◆ 1998

AMELIA BEDELIA

Parish, Peggy, and Herman Parish

HARPERCOLLINS; GREENWILLOW   E Par

GRADES K–2

HUMOR

Amelia Bedelia's literalness causes problems when she tries to follow Mrs. Rogers's instructions for household chores. She changes towels, dresses the chicken, dusts potato bugs, and sews seeds. She always does exactly as she is told, but the results are never what is expected! Laugh-out-loud funny, these books will surely entertain. Herman Parish took over writing the series following the death of his aunt, Peggy Parish, in 1988. New illustrations for some of the older books give them a fresh look.

1. Amelia Bedelia ◆ 1963
2. Thank You, Amelia Bedelia ◆ 1964
3. Amelia Bedelia and the Surprise Shower ◆ 1966
4. Come Back, Amelia Bedelia ◆ 1971
5. Play Ball, Amelia Bedelia ◆ 1972
6. Good Work, Amelia Bedelia ◆ 1976
7. Teach Us, Amelia Bedelia ◆ 1977
8. Amelia Bedelia Helps Out ◆ 1979
9. Amelia Bedelia and the Baby ◆ 1981
10. Amelia Bedelia Goes Camping ◆ 1985
11. Merry Christmas, Amelia Bedelia ◆ 1986
12. Amelia Bedelia's Family Album ◆ 1988
13. Good Driving, Amelia Bedelia (Parish, Herman) ◆ 1995
14. Bravo, Amelia Bedelia! (Parish, Herman) ◆ 1997

AMERICAN ADVENTURE

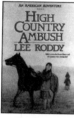

Roddy, Lee
BETHANY HOUSE
GRADES 5–8
HISTORICAL | VALUES

X ppbk

Hildy Corrigan faces many challenges during the Great Depression as she and her family move, hoping for a better life. The different locations of this series put Hildy in different situations that test her faith. Searching for a thief, adjusting to a new home, helping a girl whose father is a thief, and being accused of stealing a watch give Hildy opportunities to realize God's strength, love, and power of forgiveness. Readers looking for books in which characters struggle to be true to their values will want to read this series and other books by Lee Roddy.

1. The Overland Escape ◆ 1989
2. The Desperate Search ◆ 1989
3. Danger on Thunder Mountain ◆ 1989
4. The Secret of the Howling Cave ◆ 1990
5. The Flaming Trap ◆ 1990
6. Terror in the Sky ◆ 1991
7. Mystery of the Phantom Gold ◆ 1991
8. The Gold Train Bandits ◆ 1992
9. High Country Ambush ◆ 1992

THE AMERICAN ADVENTURE

Various authors

BARBOUR PUBLISHING

GRADES 3–6

ADVENTURE | HISTORICAL | VALUES

Ji Ame

The Smythe family travels to the New World aboard the *Mayflower* to escape religious persecution in Holland. Their adventures in reaching America and surviving the harsh first winter in Plymouth Colony are told from the point of view of twelve-year-old John Smythe in *The Mayflower Adventure* and *Plymouth Pioneers*. More than 40 additional books tell the story of the Smythe family's devout Christian relatives, descendants, and friends living through episodes in American history, all the way through World War II. There are books on the American Revolution, the World's Fair in Chicago, Irish immigration, women's suffrage, and the Ku Klux Klan. The theme of God's hand at work in American history is present throughout the series.

1. The Mayflower Adventure (Reece, Colleen L.) ◆ 1997
2. Plymouth Pioneers (Reece, Colleen L.) ◆ 1997
3. Dream Seekers (Lough, Loree) ◆ 1997
4. Fire by Night (Lough, Loree) ◆ 1997
5. Queen Anne's War (Grote, JoAnn) ◆ 1997
6. Danger in the Harbor (Grote, JoAnn) ◆ 1997
7. Smallpox Strikes! (Lutz, Norma Jean) ◆ 1997
8. Maggie's Choice (Lutz, Norma Jean) ◆ 1997
9. Boston Revolts! (Miller, Susan Martins) ◆ 1997
10. The Boston Massacre (Miller, Susan Martins) ◆ 1997
11. The American Revolution (Grote, JoAnn) ◆ 1997
12. The American Victory (Grote, JoAnn) ◆ 1997
13. Adventure in the Wilderness (Jones, Veda Boyd) ◆ 1997
14. Earthquake in Cincinnati (Hinman, Bonnie) ◆ 1997
15. Trouble on the Ohio River (Lutz, Norma Jean) ◆ 1997
16. Escape to Freedom (Lutz, Norma Jean) ◆ 1997
17. Cincinnati Epidemic (Jones, Veda Boyd) ◆ 1997
18. Riot in the Night (Hinman, Bonnie) ◆ 1997
19. Fight for Freedom (Lutz, Norma Jean) ◆ 1997
20. Enemy or Friend (Lutz, Norma Jean) ◆ 1997
21. Danger on the Railroad (Miller, Susan Martins) ◆ 1998
22. Time for Battle (Miller, Susan Martins) ◆ 1998
23. The Rebel Spy (Lutz, Norma Jean) ◆ 1998
24. War's End (Lutz, Norma Jean) ◆ 1998
25. Centennial Celebration (Grote, JoAnn) ◆ 1998
26. The Great Mill Explosion (Grote, JoAnn) ◆ 1998
27. Lights for Minneapolis (Miller, Susan Martins) ◆ 1998
28. Streetcar Riots (Miller, Susan Martins) ◆ 1998

29. Chicago World's Fair (Grote, JoAnn) ◆ 1998
30. A Better Bicycle (Grote, JoAnn) ◆ 1998
31. The New Citizen (Jones, Veda Boyd) ◆ 1998
32. The San Francisco Earthquake (Hinman, Bonnie) ◆ 1998
33. Marching with Sousa (Lutz, Norma Jean) ◆ 1998
34. Clash with the Newsboys (Lutz, Norma Jean) ◆ 1998
35. Prelude to War (Lutz, Norma Jean) ◆ 1998
36. The Great War (Lutz, Norma Jean) ◆ 1998
37. The Flu Epidemic (Grote, JoAnn) ◆ 1998
38. Women Win the Vote (Grote, JoAnn) ◆ 1998
39. Battling the Klan (Lutz, Norma Jean) ◆ 1998
40. The Bootlegger Menace (Hinman, Bonnie) ◆ 1998
41. Black Tuesday (Grote, JoAnn) ◆ 1998
42. The Great Depression (Grote, JoAnn) ◆ 1998
43. Starting Over (Miller, Susan Martins) ◆ 1998
44. Changing Times (Miller, Susan Martins) ◆ 1998
45. Rumblings of War (Lutz, Norma Jean) ◆ 1999
46. War Strikes (Lutz, Norma Jean) ◆ 1999
47. The Home Front (Hinman, Bonnie) ◆ 1999
48. Coming Home (Jones, Veda Boyd) ◆ 1999

AMERICAN DIARIES

Duey, Kathleen

ALADDIN

GRADES 4–6

HISTORICAL | REAL LIFE

Ji Due

Each book in this series features the adventures of a girl during an era of American history. After opening with a diary entry, the text describes the time and circumstances of the main character. A diary entry then closes the book. The eras and characters are diverse, providing readers with glimpses of different ways of life. Sarah Ann Hartford lives in Massachusetts in 1651 and must accept responsibility for violating Puritan standards of behavior. In Missouri in 1857, Evie Peach and her father have been emancipated by their owner and are now hoping to buy Mama's freedom. Celou Sudden Shout is the daughter of a French fur trapper and a Shoshone living in Idaho in 1826. Dramatic historical events are woven into these stories, which feature spirited female main characters.

1. Sarah Anne Hartford, Massachusetts, 1651 ◆ 1996
2. Emma Eileen Grove, Mississippi, 1865 ◆ 1996
3. Anisett Lundberg, California, 1851 ◆ 1996
4. Mary Alice Peale, Philadelphia, 1777 ◆ 1996
5. Willow Chase, Kansas Territory, 1847 ◆ 1997

   6. Ellen Elizabeth Hawkins, Texas, 1886 ◆ 1997
   7. Alexia Ellery Finsdale, San Francisco, 1905 ◆ 1997
   8. Evie Peach, St. Louis, 1857 ◆ 1997
   9. Celou Sudden Shout, Idaho, 1826 ◆ 1998
  10. Summer MacCleary, Virginia, 1720 ◆ 1998
  11. Agnes May Gleason, Walsenburg, Colorado, 1932 ◆ 1998

AMERICAN GIRLS: ADDY

Porter, Connie
PLEASANT COMPANY
GRADES 2–5
HISTORICAL | REAL LIFE

Ji Ame

Addy and her family are slaves in North Carolina. When Poppa and her brother Sam are sold, Addy and her mother leave Baby Esther on the plantation and escape to Philadelphia. Addy attends school there and learns to read and write. At a church festival, she and her friends earn money to help family members search for loved ones separated by slavery and the Civil War. Poppa and Sam find Addy and Mother, and they all try to find Baby Esther. Historical details are presented within the context of Addy's everyday life, giving readers a glimpse of life during this era. As part of the American Girls Collection, many related items are available, including an Addy doll with clothes, furniture, and artifacts.

   1. Meet Addy: An American Girl ◆ 1993
   2. Addy Learns a Lesson: A School Story ◆ 1993
   3. Addy's Surprise: A Christmas Story ◆ 1993
   4. Happy Birthday Addy: A Spring Story ◆ 1994
   5. Addy Saves the Day: A Summer Story ◆ 1994
   6. Changes for Addy: A Winter Story ◆ 1994

AMERICAN GIRLS: FELICITY

Tripp, Valerie
PLEASANT COMPANY
GRADES 2–5
HISTORICAL | REAL LIFE

Ji Ame

Felicity lives in Williamsburg in the 1770s. Her father owns one of the town's largest shops, and he has one apprentice, Ben, a patriot and friend of Felicity. In the first book, she and Ben befriend a beautiful horse that has fallen into the hands of a cruel man. They let the horse go, and Felicity hopes she will find her again some day. In subsequent books, she takes lessons in how to be a lady and meets

Elizabeth, who becomes her best friend. At Christmastime, she and Ben quarrel because she wants a new dress for a ball. Her Mother becomes ill, and Felicity is reunited with the horse. Notes at the end of each book offer information about the history of the period. Beautiful full-color paintings illustrate the books. Many related items are available, including dolls, clothes, furniture, and artifacts.

1. Meet Felicity: An American Girl ◆ 1991
2. Felicity Learns a Lesson: A School Story ◆ 1991
3. Felicity's Surprise: A Christmas Story ◆ 1991
4. Happy Birthday, Felicity! A Spring Story ◆ 1992
5. Felicity Saves the Day: A Summer Story ◆ 1992
6. Changes for Felicity: A Winter Story ◆ 1992

AMERICAN GIRLS: JOSEFINA

Tripp, Valerie
PLEASANT COMPANY
GRADES 2–5
HISTORICAL | REAL LIFE

Ji Ame

Josefina Montoya is the newest addition to the American Girls collection of books, dolls, etc. She is a Hispanic girl living in New Mexico in 1824. Although her mother is dead, Josefina is supported by her sisters and her extended family. Learning to read, celebrating her birthday and Christmas, and weaving traditional designs are some of her activities. Besides the Josefina doll, there are other related items including a small weaving loom and an adobe oven.

1. Meet Josefina: An American Girl ◆ 1997
2. Josefina Learns a Lesson: A School Story ◆ 1997
3. Josefina's Surprise: A Christmas Story ◆ 1997
4. Happy Birthday, Josefina! A Spring Story ◆ 1998
5. Josefina Saves the Day: A Summer Story ◆ 1998
6. Changes for Josefina: A Winter Story ◆ 1998

AMERICAN GIRLS: KIRSTEN

Shaw, Janet B.
PLEASANT COMPANY
GRADES 2–5
HISTORICAL | REAL LIFE

Ji Ame

The American Girls stories have a big following among intermediate readers. They portray strong young girls and women growing up in the United States during different time periods. For example, Kirsten comes from Sweden to a Minnesota farm during pioneer times. Not only does the series do a good job of describing what life was like then, it also portrays typical family life and friendships: growing up, struggles and successes, secrets, and adventures. Many related items are available, including dolls, clothes, furniture, and artifacts.

1. Meet Kirsten: An American Girl ◆ 1986
2. Kirsten Learns a Lesson: A School Story ◆ 1986
3. Kirsten's Surprise: A Christmas Story ◆ 1986
4. Happy Birthday, Kirsten! A Spring Story ◆ 1987
5. Kirsten Saves the Day: A Summer Story ◆ 1988
6. Changes for Kirsten: A Winter Story ◆ 1988

AMERICAN GIRLS: MOLLY

Tripp, Valerie

PLEASANT COMPANY

GRADES 2–5

HISTORICAL | REAL LIFE

Ji Ame

During World War II, Molly's dad is overseas working at a hospital. In *Meet Molly*, we learn about life on the home front. Victory gardens, patriotism, and waiting for the boys to come home are part of everyday life. An English refugee comes to live with Molly's family in the birthday story, and after some misunderstandings, the girls have a wonderful party together. In the school story, Molly's class has a contest to see whether the boys or the girls can do the most for the war effort. Molly's rival comes up with an idea to knit socks, which Molly and her friends Linda and Susan don't think is such a good idea. Molly and her family are excited when they learn Father is coming home. Many related items are available, including dolls, clothes, furniture, and artifacts.

1. Meet Molly: An American Girl ◆ 1986
2. Molly Learns a Lesson: A School Story ◆ 1986
3. Molly's Surprise: A Christmas Story ◆ 1986
4. Happy Birthday, Molly! A Spring Story ◆ 1987
5. Molly Saves the Day: A Summer Story ◆ 1988
6. Changes for Molly: A Winter Story ◆ 1988

AMERICAN GIRLS: SAMANTHA

Tripp, Valerie

PLEASANT COMPANY

GRADES 2–5

HISTORICAL | REAL LIFE

Ji Ame

Samantha Parkington is a young girl being raised by her grandmother in the early 1900s. The changes she experiences in her life mirror the changes the United States experienced at the time—social and economic upheavals brought about by the Industrial Revolution. In each of the six books, Samantha learns a lesson—about friendship, human nature, and generosity. These books are accompanied by a Samantha doll and accessories, as well as books of paper dolls, crafts, and recipes.

1. Meet Samantha: An American Girl ◆ 1986
2. Samantha Learns a Lesson: A School Story ◆ 1986
3. Samantha's Surprise: A Christmas Story ◆ 1986
4. Happy Birthday, Samantha! A Spring Story ◆ 1987
5. Samantha Saves the Day: A Summer Story ◆ 1988
6. Changes for Samantha: A Winter Story ◆ 1989

American Girls: Kit

AMY

Hoban, Julia

HARPERCOLLINS

GRADES K–2

FAMILY LIFE | REAL LIFE

In the four books in this series, Amy enjoys her everyday activities in each season. In the spring, Amy and Mommy go out in the rain while they go out in the car to pick up Daddy. When summer comes, Amy enjoys warm-weather activities. In the fall, Amy watches the wind tug at balloons and blow leaves off the trees. When it snows, Amy makes a snowman with the help of Daddy and Mommy.

1. Amy Loves the Sun ◆ 1988
2. Amy Loves the Wind ◆ 1988
3. Amy Loves the Rain ◆ 1989
4. Amy Loves the Snow ◆ 1989

AMY AND LAURA

Sachs, Marilyn
DOUBLEDAY
GRADES 4–6
FAMILY LIFE | REAL LIFE

Amy and her older sister Laura struggle to adjust to their new neighborhood in the Bronx in New York during the 1930s. The girls deal with more difficulties when their mother is seriously injured in an automobile accident and must be hospitalized for months. Aunt Minnie comes to live with the family and take care of the girls. It is the strength of the family that pulls the girls through these trials and all the awkward times of early adolescence in these touching stories.

1. Amy Moves In ◆ 1964
2. Laura's Luck ◆ 1965
3. Amy and Laura ◆ 1966

ANASTASIA KRUPNIK

Lowry, Lois
HOUGHTON MIFFLIN
GRADES 4–6
FAMILY LIFE | HUMOR

Ji Low

This series chronicles the life of Anastasia Krupnik beginning at age 10. Each episodic chapter relates an amusing incident in the life of this young girl as she deals with the ups and downs of growing up. Her father, an English professor, and her mother, an artist, are always supportive as she adjusts to a new brother in the first book and a move from the city to the Boston suburbs in the second. Anastasia takes on a challenging first job in *Anastasia at Your Service*, a science fair project goes awry in *Anastasia, Ask Your Analyst*, and her parents go away in *Anastasia on Her Own*. This is a humorous series that portrays a warm and loving family. There is a related series about Anastasia's brother, Sam.

1. Anastasia Krupnik ◆ 1979
2. Anastasia Again! ◆ 1981
3. Anastasia at Your Service ◆ 1982
4. Anastasia, Ask Your Analyst ◆ 1984
5. Anastasia on Her Own ◆ 1985
6. Anastasia Has the Answers ◆ 1986
7. Anastasia's Chosen Career ◆ 1987
8. Anastasia at This Address ◆ 1991
9. Anastasia, Absolutely ◆ 1996

ANATOLE

Titus, Eve

MCGRAW-HILL

GRADES K–2

ANIMAL FANTASY

EP Tit

In all of France, there is no braver mouse than Anatole, whose deeds are recounted in these ten adventures. Tired of hunting in people's homes for food, Anatole devises a plan. He travels in secret each night to the cheese factory of M'sieu Duval and begins the work of improving his cheeses. Not only do Duval's cheeses become the finest in France, but Anatole, who prefers to remain unknown, acquires a reputation as a cheese connoisseur. He befriends a cat, Gaston, travels to Italy, and develops his musical talents. Without a doubt, he is a mouse *magnifique*!

1. Anatole ◆ 1956
2. Anatole and the Cat ◆ 1957
3. Anatole and the Robot ◆ 1960
4. Anatole over Paris ◆ 1961
5. Anatole and the Poodle ◆ 1965
6. Anatole and the Piano ◆ 1966
7. Anatole and the Thirty Thieves ◆ 1969
8. Anatole and the Toyshop ◆ 1970
9. Anatole in Italy ◆ 1973
10. Anatole and the Pied Piper ◆ 1979

ANATOLE

Willard, Nancy M.

HARCOURT

GRADES 3–5

FANTASY

Anatole is an ordinary boy who lives with his cat, Plumpet. Together, they embark on fantastic adventures to magical lands, traveling on a gospel train to visit Plumpet's Aunt Pitterpat, sailing on a ship to the Island of the Grass King, and visiting Uncle Terrible. Finally, Anatole is faced with the formidable task of retrieving the thread of death from the wizard Arcimboldo.

1. Sailing to Cythera ◆ 1974
2. Island of the Grass King ◆ 1979
3. Uncle Terrible ◆ 1982

ANDIE AND THE BOYS

Harrell, Janice
POCKET BOOKS
GRADES 7–8
FAMILY LIFE

Andie faces the trials of teen life throughout this three-book series. Day-to-day high school friendships and troubles are described. Andie's new stepbrother tries to protect her from the advances of a new boyfriend in book one.

1. Andie and the Boys ◆ 1990
2. Dooley Mackenzie Is Totally Weird ◆ 1991
3. Brace Yourself ◆ 1991

ANGEL

Delton, Judy
HOUGHTON MIFFLIN
GRADES 3–5
FAMILY LIFE | HUMOR

Ji Del

Ever since their father left them, Angel O'Leary has been responsible for keeping her little brother Rags safe. It is a responsibility that weighs heavily on her. It is not until a classmate invites Angel to go to the town pool for a swim that Mrs. O'Leary realizes that Angel needs a chance to get out of the backyard and have some friends of her own. The next books introduce her mother's boyfriend, a professional clown she met on vacation, and the ensuing wedding is followed by a happy addition to the family.

1. Backyard Angel ◆ 1983
2. Angel in Charge ◆ 1985
3. Angel's Mother's Boyfriend ◆ 1986
4. Angel's Mother's Wedding ◆ 1987
5. Angel's Mother's Baby ◆ 1989

ANGEL PARK ALL STARS

Hughes, Dean
KNOPF
GRADES 4–6
REAL LIFE | RECREATION

Early books in this series follow the efforts of three rookie baseball players: Jacob Scott, Kenny Sandoval, and Harlan Sloan. In these books, the boys struggle with developing their playing skills, being accepted by their teammates, and dealing with such problems as slumps and bad grades (which keep Jacob from playing for a while). In *Championship Game*, the Angel Park Dodgers win the league title. The next book, *Superstar Team*, begins with the team feeling the pressure of being the defending champion. Coach Wilkens provides advice and playing strategies that are incorporated into the narrative. The Dodgers are a coed, multicultural team, and these fast-paced books with lots of baseball plays and action will appeal to sports enthusiasts.

1. Making the Team ◆ 1990
2. Big Base Hit ◆ 1990
3. Winning Streak ◆ 1990
4. What a Catch! ◆ 1990
5. Rookie Star ◆ 1990
6. Pressure Play ◆ 1990
7. Line Drive ◆ 1990
8. Championship Game ◆ 1990
9. Superstar Team ◆ 1991
10. Stroke of Luck ◆ 1991
11. Safe at First ◆ 1991
12. Up to Bat ◆ 1991
13. Play-Off ◆ 1991
14. All Together Now ◆ 1991

ANGEL PARK HOOP STARS

Hughes, Dean
KNOPF
GRADES 4–6
REAL LIFE | RECREATION

Ji Hug

In *Go to the Hoop!*, Harlan Sloan is the weakest player on the Angel Park Lakers. Coach Donaldson tries to encourage him, but Harlan still can't pull his game together. When he thinks about quitting the team, his friends Kenny and Miles help him realize that before he can play well he must relax and believe in himself. *Nothing but Net* features the arrival of Miles "Tip" Harris, a great player with a bad attitude. Kenny Sandoval helps him adjust to being a team player on the Lakers. Basketball statistics and plays are displayed following the story. Other books feature the concerns of different teammates as they try to play well and cope with insecurities and other problems.

1. Nothing but Net ◆ 1992
2. Point Guard ◆ 1992
3. Go to the Hoop! ◆ 1993
4. On the Line ◆ 1993

ANGEL PARK SOCCER STARS

Hughes, Dean

RANDOM HOUSE

GRADES 4–6

REAL LIFE | RECREATION

Heidi Wells is one of the best players on the coed Angel Park Pride soccer team, where she has to compete with and against boys. She is featured in several of the books in this series, making it attractive to girls as well as to boys. Other books feature other players, like Jacob Scott, who is trying to adjust to playing soccer after being successful at playing baseball; Nate Matheson, who must learn to control his temper in order to play well; and Clayton Lindsay, who has to learn to play as part of a team. Coach Toscano keeps this diverse group working together and succeeding. There is a glossary of soccer terms and some statistics and diagrams of plays at the end of each book.

1. Kickoff Time ◆ 1991
2. Defense! ◆ 1991
3. Victory Goal ◆ 1992
4. Psyched! ◆ 1992
5. Backup Goalie ◆ 1992
6. Total Soccer ◆ 1992
7. Shake Up ◆ 1993
8. Quick Moves ◆ 1993

ANGELA

Robinson, Nancy K.

SCHOLASTIC

GRADES 3–5

FAMILY LIFE | HUMOR

Six-year-old Angela is looking forward to Christmas. But all the talk about adopting an orphan is confusing and upsetting. *Oh Honestly, Angela!* is all anyone ever says to her, especially her big sister Tina. Robinson portrays the Steele children in a believable, honest, and often funny manner.

1. Oh Honestly, Angela! ◆ 1985
2. Angela, Private Citizen ◆ 1989
3. Angela and the Broken Heart ◆ 1991

ANGELINA BALLERINA

Illustrations by Helen Craig Text by Katharine Holabird

Holabird, Katherine

CROWN

GRADES K–2

ANIMAL FANTASY

EP Hol

Angelina the mouse wants nothing more than to be a ballerina. She practices every day until she finally becomes a famous ballerina. When she is not dancing, she has many other adventures. She dreams about going to the fair, but she must take along her little cousin Henry. When a new mouse baby joins the family, Angelina finds it's not easy being a big sister. Nevertheless, she and her friends always find ways to have fun—celebrating holidays and putting on special shows, for instance. Companion books include *Angelina's Birthday and Address Book* (1986) and *Angelina's Book and Doll Package* (1989).

1. Angelina Ballerina ◆ 1983
2. Angelina and the Princess ◆ 1984
3. Angelina at the Fair ◆ 1985
4. Angelina's Christmas ◆ 1985
5. Angelina on Stage ◆ 1986
6. Angelina and Alice ◆ 1987
7. Angelina's Birthday Surprise ◆ 1989
8. Angelina's Baby Sister ◆ 1991
9. Angelina Ice Skates ◆ 1993

ANIKA SCOTT

Rispin, Karen

TYNDALE HOUSE

GRADES 5–8

ADVENTURE | REAL LIFE | VALUES

When Anika Scott, 12, and her mother, father, and sister Sandy are involved in an adventure, they look to their Christian faith to guide them. On a trip to Africa, Anika finds that the elephants are in danger from poachers. Anika disobeys her parents when she leaves the camp and goes out into the Amboseli Game Preserve on her own. The strength of Anika's beliefs is tested as she faces danger and deals with the recent appearance of her half-brother Rick.

1. The Impossible Lisa Barnes ◆ 1992

2. Tianna the Terrible ◆ 1992
3. Anika's Mountain ◆ 1994
4. Ambush at Amboseli ◆ 1994
5. Sabrina the Schemer ◆ 1994

ANIMAL ARK

Baglio, Ben M.
SCHOLASTIC
GRADES 3–5
REAL LIFE

Mandy's parents are veterinarians, and she sometimes helps out at their Animal Ark Veterinary Hospital. Her interest in animals leads her to help out around the neighborhood, too. Along with her friend James, Mandy tries to find homes for stray kittens and puppies, protects a show pony, and even rescues an injured mother hedgehog and her babies. Readers who enjoy animal stories will like the additional information about veterinary practices contained in these books. They will also like reading about a character who is actively involved in helping others.

1. Kittens in the Kitchen ◆ 1994
2. Pony on the Porch ◆ 1994
3. Puppies in the Pantry ◆ 1994
4. Goat in the Garden ◆ 1994
5. Hedgehogs in the Hall ◆ 1994
6. Sheepdog in the Snow ◆ 1998
7. Badger in the Basement ◆ 1998
8. Cub in the Cupboard ◆ 1998

ANIMORPHS

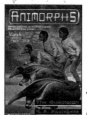

Applegate, K. A.
SCHOLASTIC
GRADES 4–8
ADVENTURE | SCIENCE FICTION

This fast-paced series involves the Yeerh—who have infected the brains of humans to control them—and the Animorphs, who have been given special powers by a dying Andalite. A special group of five friends find satisfaction in fighting the evil Yeerh. The Animorphs are able to "thought speak" and morph (for a period of two hours) into any animal they touch. A detailed discussion of the change process will hook readers as will the eye-catching covers. Short sentences plus continuous drama will keep readers involved. The *Animorph* TV series should increase the popularity of this series.

1. The Invasion ◆ 1996
2. The Visitor ◆ 1996
3. The Encounter ◆ 1996
4. The Message ◆ 1996
5. The Predator ◆ 1996
6. The Capture ◆ 1997
7. The Stranger ◆ 1997
8. The Alien ◆ 1997
9. The Secret ◆ 1997
10. The Android ◆ 1997
11. The Forgotten ◆ 1997
12. The Reaction ◆ 1998
13. The Change ◆ 1998
14. The Unknown ◆ 1998
15. The Escape ◆ 1998
16. The Warning ◆ 1998
17. The Underground ◆ 1998
18. The Decision ◆ 1998
19. The Departure ◆ 1998
20. The Discovery ◆ 1998
21. The Threat ◆ 1998
22. The Solution ◆ 1998
23. The Pretender ◆ 1998
24. The Suspicion ◆ 1998

ANNA

Kerr, Judith

BANTAM DOUBLEDAY DELL

GRADES 4–8

HISTORICAL

Anna, aged nine, flees Berlin with her family when Hitler is elected. Anna must leave behind most of her possessions, including her beloved pink rabbit. The family travels through Switzerland and France eventually to reach England. These stories of a Jewish refugee family trying to stay together with dignity and pride in the face of anti-Semitism and depression are based on the author's own childhood.

1. When Hitler Stole Pink Rabbit ◆ 1971
2. The Other Way Round ◆ 1975
3. A Small Person Far Away ◆ 1978

ANNABEL ANDREWS

Rogers, Mary
HARPERCOLLINS

GRADES 5—7

FANTASY | HUMOR

One morning Annabel wakes up to find she has turned into her mother. Annabel and her mother reverse roles for a day, and each gains a more sympathetic understanding of the other's life. Annabel blunders her way through the day and comes to appreciate her mother's daily trials, while her mother experiences life from her 13-year-old daughter's perspective. In the sequel, *A Billion for Boris*, Annabel and her 15-year-old boyfriend Boris discover a TV set that broadcasts tomorrow's news. And in *Summer Switch*, it is brother Ben's turn to switch bodies with his father.

1. Freaky Friday ◆ 1972
2. A Billion for Boris ◆ 1974
3. Summer Switch ◆ 1982

ANNIE BANANIE

Komaiko, Leah
HARPERCOLLINS

GRADES 2—4

REAL LIFE

Libby lives on a boring street with boring friends. She lives with her parents; her grandmother, who is deaf when she wants to be; and her brother Carl, who plays the piano. Her life changes completely when Annie Bananie moves to her street. Annie Bananie has a dog named Boris and wants to be friends with everyone in the neighborhood, including Bonnie, who wants to be a cat, and Nina, who thinks she's a horse. They form a club, and Libby is elected president; but then she's not sure exactly what the club is supposed to do. Annie comes to her rescue, not for the last time. Libby returns the favor when Annie gets in trouble with their eccentric neighbors and they take her to court. The first book about Annie Bananie is a picture book with a rhyming text. Subsequent books are easy chapter books for independent readers.

1. Annie Bananie ◆ 1989
2. Annie Bananie Moves to Barry Avenue ◆ 1996
3. Annie Bananie: Best Friends to the End ◆ 1997

4. Annie Bananie and the People's Court ◆ 1997
5. Annie Bananie and the Pain Sisters ◆ 1998

ANTHONY ANT

Philpot, Lorna, and Graham Philpot
RANDOM HOUSE
GRADES K–2
ANIMAL FANTASY

An amusing set of interactive picture books. Readers lift the flaps and look for clues as Anthony Ant and his creepy crawly friends have various adventures.

1. Amazing Anthony Ant ◆ 1994
2. Anthony Ant's Creepy Crawlers ◆ 1995
3. Hide and Seek with Anthony Ant ◆ 1995
4. Out and About with Anthony Ant ◆ 1995
5. Who's at Home with Anthony Ant? ◆ 1995
6. Anthony Ant's Treasure Hunt ◆ 1996

ANTHONY MONDAY

Bellairs, John
DIAL
GRADES 5–7
ADVENTURE | MYSTERY

Fourteen-year-old Anthony and his friend, librarian Miss Eells, search for a treasure rumored to have been hidden by wealthy eccentric Alpheus Winterborn. Anthony follows the clues to the Winterborn mansion and then back to the public library, where he outwits the efforts of another person who is seeking the treasure. In *The Lamp from the Warlock's Tomb*, Miss Eells buys an antique lamp and mysterious events begin to occur. There are strange voices, odd behavior, and an encounter with a ghost. These are suspenseful stories featuring supernatural events and puzzling mysteries.

1. The Treasure of Alpheus Winterborn ◆ 1978
2. The Dark Secret of Weatherend ◆ 1984
3. The Lamp from the Warlock's Tomb ◆ 1988
4. The Mansion in the Mist ◆ 1992

ANTRIAN

Wisler, G. Clifton
DUTTON
GRADES 6–8
SCIENCE FICTION

Scott looks like an ordinary teenager, but he is not. Scott is an alien with the ability to see into the future. In these books, he discovers his powers and learns their limits. He also struggles to adapt to living on Earth and to keep his abilities a secret, especially from those who would exploit him. Readers who like the Animorphs series should enjoy this series, too.

1. The Antrian Messenger ◆ 1986
2. The Seer ◆ 1988
3. The Mind Trap ◆ 1990

ARABEL AND MORTIMER

Aiken, Joan
HARPERCOLLINS
GRADES 4–6
HUMOR

From the moment Arabel's father Mr. Jones brings Mortimer, an injured raven, into their home, life for the Jones family becomes one chaotic episode after another. The irrepressible raven does as he pleases, shouting just one word, "Nevermore!" Each episode is more outrageous than the last. Fast-paced wit and humor are complemented by delightful illustrations.

1. Arabel's Raven ◆ 1974
2. Arabel and Mortimer ◆ 1981
3. Mortimer's Cross ◆ 1984
4. Mortimer Says Nothing, and Other Stories ◆ 1985

THE ARABUS FAMILY SAGA

Collier, James Lincoln, and Christopher Collier
DELL; DELACORTE
GRADES 5–8
HISTORICAL

Daniel Arabus struggles to be free during the uncertain times of the Revolutionary War. Daniel's late father was granted freedom for his service to the Continental Army, but unscrupulous men want to deny that freedom to Daniel and his mother. Two related books each feature an African American woman—Willy Freeman and Carrie—who are involved in the conflicts of the war and their desire for personal freedom. The lives of Daniel and his family intersect with each woman. Entertaining reading that aptly describes the plight of African Americans during this period.

1. Jump Ship to Freedom ◆ 1981
2. War Comes to Willy Freeman ◆ 1983
3. Who Is Carrie? ◆ 1984

ARCHIVES OF ANTHROPOS

White, John

INTERVARSITY

GRADES 4–8

FANTASY

The strange land of Anthropos is the setting for much of the action of these stories. Cousins Mary, Wesley, Lisa, and Kurt magically travel to Anthropos—a land of kings, sorcerers, and magic—to assist in the High Emperor's fight against evil. This series is modeled after the Chronicles of Narnia series and will appeal to children who enjoy allegorical fantasy stories.

1. The Tower of Geburah ◆ 1978
2. The Iron Sceptre ◆ 1981
3. The Sword Bearer ◆ 1986
4. Gaal the Conquerer ◆ 1989
5. Quest for the King ◆ 1995

ARE YOU AFRAID OF THE DARK?

Various authors

MINSTREL/POCKET BOOKS

GRADES 5–8

HORROR

Based on the *Nickelodeon* TV series, these books are similar to Goosebumps and other books in the scary-stories genre. In one book, Duncan Evans is given three wishes and finds that the adage "be careful what you wish for" is very true. Another book features Glynis Barrons, who makes a rash statement that she lives to regret. There are sinister statues, ghost riders, secret mirrors, and a virtual nightmare. This is sure to be a hit with the fans of horror books.

1. The Tale of the Sinister Statues (Peel, John) ◆ 1995
2. The Tale of Cutter's Treasure (Seidman, David L.) ◆ 1995
3. The Tale of the Restless House (Peel, John) ◆ 1995
4. The Tale of the Nightly Neighbors (Machale, D. J., and Kathleen Derby) ◆ 1995
5. The Tale of the Secret Mirror (Strickland, Brad) ◆ 1995
6. The Tale of the Phantom School Bus (Strickland, Brad) ◆ 1996
7. The Tale of the Ghost Riders (Vornholt, John) ◆ 1996
8. The Tale of the Deadly Diary (Strickland, Brad) ◆ 1996
9. The Tale of the Virtual Nightmare (Pedersen, Ted) ◆ 1996
10. The Tale of the Curious Cat (Gallagher, Diana G.) ◆ 1996
11. The Tale of the Zero Hour (Peel, John) ◆ 1997
12. The Tale of the Shimmering Shell (Weiss, David Cody, and Bobbi J. G. Weiss) ◆ 1997
13. The Tale of the Three Wishes (Peel, John) ◆ 1997
14. The Tale of the Campfire Vampires (Emery, Clayton) ◆ 1997
15. The Tale of the Bad-Tempered Ghost (Mitchell, V. E.) ◆ 1997
16. The Tale of the Souvenir Shop (Cohen, Alice E.) ◆ 1997
17. The Tale of the Ghost Cruise (Weiss, David Cody, and Bobbi J. G. Weiss) ◆ 1998
18. Tale of the Pulsating Gate (Gallagher, Diana G.) ◆ 1998
19. The Tale of the Stalking Shadow (Weiss, Bobbi J. G., and David C. Weiss) ◆ 1998
20. The Tale of the Egyptian Mummies (Mitchell, Mark) ◆ 1998
21. The Tale of the Terrible Toys (Beyers, Richard Lee) ◆ 1998
22. The Tale of the Mogul Monster (Weiss, David Cody, and Bobbi J. G. Weiss) ◆ 1998
23. The Tale of the Horrifying Hockey Team (Rodriguez, K. S.) ◆ 1999

ARNIE

Carlson, Nancy
VIKING
GRADES K–2
ANIMAL FANTASY

Arnie is a little cat who has his fears and problems. He interacts with his friends, other cats, and some dogs and rabbits and learns to get along while still being his own "person." When he becomes part of a skateboarding gang, the "cool" kid skates down a steep hill and dares the others to do it. Arnie makes the sensible choice, and the rest of the kids go along with him. Away at summer camp, Arnie is miserable at first because he doesn't know anyone and a kid in his cabin likes to play tricks. When they go on a hike, he holds a snake and decides nature is fun. Together, he and the other kids play a trick on their counselor. These are easy picture books with plenty of encouragement for solving peer problems.

1. Arnie and the Stolen Markers ◆ 1987
2. Arnie Goes to Camp ◆ 1988
3. Arnie and the New Kid ◆ 1990
4. Arnie and the Skateboard Gang ◆ 1995

ARTHUR

Brown, Marc

LITTLE, BROWN

GRADES K–3

ANIMAL FANTASY | FAMILY LIFE

E Bro

EP Bro

Marc Brown's Arthur series is well known, complete with a television series, videotapes, interactive stories on computer CDs, a fan club, a Web site, and, of course, books! Arthur is an aardvark who puts up with his sister, D.W., deals with his parents, and has fun with his friends at home and at school. Readers will identify with Arthur's everyday trials and tribulations.

1. Arthur's Nose ◆ 1976
2. Arthur's Eyes ◆ 1979
3. Arthur's Valentine ◆ 1980
4. Arthur Goes to Camp ◆ 1982
5. Arthur's Halloween ◆ 1982
6. Arthur's April Fool ◆ 1983
7. Arthur's Thanksgiving ◆ 1983
8. Arthur's Christmas ◆ 1984
9. Arthur's Tooth ◆ 1985
10. Arthur's Teacher Trouble ◆ 1986
11. Arthur's Baby ◆ 1987
12. Arthur's Birthday ◆ 1989
13. Arthur's Pet Business ◆ 1990
14. Arthur Meets the President ◆ 1991
15. Arthur Babysits ◆ 1992
16. Arthur's New Puppy ◆ 1993
17. Arthur's Chicken Pox ◆ 1994
18. Arthur's First Sleepover ◆ 1994
19. Arthur's TV Trouble ◆ 1995
20. Arthur Writes a Story ◆ 1996
21. Arthur's Computer Disaster ◆ 1997
22. Arthur Lost and Found ◆ 1998

ARTHUR READERS (RANDOM HOUSE)

1. Arthur's Reading Race ◆ 1995
2. Arthur Tricks the Tooth Fairy ◆ 1997

ARTHUR THE KID

Coren, Alan
LITTLE, BROWN
GRADES 3–5
HISTORICAL | HUMOR

Ten-year-old Arthur parodies the adventures—or misadventures—of the Lone Ranger, Custer, Sherlock Holmes, Billy the Kid, Buffalo Bill, and a Klondike gold miner in these funny historical novels.

1. Arthur the Kid ◆ 1977
2. Arthur's Last Stand ◆ 1977
3. Railroad Arthur ◆ 1977
4. Buffalo Arthur ◆ 1978
5. Lone Arthur ◆ 1978
6. Klondike Arthur ◆ 1979
7. Arthur and the Great Detective ◆ 1980
8. Arthur and the Purple Panic ◆ 1981

ARTHUR THE MONKEY

Hoban, Lillian
HARPERCOLLINS
GRADES K–2
ANIMAL FANTASY

Arthur the monkey lives with his parents and his younger sister Violet. In this series of easy-to-read books, he has many experiences that will be familiar to young readers. He goes camping, celebrates holidays (Christmas, Halloween, Valentine's Day), and loses a tooth. In one book, he learns about school bus safety and gets a surprise in his lunch box. Large print and lots of white space make this a good choice for beginning readers.

1. Arthur's Christmas Cookies ◆ 1972
2. Arthur's Honey Bear ◆ 1974
3. Arthur's Pen Pal ◆ 1976
4. Arthur's Prize Reader ◆ 1978
5. Arthur's Funny Money ◆ 1981
6. Arthur's Halloween Costume ◆ 1984
7. Arthur's Loose Tooth ◆ 1985

8. Arthur's Great Big Valentine ◆ 1989
9. Arthur's Camp Out ◆ 1993
10. Arthur's Back to School Days ◆ 1996
11. Arthur's Birthday Party ◆ 1999

ARTHUR CHAPTER BOOKS

Krensky, Stephen

LITTLE, BROWN

GRADES 3–6

ANIMAL FANTASY | FAMILY LIFE

Ji Bro

Marc Brown's Arthur books have continued with this series for the intermediate chapter book reader. Each book has some kind of dilemma or mystery. These books, based on teleplays from the television program, have a text by Stephen Krensky but feature all the popular Arthur characters, including Arthur, his sister D.W., his friends Buster and Francine, and his teacher Mr. Ratburn.

1. Arthur's Mystery Envelope ◆ 1998
2. Arthur and the Scare-Your-Pants-Off Club ◆ 1998
3. Arthur Makes the Team ◆ 1998
4. Arthur and the Crunch Cereal Contest ◆ 1998
5. Arthur Accused! ◆ 1998
6. Locked in the Library ◆ 1998
7. Buster's Dino Dilemma ◆ 1998
8. The Mystery of the Stolen Bike ◆ 1998
9. Arthur and the Lost Diary ◆ 1998
10. Who's in Love with Arthur? ◆ 1998
11. Arthur Rocks with BINKY ◆ 1998
12. Arthur and the Popularity Test ◆ 1998

ARTHURIAN KNIGHTS

Sutcliff, Rosemary

DUTTON

GRADES 6–8

ADVENTURE | HISTORICAL

The well-known legend of King Arthur—from the intrigue surrounding Arthur's conception to the quest for the Holy Grail—is dramatically retold in this series. Based on history, ballads, and Malory's *La Morte d'Arthur*, these books explain what happens to Arthur, Lancelot, Guinevere, and the others. Vivid detail describes feats of valor along with grave errors in judgment.

1. The Light Beyond the Forest: The Quest for the Holy Grail ◆ 1979
2. The Sword and the Circle: King Arthur and the Knights of the Round Table ◆ 1981
3. Road to Camlann: The Death of King Arthur ◆ 1981

AUNT EATER

Cushman, Doug

HarperCollins

Grades K–2

Animal Fantasy | Mystery

In this series of books for beginning readers, Aunt Eater is an anteater who loves to read and solve mysteries. Each book includes four different mysteries for Aunt Eater to solve, such as the case of the switched bag on the train and the mysterious torn note left in her mailbox. Aunt Eater's adventures involve various friends and neighbors in her community and on her vacations at the Hotel Bathwater.

1. Aunt Eater Loves a Mystery ◆ 1987
2. Aunt Eater's Mystery Vacation ◆ 1992
3. Aunt Eater's Mystery Christmas ◆ 1995
4. Aunt Eater's Mystery Halloween ◆ 1998

AUNT NINA

Brandenberg, Franz

Greenwillow

Grades K–2

Family Life | Humor

Aunt Nina is young and pretty and lives in a big house with no children of her own. She is visited by her six nieces and nephews, three boys and three girls ranging in age from a toddler to a boy of about ten. At Aunt Nina's house, they have a birthday party for Fluffy the cat. When the cat disappears, they search for it all over the house, finding treasures and having fun in each room. When they finally find Fluffy, they discover that she has had kittens: six, of course. On another visit, they go through all the classic stalling devices to avoid going to sleep and all end up in Aunt Nina's bed. Detailed full-color pictures capture the fun.

1. Aunt Nina and Her Nephews and Nieces ◆ 1984
2. Aunt Nina's Visit ◆ 1984
3. Aunt Nina, Good Night! ◆ 1989

AUSTIN FAMILY *see* Vicky Austin

AUSTRALIAN CHILDREN

Lester, Alison
HOUGHTON MIFFLIN
GRADES K–2
REAL LIFE

Clive, Tessa, Rosie, Frank, Ernie, Nicky, and Celeste are friends, but each has his or her way of doing things. These books celebrate their individuality. For example, they all laugh, but at different things. They earn money doing different jobs. Their differences make them unique and interesting. These books provide an entertaining way for groups of children to share information about themselves.

1. Clive Eats Alligators ◆ 1986
2. Rosie Sips Spiders ◆ 1989
3. Tessa Snaps Snakes ◆ 1991
4. When Frank Was Four ◆ 1994

AVONLEA

Montgomery, Lucy Maud
RANDOM HOUSE   *TA   Mon*
GRADES 5–8
FAMILY LIFE | HISTORICAL | REAL LIFE

Red-haired, imaginative Anne Shirley is mistakenly sent from an orphanage to live with the Cuthberts, who requested a boy to help on their farm. This series details the results. Montgomery tells Anne's life story from age 11 until well into her married years. Readers watch Anne blossom from an impetuous child into a mature woman, gaining not only physical beauty but a sense of self. Though the setting of these books is small-town Canada in the early 20th century, the themes of maturity, community, and friendship will surely resonate with today's readers. In particular, girls who enjoy imagination and creativity will become fast friends with Anne.

1. Anne of Green Gables ◆ 1908
2. Anne of Avonlea ◆ 1909
3. Chronicles of Avonlea ◆ 1912
4. Anne of the Island ◆ 1915
5. Anne's House of Dreams ◆ 1917
6. Rainbow Valley ◆ 1919

7. Further Chronicles of Avonlea ◆ 1920
8. Rilla of Ingleside ◆ 1921
9. Anne of Windy Poplars ◆ 1936
10. Anne of Ingleside ◆ 1939

B.Y. TIMES

Klein, Leah
TARGUM/FELDHEIM
GRADES 4–8
REAL LIFE

A group of girls attend the same middle school, Bais Yaakov, and work on their school newspaper, the *B.Y. Times*. The staff of the paper changes as students leave the school. In an early book, Shani Baum is the editor-in-chief; in a later book, Chani Kaufman has that job. There are references to school events and to Jewish events and holidays. An issue of the *B.Y. Times* is printed at the end of each book.

1. Shani's Scoop ◆ 1991
2. Batya's Search ◆ 1991
3. Twins in Trouble ◆ 1991
4. War! ◆ 1991
5. Spring Fever ◆ 1992
6. Party Time ◆ 1992
7. Changing Times ◆ 1992
8. Summer Daze ◆ 1992
9. Here We Go Again ◆ 1992
10. The New Kids ◆ 1992
11. Dollars and Sense ◆ 1993
12. Talking It Over ◆ 1993
13. Flying High ◆ 1993
14. Nechama on Strike ◆ 1993
15. Secrets! ◆ 1993
16. Babysitting Blues ◆ 1994
17. Jen Starts Over ◆ 1994
18. Who's Who ◆ 1994

B.Y. TIMES KID SISTERS

Various authors
TARGUM/FELDHEIM
GRADES 2–6
REAL LIFE

Sarah Chin, Naomi Kaufman, Melissa Farber, and Rivky Segal are the younger sisters of the girls who work on the Bais Yaakov middle school paper, the *B.Y. Times*. Like their older sisters, these elementary school girls enjoy friendship, school, and neighborhood adventures. There is a greater emphasis on everyday activities as the girls deal with a popular new girl, work to save a tree (and their treehouse), and endure problems between best friends. Jewish events receive much less emphasis than in the series featuring the older sisters.

1. The I-Can't-Cope Club (Harkohav-Kamins, Tamar) ◆ 1992
2. The Treehouse Kids (Harkohav-Kamins, Tamar) ◆ 1992
3. Rivky's Great Idea (Harkohav-Kamins, Tamar) ◆ 1993
4. Sarah's Room (Klein, Leah) ◆ 1993
5. Running Away (Prenzlau, Sheryl) ◆ 1993
6. Teacher's Pet (Prenzlau, Sheryl) ◆ 1993
7. Growing Up (Sutton, Esther) ◆ 1994
8. Changing Places (Prenzlau, Sheryl) ◆ 1994
9. Missing! (Prenzlau, Sheryl) ◆ 1994
10. Giant Steps (Prenzlau, Sheryl) ◆ 1995
11. The Wrong Way (Prenzlau, Sheryl) ◆ 1995
12. Ups and Downs (Prenzlau, Sheryl) ◆ 1995

BABAR

de Brunhoff, Jean, and Laurent de Brunhoff

RANDOM HOUSE

GRADES K–3

ANIMAL FANTASY

E P De B

An elephant is born in a great forest. When his mother is killed by hunters, he runs away to the big city, where he is befriended by a rich Old Lady who loves elephants. One day, his two little cousins, Arthur and Celeste, run away to the city, and Babar decides to return to the forest with them. Babar has learned so much in the city that he becomes the King of the Elephants, and he and Celeste are married. The rest of the series is about various adventures, both in the forest and in their travels. The original books were by Jean de Brunhoff. Laurent de Brunhoff continued the series, beginning with *Babar's Cousin, That Rascal Arthur* in 1948.

1. The Story of Babar the Little Elephant ◆ 1933
2. The Travels of Babar ◆ 1934
3. Babar the King ◆ 1934
4. Babar and Zephir ◆ 1937
5. Babar and His Children ◆ 1938
6. Babar and Father Christmas ◆ 1940
7. Babar's Cousin, That Rascal Arthur ◆ 1948
8. Babar's Picnic ◆ 1949
9. Babar's Fair Will Be Opened Next Sunday ◆ 1954
10. Babar and the Professor ◆ 1957
11. Babar's Castle ◆ 1962
12. Babar's French Lessons ◆ 1963

13. Babar Comes to America ◆ 1965
14. Babar's Spanish Lessons ◆ 1965
15. Babar Loses His Crown ◆ 1967
16. Babar's Birthday Surprise ◆ 1970
17. Babar Visits Another Planet ◆ 1972
18. Meet Babar and His Family ◆ 1973
19. Babar and the Wully-Wully ◆ 1975
20. Babar Saves the Day ◆ 1976
21. Babar Learns to Cook ◆ 1978
22. Babar's Mystery ◆ 1978
23. Babar and the Ghost ◆ 1981
24. Babar's ABC ◆ 1983
25. Babar's Book of Color ◆ 1984
26. Babar's Little Girl ◆ 1987
27. Babar's Little Circus Star ◆ 1988
28. Babar's Battle ◆ 1992
29. The Rescue of Babar ◆ 1993

BABY DUCK

Hest, Amy

CANDLEWICK

GRADES K–1

ANIMAL FANTASY | FAMILY LIFE

Baby Duck does not like some of the things around her, including the rain, her new eyeglasses, and the new baby. In each gentle story, Grampa helps Baby Duck accept change and inconvenience. He gives her the special attention that youngsters need.

1. In the Rain with Baby Duck ◆ 1995
2. Baby Duck and the Bad Eyeglasses ◆ 1996
3. You're the Boss, Baby Duck ◆ 1997

BABYSITTER

Stine, R. L.

SCHOLASTIC

GRADES 6–8

HORROR

Mr. Hagen hates babysitters and wants to kill them. While Jenny is babysitting for him he tries to kill her, but she kills him instead. The experience leaves her haunted and she loses her mind completely. Just as she is starting to recover, she takes another babysitting job in a haunted house. This time she confronts her fears and exorcises the ghosts. Stine's characteristic chapter endings range from the absurd to the really terrifying, and his fans will find just what they expect in this series.

1. The Babysitter ◆ 1989
2. The Babysitter II ◆ 1991
3. The Babysitter III ◆ 1993
4. The Babysitter IV ◆ 1995

BABY-SITTERS CLUB

Martin, Ann M.

SCHOLASTIC

GRADES 4–7

REAL LIFE

The Baby-sitters Club of Stoneybrook, Connecticut, is a group of five eighth-grade girls who are best friends and meet three times a week to take calls from parents who need sitters. Hardworking Kristy formed the club and tries to keep everyone in line. Quiet, sensitive Mary Anne is the secretary and sets up appointments. Stacey is the sophisticated one of the group, with a great sense of style because she comes from New York City. The club's meetings are held at Claudia's house because she has a private phone in her room. She is the artistic member of the group and a junk-food addict. Each book in the series focuses on a different girl, and as the series goes on, Dawn moves to California, divorced parents remarry (two of the girls become stepsisters), and the girls deal with problems. Stacey is diabetic, Mary Anne's father won't let her grow up, and they all occasionally don't get along with the children they babysit or the parents they work for. In every story, they work together to resolve problems with good will and humor.

1. Kristy's Great Idea ◆ 1986
2. Claudia and the Phantom Phone Calls ◆ 1986
3. The Truth About Stacey ◆ 1986
4. Mary Anne Saves the Day ◆ 1987
5. Dawn and the Impossible Three ◆ 1987
6. Kristy's Big Day ◆ 1987
7. Claudia and Mean Janine ◆ 1987
8. Boy-Crazy Stacey ◆ 1987
9. The Ghost at Dawn's House ◆ 1988
10. Logan Likes Mary Anne! ◆ 1988
11. Kristy and the Snobs ◆ 1988
12. Claudia and the New Girl ◆ 1988
13. Good-bye Stacey, Good-bye ◆ 1988
14. Hello, Mallory ◆ 1988

15. Little Miss Stoneybrook . . . and Dawn ◆ 1988
16. Jessi's Secret Language ◆ 1988
17. Mary Anne's Bad Luck Mystery ◆ 1988
18. Stacey's Mistake ◆ 1988
19. Claudia and the Bad Joke ◆ 1988
20. Kristy and the Walking Disaster ◆ 1989
21. Mallory and the Trouble with the Twins ◆ 1989
22. Jessi Ramsey, Pet-Sitter ◆ 1989
23. Dawn on the Coast ◆ 1989
24. Kristy and the Mother's Day Surprise ◆ 1989
25. Mary Anne and the Search for Tigger ◆ 1989
26. Claudia and the Sad Good-bye ◆ 1989
27. Jessi and the Superbrat ◆ 1989
28. Welcome Back, Stacey! ◆ 1989
29. Mallory and the Secret Diary ◆ 1989
30. Mary Anne and the Great Romance ◆ 1990
31. Dawn's Wicked Stepsister ◆ 1990
32. Kristy and the Secret of Susan ◆ 1990
33. Claudia and the Great Search ◆ 1990
34. Mary Anne and Too Many Boys ◆ 1990
35. Stacey and the Mystery of Stoneybrook ◆ 1990
36. Jessi's Baby-Sitter ◆ 1990
37. Dawn and the Older Boy ◆ 1990
38. Kristy's Mystery Admirer ◆ 1990
39. Poor Mallory! ◆ 1990
40. Claudia and the Middle School Mystery ◆ 1991
41. Mary Anne vs. Logan ◆ 1991
42. Jessi and the Dance School Phantom ◆ 1991
43. Stacey's Emergency ◆ 1991
44. Dawn and the Big Sleepover ◆ 1991
45. Kristy and the Baby Parade ◆ 1991
46. Mary Anne Misses Logan ◆ 1991
47. Mallory on Strike ◆ 1991
48. Jessi's Wish ◆ 1991
49. Claudia and the Genius of Elm Street ◆ 1991
50. Dawn's Big Date ◆ 1992
51. Stacey's Ex-Best Friend ◆ 1992
52. Mary Anne + 2 Many Babies ◆ 1992
53. Kristy for President ◆ 1992
54. Mallory and the Dream Horse ◆ 1992
55. Jessi's Gold Medal ◆ 1992
56. Keep Out, Claudia! ◆ 1992
57. Dawn Saves the Planet ◆ 1992
58. Stacey's Choice ◆ 1992
59. Mallory Hates Boys (and Gym) ◆ 1992
60. Mary Anne's Makeover ◆ 1993
61. Jessi and the Awful Secret ◆ 1993
62. Kristy and the Worst Kid Ever ◆ 1993

63. Claudia's—Freind—Friend ◆ 1993
64. Dawn's Family Feud ◆ 1993
65. Stacey's Big Crush ◆ 1993
66. Maid Mary Anne ◆ 1993
67. Dawn's Big Move ◆ 1993
68. Jessi and the Bad Baby-Sitter ◆ 1993
69. Get Well Soon, Mallory! ◆ 1993
70. Stacey and the Cheerleaders ◆ 1993
71. Claudia and the Perfect Boy ◆ 1994
72. Dawn and the We Love Kids Club ◆ 1994
73. Mary Anne and Miss Priss ◆ 1994
74. Kristy and the Copycat ◆ 1994
75. Jessi's Horrible Prank ◆ 1994
76. Stacey's Lie ◆ 1994
77. Dawn and Whitney, Friends Forever ◆ 1994
78. Claudia and Crazy Peaches ◆ 1994
79. Mary Anne Breaks the Rules ◆ 1994
80. Mallory Pike, #1 Fan ◆ 1994
81. Kristy and Mr. Mom ◆ 1995
82. Jessi and the Troublemaker ◆ 1995
83. Stacey vs. the BSC ◆ 1995
84. Dawn and the School Spirit War ◆ 1995
85. Claudia Kishi, Live from WSTO! ◆ 1995
86. Mary Anne and Camp BSC ◆ 1995
87. Stacey and the Bad Girl ◆ 1995
88. Farewell, Dawn ◆ 1995
89. Kristy and the Dirty Diapers ◆ 1995
90. Welcome to BSC, Abby ◆ 1995
91. Claudia and the First Thanksgiving ◆ 1995
92. Mallory's Christmas Wish ◆ 1995
93. Mary Anne and the Memory Garden ◆ 1996
94. Stacey McGill, Super Sitter ◆ 1996
95. Kristy + Bart = ? ◆ 1996
96. Abby's Lucky Thirteen ◆ 1996
97. Claudia and the World's Cutest Baby ◆ 1996
98. Dawn and Too Many Baby-Sitters ◆ 1996
99. Stacey's Broken Heart ◆ 1996
100. Kristy's Worst Idea ◆ 1996
101. Claudia Kishi, Middle School Dropout ◆ 1996
102. Mary Anne and the Little Princess ◆ 1996
103. Happy Holidays, Jessi ◆ 1996
104. Abby's Twin ◆ 1997
105. Stacey the Math Wiz ◆ 1997
106. Claudia, Queen of the Seventh Grade ◆ 1997
107. Mind Your Own Business, Kristy! ◆ 1997
108. Don't Give Up, Mallory ◆ 1997
109. Mary Anne to the Rescue ◆ 1997
110. Abby the Bad Sport ◆ 1997

111. Stacey's Secret Friend ◆ 1997
112. Kristy and the Sister War ◆ 1997
113. Claudia Makes Up Her Mind ◆ 1997
114. The Secret Life of Mary Anne Spier ◆ 1998
115. Jessi's Big Break ◆ 1998
116. Abby and the Best Kid Ever ◆ 1998
117. Claudia and the Terrible Truth ◆ 1998
118. Kristy Thomas, Dog Trainer ◆ 1998
119. Stacey's Ex-Boyfriend ◆ 1998
120. Mary Anne and the Playground Fight ◆ 1998
121. Abby in Wonderland ◆ 1998
122. Kristy in Charge ◆ 1998
123. Claudia's Big Party ◆ 1998
124. Stacey McGill . . . Matchmaker? ◆ 1998
125. Mary Anne in the Middle ◆ 1998
126. The All-New Mallory Pike ◆ 1999

BABY-SITTERS CLUB MYSTERIES

Martin, Ann M.
SCHOLASTIC
GRADES 4–7
MYSTERY | REAL LIFE

The five girls from Stoneybrook, Connecticut, who formed the Baby-sitters Club have their own mystery series. Kristy, founder and president of the group, Dawn the Californian, sophisticated Stacey, shy Mary Anne, and artistic Claudia run into mysteries involving empty houses that aren't really empty, missing rings, counterfeit money, and more—mysteries that they try to solve Nancy Drew style.

1. Stacey and the Missing Ring ◆ 1991
2. Beware Dawn! ◆ 1991
3. Mallory and the Ghost Cat ◆ 1992
4. Kristy and the Missing Child ◆ 1992
5. Mary Anne and the Secret in the Attic ◆ 1992
6. The Mystery at Claudia's House ◆ 1992
7. Dawn and the Disappearing Dogs ◆ 1993
8. Jessi and the Jewel Thieves ◆ 1993
9. Kristy and the Haunted Mansion ◆ 1993
10. Stacey and the Mystery Money ◆ 1993
11. Claudia and the Mystery at the Museum ◆ 1993
12. Dawn and the Surfer Ghost ◆ 1993
13. Mary Anne and the Library Mystery ◆ 1994
14. Stacey and the Mystery at the Mall ◆ 1994
15. Kristy and the Vampires ◆ 1994

16. Claudia and the Clue in the Photograph ◆ 1994
17. Dawn and the Halloween Mystery ◆ 1994
18. Stacey and the Mystery at the Empty House ◆ 1994
19. Kristy and the Missing Fortune ◆ 1995
20. Mary Anne and the Zoo Mystery ◆ 1995
21. Claudia and the Recipe for Danger ◆ 1995
22. Stacey and the Haunted Masquerade ◆ 1995
23. Abby and the Secret Society ◆ 1996
24. Mary Anne and the Silent Witness ◆ 1996
25. Kristy and the Middle School Vandal ◆ 1996
26. Dawn Schafer, Undercover Babysitter ◆ 1996
27. Claudia and the Lighthouse Ghost ◆ 1996
28. Abby and the Mystery Baby ◆ 1997
29. Stacey and the Fashion Victim ◆ 1997
30. Kristy and the Mystery Train ◆ 1997
31. Mary Anne and the Music Box Secret ◆ 1997
32. Claudia and the Mystery in the Painting ◆ 1997
33. Stacey and the Stolen Hearts ◆ 1998
34. Mary Anne and the Haunted Bookstore ◆ 1998
35. Abby and the Notorious Neighbor ◆ 1998
36. Kristy and the Cat Burglar ◆ 1998

SUPER MYSTERIES

1. Baby-Sitters' Haunted House ◆ 1995
2. Baby-Sitters Beware ◆ 1995
3. Baby-Sitters' Fright Night ◆ 1996
4. Baby-Sitters' Christmas Chiller ◆ 1997

BABY-SITTERS CLUB SUPER SPECIALS

Martin, Ann M.

SCHOLASTIC

GRADES 4–7

REAL LIFE

The Super Specials are about twice as long as the regular Baby-sitters Club books and deal with events such as weddings or a visit by the girls to see Dawn when she moves to California. They are narrated by all five girls, taking different chapters in turn. There are also special Super Chillers books.

1. Baby-Sitters on Board! ◆ 1988
2. Baby-Sitters' Summer Vacation ◆ 1989
3. Baby-Sitters' Winter Vacation ◆ 1989
4. Baby-Sitters' Island Adventure ◆ 1990
5. California Girls! ◆ 1990

6. New York, New York! ◆ 1991
7. Snowbound ◆ 1991
8. Baby-Sitters at Shadow Lake ◆ 1992
9. Starring the Baby-Sitters Club ◆ 1992
10. Sea City, Here We Come! ◆ 1993
11. The Baby-Sitters Remember ◆ 1994
12. Here Come the Bridesmaids ◆ 1994
13. Aloha, Baby-Sitters! ◆ 1996
14. BSC in the USA ◆ 1997

BABY-SITTERS LITTLE SISTER

Martin, Ann M.

SCHOLASTIC

GRADES 2–3

REAL LIFE

Kristy, of the famous Baby-sitters Club series, has a little stepsister who lives with her on the weekends. The series is about Karen's life, which occasionally touches Kristy and the other baby-sitters. In a typical book, Karen falls in love with her handsome baby-sitter and thinks he has asked her out on a date, when he really has a date with Kristy. There are some holiday stories involving Santa and leprechauns. Karen quarrels and makes up with her brother Andrew and with Kristy and learns to get along with her stepparents.

1. Karen's Witch ◆ 1988
2. Karen's Roller Skates ◆ 1988
3. Karen's Worst Day ◆ 1989
4. Karen's Kittycat Club ◆ 1989
5. Karen's School Picture ◆ 1989
6. Karen's Little Sister ◆ 1989
7. Karen's Birthday ◆ 1990
8. Karen's Haircut ◆ 1990
9. Karen's Sleepover ◆ 1990
10. Karen's Grandmothers ◆ 1990
11. Karen's Prize ◆ 1990
12. Karen's Ghost ◆ 1990
13. Karen's Surprise ◆ 1990
14. Karen's New Year ◆ 1991
15. Karen's in Love ◆ 1991
16. Karen's Goldfish ◆ 1991
17. Karen's Brothers ◆ 1991
18. Karen's Home Run ◆ 1991
19. Karen's Good-bye ◆ 1991
20. Karen's Carnival ◆ 1991

21. Karen's New Teacher ◆ 1991
22. Karen's Little Witch ◆ 1991
23. Karen's Doll ◆ 1991
24. Karen's School Trip ◆ 1992
25. Karen's Pen Pal ◆ 1992
26. Karen's Ducklings ◆ 1992
27. Karen's Big Joke ◆ 1992
28. Karen's Tea Party ◆ 1992
29. Karen's Cartwheel ◆ 1992
30. Karen's Kittens ◆ 1992
31. Karen's Bully ◆ 1992
32. Karen's Pumpkin Patch ◆ 1992
33. Karen's Secret ◆ 1992
34. Karen's Snow Day ◆ 1993
35. Karen's Doll Hospital ◆ 1993
36. Karen's New Friend ◆ 1993
37. Karen's Tuba ◆ 1993
38. Karen's Big Lie ◆ 1993
39. Karen's Wedding ◆ 1993
40. Karen's Newspaper ◆ 1993
41. Karen's School ◆ 1993
42. Karen's Pizza Party ◆ 1993
43. Karen's Toothache ◆ 1993
44. Karen's Big Weekend ◆ 1993
45. Karen's Twin ◆ 1994
46. Karen's Baby-Sitter ◆ 1994
47. Karen's Kite ◆ 1994
48. Karen's Two Families ◆ 1994
49. Karen's Stepmother ◆ 1994
50. Karen's Lucky Penny ◆ 1994
51. Karen's Big Top ◆ 1994
52. Karen's Mermaid ◆ 1994
53. Karen's School Bus ◆ 1994
54. Karen's Candy ◆ 1994
55. Karen's Magician ◆ 1994
56. Karen's Ice Skates ◆ 1994
57. Karen's School Mystery ◆ 1995
58. Karen's Ski Trip ◆ 1995
59. Karen's Leprechaun ◆ 1995
60. Karen's Pony ◆ 1995
61. Karen's Tattletale ◆ 1995
62. Karen's New Bike ◆ 1995
63. Karen's Movie ◆ 1995
64. Karen's Lemonade Stand ◆ 1995
65. Karen's Toys ◆ 1995
66. Karen's Monsters ◆ 1995
67. Karen's Turkey Day ◆ 1995
68. Karen's Angel ◆ 1995

69. Karen's Big Sister ◆ 1996
70. Karen's Granddad ◆ 1996
71. Karen's Island Adventure ◆ 1996
72. Karen's New Puppy ◆ 1996
73. Karen's Dinosaur ◆ 1996
74. Karen's Softball Mystery ◆ 1996
75. Karen's County Fair ◆ 1996
76. Karen's Magic Garden ◆ 1996
77. Karen's School Surprise ◆ 1996
78. Karen's Half Birthday ◆ 1996
79. Karen's Big Fight ◆ 1996
80. Karen's Christmas Tree ◆ 1996
81. Karen's Accident ◆ 1997
82. Karen's Secret Valentine ◆ 1997
83. Karen's Bunny ◆ 1997
84. Karen's Big Job ◆ 1997
85. Karen's Treasure ◆ 1997
86. Karen's Telephone Trouble ◆ 1997
87. Karen's Pony Camp ◆ 1997
88. Karen's Puppet Show ◆ 1997
89. Karen's Unicorn ◆ 1997
90. Karen's Haunted House ◆ 1997
91. Karen's Pilgrim ◆ 1997
92. Karen's Sleigh Ride ◆ 1997
93. Karen's Cooking Contest ◆ 1998
94. Karen's Snow Princess ◆ 1998
95. Karen's Promise ◆ 1998
96. Karen's Big Move ◆ 1998
97. Karen's Paper Route ◆ 1998
98. Karen's Fishing Trip ◆ 1998
99. Karen's Big City Mystery ◆ 1998
100. Karen's Book ◆ 1998
101. Karen's Chain Letter ◆ 1998
102. Karen's Black Cat ◆ 1998
103. Karen's Movie Star ◆ 1998
104. Karen's Christmas Carol ◆ 1998
105. Karen's Nanny ◆ 1998

BABY-SITTERS LITTLE SISTER SUPER SPECIALS

Martin, Ann M.

SCHOLASTIC

GRADES 2–4

REAL LIFE

Karen Brewer is the little stepsister of Kristy of the Baby-sitters Club. Karen and her brother Andrew are the children of Kristy's stepfather. Karen lives with Kristy's family on the weekends and with her mother, who has also remarried, during the week. In these Super Specials, something extra is offered. Karen flies on a plane to visit her grandmother, and there are games, activities, and recipes included at the end of each book. Karen and her three friends spend a busy summer together, and each of the girls tells part of the story.

1. Karen's Wish ◆ 1990
2. Karen's Plane Trip ◆ 1991
3. Karen's Mystery ◆ 1991
4. Karen, Hannie, and Nancy: The Three Musketeers ◆ 1992
5. Karen's Baby ◆ 1992
6. Karen's Campout ◆ 1993

BAD NEWS BALLET

Malcolm, Jahnna N.

SCHOLASTIC

GRADES 4–7

REAL LIFE

A group of girls meet when their mothers force them to try out for a ballet performance. Because they go to different schools, they decide to take ballet classes so they can see each other every week. Their rivals are girls they call the Bunheads, who love ballet and are good at it. Wiry Rocky Garcia doesn't like to be told what to do, and Mary Bubnik is something of a klutz. Gwen loves to eat and is decidedly plump, making her a special target of the Bunheads. Zan is sensitive and shy. Kathryn McGee is more of a leader than the others, and together they all try to keep the group together and get the best of the other group.

1. The Terrible Tryouts ◆ 1989
2. Battle of the Bunheads ◆ 1989
3. Stupid Cupids ◆ 1989
4. Who Framed Mary Bubnik? ◆ 1989
5. Blubberina ◆ 1989

6. Save D.A.D.! ◆ 1990
7. The King and Us ◆ 1990
8. Camp Clodhopper ◆ 1990
9. Boo Who? ◆ 1990
10. A Dog Named Toe Shoe ◆ 1991

BAD NEWS BUNNY

Saunders, Susan
SIMON & SCHUSTER
GRADES 2–4
ANIMAL FANTASY | HUMOR

Jason buys a raffle ticket and wins the third prize, which he thinks is a robot. It turns out to be a smart-mouthed rabbit with a fondness for junk food and junk television. To get back at the school bully, Jason enters the school talent show as a ventriloquist with his talking rabbit called Robot. The show is a big hit, and Robot tells Jason they will always be a team. Jason and his little sister Jenny continue to have adventures with Robot.

1. Third-Prize Surprise ◆ 1987
2. Back to Nature ◆ 1987
3. Stop the Presses ◆ 1987
4. Who's Got a Secret? ◆ 1987
5. Caught in the Act ◆ 1987
6. Narrow Escape ◆ 1987

BAGTHORPE SAGA

Cresswell, Helen
MACMILLAN
GRADES 5–6
FAMILY LIFE | HUMOR

Because every other member of the Bagthorpe family is creative and talented, Jack devises a plan to become more than an "ordinary" member of this unusual household. *Ordinary Jack* begins the humorous saga of an eccentric, lovable family whose life is never dull. The cast of characters includes the colorful, but not as brilliant, Parker family—Uncle Parker, Aunt Celia, and Daisy. Continuous drama portrays family values with comical mishaps, mix-ups, and much human interaction.

1. Ordinary Jack ◆ 1977
2. Absolute Zero ◆ 1978
3. Bagthorpes Unlimited ◆ 1978

4. Bagthorpes vs. the World ◆ 1979
5. Bagthorpes Abroad ◆ 1984
6. Bagthorpes Haunted ◆ 1985
7. Bagthorpes Liberated ◆ 1985

BAILEY CITY MONSTERS

Jones, Marcia Thornton, and Debbie Dadey
SCHOLASTIC
GRADES 2–4
FANTASY | HUMOR

There is something strange about the new family next door. Ben and
Annie have never seen such strange parents as Boris and Hilda Hauntly.
Their son Kilmer is in Ben's fourth-grade class, and he is weird, too. With
their friend Jane, Ben and Annie try to find out more about the owners of
the Hauntly Manor Inn, until they see the guests! This series, by the
authors of the Adventures of the Bailey School Kids series, combines weird
creatures with spooky situations and lots of humor. This is a good choice
for readers looking for a mild dose of monsters.

1. The Monsters Next Door ◆ 1997
2. Howling at the Hauntlys' ◆ 1998
3. Vampire Trouble ◆ 1998

BAILEY SCHOOL KIDS *see* The Adventures of the
Bailey School Kids

BAKER STREET IRREGULARS

Dicks, Terrance
DUTTON
GRADES 4–7
MYSTERY

After four London kids recover a lost painting, they are known as "The
Baker Street Irregulars" after Sherlock Holmes's gang of street kids. The
youngest, Mickey, welcomes all the attention and publicity and wants to
solve another crime. Dan, the leader of the group, and Jeff, the one with
the most common sense, are reluctant to get involved again. When a crime
wave hits their neighborhood, Dan, Jeff, and Mickey, along with their
friend Liz, find themselves drawn in almost in spite of themselves. Dan is
capable of drawing conclusions by intuitive leaps, Jeff sometimes plays the
Dr. Watson role, and Liz and Mickey are fearless in dangerous situations.

Don, a young police detective, comes to rely on their expertise as the young quartet takes on more cases. Lots of action and fairly complex clues for young mystery fans.

1. The Case of the Missing Masterpiece ◆ 1978
2. The Case of the Fagin File ◆ 1978
3. The Case of the Blackmail Boys ◆ 1979
4. The Case of the Cinema Swindle ◆ 1980
5. The Case of the Ghost Grabbers ◆ 1981
6. The Case of the Cop Catchers ◆ 1981
7. The Case of the Disappearing Diplomat ◆ 1986
8. The Case of the Comic Crooks ◆ 1986
9. The Case of the Haunted Holiday ◆ 1987
10. The Case of the Criminal Computer ◆ 1987

BAKER'S DOZEN

Various authors

TARGUM PRESS

GRADES 4–6

FAMILY LIFE

There are 14 people in the Baker family—Mr. and Mrs. Baker and their 12 children. Asher is the oldest, and he is living at a yeshivah. Bracha is the oldest girl; and while Asher is away, she is the oldest one at home. Then, there are the quintuplets—Rivka, Zahava, Dina, Tikva, and Yocheved—who receive lots of attention, not only for being quints, but also for being in such a large family. Moishy, Chezky, Donny, Saraleh, and Rachel round out this large, lively family. The activities in this house revolve around Jewish holidays and traditions, like attending a pre-Purim concert celebration or planning a bas mitzvah. Readers will enjoy the everyday problems faced by the different personalities in the Baker family.

1. On Our Own (Lazewnik, Libby) ◆ 1991
2. Ghosthunters! (Siegel, Malky) ◆ 1992
3. And the Winner Is . . . (Stein, Aidel) ◆ 1992
4. Stars in Their Eyes (Stein, Aidel) ◆ 1992
5. The Inside Story (Lazewnik, Libby) ◆ 1992
6. Trapped! (Lazewnik, Libby, et al.) ◆ 1992
7. Ima Come Home (Stein, Aidel) ◆ 1993
8. Hey Waiter! (Zitter, Emmy) ◆ 1993
9. Through Thick and Thin (Garfunkel, Debby) ◆ 1993
10. Do Not Disturb (Stein, Aidel) ◆ 1994
11. The Do-Gooders (Stein, Aidel) ◆ 1994
12. The Baker Family Circus (Rose, Miriam) ◆ 1994
13. Something's Fishy (Stein, Aidel) ◆ 1994

14. Summer Jobs (Stein, Aidel) ◆ 1995
15. Sorry About That (Steinberg, Ruth) ◆ 1995
16. Baker's Best (Lazewnik, Libby) ◆ 1996

BALLET SLIPPERS

Giff, Patricia Reilly

VIKING

GRADES 2–4

REAL LIFE

J. Gif

Rosie wants to be a ballerina. In the first book of the series, *Dance with Rosie*, she begins a class with Miss Deidre and learns how challenging ballet is. In another book, she takes her brother Andrew to see *The Sleeping Beauty*, only to have him cause a problem. Later, her ballet class performs the same ballet. In still another book, Rosie worries that her Grandpa's trip will upset her plans—and that she will miss him. The ballet activities are woven into the everyday lives of Rosie and her friends.

1. Dance with Rosie ◆ 1996
2. Rosie's Nutcracker Dreams ◆ 1996
3. Starring Rosie ◆ 1997
4. Not-So-Perfect Rosie ◆ 1997
5. Glass Slipper for Rosie ◆ 1997
6. Rosie's Big City Ballet ◆ 1998

BARKHAM STREET

Stolz, Mary

HarperCollins

GRADES 4–6

FAMILY LIFE | REAL LIFE

In *The Explorer of Barkham Street*, Martin Hastings, 13, dreams of being a hero. His everyday life is filled with problems, some involving his father, but his biggest concern is finding a way to get back his dog, Rufus. A successful baby-sitting job gives Martin a reason to feel good about himself. Earlier books show how Martin got (and lost) his dog and how he bullied Edward Frost. Martin experiences emotional growth as he deals with his anger and disappointments and begins to accept responsibility for his actions.

1. A Dog on Barkham Street ◆ 1960
2. The Bully of Barkham Street ◆ 1963
3. The Explorer of Barkham Street ◆ 1985

BASIL OF BAKER STREET

Titus, Eve

SIMON & SCHUSTER

GRADES 2–5

ANIMAL FANTASY | MYSTERY

Ji Tit

Mouse detectives Basil of Baker Street and his faithful companion Dr. David Q. Dawson live in the basement of Sherlock Holmes's house and sneak into the great detective's living room to learn from the master. When the young twins of their neighbors are mousenapped, the detective duo goes into action. They find clues about the mouse who delivered the ransom note, demanding that Basil and all his neighbors give the criminals their cozy homes in the Baker Street basement. The case is solved, and the twins are returned to their parents, but of course this is just the beginning of many adventures. The two mouse detectives travel to the United States and Mexico as their fame spreads, and their help is requested by mice all over.

1. Basil of Baker Street ◆ 1958
2. Basil and the Lost Colony ◆ 1964
3. Basil and the Pygmy Cats ◆ 1971
4. Basil in Mexico ◆ 1976
5. Basil in the Wild West ◆ 1982

BASTABLE FAMILY

Nesbit, E.

PUFFIN

GRADES 5–8

HISTORICAL | REAL LIFE

The six Bastables—Alice, Oswald, Dora, Dicky, Noel and H.O.—hunt for treasure in the opening book of this series. They don't find it, but they do end up living in an old house in the country. They form a club called the Would-Be-Goods as they try to behave themselves. They have a hard time, and can't seem to help getting into trouble, from falling in the millpond to messing up the house just in time for important visitors. Unlike the Five Children and It series, there is no fantasy element, but Nesbit fans will enjoy the similar characters and turn-of-the-century British setting. Some of the books are available in paperback.

1. The Story of the Treasure Seekers ◆ 1899
2. Wouldbegoods ◆ 1901
3. New Treasure Seekers ◆ 1904
4. Oswald Bastable and Others ◆ 1904

BEANY MALONE

Weber, Lenora Mattingly
THOMAS Y. CROWELL
GRADES 4–8
FAMILY LIFE | HUMOR

Denver, Colorado, is the home to the noisy, active Malone family. The father, Martie, is a newspaper columnist and crusader. Son Johnny is in love with the history of the state. Mary Fred loves horses and wins prizes with her beloved Mr. Chips. Beany, the youngest, takes care of the house because their mother is dead, and her helpful nature makes her the "little mother" to them all. Beany's love interest is Norbett, a cub reporter at a paper that is rival to her father's. The series follows her through high school, where she and Norbett have a stormy, on-again off-again relationship. When Martie decides to remarry, Beany has trouble getting along with her stepmother. Beany gets great satisfaction from a part-time job helping out with an advice column on her father's paper.

1. Meet the Malones ◆ 1944
2. Beany Malone ◆ 1948
3. Leave It to Beany ◆ 1950
4. Beany and the Beckoning Road ◆ 1952
5. Beany Has a Secret Life ◆ 1955
6. Make a Wish for Me ◆ 1956
7. Happy Birthday, Dear Beany ◆ 1957
8. The More the Merrier ◆ 1958
9. A Bright Star Falls ◆ 1959
10. Welcome Stranger ◆ 1960
11. Pick a New Dream ◆ 1961
12. Tarry Awhile ◆ 1962
13. Something Borrowed, Something Blue ◆ 1963
14. Come Back, Wherever You Are ◆ 1969

BEAR

Asch, Frank
PARENTS MAGAZINE PRESS
GRADES K–2
ANIMAL FANTASY | FAMILY LIFE

This series of books features a young bear, usually with his parents. In *Popcorn*, Bear is left home while his parents go to a Halloween party. He has his own party, but must clean up a mess of popcorn. For a surprise, his parents bring him more popcorn. These stories have gentle humor that appeals to young children. Frank Asch also features bears in his Moonbear series.

1. Sandcake ◆ 1978
2. Popcorn ◆ 1979
3. Bread and Honey ◆ 1981
4. Milk and Cookies ◆ 1982

BEAR

Winthrop, Elizabeth

HOLIDAY HOUSE

GRADES K–1

ANIMAL FANTASY | HUMOR

Young children will relate to the feeling of anxiety that Bear (a teddy bear who acts like a child) feels when Nora leaves him with a baby-sitter, Mrs. Duck. While Nora is away, Bear plans to be difficult, but Mrs. Duck—who is a duck—proves to be a very wise baby-sitter. At Christmas, Mrs. Duck returns while Nora goes shopping, and Bear learns a lesson about peeking into presents. In another book, Nora brings home a new bear who is to be Bear's sister. It takes Bear a while to accept this big new panda bear into his heart, but he does. Like Amy Hest's books about Baby Duck, this series is right on target with the fears and simple concerns of young children. Charming illustrations add to the warmth of this picture book series.

1. Bear and Mrs. Duck ◆ 1988
2. Bear's Christmas Surprise ◆ 1991
3. Bear and Roly-Poly ◆ 1996

BEECHWOOD BUNNY TALES

Huriet, Genevieve

GARETH STEVENS

GRADES K–3

ANIMAL FANTASY

Joyful bunnies and other creatures of Beechwood Grove romp across the pages of this series. Younger children will enjoy the cheerful illustrations of the Bellflower family and their friends. Adventures include gardening, moving, encountering strangers, and attending the Full Moon Ball. The bunnies learn important life lessons in each book.

1. Dandelion's Vanishing Vegetable Garden ◆ 1991
2. Mistletoe and the Baobab Tree ◆ 1991

3. Periwinkle at the Full Moon Ball ◆ 1991
4. Poppy's Dance ◆ 1991
5. Aunt Zinnia and the Ogre ◆ 1992
6. Family Moving Day ◆ 1992
7. Violette's Daring Adventure ◆ 1992

BEEZUS AND RAMONA *see* Ramona Quimby

BEEZY

McDonald, Megan
ORCHARD BOOKS
GRADES 1–2
FAMILY LIFE | HUMOR

E McD

Beezy enjoys many of the everyday activities that will be familiar to readers. She plays with her dog, Funnybone; enjoys Gran's baking and stories; and plays softball with her friend Sarafina. Picking blackberries, waiting out a big storm, and enjoying the company of her friend Merlin are also described. Short chapters, each a complete story, make this an accessible series for younger readers. The humor and realistic situations will also be appealing.

1. Beezy ◆ 1997
2. Beezy Magic ◆ 1998
3. Beezy at Bat ◆ 1998

BENJAMIN

Baker, Alan
LOTHROP, LEE & SHEPARD
GRADES K–1
ANIMAL FANTASY | HUMOR

Benjamin the hamster gets involved in many adventures. He experiments with art in *Benjamin's Portrait*. He goes aloft in *Benjamin's Balloon*. When he needs new glasses and does not read an important sign, he goes for a wild ride in *Benjamin Bounces Back*. In every book, Benjamin displays his intrepid spirit and energy.

1. Benjamin and the Box ◆ 1978
2. Benjamin Bounces Back ◆ 1978
3. Benjamin's Dreadful Dream ◆ 1980
4. Benjamin's Book ◆ 1983

5. Benjamin's Portrait ◆ 1987
6. Benjamin's Balloon ◆ 1990

BENJY

Van Leeuwen, Jean
DIAL
GRADES 3–4
REAL LIFE

Benjy is an average boy who experiences the typical ups and downs of childhood. He deals with them with a determination that endears him to readers. He works hard to get bigger so he can stand up to the class bully and play kickball better. He tries every kind of odd job to earn money for a baseball mitt. No matter what the situation, Benjy—with his friend Jason's help—rises to the occasion.

1. Benjy and the Power of Zingies ◆ 1982
2. Benjy in Business ◆ 1983
3. Benjy the Football Hero ◆ 1985

BENNY AND WATCH *see* Boxcar Children: Adventures of Benny and Watch

BERENSTAIN BEARS

Berenstain, Stan, and Jan Berenstain
RANDOM HOUSE
GRADES K–2
ANIMAL FANTASY | HUMOR

Papa and Mama Bear live with their children, Brother and Sister Bear, in a tree house in Bear Country. They have a happy family life and get along well together. Most of the books in the series teach a lesson in healthy, safe, and sensible living. In a story about eating well, the young bears and their father have been eating too much junk food. The mother tries to get them on a better diet and insists that they go to see the doctor. The doctor tells them all about their bodies and why a proper diet is important. Similar books discuss TV, talking to strangers, and peer pressure. There are different formats featuring the Berenstain Bears. There are lift-the-flap, activity, and sticker books for very young children. There are board books, workbooks, "Do-It" books, and mini-books for toddlers. The longer chapter books and Bear Scouts books are listed separately. Listed below are other groupings of these popular books.

BRIGHT AND EARLY BOOKS

Very few words; designed for beginning readers.   EP Ber

1. Inside Outside Upside Down ◆ 1968
2. Bears on Wheels ◆ 1969
3. The Bears' Christmas ◆ 1970
4. Old Hat, New Hat ◆ 1970
5. Bears in the Night ◆ 1971
6. The Berenstains' B Book ◆ 1971
7. He Bear, She Bear ◆ 1974
8. The Berenstain Bears and the Spooky Old Tree ◆ 1978
9. The Berenstain Bears on the Moon ◆ 1985
10. The Berenstains' C Book ◆ 1997

BEGINNER BOOKS

Few words; designed for beginning readers.   E Ber

1. The Big Honey Hunt ◆ 1962
2. The Bike Lesson ◆ 1964
3. The Bears' Picnic ◆ 1966
4. The Bear Scouts ◆ 1967
5. The Bears' Vacation ◆ 1968
6. The Bear Detectives ◆ 1975
7. The Berenstain Bears and the Missing Dinosaur Bones ◆ 1980

BERENSTAIN BEARS FIRST TIME BOOK

Longer story; picture book format.   EP Ber

1. The Berenstain Bears' New Baby ◆ 1974
2. The Berenstain Bears Go to School ◆ 1978
3. The Berenstain Bears and the Homework Hassle ◆ 1979
4. The Berenstain Bears and the Sitter ◆ 1981
5. The Berenstain Bears Go to the Doctor ◆ 1981
6. The Berenstain Bears' Moving Day ◆ 1981
7. The Berenstain Bears Visit the Dentist ◆ 1981
8. The Berenstain Bears Get in a Fight ◆ 1982
9. The Berenstain Bears Go to Camp ◆ 1982
10. The Berenstain Bears in the Dark ◆ 1982
11. The Berenstain Bears and the Messy Room ◆ 1983
12. The Berenstain Bears and the Truth ◆ 1983
13. The Berenstain Bears' Trouble with Money ◆ 1983
14. The Berenstain Bears and Mama's New Job ◆ 1984
15. The Berenstain Bears and Too Much TV ◆ 1984
16. The Berenstain Bears Meet Santa Bear ◆ 1984
17. The Berenstain Bears and Too Much Junk Food ◆ 1985
18. The Berenstain Bears Forget Their Manners ◆ 1985
19. The Berenstain Bears Learn about Strangers ◆ 1985
20. The Berenstain Bears and the Bad Habit ◆ 1986
21. The Berenstain Bears and the Trouble with Friends ◆ 1986

22. The Berenstain Bears and the Week at Grandma's ◆ 1986
23. The Berenstain Bears and Too Much Birthday ◆ 1986
24. The Berenstain Bears Get Stage Fright ◆ 1986
25. The Berenstain Bears Go Out for the Team ◆ 1986
26. The Berenstain Bears: No Girls Allowed ◆ 1986
27. The Berenstain Bears' Trouble at School ◆ 1986
28. The Berenstain Bears and the Bad Dream ◆ 1988
29. The Berenstain Bears and the Double Dare ◆ 1988
30. The Berenstain Bears Get the Gimmies ◆ 1988
31. The Berenstain Bears and the In-Crowd ◆ 1989
32. The Berenstain Bears and Too Much Vacation ◆ 1989
33. The Berenstain Bears Trick or Treat ◆ 1989
34. The Berenstain Bears and the Prize Pumpkin ◆ 1990
35. The Berenstain Bears and the Slumber Party ◆ 1990
36. The Berenstain Bears' Trouble with Pets ◆ 1990
37. The Berenstain Bears Don't Pollute (Anymore) ◆ 1991
38. The Berenstain Bears and the Trouble with Grownups ◆ 1992
39. The Berenstain Bears and Too Much Pressure ◆ 1992
40. The Berenstain Bears and the Bully ◆ 1993
41. The Berenstain Bears and the Green-Eyed Monster ◆ 1994
42. The Berenstain Bears' New Neighbors ◆ 1994
43. The Berenstain Bears and Too Much Teasing ◆ 1995
44. The Berenstain Bears Count Their Blessings ◆ 1995
45. The Berenstain Bears and the Blame Game ◆ 1997
46. The Berenstain Bears Get Their Kicks ◆ 1998
47. The Berenstain Bears Lend a Helping Hand ◆ 1998

BERENSTAIN BEARS FIRST TIME READERS

Similar to the picture books but a little easier for children to read.

1. The Berenstain Bears and the Big Road Race ◆ 1987
2. The Berenstain Bears and the Missing Honey ◆ 1987
3. The Berenstain Bears Blaze a Trail ◆ 1987
4. The Berenstain Bears on the Job ◆ 1987
5. The Day of the Dinosaur ◆ 1987
6. After the Dinosaurs ◆ 1988
7. The Berenstain Bears and the Ghost of the Forest ◆ 1988
8. The Berenstain Bears Ready, Get Set, Go! ◆ 1988

STEP INTO READING BOOKS

Simple text with different levels for beginning readers.

1. The Berenstain Bears' Big Bear, Small Bear ◆ 1998
2. The Berenstain Bears Ride the Thunderbolt ◆ 1998
3. The Berenstain Bears by the Sea ◆ 1998

BERENSTAIN BEARS: BEAR SCOUTS

Berenstain, Stan, and Jan Berenstain

LITTLE APPLE / SCHOLASTIC

GRADES 1–3

ANIMAL FANTASY | HUMOR

The Bear Scouts work as a team, but each has individual skills. Scout Lizzy has an affinity for animals; Scout Fred is smart; Scout Sister is high-spirited and full of energy; and Scout Brother is the sensible, thoughtful leader. As in the picture books and easy readers about the Bear family, Papa Q. Bear is a bit of a buffoon whose decisions often cause problems. In *The Berenstain Bear Scouts and the Humongous Pumpkin*, Papa is duped by Ralph Ripoff and Weasel McGreed, who also cause problems in other books in the series. Good triumphs, however, as the Bear Scouts outwit the smarmy bad guys. The slapstick humor in these somewhat predictable chapter books will meet the expectations of fans of the books for younger readers.

1. The Berenstain Bear Scouts and the Humongous Pumpkin ◆ 1995
2. The Berenstain Bear Scouts in Giant Bat Cave ◆ 1995
3. The Berenstain Bear Scouts Meet Bigpaw ◆ 1995
4. The Berenstain Bear Scouts and the Coughing Catfish ◆ 1996
5. The Berenstain Bear Scouts and the Sci-Fi Pizza ◆ 1996
6. The Berenstain Bear Scouts and the Terrible Talking Termite ◆ 1996
7. The Berenstain Bear Scouts Ghost Versus Ghost ◆ 1996
8. The Berenstain Bear Scouts Save That Backscratcher ◆ 1996
9. The Berenstain Bear Scouts and the Ice Monster ◆ 1997
10. The Berenstain Bear Scouts and the Magic Crystal Caper ◆ 1997
11. The Berenstain Bear Scouts and the Run-Amuck Robot ◆ 1997
12. The Berenstain Bear Scouts and the Sinister Smoke Ring ◆ 1997
13. The Berenstain Bear Scouts and the Missing Merit Badge ◆ 1998
14. The Berenstain Bear Scouts and the Really Big Disaster ◆ 1998
15. The Berenstain Bear Scouts and the Search for Naughty Ned ◆ 1998
16. The Berenstain Bear Scouts Scream Their Heads Off ◆ 1998

BERENSTAIN BEARS: BIG CHAPTER BOOKS

Berenstain, Stan, and Jan Berenstain

RANDOM HOUSE

GRADES 1–3

ANIMAL FANTASY | HUMOR

Ji Ber

These books feature the Bear County cubs in a variety of entertaining situations. Some of the stories take place at

Bear County School. For example, Queenie McBear gets a crush on the new art teacher, Mr. Smock, making Too-Tall Grizzly jealous. Other stories take place in locations in the area, such as a Halloween Festival at Farmer Ben's farm and a visit to the Freaky Funhouse. Brother and Sister often have ideas that involve their friends Queenie McBear, Barry Bruin, and Too-Tall Grizzly. Readers who loved the picture books about the Bears will want to read these Big Chapter books, which also connect with the Berenstain Bear Scouts series.

1. The Berenstain Bears and the Drug Free Zone ◆ 1993
2. The Berenstain Bears and the New Girl in Town ◆ 1993
3. The Berenstain Bears Gotta Dance! ◆ 1993
4. The Berenstain Bears and the Nerdy Nephew ◆ 1993
5. The Berenstain Bears Accept No Substitutes ◆ 1993
6. The Berenstain Bears and the Female Fullback ◆ 1994
7. The Berenstain Bears and the Red-Handed Thief ◆ 1994
8. The Berenstain Bears and the Wheelchair Commando ◆ 1994
9. The Berenstain Bears and the School Scandal Sheet ◆ 1994
10. The Berenstain Bears and the Galloping Ghost ◆ 1994
11. The Berenstain Bears at Camp Crush ◆ 1994
12. The Berenstain Bears and the Giddy Grandma ◆ 1994
13. The Berenstain Bears and the Dress Code ◆ 1995
14. The Berenstain Bears' Media Madness ◆ 1995
15. The Berenstain Bears in the Freaky Funhouse ◆ 1995
16. The Berenstain Bears and the Showdown at Chainsaw Gap ◆ 1995
17. The Berenstain Bears at the Teen Rock Café ◆ 1996
18. The Berenstain Bears in Maniac Mansion ◆ 1996
19. The Berenstain Bears and the Bermuda Triangle ◆ 1997
20. The Berenstain Bears and the Ghost of the Auto Graveyard ◆ 1997
21. The Berenstain Bears and the Haunted Hayride ◆ 1997
22. The Berenstain Bears and Queenie's Crazy Crush ◆ 1997
23. The Berenstain Bears and the Big Date ◆ 1998
24. The Berenstain Bears and the Love Match ◆ 1998
25. The Berenstain Bears and the Perfect Crime (Almost) ◆ 1998
26. The Berenstain Bears Go Platinum ◆ 1998

BERNARD

Freschet, Berniece
SCRIBNER'S
GRADES 2–4
ANIMAL FANTASY

Bernard lives with his mouse family at the top of Beacon Hill in Boston. He has traveled all the world and had wonderful adventures. Disturbed by the provincialism of his family, he sets out to see Switzerland and France, but instead he becomes a stowaway on a spaceship, sees the world, and makes it home for Christmas. At the invitation of his Aunt, he goes to London and helps his cousin Foster catch a thieving gang of moles. Back at home, he rescues a cat. Black-and-white drawings on every page highlight the aristocratic mouse's adventures.

1. Bernard Sees the World ◆ 1976
2. Bernard of Scotland Yard ◆ 1978
3. Bernard and the Catnip Caper ◆ 1981

BESSLEDORF HOTEL

Naylor, Phyllis Reynolds
SIMON & SCHUSTER

GRADES 5–7

FAMILY LIFE | MYSTERY

The Magruder family lives in an apartment at the Bessledorf Hotel. The father, Theodore, manages the hotel. Alma helps out, but she dreams of writing romance novels. Son Joseph goes to veterinary college, and daughter Delores works at a parachute factory. Bernie likes to solve mysteries, and the old hotel provides plenty of them. A ghost appears to Bernie in one book, and he must figure out what it wants so that it will rest in peace.

1. The Mad Gasser of Bessledorf Street ◆ 1983
2. The Bodies in the Bessledorf Hotel ◆ 1986
3. Bernie and the Bessledorf Ghost ◆ 1990
4. The Face in the Bessledorf Funeral Parlor ◆ 1993
5. The Bomb in the Bessledorf Bus Depot ◆ 1996
6. The Treasure of Bessledorf Hill ◆ 1997

BEST ENEMIES

Leverich, Kathleen
GREENWILLOW

GRADES 2–3

HUMOR | REAL LIFE

With an easily read format of four short chapters in each title, this series focuses on school rivalry. In *Best Enemies*, Priscilla Robin begins primary school with all new classmates. Her hope to make friends fades when she meets Felicity Doll, described by her sister Eve as "a snake." Felicity is a bully and braggart whose obnoxious tricks make Priscilla's life miserable. Patient and long-suffering, Priscilla finally uses her wits to outsmart her archenemy and continues to successfully turn the tables in each new title. The behavior of the main characters might provide worthwhile discussions for teachers and parents.

1. Best Enemies ◆ 1989
2. Best Enemies Again ◆ 1991
3. Best Enemies Forever ◆ 1995

BEST FRIENDS

Smith, Susan

POCKET BOOKS

GRADES 4–7

REAL LIFE

Sonya moves back to California after living with her father in New York for two years. She renews her friendship with Terri, Angela, and Dawn, her best friends from fourth grade. Celia, a pretty and popular girl, takes an interest in her, and Sonya starts seeing faults in her old friends. Sonya decides to stick with them, though, after Celia asks her to cheat on a test. The rest of the series sees the friends through their middle school years. Celia remains the "enemy," and she and her friends are a rival crowd. A fifth girl, Linda, becomes one of the Best Friends. There are boyfriends and school activities as the girls pursue their various interests.

1. Sonya Begonia and the Eleventh Birthday Blues ◆ 1988
2. Angela and the King-Size Crusade ◆ 1988
3. Dawn Selby, Super Sleuth ◆ 1988
4. Terri the Great ◆ 1989
5. Sonya and the Chain Letter Gang ◆ 1989
6. Angela and the Greatest Guy in the World ◆ 1989
7. One Hundred Thousand Dollar Dawn ◆ 1990
8. The Terrible Terri Rumors ◆ 1990
9. Linda and the Little White Lies ◆ 1990
10. Sonya and the Haunting of Room 16A ◆ 1990
11. Angela and the Great Book Battle ◆ 1990
12. Dynamite Dawn vs. Terrific Terri ◆ 1991
13. Who's Out to Get Linda ◆ 1991
14. Terri and the Shopping Mall Disaster ◆ 1991
15. The Sonya and Howard Wars ◆ 1991
16. Angela and the Accidental-on-Purpose Romance ◆ 1991

BEST FRIENDS

Stahl, Hilda
CROSSWAY BOOKS
GRADES 4–6
REAL LIFE | VALUES

Ji Sta

Four middle school girls live in a comfortable suburb and have formed the "Best Friends" club. They meet regularly to study the Bible and pray together. They encourage each other and work through problems together. Hannah is Native American, and the problem of racism is addressed in several books. The girls have problems with boys and families that are resolved using scriptural guidelines.

 1. Chelsea and the Outrageous Phone Bill ◆ 1992
 2. Big Trouble for Roxie ◆ 1992
 3. Kathy and the Babysitting Hassle ◆ 1992
 4. Hannah and the Special Fourth of July ◆ 1992
 5. Roxie and Red Rose Mystery ◆ 1992
 6. Kathy's New Brother ◆ 1992
 7. A Made-Over Chelsea ◆ 1992
 8. No Friends for Hannah ◆ 1992
 9. Tough Choices for Roxie ◆ 1993
10. Chelsea's Special Touch ◆ 1993
11. Mystery at Bellwood Estate ◆ 1993
12. Hannah and the Daring Escape ◆ 1993
13. Hannah and the Snowy Hideaway ◆ 1993
14. Chelsea and the Alien Invasion ◆ 1993
15. Roxie's Mall Madness ◆ 1993
16. The Secret Tunnel Mystery ◆ 1994

BETSY

Haywood, Carolyn
MORROW
GRADES 1–3
FAMILY LIFE | HUMOR

Betsy lives with her mother and father and little sister Star in the United States of the 1950s. The series centers around

Betsy and her neighborhood friends as they play in the summerhouse that Betsy's father builds for them, find stray cats that they want to keep, and put on shows for the neighbors, sometimes with funny results. In the winter-time, Father turns the basement into a "winterhouse" for the children. When they build a dollhouse by themselves, they forget to add a door and Billy is trapped inside. Occasional black-and-white drawings decorate the series.

1. B Is for Betsy ◆ 1939
2. Betsy and Billy ◆ 1941
3. Back to School with Betsy ◆ 1943
4. Betsy and the Boys ◆ 1945
5. Betsy's Little Star ◆ 1950
6. Betsy and the Circus ◆ 1954
7. Betsy's Busy Summer ◆ 1956
8. Betsy's Winterhouse ◆ 1958
9. Snowbound with Betsy ◆ 1962
10. Betsy and Mr. Kilpatrick ◆ 1967
11. Merry Christmas from Betsy ◆ 1970
12. Betsy's Play School ◆ 1977

BETSY-TACY

Lovelace, Maud Hart
HARPERCOLLINS
GRADES 2–5
HISTORICAL | REAL LIFE

Little Betsy lives with her family in a pleasant house in a Minnesota town in the early part of the century. She is the only girl on her street, so she is glad when a new family moves in with a daughter, Tacy. Betsy and Tacy become such good friends that people refer to them in the same breath as Betsy-Tacy. Tib, a blond-haired girl from a German family, comes along in the second book, and from then on the three girls are inseparable. They grow up together, go to high school, are part of a good "crowd," decide about careers, have beaus, and eventually get married. Lois Lenski's illustrations and the girls' adventures give a good sense of the flavor of the times.

1. Betsy-Tacy ◆ 1940
2. Betsy-Tacy and Tib ◆ 1941
3. Betsy and Tacy Go Over the Big Hill ◆ 1942
4. Betsy and Tacy Go Down Town ◆ 1943
5. Heaven to Betsy ◆ 1945
6. Betsy in Spite of Herself ◆ 1946
7. Betsy Was a Junior ◆ 1947
8. Betsy and Joe ◆ 1948

9. Betsy and the Great World ◆ 1952
10. Betsy's Wedding ◆ 1955

BEWARE

Haas, Jessie

GREENWILLOW

GRADES 3–5

REAL LIFE

Lily has outgrown her pony, and her grandfather, a livestock dealer, buys her a mare named Beware. Despite Beware's ominous name, Lily discovers that she just likes to have her belly scratched, and she will bump up against her owners when she wants them to do it. In the second book of this series, Lily competes on Beware against her best friend, Mandy. They both win some ribbons and stay friends, even though they are rivals. In another book, Beware becomes sick and Lily, her Mom, and Gramp try to save her. Even Gran, who doesn't like horses, is concerned.

1. Beware the Mare ◆ 1993
2. A Blue for Beware ◆ 1995
3. Be Well, Beware ◆ 1996
4. Beware and Stogie ◆ 1998

BILL AND PETE

dePaola, Tomie

PUTNAM

GRADES K–2

ANIMAL FANTASY

Bill is a crocodile whose full name is William Everett Crocodile. Pete is his toothbrush bird and buddy. In these picture books, the two friends have adventures around the world. Along the way, they outwit the Bad Guy from Cairo and his Big Bad Brother and rescue little Jane Alison Crocodile. The colorful illustrations show dePaola's skill at creating humorous personalities.

1. Bill and Pete ◆ 1978
2. Bill and Pete Go Down the Nile ◆ 1987
3. Bill and Pete to the Rescue ◆ 1998

BILLY AND BLAZE *see* Blaze

BINGO BROWN

Byars, Betsy
VIKING
GRADES 4–7
HUMOR | REAL LIFE

Bingo Brown is in sixth grade at the beginning of this series and is just discovering "mixed-sex conversations." He falls in and out of love many times but ends up being in love with Melissa. He is devastated when she moves to Oklahoma. That summer, he racks up a huge phone bill calling her and is pursued by her best friend. His parents go through a crisis of their own when his mother discovers she is pregnant. As Bingo enters seventh grade, he has a new baby brother, and is an acknowledged authority on romance among his friends.

1. The Burning Questions of Bingo Brown ◆ 1988
2. Bingo Brown and the Language of Love ◆ 1989
3. Bingo Brown, Gypsy Lover ◆ 1990
4. Bingo Brown's Guide to Romance ◆ 1992

BISCUIT

Capucilli, Alyssa Satin
HARPERCOLLINS
GRADES K–1
REAL LIFE

E Cap

This series is just right for beginning readers. The words are simple and the print is large enough for young children who are just learning to focus on the text and decode it. Young readers will be delighted by the antics of Biscuit the puppy—avoiding his bedtime, finding a duckling, and going on a picnic. Watch for more books about this delightful puppy.

1. Biscuit ◆ 1996
2. Biscuit Finds a Friend ◆ 1997
3. Biscuit's Picnic ◆ 1998
4. Hello, Biscuit! ◆ 1998
5. Bathtime for Biscuit ◆ 1998

BIZZY BONES

Martin, Jacqueline Briggs

LOTHROP, LEE & SHEPARD

GRADES K–2

ANIMAL FANTASY | FAMILY LIFE

Two mice, Bizzy Bones and Uncle Ezra, live together in an old shoe house near the edge of Piney Woods. Uncle Ezra tries very hard to remember how it was to be a very young mouse and reacts with kindness to all of young Bizzy's fears. Fierce winds, losing a beloved blanket, and staying with Uncle's friend, Mouse Mouse, are plots explored in this series. The softly detailed illustrations add to the gentle charm and depict Bizzy's fears and Uncle Ezra's wisdom.

1. Bizzy Bones and Uncle Ezra ◆ 1984
2. Bizzy Bones and Mouse Mouse ◆ 1986
3. Bizzy Bones and the Lost Quilt ◆ 1988

BLACK CAT CLUB

Saunders, Susan

HARPERCOLLINS

GRADES 2–4

HUMOR

In Maplewood, things are pretty quiet—that is, until Robert, Belinda, Andrew, and Sam decide to form the Black Cat Club and investigate supernatural events. They end up adding a new member to their club—Alice, who is a ghost! These mild horror books are more humorous than frightening. For example, when the friends want to change the food in the cafeteria, they find that the new food is even worse—eyeballs and worms! Another book takes place in a haunted movie theater. Still another involves a creepy camping trip. Ghosts, phantoms, mummies, and other creatures add to the appeal of this series.

1. The Ghost Who Ate Chocolate ◆ 1996
2. The Haunted Skateboard ◆ 1996
3. The Curse of the Cat Mummy ◆ 1997
4. The Ghost of Spirit Lake ◆ 1997

5. The Revenge of the Pirate Ghost ◆ 1997
6. The Phantom Pen Pal ◆ 1997
7. The Case of the Eyeball Surprise ◆ 1997
8. The Chilling Tale of Crescent Pond ◆ 1998
9. The Creature Double Feature ◆ 1998
10. The Creepy Camp-Out ◆ 1998

BLACK LAGOON

Thaler, Mike

SCHOLASTIC

GRADES K–3

HUMOR

EP Tha

A small boy relates the horrific stories he has heard about school, the teachers, the principal, and other school officials. The stories are all illustrated with cartoonlike exaggeration on each page. Teachers are portrayed as monsters of one sort or another, and the children are cut in half, put in freezers, or reduced to piles of ashes. On the last few pages, the boy meets the real adults, who turn out to be kind and helpful. For instance, the school nurse cures the blue spots on his hand by wiping off the ink, and his teacher is young, pretty, and loving.

1. The Teacher from the Black Lagoon ◆ 1989
2. The Principal from the Black Lagoon ◆ 1993
3. The Gym Teacher from the Black Lagoon ◆ 1994
4. The School Nurse from the Black Lagoon ◆ 1995
5. The Librarian from the Black Lagoon ◆ 1997
6. The Cafeteria Lady from the Black Lagoon ◆ 1998

BLACK STALLION

Farley, Walter, and Steven Farley

RANDOM HOUSE

GRADES 4–6

ADVENTURE

On his way home from visiting his missionary uncle, Alec Ramsey is shipwrecked along with a wild black stallion. They are rescued, and Alec takes the horse back to New York where he boards the horse at a nearby farm to be trained by Henry Dailey. Because there are no official papers on "the

Black," Alec cannot enter him in races. However, in a special race for the fastest horse in the country, Alec and "the Black" earn the respect they deserve. In another book, Alec travels to Arabia to research the claim of a man who is trying to take away his horse. The series continues as the stallion sires foals that Alec and Henry train and race. Walter Farley wrote the early books in the series. Walter and Steven Farley wrote The Young Black Stallion, and Steven Farley is continuing the series. The Island Stallion series features another young man and a horse.

1. The Black Stallion ◆ 1941
2. The Black Stallion Returns ◆ 1945
3. Son of the Black Stallion ◆ 1947
4. The Black Stallion and Satan ◆ 1949
5. The Blood Bay Colt ◆ 1950
6. The Black Stallion's Filly ◆ 1952
7. The Black Stallion Revolts ◆ 1953
8. The Black Stallion's Sulky Colt ◆ 1954
9. The Black Stallion's Courage ◆ 1956
10. The Black Stallion Mystery ◆ 1957
11. The Black Stallion and Flame ◆ 1960
12. The Black Stallion Challenged ◆ 1964
13. The Black Stallion's Ghost ◆ 1969
14. The Black Stallion and the Girl ◆ 1971
15. The Black Stallion Legend ◆ 1983
16. The Young Black Stallion ◆ 1989
17. The Black Stallion's Shadow ◆ 1996

BLACKBOARD BEAR

Alexander, Martha
DIAL
GRADES K–1
ANIMAL FANTASY

"Take your bear and go home," the older boys tell the small hero, and so he does. Then he decides to toss the bear out the window and draw a better one on the blackboard. This bear is huge and wears a red collar. He comes to life, and the two have many adventures.

1. Blackboard Bear ◆ 1969
2. And My Mean Old Mother Will Be Sorry, Blackboard Bear ◆ 1972
3. I Sure Am Glad to See You, Blackboard Bear ◆ 1976
4. We're in Big Trouble, Blackboard Bear ◆ 1980
5. You're a Genius, Blackboard Bear ◆ 1995

BLAZE

Anderson, C.W.   *E And*

SIMON & SCHUSTER

GRADES K–2

REAL LIFE

Billy loves horses. For his birthday, Billy's parents give him a pony that he names Blaze. Billy takes very good care of Blaze, while learning to ride him and to jump. When they enter a horse show, they win the silver cup, jumping over all the fences without a fault. Even Billy's dog, Rex, jumps with them. Each book features a new adventure: Billy and Blaze dramatically ride across fields, streams, and fences to warn about a brush fire and they rescue a lost calf from a mountain lion, for example.

1. Billy and Blaze: A Boy and His Pony ◆ 1936
2. Blaze and the Gypsies ◆ 1937
3. Blaze and the Forest Fire ◆ 1938
4. Blaze Finds the Trail ◆ 1950
5. Blaze and Thunderbolt ◆ 1955
6. Blaze and the Mountain Lion ◆ 1959
7. Blaze and the Indian Cave ◆ 1964
8. Blaze and the Lost Quarry ◆ 1966
9. Blaze and the Gray Spotted Pony ◆ 1968
10. Blaze Shows the Way ◆ 1969
11. Blaze Finds Forgotten Roads ◆ 1970

BLOSSOM CULP

Peck, Richard

DELL

GRADES 5–7

FANTASY | MYSTERY

Blossom Culp lives on the wrong side of the tracks in a small Midwestern town at the turn of the century. Her mother is a fortune teller, who is jealous when it seems that Blossom has "the gift." Alexander, the son of a wealthy and prominent family, lives right across the tracks and his barn is right in Blossom's back yard. The barn is inhabited by a ghost that Blossom can see. Alexander is reluctantly drawn into this adventure, only the first of many inspired by Blossom's gift. Blossom's contacts with the dead bring her fame and a certain social standing in the town. She moves into her high school years, she has more encounters with the beyond, including an Egyptian princess and time travel 70 years into the future.

1. The Ghost Belonged to Me ◆ 1975
2. Ghosts I Have Been ◆ 1977
3. The Dreadful Future of Blossom Culp ◆ 1983
4. Blossom Culp and the Sleep of Death ◆ 1986

THE BLOSSOM FAMILY

Byars, Betsy

DELL

GRADES 4–7

FAMILY LIFE | HUMOR

Maggie, Junior, and Vern Blossom live with their mother, Vicki, and their grandfather, Pap. Their father, Cotton, was killed riding a bull in the rodeo when the children were small. Vicki is a trick rider and goes out on the rodeo circuit, leaving the children behind with Pap in a rural section of the eastern United States. They make friends with a lady who lives a hermit's life in a cave. One of the boys almost drowns making a raft to float on the river. Two of the children break into prison when Pap is arrested, and Maggie makes her debut in trick riding. In each book, the stories of each family member intersect.

1. The Not-Just-Anybody Family ◆ 1986
2. The Blossoms Meet the Vulture Lady ◆ 1986
3. The Blossoms and the Green Phantom ◆ 1987
4. A Blossom Promise ◆ 1987
5. Wanted—Mud Blossom ◆ 1991

BLUE MOOSE

Pinkwater, Daniel Manus

LITTLE, BROWN

GRADES 2–3

ANIMAL FANTASY | HUMOR

During a very cold winter, Mr. Breton, who owns a restaurant at the edge of the woods, encounters an unusual animal—a very large blue moose that talks! While waiting for the spring thaw, the moose moves in to become the headwaiter and a friendship develops. Silly episodes are featured in each title, including one with a report of a vampire moose.

1. Blue Moose ◆ 1975
2. Return of the Moose ◆ 1979
3. The Moosepire ◆ 1986

BOBBSEY TWINS

Hope, Laura Lee

PUTNAM

GRADES 3–5

FAMILY LIFE

Stratemeyer's first series, the Bobbsey Twins, was first published in 1904. The books feature two sets of twins. Flossie and Freddie Bobbsey, the younger twins, are blond, blue-eyed four-year-olds. Then there are the eight-year-old twins, Nan and Bert, who are dark-haired, dark-eyed, and responsible. The twins' father owns a lumber company, and Mrs. Bobbsey is a housewife, involved in social and charitable activities. The Bobbseys are always doing exciting things, such as acquiring an actual miniature railroad. By the 1960s the Bobbseys had aged slightly—Nan and Bert are 12 and Flossie and Freddie are 6—and they have become amateur detectives. Continuing to keep up with the times, by the 1980s the twins occasionally play in a rock band.

1. Bobbsey Twins ◆ 1904
2. Bobbsey Twins in the Country ◆ 1904
3. Bobbsey Twins at the Seashore ◆ 1907
4. Bobbsey Twins at School ◆ 1913
5. Bobbsey Twins at Snow Lodge ◆ 1913
6. Bobbsey Twins on a Houseboat ◆ 1915
7. Bobbsey Twins at Meadow Brook ◆ 1915
8. Bobbsey Twins at Home ◆ 1916
9. Bobbsey Twins in a Great City ◆ 1917
10. Bobbsey Twins on Blueberry Island ◆ 1917
11. Bobbsey Twins on the Deep Blue Sea ◆ 1918
12. Bobbsey Twins in Washington ◆ 1919
13. Bobbsey Twins in the Great West ◆ 1920
14. Bobbsey Twins at Cedar Camp ◆ 1921
15. Bobbsey Twins at the Country Fair ◆ 1922
16. Bobbsey Twins Camping Out ◆ 1923
17. Bobbsey Twins and Baby May ◆ 1924
18. Bobbsey Twins Keeping House ◆ 1925
19. Bobbsey Twins at Cloverbank ◆ 1926
20. Bobbsey Twins at Cherry Corners ◆ 1927
21. Bobbsey Twins and Their Schoolmates ◆ 1928
22. Bobbsey Twins Treasure Hunting ◆ 1929
23. Bobbsey Twins at Spruce Lake ◆ 1930
24. Bobbsey Twins' Wonderful Secret ◆ 1931
25. Bobbsey Twins at the Circus ◆ 1932
26. Bobbsey Twins on an Airplane Trip ◆ 1933
27. Bobbsey Twins Solve a Mystery ◆ 1934
28. Bobbsey Twins on a Ranch ◆ 1935

29. Bobbsey Twins in Eskimo Land ◆ 1936
30. Bobbsey Twins in a Radio Play ◆ 1937
31. Bobbsey Twins at Windmill Cottage ◆ 1938
32. Bobbsey Twins at Lighthouse Point ◆ 1939
33. Bobbsey Twins at Indian Hollow ◆ 1940
34. Bobbsey Twins at the Ice Carnival ◆ 1941
35. Bobbsey Twins in the Land of Cotton ◆ 1942
36. Bobbsey Twins in Echo Valley ◆ 1943
37. Bobbsey Twins on the Pony Trail ◆ 1944
38. Bobbsey Twins at Mystery Mansion ◆ 1945
39. Bobbsey Twins at Sugar Maple Hill ◆ 1946
40. Bobbsey Twins in Mexico ◆ 1947
41. Bobbsey Twins' Toy Shop ◆ 1948
42. Bobbsey Twins in Tulip Land ◆ 1949
43. Bobbsey Twins in Rainbow Valley ◆ 1950
44. Bobbsey Twins' Own Little Railroad ◆ 1951
45. Bobbsey Twins at Whitesail Harbor ◆ 1952
46. Bobbsey Twins and the Horseshoe Riddle ◆ 1953
47. Bobbsey Twins at Big Bear Pond ◆ 1954
48. Bobbsey Twins on a Bicycle Trip ◆ 1955
49. Bobbsey Twins' Own Little Ferryboat ◆ 1956
50. Bobbsey Twins at Pilgrim Rock ◆ 1957
51. Bobbsey Twins' Forest Adventure ◆ 1958
52. Bobbsey Twins at London Tower ◆ 1959
53. Bobbsey Twins in the Mystery Cave ◆ 1960
54. Bobbsey Twins in Volcano Land ◆ 1961
55. Bobbsey Twins and the Goldfish Mystery ◆ 1962
56. Bobbsey Twins and the Big River Mystery ◆ 1963
57. Bobbsey Twins and the Greek Hat Mystery ◆ 1963
58. Bobbsey Twins' Search for the Green Rooster ◆ 1965
59. Bobbsey Twins and Their Camel Adventure ◆ 1966
60. Bobbsey Twins and the Mystery of the King's Puppet ◆ 1967
61. Bobbsey Twins and the Secret of Candy Castle ◆ 1968
62. Bobbsey Twins and the Doodlebug Mystery ◆ 1969
63. Bobbsey Twins and the Talking Fox Mystery ◆ 1970
64. Bobbsey Twins and the Blue Mystery ◆ 1971
65. Bobbsey Twins and Doctor Funnybone's Secret ◆ 1972
66. Bobbsey Twins and the Tagalong Giraffe ◆ 1973
67. Bobbsey Twins and the Flying Clown ◆ 1974
68. Bobbsey Twins and the Sun-Moon Cruise ◆ 1975
69. Bobbsey Twins and the Freedom Bell Mystery ◆ 1976
70. Bobbsey Twins and the Smoky Mountain Mystery ◆ 1977
71. Bobbsey Twins in a TV Mystery Show ◆ 1978
72. Bobbsey Twins and the Coral Turtle Mystery ◆ 1979
73. Bobbsey Twins and the Blue Poodle Mystery ◆ 1980
74. Bobbsey Twins and the Secret in the Pirate's Cave ◆ 1980
75. Bobbsey Twins and the Dune Buggy Mystery ◆ 1980
76. Bobbsey Twins and the Missing Pony Mystery ◆ 1981

77. Bobbsey Twins and the Rose Parade Mystery ◆ 1981
78. Bobbsey Twins and the Camp Fire Mystery ◆ 1981
79. Bobbsey Twins and Double Trouble ◆ 1982
80. Bobbsey Twins and the Mystery of the Laughing Dinosaur ◆ 1983
81. Bobbsey Twins and the Music Box Mystery ◆ 1983
82. Bobbsey Twins and the Ghost in the Computer ◆ 1984
83. Bobbsey Twins and the Scarecrow Mystery ◆ 1984
84. Bobbsey Twins and the Haunted House Mystery ◆ 1985
85. Bobbsey Twins and the Mystery of the Hindu Temple ◆ 1985
86. Bobbsey Twins and the Grinning Gargoyle Mystery ◆ 1986

BOBBSEY TWINS: THE NEW BOBBSEY TWINS

Hope, Laura Lee
POCKET BOOKS
GRADES 3–5
FAMILY LIFE | MYSTERY

Nan and Bert, the older twins, and Freddie and Flossie, the younger twins, continue sleuthing in the New Bobbsey Twins series. This intuitive foursome solves big and small mysteries, from burglaries in their town to missing documents. The Bobbseys sometimes make mistakes when several people seem suspicious. However, by cooperating with each other and using thinking skills, these siblings always discover the culprit.

1. The Secret of Jungle Park ◆ 1987
2. The Case of the Runaway Money ◆ 1987
3. The Clue that Flew Away ◆ 1987
4. The Secret of the Sand Castle ◆ 1988
5. The Case of the Close Encounter ◆ 1988
6. Mystery on the Mississippi ◆ 1988
7. Trouble in Toyland ◆ 1988
8. The Secret of the Stolen Puppies ◆ 1988
9. The Clue in the Classroom ◆ 1988
10. The Chocolate-Covered Clue ◆ 1989
11. The Case of the Crooked Contest ◆ 1989
12. The Secret of the Sunken Treasure ◆ 1989
13. The Case of the Crying Clown ◆ 1989
14. The Mystery of the Missing Mummy ◆ 1989
15. Secret of the Stolen Clue ◆ 1989
16. The Case of the Missing Dinosaur ◆ 1990
17. The Case at Creepy Castle ◆ 1990
18. The Secret at Sleepaway Camp ◆ 1990
19. Show and Tell Mystery ◆ 1990
20. The Weird Science Mystery ◆ 1990

21. The Great Skate Mystery ◆ 1990
22. The Super-Duper Cookie Caper ◆ 1991
23. The Monster Mouse Mystery ◆ 1991
24. The Case of the Goofy Game Show ◆ 1991
25. The Case of the Crazy Collections ◆ 1991
26. The Clue at Casper Creek ◆ 1991
27. The Big Pig Puzzle ◆ 1991
28. The Case of the Vanishing Video ◆ 1992
29. The Case of the Tricky Trickster ◆ 1992
30. Mystery of the Mixed-Up Mail ◆ 1992

BONE CHILLERS

TIKI DOLL OF DOOM

Haynes, Betsy

HARPERCOLLINS

GRADES 5–8

HORROR | HUMOR

The covers of these books make statements like "Bone Chillers: They'll make your skin crawl!" and "Bone Chillers: They'll scare the words right out of your mouth!" With spooky situations and creepy creatures, this series is similar to others in the horror genre. The books feature different characters, like Azie Appleton, who always tells lies, until one day her claim about giant termites comes true. Another book features Isabella Richmond, who thinks that gargoyles are kidnapping neighborhood kids. Some books are not just spooky but gross. In one, Jeremy Wilson sneezes and his mucus becomes a slimy green glob. Readers who want horror and humor will devour this series.

1. Beware the Shopping Mall! ◆ 1994
2. Little Pet Shop of Horrors ◆ 1994
3. Back to School ◆ 1994
4. Frankenturkey ◆ 1994
5. Strange Brew ◆ 1995
6. Teacher Creature ◆ 1995
7. Frankenturkey I ◆ 1995
8. Welcome to Alien Inn ◆ 1995
9. Attack of the Killer Ants ◆ 1996
10. Slime Time ◆ 1996
11. Toilet Terror ◆ 1996
12. Night of the Living Clay ◆ 1996
13. The Thing Under the Bed ◆ 1997
14. A Terminal Case of the Uglies ◆ 1997
15. Tiki Doll of Doom ◆ 1997
16. The Queen of the Gargoyles ◆ 1997
17. Why I Quit the Baby-Sitter's Club ◆ 1997

18. blowtorch@psycho.com ◆ 1997
19. The Night Squawker ◆ 1997
20. Scare Bear ◆ 1997
21. The Dog Ate My Homework ◆ 1997
22. Killer Clown of Kings County ◆ 1998
23. Romeo and Ghouliette ◆ 1998

BONNETS AND BUGLES

Morris, Gilbert

MOODY PRESS

GRADES 5–7

HISTORICAL

The Civil War splits neighbors and friends and provides opportunities for spiritual growth for five young people and their families. Tom and Jeff and their parents decide to move to Virginia and fight for the Confederacy, leaving Leah and Sarah and their parents in Kentucky as Union sympathizers. Mrs. Majors dies giving birth to Esther, and, with all the men off to war, there is no one to care for the baby. They turn to the Carters, who take her in to raise as their own. Throughout the course of the war, Jeff is a drummer boy and the other two boys are soldiers seeing action in major battles. They manage to get back to the girls often as Jeff courts Leah and Tom and Sarah become engaged. Tom loses his leg in Gettysburg and comes close to losing his faith in God, but the others help him back to spiritual health.

1. Drummer Boy at Bull Run ◆ 1995
2. Yankee Belles in Dixie ◆ 1995
3. The Secret of Richmond Manor ◆ 1995
4. The Soldier Boy's Discovery ◆ 1996
5. Blockade Runner ◆ 1996
6. The Gallant Boys of Gettysburg ◆ 1996
7. The Battle of Lookout Mountain ◆ 1996
8. Encounter at Cold Harbor ◆ 1997
9. Fire over Atlanta ◆ 1997
10. Bring the Boys Home ◆ 1997

THE BORROWERS

Norton, Mary

HARCOURT

GRADES 3–7

FANTASY

Under the floor of an old house, the little Borrowers live by borrowing from the family. They are the reason, Kate realizes, why there is never a needle when you need one. Pod, Homily, and their daughter, little Arrietty, live a quiet life by themselves, but once there had been many other Borrowers in the old house. Arrietty is "seen" by a boy who comes to live in the house, and he tells her that her family may be the last Borrowers left. He begins to bring them things from a doll-house, and that leads to the little family being discovered by the adults and harassed out of the house. As the series continues, the Borrowers find a little creature named Spiller who helps them find their relatives, who are living in a cottage. They stay with them until the cottage is sold. The rest of the series is about their attempts to find a new place to live as they travel by raft and hot-air balloon.

1. The Borrowers ◆ 1952
2. The Borrowers Afield ◆ 1955
3. The Borrowers Afloat ◆ 1959
4. The Borrowers Aloft ◆ 1961
5. Poor Stainless ◆ 1966
6. The Borrowers Avenged ◆ 1982

BOXCAR CHILDREN

Warner, Gertrude Chandler
WHITMAN
GRADES 2–5
FAMILY LIFE | MYSTERY

Ji War

Four children run away because their parents have died and they are being sent to their grandfather, who they think doesn't like them. They find an abandoned boxcar in the woods and fix it up to live in. Henry, the oldest, goes into a nearby town to find work; and Jessie, the oldest girl, tries to keep house with help from Violet and little Benny. When Violet becomes ill, Henry and Jessie seek help from the elderly gentleman for whom Henry has been working. The gentleman turns out to be their grandfather. In the rest of the series, the children live happily with their wealthy grandfather and get involved in a number of mysteries. The special books include pages with games and activities.

1. The Boxcar Children ◆ 1924
2. Surprise Island ◆ 1949
3. The Yellow House Mystery ◆ 1953
4. Mystery Ranch ◆ 1958
5. Mike's Mystery ◆ 1960
6. Blue Bay Mystery ◆ 1961
7. The Woodshed Mystery ◆ 1962
8. The Lighthouse Mystery ◆ 1963
9. Mountain Top Mystery ◆ 1964
10. Schoolhouse Mystery ◆ 1965
11. Caboose Mystery ◆ 1966
12. Houseboat Mystery ◆ 1967

13. Snowbound Mystery ◆ 1968
14. Tree House Mystery ◆ 1969
15. Bicycle Mystery ◆ 1970
16. Mystery in the Sand ◆ 1971
17. Mystery Behind the Wall ◆ 1973
18. The Bus Station Mystery ◆ 1974
19. Benny Uncovers a Mystery ◆ 1976
20. The Haunted Cabin Mystery ◆ 1991
21. The Deserted Library Mystery ◆ 1991
22. The Animal Shelter Mystery ◆ 1991
23. The Old Motel Mystery ◆ 1991
24. The Mystery of the Hidden Painting ◆ 1992
25. The Amusement Park Mystery ◆ 1992
26. The Mystery of the Mixed-Up Zoo ◆ 1992
27. The Camp-Out Mystery ◆ 1992
28. The Mystery Girl ◆ 1992
29. The Mystery Cruise ◆ 1992
30. The Disappearing Friend Mystery ◆ 1992
31. The Mystery of the Singing Ghost ◆ 1992
32. The Mystery in the Snow ◆ 1992
33. The Pizza Mystery ◆ 1993
34. The Mystery Horse ◆ 1993
35. The Mystery at the Dog Pound ◆ 1993
36. The Castle Mystery ◆ 1993
37. The Mystery of the Lost Village ◆ 1993
38. The Mystery of the Purple Pool ◆ 1994
39. The Ghost Ship Mystery ◆ 1994
40. The Canoe Trip Mystery ◆ 1994
41. The Mystery of the Hidden Beach ◆ 1994
42. The Mystery of the Missing Cat ◆ 1994
43. The Mystery on Stage ◆ 1994
44. The Dinosaur Mystery ◆ 1995
45. The Mystery of the Stolen Music ◆ 1995
46. The Chocolate Sundae Mystery ◆ 1995
47. The Mystery of the Hot Air Balloon ◆ 1995
48. The Mystery Bookstore ◆ 1995
49. The Mystery of the Stolen Boxcar ◆ 1995
50. The Mystery in the Cave ◆ 1996
51. The Mystery on the Train ◆ 1996
52. The Mystery of the Lost Mine ◆ 1996
53. The Guide Dog Mystery ◆ 1996
54. The Hurricane Mystery ◆ 1996
55. The Mystery of the Secret Message ◆ 1996
56. The Firehouse Mystery ◆ 1997
57. The Mystery in San Francisco ◆ 1997
58. The Mystery at the Alamo ◆ 1997

59. The Outer Space Mystery ◆ 1998
60. The Soccer Mystery ◆ 1998
61. The Growling Bear Mystery ◆ 1997
62. The Mystery of the Lake Monster ◆ 1997
63. The Mystery at Peacock Hall ◆ 1998
64. The Black Pearl Mystery ◆ 1998
65. The Cereal Box Mystery ◆ 1998
66. The Panther Mystery ◆ 1998
67. The Mystery of the Stolen Sword ◆ 1998
68. The Basketball Mystery ◆ 1999

BOXCAR CHILDREN SPECIALS

1. The Mystery on the Ice ◆ 1994
2. The Mystery in Washington, D.C. ◆ 1994
3. The Mystery at Snowflake Inn ◆ 1995
4. The Mystery at the Ballpark ◆ 1995
5. The Pilgrim Village Mystery ◆ 1995
6. The Mystery at the Fair ◆ 1996
7. The Pet Shop Mystery ◆ 1996
8. The Niagara Falls Mystery ◆ 1997
9. The Mystery in the Old Attic ◆ 1997
10. The Windy City Mystery ◆ 1998
11. The Mystery of the Queen's Jewels ◆ 1998

BOXCAR CHILDREN: ADVENTURES OF BENNY AND WATCH

Warner, Gertrude Chandler
WHITMAN
GRADES 1–3
FAMILY LIFE

The Boxcar Children books by Gertude Chandler Warner have been popular for many years. This new series, based on the books she created, is designed for younger readers. The text is not as long as in the original mysteries and there are more illustrations to provide support for beginning readers. Benny Alden, the youngest of the Boxcar Children, is featured in these books, which include stories of family, friendship, and simple mysteries. Watch, the family dog, also plays a prominent role in these stories.

1. Meet the Boxcar Children ◆ 1998
2. A Present for Grandfather ◆ 1998
3. Benny's New Friend ◆ 1998
4. The Magic Show Mystery ◆ 1998
5. Benny Goes Into Business ◆ 1999

BRAMBLY HEDGE

Barklem, Jill

PUTNAM

GRADES 3–5

ANIMAL FANTASY

A colony of mice live a sort of 19th-century idyllic life in a hedge, illustrated in great detail. They have a dairy, a mill, and a storehouse where everyone can help themselves to what they need. Lord and Lady Woodmouse live in a palace with their daughter Primrose and take care of everyone. The first four stories follow the mice through the seasons. The series continues with more stories about the mouse community. Companion book *The Four Seasons of Brambly Hedge* collects the seasonal stories.

1. Winter Story ◆ 1980
2. Autumn Story ◆ 1980
3. Spring Story ◆ 1980
4. Summer Story ◆ 1980
5. The Secret Staircase ◆ 1983
6. The High Hills ◆ 1986
7. The Sea Story ◆ 1991
8. Poppy's Babies ◆ 1995

BRIAN AND PEA BRAIN

Levy, Elizabeth

HARPERCOLLINS

GRADES 2–4

HUMOR | MYSTERY

Combining humor and mysterious circumstances, this series will appeal to middle grade readers. Brian Casanova is in the second grade, and he is often annoyed by his little sister Penny. She is in kindergarten, and Brian calls her "Pea Brain." Yet Brian needs her help to unravel events. In one book, they investigate who is sabotaging School Spirit Week, revealing that a new student who misses her old school is causing the disruptions. In another, Brian is the victim of some cruel rumors, and Pea Brain is able to find out why. Familiar locations like school and the science museum and everyday activities like playing soccer and face painting will attract readers.

1. Rude Rowdy Rumors ◆ 1994

2. School Spirit Sabotage ◆ 1994
3. A Mammoth Mix-Up ◆ 1995

BRIAN ROBESON

Paulsen, Gary

DELACORTE

GRADES 4–8

ADVENTURE | REAL LIFE

In *Hatchet*, 13-year-old Brian Robeson is stranded in the Canadian wilderness after a plane crash. He struggles to survive before being rescued just as winter approaches. *The River* features Brian returning to the site of his adventure with a psychologist, Derek Holtzer, who plans to observe and record the experience. Their trip turns into another struggle to survive. *Brian's Winter* is a continuation of *Hatchet*, but with the premise that Brian is not rescued before winter arrives and must struggle to survive even harsher conditions. Fast-paced action—told in short, direct sentences—could appeal to reluctant readers.

1. Hatchet ◆ 1987
2. The River ◆ 1991
3. Brian's Winter ◆ 1996
4. Brian's Return ◆ 1999

BRIGID THRUSH BOOKS

Leverich, Kathleen

RANDOM HOUSE

GRADES 2–3

FANTASY

Brigid Thrush is an average nine-year-old who wishes for a fairy godmother. She gets one, but not exactly what she was expecting: her fairy godmother is another nine-year-old who also turns into a large cat and appears at the most unexpected moments. In one story she magically helps Brigid overcome her fear of the new high dive at the local pool. An entertaining series for young chapter book readers.

1. Brigid Bewitched ◆ 1994
2. Brigid Beware ◆ 1995
3. Brigid the Bad ◆ 1995

BRIMHALL

Delton, Judy

LOTHROP, LEE & SHEPARD; CAROLRHODA

GRADES K–2

ANIMAL FANTASY | HUMOR

In *Brimhall Comes to Stay*, Bear is looking forward to having his cousin Brimhall live with him. Brimhall's eccentricities wreak havoc with Bear's orderly routine until Bear remembers the importance of family. These easy-to-read books feature likable characters, particularly Brimhall, who is somewhat bumbling but has the best intentions.

1. Brimhall Comes to Stay ◆ 1978
2. Brimhall Turns to Magic ◆ 1979
3. Brimhall Turns Detective ◆ 1983
4. A Birthday Bike for Brimhall ◆ 1985
5. Christmas Gift for Brimhall ◆ 1986

BROMELIAD

Pratchett, Terry

DELACORTE

GRADES 5–8

FANTASY

A tiny race of beings called nomes came from outer space to earth centuries ago and showed man how to use metal. Then they forgot everything they knew. Some of them ended up living in the floorboards of a department store and developed a religion based on the founders of the store. "Outside" is a myth, they believe, and the whole universe is the store. Then one day everything changes, when nomes from the Outside show up carrying the Thing, the on-board computer from the spaceship. Fans of all kinds of fantasy will love the satire and inventiveness of this series.

1. Truckers ◆ 1989
2. Diggers: The Second Book of the Bromeliad ◆ 1991
3. Wings: The Last Book of the Bromeliad ◆ 1991

THE BROOKFIELD YEARS *see* Little House: The Caroline Years

BROWNIE GIRL SCOUT BOOKS *see* Here Come the Brownies

BRUNO AND BOOTS

> Korman, Gordon
> SCHOLASTIC
> GRADES 5–8
> HUMOR

Bruno and Boots are pranksters at an exclusive boys boarding school in Canada. They replace the Canadian flag with the flag of Malbonia and steal a rival school's mascot. The school's headmaster, Mr. Sturgeon ("The Fish") knows they are the culprits and decides to separate them. But when they manage to rescue the son of the Malbonian ambassador, who is stuck in a tree in a hot-air balloon, they are allowed to room together again. In their further adventures, they drive "The Fish" crazy, delight their classmates, and plan mayhem with the girls from the finishing school across the street.

1. This Can't Be Happening at Macdonald Hall! ◆ 1990
2. Beware the Fish! ◆ 1991
3. The Zucchini Warriors ◆ 1991
4. Something Fishy at Macdonald Hall ◆ 1995

BUDGIE

> The Duchess of York
> ALADDIN
> GRADES K–1
> FANTASY

Budgie is a small helicopter with a big heart. He is always ready to help. In an adventure at sea, he delivers the mail and helps in a rescue. During a blizzard, Budgie brings a young couple to a medical facility just in time for the arrival of their new baby. Budgie and his friend Pippa the Piper Warrior leave the air show to rescue two boys at Bendick's Point. Budgie is an endearing character, and these simple stories will attract readers who want mild adventure and predictable, satisfying conclusions.

1. Budgie at Bendick's Point ◆ 1989
2. Budgie the Little Helicopter ◆ 1989
3. Budgie and the Blizzard ◆ 1991
4. Budgie Goes to Sea ◆ 1991

BUFFY, THE VAMPIRE SLAYER

Various authors

ARCHWAY/POCKET BOOKS

GRADES 6–8

ADVENTURE | HORROR

Buffy the Vampire Slayer has an intensely loyal following among preteens and adolescents who enjoy violent encounters involving vampires and their victims. Buffy Summers leads a group of high school friends to try to destroy the creatures that have targeted Sunnydale. These books parallel some of the episodes from the television series by the same name. The teens, aided by the Giles, the school librarian, try to stop the zombies, vampires, and other ghouls. This is not for the fainthearted. Buffy uses her wits and her physical skills to protect her friends and the world.

1. The Harvest (Cusick, Richie Tankersley) ◆ 1997
2. Halloween Rain (Golden, Christopher, and Nancy Holder) ◆ 1997
3. Coyote Moon (Vornholt, John) ◆ 1998
4. The Night of the Living Rerun (Cover, Arthur Byron) ◆ 1998
5. Blooded (Golden, Christopher, and Nancy Holder) ◆ 1998
6. Child of the Hunt (Golden, Christopher, and Nancy Holder) ◆ 1998

BULLFROG BOOKS

Dauer, Rosamond

GREENWILLOW

GRADES 1–3

ANIMAL FANTASY | HUMOR

Easy readers about a tadpole who is adopted by a mouse family and grows up to be a very large bullfrog. When he begins to take over their lives, the mice realize it is time for him to set out to make a life and family of his own. In the second book, he meets Gertrude, who will become his companion; and in the third book, they meet and adopt Itsa Snake, a harmless, lonely snake. Droll situations with silly dialogue and totally impossible scenarios will appeal to slightly older reluctant readers.

1. Bullfrog Grows Up ◆ 1976
2. Bullfrog Builds a House ◆ 1977
3. Bullfrog and Gertrude Go Camping ◆ 1980

BUNNICULA

Howe, James, and Deborah Howe

ATHENEUM; MORROW

GRADES 3–5

ANIMAL FANTASY | HUMOR | MYSTERY

Harold the dog and Chester the cat are living happily with their family until one day when their boy, Toby, brings home a rabbit. Chester, who can read and knows things about the world, decides that the bunny is a vampire when they find vegetables drained dry and an empty cage at night. Harold makes friends with the little rabbit and decides that he is harmless, but Chester tries to starve him. In the end, Chester decides that Bunnicula is a vampire all right, but a modern one who wants only vegetable juice. The three animals become friends, and later in the series a puppy, Howie, is added to the household. They all go on to have adventures together. The first Bunnicula book was written by Deborah and James Howe; the remaining books are by James Howe. This series includes both picture books and chapter books for older readers.

CHAPTER BOOKS (ATHENEUM)

1. Bunnicula: A Rabbit-Tale of Mystery ◆ 1979
2. Howliday Inn ◆ 1982
3. The Celery Stalks at Midnight ◆ 1983
4. Nighty-Nightmare ◆ 1987
5. Return to Howliday Inn ◆ 1992

PICTURE BOOKS (MORROW)

1. Harold and Chester in the Fright Before Christmas ◆ 1989
2. Harold and Chester in Scared Silly: A Halloween Treat ◆ 1989
3. Harold and Chester in Hot Fudge ◆ 1990
4. Harold and Chester in Creepy-Crawly Birthday ◆ 1991
5. Harold and Chester in Rabbit-Cadabra ◆ 1993

BUNNY TROUBLE

Wilhelm, Hans

SCHOLASTIC

GRADES K–2

ANIMAL FANTASY | HUMOR | RECREATION

Ralph is a rabbit who is supposed to work with other rabbits decorating eggs for the Easter Bunny. Unfortunately, Ralph likes playing soccer more than doing his job. Luckily, Ralph's soccer skills do come in handy. In one book, Ralph uses his soccer kicking ability to stop some foxes from turning bunnies into rabbit stew. This is an entertaining series of books that should attract readers who like sports and cute bunnies.

1. Bunny Trouble ◆ 1980
2. More Bunny Trouble ◆ 1990
3. Bad, Bad Bunny Trouble ◆ 1995

BUSYBODY NORA *see* Nora and Teddy

BUTTERFIELD SQUARE *see* Miss Know It All

CALICO CAT

Charles, Donald
CHILDREN'S PRESS
GRADES K–1
HUMOR

The Calico Cat books often feature concepts that would be appropriate for preschool and primary grade children. Seasons, colors, telling time, and animals are among the topics presented. Most of the books have a brief text with some rhyming elements, which would make them more accessible to struggling readers. The colorful illustrations also add to their appeal.

1. Count on Calico Cat ◆ 1974
2. Letters from Calico Cat ◆ 1974
3. Calico Cat Looks Around ◆ 1975
4. Calico Cat's Rainbow ◆ 1975
5. Fat, Fat Calico Cat ◆ 1977
6. Calico Cat Meets Bookworm ◆ 1978
7. Time to Rhyme with Calico Cat ◆ 1978
8. Calico Cat at School ◆ 1981
9. Calico Cat at the Zoo ◆ 1981
10. Calico Cat's Exercise Book ◆ 1982
11. Calico Cat's Year ◆ 1984
12. Calico Cat's Sunny Smile ◆ 1990

CALIFORNIA DIARIES

Martin, Ann M.
SCHOLASTIC
GRADES 6–8
REAL LIFE

These books feature various girls who are facing problems that will be familiar to young teens. Sunny's family is trying to cope with the reality of her mother's cancer. Even with this trauma, Sunny must deal with issues involving school, boys, and friends. Maggie has a goal: She wants to weigh 90 pounds. That means she must lose 13 pounds. She also must face her mother's drinking problem and her father being away from home so much. The girls in the series know each other, so sometimes they refer to each other's circumstances. The diary format, which sometimes includes hand-printed words, may make them attractive to reluctant readers.

1. Dawn ◆ 1997
2. Sunny ◆ 1997
3. Maggie ◆ 1997
4. Amalia ◆ 1997
5. Ducky ◆ 1998
6. Sunny, Diary Two ◆ 1998
7. Dawn, Diary Two ◆ 1998
8. Maggie, Diary Two ◆ 1998
9. Amalia, Diary Two ◆ 1998
10. Ducky, Diary Two ◆ 1998

CAM JANSEN *see also* Young Cam Jansen

Adler, David A.

VIKING

GRADES 2–4

MYSTERY

Ji Adl

When Cam Jansen closes her eyes and says "click," her friends know she is using her photographic memory to solve crimes. Her friend Eric offers help and support to the elementary school sleuth. When they go shopping at the mall, they learn that someone is stealing shopping bags. Cam takes a mental picture of the people who were around at the time of the crime and leads police to the culprit. Standing in line to buy tickets to a rock concert, Eric and Cam see a person dressed as a ghost who is scaring people. Cam's skills lead them to the person, who is trying to sabotage the band. Includes short, easy-reading chapters and black-and-white illustrations for beginning readers.

1. Cam Jansen and the Mystery of the Stolen Diamonds ◆ 1980
2. Cam Jansen and the Mystery of the UFO ◆ 1980
3. Cam Jansen and the Mystery of the Dinosaur Bones ◆ 1981
4. Cam Jansen and the Mystery of the Television Dog ◆ 1981
5. Cam Jansen and the Mystery of the Gold Coins ◆ 1982
6. Cam Jansen and the Mystery of the Babe Ruth Baseball ◆ 1982
7. Cam Jansen and the Mystery of the Circus Clown ◆ 1983
8. Cam Jansen and the Mystery of the Monster Movie ◆ 1984
9. Cam Jansen and the Mystery of the Carnival Prize ◆ 1984
10. Cam Jansen and the Mystery at the Monkey House ◆ 1985
11. Cam Jansen and the Mystery of the Stolen Corn Popper ◆ 1986
12. Cam Jansen and the Mystery of Flight 54 ◆ 1989

13. Cam Jansen and the Mystery at the Haunted House ◆ 1992
14. Cam Jansen and the Chocolate Fudge Mystery ◆ 1993
15. Cam Jansen and the Triceratops Pops Mystery ◆ 1995
16. Cam Jansen and the Ghostly Mystery ◆ 1996
17. Cam Jansen and the Scary Snake Mystery ◆ 1997
18. Cam Jansen and the Catnapping Mystery ◆ 1998

CAMP HAUNTED HILLS

Coville, Bruce
POCKET BOOKS
GRADES 4–7
FANTASY | HUMOR

Camp Haunted Hills is not like any ordinary camp. It is a movie camp where there are weird characters and special effects, but it is all part of the movies . . . or is it? Stuart Glassman and the other campers find out that there is often more than meets the eye. Like when Lucius Colton, the camp bully, turns into a hairy monster or when the campers travel back to the time of the dinosaurs. This series is full of fantastic fun that will attract many elementary and middle school readers.

1. How I Survived My Summer Vacation ◆ 1988
2. Some of My Best Friends Are Monsters ◆ 1988
3. The Dinosaur That Followed Me Home ◆ 1990

CAMP SUNNYSIDE

Kaye, Marilyn
AVON
GRADES 4–7
REAL LIFE

Five girls from different parts of the country and with very different personalities meet every summer at Camp Sunnyside. Katie is the born leader, and she always has a scheme up her sleeve. Trina is more mature and thoughtful, while Erin is the sophisticated one in the group. Rounding out the complement of characters are Sarah, the intellectual, and Megan, the daydreamer. In *No Boys Allowed*, a neighboring boys camp has been destroyed by fire, and plans are made for the campers to stay at Camp Sunnyside temporarily. Katie, who has obnoxious older brothers, is vehemently opposed to the idea and plans to let the boys know they are not welcome. She recruits the other girls to join her, but one by one they meet boys they like who share their interests. Everyone tries to hide this fact from everyone else, but eventually even Katie succumbs to a boy's interest and all is revealed. The series continues for several summers, until the girls are in junior high.

1. No Boys Allowed ◆ 1989
2. Cabin Six Plays Cupid ◆ 1989
3. Color War! ◆ 1989
4. New Girl in Cabin Six ◆ 1989
5. Looking for Trouble ◆ 1990
6. Katie Steals the Show ◆ 1990
7. A Witch in Cabin Six ◆ 1990
8. Too Many Counselors ◆ 1990
9. The New and Improved Sarah ◆ 1990
10. Erin and the Movie Star ◆ 1991
11. The Problem with Parents ◆ 1991
12. The Tennis Trap ◆ 1991
13. Big Sister Blues ◆ 1991
14. Megan's Ghost ◆ 1991
15. Christmas Break ◆ 1991
16. Happily Ever After ◆ 1992
17. Camp Spaghetti ◆ 1992
18. Balancing Act ◆ 1992

CAMP ZOMBIE

Stine, Megan, and H. William Stine
RANDOM HOUSE
GRADES 5–7
HORROR

Five people once drowned in the lake at Camp Harvest Moon in Maine. Years later, the camp reopens and Corey and his sister Amanda are among the first new campers. But something very strange is going on. Amanda, an excellent swimmer, is almost drowned, and she is sure something grabbed her. Corey and Amanda and some other campers confront the five zombies from the lake and a new zombie—a dead camp counselor. The next summer, their cousin Griffen is sent to the same camp! And the next summer, on a trip with their grandparents, the cousins meet the zombies again. There are plot twists and dramatic moments when the zombies are just inches away that will provide readers with moments of spine-tingling suspense.

1. Camp Zombie ◆ 1994
2. Camp Zombie: The Second Summer ◆ 1995
3. Camp Zombie: The Lake's Revenge ◆ 1996

CAPE HATTERAS TRILOGY *see* Outer Banks Trilogy

CARL

Day, Alexandra
FARRAR, STRAUS & GIROUX
GRADES K–1
ANIMAL FANTASY | HUMOR

In these almost wordless picture books, Carl, a huge rottweiler, takes care of a baby in unique ways. In a typical book, the mother takes them shopping and tells Carl on the first page to "take good care of the baby" while she goes upstairs. The baby promptly climbs on the dog's back and away they go, wreaking havoc on the toy department, reading *Rottweilers I Have Known* in the book department, and watching themselves on camera in the electronics department. Chaos continues as they let all the animals out of their cages in the pet shop. The baby's mother never suspects the mischief these two get into. In other books, Carl watches the baby at home, where they play dress-up and feast in the kitchen; and at a daycare center, where Carl again takes charge.

1. Good Dog, Carl ◆ 1987
2. Carl Goes Shopping ◆ 1990
3. Carl's Christmas ◆ 1990
4. Carl's Afternoon in the Park ◆ 1991
5. Carl's Masquerade ◆ 1992
6. Carl Goes to Daycare ◆ 1993
7. Carl Makes a Scrap-Book ◆ 1994
8. Carl's Birthday ◆ 1995
9. Follow Carl! ◆ 1998

CARMEN SANDIEGO MYSTERIES

Various authors
HARPERTROPHY
GRADES 4–6
MYSTERY

Maya's aunt is the head of a world-famous crime-fighting organization called ACME. Maya and Ben are her youngest and best secret agents and they travel the world mostly in pursuit of one master criminal—Carmen Sandiego. Carmen is a former ACME agent who now commits outrageous crimes just for the fun of pitting her wits against theirs. She dresses in red and flies in a red jet, and she often leaves a calling card at the scene of the crime. Maya and Ben use his computer knowledge and her athletic skill to solve the crimes, but they never quite catch Carmen.

1. Hasta La Vista, Blarney (Peterson, Melissa) ◆ 1997
2. Color Me Criminal (Weiss, Ellen, and Mel Friedman) ◆ 1997
3. The Cocoa Commotion (Peterson, Melissa) ◆ 1997
4. One T. Rex Over Easy (Bader, Bonnie, and Tracey West) ◆ 1997
5. Take the Mummy and Run (Weiss, Ellen, and Mel Friedman) ◆ 1997
6. Highway Robbery (Bader, Bonnie, and Tracey West) ◆ 1997

THE CAROLINE YEARS *see* Little House: The Caroline Years

CASEBUSTERS

Nixon, Joan Lowery
DISNEY PRESS
GRADES 2–4
MYSTERY

Brian and his younger brother Sean are the sons of a private detective, and they help with his cases and sometimes work on cases of their own. In *Beware the Pirate Ghost*, they help their father find a spoiled young boy who fakes his own kidnapping and then finds himself in real danger. On their own in *The Internet Escapade*, they find out who has been sabotaging the school computers and shifting the blame to Sean. The boys have friends who are intrigued by their detective work and want to help, and their parents and other adults in town are supportive. Their frequent use of computers makes their stories up to date. Boys who are too young for the Hardy Boys will enjoy this series.

1. The Statue Walks at Night ◆ 1995
2. The Legend of the Deadman's Mine ◆ 1995
3. Backstage with a Ghost ◆ 1995
4. Check in to Danger ◆ 1995
5. The House Has Eyes ◆ 1996
6. The Secret of the Time Capsule ◆ 1996
7. Beware the Pirate Ghost ◆ 1996
8. Catch a Crooked Clown ◆ 1996
9. Fear Stalks Grizzly Hill ◆ 1996
10. Sabotage on the Set ◆ 1996
11. The Internet Escapade ◆ 1997
12. Bait for a Burglar ◆ 1997

CASEY, JENNY, AND KATE

Hest, Amy

MORROW

GRADES 2–4

REAL LIFE

The emphasis in this series is on friendship and fun. The books are narrated in the first person by Casey, who provides insights and side comments throughout the books. Sometimes, because there are three friends, problems develop, as at the three-girl pajama party where Kate gets homesick and Jenny and Casey try not to think she is a baby. Or when the girls watch Baby Daisy and don't always agree on what to do. In each book, the girls experience familiar activities, including ice skating and a birthday party. Many readers will relate to and enjoy their lives.

1. Pajama Party ◆ 1992
2. Nannies for Hire ◆ 1994
3. Party on Ice ◆ 1995

CASEY, TRACEY AND COMPANY

Giff, Patricia Reilly

DELACORTE; DELL YEARLING

GRADES 3–6

REAL LIFE

Casey and her friends have various difficulties to overcome in each of these books, and manage to do so in adventurous and humorous ways. Raising worms to sell and trying to outdo a cousin, experiencing divorce and dealing with being called names, even putting a cast on an arm to get out of playing a game, all are told with tenderness and humor.

1. Fourth Grade Celebrity ◆ 1979
2. Left-Handed Shortstop ◆ 1980
3. The Winter Worm Business ◆ 1981
4. The Girl Who Knew It All ◆ 1984
5. Rat Teeth ◆ 1984
6. Love, from the Fifth-Grade Celebrity ◆ 1986
7. Poopsie Pomerantz, Pick Up Your Feet ◆ 1989

CASSIE PERKINS

Hunt, Angela Elwell
TYNDALE HOUSE
GRADES 4–7
REAL LIFE | VALUES

Cassie Perkins thinks she has the perfect life until her father walks out on her family. Later, her parents tell Cassie and her beloved little brother Max that he is going to live with their father. Cassie lands the lead in her school's production of *Oklahoma*. This makes her friend Andrea envious because she has a crush on Chip, the male lead. He becomes a good friend to Cassie and leads her to faith in Christ. Her music teacher recommends her to a performing arts high school, but her mother doesn't think they can afford it. Cassie learns to trust in God for this and everything else.

1. No More Broken Promises ◆ 1991
2. A Forever Friend ◆ 1991
3. A Basket of Roses ◆ 1991
4. A Dream to Cherish ◆ 1992
5. The Much-Adored Sandy Shore ◆ 1992
6. Love Burning Bright ◆ 1992
7. Star Light, Star Bright ◆ 1993
8. The Chance of a Lifetime ◆ 1993
9. The Glory of Love ◆ 1993

CASTLE COURT KIDS

Snyder, Zilpha Keatley
DELL YEARLING
GRADES 3–5
REAL LIFE

The kids who live on the cul-de-sac at the end of Castle Court are friends who have banded together to do neighborhood projects. In one book, Carlos Garcia helps them get organized to build a baseball diamond, but two of the friends, Kate Nicely and Aurora Pappas, don't want a special grove of trees cut down for the field. In another book, Carlos and his friends Eddy Wong and Bucky Brockhurst have found a buried treasure, but when they look for it again, it is gone! Although the group often works together as friends, they have their differences—for instance when the boys surprise the girls who are ghost hunting. This is an easy-to-read series for middle grade children who enjoy books featuring familiar neighborhood activities.

1. The Diamond War ◆ 1995
2. The Box and the Bone ◆ 1995
3. Ghost Invasion ◆ 1995
4. Secret Weapons ◆ 1995

CATWINGS

LeGuin, Ursula K.

FRANKLIN WATTS

GRADES 4–7

ANIMAL FANTASY

In a rough city neighborhood, four kittens are born with wings. Their mother does not know why until she realizes that the wings will enable her children to leave the city and find a better life elsewhere. The kittens—Roger, Thelma, Harriet, and James—say good-bye to their mother and fly to the country, where they must adjust to a new life with new risks, including the Owl. Eventually, they meet two children, Susan and Hank Brown, who convince the kittens to live in an abandoned barn. The series continues with the "Catwings" returning to visit their mother in the city and helping a normal kitten, Alexander Furby, who is lost in the woods.

1. Catwings ◆ 1988
2. Catwings Return ◆ 1989
3. Wonderful Alexander and the Catwings ◆ 1994

¡CHANA!

Ramirez, Michael Rose

AVON

GRADES 3–5

FAMILY LIFE | REAL LIFE

Chana and her family have moved to California. There are so many adjustments—new home, new friends, new school. Chana misses her old friends in the Puerto Rican neighborhood in New York City. This series describes how she learns to fit in. Many readers will appreciate the Spanish words and phrases that are incorporated into these stories.

1. Hola, California! ◆ 1997

2. Hoppin' Halloween ◆ 1997
3. Gingerbread Sleepover ◆ 1997
4. Live from Cedar Hills! ◆ 1998

CHARLOTTE CHEETHAM

Holmes, Barbara Ware
HARPERCOLLINS
GRADES 4–6
HUMOR | REAL LIFE

Charlotte Cheetham has a great imagination. Her favorite character is Pippi Longstocking. Sometimes Charlotte's impetuous nature gets her into trouble, especially when she stretches the truth to fit her needs. When she wants to make friends with the popular girls in sixth grade, she tells a lie to show off. As a result, she almost loses her one real friend, Annie. Charlotte and Annie's friendship is tested again when Charlotte writes a play and Annie gets the lead. Charlotte becomes jealous and angry at the attention that Annie receives, but it is Charlotte who helps Annie overcome her shyness and be the star. This is a fun, light-hearted series that will appeal to readers who enjoy lively female main characters.

1. Charlotte Cheetham: Master of Disaster ◆ 1985
2. Charlotte the Starlet ◆ 1988
3. Charlotte Shakespeare and Annie the Great ◆ 1989

CHEER SQUAD

Singleton, Linda Joy
AVON CAMELOT
GRADES 6–8
REAL LIFE | RECREATION

Oh, no! Darlene and her megapopular friends have been chosen to be seventh-grade cheerleaders. Will Wendi and Tabby always be popularity rejects? Not when a new cheer squad is formed for the basketball team. Now Wendi and Tabby and their classmates Krystal, Anna, Celine, and Rachel have a chance. Girls who like to read about regular girls who succeed against the "in" crowd will enjoy this series. There is even a bit of budding romance when boys join the cheer squad.

1. Crazy for Cartwheels ◆ 1996
2. Spirit Song ◆ 1996
3. Stand Up and Cheer ◆ 1996
4. Boys Are Bad News ◆ 1997

5. Spring to Stardom ◆ 1997
6. Camp Confessions ◆ 1997

CHESTER CRICKET

Selden, George

FARRAR, STRAUS & GIROUX

GRADES 3–6

ANIMAL FANTASY | HUMOR

Chester Cricket travels unwillingly in a picnic basket from the country to New York City. There he meets Mario Bellini and his family, who run a newsstand in Times Square. His musical talent is discovered, and he plays wonderful concerts that bring large crowds to the Bellinis' newsstand. Eventually, he tires of city life and wants to go back to his home in the country, so Harry Kitten and Tucker Mouse put him on a train for Connecticut. The rest of the series includes some picture books and some novel-length books, all about the further adventures of one or all of the animals. *Harry Kitten and Tucker Mouse* is a prequel to *The Cricket in Times Square*.

1. The Cricket in Times Square ◆ 1960
2. Tucker's Countryside ◆ 1969
3. Harry Cat's Pet Puppy ◆ 1974
4. Chester Cricket's Pigeon Ride ◆ 1981
5. Chester Cricket's New Home ◆ 1983
6. Harry Kitten and Tucker Mouse ◆ 1986
7. The Old Meadow ◆ 1987

CHICAGO AND THE CAT

Koontz, Robin Michal

DUTTON

GRADES K–2

ANIMAL FANTASY

One day, Chicago the rabbit finds that a cat is living in her house. Chicago wonders how soon the cat will leave. Then, she eats the carrot pancakes that the cat has made for her. Delicious! The cat does not like being outdoors at night. She does not like getting wet when the she goes rafting with Chicago. *The Family Reunion* describes how the cat deals with the crowd of rabbits when Chicago's family comes to visit. With simple chapters and controlled vocabulary, this is a great choice for beginning readers.

1. Chicago and the Cat ◆ 1993
2. Chicago and the Cat: The Camping Trip ◆ 1994
3. Chicago and the Cat: The Halloween Party ◆ 1994
4. Chicago and the Cat: The Family Reunion ◆ 1996
5. Chicago and the Cat at the Country Fair ◆ 1998

CHILDREN OF AMERICA

Armstrong, Jennifer
RANDOM HOUSE
GRADES 2–4
HISTORICAL

Each book in this series focuses on the immigration experiences of different children. Patrick Doyle is growing up in the Hell's Kitchen area of New York, enjoying his new life, new friends, and a new sport—baseball. *Foolish Gretel* describes the life of a ten-year-old German-American girl in Texas. And, although Lili Alesund loves Norway, she must travel on a huge ship when her parents decide to go to Minnesota. The characters are high-spirited as they face their new lives in America.

1. Patrick Doyle Is Full of Blarney ◆ 1996
2. Lili the Brave ◆ 1997
3. Foolish Gretel ◆ 1997

CHINA TATE

Johnson, Lissa Halls
FOCUS ON THE FAMILY
GRADES 5–8
REAL LIFE | VALUES

At Camp Crazy Bear, China Tate and her best friend Deedee Kiersey have adventures involving bear cubs, a lost dog, and the beginning of romance. China is the daughter of missionaries and many of her actions are guided by her faith in God. In one book, China befriends a charismatic young man and her interest in him makes her question the importance of her beliefs. In another book, China and Deedee learn a lesson about disobedience after they feed some wild bear cubs. Values and Christian beliefs are incorporated into each story.

1. Sliced Heather on Toast ◆ 1994
2. The Secret in the Kitchen ◆ 1994
3. Project Black Bear ◆ 1994
4. Wishing Upon a Star ◆ 1995

5. Comedy of Errors ◆ 1995
6. The Ice Queen ◆ 1996
7. The Never-Ending Day ◆ 1997

CHINCOTEAGUE

Henry, Marguerite
SIMON & SCHUSTER
GRADES 3–6
REAL LIFE

Beginning with the shipwreck that marooned the wild horses on an island just off the coast of Virginia, these books trace the story of Misty, who began her life on Assateague Island and was captured and brought to Chincoteague, and of her descendants. In each, there is the drama of real life: a tidal wave, the need to sell Misty to raise money, and the hard work of training and caring for horses.

1. Misty of Chincoteague ◆ 1947
2. Sea Star, Orphan of Chincoteague ◆ 1949
3. Stormy, Misty's Foal ◆ 1963
4. Misty's Twilight ◆ 1992

CHOOSE YOUR OWN ADVENTURE

Various authors
BANTAM
GRADES 4–8
ADVENTURE | MYSTERY

With nearly 200 titles, this series has attracted a large audience. The format allows readers to make choices at key moments in the plot. Should you go left? Go right? Should you turn around? Each choice leads to a different page, more choices, and your own story. Then you can go back to an earlier choice, make different selections, and create a different story. Newer adventures feature ninjas, computers, aliens, cyber-hacking, and mutant spider ants. This is a popular series with a fairly accessible reading level. See also the Choose Your Own Nightmare series.

1. The Cave of Time (Packard, Edward) ◆ 1979
2. Journey Under the Sea (Mountain, Robert) ◆ 1977
3. By Balloon to the Sahara (Terman, Douglas) ◆ 1979
4. Space and Beyond (Montgomery, Raymond) ◆ 1980
5. Mystery of Chimney Rock (Packard, Edward) ◆ 1980
6. Your Code Name Is Jonah (Packard, Edward) ◆ 1979

7. Third Planet from Altair (Packard, Edward) ◆ 1979
8. Deadwood City (Packard, Edward) ◆ 1978
9. Who Killed Harlowe Thrombey? (Packard, Edward) ◆ 1981
10. Lost Jewels of Nabooti (Montgomery, Raymond) ◆ 1981
11. Mystery of the Maya (Montgomery, Raymond) ◆ 1981
12. Inside UFO 54-40 (Packard, Edward) ◆ 1982
13. Abominable Snowman (Montgomery, Raymond) ◆ 1982
14. Forbidden Castle (Packard, Edward) ◆ 1982
15. House of Danger (Montgomery, Raymond) ◆ 1982
16. Survival at Sea (Packard, Edward) ◆ 1983
17. Race Forever (Montgomery, Raymond) ◆ 1983
18. Underground Kingdom (Packard, Edward) ◆ 1983
19. Secret of the Pyramids (Brightfield, Richard) ◆ 1983
20. Escape (Montgomery, Raymond) ◆ 1983
21. Hyperspace (Packard, Edward) ◆ 1983
22. Space Patrol (Goodman, Julius) ◆ 1983
23. Lost Tribe (Foley, Louise Munro) ◆ 1983
24. Lost on the Amazon (Montgomery, Raymond) ◆ 1983
25. Prisoner of the Ant People (Montgomery, Raymond) ◆ 1983
26. Phantom Submarine (Brightfield, Richard) ◆ 1983
27. Horror of High Ridge (Goodman, Julius) ◆ 1983
28. Mountain Survival (Packard, Edward) ◆ 1984
29. Trouble on Planet Earth (Montgomery, Raymond) ◆ 1984
30. Curse of Batterslea Hall (Brightfield, Richard) ◆ 1984
31. Vampire Express (Koltz, Tony) ◆ 1984
32. Treasure Diver (Goodman, Julius) ◆ 1984
33. Dragons' Den (Brightfield, Richard) ◆ 1984
34. Mystery of the Highland Crest (Foley, Louise Munro) ◆ 1984
35. Journey to Stonehenge (Graver, Fred) ◆ 1984
36. Secret Treasure of Tibet (Brightfield, Richard) ◆ 1984
37. War with the Evil Power Master (Montgomery, Raymond) ◆ 1984
38. Sabotage (Leibold, Jay) ◆ 1984
39. Supercomputer (Packard, Edward) ◆ 1984
40. Throne of Zeus (Goodman, Deborah Lerne) ◆ 1985
41. Search for the Mountain Gorillas (Wallace, Jim) ◆ 1985
42. Mystery of Echo Lodge (Foley, Louise Munro) ◆ 1985
43. Grand Canyon Odyssey (Leibold, Jay) ◆ 1985
44. Mystery of Ura Senke (Gilligan, Shannon) ◆ 1985
45. You Are a Shark (Packard, Edward) ◆ 1985
46. Deadly Shadow (Brightfield, Richard) ◆ 1985
47. Outlaws of Sherwood Forest (Kushner, Ellen) ◆ 1985
48. Spy for George Washington (Leibold, Jay) ◆ 1985
49. Danger at Anchor Mine (Foley, Louise Munro) ◆ 1985
50. Return to the Cave of Time (Packard, Edward) ◆ 1985
51. Magic of the Unicorn (Goodman, Deborah Lerne) ◆ 1985
52. Ghost Hunter (Packard, Edward) ◆ 1986
53. Case of the Silk King (Gilligan, Shannon) ◆ 1986
54. Forest of Fear (Foley, Louise Munro) ◆ 1986

55. Trumpet of Terror (Goodman, Deborah Lerne) ◆ 1986
56. Enchanted Kingdom (Kushner, Ellen) ◆ 1986
57. Antimatter Formula (Leibold, Jay) ◆ 1986
58. Statue of Liberty Adventure (Kushner, Ellen) ◆ 1986
59. Terror Island (Koltz, Tony) ◆ 1986
60. Vanished! (Goodman, Deborah Lerne) ◆ 1986
61. Beyond Escape! (Montgomery, Raymond) ◆ 1986
62. Sugarcane Island (Packard, Edward) ◆ 1986
63. Mystery of the Secret Room (Kushner, Ellen) ◆ 1986
64. Volcano! (Siegman, Meryl) ◆ 1987
65. Mardi Gras Mystery (Foley, Louise Munro) ◆ 1987
66. Secret of the Ninja (Leibold, Jay) ◆ 1987
67. Seaside Mystery (Hodgman, Ann) ◆ 1987
68. Secret of the Sun God (Packard, Andrea) ◆ 1987
69. Rock and Roll Mystery (Wallace, Jim) ◆ 1987
70. Invaders of Planet Earth (Brightfield, Richard) ◆ 1987
71. Space Vampire (Packard, Edward) ◆ 1987
72. Brilliant Doctor Wogan (Montgomery, Raymond) ◆ 1987
73. Beyond the Great Wall (Leibold, Jay) ◆ 1987
74. Longhorn Territory (Newman, Marc) ◆ 1987
75. Planet of the Dragons (Brightfield, Richard) ◆ 1988
76. Mona Lisa Is Missing (Montgomery, Ramsey) ◆ 1988
77. First Olympics (Baglio, Ben) ◆ 1988
78. Return to Atlantis (Montgomery, Raymond) ◆ 1988
79. Mystery of the Sacred Stones (Foley, Louise Munro) ◆ 1988
80. Perfect Planet (Packard, Edward) ◆ 1988
81. Terror in Australia (Gilligan, Shannon) ◆ 1988
82. Hurricane! (Brightfield, Richard) ◆ 1988
83. Track of the Bear (Montgomery, Raymond) ◆ 1988
84. You Are a Monster (Packard, Edward) ◆ 1988
85. Inca Gold (Beckett, Jim) ◆ 1988
86. Knights of the Round Table (Kushner, Ellen) ◆ 1988
87. Exiled to Earth (Montgomery, Raymond) ◆ 1989
88. Master of Kung Fu (Brightfield, Richard) ◆ 1989
89. South Pole Sabotage (Johnson, Seddon) ◆ 1989
90. Mutiny in Space (Packard, Edward) ◆ 1989
91. You Are a Superstar (Packard, Edward) ◆ 1989
92. Return of the Ninja (Leibold, Jay) ◆ 1989
93. Captive! (Hampton, Bill) ◆ 1989
94. Blood on the Handle (Montgomery, Raymond) ◆ 1989
95. You Are a Genius (Packard, Edward) ◆ 1989
96. Stock Car Champion (Montgomery, Raymond) ◆ 1989
97. Through the Black Hole (Packard, Edward) ◆ 1990
98. You Are a Millionaire (Leibold, Jay) ◆ 1990
99. Revenge of the Russian Ghost (Leibold, Jay) ◆ 1990
100. Worst Day of Your Life (Packard, Edward) ◆ 1990
101. Alien, Go Home! (Johnson, Seddon) ◆ 1990
102. Master of Tae Kwon Do (Brightfield, Richard) ◆ 1990

151. Gunfire at Gettysburg (Wilhelm, Doug) ◆ 1994
152. War with the Mutant Spider Ants (Packard, Edward) ◆ 1994
153. Last Run (Montgomery, R. A.) ◆ 1994
154. Cyberspace Warrior (Packard, Edward) ◆ 1994
155. Ninja Cyborg (Leibold, Jay) ◆ 1995
156. You Are an Alien (Packard, Edward) ◆ 1995
157. U.N. Adventure (Brightfield, Richard) ◆ 1995
158. Sky-jam! (Packard, Edward) ◆ 1995
159. Tattoo of Death (Montgomery, R. A.) ◆ 1995
160. The Computer Takeover (Packard, Edward) ◆ 1995
161. Possessed! (Montgomery, R. A.) ◆ 1995
162. Typhoon! (Packard, Edward) ◆ 1995
163. Shadow of the Swastika (Wilhelm, Doug) ◆ 1995
164. Fright Night (Packard, Edward) ◆ 1995
165. Snowboard Racer (Montgomery, Anson) ◆ 1995
166. Master of Aikido (Brightfield, Richard) ◆ 1995
167. Moon Quest (Montgomery, Anson) ◆ 1996
168. Hostage! (Packard, Edward) ◆ 1996
169. Terror on the Titanic (Brightfield, Richard) ◆ 1996
170. Greed, Guns, and Gold (Packard, Edward) ◆ 1996
171. Death in the Dorm (Montgomery, R. A.) ◆ 1996
172. Mountain Biker (Packard, Edward) ◆ 1996
173. The Gold Medal Secret (Wilhelm, Doug) ◆ 1996
174. The Underground Railroad (Wilhelm, Doug) ◆ 1996
175. Master of Kendo (Brightfield, Richard) ◆ 1997
176. Killer Virus (Montgomery, R. A.) ◆ 1997
177. River of No Return (Lahey, Vince) ◆ 1997
178. Ninja Avenger (Leibold, Jay) ◆ 1997
179. Stampede! (Hill, Laban Carrick) ◆ 1997
180. Fire on Ice (Packard, Edward) ◆ 1998
181. Fugitive (Packard, Edward) ◆ 1998
182. CyberHacker (Montgomery, Anson) ◆ 1998
183. Mayday! (Packard, Edward, and Andrea Packard) ◆ 1998

CHOOSE YOUR OWN ADVENTURE: PASSPORT *see* Passport

CHOOSE YOUR OWN ADVENTURE: YOUNG INDIANA JONES *see* Young Indiana Jones Chronicles: Choose Your Own Adventure

CHOOSE YOUR OWN NIGHTMARE

Various authors

BANTAM

GRADES 4–8

ADVENTURE I HORROR

A spin-off of the Choose Your Own Adventure series, these books capitalize on the popularity of horror fiction. From *Night of the Werewolf* onward, these books are filled with venomous snakes, killer insects, mummies, and haunted babies. With twists and turns, doom and demons, they are sure to appeal to the scary-story crowd.

1. Night of the Werewolf (Packard, Edward) ◆ 1995
2. Beware the Snake's Venom (McMurtry, Ken) ◆ 1995
3. Island of Doom (Brightfield, Richard) ◆ 1995
4. Castle of Darkness (Montgomery, R. A.) ◆ 1995
5. The Halloween Party (Jakab, E.A.M.) ◆ 1995
6. Risk Your Life Arcade (McMurtry, Ken) ◆ 1995
7. Biting for Blood (Packard, Edward) ◆ 1996
8. Bugged Out! (Hill, Laban Carrick) ◆ 1996
9. The Mummy Who Wouldn't Die (Jakab, E.A.M.) ◆ 1996
10. It Happened at Camp Pine Tree (Montgomery, R. A., and Janet Hubbard-Brown) ◆ 1996
11. Watch Out for Room 13 (Hill, Laban Carrick) ◆ 1996
12. Something's in the Woods (Brightfield, Richard) ◆ 1996
13. The Haunted Baby (Packard, Edward) ◆ 1997
14. The Evil Pen Pal (Hill, Laban Carrick) ◆ 1997
15. How I Became a Freak (Brightfield, Richard) ◆ 1997
16. Welcome to Horror Hospital (Hill, Laban Carrick) ◆ 1997
17. Attack of the Living Mask (Hirschfeld, Robert) ◆ 1997
18. The Toy Shop of Terror (Hill, Laban Carrick) ◆ 1997

CHOOSE YOUR OWN STAR WARS ADVENTURES

Golden, Christopher

BANTAM

GRADES 4–8

ADVENTURE I SCIENCE FICTION

This series links two popular items: the *Star Wars* movies, plots, and characters and the Choose Your Own Adventure format. The familiar characters—Luke Skywalker, Princess Leia, Han Solo, and Darth Vader—are embroiled in more intergalactic intrigues, and the reader gets to make choices about which direction the plot will take. Will there be rebellion or destruction? Will you be loyal to the Jedi or embrace the dark side? The 3-D hologram on the cover of each book will attract many readers. This is sure to be a great choice for fans of movies and participatory fiction.

1. Star Wars: A New Hope ◆ 1998
2. Star Wars: The Empire Strikes Back ◆ 1998
3. Star Wars: Return of the Jedi ◆ 1998

CHRISTIE & COMPANY

Page, Katherine Hall

AVON

GRADES 5–7

MYSTERY

Three girls—Christie, Maggie, and Vicky—meet at the boarding school where they begin eighth grade. They are from different backgrounds but they share an interest in mysteries. Christie Montgomery is the main character and she directs the trio's activities, solving thefts at school, finding those responsible for the sabotage of an inn owned by Maggie's parents, and helping a family being threatened by a Chinese gang. While seeking solutions to these mysteries, the girls continue to grow and mature. There is lots of dialogue, making this fairly accessible. Children who enjoy mystery and adventure books featuring girls will like this series.

1. Christie & Company ◆ 1996
2. Christie & Company Down East ◆ 1997
3. Christie & Company in the Year of the Dragon ◆ 1998

CHRISTINA KATERINA

Gauch, Patricia Lee

PUTNAM

GRADES K–3

FAMILY LIFE | REAL LIFE

In this picture book series, Christina Katerina quarrels and makes up with her family, loves her bears, and has a neighborhood war. When her parents come home with a baby sister, she gets her bears together for a journey. Caught in a seedy neighborhood in the rain, she is glad to see her father coming to get her. The best part of a journey, she tells the bears, is going home, especially if you have a baby sister waiting. When she is a little older, she has a falling out with her best friend, the rest of the neighborhood takes sides, and war is declared. Christina is a feisty and determined heroine in a loving family.

1. Christina Katerina and the Box ◆ 1971
2. Christina Katerina and the First Annual Grand Ballet ◆ 1973
3. Christina Katerina and the Time She Quit the Family ◆ 1987
4. Christina Katerina and the Great Bear Train ◆ 1990
5. Christina Katerina and Fats and the Great Neighborhood War ◆ 1997

CHRISTOPHER

Carrick, Carol
HOUGHTON MIFFLIN
GRADES K–2
FAMILY LIFE | REAL LIFE

EP Car

This series of books chronicles the everyday experiences of Christopher and his family. Several books focus on Christopher and his dog, Bodger, with *The Accident* describing Christopher's sense of loss when Bodger is hit by a truck and killed. Finding a stray puppy and accepting him is presented in *The Foundling*. One book shows how Christopher overcomes his fear of swimming in the pond; another describes a sleep-out; still another shows an encounter between Christopher's new dog, Ben, and a porcupine. The stories in this series convey a strong sense of family togetherness and respect for the beauty of nature.

1. Sleep Out ◆ 1973
2. Lost in the Storm ◆ 1974
3. The Accident ◆ 1976
4. The Foundling ◆ 1977
5. The Washout ◆ 1978
6. Ben and the Porcupine ◆ 1981
7. Dark and Full of Secrets ◆ 1984
8. Left Behind ◆ 1988

CHRISTY

Marshall, Catherine
TOMMY NELSON WORDKIDS
GRADES 5–8
HISTORICAL | REAL LIFE | VALUES

Christy Huddleston, 19, goes to teach in the Great Smoky Mountains where she finds hardships, heartache, and hope. Christy's idealism and energy often put her in conflict with people in the community, but she has the ongoing support of Dr. Neil MacNeill and the admiration of David Grantland. Christy meets Miss Alice, a veteran missionary who understands the mountain people and helps her adjust to their ways. The stories have an element of romance and are filled with Christy's commitment to her religion and her values. The series follows the format of the popular TV series. Catherine Marshall based these stories on the real life of her mother around the turn of the century.

1. The Bridge to Cutter Gap ◆ 1995
2. Silent Superstitions ◆ 1995
3. The Angry Intruder ◆ 1995
4. Midnight Rescue ◆ 1995
5. The Proposal ◆ 1995
6. Christy's Choice ◆ 1996
7. The Princess Club ◆ 1996
8. Family Secrets ◆ 1996
9. Mountain Madness ◆ 1997
10. Stage Fright ◆ 1997
11. Goodbye, Sweet Prince ◆ 1997
12. Brotherly Love ◆ 1997

CHRISTY MILLER

Gunn, Robin Jones
FOCUS ON THE FAMILY
GRADES 6–8
REAL LIFE | VALUES

Christy Miller's faith in God and the support of her family help her deal with many teenage traumas. Making new friends in California, expressing her interest in Todd, being attracted by another boy (Rick), and almost losing her best friend Katie are some of Christy's concerns. Christy seeks guidance from the Lord as she tries to reconcile her personal wants with the needs of her faith. Opportunities for Biblical explications are provided as the characters attend study groups and seek guidance. Christy's romantic dilemmas will appeal to many girls. This series will connect with other values-related books.

1. Summer Promise ◆ 1988
2. A Whisper and a Wish ◆ 1989
3. Yours Forever ◆ 1990
4. Surprise Endings ◆ 1991
5. Island Dreamer ◆ 1992
6. A Heart Full of Hope ◆ 1992
7. True Friends ◆ 1993
8. Starry Night ◆ 1993
9. Seventeen Wishes ◆ 1993

10. A Time to Cherish ◆ 1993
11. Sweet Dreams ◆ 1994
12. A Promise Is Forever ◆ 1994

CHRONICLES OF NARNIA

Lewis, C. S.

MACMILLAN

GRADES 4–8

ADVENTURE | FANTASY

Lucy, Peter, Susan, and Edmund are British schoolchildren during World War II in this series of fantasy adventures. Entering a mirrored wardrobe, they find a magical world called Narnia, peopled by fauns, witches, nymphs, dwarves, and talking animals. The children fight many battles against evil and eventually become rulers of the land. Quirks in the chronicles include the facts that Narnia's inhabitants have always supposed humans to be mythical creatures and that the adventures that seem to last forever in Narnia only fill a split second at home. There is debate about the best order in which to read these books. Many prefer the order in which they were published, but boxed sets now present the books in chronological sequence: *The Magician's Nephew; The Lion, the Witch, and the Wardrobe; The Horse and His Boy; Prince Caspian; The Voyage of the Dawn Treader; The Silver Chair;* and *The Last Battle.*

1. The Lion, the Witch, and the Wardrobe ◆ 1950
2. Prince Caspian ◆ 1951
3. The Voyage of the Dawn Treader ◆ 1952
4. The Silver Chair ◆ 1953
5. The Horse and His Boy ◆ 1954
6. The Magician's Nephew ◆ 1955
7. The Last Battle ◆ 1956

CLAUDE

Nixon, Joan Lowery

VIKING

GRADES 1–3

HUMOR

Set in Texas, this series has the flavor of a tall tale with lots of humor and outlandish situations. Claude and Shirley are loners who find each other and fall in love. Once they are married, they adopt a little boy named Tom. After they meet Tom's sister Bessie, they adopt her, too. There are encounters with desperadoes and searches for gold, but there are also poignant moments. Lively illustrations make these unusual characters come to life.

1. If You Say So, Claude ◆ 1980
2. Beats Me, Claude ◆ 1986
3. Fat Chance, Claude ◆ 1987
4. You Bet Your Britches, Claude ◆ 1989
5. That's the Spirit, Claude ◆ 1992

CLAUDE THE DOG

Gackenbach, Dick

HOUGHTON MIFFLIN

GRADES K–2

ANIMAL FANTASY

Claude is a sad-eyed dog who cares about others. In *Claude the Dog*, he gives away his presents to a friend in need. *Claude and Pepper* shows Claude reaching out to help another of his friends. These picture books are enhanced by the author's illustrations, which convey Claude's gentle spirit.

1. Claude the Dog: A Christmas Story ◆ 1974
2. Claude and Pepper ◆ 1976
3. What's Claude Doing? ◆ 1984
4. Claude Has a Picnic ◆ 1993

CLEARWATER CROSSING

Roberts, Laura Peyton

BANTAM DOUBLEDAY DELL

GRADES 5–8

REAL LIFE | VALUES

In this series, good friends Melanie, Peter, Jenna, Jesse, Nicole, Miguel, Ben, and Leah face high school with the support of each other and their faith in God. Concerns including boyfriends, sports, school events—even hardship and tragedy—are resolved through the guidance of Christian friends and family. Modern photographic covers give these books an appeal similar to that of the Sweet Valley series.

1. Get a Life ◆ 1998
2. Reality Check ◆ 1998
3. Heart & Soul ◆ 1998
4. Promises, Promises ◆ 1998
5. Just Friends ◆ 1998
6. Keep the Faith ◆ 1998

CLIFFORD

Bridwell, Norman

SCHOLASTIC

GRADES K–2

ANIMAL FANTASY | HUMOR

Everyone loves Clifford. The big red dog and his little girl, Emily Elizabeth, have enchanted children for more than 30 years. There are many books about Clifford, including ones celebrating holidays and seasons and others building on the humor of a huge dog (bigger than a house) in awkward situations. Related books include riddle books, board books, scratch-and-sniff books, even a barking book. There are cookie cutters, cassettes, a puppet, and a stuffed animal.

1. Clifford, the Big Red Dog ◆ 1962
2. Clifford Gets a Job ◆ 1965
3. Clifford Takes a Trip ◆ 1966
4. Clifford's Halloween ◆ 1967
5. Clifford's Tricks ◆ 1969
6. Clifford, the Small Red Puppy ◆ 1972
7. Clifford's Riddles ◆ 1974
8. Clifford's Good Deeds ◆ 1975
9. Clifford at the Circus ◆ 1977
10. Clifford Goes to Hollywood ◆ 1980
11. Clifford's ABC ◆ 1983
12. Clifford and the Grouchy Neighbors ◆ 1984
13. Clifford's Christmas ◆ 1984
14. Clifford's Family ◆ 1984
15. Clifford's Kitten ◆ 1984
16. Clifford's Pals ◆ 1985
17. Clifford's Manners ◆ 1985
18. Count on Clifford ◆ 1985
19. Clifford's Birthday Party ◆ 1988
20. Clifford's Puppy Days ◆ 1989
21. Clifford's Word Book ◆ 1990
22. Clifford, We Love You ◆ 1991
23. Clifford's Noisy Day ◆ 1992
24. Clifford's Thanksgiving Visit ◆ 1993
25. Clifford the Fire House Dog ◆ 1994
26. Clifford's First Christmas ◆ 1994
27. Clifford's Happy Easter ◆ 1994
28. Clifford and the Big Storm ◆ 1995
29. Clifford's First Halloween ◆ 1995
30. Clifford's Sports Day ◆ 1996
31. Clifford's First Autumn ◆ 1997
32. Clifford's First Valentine's Day ◆ 1997

33. Clifford's Spring Clean-Up ◆ 1997
34. Clifford and the Big Parade ◆ 1998
35. Clifford Makes a Friend ◆ 1998
36. Clifford's First Snow Day ◆ 1998

CLUE

Various authors

SCHOLASTIC

GRADES 3–6

MYSTERY

The characters from the popular Parker Brothers board game are suspects in short mysteries, ten in each book. The solution for each one appears upside down at the end. The stories are filled with insults and puns. The characters maintain their distinct personalities. In each of the stories, they are all guests of Reginald Boddy, except Mrs. White, who is his maid. Typically, he shows them a certain treasure or engages them in a get-rich-quick scheme, and then one of them steals something. Readers are asked which one did it, in what room, and with what weapon, as in the game. A facsimile of the game's worksheet is shown to keep track of things. The mysteries are challenging enough for older children, and the dialogue is amusing.

1. Who Killed Mr. Boddy? (Weiner, Eric) ◆ 1992
2. The *Secret* Secret Passage (Weiner, Eric) ◆ 1992
3. The Case of the Invisible Cat (Weiner, Eric) ◆ 1992
4. Mystery at the Masked Ball (Weiner, Eric) ◆ 1993
5. Midnight Phone Calls (Weiner, Eric) ◆ 1994
6. Booby-Trapped! (Weiner, Eric) ◆ 1994
7. The Picture-Perfect Crime (Malcolm, Jahnna N.) ◆ 1994
8. The Clue in the Shadows (Malcolm, Jahnna N.) ◆ 1995
9. Mystery in the Moonlight (Jacks, Marie) ◆ 1995
10. The Screaming Skeleton (Jacks, Marie) ◆ 1995
11. Death by Candlelight (Jacks, Marie) ◆ 1995
12. The Haunted Gargoyle (Jacks, Marie) ◆ 1996
13. Revenge of the Mummy (Jacks, Marie) ◆ 1996
14. The Dangerous Diamond (Jacks, Marie) ◆ 1996
15. The Vanishing Vampire (Jacks, Marie) ◆ 1997
16. Danger After Dark (Smith, Dona) ◆ 1997
17. The Clue in the Crystal Ball (Smith, Dona) ◆ 1997
18. Footprints in the Fog (Smith, Dona) ◆ 1997

CLUE JR.

Various authors

SCHOLASTIC

GRADES 2–4

MYSTERY

Four fourth-grade kids form a Clue Club to talk about mysteries and to solve their own. The mysteries are all easy to solve using a little logic. Each two- or three-page chapter contains a separate case, and the solution is given upside down at the end. Peter, Samantha, Greta, and Mortimer are the "good guys" and use their skills to catch others in their class misbehaving. This series is for much younger children than the Clue series. The characters are not the ones from the popular Parker Brothers game, and the crimes are much more easily solved.

1. The Case of the Secret Message (Teitelbaum, Michael, and Steve Morganstern) ◆ 1994
2. The Case of the Stolen Jewel (Teitelbaum, Michael, and Steve Morganstern) ◆ 1995
3. The Case of the Chocolate Fingerprints (Rowland, Della) ◆ 1995
4. The Case of the Missing Movie (Rowland, Della) ◆ 1995
5. The Case of the Zoo Clue (Rowland, Della) ◆ 1996
6. The Case of the Runaway Turtle (Rowland, Della) ◆ 1996
7. The Case of the Mystery Ghost (Rowland, Della) ◆ 1996
8. The Case of the Clubhouse Thief (Rowland, Della) ◆ 1997
9. The Case of the Karate Chop (Rowland, Della) ◆ 1997
10. The Case of the Secret Password (Rowland, Della) ◆ 1997
11. The Case of the Barking Dog (Rowland, Della) ◆ 1997
12. The Case of the Winning Skateboard (Rowland, Della) ◆ 1998
13. The Case of the Soccer Camp Mystery (Rowland, Della) ◆ 1998

CLUELESS

Various authors

ARCHWAY

GRADES 6–9

REAL LIFE

This series is based on the original "Clueless" movie which later evolved into a television program. Cher has been named for the famous singer and actress. She is the ultimate princess, daughter of an indulgent and busy father. Her goals while in high school include dressing appropriately in designer fashions, hanging out at the mall, and keeping up with popular friends. The plots change a little from title to title, but the theme remains the same.

1. Cher Negotiates New York (Baker, Jennifer) ◆ 1995
2. Cher's Guide to . . . Whatever (Gilmour, H. B., and Amy Heckerling) ◆ 1995
3. Clueless: A Novel (Gilmour, H. B., and H. R. Gilmour) ◆ 1995
4. Achieving Personal Perfection (Gilmour, H. B.) ◆ 1996
5. An American Betty in Paris (Reisfeld, Randi) ◆ 1996
6. Cher Goes Enviro-mental (Reisfeld, Randi) ◆ 1996
7. Cher's Furiously Fit Workout (Reisfeld, Randi) ◆ 1996
8. Friend or Faux (Gilmour, H. B.) ◆ 1996
9. Baldwin from Another Planet (Gilmour, H. B.) ◆ 1997
10. Cher and Cher Alike (Gilmour, H. B.) ◆ 1997
11. Romantically Correct (Gilmour, H. B.) ◆ 1997
12. Too Hottie to Handle (Reisfeld, Randi) ◆ 1997
13. True Blue Hawaii (Reisfeld, Randi) ◆ 1997
14. Babes in Boyland (Gilmour, H. B.) ◆ 1998
15. Cher's Frantically Romantic Assignment (Gilmour, H. B.) ◆ 1998
16. Chronically Crushed (Reisfeld, Randi) ◆ 1998
17. Dude With a 'Tude (Reisfeld, Randi) ◆ 1998
18. A Totally Cher Affair (Gilmour, H. B.) ◆ 1998
19. Extreme Sisterhood (Reisfeld, Randi) ◆ 1999

CODY

Duffey, Betsy

VIKING

GRADES 2–4

FAMILY LIFE | REAL LIFE

Cody Michaels, the new kid at school, invents outrageous stories about his family, calling himself Super Cody to impress the class. In *Virtual Cody*, he tries to discover the origin of his name for a class project. In *Spotlight on Cody*, all of the third-graders seem to have a talent for the talent show—except Cody. Cody's friends, Chip and Holly, are supportive and realistic. The easy chapters, funny and perceptive characters, and realistic dialogue make this a good choice for middle grade readers.

1. Hey, New Kid! ◆ 1996
2. Virtual Cody ◆ 1997
3. Cody's Secret Admirer ◆ 1998
4. Spotlight on Cody ◆ 1998

COLLETTE MURPHY *see* Murphy Family

COMMANDER TOAD

Yolen, Jane

PUTNAM

GRADES K–3

ANIMAL FANTASY | HUMOR | SCIENCE FICTION

The "brave and bright" Commander Toad sails through the galaxy with his faithful crew in a parody of *Star Trek* and *Star Wars*. Mr Hop looks solemn and thinks a lot, Doc Peeper is crotchety, and the eager Jake Skyjumper reads a lot of comics. As they go from one adventure to another, puns abound, especially relating to frogs and toads. They bravely save aliens from disasters, and in one episode they go after intergalactic spy 007 1/2. He is Commander Toad's cousin, and they are both "toadally handsome." Lieutenant Lily puts the ship in "high wart speed," and they take off. Adults and older children will enjoy the satire, while younger children will enjoy the adventures.

1. Commander Toad in Space ◆ 1980
2. Commander Toad and the Planet of the Grapes ◆ 1982
3. Commander Toad and the Big Black Hole ◆ 1983
4. Commander Toad and the Dis-asteroid ◆ 1985
5. Commander Toad and the Intergalactic Spy ◆ 1986
6. Commander Toad and the Space Pirates ◆ 1987
7. Commander Toad and the Voyage Home ◆ 1998

CONTENDER

Lipsyte, Robert

HARPERCOLLINS

GRADES 6–8

REAL LIFE

Alfred is an orphaned inner-city boy who lives with his aunt and three cousins. When the series opens, he has dropped out of school and works in a grocery store. His best friend has fallen in with a crowd of punks and gets arrested for robbing a store. Alfred decides to start working out at Donatelli's Gym to become a boxer. Donatelli convinces him to try to become a contender. As the series continues, Alfred succeeds as a boxer, becomes a policeman, and teaches a young Native American, Sonny, the lessons he learned from Donatelli.

1. The Contender ◆ 1967

2. The Brave ◆ 1991
3. The Chief ◆ 1993

COOPER KIDS

Peretti, Frank

TOMMY NELSON WORDKIDS

GRADES 5–7

ADVENTURE | VALUES

Dr. Cooper, a biblical archeologist, travels all over the world with his two children, getting in and out of all sorts of danger and solving mysteries. Smart and competent, Jay and Lila help him out. Lila, traveling back to the United States from an assignment in Japan, is trapped at the bottom of the ocean. Her rescue is hampered by a conflict with Communist guerrillas in the Philippines. A hint of the supernatural is introduced in an episode involving a space-time warp, where the children are trapped in an old Western town and solve a century-old murder mystery. This series features lots of excitement and Christian characters, for whom prayer and trust in God is a part of life.

1. The Door in the Dragon's Throat ◆ 1985
2. Escape from the Island of Aquarius ◆ 1986
3. Tombs of Anak ◆ 1987
4. Trapped at the Bottom of the Sea ◆ 1988
5. The Secret of the Desert Stone ◆ 1996
6. The Deadly Curse of Toco-Rey ◆ 1996
7. The Legend of Annie Murphy ◆ 1997
8. Flying Blind ◆ 1997

CORDUROY

Freeman, Don, and Barbara G. Hennessy

VIKING

GRADES K–1

FANTASY

The two original books about Corduroy—*Corduroy* and *A Pocket for Corduroy*—feature a toy bear and his owner-friend Lisa. When he is left on his own, Corduroy can move around and has adventures in a department store and a laundromat. These books by Freeman have been extended by celebration stories (birthday and holiday) by Hennessy. There are also board books featuring Corduroy that are suitable for toddlers.

1. Corduroy (Freeman, Don) ◆ 1968
2. A Pocket for Corduroy (Freeman, Don) ◆ 1978
3. Corduroy's Christmas (Hennessy, Barbara G.) ◆ 1992
4. Corduroy's Halloween (Hennessy, Barbara G.) ◆ 1995
5. Corduroy's Birthday (Hennessy, Barbara G.) ◆ 1997

COUSINS CLUB

Hermes, Patricia
POCKET BOOKS
GRADES 4–6
FAMILY LIFE

Meghann and Marcie are next-door neighbors and cousins. They are glad to see some of their relatives, but not to play hostess to William, a whining, accident-prone pest. They start a pet-sitting service so they will have an excuse not to spend time with him. Babysitting a couple of snakes and a ferret gets the girls in some funny situations, and when William begins spying on them, the war really begins. In another book, her parents are getting a divorce, and must enlist the help of a hated boy to help her get her parents back together.

1. I'll Pulverize You, William ◆ 1994
2. Everything Stinks ◆ 1995
3. Thirteen Things Not to Tell a Parent ◆ 1995
4. Boys Are Even Worse than I Thought ◆ 1996

COUSINS QUARTET

Mahy, Margaret
DELACORTE
GRADES 4–6
FAMILY LIFE

Pete Fortune and his family (mother, father, brother Simon, and baby sister Bombshell) leave Australia and return to the home of the father's family in Fairfield, New Zealand. There, Pete meets his cousins and must try to fit in with the Good Fortunes Gang. Each book of the quartet features a different cousin and the struggle to both belong and be independent. There are meetings in a treehouse, a visit to a graveyard, concerns about parents with problems, and a wedding. These are lively books with lots of entertaining dialogue and adventures.

1. The Good Fortunes Gang ◆ 1993
2. A Fortunate Name ◆ 1993
3. A Fortune Branches Out ◆ 1994
4. Tangled Fortunes ◆ 1994

COVEN TREE

Brittain, Bill
HARPERCOLLINS
GRADES 3–6
FANTASY

Adventures both amusing and amazing await the readers of this series. When the Wish Giver comes to Coven Tree, four people find out that wishes aren't always what they expect. Professor Popkin promises an equally amazing product, and Dr. Dredd brings much more than the services of Bufu the Rainmaker.

1. The Wish Giver: Three Tales of Coven Tree ◆ 1983
2. Dr. Dredd's Wagon of Wonders ◆ 1987
3. Professor Popkin's Prodigious Polish: A Tale of Coven Tree ◆ 1990

CRANBERRYPORT

Devlin, Wende, and Harry Devlin
MACMILLAN
GRADES 1–3
MYSTERY

The residents of the small town of Cranberryport certainly keep busy solving mysteries, raising funds for good causes, and celebrating special holidays. Grandma is a prominent citizen, as is her granddaughter Maggie. Along with Mr. Whiskers, an old sea captain, Maggie solves minor mysteries. With full-page, comical illustrations, simple problems, and quick solutions, this series is fun for reading aloud or alone. Cranberry recipes are included in each title.

1. Cranberry Thanksgiving ◆ 1971
2. Cranberry Christmas ◆ 1976
3. Cranberry Mystery ◆ 1978
4. Cranberry Halloween ◆ 1982
5. Cranberry Valentine ◆ 1986
6. Cranberry Birthday ◆ 1988
7. Cranberry Easter ◆ 1990
8. Cranberry Summer ◆ 1992
9. Cranberry Autumn ◆ 1993
10. Cranberry First Day of School ◆ 1995

CRICKET KAUFMAN *see* Edison-Armstrong School

CRITTERS OF THE NIGHT *see* Mercer Mayer's
Critters of the Night

CUCUMBERS TRILOGY

Moore, Lilian

ATHENEUM

GRADES 2–4

ADVENTURE | ANIMAL FANTASY

Adam Mouse is an introspective young mouse who observes the world around him and creates poetry from his reflections. His friend Junius is more lively and risk-taking. In *I'll Meet You at the Cucumbers*, Adam and Junius leave the security of their rural home and travel to the city, where they meet Adam's pen friend Amanda. The second book describes Amanda's adventures when she visits the country. The third book is a collection of Adam's poems, which capture his feelings about nature, his home, his friends, and his hopes.

1. I'll Meet You at the Cucumbers ◆ 1988
2. Don't Be Afraid, Amanda ◆ 1992
3. Adam Mouse's Book of Poems ◆ 1992

CULPEPPER ADVENTURES

Paulsen, Gary

YEARLING

GRADES 3–5

ADVENTURE | MYSTERY

Amos Binder and Duncan "Dunc" Culpepper are best friends who stumble into mysteries and adventures. In one book, the friends are in a haunted castle in Scotland; in another, they are in Santa Fe to find out who is rustling Uncle Woody's prize cattle. *Dunc and Amos Go to the Dogs* finds them investigating a dognapping scheme. Melissa Hansen is in some of the books, causing problems for Amos, who finds her very special (see *Amos Gets Married*). These books offer fast-paced adventure with zippy dialogue. They are a good choice for middle elementary grades and reluctant readers.

1. The Case of the Dirty Bird ◆ 1992
2. Dunc's Doll ◆ 1992
3. Culpepper's Cannon ◆ 1992
4. Dunc Gets Tweaked ◆ 1992
5. Dunc's Halloween ◆ 1992

6. Dunc Breaks the Record ◆ 1992
7. Dunc and the Flaming Ghost ◆ 1992
8. Amos Gets Famous ◆ 1993
9. Dunc and Amos Hit the Big Top ◆ 1993
10. Dunc's Dump ◆ 1993
11. Amos's Last Stand ◆ 1993
12. Dunc and Amos and the Red Tattoos ◆ 1993
13. Dunc's Undercover Christmas ◆ 1993
14. The Wild Culpepper Cruise ◆ 1993
15. Dunc and the Haunted Castle ◆ 1993
16. Cowpokes and Desperadoes ◆ 1994
17. Prince Amos ◆ 1994
18. Coach Amos ◆ 1994
19. Amos and the Alien ◆ 1994
20. Dunc and Amos Meet the Slasher ◆ 1994
21. Dunc and the Greased Sticks of Doom ◆ 1994
22. Amos's Killer Concert Caper ◆ 1995
23. Amos Gets Married ◆ 1995
24. Amos Goes Bananas ◆ 1996
25. Dunc and Amos Go to the Dogs ◆ 1996
26. Amos and the Vampire ◆ 1996
27. Amos and the Chameleon Caper ◆ 1996
28. Amos Binder, Secret Agent ◆ 1997
29. Dunc and Amos on Thin Ice ◆ 1997
30. Super Amos ◆ 1997

CURIOUS GEORGE

Rey, Hans Augusto, and Margret Rey
HOUGHTON MIFFLIN

GRADES K–2

ANIMAL FANTASY | HUMOR

The man in the yellow hat brings George, a little monkey, home from the jungle to live with him. George is very curious and is always getting into trouble, but he always ends up making people laugh or solving a problem. When he goes to a friend's house to help bake a cake, he gets into everything and makes a terrible mess; but when the cake is done, his hostess finds her lost necklace inside. He takes a job delivering papers, but he ends up making paper boats out of them. In one of the longest books, a scientist wants him to go up in a space capsule and parachute back down, which he does successfully, earning himself a medal. This series is all in picture book format, but the books vary quite a bit in length. There are three groups of Curious George books. The original Curious George books were by H. A. Rey (assisted by Margret Rey on *Curious George Flies a Kite* and *Curious George Goes to the Hospital*). Margret Rey and Alan Shalleck produced a series of books that correlated with the release of movies about Curious George. Houghton Mifflin has released a new series of books that feature Margret and H. A. Rey's Curious George. There are some board books, big books, and CD-ROM tie-ins, as well.

ORIGINAL CURIOUS GEORGE BOOKS

1. Curious George ◆ 1941
2. Curious George Takes a Job ◆ 1947
3. Curious George Rides a Bike ◆ 1952
4. Curious George Gets a Medal ◆ 1957
5. Curious George Flies a Kite ◆ 1958
6. Curious George Learns the Alphabet ◆ 1963
7. Curious George Goes to the Hospital ◆ 1966

CURIOUS GEORGE MOVIE BOOKS

1. Curious George and the Dump Truck ◆ 1984
2. Curious George Goes Sledding ◆ 1984
3. Curious George Goes to the Aquarium ◆ 1984
4. Curious George Goes to the Circus ◆ 1984
5. Curious George and the Pizza ◆ 1985
6. Curious George at the Fire Station ◆ 1985
7. Curious George Goes Hiking ◆ 1985
8. Curious George Visits the Zoo ◆ 1985
9. Curious George at the Ballet ◆ 1985
10. Curious George Goes to a Costume Party ◆ 1986
11. Curious George Plays Baseball ◆ 1986
12. Curious George Walks the Pets ◆ 1986
13. Curious George at the Airport ◆ 1986
14. Curious George at the Laundromat ◆ 1987
15. Curious George Goes Fishing ◆ 1987
16. Curious George Visits the Police Station ◆ 1987
17. Curious George at the Beach ◆ 1988
18. Curious George at the Railroad Station ◆ 1988
19. Curious George Goes to a Restaurant ◆ 1988
20. Curious George Visits an Amusement Park ◆ 1988
21. Curious George and the Dinosaur ◆ 1989
22. Curious George Goes to an Ice Cream Shop ◆ 1989
23. Curious George Goes to School ◆ 1989
24. Curious George Goes to the Dentist ◆ 1989
25. Curious George Bakes a Cake ◆ 1990
26. Curious George Goes Camping ◆ 1990
27. Curious George Goes to a Toy Store ◆ 1990
28. Curious George Goes to an Air Show ◆ 1990

MARGRET AND H. A. REY'S CURIOUS GEORGE BOOKS

1. Curious George and the Hot Air Balloon ◆ 1998
2. Curious George and the Puppies ◆ 1998
3. Curious George Feeds the Animals ◆ 1998
4. Curious George Goes to the Chocolate Factory ◆ 1998
5. Curious George Goes to a Movie ◆ 1998
6. Curious George in the Snow ◆ 1998
7. Curious George Makes Pancakes ◆ 1998
8. Curious George's Dream ◆ 1998

THE CUT-UPS

Marshall, James
PENGUIN
GRADES K–3
HUMOR

Spud Jenkins and Joe Turner are a couple of "cut-ups" who terrorize their mothers and the neighborhood. Sitting in the movie theater, one says out loud to the other, "I thought you had the snake." They snorkle in the flooded bathroom and hook Spud's little brother to a kite. But they meet their match in Mary Frances, who catapults them into the yard of the kid-hating Lamar Spurgle. Full-color cartoony illustrations on every page add to the zany humor.

1. The Cut-Ups ◆ 1984
2. The Cut-Ups Cut Loose ◆ 1987
3. The Cut-Ups at Camp Custer ◆ 1989
4. The Cut-Ups Carry On ◆ 1990
5. The Cut-Ups Crack Up ◆ 1992

CYBER.KDZ

Balan, Bruce
AVON
GRADES 4–6
ADVENTURE | MYSTERY

Seven friends—Josh, Tereza, Sanjeev, Deeder, Becky, Loren, and Paul—use their Cyber.kdz chat line to solve high-tech mysteries. In one book, Tereza and Josh vacation in the Amazon rainforest and are at risk from poachers. Using their computer skills, they contact friends who hack into a government computer network. In another book, the Cyber.kdz have added video cameras to their systems, which allows them to find out who is changing Becky's grades in the school's database. In addition to the text, there are e-mail messages and data transfers that add to the action. With each kid living in a different location, there are many opportunities to link up with events around the world.

1. In Search of Scum ◆ 1997
2. A Picture's Worth ◆ 1997
3. The Great NASA Flu ◆ 1997
4. Blackout in the Amazon ◆ 1997
5. In Pursuit of Picasso ◆ 1998
6. When the Chips Are Down ◆ 1998

CYBERSURFERS

Pedersen, Ted, and Mel Gilden
PRICE STERN SLOAN
GRADES 5–7
ADVENTURE

Mr. Madison, the computer lab teacher at Fort Benson High School, engages two young computer students to explore the Internet in a special program. Fourteen-year-old techno-wizard Athena Bergstrom and computer hacker Jason Kane share adventures both dangerous and exciting. Internet notes plus a user-friendly glossary explain terms for "Newbies" to the technology. This series would have a particular appeal to kids with an interest in computers.

1. Pirates on the Internet ◆ 1995
2. Cyberspace Cowboy ◆ 1995
3. Ghost on the Net ◆ 1996
4. Cybercops and Flame Wars ◆ 1996

D.J. DILLON ADVENTURES

Roddy, Lee
VICTOR BOOKS
GRADES 4–6
ADVENTURE | VALUES

D.J. Dillon, 13, balances his Christian values with an adventurous life in the Sierra Nevada mountains. He searches for an arsonist, investigates the dumping of hazardous waste materials, goes on a bear hunt, and helps cope with a mudslide. One crisis of faith occurs when D.J. wants to seek revenge against the dog that attacked D.J.'s dog. D.J. is a loyal friend who overcomes efforts to undermine his devotion to God.

1. Dooger, the Grasshopper Hound ◆ 1985
2. The City Bear's Adventure ◆ 1985
3. The Ghost Dog of Stoney Ridge ◆ 1985
4. The Hair-Pulling Bear Dog ◆ 1985
5. Mad Dog of Lobo Mountain ◆ 1986
6. The Legend of the White Raccoon ◆ 1986
7. Ghost of the Moaning Mansion ◆ 1987
8. The Mystery of the Black Hole Mine ◆ 1987
9. Escape Down the Raging Rapids ◆ 1989
10. The Bear Cub Disaster ◆ 1996

D.W.

Brown, Marc

LITTLE, BROWN

GRADES K–2

ANIMAL FANTASY | FAMILY LIFE | HUMOR

Meet adventurous D.W., who always finds herself in trouble with her older brother Arthur and the rest of her family. With determination and much confidence, D.W. is always ready to tackle new situations, from learning to try new foods to riding a two-wheeler. No matter how difficult the challenge, D.W. plows her way through and lands on her feet. Laced with humor, these situations are very familiar to youngsters. They will laugh out loud at D.W.'s hilarious antics. *Glasses for D.W.* (1996) is part of the Random House Step into Reading series.

1. D.W. Flips! ◆ 1987
2. D.W. All Wet ◆ 1988
3. D.W. Rides Again ◆ 1993
4. D.W. Thinks Big ◆ 1993
5. D.W. the Picky Eater ◆ 1995
6. D.W.'s Lost Blankie ◆ 1997

DAGMAR SCHULTZ

Hall, Lynn

SCRIBNER'S; MACMILLAN

GRADES 4–6

FAMILY LIFE | HUMOR

Dagmar Schultz, 12, finds life almost unbearable in a small Midwestern town. She manages to keep busy with her many dreams and aspirations. In her first adventure, Dagmar looks forward to her 13th birthday and having a secret life and a boyfriend. She almost turns the town inside out as she works to make her dreams come true. In further adventures, she makes a deal with a warlock, ignores a ghost, and fights feelings of jealousy—all in the name of love. Preteen girls will enjoy the lighthearted, humorous sagas.

1. The Secret Life of Dagmar Schultz ◆ 1988
2. Dagmar Schultz and the Angel Edna ◆ 1989
3. Dagmar Schultz and the Powers of Darkness ◆ 1989
4. Dagmar Schultz and the Green-Eyed Monster ◆ 1991

DALLAS O'NEIL AND THE BAKER STREET SPORTS CLUB

Jenkins, Jerry B.
MOODY
GRADES 4–6
MYSTERY | REAL LIFE | VALUES

Dallas and his friend Jimmy are members of the Baker Street Sports Club, an informal group of boys who share a love of sports and end up solving mysteries and helping others. The boys are Christians and turn to prayer for help with the mysteries.

1. The Secret Baseball Challenge ◆ 1986
2. The Scary Baseball Player ◆ 1986
3. The Mysterious Football Team ◆ 1986
4. The Weird Soccer Match ◆ 1986
5. The Strange Swimming Coach ◆ 1986
6. The Silent Track Star ◆ 1986
7. The Bizarre Hockey Tournament ◆ 1986
8. The Angry Gymnast ◆ 1986

DALLAS O'NEIL MYSTERIES

Jenkins, Jerry B.
MOODY
GRADES 4–8
MYSTERY | REAL LIFE | VALUES

Dallas O'Neil and his friends return to solve more mysteries. In *Mystery of the Kidnapped Kid*, an unfriendly boy moves into the neighborhood and is the victim of kidnap threats. Dallas and Jimmy find out that the boy is staging the incidents himself to get his parents' attention. *Mystery of the Mixed Up Teacher* deals with Alzheimer's, as a favorite teacher suffers from confusion. Christian values help the boys meet their challenges.

1. Mystery of the Scorpion Threat ◆ 1988
2. Mystery of the Mixed Up Teacher ◆ 1988
3. Mystery of the Missing Sister ◆ 1988
4. Mystery of the Kidnapped Kid ◆ 1988
5. Mystery on the Midway ◆ 1989
6. Mystery of the Golden Palomino ◆ 1989
7. Mystery of the Skinny Sophomore ◆ 1989
8. Mystery of the Phony Murder ◆ 1989

DAMAR CHRONICLES

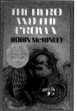

McKinley, Robin

GREENWILLOW

GRADES 5–8

ADVENTURE | FANTASY

Two of the three books in this wonderful fantasy series are Newbery award-winning titles. *The Blue Sword* is the story of Harry Crewe, who leaves her homeland and travels to the outpost of the Homelander empire when her father dies. She is kidnapped by a native king with mysterious powers. *The Hero and the Crown* is the prequel to *The Blue Sword*, and gives the reader historical background on the magical powers of the kingdom. Aerin, the main character of this story, wins her birthright with the help of a wizard and the blue sword. The third volume in the series, *A Knot in the Grain*, is a collection of short stories set in the kingdom of Damar. The most recent addition to the series is *The Stone Fey*. Maddy, the main character, is as strong-willed and independent as the women in the earlier books. Maddy's fascination with the Fey threatens her future.

1. The Blue Sword ◆ 1982
2. The Hero and the Crown ◆ 1984
3. A Knot in the Grain and Other Stories ◆ 1994
4. The Stone Fey ◆ 1998

DANA GIRLS

Keene, Carolyn

GROSSET & DUNLAP

GRADES 3–5

MYSTERY

Published from 1934 to 1979 by the Stratemeyer Syndicate under the pseudonym of Carolyn Keene, this mystery series features two sisters: 17-year-old Louise, who is dark-haired and serious, and 16-year-old Jean, who is fair-haired and more impetuous. They are orphans who live with their Uncle Ned, a ship's captain, and his sister, Aunt Harriet. Because the Danas attend a boarding school, most of the mysteries take place in a school setting.

1. By the Light of the Study Lamp ◆ 1934
2. Secret at Lone Tree Cottage ◆ 1934
3. In the Shadow of the Tower ◆ 1934
4. Three-Cornered Mystery ◆ 1935
5. Secret at the Hermitage ◆ 1936
6. Circle of Footprints ◆ 1937
7. Mystery of the Locked Room ◆ 1938
8. Clue in the Cobweb ◆ 1939
9. Secret at the Gatehouse ◆ 1940
10. Mysterious Fireplace ◆ 1941
11. Clue of the Rusty Key ◆ 1942
12. Portrait in the Sand ◆ 1943
13. Secret in the Old Well ◆ 1944
14. Clue in the Ivy ◆ 1952
15. Secret of the Jade Ring ◆ 1953
16. Mystery at the Crossroads ◆ 1954
17. Ghost in the Gallery ◆ 1955
18. Clue of the Black Flower ◆ 1956
19. Winking Ruby Mystery ◆ 1957
20. Secret of the Swiss Chalet ◆ 1958
21. Haunted Lagoon ◆ 1959
22. Mystery of the Bamboo Bird ◆ 1960
23. Sierra Gold Mystery ◆ 1961
24. Secret of the Lost Lake ◆ 1963
25. Mystery of the Stone Tiger ◆ 1963
26. Riddle of the Frozen Mountain ◆ 1964
27. Secret of the Silver Dolphin ◆ 1965
28. Mystery of the Wax Queen ◆ 1966
29. Secret of the Minstrel's Guitar ◆ 1967
30. Phantom Surfer ◆ 1968
31. Hundred-Year Mystery ◆ 1977
32. Mountain-Peak Mystery ◆ 1978
33. Witch's Omen ◆ 1979

DANGER.COM

Cray, Jordan
SIMON & SCHUSTER
GRADES 5–8
ADVENTURE | MYSTERY

These books use communication on the Internet to establish the plots and then have the characters solve the mystery. In one book, Annie and her brother Nick send messages to a cute girl who has stolen Annie's boyfriend. When the messages fall into the wrong hands, there is danger, and Annie and Nick must use their computer skills to prevent even more trouble. Annie and Nick return in another book to solve a murder while on vacation in Florida. Internet dating, cyber-terrorists, chat rooms, and a web of lies enhance the action-packed stories.

1. Gemini 7 ◆ 1997
2. Firestorm ◆ 1997
3. Shadow Man ◆ 1997
4. Hot Pursuit ◆ 1997
5. Stalker ◆ 1998
6. Bad Intent ◆ 1998
7. Most Wanted ◆ 1998
8. Dead Man's Hand ◆ 1998
9. Shiver ◆ 1998

DANGER GUYS

Abbott, Tony
HARPERTROPHY
GRADES 3–5
ADVENTURE | MYSTERY

Noodle Newton and Zeek Pilinsky are best friends who attend the grand opening of Danger Guy, an adventure store. They buy such Danger Guy paraphernalia as jackets and backpacks and are ready for action. Far-fetched plots and exotic locations, such as Central America and Hollywood, add to the drama. The boys face thieves, smugglers, prehistoric ice men, human-eating plants, and even a cyborg. Snappy dialogue and lots of action will attract some reluctant readers. The fact that Noodle is white and Zeek is African American may broaden the appeal.

1. Danger Guys ◆ 1994
2. Danger Guys: Hollywood Halloween ◆ 1994
3. Danger Guys Blast Off ◆ 1994
4. Danger Guys Hit the Beach ◆ 1995
5. Danger Guys on Ice ◆ 1995
6. Danger Guys and the Golden Lizard ◆ 1996

DANNY AND THE DINOSAUR

Hoff, Syd
HARPERCOLLINS
GRADES K–3
ANIMAL FANTASY

This series is an all-time favorite with beginning readers. Danny goes to the museum one day and finds the dinosaur area. He is wishing that they were alive when one of the dinosaurs speaks to him! They play together and have many amusing adventures throughout the series.

1. Danny and the Dinosaur ◆ 1958
2. Danny and the Dinosaur Go to Camp ◆ 1958
3. Happy Birthday, Danny and the Dinosaur! ◆ 1995

DANNY DUNN

Williams, Jay, and Raymond Abrashkin
MCGRAW-HILL
GRADES 3–6
ADVENTURE | SCIENCE FICTION

Young readers who enjoy science will be especially interested in the Danny Dunn series. Danny is a boy who wants to become a scientist, and he has all kinds of adventures as a result of his curiosity. He is joined by local scientist Euclid Bullfinch, Dr. Grimes (another scientist), and friend Joe Pearson. This series has the potential to spark scientific interest by showing readers that science is exciting and fun.

1. Danny Dunn and the Anti-Gravity Paint ◆ 1956
2. Danny Dunn on a Desert Island ◆ 1957
3. Danny Dunn and the Homework Machine ◆ 1958
4. Danny Dunn and the Weather Machine ◆ 1959
5. Danny Dunn on the Ocean Floor ◆ 1960
6. Danny Dunn and the Fossil Cave ◆ 1961
7. Danny Dunn and the Heat Ray ◆ 1962
8. Danny Dunn, Time Traveller ◆ 1963
9. Danny Dunn and the Automatic House ◆ 1965
10. Danny Dunn and the Voice from Space ◆ 1967
11. Danny Dunn and the Smallifying Machine ◆ 1969
12. Danny Dunn and the Swamp Monster ◆ 1971
13. Danny Dunn, Invisible Boy ◆ 1974
14. Danny Dunn, Scientific Detective ◆ 1975
15. Danny Dunn and the Universal Glue ◆ 1977

DARCI DANIELS

Tolles, Martha
SCHOLASTIC; DUTTON/ LODESTAR
GRADES 4–6
ADVENTURE | FAMILY LIFE | HUMOR

Darci Daniels, a typical sixth-grade girl, just wants to be accepted by her peers. In California, she writes in her diary about her dreams and is dismayed when the diary is misplaced. At camp, she tries to fit in with the other girls. When she moves East, she tries to adjust to her new school by entering a dance contest. Predictable plots and easy-to-read text make this popular with reluctant readers.

1. Who's Reading Darci's Diary? ◆ 1984
2. Darci and the Dance Contest ◆ 1985
3. Darci in Cabin Thirteen ◆ 1989

DARCY J. DOYLE, DARING DETECTIVE

Maifair, Linda Lee
ZONDERVAN
GRADES 1–3
MYSTERY

Darcy J. Doyle, who also goes by D.J., likes to consider herself a "Daring Detective." Her dog Max is supposed to be her helper, but his efforts are not always fruitful. For example, when Darcy is on the trail of a Halloween prankster and orders Max to chase the costumed culprit, Max runs in the other direction and Darcy must chase the suspect herself. The problems that Darcy solves are fairly simple—finding missing homework and solving neighborhood problems. Darcy's brother Willie is sometimes involved, as are her friends and classmates. Young readers who want longer chapter books will enjoy these easy mysteries.

1. The Case of the Mixed-Up Monsters ◆ 1993
2. The Case of the Choosey Cheater ◆ 1993
3. The Case of the Giggling Ghost ◆ 1993
4. The Case of the Pampered Poodle ◆ 1993
5. The Case of the Creepy Campout ◆ 1994
6. The Case of the Bashful Bully ◆ 1994
7. The Case of the Angry Actress ◆ 1994
8. The Case of the Missing Max ◆ 1994
9. The Case of the Troublesome Treasure ◆ 1996
10. The Case of the Sweet-Toothed Shoplifter ◆ 1996
11. The Case of the Bashed-Up Bicycle ◆ 1996
12. The Case of the Near-Sighted Neighbor ◆ 1996

DARK IS RISING

Cooper, Susan
COLLIER
GRADES 4–8
ADVENTURE | FANTASY

This is a classic fantasy series. Two of the five books are Newbery award winners. The story starts out with the three Drew children: Simon, Jane, and Barney. While on holiday, they discover an ancient manuscript that will reveal the true story of King Arthur. In the second book, Will Stanton, age 11, discovers that he is the last of the Old Ones, who are able to triumph over the evil forces of the Dark. In *Greenwitch*, Jane and her brothers help the Old Ones uncover the grail. As the quest continues, Will and his companions must uncover the items necessary to vanquish the rising forces of the Dark. Fantasy lovers will be absorbed by this series and will also enjoy C. S. Lewis's Chronicles of Narnia and Tolkien's Lord of the Rings trilogy, which plunge readers into mysterious fantasy worlds.

1. Over Sea, Under Stone ◆ 1965
2. The Dark Is Rising ◆ 1973
3. Greenwitch ◆ 1974
4. The Grey King ◆ 1975
5. Silver on the Tree ◆ 1977

DAUGHTERS OF LIBERTY

Massie, Elizabeth

POCKET BOOKS

GRADES 3–6

HISTORICAL

Patsy Black and Barbara Layman, two young girls living in Philadelphia at the time of the Revolution, form a club called Daughters of Liberty. They never dream that they will actually be involved in the fight for freedom. Each book finds the girls in the middle of a different adventure. British spies, runaway slaves, and secret notes make for entertaining reading as the girls become accidentally involved in the Revolution.

1. Barbara's Escape ◆ 1997
2. Patsy's Discovery ◆ 1997
3. Patsy and the Declaration ◆ 1997

DAVID AND GOLIATH

Dicks, Terrance

SCHOLASTIC

GRADES 1–3

REAL LIFE

Pet-loving David rescues Goliath from his lonely existence as the only mongrel in the pet store when Goliath is just a puppy. Soon Goliath grows big enough to live up to his name. Though David's parents are not initially enthusiastic about Goliath's presence in the house, they do grow to love him. David, who is an only child and small for his age, enjoys the companionship and confidence that Goliath gives him. This series will appeal to all children who have experienced a special bond with a pet.

1. Goliath and the Dognappers ◆ 1985
2. Goliath in the Snow ◆ 1986
3. Goliath and the Burglar ◆ 1987
4. Goliath and the Buried Treasure ◆ 1987
5. Goliath at the Dog Show ◆ 1987
6. Goliath on Vacation ◆ 1987
7. Goliath's Christmas ◆ 1987
8. Goliath at Sports Day ◆ 1988
9. Goliath's Easter Parade ◆ 1988
10. Goliath at the Seaside ◆ 1989
11. Goliath Goes to Summer School ◆ 1989
12. Goliath and the Cub Scouts ◆ 1990
13. Big Match ◆ 1991
14. Goliath Gets a Job ◆ 1991
15. Goliath's Birthday ◆ 1992
16. Teacher's Pet ◆ 1992
17. David and Goliath on Their Own ◆ 1993
18. Goliath and the School Bully ◆ 1993

DAVY

Weninger, Brigitte

NORTH-SOUTH BOOKS

GRADES K–2

ANIMAL FANTASY

Davy the rabbit seems to find trouble wherever he goes, although he always means well. He gives away his family's Christmas dinner to some other hungry animals, loses his favorite stuffed rabbit, and reluctantly helps out by looking after the baby. Davy and his huge lop ears (he has a special red hood to cover them up) are charmingly painted in watercolors.

1. What Have You Done, Davy? ◆ 1996
2. Where Have You Gone, Davy? ◆ 1996
3. Will You Mind the Baby, Davy? ◆ 1997
4. What's the Matter, Davy? ◆ 1998
5. Merry Christmas, Davy! ◆ 1998

DEADTIME STORIES

Cascone, A. G.

TROLL

GRADES 4–7

HORROR

What would you do if you encountered a man-eating spider? Has a ghost ever communicated with you through your cell phone? Have you ever wondered if your toys are planning a coup? These are some of the circumstances that occur in this series of books. Like others in the horror genre, this series features different characters in bizarre situations, often with spooky creatures. Applehead dolls that take the place of parents, magic tricks that can't be undone, and mutant sea creatures should capture the interest of horror fans.

1. Along Came a Spider ◆ 1996
2. Ghost Knight ◆ 1996
3. Invasion of the Appleheads ◆ 1996
4. Terror in Tiny Town ◆ 1996
5. Revenge of the Goblins ◆ 1996
6. Little Magic Shop of Horrors ◆ 1996
7. It Came from the Deep ◆ 1997
8. Grave Secrets ◆ 1997
9. Mirror Mirror ◆ 1997
10. Grandpa's Monster Movies ◆ 1997
11. Nightmare on Planet X ◆ 1997
12. Welcome to the Terror-Go-Round ◆ 1997

DEAR AMERICA

Various authors

SCHOLASTIC

GRADES 4–6

HISTORICAL | REAL LIFE

Well-known authors, including Kathryn Lasky, Joyce Hansen, Patricia McKissack, and Jim Murphy create fictional characters to present historical information. Using a diary format, each author describes people, places, and events through the eyes of a young girl. On the Oregon Trail, Hattie

Campbell describes the hardships and dangers of American pioneers. Another diary features the reflections of a freed slave girl, Patsy, while another diary gives the insights of a Jewish girl whose family is emigrating from Russia to the United States. A companion series featuring boys, My Name Is America, is also available. Readers who enjoy this series will also enjoy the Once Upon America books.

1. When Will This Cruel War Be Over? The Civil War Diary of Emma Simpson (Denenberg, Barry) ◆ 1996
2. The Winter of Red Snow: The Revolutionary War Diary of Abigail Jane Stewart (Gregory, Kristiana) ◆ 1996
3. Across the Wide and Lonesome Prairie: The Oregon Trail Diary of Hattie Campbell (Gregory, Kristiana) ◆ 1997
4. I Thought My Soul Would Rise and Fly: The Diary of Patsy, a Freed Girl (Hansen, Joyce) ◆ 1997
5. A Journey to the New World: The Diary of Remember Patience Whipple (Lasky, Kathryn) ◆ 1997
6. A Picture of Freedom: The Diary of Clotee, a Slave Girl (McKissack, Patricia C.) ◆ 1997
7. So Far from Home: The Diary of Mary Driscoll, a Mill Girl (Denenberg, Barry) ◆ 1997
8. Dreams in the Golden Country: The Diary of Zipporah Feldman, a Jewish Immigrant Girl (Lasky, Kathryn) ◆ 1998
9. A Line in the Sand: The Alamo Diary of Lucinda Lawrence (Garland, Sherry) ◆ 1998
10. Standing in the Light: The Captive Diary of Catherine Casey Logan (Osborne, Mary P.) ◆ 1998
11. Voyage on the Great Titanic: The Diary of Margaret Ann Brady (White, Ellen Emerson) ◆ 1998
12. West to a Land of Plenty: The Diary of Teresa Angelino Viscardi (Murphy, Jim) ◆ 1998

DEAR DRAGON

Hillert, Margaret
MODERN CURRICULUM PRESS
GRADES K–3
FANTASY

A little boy and his dragon have various adventures as they go to the circus, celebrate holidays, and take care of each other. At the end of each book is a list of all the words contained in the story. Beginning readers will have much success with this series.

1. Happy Birthday, Dear Dragon ◆ 1977
2. Happy Easter, Dear Dragon ◆ 1981
3. Help for Dear Dragon ◆ 1981

4. I Love You, Dear Dragon ◆ 1981
5. It's Halloween Time, Dear Dragon ◆ 1981
6. Let's Go, Dear Dragon ◆ 1981
7. Merry Christmas, Dear Dragon ◆ 1981
8. Come to School, Dear Dragon ◆ 1985
9. A Friend for Dear Dragon ◆ 1985
10. Go to Sleep, Dear Dragon ◆ 1985
11. I Need You, Dear Dragon ◆ 1985
12. It's Circus Time, Dear Dragon ◆ 1985

DEEP SPACE NINE *see* Star Trek: Deep Space Nine

DESDEMONA

Keller, Beverly
SIMON & SCHUSTER
GRADES 4–6
FAMILY LIFE | HUMOR

Desdemona Blank must cope with great changes in her life when her mother leaves the family to "find herself" (*No Beasts! No Children!*). After ten months without a mother, the Blank family begins to adjust by moving to the only place that will accept three children and three dogs. They get a housekeeper to help with the five-year-old twins, Aida and Anthony, and life begins to get better. Desdemona worries about animal rights issues, new friends, and Dad beginning to date. The plot development and humor are similar to Lowry's Anastasia series, providing light reading on issues that are still relevant today.

1. No Beasts! No Children! ◆ 1983
2. Desdemona: Twelve Going on Desperate ◆ 1986
3. Fowl Play, Desdemona ◆ 1989
4. Desdemona Moves On ◆ 1992

DESMOND

Best, Herbert
VIKING
GRADES 2–5
MYSTERY

Gus is a young boy living in a small coastal town in the mid-20th-century United States. Desmond is his mystery-solving dog. Together, they have numerous adventures and solve numerous crimes. A typical plot follows

Gus and Desmond as they find a dog that has strayed from its owner and cooperate with the police department to reunite owner and dog. This series will appeal to children who enjoy animal stories and those who enjoy mysteries.

1. Desmond's First Case ◆ 1961
2. Desmond the Dog Detective (The Case of the Lone Stranger) ◆ 1962
3. Desmond and the Peppermint Ghost ◆ 1965
4. Desmond and Dog Friday ◆ 1968

DETECTIVE MOLE

Quackenbush, Robert
LOTHROP, LEE & SHEPARD
GRADES 1–3
ANIMAL FANTASY | MYSTERY

Armed with a diploma from detective school, a how-to manual, a magnifying glass, and his wits, Detective Maynard Mole begins his career solving puzzling crimes for the animals in his neighborhood. The reading level becomes more difficult as the series progresses. Colorful illustrations add to the interest.

1. Detective Mole ◆ 1976
2. Detective Mole and the Secret Clues ◆ 1977
3. Detective Mole and the Tip-Top Mystery ◆ 1978
4. Detective Mole and the Seashore Mystery ◆ 1979
5. Detective Mole and the Circus Mystery ◆ 1980
6. Detective Mole and the Halloween Mystery ◆ 1981
7. Detective Mole and the Haunted Castle Mystery ◆ 1985

DETERMINED DETECTIVES

Christian, Mary Blount
DUTTON
GRADES 2–4
MYSTERY

Real-life crimes are no trouble for the Determined Detectives, who are main sleuth Fenton P. Smith and his junior partner Gerald Grubbs. In fact, these two search for mysteries to solve. Sometimes, a newspaper tip leads to a possible crime. Then, there was the strange cat with a message for help stuck in its collar. Another book features a problem at a construction company. The boys are quick-thinking sleuths whose cleverness leads them into a lot of action that should appeal to mystery fans.

1. The Mysterious Case Case ◆ 1985
2. Merger on the Orient Expressway ◆ 1986
3. The Phantom of the Operetta ◆ 1986
4. The Maltese Feline ◆ 1988

DIADEM

Peel, John

SCHOLASTIC

GRADES 6–8

ADVENTURE | FANTASY

Three characters from diverse backgrounds and eras are drawn into adventures in another dimension. Score is an orphan from the streets of New York City. Renald is a girl warrior from medieval times. Pixel exists in virtual reality. They are kidnapped by an unknown force and drawn toward the Diadem. To survive, they seek the help of magicians, both good and evil, and they try to understand the reason for their selection.

1. Book of Names ◆ 1997
2. Book of Signs ◆ 1997
3. Book of Magic ◆ 1997
4. Book of Thunder ◆ 1997
5. Book of Earth ◆ 1998
6. Book of Nightmares ◆ 1998

DIDO TWITE *see* Wolves Chronicles

DIGBY AND KATE

Baker, Barbara

DUTTON

GRADES 1–2

ANIMAL FANTASY

Digby the dog and Kate the cat are friends. In these brief chapter books for beginning readers, the two friends share simple activities. When Digby wants to paint his walls, Kate asks to help, only to fill Digby's wall with drawings of animals. Digby finds a way to finish covering his walls with paint without hurting Kate's feelings. In another story, the two friends rake leaves together, only to jump into them. Digby and Kate enjoy many familiar activities, like playing checkers and walking in the rain. These are pleasant, easy-to-read books with simple chapters that are just right for beginning readers.

1. Digby and Kate ◆ 1988
2. Digby and Kate Again ◆ 1989
3. Digby and Kate and the Beautiful Day ◆ 1998

DINAH

Mills, Claudia
MACMILLAN
GRADES 3–6
HUMOR

So far in this series, Dinah has gone from being an irrepressible ten-year-old to her eighth-grade year. Nothing but fun, these stories of school (and especially the trials and tribulations of middle school) will delight readers. Class elections, the school play, confusing substitute teachers, eating 14 cups of ice cream at lunch—all these make for entertaining reading.

1. Dynamite Dinah ◆ 1990
2. Dinah for President ◆ 1992
3. Dinah in Love ◆ 1993
4. Dinah Forever ◆ 1995

DINOSAURS

Donnelly, Liza
SCHOLASTIC
GRADES K–2
ANIMAL FANTASY

A small boy has adventures with dinosaur friends in a very simple picture book series. On Halloween, the boy goes out dressed as a dinosaur and is joined by another trick-or-treater in a strikingly realistic dino costume. When some bullies attack and demand their candy, the little dinosaur's friends rush to the rescue. At Christmas time, he and his dog go sledding, right over a friendly Plateosaurus. Santa's helpers are trying to make dinosaurs, he explains, and they're making them all wrong. The boy straightens everything out, but then Santa's reindeer get the flu. Dinosaurs to the rescue again. Each book has dinosaur information at the end.

1. Dinosaur Day ◆ 1987
2. Dinosaurs' Halloween ◆ 1987
3. Dinosaur Beach ◆ 1989
4. Dinosaur Garden ◆ 1990
5. Dinosaurs' Christmas ◆ 1991

6. Dinosaur Valentine ◆ 1994
7. Dinosaurs' Thanksgiving ◆ 1995

DINOTOPIA

Various authors

RANDOM HOUSE

GRADES 3–6

FANTASY

Inspired by James Gurney's popular 1992 picture book *Dinotopia*, this series of short novels portrays life on a hidden island where dinosaurs still roam. The only human inhabitants are shipwreck survivors and they have cooperated with the dinosaurs to build a beautiful paradise. Newly shipwrecked island-dwellers learn the true meaning of friendship from the idyllic relationships between the dinosaurs and humans.

1. Windchaser (Ciencin, Scott) ◆ 1995
2. River Quest (Vornholt, John) ◆ 1995
3. Hatchling (Snyder, Midori) ◆ 1995
4. Lost City (Ciencin, Scott) ◆ 1996
5. Sabertooth Mountain (Vornholt, John) ◆ 1996
6. Thunder Falls (Ciencin, Scott) ◆ 1996
7. Firestorm (DeWeese, Eugene) ◆ 1997
8. The Maze (David, Peter) ◆ 1998

DISNEY GIRLS

Charbonnet, Gabrielle

DISNEY PRESS

GRADES 3–5

REAL LIFE

Each girl in this series has a special affinity for a favorite Disney character. Isabelle relates to Belle in *Beauty and the Beast*; Ella with Cinderella; Ariel with the Little Mermaid; Jasmine with the princess in *Aladdin*; Yukiko with Snow White; and Paula with Pocahontas. The stories sometimes mirror the experiences of their favorite characters—Isabelle's neighbor Kenny acts like a beast and Ella makes gingerbread castles and needs the help of her stepfamily. The Disney Girls even dress up as their favorite characters and participate in the Magic Kingdom Princess Parade. Fans of the Disney films, videos, and TV programs will also enjoy these stories of friendship.

1. One of Us ◆ 1998
2. Attack of the Beast ◆ 1998
3. And Sleepy Makes Seven ◆ 1998
4. A Fish Out of Water ◆ 1998
5. Cinderella's Castle ◆ 1998
6. One Pet Too Many ◆ 1999
7. Adventure in Walt Disney World ◆ 1999

DIXON TWINS

Markham, Marion M.
HOUGHTON MIFFLIN
GRADES 1–3
MYSTERY

Mickey is interested in being a detective. Kate is interested in science. Together, the twins solve mysteries in their neighborhood. Their cases often occur at holidays or special occasions. For April Fool's Day, the twins look for a practical joker. Easy-to-read, this series will be enjoyed by children who like Nate the Great books.

1. The Halloween Candy Mystery ◆ 1982
2. The Christmas Present Mystery ◆ 1984
3. The Thanksgiving Day Parade Mystery ◆ 1986
4. The Birthday Party Mystery ◆ 1989
5. The April Fool's Day Mystery ◆ 1991
6. The Valentine's Day Mystery ◆ 1992
7. The St. Patrick's Day Shamrock Mystery ◆ 1995

DOCTOR DOLITTLE

Lofting, Hugh
DELACORTE
GRADES 4–6
ANIMAL FANTASY

Doctor Dolittle is an extraordinarily gifted man who can communicate with any animal. As one would imagine, this talent leads to an eccentric reputation and some amazing adventures. The doctor takes expert care of sick and wounded animals and, along with his animals, travels to exotic places, including the moon. Companion volumes include *Doctor Dolittle, a Treasury* (1967) and *Gub-Gub's Book, an Encyclopaedia of Food* (1932). This classic series will delight avid readers who are animal lovers. In one reissue of *The Story of Doctor Dolittle* (Morrow, 1997), Patricia C. McKissack and Fredrick

L. McKissack discuss the controversy surrounding the stereotypical elements in the original book and the rationale for the revisions they made.

1. The Story of Doctor Dolittle (Doctor Dolittle) ◆ 1920
2. The Voyages of Doctor Dolittle (Doctor Dolittle and the Pirates) ◆ 1922
3. Doctor Dolittle's Post Office ◆ 1923
4. Doctor Dolittle's Circus ◆ 1924
5. Doctor Dolittle's Zoo ◆ 1925
6. Doctor Dolittle's Caravan ◆ 1926
7. Doctor Dolittle's Garden ◆ 1927
8. Doctor Dolittle in the Moon ◆ 1928
9. Doctor Dolittle's Return ◆ 1933
10. Doctor Dolittle and the Secret Lake ◆ 1948
11. Doctor Dolittle and the Green Canary ◆ 1950
12. Doctor Dolittle's Puddleby Adventures ◆ 1952

DOGTOWN GHETTO

Bonham, Frank
DELL
GRADES 6–8
REAL LIFE

This series depicts the tough life of kids who grow up in housing projects. Keeny is proud of his Mexican heritage and wants to live up to his dead father's expectations, but he is often led astray by circumstances in his environment. The theme of feeling misunderstood may resonate with readers, and the almost journalistic depiction of street life is admirable, but readers may find much of the material dated.

1. Durango Street ◆ 1965
2. Mystery of the Fat Cat ◆ 1968
3. Golden Bees of Tulami ◆ 1974

DORIS FEIN

Bethancourt, T. Ernesto
HOLIDAY HOUSE
GRADES 7–8
MYSTERY

The character of Doris Fein made her debut in *Dr. Doom: Superstar* as a feisty young adult capable of quick thinking and instant response to danger. Doris's hometown is Santa Amelia, California, but the location of the mysteries varies. In all of the Doris Fein spy or mystery stories there is a romantic involvement that will pique the interest of female readers. Doris is the narrator in this series, which is full of nonstop action, clues for the reader to ponder, some humor, and many cliff-hanging moments.

1. Dr. Doom: Superstar ◆ 1978
2. Doris Fein: Superspy ◆ 1979
3. Doris Fein: Quartz Boyar ◆ 1980
4. Doris Fein: Phantom of the Casino ◆ 1981
5. Doris Fein: The Mad Samurai ◆ 1981
6. Doris Fein: Deadly Aphrodite ◆ 1982
7. Doris Fein: Murder Is No Joke ◆ 1982
8. Doris Fein: Dead Heat at Long Beach ◆ 1983
9. Doris Fein: Legacy of Terror ◆ 1984

DORRIE

Coombs, Patricia
HOUGHTON MIFFLIN
GRADES K–3
FANTASY

Young readers can follow the adventures of a witch in training in this amusing series. Dorrie, a young witch, is earnest in her desire to learn, but sometimes gets carried away. In a typical plot, Dorrie tries to use her powers to stop the rain, but bungles the spell and succeeds in creating a more severe storm. Dorrie's mother is understanding but firm in her reaction. Younger children fascinated by magic will enjoy this series.

1. Dorrie's Magic ◆ 1962
2. Dorrie and the Blue Witch ◆ 1964
3. Dorrie's Play ◆ 1965
4. Dorrie and the Weather Box ◆ 1966
5. Dorrie and the Witch Doctor ◆ 1967
6. Dorrie and the Wizard's Spell ◆ 1968
7. Dorrie and the Haunted House ◆ 1970
8. Dorrie and the Birthday Eggs ◆ 1971
9. Dorrie and the Goblin ◆ 1972
10. Dorrie and the Fortune Teller ◆ 1973
11. Dorrie and the Amazing Magic Elixir ◆ 1974
12. Dorrie and the Witch's Imp ◆ 1975
13. Dorrie and the Hallowe'en Plot ◆ 1976
14. Dorrie and the Dreamyard Monsters ◆ 1977
15. Dorrie and the Screebit Ghost ◆ 1979
16. Dorrie and the Witchville Fair ◆ 1980
17. Dorrie and the Witch's Camp ◆ 1983
18. Dorrie and the Museum Case ◆ 1986

19. Dorrie and the Pin Witch ◆ 1989
20. Dorrie and the Haunted Schoolhouse ◆ 1992

DOUG CHRONICLES

Various authors

DISNEY PRESS

GRADES 2–4

HUMOR

Kids love their Saturday morning cartoons, and Doug and his friends attract many viewers. This series capitalizes on the interest in the TV programs and related media materials like home videos and the Web site Disney.com. The books feature everyday experiences of the familiar characters—Doug serving on the safety patrol and giving Patti a detention and Roger's investments going down after he follows Doug's advice. The humor of this series is balanced by messages about friendship and fairness. There is also a picture book series featuring Doug and his pals including *Doug's Big Shoe Disaster, Doug's Secret Christmas, Doug Counts Down,* and *Doug's Twelve Days of Christmas.*

1. Lost in Space (Grundmann, Tim) ◆ 1998
2. Porkchop to the Rescue (Rubin, Jim) ◆ 1998
3. A Picture for Patti (Garvey, Linda K.) ◆ 1998
4. A Day with Dirtbike (Goldman, Lisa) ◆ 1998
5. Power Trip (Nodelman, Jeffrey) ◆ 1998
6. The Funnie Haunted House (Grundmann, Tim) ◆ 1998
7. Poor Roger (Gross, Bill) ◆ 1998
8. Winter Games (Grundmann, Tim) ◆ 1999

DR. MERLIN

Corbett, Scott

LITTLE, BROWN

GRADES 1–3

FANTASY | HUMOR

On a very foggy day, while walking his dog Bert, Nick sees a new store: Dr. Merlin's Magic Shop. Although it is closed, Bert finds a way in and Nick follows. There he meets Dr. Merlin, who wreaks havoc with his magic. Using his wits, Nick is able to rescue Bert and they escape. Outside, the fog has cleared and Dr. Merlin's shop has disappeared. On other foggy days, Nick and Bert find Dr. Merlin in a bakery and they travel to Dinosaur Land. The books in this series combine zany magic, humorous situations, and a text that is accessible to younger readers.

1. Dr. Merlin's Magic Shop ◆ 1973
2. The Great Custard Pie Panic ◆ 1974
3. The Foolish Dinosaur Fiasco ◆ 1978

DRAGON

Gannett, Ruth Stiles

KNOPF

GRADES 1–3

ADVENTURE | FANTASY

This series is recommended for younger readers who enjoy adventure stories. It concerns the exploits of a curious, fearless young boy and a baby dragon. The dragon has a human personality, and he and the boy, Elmer, become good friends. They travel to far-off lands and arrive home with some very special souvenirs. The series is light and humorous, and the illustrations are lively and fun. There is even a map at the back of each book so that readers can see where the adventures take place.

1. My Father's Dragon ◆ 1948
2. Elmer and the Dragon ◆ 1950
3. The Dragons of Blueland ◆ 1951

DRAGON

Pilkey, Dav

ORCHARD

GRADES 1–2

FANTASY | HUMOR

Dragon's silliness and his blue appearance will appeal to beginning readers, who will enjoy the creative solutions to problem situations, such as finding a friend. Dragon's selection of an apple to be his friend will seem absurd to kids. In the holiday titles, Dragon shows kindness and caring when he does things like share his Christmas presents with the animals. Comical, bold illustrations add to the humor of the series.

1. A Friend for Dragon ◆ 1991
2. Dragon Gets By ◆ 1991

3. Dragon's Merry Christmas ◆ 1991
4. Dragon's Fat Cat ◆ 1992
5. Dragon's Halloween ◆ 1993

DRAGON CHRONICLES

Fletcher, Susan
ATHENEUM; ALADDIN
GRADES 5–8
ADVENTURE | FANTASY

Each book in this series features a strong female main character working to overcome the forces of evil and protect the dragons. *Flight of the Dragon Kyn* is listed as the second book, but it is really a prequel to *Dragon's Milk* and deals with an earlier time. In *Flight of the Dragon Kyn*, the king hopes to use Kara's ability to call the dragons so that he can kill them. Kaeldra saves the draclings from the dragonslayer in *Dragon's Milk*. The saga continues in *Sign of the Dove*, as Lyf protects the draclings and takes them on a dangerous journey. Fans of Robin McKinley will also enjoy this series.

1. Dragon's Milk ◆ 1969
2. Flight of the Dragon Kyn ◆ 1993
3. Sign of the Dove ◆ 1996

DRAGON OF THE LOST SEA FANTASIES

Yep, Laurence
HARPERCOLLINS
GRADES 7–8
FANTASY

Shimmer is able to leave the human world and transform herself into dragon form. In the first novel, she tries to redeem herself by capturing a witch with the help of Thorn, her human companion. Each book consists of a quest or adventure for Shimmer and her companions.

1. Dragon Steel ◆ 1985
2. Dragon of the Lost Sea ◆ 1988
3. Dragon Cauldron ◆ 1991
4. Dragon War ◆ 1992

THE DRAGONLING

Koller, Jackie French

LITTLE, BROWN

GRADES 2–4

ADVENTURE | FANTASY

After Darek rescues and raises a dragonling, he faces many problems. Dragons are feared in Darek's village and Zantor (the dragonling) is in danger. Darek must convince the townspeople, especially his family, that dragons can be trusted. Further adventures take Darek and his friends Rowena and Pol to Krad where they risk their lives to save Darek's father. With a quick-moving plot and lots of action, these books appeal to many readers, including reluctant readers.

1. The Dragonling ◆ 1990
2. A Dragon in the Family ◆ 1993
3. Dragon Quest ◆ 1997
4. Dragons of Krad ◆ 1997
5. Dragon Trouble ◆ 1997
6. Dragons and Kings ◆ 1998

DUCK

Gretz, Susanna

FOUR WINDS

GRADES K–2

ANIMAL FANTASY

Duck and her good friends Frog and Rabbit have a lot of fun together but occasionally squabble as all children do. Duck gets too bossy, so Frog and Rabbit find a way to help her. Rabbit is boastful, so Duck and Frog find a way to make him stop . . . and the fun continues.

1. Duck Takes Off ◆ 1991
2. Frog in the Middle ◆ 1991
3. Frog, Duck, and Rabbit ◆ 1992
4. Rabbit Rambles On ◆ 1992

DUMB BUNNIES

Denim, Sue

SCHOLASTIC

GRADES 1–3

ANIMAL FANTASY | HUMOR

Momma Bunny is dumb. Papa Bunny is dumber. And Baby Bunny is the dumbest bunny of all. They live is a log cabin made of bricks. One day while they are eating porridge, Momma's is too cold so she blows on it. Papa's is too hot so he puts it in the oven. Then they go to town and go ice skating in the lake, even though, as young readers will see, it isn't frozen and they are skating on the bottom. Next they have a picnic at the car wash. When they get home, they find Little Red Goldilocks, and they like her so much that they flush her down the toilet. On another day, it is so stormy that the bunnies decide it's a perfect day for the beach; and when they want to see sculptures and paintings, they go to the zoo. Sight gags in the drawings are a good part of the fun, and young readers will find new ones each time they return to this series.

1. The Dumb Bunnies ◆ 1994
2. The Dumb Bunnies' Easter ◆ 1995
3. Make Way for Dumb Bunnies ◆ 1996
4. The Dumb Bunnies Go to the Zoo ◆ 1997

DUNCAN AND DOLORES

Samuels, Barbara

MACMILLAN, ORCHARD BOOKS

GRADES K–3

FAMILY LIFE | HUMOR

Faye and Dolores are sisters with different personalities. Faye is sensible while Dolores is boisterous. When Dolores decides she wants Duncan the cat to be her pet, she wants him to like her right away. Dolores must develop patience before Duncan will show he likes her. These are entertaining stories about sisters and a pet with personality.

1. Faye and Dolores ◆ 1985
2. Duncan & Dolores ◆ 1986
3. Happy Birthday, Dolores ◆ 1989

EAGLE-EYE ERNIE

Pearson, Susan

SIMON & SCHUSTER

GRADES 1–3

MYSTERY

Moving from Virginia to Minnesota was hard enough for Ernestine Jones, whose nickname is Ernie, but getting blamed for stealing lunches on her first day of school is an outrage. Ernie uses her expert deductive powers and a good eye for detail to solve the lunch box thefts and is able to make friends and win the admiration of the whole school. The series continues with simple school situations that require the detective work of Ernie and her friends Rachel (R.T.), Michael, and William.

1. The Bogeyman Caper ◆ 1990
2. The Campfire Ghosts ◆ 1990
3. Eagle-Eye Ernie Comes to Town ◆ 1990
4. The Tap Dance Mystery ◆ 1990
5. The Green Magician Puzzle ◆ 1991
6. The 123 Zoo Mystery ◆ 1991
7. The Spooky Sleepover ◆ 1991
8. The Spy Code Caper ◆ 1991

EARTHSEA

LeGuin, Ursula K.

ATHENEUM

GRADES 7–8

FANTASY

Readers who enjoy Tolkien's Middle Earth books and the Narnia books by C. S. Lewis will enjoy this journey into the realm of wizards and dragons. This fantasy world is full of strong characters and powerful language featuring Sparrowhawk, apprentice to a master wizard. As in many fantasies, there is a confrontation with the powers of darkness, and the realization that some of the most dangerous evils come from within. Often considered a trilogy, *Tehanu* is linked to the original books with a strong female main character who continues the struggles in Earthsea.

1. A Wizard of Earthsea ◆ 1968
2. The Tombs of Atuan ◆ 1971
3. The Farthest Shore ◆ 1972
4. Tehanu ◆ 1990

ECO KIDS

Makris, Kathryn
AVON CAMELOT
GRADES 3–5
REAL LIFE

Three friends decide that they want to do things to help their community. Sienna, Jess, and Cary become involved in recycling by cleaning up their schoolyard. They start a group to help homeless pets find good homes. They work to stop a developer from building on a wetlands area. These girls are spunky and their desire to get involved could serve as a model for readers.

1. The Five Cat Club ◆ 1994
2. The Clean-Up Crew ◆ 1994
3. The Green Team ◆ 1994

EDDIE WILSON

Haywood, Carolyn
MORROW
GRADES 1–3
REAL LIFE

Eddie Wilson and Boodles Carey are best friends in this series that chronicles their lives in a typical American town. Author Carolyn Haywood, also known for the Betsy series, has a knack for creating timeless characters, so the age of some of this material will not affect its impact on readers. Readers will recognize the adventures of Eddie and Boodles and will appreciate the crazy schemes that are the characters' trademarks.

1. Little Eddie ◆ 1947
2. Eddie and the Fire Engine ◆ 1949
3. Eddie and Gardenia ◆ 1951
4. Eddie's Pay Dirt ◆ 1953
5. Eddie and His Big Deals ◆ 1955
6. Eddie Makes Music ◆ 1957
7. Eddie and Louella ◆ 1959
8. Annie Pat and Eddie ◆ 1960
9. Eddie's Green Thumb ◆ 1964
10. Eddie the Dog Holder ◆ 1966
11. Ever-ready Eddie ◆ 1968
12. Eddie's Happenings ◆ 1971
13. Eddie's Valuable Property ◆ 1975
14. Eddie's Menagerie ◆ 1978
15. Merry Christmas from Eddie ◆ 1986
16. Eddie's Friend Boodles ◆ 1991

EDISON-ARMSTRONG SCHOOL

Hurwitz, Johanna

MORROW

GRADES 3–5

REAL LIFE

The students at Edison-Armstrong school are introduced in *Class Clown*. Lucas Cott is very smart, but he is sometimes too smart for his own good. Other books feature Cricket Kaufman, who is used to being the teacher's favorite until Zoe Mitchell moves into town. Julio Sanchez tries to help Lucas be elected *Class President*, but his classmates choose him instead. In newer books, the friends are on summer vacation and then work together to keep their school from closing. The series expands with *Starting School*, in which Lucas's twin brothers, Marius and Marcus, enter the school's kindergarten. As with Hurwitz's books about Aldo and those featuring Ali Baba Bernstein, these are lots of fun and very popular.

1. Class Clown ◆ 1987
2. Teacher's Pet ◆ 1988
3. Class President ◆ 1990
4. School's Out ◆ 1991
5. School Spirit ◆ 1994
6. Starting School ◆ 1998

EDWARD THE UNREADY

Wells, Rosemary

DIAL

GRADES K–1

ANIMAL FANTASY | FAMILY LIFE | HUMOR

Edward is a little bear who takes his time getting ready for familiar activities—going to school, learning to swim, and staying overnight with a friend. Refreshingly, his parents allow him to reject the activity until he's really ready. Droll pictures show a wide-eyed, sometimes mystified little bear who could be any child who's "not quite ready."

1. Edward Unready for School ◆ 1995
2. Edward in Deep Water ◆ 1995
3. Edward's Overwhelming Overnight ◆ 1995

EERIE INDIANA

Various authors

AVON CAMELOT

GRADES 5–8

HORROR | MYSTERY

Marshall Teller and his family have left the crowded, noisy, crime-filled streets of a New Jersey city to live the bucolic small-town life in Eerie, Indiana. What a mistake! This town is not normal. Weird things happen here, like the release of characters from a cryogenic store—including Jesse James. Then, there is a dollhouse that looks like a real house and a doll that looks like a real girl and Marshall seems to be getting smaller. This series mixes the horror genre with bizarre situations that many readers will find amusing.

1. Return to Foreverware (Ford, Mike) ◆ 1997
2. Bureau of Lost (Peel, John) ◆ 1997
3. The Eerie Triangle (Ford, Mike) ◆ 1997
4. Simon and Marshall's Excellent Adventure (Peel, John) ◆ 1997
5. Have Yourself an Eerie Little Christmas (Ford, Mike) ◆ 1997
6. Fountain of Weird (Shahan, Sherry) ◆ 1998
7. Attack of the Two-Ton Tomatoes (Ford, Mike) ◆ 1998
8. Who Framed Alice Prophet? (Ford, Mike) ◆ 1998
9. Bring Me a Dream (James, Robert) ◆ 1998
10. Finger-Lickin' Strange (Roberts, Jeremy) ◆ 1998
11. The Dollhouse that Time Forgot (Ford, Mike) ◆ 1998
12. They Say (Ford, Mike) ◆ 1998
13. Switching Channels (Ford, Mike) ◆ 1998
14. The Incredible Shrinking Stanley (James, Robert) ◆ 1998
15. Halloweird (Ford, Mike) ◆ 1998
16. Eerie in the Mirror (James, Robert) ◆ 1998
17. We Wish You an Eerie Christmas (James, Robert) ◆ 1998

EGERTON HALL NOVELS

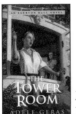

Geras, Adèle

HARCOURT

GRADES 7–8

REAL LIFE

Megan, Bella, and Alice become friends at an exclusive British girls school in the early 1960s. The clash between their secluded school surroundings and the often harsh nature of the outside world provides the basis for many of the plots. The girls confront jealous stepmothers, family curses, and first loves over the course of the series.

1. The Tower Room ◆ 1991
2. Watching the Roses ◆ 1992
3. Pictures of the Night ◆ 1993

EINSTEIN ANDERSON

Simon, Seymour

VIKING; MORROW

GRADES 3–6

MYSTERY

Fans of the Encyclopedia Brown series may also enjoy this humorous series about a boy genius who solves mysteries. Einstein uses his precocious knowledge of science to baffle even his teachers and his mother. Though Einstein loves science, children will also identify with his interest in sports. Readers have the opportunity to solve the several mysteries in each book along with Einstein. The Einstein Anderson, Science Sleuth books have been reformatted into the Einstein Anderson, Science Detective series (with some updated information, too). Both series are listed below.

EINSTEIN ANDERSON, SCIENCE SLEUTH (VIKING)

1. Einstein Anderson, Science Sleuth ◆ 1980
2. Einstein Anderson Shocks His Friends ◆ 1980
3. Einstein Anderson Makes Up for Lost Time ◆ 1981
4. Einstein Anderson Tells a Comet's Tale ◆ 1981
5. Einstein Anderson Goes to Bat ◆ 1982
6. Einstein Anderson Lights Up the Sky ◆ 1982
7. Einstein Anderson Sees Through the Invisible Man ◆ 1983

EINSTEIN ANDERSON, SCIENCE DETECTIVE (MORROW)

1. The Howling Dog and Other Cases ◆ 1997
2. The Halloween Horror and Other Cases ◆ 1997
3. The Gigantic Ants and Other Cases ◆ 1997
4. The Time Machine and Other Cases ◆ 1997
5. The On-Line Spaceman and Other Cases ◆ 1997
6. Wings of Darkness and Other Cases ◆ 1998

7. The Invisible Man and Other Cases ◆ 1998
8. The Mysterious Lights and Other Cases ◆ 1998

ELISA

Hurwitz, Johanna
MORROW
GRADES 1–3
FAMILY LIFE | HUMOR

Elisa Michaels is Russell's little sister. These books show her growing up: from a toddler to adjusting to a new baby brother to getting her own room to entering first grade. Elisa faces many situations that will be familiar to young readers. Children will also want to read the Russell books and the series about Elisa's friends, Nora and Teddy.

1. Rip-Roaring Russell ◆ 1983
2. Russell Rides Again ◆ 1985
3. Russell Sprouts ◆ 1987
4. Russell and Elisa ◆ 1989
5. "E" Is for Elisa ◆ 1991
6. Make Room for Elisa ◆ 1993
7. Elisa in the Middle ◆ 1995
8. Ever-Clever Elisa ◆ 1997

ELLEN GRAE

Cleaver, Vera, and Bill Cleaver
J.B. LIPPINCOTT
GRADES 3–6
REAL LIFE

Ellen Grae Derryberry is a girl who loves to tell strange, funny stories. She is irreverent and real. This series follows her adventures when her divorced parents send her to live with Mrs. McGruder. She struggles with authority figures and attempts to decipher such issues as the meaning of honesty and telling right from wrong. Told in the first person, this series should appeal especially to imaginative girls. Ellen Grae has the rare combination of being both humorous and thought-provoking.

1. Ellen Grae ◆ 1967
2. Lady Ellen Grae ◆ 1968
3. Grover ◆ 1970

THE ELLIOTT COUSINS

Thesman, Jean
AVON
GRADES 7–8
REAL LIFE

Jamie, Meredith, and Teresa are cousins and very close friends. They meet at an annual family reunion and help each other with problems, especially those with boys. Teresa is shy and her mother is overprotective, so when she meets a new boy named Ian, her insecurities almost keep her from making friends with him and getting her first kiss. Jamie is afraid to tell her boyfriend that she wants to see other people. Meredith is still getting over being betrayed by her boyfriend and her (former) best friend. These are romances that will appeal to junior high girls.

1. Jamie ◆ 1998
2. Meredith ◆ 1998
3. Teresa ◆ 1998

ELLIS ISLAND

Nixon, Joan Lowery
BANTAM; DELACORTE
GRADES 6–8
FAMILY LIFE | HISTORICAL

Each title in this series features a different young girl arriving in America with dreams of a new life better than the one left behind. Rebekah Levinsky arrives with her family after the Russian pogroms in the early 1900s. Rebekah befriends two other girls, Kristin Swenson and Rose Carney, who are the main characters in subsequent titles. The theme of the search for a better life and freedom is coupled with the hardships and difficult decisions that were faced by the immigrants. Ellis Island is where the girls separated and where each fictionalized account really begins. This historical portrayal will give readers an accurate glimpse of a very special era in American history.

1. Land of Hope ◆ 1992
2. Land of Promise ◆ 1993
3. Land of Dreams ◆ 1994

ELMER

McKee, David

LOTHROP, LEE & SHEPARD

GRADES K–2

ANIMAL FANTASY | HUMOR

Elmer does not look like other elephants. His colorful patchwork skin is a perfect match for his bright, creative personality. Elmer can always find a way to enliven the lives of the other elephants. In one book, Elmer's friend Harold pretends he is Elmer. In another, Elmer's cousin Wilbur (who is covered in black-and-white patchwork) comes to visit. There are companion board books for younger children that focus on friends, colors, days, and the weather.

1. Elmer ◆ 1989
2. Elmer Again ◆ 1992
3. Elmer in the Snow ◆ 1995
4. Elmer and Wilbur ◆ 1996
5. Elmer Takes Off ◆ 1998
6. Hide-and-Seek Elmer ◆ 1998

ELSIE EDWARDS

DeClements, Barthe

VIKING

GRADES 4–8

REAL LIFE

Elsie Edwards and Jenny Sawyer become friends in fifth grade. This series chronicles their transitions in the awkward middle school years. Elsie grows from an overweight fifth-grader to a slim ninth-grader, gaining self-confidence along the way. The girls in this series have typical concerns—school, family, and "fitting in" —and the books reinforce the importance of self-esteem and the value of friendship. Elsie and Jenny make cameo appearances in *Sixth Grade Can Really Kill You* (1985), which may attract readers to that book, too.

1. Nothing's Fair in Fifth Grade ◆ 1981
2. How Do You Lose Those Ninth Grade Blues? ◆ 1983
3. Seventeen and In-Between ◆ 1984

EMILY EYEFINGER

Ball, Duncan
SIMON & SCHUSTER
GRADES 2–4
ADVENTURE | FANTASY | HUMOR

Emily was born with an extra eye, right on the end of her finger. Despite the nuisance of getting dirt in it or keeping soap out of it, Emily enjoys being able to help others find things by seeing around corners or into difficult places. In the first volume, several chapters are devoted to establishing how Emily handles this oddity. Subsequent stories involve her in problem-solving adventures, including finding a lost treasure.

1. Emily Eyefinger ◆ 1992
2. Emily Eyefinger, Secret Agent ◆ 1993
3. Emily Eyefinger and the Lost Treasure ◆ 1994

EMMA

McPhail, David
DUTTON
GRADES K–2
ANIMAL FANTASY | HUMOR

Emma, a young bear, often sets her parents straight. When they go on vacation, it is Emma who shows her parents how to have fun. When Emma begins looking for a new pet, there is a surprise ending for all. Young children will enjoy these warm stories.

1. Fix It! ◆ 1984
2. Emma's Pet ◆ 1985
3. Emma's Vacation ◆ 1987

EMMA

Stevenson, James
GREENWILLOW
GRADES K–3
FANTASY | HUMOR

Dolores and Lavinia, two witches, are constantly thinking of ways to torment Emma, a young and amiable witch. Throughout the series, Emma manages to outwit them with the help of her friends Roland the owl and Botsford the cat.

1. Yuck! ◆ 1984
2. Emma ◆ 1985
3. Fried Feathers for Thanksgiving ◆ 1986
4. Happy Valentine's Day, Emma! ◆ 1987
5. Un-happy New Year, Emma! ◆ 1989
6. Emma at the Beach ◆ 1990

ENCHANTED FOREST CHRONICLES

Wrede, Patricia C.

HARCOURT; SCHOLASTIC

GRADES 4–7

FANTASY

Sensing the boredom that awaits her if she marries Prince Therandil as her parents require, reluctant princess Cimorene escapes to the Enchanted Forest to meet Kazul, King of the Dragons. With the dragons, Cimorene finally experiences the adventure she craves. Throughout the series, Cimorene and Kazul confront wicked wizards to save the forest.

1. Dealing with Dragons ◆ 1990
2. Searching for Dragons ◆ 1991
3. Calling on Dragons ◆ 1993
4. Talking to Dragons ◆ 1993

ENCYCLOPEDIA BROWN

Sobol, Donald J.

BANTAM

GRADES 2–6

MYSTERY | REAL LIFE

Encyclopedia Brown earned his nickname for his vast knowledge of just about everything, which is even more impressive when one considers that Encyclopedia is only ten years old. He uses this knowledge to fight crime in his hometown of Idaville, where his father is the police chief. Encyclopedia often confronts arch rival Bugs Meany and is always able to outsmart him, especially with the help of his assistant, Sally Kimball. The series allows readers to figure out the cases for themselves before Encyclopedia's answer is revealed, so it may make children want to do some detective work of their own.

1. Encyclopedia Brown, Boy Detective ◆ 1963
2. Encyclopedia Brown and the Case of the Secret Pitch ◆ 1965

3. Encyclopedia Brown Finds the Clues ◆ 1966
4. Encyclopedia Brown Gets His Man ◆ 1967
5. Encyclopedia Brown Solves Them All ◆ 1968
6. Encyclopedia Brown Keeps Peace ◆ 1969
7. Encyclopedia Brown Saves the Day ◆ 1970
8. Encyclopedia Brown Tracks Them Down ◆ 1971
9. Encyclopedia Brown Shows the Way ◆ 1972
10. Encyclopedia Brown Takes the Case ◆ 1973
11. Encyclopedia Brown Lends a Hand ◆ 1974
12. Encyclopedia Brown and the Case of the Dead Eagles ◆ 1975
13. Encyclopedia Brown and the Case of the Midnight Visitor ◆ 1977
14. Encyclopedia Brown Carries On ◆ 1980
15. Encyclopedia Brown Sets the Pace ◆ 1981
16. Encyclopedia Brown and the Case of the Mysterious Handprints ◆ 1985
17. Encyclopedia Brown and the Case of the Treasure Hunt ◆ 1988
18. Encyclopedia Brown and the Case of the Disgusting Sneakers ◆ 1990
19. Encyclopedia Brown and the Case of the Two Spies ◆ 1994
20. Encyclopedia Brown and the Case of Pablo's Nose ◆ 1996
21. Encyclopedia Brown and the Case of the Sleeping Dog ◆ 1998

Eric Sterling, Secret Agent

Herndon, Ernest
Zondervan
Grades 4–6
Adventure

Eric Sterling and his friends Ax and Sharon work for Wildlife Special Investigations, a branch of the CIA. Eric is an unlikely hero: He is easily scared and doesn't like to take chances. Ax and Sharon are both more daring and athletic. Eric is recruited into the organization by mistake but he proves his worth on a mission to prevent genetic engineering of gigantic lizards. Their adventures take them to 'gator country to catch whoever has been butchering the alligators and to Central America and Alaska, with Eric and his friends falling in and out of trouble and facing villains of all kinds. Eric can't even escape danger on vacation: When his family goes to Hawaii, he runs into a girl desperate to protect her family farm, which is now on public land.

1. The Secret of Lizard Island ◆ 1994
2. Double-Crossed in Gator Country ◆ 1994
3. Night of the Jungle Cat ◆ 1994
4. Smugglers on Grizzly Mountain ◆ 1994
5. Sisters of the Wolf ◆ 1996
6. Trouble at Bamboo Bay ◆ 1996

7. Deathbird of Paradise ◆ 1997
8. Little People of the Lost Coast ◆ 1997

ERNEST AND CELESTINE

Vincent, Gabrielle

GREENWILLOW

GRADES K–3

ANIMAL FANTASY

Ernest the bear and Celestine, the young mouse he looks after, have a warm and wonderful relationship. When Celestine gets lost in a museum, Ernest finds her and comforts her. When Ernest is sick, Celestine does her best to take care of him. Young children will identify with Celestine and the lovable, caring Ernest.

1. Ernest and Celestine ◆ 1982
2. Bravo, Ernest and Celestine! ◆ 1982
3. Ernest and Celestine's Picnic ◆ 1982
4. Smile, Ernest and Celestine ◆ 1982
5. Merry Christmas, Ernest and Celestine! ◆ 1984
6. Ernest and Celestine's Patchwork Quilt ◆ 1985
7. Breakfast Time, Ernest and Celestine ◆ 1985
8. Where Are You, Ernest and Celestine? ◆ 1986
9. Feel Better, Ernest! ◆ 1988
10. Ernest and Celestine at the Circus ◆ 1989

ERNESTINE AND AMANDA

Belton, Sandra

SIMON & SCHUSTER

GRADES 4–5

REAL LIFE

When Ernestine Harris and Amanda Clay are fifth-graders, they are more antagonistic than friendly at school, dance class, and neighborhood functions. These books follow the girls into sixth grade, describing their growth as their families change. Both girls are talented—Ernestine as a pianist and Amanda as a dancer. They are often rivals and sometimes friends willing to engage in girlish gossip and rumors. By the last title of the series, they are beginning to mature and accept more responsibilities. These books take place in the 1950s, and segregation is an issue for these two African American girls.

1. Ernestine and Amanda ◆ 1996

2. Ernestine and Amanda: Summer Camp, Ready or Not! ◆ 1997
3. Ernestine and Amanda, Members of the Club ◆ 1997
4. Ernestine and Amanda, Mysteries on Monroe Street ◆ 1998

EVERETT ANDERSON

Clifton, Lucille

HENRY HOLT

GRADES K–2

FAMILY LIFE | REAL LIFE

Many of the books about Everett Anderson incorporate such concepts as numbers and counting, days of the week, and months of the year. One book, *Everett Anderson's Goodbye* describes his grief at the death of his father; another, *Everett Anderson's Nine Month Long*, tells of his mother's remarriage to Mr. Perry and the excitement of waiting for a new baby. Friendship, holidays, and seasons are topics in some of the other books. The rhyming text in these books captures the joys, humor, worries, and fears of a young African American boy. *Everett Anderson's Christmas Coming* was updated in 1991 with new illustrations.

1. Some of the Days of Everett Anderson ◆ 1970
2. Everett Anderson's Christmas Coming ◆ 1971
3. Everett Anderson's Year ◆ 1974
4. Everett Anderson's Friend ◆ 1976
5. Everett Anderson's 1-2-3 ◆ 1977
6. Everett Anderson's Nine Month Long ◆ 1978
7. Everett Anderson's Goodbye ◆ 1983

EXILES

McKay, Hilary

SIMON & SCHUSTER

GRADES 4–6

FAMILY LIFE | HUMOR

The author's own family could have been the model for this humorous series about four sisters. The Conroy sisters range in age from 6 to 13 and have very different personalities. A larger-than-life character is Big Grandma, who is as rough and strict as a drill sergeant. In *The Exiles*, the girls are sent to Big Grandma's for the summers and she attempts to change her book-loving, lazy granddaughters into industrious and productive girls. The sisters grow older with each new book, and in

The Exiles in Love a French boy is introduced and a romantic dilemma occurs. The series is similar to Helen Cresswell's Bagthorpes family saga.

1. The Exiles ◆ 1992
2. The Exiles at Home ◆ 1994
3. The Exiles in Love ◆ 1998

FABULOUS FIVE

Haynes, Betsy

BANTAM

GRADES 5–8

REAL LIFE

Five junior high girls experience ups and downs in relationships with boys, school activities, other groups, and their friendships with each other. Each book features one of the girls, who all excel in different areas. This is the same group of girls that united in elementary school against the snobby Taffy Sinclair in the series by that name.

1. Seventh Grade Rumors ◆ 1988
2. The Trouble with Flirting ◆ 1988
3. The Popularity Trap ◆ 1988
4. Her Honor, Katie Shannon ◆ 1988
5. The Bragging War ◆ 1989
6. Parent Game ◆ 1989
7. The Kissing Disaster ◆ 1989
8. The Runaway Crisis ◆ 1989
9. The Boyfriend Dilemma ◆ 1989
10. Playing the Part ◆ 1989
11. Hit and Run ◆ 1989
12. Katie's Dating Tips ◆ 1989
13. The Christmas Countdown ◆ 1989
14. Seventh-Grade Menace ◆ 1989
15. Melanie's Identity Crisis ◆ 1990
16. The Hot-Line Emergency ◆ 1990
17. Celebrity Auction ◆ 1990
18. Teen Taxi ◆ 1990
19. Boys Only Club ◆ 1990
20. The Witches of Wakeman ◆ 1990
21. Jana to the Rescue ◆ 1990
22. Melanie's Valentine ◆ 1991
23. Mall Mania ◆ 1991
24. The Great TV Turnoff ◆ 1991
25. Fabulous Five Minus One ◆ 1991
26. Laura's Secret ◆ 1991
27. The Scapegoat ◆ 1991

28. Breaking Up ◆ 1991
29. Melanie Edwards, Super Kisser ◆ 1992
30. Sibling Rivalry ◆ 1992
31. The Fabulous Five Together Again ◆ 1992
32. Class Trip Calamity ◆ 1992

THE FAMOUS FIVE

Blyton, Enid
HODDER AND STOUGHTON; CHIVERS NORTH AMERICA
GRADES 4–6
ADVENTURE

Julian, Dick, and Anne Kirrin, along with their cousin George and their dog Timmy, are an adventurous group, making up the Famous Five. Immensely popular in Great Britain in the 1940s and 1950s, this series can be difficult to find in the United States, but is well loved by readers who have discovered it. The characters fall into traditional roles, with Julian, the older boy, the strong and brave leader of the group, and Anne, his little sister, timid and hesitant. But George (whose real name is Georgina), an only child who has her very own island, gives readers another view of an adventurous girl.

1. Five on a Treasure Island ◆ 1942
2. Five Go Adventuring Again ◆ 1943
3. Five Run Away Together ◆ 1944
4. Five Go to Smuggler's Top ◆ 1945
5. Five Go Off in a Caravan ◆ 1946
6. Five on Kirrin Island Again ◆ 1947
7. Five Go Off to Camp ◆ 1948
8. Five Get Into Trouble ◆ 1949
9. Five Fall Into Adventure ◆ 1950
10. Five on a Hike Together ◆ 1951
11. Five Have a Wonderful Time ◆ 1952
12. Five Go Down to the Sea ◆ 1953
13. Five Go to Mystery Moor ◆ 1954
14. Five Have Plenty of Fun ◆ 1955
15. Five on a Secret Trail ◆ 1956
16. Five Go to Billycock Hill ◆ 1957
17. Five Get Into a Fix ◆ 1958
18. Five on Finniston Farm ◆ 1960
19. Five Go to Demon's Rocks ◆ 1961
20. Five Have a Mystery to Solve ◆ 1962
21. Five Are Together Again ◆ 1963

FAT GLENDA

Perl, Lila
CLARION
GRADES 4–8
REAL LIFE

Overweight Glenda gains and loses pounds over the course of the series. She loses weight and finds a boyfriend, only to gain it back when he doesn't call. Later, she meets an even more obese teen who interests her in plus-size modeling. Throughout, her mother makes things more difficult for her by denying that she has a problem.

1. Me and Fat Glenda ◆ 1972
2. Hey, Remember Fat Glenda? ◆ 1981
3. Fat Glenda's Summer Romance ◆ 1986
4. Fat Glenda Turns 14 ◆ 1991

FELICITY *see* American Girls: Felicity

FIENDLY CORNERS

Leroe, Ellen W.
HYPERION
GRADES 5–8
HORROR

In this small town, strange things happen. Like when the pizza parlor sends out toy robots with each pizza. The robots turn the residents into *Pizza Zombies* and Bryan Hartley must try to undo the damage and save the town. Another book features Jamie, who receives the contact lenses of a dead magician and is haunted by his ghost. A werewolf and an evil snowman cause problems in other books. Action, suspense, horror, and creatures make these a choice for the Goosebumps and Fear Street fans.

1. Monster Vision ◆ 1996
2. Pizza Zombies ◆ 1996
3. Revenge of the Hairy Horror ◆ 1996
4. Nasty the Snowman ◆ 1996

FIFTH GRADE STARS *see* Stars

FIREBALL

Christopher, John

DUTTON

GRADES 5–7

FANTASY

Two cousins encounter a "fireball," which proves to be an entry into a parallel, "what-if" world. In this world, the Roman Empire has endured, and European society has been static for two thousand years. In our hemisphere, without interference from the white man, the Aztecs have conquered the Incas and taken over North and South America. Brad and Simon travel all over this world having one adventure after another. They provoke a revolution against the Empire in Britain, but then are victims of persecution by the new regime. They flee to the New World and become the heroes of an Aztec game. Then they run into a Chinese civilization that has also remained static. In all their adventures, they use their superior technical knowledge to come out on top. In the end, given the opportunity to go home, they decide to explore other possible worlds.

1. Fireball ◆ 1981
2. New Found Land ◆ 1983
3. Dragon Dance ◆ 1986

FIRST GRADE

Cohen, Miriam

GREENWILLOW

GRADES K–2

REAL LIFE

In *Will I Have a Friend?* Jim is worried about the first day of school. By the end of the day, he has made a friend, Paul. Their adventure continues in *Best Friends.* The children in this class have many experiences that young readers will relate to—taking a test, getting lost, enjoying holidays, and performing in a play.

1. Will I Have a Friend? ◆ 1967
2. Best Friends ◆ 1971
3. The New Teacher ◆ 1972
4. Tough Jim ◆ 1974
5. When Will I Read? ◆ 1977
6. "Bee My Valentine!" ◆ 1978
7. Lost in the Museum ◆ 1979
8. No Good in Art ◆ 1980
9. First Grade Takes a Test ◆ 1980

10. Jim Meets the Thing ◆ 1981
11. So What? ◆ 1982
12. See You Tomorrow, Charles ◆ 1983
13. Jim's Dog Muffins ◆ 1984
14. Starring First Grade ◆ 1985
15. Liar, Liar, Pants on Fire! ◆ 1985
16. Don't Eat Too Much Turkey! ◆ 1987
17. It's George! ◆ 1988
18. See You in Second Grade! ◆ 1989
19. The Real-Skin Rubber Monster Mask ◆ 1990

FIRST GRADE IS THE BEST

Ryder, Joanne

TROLL

GRADES K–2

REAL LIFE

This series deals with the everyday events and concerns of a class of first-graders. From the first day of school to secret pals for Christmas to making valentines and growing plants, the students in Ms. Lee's class share special times and show they care.

1. Hello, First Grade ◆ 1993
2. First Grade Elves ◆ 1993
3. First Grade Ladybugs ◆ 1993
4. First Grade Valentines ◆ 1993

FIVE CHILDREN

Nesbit, E.

SCHOLASTIC

GRADES 4–8

FANTASY

Four children in England find a sand-fairy called Psammead, a strange-looking creature with telescope eyes that can grant wishes. Jane, Robert, Anthea, and Cyril find it's not easy to think of good wishes, and their attempts have some very funny results, as when they wish to fly or to be as "beautiful as the day." The next book in the series finds the children having adventures with a magic carpet, and in the last book they save the sand-fairy from a pet shop. He can't grant them any wishes, but he leads them to a mysterious amulet that can grant them their hearts' desires, which is to be reunited with their sick mother and the Lamb, their little brother.

1. Five Children and It ◆ 1902
2. The Phoenix and the Carpet ◆ 1904
3. The Story of the Amulet ◆ 1906

FIVE MONKEYS

Christelow, Eileen

CLARION

GRADES K–3

ANIMAL FANTASY | HUMOR

The popular rhyme and fingerplay is expanded in these stories featuring a lively group of monkeys. They jump on a bed, tease an alligator, and narrowly miss being eaten. They even celebrate Mama's birthday. The hijinks and hilarity will delight young readers.

1. Five Little Monkeys Jumping on the Bed ◆ 1989
2. Five Little Monkeys Sitting in a Tree ◆ 1991
3. Don't Wake Up Mama! Another Five Little Monkeys Story ◆ 1992
4. Five Little Monkeys with Nothing to Do ◆ 1996

FLAMBARDS

Peyton, K. M.

PHILOMEL

GRADES 7–8

FAMILY LIFE | HISTORICAL

This saga of the Russell family and Flambards, their historic mansion in rural England, begins in 1908. Christina comes to the family as an orphan, sent to live at Flambards with her uncle and two cousins. This series is filled with historical details and provides a glimpse into the social conventions of this era. This saga was produced as a 12-part series for public television in the 1980s and is still popular with many readers, especially those who enjoy English historical fiction.

1. Flambards ◆ 1967
2. The Edge of the Cloud ◆ 1969
3. Flambards in Summer ◆ 1969
4. Flambards Divided ◆ 1981

FLATFOOT FOX

Clifford, Eth

HOUGHTON MIFFLIN

GRADES 2–4

ANIMAL FANTASY | HUMOR | MYSTERY

Flatfoot Fox is the smartest and greatest detective in the world, by his own admission and that of his faithful friend and companion, Secretary Bird. Principal Porcupine comes to Flatfoot needing his help to find a missing schoolhouse. Flatfoot decides that he knows who stole it and just needs to find out how. Secretary Bird is shocked and thinks he should go about things in the usual way by finding clues and interviewing suspects. In the end, they find that Wackey Weasel caused the schoolhouse to be lost by moving the sign that pointed the way to it. In another case, Bashful Beaver and other animals are missing things that have been replaced by something else. This turns out to be the work of Rat a Tat Rat, who doesn't see anything wrong in "trading" things.

1. Flatfoot Fox and the Case of the Missing Eye ◆ 1990
2. Flatfoot Fox and the Case of the Nosy Otter ◆ 1992
3. Flatfoot Fox and the Case of the Missing Whooo ◆ 1993
4. Flatfoot Fox and the Case of the Bashful Beaver ◆ 1995
5. Flatfoot Fox and the Case of the Missing Schoolhouse ◆ 1997

FLICKA

O'Hara, Mary

HARPERCOLLINS

GRADES 5–8

REAL LIFE

A dreamy young boy living on a ranch in Wyoming has trouble getting along with his practical father. His mother persuades his father to let him have a colt, hoping it will change things for him. Ken's devotion to Flicka, as she sickens and almost dies, almost kills him, too. His father is ready to shoot the ailing horse rather than see it suffer, but Ken persuades him to let her live. Ken wins his admiration in the end. The sequel, *Thunderhead*, is about Flicka's colt. Ken dreams of Thunderhead being a race horse. The 1940s setting provides historical interest, and the relationships between the family members are complex and emotional.

1. My Friend Flicka ◆ 1941
2. Thunderhead ◆ 1943
3. Green Grass of Wyoming ◆ 1946

FLOWER GIRLS

Leverich, Kathleen

HARPERCOLLINS

GRADES 2–4

REAL LIFE

Four girls with flower names all want to be flower girls, and each gets her chance, sometimes in a surprising way. Shy Violet ends up in a "punk" wedding, and Rose does the honors for her single mom. Each of the girls grows in an important way in "her" book.

1. Violet ◆ 1997
2. Daisy ◆ 1997
3. Heather ◆ 1997
4. Rose ◆ 1997

FOREVER ANGELS

Weyn, Suzanne

TROLL

GRADES 4–7

FANTASY

Molly, Katie, Ashley, and Christina all have guardian angels. The books in this series generally feature one of the girls, like *Angel for Molly* in which Molly finds her angel on a trip to Ireland. *Katie's Angel* describes Katie's loneliness after the death of her parents and how she finds and accepts her guardian angel. This is a series that will appeal to readers who like magic and who are reassured by the idea that someone is watching over them.

1. Ashley's Lost Angel ◆ 1995
2. The Baby Angel ◆ 1995
3. Christina's Dancing Angel ◆ 1995
4. Katie's Angel ◆ 1995
5. An Angel for Molly ◆ 1996
6. Ashley's Love Angel ◆ 1996
7. The Blossom Angel ◆ 1996
8. The Forgotten Angel ◆ 1996
9. The Golden Angel ◆ 1997
10. The Snow Angel ◆ 1997
11. The Movie Star Angel ◆ 1998

THE FOURTEEN FOREST MICE

Iwamura, Kazuo

GARETH STEVENS

GRADES K–3

ANIMAL FANTASY | FAMILY LIFE

The fourteen members of the Forest Mice family work and play together in the outdoors. There are four books in this series, one for each season. In the winter, the mice go sledding; in the spring, they picnic in the meadow; summer finds them doing their laundry in a stream; they admire the harvest moon in the fall. Readers will enjoy finding their favorite mice in each of these books about family togetherness and nature's beauty.

1. The Fourteen Forest Mice and the Harvest Moon Watch ◆ 1991
2. The Fourteen Forest Mice and the Spring Meadow Picnic ◆ 1991
3. The Fourteen Forest Mice and the Summer Laundry Day ◆ 1991
4. The Fourteen Forest Mice and the Winter Sledding Day ◆ 1991

FOURTH FLOOR TWINS

Adler, David A.

VIKING

GRADES 1–4

MYSTERY

Two sets of twins who live on the fourth floor of an apartment building solve neighborhood mysteries by carefully observing and drawing conclusions. Their sleuthing leads them into many funny situations in these easy chapter books.

1. The Fourth Floor Twins and the Fish Snitch Mystery ◆ 1985
2. The Fourth Floor Twins and the Fortune Cookie Chase ◆ 1985
3. The Fourth Floor Twins and the Disappearing Parrot Trick ◆ 1986
4. The Fourth Floor Twins and the Silver Ghost Express ◆ 1986
5. The Fourth Floor Twins and the Talking Bird Trick ◆ 1986
6. The Fourth Floor Twins and the Skyscraper Parade ◆ 1987
7. The Fourth Floor Twins and the Sand Castle Contest ◆ 1988

FOX

Marshall, James, a.k.a. Edward Marshall

DIAL

GRADES K–3

ANIMAL FANTASY | HUMOR

This series offers the hilarious adventures of a lovable, egotistical Fox and his friends Carmen the alligator and Dexter the pig. Fox's sister Louise, cool and collected, is the perfect foil to the dramatic Fox. During the series Fox falls in love with the lovely Raisin, makes a video of himself, and learns how to twirl a baton, among other adventures.

1. Fox and His Friends ◆ 1982
2. Fox in Love ◆ 1982
3. Fox on Wheels ◆ 1983
4. Fox at School ◆ 1983
5. Fox All Week ◆ 1984
6. Fox on the Job ◆ 1988
7. Fox Be Nimble ◆ 1990
8. Fox Outfoxed ◆ 1992
9. Fox on Stage ◆ 1993

FOXFIRE

Yep, Laurence

HARPERCOLLINS

GRADES 7–8

HISTORICAL

Each of these books has a different main character, but they are all intertwined by family ties. In the first book, *Serpent's Children*, Foxfire and Cassia are a brother and sister in China whose father, Gallant, has gone to war against the British invaders. Cassia struggles to hold her family together. In the second novel, *Mountain Light*, another character, Squeaky, loses his home in one of the rebellions and goes off to America to seek his fortune. Finally, in *Dragon's Gate*, Otter goes to join his Uncle Foxfire in America to become rich and then return to China and continue fighting against the Manchu. Instead, he discovers that Foxfire is not the man he thought he was and that the Chinese working on the railroad are little more than slaves. With much historical detail, these books make for great reads.

1. The Serpent's Children ◆ 1984
2. Mountain Light ◆ 1985
3. Dragon's Gate ◆ 1993

FOXWOOD

Paterson, Cynthia, and Brian Paterson

BARRON'S

GRADES 3–5

ANIMAL FANTASY | MYSTERY

A group of little animals, dressed and illustrated in Beatrix Potter style, have adventures in the idyllic land of Foxwood. Every page is illustrated in full-color, intricate detail as Rue Rabbit, Harvey Mouse, and Willy Hedgehog battle the evil rats. When Rue's brilliant Uncle Willy is kidnapped and held by the rats, the three young animals save him with the help of a hot-air balloon and see the train Uncle Willy has rebuilt for everyone in Foxwood to use. In another story, the unscrupulous rats cheat to win the Foxwood regatta every year, but Rue plans to use cunning and strategy to defeat them. In spite of their best efforts, the rats cheat again and win, but the friends are cheered by winning second prize overall and first prize for the prettiest boat.

1. Robbery at Foxwood ◆ 1985
2. The Foxwood Treasure ◆ 1985
3. The Foxwood Kidnap ◆ 1986
4. The Foxwood Regatta ◆ 1986
5. The Foxwood Smugglers ◆ 1988

FRANCES

Hoban, Russell

HARPERCOLLINS

GRADES K–3

ANIMAL FANTASY | FAMILY LIFE | HUMOR

Frances is a little badger living with her mother and father and younger sister Gloria. She quarrels and makes up with her friend Albert, adjusts to having a little sister, hides under the dining room table, and has a little song to sing for every occasion.

1. Bedtime for Frances ◆ 1960
2. A Baby Sister for Frances ◆ 1964
3. Bread and Jam for Frances ◆ 1964
4. A Birthday for Frances ◆ 1968
5. Best Friends for Frances ◆ 1969
6. A Bargain for Frances ◆ 1970
7. Eggs, Thoughts, and Other Frances Songs ◆ 1972

FRANCES IN THE FOURTH GRADE

Cooper, Ilene

KNOPF

GRADES 3–5

FAMILY LIFE | REAL LIFE

Frances lives in a small town in Wisconsin, leading the ordinary life of an American schoolgirl. She likes to read and take ballet lessons, and although she has two friends, Lena and Polly, they are not part of the popular crowd. Her family—Mom, Dad, and older siblings Elizabeth and Mike—are loving and supportive. During the series, she becomes less shy, makes new friends, and discovers new interests.

1. Frances Takes a Chance ◆ 1991
2. Frances Dances ◆ 1991
3. Frances Four-Eyes ◆ 1991
4. Frances and Friends ◆ 1991

FRANK AND ERNEST

Day, Alexandra

SCHOLASTIC

GRADES 2–5

ANIMAL FANTASY | HUMOR

Frank, a bear, and his friend Ernest, an elephant, dress in normal human clothes and take a variety of temporary jobs. They take over a diner and a truck route and become managers of a baseball team. As they take on each new endeavor, they diligently learn the colorful slang of the trade. When they work at the diner, they learn, among other things, that apple pie is "Eve with a lid" and milk is "cow juice." In the subsequent books, the new words they have learned are featured in boxes and are also listed at the end.

1. Frank and Ernest ◆ 1988
2. Frank and Ernest Play Ball ◆ 1990
3. Frank and Ernest on the Road ◆ 1994

FRANK AND JOE HARDY—THE CLUES BROTHERS *see* Hardy Boys: Frank and Joe Hardy: The Clues Brothers

FRANKLIN

Bourgeois, Paulette
SCHOLASTIC
GRADES K–3
ANIMAL FANTASY

Franklin is a young turtle who goes through the trials and tribulations of childhood: making new friends, having sleep-overs, being afraid of the dark. Franklin always finds a way out of his problems and has fun along the way. This has been such a popular series with children that there are even related items such as Franklin puppets.

1. Franklin in the Dark ◆ 1987
2. Hurry Up, Franklin ◆ 1991
3. Franklin Fibs ◆ 1992
4. Franklin Is Lost ◆ 1993
5. Franklin Is Bossy ◆ 1994
6. Franklin and Me ◆ 1995
7. Franklin Goes to School ◆ 1995
8. Franklin Is Messy ◆ 1995
9. Franklin Plays the Game ◆ 1995
10. Franklin Wants a Pet ◆ 1995
11. Franklin and the Tooth Fairy ◆ 1996
12. Franklin Has a Sleepover ◆ 1996
13. Franklin's Halloween ◆ 1996
14. Franklin's School Play ◆ 1996
15. Franklin Rides a Bike ◆ 1997
16. Franklin's Bad Day ◆ 1997
17. Franklin's Blanket ◆ 1997
18. Franklin's New Friend ◆ 1997
19. Finders Keepers for Franklin ◆ 1998
20. Franklin and the Thunderstorm ◆ 1998
21. Franklin Goes to Day Care ◆ 1998
22. Franklin's Christmas Gift ◆ 1998
23. Franklin's Secret Club ◆ 1998

FRED BEAR

Hayes, Sarah
LITTLE, BROWN
GRADES K–1
FANTASY | HUMOR

Fred is a toy bear who has several exciting adventures. He is lost in the dump and left in the park overnight. His owner's dog tries to spoil Fred's picnic and a naughty little girl tries to steal Fred. Through it all, Fred is unflappable and children are delighted.

1. This Is the Bear ◆ 1986
2. This Is the Bear and the Picnic Lunch ◆ 1988
3. This Is the Bear and the Scary Night ◆ 1992
4. This Is the Bear and the Bad Little Girl ◆ 1995

FREDDY

Brooks, Walter R.
OVERLOOK PRESS
GRADES 3–5
ANIMAL FANTASY

Freddy is a truly remarkable pig. In this series, he is by turns a cowboy, a detective, and a balloon rider. He has all these adventures at the Bean farm with his friends Jinx the cat, Mrs. Wiggins the cow, Charles the rooster, and the ducks Alice and Emma. Their relationships and humanlike qualities lead to some very funny situations.

1. To and Again ◆ 1927
2. More To and Again ◆ 1930
3. Freddy the Detective ◆ 1932
4. Story of Freginald ◆ 1936
5. The Clockwork Twin ◆ 1937
6. Wiggins for President ◆ 1939
7. Freddy the Politician ◆ 1939
8. Freddy's Cousin Weedly ◆ 1940
9. Freddy and the Ignoramus ◆ 1941
10. Freddy and the Perilous Adventure ◆ 1942
11. Freddy and the Bean Home News ◆ 1943
12. Freddy and Mister Camphor ◆ 1944
13. Freddy and the Popinjay ◆ 1945
14. Freddy the Pied Piper ◆ 1946
15. Freddy the Magician ◆ 1947
16. Freddy Goes Camping ◆ 1948
17. Freddy Plays Football ◆ 1949
18. Freddy the Cowboy ◆ 1950
19. Freddy Rides Again ◆ 1951
20. Freddy the Pilot ◆ 1952
21. Freddy and the Space Ship ◆ 1953
22. Freddy and the Men from Mars ◆ 1954
23. Freddy and the Baseball Team from Mars ◆ 1955
24. Freddy and Simon the Dictator ◆ 1956

25. Freddy and the Flying Saucer Plans ◆ 1957
26. Freddy and the Dragon ◆ 1958

FRIENDS AND AMIGOS

Giff, Patricia Reilly
BANTAM DOUBLEDAY DELL
GRADES 2–4
REAL LIFE

Sarah and Anna are best friends who are often bothered by a pesky classmate, Benjamin. In one book, Sarah tries to learn Spanish while Anna is at camp. In another, the girls organize a program for Columbus Day and plan for a visit from Anna's cousin from Colombia. Their librarian, Mrs. Muñoz, helps them with many of their projects. Anna and her family are bilingual (speaking English and Spanish), and the series incorporates simple Spanish words, phrases, and lessons into the text.

1. Adios, Anna ◆ 1995
2. Say Hola, Sarah ◆ 1995
3. Ho, Ho Benjamin, Feliz Navidád ◆ 1995
4. Happy Birthday Anna, Sorpresa! ◆ 1996
5. It's a Fiesta, Ben ◆ 1996
6. Good Dog, Bonita ◆ 1996

THE FRIENDSHIP RING

Vail, Rachel
SCHOLASTIC
GRADES 5–8
REAL LIFE

A trio of books about a trio of seventh-grade friends. Each book tells the story of one of the girls: her problems, her family, and how she feels about the other two friends. The girls have very different families, very different talents, and very different likes and dislikes. Preteen and adolescent girls will enjoy these stories about friendship and its ups and downs.

1. Please, Please, Please ◆ 1998
2. If You Only Knew ◆ 1998
3. Not That I Care ◆ 1998

FRIGHTMARES

Kehret, Peg
MINSTREL/POCKET BOOKS
GRADES 2–6
ADVENTURE | MYSTERY

Rosie and Kayo have a Care Club to look after animals, which keeps getting them into dangerous situations that give their parents "frightmares." An elderly neighbor has to find a new home for her cat because her nephew is allergic to it. Naturally, the girls try to help her, and in the process they discover that someone is trying to poison the old woman. As the plot unfolds, the girls get into ever deeper trouble, and even the police can't help. A similar situation occurs when the girls go camping with Rosie's parents. Everything always ends happily, but readers are in for some scares.

1. Cat Burglar on the Prowl ◆ 1995
2. Bone Breath and the Vandals ◆ 1995
3. Don't Go Near Mrs. Tallie ◆ 1995
4. Desert Danger ◆ 1995
5. The Ghost Followed Us Home ◆ 1996
6. Race to Disaster ◆ 1996
7. Screaming Eagles ◆ 1996
8. Backstage Fright ◆ 1996

FROG

Mayer, Mercer
DIAL
GRADES K–1
ANIMAL FANTASY | HUMOR

A boy and his dog go out to catch a frog. They give up in disgust, but the frog has been having fun and decides to go home with them. When the frog stows away in the boy's pocket for a family visit to a fancy restaurant, the words "fancy restaurant" are there on a sign. The boy, the dog, and the frog acquire a turtle, who joins their adventures. One day, the frog runs away, and the boy and dog have several mishaps looking for him. These books are wordless except for occasional signposts in the illustrations.

1. A Boy, a Dog, and a Frog ◆ 1967
2. Frog, Where Are You? ◆ 1969
3. A Boy, a Dog, a Frog, and a Friend ◆ 1971
4. Frog on His Own ◆ 1973
5. Frog Goes to Dinner ◆ 1974
6. One Frog Too Many ◆ 1975

FROG

Velthuijs, Max

MORROW

GRADES K–2

ANIMAL FANTASY | VALUES

Four animal friends deal with life issues in these gentle stories. Hare is the one who is wise and mentors the other three. When Frog feels very strange, "hot and cold and something going thump thump inside," Hare decides he must be in love with the white duck. Pig says they can't be in love because "you're green and she's white." Frog doesn't let that bother him, and they fall in love. When a stranger moves into their neighborhood, Pig says he is just a dirty rat, but Hare pleads for tolerance. Rat proves to be hard-working, helpful, and clever. In another book, when a blackbird dies, the four friends find comfort in the continuance of everyday life.

1. Frog in Love ◆ 1989
2. Frog and the Birdsong ◆ 1991
3. Frog in Winter ◆ 1993
4. Frog and the Stranger ◆ 1994
5. Frog Is Frightened ◆ 1995
6. Frog Is a Hero ◆ 1996

FROG AND TOAD

Lobel, Arnold

HARPERCOLLINS

GRADES K–3

ANIMAL FANTASY | HUMOR

Frog and Toad live in little houses in the forest, and they like to visit each other, take walks, and enjoy the seasons together. Frog is the more sensible of the two and gently helps out as Toad worries about how his bathing suit looks or doing things on his list. In each of the five little stories that make up these easy readers, the animals express their friendship with humor and affection. Companion volumes include *The Frog and Toad Coloring Book* and *The Frog and Toad Pop-up Book*.

1. Frog and Toad Are Friends ◆ 1970
2. Frog and Toad Together ◆ 1972
3. Frog and Toad All Year ◆ 1976
4. Days with Frog and Toad ◆ 1979

FROGGY

London, Jonathan
VIKING
GRADES K–3
ANIMAL FANTASY | HUMOR

Froggy and his parents go through the simple routines of living and learning, with amusing takes on the parent-child relationship. Froggy doesn't want to learn to swim; but when he finally does learn, he doesn't want to stop. He has a terrible dream the night before his first day of school—he goes to school in his underwear. All ends happily when he wakes up and leapfrogs with his parents out to the bus stop.

1. Froggy Gets Dressed ◆ 1992
2. Let's Go, Froggy! ◆ 1994
3. Froggy Learns to Swim ◆ 1995
4. Froggy Goes to School ◆ 1996
5. Froggy's First Kiss ◆ 1998
6. Froggy Plays Soccer ◆ 1999

FUDGE

Blume, Judy
BANTAM
GRADES 3–5
HUMOR | REAL LIFE

Peter Hatcher is a fairly ordinary middle school kid with an extraordinary nuisance of a little brother known as Fudge. (Besides saying embarrassing things in public and ruining Peter's school projects, Fudge swallows Peter's pet turtle whole.) The Hatchers spend a summer sharing a house with Sheila Tubman's family at a rented house in Maine. Peter hates Sheila when the summer begins; but after some shared adventures babysitting Fudge, they begin to get along. Sheila is featured in a related book, *Otherwise Known as Sheila the Great* (1972).

1. Tales of a Fourth Grade Nothing ◆ 1972
2. Superfudge ◆ 1980
3. Fudge-a-mania ◆ 1990

FULL HOUSE: CLUB STEPHANIE

Various authors

POCKET BOOKS

GRADES 4–6

REAL LIFE

In the other Full House series books, the focus is on the activities of the Tanner family. In this group, the focus is on Stephanie and her friends Darcy, Anna, Kayla, and Allie and their interests: friendship, boys, projects, boys, summertime, and boys. Stephanie and her friends are often bothered by a group of snobby, popular girls called the Flamingoes. Readers who enjoy the television show will like seeing Stephanie in her own adventures. They will also like the breezy style of writing and the light, entertaining plots.

1. Fun, Sun, and Flamingoes (Quin-Harkin, Janet) ◆ 1997
2. Fireworks and Flamingoes (Ecco, Emily) ◆ 1997
3. Flamingo Revenge (Quin-Harkin, Janet) ◆ 1997
4. Too Many Flamingoes (Eisenberg, Lisa) ◆ 1998
5. Friend Or Flamingo? (Haley, Wendy) ◆ 1998
6. Flamingoes Overboard! (Alexander, Brandon) ◆ 1998

FULL HOUSE: MICHELLE

Various authors

POCKET BOOKS

GRADES 2–4

FAMILY LIFE | REAL LIFE

As the youngest child in the main family in the *Full House* TV series, Michelle is cute and sassy. The books in this series put her in situations involving her older sisters, D.J. and Stephanie, and her dad, Danny. Other regulars include Joey Gladstone and Uncle Jesse. Familiar situations such as sleep-overs, ballet, science fair projects, and being cool are featured.

1. The Great Pet Project (Carroll, Jacqueline) ◆ 1995
2. The Super-Duper Sleepover Party (Stine, Megan) ◆ 1995
3. My Two Best Friends (Dubowski, Cathy East) ◆ 1995

4. Lucky, Lucky Day (O'Neill, Laura) ◆ 1995
5. The Ghost in My Closet (Dubowski, Cathy East) ◆ 1995
6. Ballet Surprise (Waricha, Jean) ◆ 1996
7. Major League Trouble (O'Neill, Laura) ◆ 1996
8. My Fourth-Grade Mess (Dubowski, Cathy East) ◆ 1996
9. Bunk 3, Teddy and Me (Dubowski, Cathy East) ◆ 1996
10. My Best Friend Is a Movie Star! (Dubowski, Cathy East) ◆ 1996
11. The Big Turkey Escape (Waricha, Jean) ◆ 1996
12. The Substitute Teacher (Dubowski, Cathy East) ◆ 1997
13. Calling All Planets (Verney, Sarah) ◆ 1997
14. I've Got a Secret (Dubowski, Cathy East) ◆ 1997
15. How to Be Cool (Weyn, Suzanne) ◆ 1997
16. The Not-So-Great Outdoors (Waricha, Jean) ◆ 1997
17. My Ho-Ho Horrible Christmas (Preiss, Pauline) ◆ 1997
18. My Almost Perfect Plan (Verney, Sarah) ◆ 1998
19. April Fools! (Alexander, Nina) ◆ 1998
20. My Life Is a Three-Ring Circus (Dubowski, Cathy East) ◆ 1998
21. Welcome to My Zoo (Waricha, Jean) ◆ 1998
22. The Problem with Pen Pals (McMahon, Maggie) ◆ 1998
23. Merry Christmas, World! (Davis, Gibbs) ◆ 1998

FULL HOUSE: STEPHANIE

Various authors
POCKET BOOKS
GRADES 4–6
FAMILY LIFE | REAL LIFE

Fans of the TV comedy *Full House* will enjoy reading these books about Stephanie. As the middle daughter (D.J. is older; Michelle is younger), Stephanie sometimes struggles to get attention and cope with problems. After the death of Stephanie's mom, her dad, Danny, tries to deal with raising three daughters. His friend Joey Gladstone and the girls' Uncle Jesse aid him. Plots include Stephanie wanting to be on her school's TV show and what happens when she takes riding lessons. Girlfriends and the beginning of relationships with boys are also featured. These are light-hearted problems that are neatly wrapped up at the end of each book.

1. Phone Call from a Flamingo (Speregen, Devra Newberger) ◆ 1993
2. The Boy-Oh-Boy Next Door (Miami, Rita) ◆ 1993
3. Twin Troubles (Wright, Mary) ◆ 1994
4. Hip Hop Till You Drop (Speregen, Devra Newberger) ◆ 1994
5. Here Comes the Brand-New Me (Carroll, Jacqueline) ◆ 1994
6. The Secret's Out (Kimball, Katie) ◆ 1994

7. Daddy's Not-So-Little Girl (Thomas, Lucinda) ◆ 1995
8. P.S. Friends Forever (Speregen, Devra Newberger) ◆ 1995
9. Getting Even With the Flamingoes (Umansky, Diane) ◆ 1995
10. The Dude of My Dreams (Bentley, Karen) ◆ 1995
11. Back-to-School Cool (Speregen, Devra Newberger) ◆ 1995
12. Picture Me Famous (Simon, Lisa) ◆ 1995
13. Two-For-One Christmas Fun (Landesman, Peter) ◆ 1995
14. The Big Fix-up Mix-up (Speregen, Devra Newberger) ◆ 1996
15. Ten Ways to Wreck a Date (Landesman, Peter) ◆ 1996
16. Wish Upon a VCR (Speregen, Devra Newberger) ◆ 1996
17. Doubles or Nothing (West, Eliza) ◆ 1996
18. Sugar and Spice Advice (Speregen, Devra Newberger) ◆ 1996
19. Never Trust a Flamingo (Speregen, Devra Newberger) ◆ 1996
20. The Truth About Boys (Costello, Emily) ◆ 1997
21. Crazy About the Future (Speregen, Devra Newberger) ◆ 1997
22. My Secret Secret Admirer (Umansky, Diane) ◆ 1997
23. Blue Ribbon Christmas (Costello, Emily) ◆ 1997
24. The Story on Older Boys (Weyn, Suzanne) ◆ 1998
25. My Three Weeks as a Spy (Steiber, Ellen) ◆ 1998
26. No Business Like Show Business (Herman, Gail) ◆ 1998
27. Mail-Order Brother (O'Neill, Laura) ◆ 1998
28. To Cheat or Not to Cheat (Speregen, Devra Newberger) ◆ 1998

FUNNY FIRSTS

Thaler, Mike
TROLL
GRADES K–1
HUMOR

How did you cope with your first trip to the dentist? Or with the first time you went to camp? Snarvey Gooper faces these first-time events and finds the humor in them. Taking his pet to the vet, moving to a new neighborhood, even trick-or-treating for the first time are anxious moments for Snarvey. Readers will be reassured by how he worries and frets before finding a way to overcome his fears.

1. Camp Rotten Time ◆ 1993
2. Fang the Dentist ◆ 1993
3. My Cat Is Going to the Dogs ◆ 1993
4. The Schmo Must Go On ◆ 1994
5. Love Stinks ◆ 1996
6. Moving to Mars ◆ 1996
7. I'm Dracula, Who Are You? ◆ 1997

FUNNYBONES

Ahlberg, Allan
GREENWILLOW; MULBERRY
GRADES K–2
FANTASY | HUMOR

Colorful cartoon-style illustrations show big skeleton, little skeleton, and their dog skeleton. In one book, they go for a late night walk, hoping to frighten someone. No one is out, so they play in the park and visit the skeleton animals in the zoo. In another book, they solve some mini-mysteries as they drive around town. There is lots of fun with these not-so-scary skeletons.

1. Funnybones ◆ 1980
2. The Black Cat ◆ 1990
3. The Pet Shop ◆ 1990
4. Dinosaur Dreams ◆ 1991
5. Mystery Tour ◆ 1991
6. Skeleton Crew ◆ 1991
7. Bumps in the Night ◆ 1991
8. Give the Dog a Bone ◆ 1991
9. Ghost Train ◆ 1992

FUZZY RABBIT

Billam, Rosemary
RANDOM HOUSE
GRADES K–1
FAMILY LIFE | FANTASY

Ellen loves her toy rabbit, Fuzzy Rabbit. Sometimes, Ellen's brother Robert wants to get his hands on Fuzzy Rabbit. In one book Fuzzy Rabbit saves Christmas when he wakes Santa up on Christmas Eve. Fuzzy Rabbit is a sweet character, and children who like reading about favorite toys enjoy these books.

1. Fuzzy Rabbit ◆ 1984
2. Fuzzy Rabbit in the Park ◆ 1986
3. Fuzzy Rabbit and the Little Brother Problem ◆ 1988
4. Fuzzy Rabbit Saves Christmas ◆ 1991

GARY PAULSEN'S WORLD OF ADVENTURE *see* World of Adventure

GATOR GIRLS

Calmenson, Stephanie, and Joanna Cole

MORROW

GRADES 1–3

ANIMAL FANTASY | HUMOR

Easy-to-read, humorous stories feature likable friends Amy and Allie Gator and a pest, Marvin Gator. The short, fast-paced chapters involve childlike problems with predictable endings that leave the characters and the readers happy. Camp Wogga-Bog almost ruins the summer for the Gator girls, especially when Allie gets accepted at the last minute—without her friend Amy. Quick thinking averts that near disaster. Lots of action and laughter along with strong friendship models will entertain early readers.

   1. The Gator Girls ◆ 1995
   2. Rockin' Reptiles ◆ 1997
   3. Get Well, Gators! ◆ 1998

GENGHIS KHAN

Sharmat, Marjorie Weinman

RANDOM HOUSE

GRADES 2–3

HUMOR

The Shedd family's life changes dramatically when young Fred brings home a stray dog, Duz. The dog only *looks* mean and scary, resembling Dracula with fanglike teeth. Duz wins a lookalike contest and is chosen to replace a famous movie star dog. The family moves to Hollywood for more adventures with Duz, alias Genghis Khan. Short sentences, quick action, and easy chapters will make this series attractive to early readers.

   1. The Great Genghis Khan Look-Alike Contest ◆ 1993
   2. Genghis Khan: A Dog Star Is Born ◆ 1994
   3. Genghis Khan: Dog-Gone Hollywood ◆ 1995

GEORGE AND MARTHA

Marshall, James
HOUGHTON MIFFLIN
GRADES K–2
ANIMAL FANTASY | HUMOR

Two hippos are best friends in this easy-reader series. They have many little quarrels caused by miscommunication, but all comes out happily in the end. In one story, Martha doesn't want to use suntan lotion and gets sunburned. George doesn't say "I told you so" because "that's not what friends do." Most of the stories end with this kind of twist. In one, George has a secret club, and Martha is furious until she finds out it's her fan club. Each book has several self-contained stories, with full-color cartoonlike illustrations on every other page.

1. George and Martha ◆ 1972
2. George and Martha Encore ◆ 1973
3. George and Martha Rise and Shine ◆ 1976
4. George and Martha One Fine Day ◆ 1978
5. George and Martha, Tons of Fun ◆ 1980
6. George and Martha Back in Town ◆ 1984
7. George and Martha 'Round and 'Round ◆ 1988

GEORGE AND MATILDA MOUSE

Buchanan, Heather S.
SIMON & SCHUSTER
GRADES K–3
ANIMAL FANTASY

George and Matilda are lovable and adventurous mice who live in an old dollhouse with their family. Readers are able to look at the world through the eyes of small mice and watch their escapades.

1. George Mouse's First Summer ◆ 1985
2. Emily Mouse's First Adventure ◆ 1985
3. George Mouse Learns to Fly ◆ 1985
4. Emily Mouse Saves the Day ◆ 1985
5. George Mouse's Covered Wagon ◆ 1987
6. George Mouse's Riverboat Band ◆ 1987
7. Emily Mouse's Beach House ◆ 1987
8. Emily Mouse's Garden ◆ 1987
9. George and Matilda Mouse and the Doll's House ◆ 1988
10. George and Matilda Mouse and the Floating School ◆ 1990
11. George and Matilda Mouse and the Moon Rocket ◆ 1992
12. George and Matilda Mouse's Christmas Journey ◆ 1993

GEORGIE

Bright, Robert
DOUBLEDAY

GRADES 1–3

FANTASY | HUMOR

Georgie is a polite, kind little ghost who lives in the Whittakers' attic. With his friends Herman the cat and Miss Oliver the owl, he does what he can to help out the Whittakers and their friends. When they go out west, he catches a gang of horse thieves and recovers a stolen pony. In the Christmas book, he plays Santa Claus to the town Scrooge.

1. Georgie ◆ 1944
2. Georgie to the Rescue ◆ 1956
3. Georgie's Halloween ◆ 1958
4. Georgie and the Robbers ◆ 1963
5. Georgie and the Magician ◆ 1966
6. Georgie and the Noisy Ghost ◆ 1971
7. Georgie Goes West ◆ 1973
8. Georgie's Christmas Carol ◆ 1975
9. Georgie and the Buried Treasure ◆ 1979
10. Georgie and the Ball of Yarn ◆ 1983
11. Georgie and the Baby Birds ◆ 1983
12. Georgie and the Little Dog ◆ 1983
13. Georgie and the Runaway Balloon ◆ 1983

GERALDINE

Keller, Holly
GREENWILLOW

GRADES K–2

ANIMAL FANTASY | FAMILY LIFE | HUMOR

Geraldine is a young pig who has the same concerns as many children. Why does she have to give up her blanket? When will the snow come so she can use her new sled? Why is her new baby brother, Willie, such a nuisance? Each simple story has a reassuring ending as Mama and Papa understand Geraldine's frustrations and help her solve her problems. Additional books deal with being an older sister and celebrating Christmas.

1. Geraldine's Blanket ◆ 1984
2. Geraldine's Big Snow ◆ 1988
3. Geraldine's Baby Brother ◆ 1994
4. Geraldine First ◆ 1996
5. Merry Christmas, Geraldine ◆ 1997

GERMY

Jones, Rebecca C.

DUTTON

GRADES 3–6

HUMOR | REAL LIFE

Jeremy Bluett, called "Germy Blew It" by everyone except adults and new kids, wants to be on TV. He organizes a strike at school when field trips are canceled, but no one else participates. When he finds out that TV cameras came to school while he was gone, he tries one scheme after another to be famous. Finally, with the help of his friend Squirrel, he organizes a bubblegum-blowing contest at his house. He gets his wish to be on TV, but ends up owing the school money. In subsequent books, he tries a variety of get-rich-quick schemes to pay back the school, starts a school newspaper, and is elected to student council.

1. Germy Blew It ◆ 1987
2. Germy Blew It—Again ◆ 1988
3. Germy Blew the Bugle ◆ 1990
4. Germy in Charge ◆ 1993

GHOST SQUAD

Hildick, E. W.

DUTTON

GRADES 5–8

FANTASY | MYSTERY

Joe, Danny, Karen, and Carlos are ghosts who have learned how to communicate with living people using a computer. They make contact with Carlos and Danny's best friends, Buzz and Wacko, and together the four ghosts and two boys form the Ghost Squad to solve crimes. Joe, the group's leader, was murdered and wants to find out who did it and assure his wife that it was not a suicide. Karen and Danny also want to help their families, but Carlos's family has adjusted to his death. His concern is with computers, and he figures out how to use a ghost's "micro-micro energy" to operate a word processor. The Ghost Squad battles both living enemies and Malevs (ghosts who try to harm living people) in their adventures, which include plenty of action.

1. The Ghost Squad Breaks Through ◆ 1984
2. The Ghost Squad and the Halloween Conspiracy ◆ 1985
3. The Ghost Squad Flies Concorde ◆ 1985
4. The Ghost Squad and the Ghoul of Grunberg ◆ 1986
5. The Ghost Squad and the Prowling Hermits ◆ 1987
6. The Ghost Squad and the Menace of the Malevs ◆ 1988

GHOST STORIES

Coville, Bruce

BANTAM

GRADES 5–6

MYSTERY

The active involvement of a ghost in each of these titles creates special mysteries for sixth-grade friends Nina and Chris. The girls meet during an audition in a theater said to be haunted by an actress who was murdered on stage fifty years ago. Of course, only the girls can see the ghostly apparitions and it becomes their responsibility to unravel the strange adventures.

1. The Ghost in the Third Row ◆ 1987
2. The Ghost Wore Gray ◆ 1988
3. The Ghost in the Big Brass Bed ◆ 1991

GHOSTS OF FEAR STREET

Stine, R. L.

POCKET BOOKS

GRADES 4–8

HORROR

Shadow people, ooze, the bugman, the werecat, ghouls, ghosts, and other creatures populate these horror books. The unsuspecting characters experience nightmares; they encounter body switchers and screaming jokers; and they have frightening Christmas celebrations and are attacked by aqua apes. There are many cliff-hanging chapters, like one that ends with a scream and another that ends with fingers grabbing the character's neck, so readers have many scary moments. R. L. Stine has expanded his successful horror books with this series.

1. Hide and Shriek ◆ 1995
2. Who's Been Sleeping in My Grave? ◆ 1995
3. The Attack of the Aqua Apes ◆ 1995
4. Nightmare in 3-D ◆ 1996
5. Stay Away from the Treehouse ◆ 1996
6. The Eye of the Fortuneteller ◆ 1996
7. Fright Knight ◆ 1996
8. The Ooze ◆ 1996
9. The Revenge of the Shadow People ◆ 1996
10. The Bugman Lives! ◆ 1996
11. The Boy Who Ate Fear Street ◆ 1996
12. Night of the Werecat ◆ 1996
13. How to Be a Vampire ◆ 1996
14. Body Switchers from Outer Space ◆ 1996

15. Fright Christmas ◆ 1996
16. Don't Ever Get Sick at Granny's ◆ 1997
17. House of a Thousand Screams ◆ 1997
18. Camp Fear Ghouls ◆ 1997
19. Three Evil Wishes ◆ 1997
20. Spell of the Screaming Jokers ◆ 1997
21. The Creature from Club Lagoona ◆ 1997
22. Field of Screams ◆ 1997
23. Why I'm Not Afraid of Ghosts ◆ 1997
24. Monster Dog ◆ 1997
25. Halloween Bugs Me! ◆ 1997
26. Go to Your Tomb—Right Now! ◆ 1997
27. Parents from the 13th Dimension ◆ 1997
28. Hide and Shriek II ◆ 1998
29. The Tale of the Blue Monkey ◆ 1998
30. I Was a Sixth-Grade Zombie ◆ 1998
31. Escape of the He-Beast ◆ 1998
32. Caution: Aliens at Work ◆ 1998
33. Attack of the Vampire Worms ◆ 1998
34. Horror Hotel: The Vampire Checks In ◆ 1998

GHOSTS OF FEAR STREET CREEPY COLLECTION

1. Happy Hauntings ◆ 1998
2. Beastly Tales ◆ 1998
3. The Scream Team ◆ 1998
4. Big Bad Bugs ◆ 1998
5. Ghoul Friends ◆ 1998

GHOSTWRITER

Various authors
BANTAM
GRADES 4–6
MYSTERY | SCIENCE FICTION

Four children living in the inner city make contact with a ghost who communicates by rearranging letters into messages that only the children can see. The children and the ghost form a crime-fighting team, using the ghost's unique skills and the children's expertise with codes and secret writing. Over the course of the series, new members are added to the team and the adventures become more fantastic. The series is a companion to the PBS series of the same name, which stresses the importance of literacy.

1. A Match of Wills (Weiner, Eric) ◆ 1992
2. Courting Danger and Other Stories (Anastasio, Dina) ◆ 1992
3. Dress Code Mess (St. Antoine, Sara) ◆ 1992
4. Steer Clear of Haunted Hill (Weiner, Eric) ◆ 1993

5. Amazement Park Adventure (Chevat, Richie) ◆ 1994
6. Alias Diamond Jones (Salat, Cristina) ◆ 1993
7. Blackout! (Weiner, Eric) ◆ 1993
8. A Blast with the Past (Wilsdon, Christina) ◆ 1994
9. Digging for Clues (Keyishian, Amy) ◆ 1994
10. Disappearing Act (Blundell, Judy) ◆ 1994
11. The Book Chase (Woodson, Jacqueline) ◆ 1994
12. Clinton Street Crime Wave (Hill, Laban C.) ◆ 1994
13. Ghost Story (Kleinbaum, N. H.) ◆ 1995
14. The Big Stink & Five Other Mysteries (Chevat, Richie) ◆ 1995
15. The Chocolate Bar Bust (Barry, Miranda) ◆ 1995
16. Daycamp Nightmare: Camp at Your Own Risk #1 (Butcher, Nancy) ◆ 1995
17. Disaster on Wheels: Camp at Your Own Risk #2 (Butcher, Nancy) ◆ 1995
18. Creepy Sleepaway: Camp at Your Own Risk #3 (Butcher, Nancy) ◆ 1995
19. Night of the Living Cavemen (Weiner, Eric) ◆ 1995
20. A Crime of Two Cities (Leeden, Ivy D., and Kermit Frazier) ◆ 1995
21. Just in Time (Hyman, Fracaswell) ◆ 1996
22. Deadline (Weiner, Eric) ◆ 1996
23. Attack of the Slime Monster (Baker, Carin Greenberg) ◆ 1996
24. The Man Who Vanished (Keyishian, Amy) ◆ 1996
25. Alien Alert (Korman, Susan) ◆ 1996
26. Caught in the Net (Butcher, Nancy) ◆ 1997
27. Hector's Haunted House (Korman, Susan) ◆ 1997

GIRLHOOD JOURNEYS: JULIET

Kirwan, Anna
SIMON & SCHUSTER
GRADES 4–6
FAMILY LIFE | HISTORICAL

Juliet lives in England in the 14th century. Her father, a freeman, works for Sir Pepin D'Arsy, and her best friend is Sir Pepin's daughter, Marguerite. There is intrigue involving mysterious guests, Marguerite's betrothal, and a lost falcon. Juliet is an energetic character who solves problems on her own, even given the restrictions of her era. For example, when her little brother, Alban, accidentally releases the falcon, Juliet searches for it, finds it, and returns it. There is an afterword describing daily life in the Middle Ages.

1. A Dream Takes Flight ◆ 1996
2. Rescue at Marlehead Manor ◆ 1997
3. Midsummer at Greenchapel ◆ 1997

GIRLHOOD JOURNEYS: KAI

Various authors
SIMON & SCHUSTER
GRADES 4–6
FAMILY LIFE | HISTORICAL

It is 1440, and Kai lives in a Yoruba village in Africa (in the area that is now Nigeria). Each book portrays Kai as a strong-willed, resourceful young woman. In one book, she and her sister Jamila help their people during a time of famine. In another book, Kai, Jamila, and their friend Aisha travel to Oyo, where Kai works with the master sculptor Akibu. Her efforts to fulfill her artistic dreams take her away from her home, and she must develop self-reliance and confidence. There is a glossary of terms as well as a section of information about the Yoruba in history and today.

1. A Mission for Her Village (Thomas, Dawn C. Gill) ◆ 1996
2. A Big Decision (Gayle, Sharon Shavers) ◆ 1997
3. The Lost Statue (Welch, Leona Nicholas) ◆ 1997

GIRLHOOD JOURNEYS: MARIE

Various authors
SIMON & SCHUSTER
GRADES 4–6
FAMILY LIFE | HISTORICAL

Marie La Marche and her family live in Paris in the years just before the French Revolution. Marie's interest in ballet seems destined to be unfulfilled until she receives some attention and support. The first two books of this series focus on Marie's interest in the world of dance and on the behaviors and intrigues of 18th-century Paris. These adventures involve her friend Joelle. The third book follows the family to the country for the summer, where Marie makes friends with her cousin Jeannette. When Jeannette must leave the family to find work, Marie's resourcefulness helps her use her talents to earn money and stay at home. This is a lively series with an emphasis on relationships. A glossary of French words opens the book and helps with the reading; an afterword focuses on French life in this era.

1. An Invitation to Dance (Kudlinski, Kathleen V.) ◆ 1996
2. Mystery at the Paris Ballet (Greene, Jacqueline D.) ◆ 1997
3. Summer in the Country (Greene, Jacqueline D.) ◆ 1997

GIRLHOOD JOURNEYS: SHANNON

Kudlinski, Kathleen V.
SIMON & SCHUSTER
GRADES 4–6
FAMILY LIFE | HISTORICAL

Arriving in San Francisco from Ireland, Shannon O'Brien and her family must adjust to new customs in this lively new home. It is 1880, and Shannon meets a Chinese immigrant, Mi Ling, who involves her in several mysteries. Shannon finds out about prejudice toward Mi Ling as well as narrow attitudes about her Irish heritage when she attends school. These stories have adventure and are fast-paced. There is an afterword describing California in the 1880s.

1. A Chinatown Adventure ◆ 1996
2. Lost and Found ◆ 1997
3. The Schoolmarm Mysteries ◆ 1997

GIRLS R.U.L.E.

Lowe, Kris
BERKLEY
GRADES 6–8
ADVENTURE | REAL LIFE

Cayenga Park is adding a girls' division of junior rangers. The tryouts will be difficult, especially since the boys' division of junior rangers is not totally in favor of this new group. Five girls— Kayla Adams, Carson McDonald, Sophie Schultz, Becca Fisher, and Alex Loomis-Drake—tell their own stories about their lives and interest in the park program. The first book establishes the personality of each girl, her strengths, insecurities, and special needs. Sophie is stubborn and outspoken; Carson does not let her hearing disability limit her accomplishments; Becca's jokes and sarcasm sometimes cause problems. This adventure series will appeal to girls who like intrepid, strong-willed, female main characters.

1. Girls R.U.L.E. ◆ 1998
2. Trail of Terror ◆ 1998
3. Seal Island Scam ◆ 1998

GIVE YOURSELF GOOSEBUMPS *see*

Goosebumps: Give Yourself Goosebumps

GOLIATH *see* David and Goliath

GOLLY SISTERS

Byars, Betsy
HARPERCOLLINS
GRADES K–2
HISTORICAL | HUMOR

Rose and May-May Golly have a traveling road show that takes them across the western frontier. Their show is funny and so are the predicaments that they experience. In one story, they put on a show for an audience of dogs; in another, May-May decides to use pigs in her magic act instead of rabbits ("Everyone uses rabbits"); in still another, the sisters visit a talking rock. The appealing illustrations, brief chapters, and simple text make this a good choice for beginning readers, and the humor would attract reluctant readers.

1. The Golly Sisters Go West ◆ 1985
2. Hooray for the Golly Sisters! ◆ 1990
3. The Golly Sisters Ride Again ◆ 1994

GONERS

Simons, Jamie, and E. W. Scollon
AVON CAMELOT
GRADES 4–6
ADVENTURE | SCIENCE FICTION

The books in this series link the creatures on a planetoid in the future with past events on Earth. Dr. Autonomou has identified some Goners—interplanetary diplomats who were sent to various times and places on Earth but were lost when the transport system was destroyed. The doctor is now experimenting with ways to bring them back, including sending other creatures from Planetoid Roma to Planet RU1:2 (a.k.a. Earth). After undergoing "biological osmosis" to look like earthlings, Rubidoux, Xela, Gogol, and Arms Akimbo experience adventures with Thomas Jefferson, Christopher Columbus, and Edward VI.

1. RU 1:2 ◆ 1998
2. The Hunt Is On ◆ 1998
3. All Hands on Deck ◆ 1998
4. Spitting Image ◆ 1998
5. Rabid Transit ◆ 1998
6. Under Loch and Key ◆ 1998

GOOSEBUMPS

Stine, R. L.

SCHOLASTIC

GRADES 4–8

HORROR

According to the publisher, more than 200 million copies of Goosebumps have been sold. There are spin-off series, TV tie-ins, and a Web site (http://www.scholastic.com/goosebumps). The books are filled with creatures and gore, with implausible situations and frightening circumstances. The characters are often unsuspecting innocents—just like your neighbors and friends, or even yourself—caught in the clutches of gnomes, werewolves, monsters, vampires, and other creatures. The locations include a mummy's tomb, Camp Nightmare, Horrorland, and the Haunted School. This popular series brings the horror genre to a younger audience, giving them dripping blood, shrunken heads, and monsters awaiting their next victim.

1. Welcome to Dead House ◆ 1992
2. Stay Out of the Basement ◆ 1992
3. Monster Blood ◆ 1992
4. Say Cheese and Die! ◆ 1992
5. Curse of the Mummy's Tomb ◆ 1993
6. Let's Get Invisible! ◆ 1993
7. Night of the Living Dummy ◆ 1993
8. The Girl Who Cried Monster ◆ 1993
9. Welcome to Camp Nightmare ◆ 1993
10. The Ghost Next Door ◆ 1993
11. The Haunted Mask ◆ 1993
12. Be Careful What You Wish For ◆ 1993
13. Piano Lessons Can Be Murder ◆ 1993
14. The Werewolf of Fever Swamp ◆ 1993
15. You Can't Scare Me! ◆ 1994
16. One Day at Horrorland ◆ 1994
17. Why I'm Afraid of Bees ◆ 1994
18. Monster Blood II ◆ 1994
19. Deep Trouble ◆ 1994
20. The Scarecrow Walks at Midnight ◆ 1994
21. Go Eat Worms! ◆ 1994
22. Ghost Beach ◆ 1994
23. Return of the Mummy ◆ 1994
24. Phantom of the Auditorium ◆ 1994
25. Attack of the Mutant ◆ 1994
26. My Hairiest Adventure ◆ 1994
27. A Night in Terror Tower ◆ 1995
28. The Cuckoo Clock of Doom ◆ 1995

29. Monster Blood III ◆ 1995
30. It Came from Beneath the Sink! ◆ 1995
31. Night of the Living Dummy II ◆ 1995
32. The Barking Ghost ◆ 1995
33. The Horror at Camp Jellyjam ◆ 1995
34. Revenge of the Lawn Gnomes ◆ 1995
35. A Shocker on Shock Street ◆ 1995
36. The Haunted Mask II ◆ 1995
37. The Headless Ghost ◆ 1995
38. The Abominable Snowman of Pasadena ◆ 1995
39. How I Got My Shrunken Head ◆ 1996
40. Night of the Living Dummy III ◆ 1996
41. Bad Hare Day ◆ 1996
42. Egg Monsters from Mars ◆ 1996
43. The Beast from the East ◆ 1996
44. Say Cheese and Die—Again! ◆ 1996
45. Ghost Camp ◆ 1996
46. How to Kill a Monster ◆ 1996
47. Legend of the Lost Legend ◆ 1996
48. Attack of the Jack-O'-Lanterns ◆ 1996
49. Vampire Breath ◆ 1996
50. Calling All Creeps! ◆ 1996
51. Beware, the Snowman ◆ 1997
52. How I Learned to Fly ◆ 1997
53. Chicken Chicken ◆ 1997
54. Don't Go to Sleep! ◆ 1997
55. The Blob That Ate Everyone ◆ 1997
56. The Curse of Camp Cold Lake ◆ 1997
57. My Best Friend Is Invisible ◆ 1997
58. Deep Trouble II ◆ 1997
59. The Haunted School ◆ 1997
60. Werewolf Skin ◆ 1997
61. I Live in Your Basement! ◆ 1997
62. Monster Blood IV ◆ 1998

GOOSEBUMPS: GIVE YOURSELF GOOSEBUMPS

Stine, R. L.

SCHOLASTIC

GRADES 4–8

HORROR

What do you get when you cross the incredibly popular horror stories of Goosebumps with the popular format of Choose Your Own Adventure? You get Give Yourself Goosebumps. The cover of each book announces

"Choose from over 20 different scary endings," giving readers many different ways to direct the adventures. Like the basic Goosebumps books, these are scary stories where characters try to escape from weird creatures or are attacked by monsters or lost in a swamp. You meet werewolves, vampires, and terrible toys. You visit places like the Carnival of Horrors and the Dead-End Hotel. Depending on the choices, the reader can triumph over the evil creatures, just barely escape, or be swallowed by a sea monster. The two popular genres represented in this series are sure to capture the interest of even the most reluctant readers.

1. Escape from the Carnival of Horrors ◆ 1995
2. Tick Tock, You're Dead! ◆ 1995
3. Trapped in Bat Wing Hall ◆ 1995
4. The Deadly Experiments of Dr. Eek ◆ 1996
5. Night in Werewolf Woods ◆ 1996
6. Beware of the Purple Peanut Butter ◆ 1996
7. Under the Magician's Spell ◆ 1996
8. The Curse of the Creeping Coffin ◆ 1996
9. The Knight in Screaming Armor ◆ 1996
10. Diary of a Mad Mummy ◆ 1996
11. Deep in the Jungle of Doom ◆ 1996
12. Welcome to the Wicked Wax Museum ◆ 1996
13. Scream of the Evil Genie ◆ 1997
14. The Creepy Creations of Professor Shock ◆ 1997
15. Please Don't Feed the Vampire! ◆ 1997
16. Secret Agent Grandma ◆ 1997
17. Little Comic Shop of Horrors ◆ 1997
18. Attack of the Beastly Baby-Sitter ◆ 1997
19. Escape from Camp Run-for-Your-Life ◆ 1997
20. Toy Terror: Batteries Included ◆ 1997
21. The Twisted Tale of Tiki Island ◆ 1997
22. Return to the Carnival of Horrors ◆ 1997
23. Zapped in Space ◆ 1997
24. Lost in Stinkeye Swamp ◆ 1997
25. Shop 'Till You Drop . . . Dead! ◆ 1998
26. Alone in Snakebite Canyon ◆ 1998
27. Checkout Time at the Dead-End Hotel ◆ 1998
28. Night of a Thousand Claws ◆ 1998
29. Invaders from the Big Screen ◆ 1998
30. You're Plant Food! ◆ 1998
31. The Werewolf of Twisted Tree Lodge ◆ 1998
32. It's Only a Nightmare ◆ 1998

GIVE YOURSELF GOOSEBUMPS SPECIAL EDITIONS

1. Into the Jaws of Doom ◆ 1998
2. Return to Terror Tower: The Nightmare Continues ◆ 1998
3. Power Play: Trapped in the Circus of Fear ◆ 1998
4. The Ultimate Challenge: One Night in Payne House ◆ 1998

GOOSEBUMPS PRESENTS

Stine, R. L.

SCHOLASTIC

GRADES 3–6

HORROR

This TV tie-in series features adaptations of plots that were shown as part of the *Goosebumps* program. The plots include encounters with a headless ghost, mutants, and avenging lawn gnomes. In the middle of the books, there are color photographs from the TV show. Some of these books are much shorter adaptations of books in the original Goosebumps series, but the addition of photographs from the show will attract many readers.

1. The Girl Who Cried Monster ◆ 1996
2. The Cuckoo Clock of Doom ◆ 1996
3. Welcome to Camp Nightmare ◆ 1996
4. Return of the Mummy ◆ 1996
5. Night of the Living Dummy II ◆ 1996
6. My Hairiest Adventure ◆ 1996
7. The Headless Ghost ◆ 1996
8. Be Careful What You Wish For ◆ 1997
9. Go Eat Worms! ◆ 1997
10. Bad Hare Day ◆ 1997
11. Let's Get Invisible ◆ 1997
12. Attack of the Mutant ◆ 1997
13. Ghost Beach ◆ 1997
14. You Can't Scare Me! ◆ 1997
15. Monster Blood ◆ 1997
16. Attack of the Jack-O'-Lanterns ◆ 1997
17. Calling All Creeps ◆ 1997
18. Revenge of the Lawn Gnomes ◆ 1998

GOOSEBUMPS SERIES 2000

Stine, R. L.

SCHOLASTIC

GRADES 4–8

HORROR

Advertised as having a "scarier edge," Goosebumps 2000 capitalizes on the popularity of the horror genre and the familiar name of Goosebumps. The danger in these books is a bit more intense and could appeal to an older audience. As with the related series, there are weird creatures and slime, ghosts and gore. This series could provide a transition to YA horror titles.

1. Cry of the Cat ◆ 1998
2. Bride of the Living Dummy ◆ 1998
3. Creature Teacher ◆ 1998
4. Invasion of the Body Squeezers, Part 1 ◆ 1998
5. Invasion of the Body Squeezers, Part 2 ◆ 1998
6. I Am Your Evil Twin ◆ 1998
7. Revenge R Us ◆ 1998
8. Fright Camp ◆ 1998
9. Are You Terrified Yet? ◆ 1998
10. Headless Halloween ◆ 1998
11. Attack of the Graveyard Ghouls ◆ 1998
12. Brain Juice ◆ 1998

GORDY SMITH

Hahn, Mary Downing
CLARION
GRADES 5–7
FAMILY LIFE | HISTORICAL

This series begins during World War II when best friends Elizabeth and Margaret spy on their sixth-grade classmate—a bully named Gordy Smith. They discover that he is hiding his brother Stu, who is an Army deserter. This is a grave moral dilemma for these patriotic friends. The sequels focus on Gordy as he is separated from his abusive family and sent to live with a grandmother in North Carolina. On her sudden death, Gordy returns to his hometown and the lingering perceptions of his being a bully from a "trashy" family. These are thoughtfully written books with realistic insights into the era and the characters.

1. Stepping on the Cracks ◆ 1991
2. Following My Own Footsteps ◆ 1996
3. As Ever Gordy ◆ 1998

GRANDADDY

Griffith, Helen V.
GREENWILLOW
GRADES 2–4
FAMILY LIFE | REAL LIFE

Janetta's Grandaddy lives in the country in Georgia and Janetta and her Mom live in Baltimore. When Janetta is about six, her Mom decides it is time they met, so they take the train down to the farm. At first, Janetta isn't sure about Grandaddy and his animals, and she is sure they don't like her. She is especially afraid of his mule. Sitting on the porch that night, Grandaddy tells a story about a star that fell to the Earth and wanted to go back to the sky. The mule jumped up with the star on its back. The story is the beginning of a friendship between Janetta, Grandaddy, and his animals. As the series continues, they share more stories and love in these picture books.

1. Georgia Music ◆ 1986
2. Grandaddy's Place ◆ 1987
3. Grandaddy and Janetta ◆ 1993
4. Grandaddy's Stars ◆ 1995

GRANDMA

McCully, Emily Arnold
HARPERCOLLINS
GRADES K–3
FAMILY LIFE

A delightful beginning-to-read series that illustrates how very different people can learn to compromise. Pip's two grandmas are exactly opposite: One is very strict, one is too lenient. His parents are exactly right: in between both extremes. Pip, and sometimes his friend Ski, try to set the grandmas straight on what is really acceptable for children his age. Told in a humorous and gentle way, young readers will enjoy the way Pip tackles his grandmothers.

1. The Grandma Mix-Up ◆ 1988
2. Grandmas at the Lake ◆ 1990
3. Grandmas at Bat ◆ 1993

GRANDMA'S ATTIC

Richardson, Arleta
DAVID C. COOK
GRADES 3–6
FAMILY LIFE | VALUES

A little girl visits her grandmother and hears stories about her childhood, prompted by items found in her attic or around the house The grandmother was a girl in the late 1800s, and all the stories are nostalgic and idealistic portrayals of that time. The family is Christian, and Christian values permeate the stories. The format is the same throughout the series: short anecdotes tied together by the child's questions. The grandmother may comment on the moral.

1. In Grandma's Attic ◆ 1974
2. More Stories from Grandma's Attic ◆ 1979
3. Still More Stories from Grandma's Attic ◆ 1980
4. Treasures from Grandma ◆ 1984
5. Sixteen and Away from Home ◆ 1985
6. Eighteen and on Her Own ◆ 1986
7. Nineteen and Wedding Bells Ahead ◆ 1987
8. At Home in North Branch ◆ 1988
9. New Faces New Friends ◆ 1989
10. Stories from the Growing Years ◆ 1991
11. The Grandma's Attic Story Book ◆ 1993
12. Christmas Stories from Grandma's Attic ◆ 1994
13. Letters from Grandma's Attic ◆ 1995
14. A School of Her Own ◆ 1995
15. Still More Stories from Grandma's Attic ◆ 1995

GRANDPA

Stevenson, James
GREENWILLOW
GRADES 1–4
FAMILY LIFE | HUMOR

When Mary Ann and Louie visit Grandpa, they try to tell him interesting things. He responds with exaggerated slapstick stories of similar situations from his own childhood. If Mary Ann and Louie look forward to their Easter egg hunt, then Grandpa tells them about his trip to the Frammistan Mountains to hunt for an enormous Easter egg. And, of course, when Mary Ann and Louie are bored, Grandpa describes an even more boring time (sort of). Some of Grandpa's stories involve his brother Wainwright (Wainey). Children love these wild stories and great illustrations.

1. Could Be Worse! ◆ 1977
2. That Terrible Halloween Night ◆ 1980
3. What's Under My Bed? ◆ 1983
4. Grandpa's Great City Tour ◆ 1983
5. The Great Big Especially Beautiful Easter Egg ◆ 1983
6. Worse Than Willie! ◆ 1984
7. That Dreadful Day ◆ 1985
8. No Friends ◆ 1986
9. There's Nothing to Do! ◆ 1986
10. Will You Please Feed Our Cat? ◆ 1987
11. We Hate Rain! ◆ 1988
12. Grandpa's Too-Good Garden ◆ 1989
13. Brrr! ◆ 1991
14. That's Exactly the Way It Wasn't ◆ 1991

GRANNY

Parish, Peggy

MACMILLAN; SIMON & SCHUSTER

GRADES K–3

HUMOR

This series for early readers is by the author of the humorous Amelia Bedelia stories. Granny Guntry is actually harmless enough, but the Indians, wolves, and desperadoes that she takes care of never find that out until it's too late. Children will chuckle at the predicaments that they all get into.

1. Granny and the Indians ◆ 1969
2. Granny and the Desperadoes ◆ 1970
3. Granny, the Baby, and the Big Gray Thing ◆ 1972

GRAVEYARD SCHOOL

Stone, Tom B.

BANTAM

GRADES 4–7

HORROR

Grove School is right next to a graveyard. So, naturally, the kids call it Graveyard School. Park, who considers himself a detective, and his friend Stacey solve mysteries and get into some terrifying situations. At the beginning of their sixth-grade year, the principal, Dr. Morehouse, introduces a new lunch room supervisor who promises tasty meals at low cost. Soon after, pets start disappearing all over town. The series continues as the friends solve more scary mysteries at the school.

1. Don't Eat the Mystery Meat ◆ 1994
2. The Skeleton on the Skateboard ◆ 1994
3. The Headless Bicycle Rider ◆ 1994
4. Little Pet Werewolf ◆ 1995
5. Revenge of the Dinosaurs ◆ 1995
6. Camp Dracula ◆ 1995
7. Slime Lake ◆ 1995
8. Let's Scare the Teacher to Death ◆ 1995
9. The Abominable Snow Monster ◆ 1995
10. There's a Ghost in the Boys' Bathroom ◆ 1996
11. April Ghoul's Day ◆ 1996

12. Scream, Team! ◆ 1996
13. Tales Too Scary to Tell at Camp ◆ 1996
14. The Tragic School Bus ◆ 1996
15. The Fright Before Christmas ◆ 1996
16. Don't Tell Mummy ◆ 1997
17. Jack and the Beanstalker ◆ 1997
18. The Dead Sox ◆ 1997
19. The Gator Ate Her ◆ 1997
20. Creature Teacher ◆ 1997
21. The Skeleton's Revenge ◆ 1997
22. Boo Year's Eve ◆ 1998
23. The Easter Egg Haunt ◆ 1998
24. Scream Around the Campfire ◆ 1998
25. Escape from Vampire Park ◆ 1998
26. Little School of Horrors ◆ 1998
27. Here Comes Santa Claws ◆ 1998
28. The Spider Beside Her ◆ 1998

THE GREAT BRAIN

Fitzgerald, John D.
DIAL
GRADES 5–7
HISTORICAL | HUMOR | REAL LIFE

Tom, Sweyn, and J.D. are three brothers growing up in a small Utah town in the late 1800s. Tom has a great brain and an insatiable love for money, a combination that leads him to concoct endless schemes for swindling his friends and family. One of his first enterprises is to charge the neighborhood kids to see his family's toilet, the first in town. Occasionally, he has fits of conscience and promises to reform, most notably when the neighborhood kids decide to stop speaking to him. Sweyn, the oldest brother, is amused by Tom's schemes, but J.D., the youngest brother and narrator, always seems to be taken in.

1. The Great Brain ◆ 1967
2. More Adventures of the Great Brain ◆ 1969
3. Me and My Little Brain ◆ 1971
4. The Great Brain at the Academy ◆ 1972
5. The Great Brain Reforms ◆ 1973
6. The Return of the Great Brain ◆ 1974
7. The Great Brain Does It Again ◆ 1975
8. The Great Brain Is Back ◆ 1995

THE GREAT MCGONIGGLE

Corbett, Scott

LITTLE, BROWN

GRADES 2–3

ADVENTURE | MYSTERY

Mac McGoniggle and his friend Ken Wetzel manage to solve crimes more quickly than the police. They foil a jewel thief, retrieve a valuable prize, and outsmart a player on their ball team in this fast-paced mystery series. Two of the books deal with sports, which could be attractive to reluctant readers. Cartoonlike line drawings will appeal to this audience, too.

1. The Great McGoniggle's Gray Ghost ◆ 1975
2. The Great McGoniggle's Key Play ◆ 1976
3. The Great McGoniggle Rides Again ◆ 1978
4. The Great McGoniggle Switches Pitches ◆ 1980

THE GREAT SKINNER

Tolan, Stephanie S.

MACMILLAN

GRADES 4–7

FAMILY LIFE | HUMOR

Jennifer Skinner narrates the hilarious adventures of the not-quite-normal Skinner family. The slide from normalcy begins when her mother decides to go on strike to get her family to do more of the housework. The strike gains national attention, much to the disgust of Jennifer and her siblings. The strike is finally settled when everyone in the family agrees to do more around the house. But Mr. Skinner has been irrevocably changed by the whole business. He decides to quit his job and start a family business, which turns out to be too successful. Just as the family is hoping to settle down again, he buys a motor home and they start off on a trip across the country.

1. The Great Skinner Strike ◆ 1983
2. The Great Skinner Enterprise ◆ 1986
3. The Great Skinner Getaway ◆ 1987
4. The Great Skinner Homestead ◆ 1988

GREEN KNOWE

Boston, L. M.

HARCOURT

GRADES 4–8

FANTASY

An ancient house in Great Britain is rich with history and stories of the children who have lived there over the centuries. Lonely young Tolly goes to live there with his Great-Grandmother Oldknow in the early 1930s. Tolly soon discovers that his great-grandmother's stories about the children who used to live there literally come to life. We are not sure at first whether he is time-traveling or seeing the children's ghosts, but it soon becomes clear that all time blends together in this house. The series continues with more stories of children from different eras and with mysteries about the house, including hidden treasure.

1. The Children of Green Knowe ◆ 1954
2. The Treasure of Green Knowe ◆ 1958
3. The River at Green Knowe ◆ 1959
4. A Stranger at Green Knowe ◆ 1961
5. An Enemy at Green Knowe ◆ 1964
6. Memory in a House ◆ 1973
7. The Guardians of the House ◆ 1974
8. The Stones of Green Knowe ◆ 1976
9. Adventure at Green Knowe ◆ 1979

GRUMPY BUNNY

Korman, Justine

TROLL

GRADES K–1

ANIMAL FANTASY | HUMOR

Hopper is a grumpy bunny, even on holidays and other special occasions. At Easter, he is a grumpy bunny because he must give away so many Easter treats. On Valentine's Day, he does not like all that mushy stuff. On the first day of school, he dreads his kinderbunny class. Cute illustrations add to the appeal of these stories.

1. The Grumpy Bunny Goes to School ◆ 1996
2. The Grumpy Easter Bunny ◆ 1996

3. I Love You, Grumpy Bunny ◆ 1996
4. The Grumpy Bunny Goes West ◆ 1997
5. The Grumpy Bunny's Snowy Day ◆ 1997
6. The Grumpy Bunny Joins the Team ◆ 1998
7. The Grumpy Bunny's Field Trip ◆ 1998

GUS AND GRANDPA

Mills, Claudia
FARRAR, STRAUS & GIROUX
GRADES K–2
FAMILY LIFE | REAL LIFE

This is a charming series highlighting the special, loving relationship between Gus, who is almost seven, and his grandfather, who is almost seventy. They love spending time together, playing with Grandpa's dog, Skipper, celebrating their birthdays, and baking Christmas cookies. Because Gus is young and Grandpa is old, they sometimes forget things, but they help each other cope. They both love trains and one book features a special ride on a steam engine. Another book describes how Gus visits and helps Grandpa in the hospital after a heart attack. Beginning readers will find the larger print and simple sentences very accessible.

1. Gus and Grandpa ◆ 1996
2. Gus and Grandpa Ride the Train ◆ 1997
3. Gus and Grandpa and the Christmas Cookies ◆ 1997
4. Gus and Grandpa at the Hospital ◆ 1998

GYMNASTS

Levy, Elizabeth
SCHOLASTIC
GRADES 4–6
REAL LIFE | RECREATION

Six girls—Cindi, Darlene, Lauren, Jodi, Ti An, and Ashley—are on a gymnastics team called the Pinecones. They aren't the best team, but they stick together and learn from each other and their coach, Patrick. There's a lot of information about gymnastics woven in, but the girls also deal with situations in their families and with boys and friends.

1. The Beginners ◆ 1988
2. First Meet ◆ 1988
3. Nobody's Perfect ◆ 1988
4. The Winner ◆ 1989

5. Trouble in the Gym ◆ 1989
6. Bad Break ◆ 1989
7. Tumbling Ghosts ◆ 1989
8. The Captain of the Team ◆ 1989
9. Crush on the Coach ◆ 1990
10. Boys in the Gym ◆ 1990
11. Mystery at the Meet ◆ 1990
12. Out of Control ◆ 1990
13. First Date ◆ 1990
14. World Class Gymnast ◆ 1990
15. Nasty Competition ◆ 1991
16. Fear of Falling ◆ 1991
17. Gymnast Commandoes ◆ 1991
18. The New Coach ◆ 1991
19. Tough at the Top ◆ 1991
20. The Gymnasts' Gift ◆ 1991
21. Team Trouble ◆ 1992
22. Go for the Gold ◆ 1992

HANK THE COWDOG

Erickson, John R.
MAVERICK
GRADES 4–6
ANIMAL FANTASY | HUMOR

Hank is the "Head of Ranch Security" at Sally May and Loper's ranch. He
bosses around his fellow guard dog, Drover, and quarrels with Pete the cat.
In the first book, he is falsely accused of killing a chicken. He runs away
and decides to become an outlaw. After outwitting a pack of coyotes, he
returns to the ranch and tracks a "badger," who turns out to be a skunk.
In subsequent books, Hank gets involved in other mysteries around the
ranch. The humor in the series comes from Hank's buffoonery as he swag-
gers and boasts, but actually does very little guarding.

1. Hank the Cowdog ◆ 1983
2. Further Adventures of Hank the Cowdog ◆ 1983
3. It's a Dog's Life ◆ 1984
4. Murder in the Middle Pasture ◆ 1984
5. Faded Love ◆ 1985
6. Let Sleeping Dogs Lie ◆ 1986
7. The Curse of the Incredible Priceless Corncob ◆ 1989
8. The Case of the One-Eyed Killer Stud Horse ◆ 1989
9. The Case of the Halloween Ghost ◆ 1989
10. Every Dog Has His Day ◆ 1989
11. Lost in the Dark Enchanted Forest ◆ 1989

12. The Case of the Fiddle-Playing Fox ◆ 1989
13. The Case of the Wounded Buzzard on Christmas Eve ◆ 1989
14. Monkey Business ◆ 1990
15. The Case of the Missing Cat ◆ 1990
16. Lost in the Blinded Blizzard ◆ 1991
17. The Case of the Car-Barkaholic Dog ◆ 1991
18. The Case of the Hooking Bull ◆ 1992
19. The Case of the Midnight Rustler ◆ 1992
20. The Phantom in the Mirror ◆ 1993
21. The Case of the Vampire Cat ◆ 1993
22. The Case of the Double Bumblebee Sting ◆ 1994
23. Moonlight Madness ◆ 1994
24. The Case of the Black-Hooded Hangman ◆ 1995
25. The Case of the Swirling Tornado ◆ 1995
26. The Case of the Kidnapped Collie ◆ 1996
27. The Case of the Night-Stalking Bone Monster ◆ 1996
28. The Mopwater Flies ◆ 1997
29. The Case of the Vampire Vacuum Sweeper ◆ 1997
30. The Case of the Haystack Kitties ◆ 1998
31. The Case of the Vanishing Fishhook ◆ 1998
32. The Garbage Monster from Outer Space ◆ 1999
33. The Case of the Measled Cowboy ◆ 1999

HANNAH AND THE ANGELS

Keep, Linda Lowery

RANDOM HOUSE

GRADES 3–5

ADVENTURE | FANTASY

Hannah is an intrepid girl who is aided by angels as she confronts problems around the world. She faces poachers in Australia, disease in Africa, thieves in Mexico, and a kidnapping in the Appalachian Mountains. Throughout, she is guided by angels, who choose her adventures and provide her with help as she deals with the problems.

1. Mission Down Under ◆ 1998
2. Searching for Lulu ◆ 1998
3. Mexican Treasure Hunt ◆ 1998
4. Notes from Blue Mountain ◆ 1998

HARDY BOYS

Dixon, Franklin W.

SIMON & SCHUSTER

GRADES 5–7

MYSTERY

Frank and Joe Hardy, the sons of famous detective Fenton Hardy, have become well-known detectives in their own right, even though they are still in their teens. In each book, the two boys are pursuing their various interests when they are confronted with a crime or mystery. After much action and adventure, the mystery is solved, the criminal is caught, and all is well again in Bayport. Frank is cast as the serious and thoughtful one, while Joe is more athletic and impulsive. They are aided occasionally by their friend Chet and their father's sister Gertrude.

1. The Tower Treasure ◆ 1927
2. The House on the Cliff ◆ 1927
3. The Secret of the Old Mill ◆ 1927
4. The Missing Chums ◆ 1928
5. Hunting for Hidden Gold ◆ 1928
6. The Shore Road Mystery ◆ 1928
7. Secret of the Caves ◆ 1929
8. Mystery of Cabin Island ◆ 1929
9. Great Airport Mystery ◆ 1930
10. What Happened at Midnight? ◆ 1931
11. While the Clock Ticked ◆ 1932
12. Footprints Under the Window ◆ 1933
13. The Mark on the Door ◆ 1934
14. The Hidden Harbor Mystery ◆ 1935
15. Sinister Signpost ◆ 1936
16. Figure in Hiding ◆ 1937
17. Secret Warning ◆ 1938
18. The Twisted Claw ◆ 1939
19. The Disappearing Floor ◆ 1940
20. Mystery of the Flying Express ◆ 1941
21. The Clue of the Broken Blade ◆ 1942
22. The Flickering Torch Mystery ◆ 1943
23. The Melted Coins ◆ 1944
24. Short-Wave Mystery ◆ 1945
25. The Secret Panel ◆ 1946

26. The Phantom Freighter ◆ 1947
27. The Secret of Skull Mountain ◆ 1948
28. The Sign of the Crooked Arrow ◆ 1949
29. The Secret of the Lost Tunnel ◆ 1950
30. The Wailing Siren Mystery ◆ 1951
31. The Secret of Wildcat Swamp ◆ 1952
32. The Yellow Feather Mystery ◆ 1953
33. The Crisscross Shadow ◆ 1953
34. The Hooded Hawk Mystery ◆ 1954
35. The Clue in the Embers ◆ 1955
36. The Secret of Pirates' Hill ◆ 1957
37. The Ghost at Skeleton Rock ◆ 1957
38. Mystery at Devil's Paw ◆ 1959
39. Mystery of the Chinese Junk ◆ 1960
40. Mystery of the Desert Giant ◆ 1961
41. Clue of the Screeching Owl ◆ 1962
42. The Viking Symbol Mystery ◆ 1963
43. Mystery of the Aztec Warrior ◆ 1964
44. The Haunted Fort ◆ 1965
45. Mystery of the Spiral Bridge ◆ 1966
46. Secret Agent on Flight 101 ◆ 1967
47. Mystery of the Whale Tattoo ◆ 1968
48. The Arctic Patrol Mystery ◆ 1969
49. Bombay Boomerang ◆ 1970
50. Danger on Vampire Trail ◆ 1971
51. The Masked Monkey ◆ 1972
52. The Shattered Helmet ◆ 1973
53. The Clue of the Hissing Serpent ◆ 1974
54. The Mysterious Caravan ◆ 1975
55. The Witchmaster's Key ◆ 1976
56. The Jungle Pyramid ◆ 1977
57. Firebird Rocket ◆ 1978
58. The Sting of the Scorpion ◆ 1979
59. Night of the Werewolf ◆ 1979
60. The Mystery of the Samurai Sword ◆ 1979
61. The Pentagon Spy ◆ 1980
62. The Apeman's Secret ◆ 1980
63. The Mummy Case ◆ 1980
64. Mystery of Smuggler's Cove ◆ 1980
65. The Stone Idol ◆ 1981
66. The Vanishing Thieves ◆ 1981
67. The Outlaw's Silver ◆ 1981
68. Deadly Chase ◆ 1981
69. The Four-Headed Dragon ◆ 1981
70. The Infinity Clue ◆ 1981
71. Track of the Zombie ◆ 1982
72. The Voodoo Plot ◆ 1982
73. The Billion Dollar Ransom ◆ 1982

74. Tic-Tac Terror ◆ 1982
75. Trapped at Sea ◆ 1982
76. Game Plan for Disaster ◆ 1982
77. The Crimson Flame ◆ 1983
78. Cave-In! ◆ 1983
79. Sky Sabotage ◆ 1983
80. The Roaring River Mystery ◆ 1984
81. The Demon's Den ◆ 1984
82. The Blackwing Puzzle ◆ 1984
83. The Swamp Monster ◆ 1985
84. Revenge of the Desert Phantom ◆ 1985
85. The Skyfire Puzzle ◆ 1985
86. The Mystery of the Silver Star ◆ 1987
87. Program for Destruction ◆ 1987
88. Tricky Business ◆ 1988
89. Sky Blue Frame ◆ 1988
90. Danger on the Diamond ◆ 1988
91. Shield of Fear ◆ 1988
92. The Shadow Killers ◆ 1988
93. The Serpent's Tooth Mystery ◆ 1988
94. Breakdown in Axeblade ◆ 1989
95. Danger on the Air ◆ 1989
96. Wipeout ◆ 1989
97. Cast of Criminals ◆ 1989
98. Spark of Suspicion ◆ 1989
99. Dungeon of Doom ◆ 1989
100. The Secret of the Island Treasure ◆ 1990
101. The Money Hunt ◆ 1990
102. Terminal Shock ◆ 1990
103. The Million-Dollar Nightmare ◆ 1990
104. Tricks of the Trade ◆ 1990
105. The Smoke Screen Mystery ◆ 1990
106. Attack of the Video Villains ◆ 1991
107. Panic on Gull Island ◆ 1991
108. Fear on Wheels ◆ 1991
109. The Prime-Time Crime ◆ 1991
110. Secret of Sigma Seven ◆ 1991
111. Three-Ring Terror ◆ 1991
112. The Demolition Mission ◆ 1992
113. Radical Moves ◆ 1992
114. Case of the Counterfeit Criminals ◆ 1992
115. Sabotage at Sports City ◆ 1992
116. Rock 'n' Roll Renegades ◆ 1992
117. The Baseball Card Conspiracy ◆ 1992
118. Danger in the Fourth Dimension ◆ 1993
119. Trouble at Coyote Canyon ◆ 1993
120. Case of the Cosmic Kidnapping ◆ 1993
121. The Mystery in the Old Mine ◆ 1993

122. Carnival of Crime ◆ 1993
123. The Robot's Revenge ◆ 1993
124. Mystery with a Dangerous Beat ◆ 1993
125. Mystery on Makatunk Island ◆ 1994
126. Racing to Disaster ◆ 1994
127. Reel Thrills ◆ 1994
128. Day of the Dinosaur ◆ 1994
129. The Treasure at Dolphin Bay ◆ 1994
130. Sidetracked to Danger ◆ 1995
131. Crusade of the Flaming Sword ◆ 1995
132. Maximum Challenge ◆ 1995
133. Crime in the Kennel ◆ 1995
134. Cross-Country Crime ◆ 1995
135. The Hypersonic Secret ◆ 1995
136. The Cold Cash Caper ◆ 1996
137. High-Speed Showdown ◆ 1996
138. The Alaskan Adventure ◆ 1996
139. The Search for the Snow Leopard ◆ 1996
140. Slam Dunk Sabotage ◆ 1996
141. The Desert Thieves ◆ 1996
142. Lost in the Gator Swamp ◆ 1997
143. The Giant Rat of Sumatra ◆ 1997
144. The Secret of Skeleton Reef ◆ 1997
145. Terror at High Tide ◆ 1997
146. The Mark of the Blue Tattoo ◆ 1997
147. Trial and Terror ◆ 1998
148. The Ice-Cold Case ◆ 1998
149. The Chase for the Mystery Twister ◆ 1998
150. The Crisscross Crime ◆ 1998
151. The Rocky Road to Revenge ◆ 1998
152. Danger in the Extreme ◆ 1998
153. Eye on Crime ◆ 1998

HARDY BOYS: FRANK AND JOE HARDY: THE CLUES BROTHERS

Dixon, Franklin W.

POCKET BOOKS

GRADES 2–3

MYSTERY

Younger versions of the popular Hardy Boys characters are presented in this series. Nine-year-old Frank and his eight-year-old brother Joe move from New York City to the suburb of Bayport when their father resigns from his position as police detective to take an office job. Along with their friends Chet and Mike, the brothers solve all kinds of mysteries. Joe loves ghost stories and always looks for paranormal explanations for their cases. While sleuthing, the boys confront bullies and adapt to their new town.

1. The Gross Ghost Mystery ◆ 1997
2. The Karate Clue ◆ 1997
3. First Day, Worst Day ◆ 1997
4. Jump Shot Detectives ◆ 1998
5. Dinosaur Disaster ◆ 1998
6. Who Took the Book? ◆ 1998
7. The Abracadabra Case ◆ 1998
8. The Doggone Detectives ◆ 1998

HARDY BOYS CASEFILES

Dixon, Franklin W.
ARCHWAY

GRADES 6–8

MYSTERY

The Hardy Boys Casefiles series is for an older audience of readers. Frank and Joe Hardy have girlfriends and face more serious crimes than in the original series. Corruption, organized crime, hired thugs, conspiracies, and even the threat of murder are included in the action. Even though Frank and Joe always succeed, the increased realism of the danger and violence make this a choice for middle school and older.

1. Dead on Target ◆ 1987
2. Evil, Inc. ◆ 1987
3. Cult of Crime ◆ 1987
4. The Lazarus Plot ◆ 1988
5. Edge of Destruction ◆ 1988
6. The Crowning Terror ◆ 1988
7. Deathgame ◆ 1988
8. See No Evil ◆ 1988
9. The Genius Thieves ◆ 1988
10. Hostages of Hate ◆ 1988
11. Brother Against Brother ◆ 1988
12. Perfect Getaway ◆ 1988
13. The Borgia Dagger ◆ 1988
14. Too Many Traitors ◆ 1989
15. Blood Relations ◆ 1989
16. Line of Fire ◆ 1989
17. The Number File ◆ 1989
18. A Killing in the Market ◆ 1989
19. Nightmare in Angel City ◆ 1989
20. Witness to Murder ◆ 1989
21. Street Spies ◆ 1989

22. Double Exposure ◆ 1989
23. Disaster for Hire ◆ 1989
24. Scene of the Crime ◆ 1989
25. The Borderline Case ◆ 1989
26. Trouble in the Pipeline ◆ 1989
27. Nowhere to Run ◆ 1989
28. Countdown to Terror ◆ 1989
29. Thick as Thieves ◆ 1989
30. The Deadliest Dare ◆ 1989
31. Without a Trace ◆ 1989
32. Blood Money ◆ 1989
33. Collision Course ◆ 1989
34. Final Cut ◆ 1989
35. The Dead Season ◆ 1990
36. Running on Empty ◆ 1990
37. Danger Zone ◆ 1990
38. Diplomatic Deceit ◆ 1990
39. Flesh and Blood ◆ 1991
40. Fright Wave ◆ 1991
41. Highway Robbery ◆ 1990
42. The Last Laugh ◆ 1990
43. Strategic Moves ◆ 1990
44. Castle Fear ◆ 1991
45. In Self-Defense ◆ 1990
46. Foul Play ◆ 1990
47. Flight into Danger ◆ 1991
48. Rock 'n' Revenge ◆ 1991
49. Dirty Deeds ◆ 1991
50. Power Play ◆ 1991
51. Choke Hold ◆ 1991
52. Uncivil War ◆ 1991
53. Web of Horror ◆ 1991
54. Deep Trouble ◆ 1991
55. Beyond the Law ◆ 1991
56. Height of Danger ◆ 1991
57. Terror on Track ◆ 1991
58. Spiked! ◆ 1991
59. Open Season ◆ 1992
60. Deadfall ◆ 1992
61. Grave Danger ◆ 1992
62. Final Gambit ◆ 1992
63. Cold Sweat ◆ 1992
64. Endangered Species ◆ 1992
65. No Mercy ◆ 1992
66. The Phoenix Equation ◆ 1992
67. Lethal Cargo ◆ 1992
68. Rough Riding ◆ 1992
69. Mayhem in Motion ◆ 1992

70. Rigged for Revenge ◆ 1992
71. Real Horror ◆ 1993
72. Screamers ◆ 1993
73. Bad Rap ◆ 1993
74. Road Pirates ◆ 1993
75. No Way Out ◆ 1993
76. Tagged for Terror ◆ 1993
77. Survival Run ◆ 1993
78. The Pacific Conspiracy ◆ 1993
79. Danger Unlimited ◆ 1993
80. Dead of Night ◆ 1993
81. Sheer Terror ◆ 1993
82. Poisoned Paradise ◆ 1993
83. Toxic Revenge ◆ 1994
84. False Alarm ◆ 1994
85. Winner Take All ◆ 1994
86. Virtual Villainy ◆ 1994
87. Dead Man in Deadwood ◆ 1994
88. Inferno of Fear ◆ 1994
89. Darkness Falls ◆ 1994
90. Deadly Engagement ◆ 1994
91. Hot Wheels ◆ 1994
92. Sabotage at Sea ◆ 1994
93. Mission: Mayhem ◆ 1994
94. A Taste for Terror ◆ 1994
95. Illegal Procedure ◆ 1995
96. Against All Odds ◆ 1995
97. Pure Evil ◆ 1995
98. Murder by Magic ◆ 1995
99. Frame-Up ◆ 1995
100. True Thriller ◆ 1995
101. Peak of Danger ◆ 1995
102. Wrong Side of the Law ◆ 1995
103. Campaign of Crime ◆ 1995
104. Wild Wheels ◆ 1995
105. Law of the Jungle ◆ 1995
106. Shock Jock ◆ 1995
107. Fast Break ◆ 1996
108. Blown Away ◆ 1996
109. Moment of Truth ◆ 1996
110. Bad Chemistry ◆ 1996
111. Competitive Edge ◆ 1996
112. Cliff-Hanger ◆ 1996
113. Sky High ◆ 1996
114. Clean Sweep ◆ 1996
115. Cave Trap ◆ 1996
116. Acting Up ◆ 1996
117. Blood Sport ◆ 1996

118. The Last Leap ◆ 1996
119. The Emperor's Shield ◆ 1997
120. Survival of the Fittest ◆ 1997
121. Absolute Zero ◆ 1997
122. River Rats ◆ 1997
123. High–Wire Act ◆ 1997
124. The Viking's Revenge ◆ 1997
125. Stress Point ◆ 1997
126. Fire in the Sky ◆ 1997
127. Dead in the Water ◆ 1998

HAROLD AND CHESTER *see* Bunnicula

HAROLD AND THE PURPLE CRAYON

Johnson, Crockett
HARPERCOLLINS
GRADES K–2
FANTASY

Whatever Harold draws with his purple crayon becomes real. He draws a highway and then a forest. When a dragon that he draws to guard the apple tree in the forest scares him, his hand shakes and makes the ocean. To solve this problem, he just draws a boat. One night, he gets up from bed and draws a castle with a garden. A garden fairy he draws gives him a wish, and with that and a magic carpet he draws, he makes it home in time for a story.

1. Harold and the Purple Crayon ◆ 1955
2. Harold's Fairy Tale ◆ 1956
3. Harold's Trip to the Sky ◆ 1957
4. Harold's Circus ◆ 1959
5. A Picture for Harold's Room ◆ 1960
6. Harold's ABC ◆ 1963

HARPER WINSLOW

Trembath, Don
ORCA
GRADES 7–8
REAL LIFE

Harper Winslow, 15, tells his own stories in this series of books which are set in Canada, near Toronto. In *The Tuesday Cafe*, Harper describes his problems with his parents and his school, problems which have resulted in an appearance in juvenile court. He is assigned to write an essay about changing his life, so he enrolls in a writing class called "The Tuesday Cafe." Harper grows and changes as a character, developing insights into his personality and choices that will resonate with junior high school readers. The essay that he writes appears toward the end of the book and it provides a wonderful look at a character's development. Subsequent books allow Harper to continue to change by writing for the school newspaper and beginning a romantic friendship.

1. The Tuesday Cafe ◆ 1996
2. A Fly Named Alfred ◆ 1997
3. A Beautiful Place on Yonge Street ◆ 1998

HARRIET

Carlson, Nancy

CAROLRHODA

GRADES K–2

ANIMAL FANTASY | REAL LIFE

Harriet is a dog who faces everyday situations, such as watching out for her little brother, Walt, when she really wants to play, or being honest about spoiling a neighbor's prize flower. There is a gentle lesson in each book as Harriet solves simple problems.

1. Harriet's Recital ◆ 1982
2. Harriet's Halloween Candy ◆ 1982
3. Harriet and the Roller Coaster ◆ 1982
4. Harriet and Walt ◆ 1982
5. Harriet and the Garden ◆ 1982

HARRIET

Maestro, Betty, and Giulio Maestro

CROWN

GRADES K–1

ANIMAL FANTASY

A perky young elephant demonstrates important concepts to very young children. One simple line of text on each page is accompanied by a brightly colored illustration featuring a posterlike Harriet. Some of the concepts illustrated include time, ordinal numbers, reading signs, and prepositions.

1. Harriet Goes to the Circus ◆ 1977
2. Harriet Reads Signs and More Signs ◆ 1981

3. Around the Clock with Harriet ◆ 1984
4. Harriet at Play ◆ 1984
5. Harriet at School ◆ 1984
6. Harriet at Home ◆ 1984
7. Harriet at Work ◆ 1984
8. Throughout the Year with Harriet ◆ 1985
9. Dollars and Cents for Harriet ◆ 1988

HARRIET M. WELSH

Fitzhugh, Louise
HARPERCOLLINS
GRADES 4–6
REAL LIFE

The award-winning first book in this trilogy introduces us to Harriet Welsh, a student at a private school in New York in the 1960s. She fancies herself a spy and keeps a notebook in which she records her impressions of her friends. When the notebook is found and read, she learns some valuable lessons about herself and others. The second book focuses on her friend Beth Ellen. They are spending the summer in a small town in upstate New York. Harriet is still keeping her notebook, trying to find out who is leaving strange notes all over town. The last book is about one of Harriet's friends, Sport, a boy who takes care of his absentminded father.

1. Harriet the Spy ◆ 1964
2. The Long Secret ◆ 1965
3. Sport ◆ 1979

HARRIET THE TROUBLEMAKER

Waddell, Martin
LITTLE, BROWN
GRADES 3–5
HUMOR

Harriet, who lives in England, wreaks havoc wherever she goes. Harriet doesn't mean to cause trouble—she just does. Miss Granston, Headmistress of Slow Street School, often deals with the havoc that Harriet has caused. When Harriet's pet snail is lost, she chooses a new pet from the zoo—a crocodile. When Harriet builds a robot named Dolly, she is surprised by the damage that a runaway robot can do. And Harriet causes great confusion when she helps a circus horse by hiding it in the school. The British school setting does not interfere with the humor. Harriet is incorrigible and should appeal to the fans of Ramona.

1. Harriet and the Crocodiles ◆ 1984
2. Harriet and the Haunted School ◆ 1985
3. Harriet and the Robot ◆ 1987

HARRY

Porte, Barbara Ann
GREENWILLOW
GRADES 1–3
HUMOR | REAL LIFE

Harry lives with his widowed father. This fully illustrated easy-reader series is about everyday events in their lives. Harry's Aunt Rose gets married in one book, and in another Harry wins a pony. Harry is surrounded by wise and loving grown-ups and good friends.

1. Harry's Visit ◆ 1983
2. Harry's Dog ◆ 1984
3. Harry's Mom ◆ 1985
4. Harry in Trouble ◆ 1989
5. Harry Gets an Uncle ◆ 1991
6. Harry's Birthday ◆ 1994
7. Harry's Pony ◆ 1997

HARRY AND CHICKEN

Sheldon, Dyan
CANDLEWICK
GRADES 3–5
FAMILY LIFE | FANTASY | HUMOR

Harry is a talking cat—actually, he's an alien being from the planet Arcana who has taken on the form of a cat. In the first book, we watch Chicken— a girl—try to keep her new friend Harry secret until he insinuates himself into her family: a mother who doesn't like cats, a sister who is allergic to them, and a brother who has two birds. In the following two books, Harry uses a little space magic to transport them to a small boat in the middle of a strange lake (*Harry the Explorer*) and takes his revenge on Chicken's bullying siblings (*Harry on Vacation*).

1. Harry and Chicken ◆ 1992
2. Harry the Explorer ◆ 1992
3. Harry on Vacation ◆ 1993

Harry the Dirty Dog

Zion, Gene
HarperCollins
Grades K–3
Humor

Harry is a white dog with black spots who gets into one funny scrape after another. At the beach, he becomes entangled in seaweed so that everyone thinks he is a sea monster. A relative sends him an ugly sweater that he can't get rid of. At the end of every misadventure, Harry is reunited with his loving family.

1. Harry the Dirty Dog ◆ 1956
2. No Roses for Harry ◆ 1958
3. Harry and the Lady Next Door ◆ 1960
4. Harry by the Sea ◆ 1965

Harry the Hippo

Gaban, Jesús
Gareth Stevens
Grades K–2
Animal Fantasy

Harry is a bright pink hippo who can count on the help of Mama and Papa when he tries to do big things, like dress himself, feed himself, and take a bath. Very young children will enjoy reading or hearing about Harry's adventures.

1. Harry's Mealtime Mess ◆ 1992
2. Harry Dresses Himself ◆ 1992
3. Tub Time for Harry ◆ 1992
4. Harry's Sandbox Surprise ◆ 1992

Harvey

Clifford, Eth
Houghton Mifflin
Grades 3–5
Humor | Mystery

Whenever Harvey's cousin Nora comes for a visit, Harvey knows he's in for a wacky adventure, probably involving a strange mystery. When Nora visits Harvey for spring break they catch a prowler and a raccoon. The raccoon leads them to counterfeiters and the cousins are heroes. Nora is flamboyant and loves animals. Harvey is more low key, which adds to the humor of their adventures.

1. Harvey's Horrible Snake Disaster ◆ 1984
2. Harvey's Marvelous Monkey Mystery ◆ 1987
3. Harvey's Wacky Parrot Adventure ◆ 1990
4. Harvey's Mystifying Raccoon Mix-Up ◆ 1994

HATCHET *see* Brian Robeson

HATFORD BOYS

Naylor, Phyllis Reynolds
DELACORTE; DELL
GRADES 3–5
HUMOR | REAL LIFE

The Hatford boys and the Malloy girls just can't seem to get along. The boys think they are smarter and try to prove it by tricking the girls. Will the girls fall for their schemes? Disgusting gifts (neatly wrapped), trading places, and creating a creature are some of the antics in these funny books.

1. The Boys Start the War ◆ 1993
2. The Girls Get Even ◆ 1993
3. Boys Against the Girls ◆ 1994
4. The Girls' Revenge ◆ 1998

HATTIE RABBIT

Gackenbach, Dick
HARPERCOLLINS
GRADES K–2
ANIMAL FANTASY | HUMOR

Little Hattie Rabbit spars with the adults and friends in her life and sometimes comes out on top in this easy-reader series. In one story, she wishes her Mom had a neck like a giraffe, feet like a chicken, and a nose like an elephant—until she realizes how silly she would look. In another, when she has to go to bed in the summer light, she persuades her Mom to paint a night scene on her window shade.

1. Hattie Rabbit ◆ 1976
2. Hattie Be Quiet, Hattie Be Good ◆ 1977

3. Mother Rabbit's Son Tom ◆ 1977
4. Hattie, Tom, and the Chicken Witch: A Play and a Story ◆ 1980
5. Hurray for Hattie Rabbit ◆ 1986

HAUNTING WITH LOUISA

Cates, Emily
BANTAM
GRADES 5–8
MYSTERY

Dee Forest comes to Misty Island to live with her Aunt Winnifred after her mother dies and her father cannot cope with his grief. There she meets Louisa, a young ghost who must help four of her living relatives before she can go on to the next life. With Dee's help and after many adventures, Louisa finds three of them. In the last book, they discover that Dee is Louisa's distant cousin, and Louisa saves her life. Meanwhile, Louisa is concerned that Dee doesn't have any living friends and urges her to make some. At the same time, Dee's father finds a new romance, which Dee comes to accept.

1. The Ghost in the Attic ◆ 1990
2. The Mystery of Misty Island Inn ◆ 1991
3. The Ghost Ferry ◆ 1991

HEART BEATS

Rees, Elizabeth M.
ALADDIN
GRADES 7–8
REAL LIFE

The students at Dance Tech are devoted to their dreams of success in dancing. They are also devoted to being friends, including boyfriends. Sophy likes having Carlos for her dance partner, but she is also interested in him romantically. Ray is worried about Daly's commitment to losing weight. Can he help her and still be her boyfriend? The dance school setting provides a background for stories of jealousy, both personal and professional.

1. Moving as One ◆ 1998
2. Body Lines ◆ 1998
3. In the Spotlight ◆ 1998
4. Latin Nights ◆ 1998
5. Face the Music ◆ 1999

HEARTLAND

Lawlor, Laurie
MINSTREL/POCKET BOOKS
GRADES 3–6
FAMILY LIFE | HISTORICAL

In Luck, Wisconsin, in the early 1900s, Madeline "Moe" McDonohugh longs for adventure. Her life seems so restricted. There are the expectations of her parents and grandparents. There are the social conventions of her era. Moe is high-spirited, which sometimes lands her in trouble. Her adventures include encounters with gypsies, a visit from her cousins, finding a tarantula, and taking a trip to her grandparents' farm to view Halley's Comet. This book will appeal to girls who like historical fiction and who enjoy energetic female main characters.

1. Come Away with Me ◆ 1996
2. Take to the Sky ◆ 1996
3. Luck Follows Me ◆ 1996

HELP, I'M TRAPPED

Strasser, Todd
SCHOLASTIC
GRADES 5–8
FANTASY | HUMOR

Jake Sherman seems like an ordinary middle school student, but he has a secret. He can body switch. He has been trapped in his teacher's body, his sister's body, the President's body, and his gym teacher's body. He has even been trapped in a dog's body. In some of the books, he is trapped in repeating events. For example, he has to live through the first day of school until he makes the right choices that break the cycle. Readers will like the implausible situations and the ensuing confusion. These are fun books with lots of clever dialogue, albeit at the humor level of a junior high school audience.

1. Help! I'm Trapped in My Teacher's Body ◆ 1994
2. Help! I'm Trapped in the First Day of School ◆ 1994
3. Help! I'm Trapped in Obedience School ◆ 1995
4. Help! I'm Trapped in Obedience School Again ◆ 1995
5. Help! I'm Trapped in Santa's Body ◆ 1996
6. Help! I'm Trapped in My Gym Teacher's Body ◆ 1997
7. Help! I'm Trapped in My Sister's Body ◆ 1997
8. Help! I'm Trapped in the President's Body ◆ 1997
9. Help! I'm Trapped in an Alien's Body ◆ 1998

    10. Help! I'm Trapped in the First Day of Summer Camp ◆ 1998
    11. Help! I'm Trapped in a Movie Star's Body ◆ 1999

HENRIETTA

Hoff, Syd

GARRARD

GRADES K–2

ANIMAL FANTASY

Henrietta the hen is dissatisfied with her life, so she runs away from the farm. In the city, she is able to organize a special egg hunt for the children. Henrietta goes on to have adventures at the circus and on holidays. The simple text of these books is designed for beginning readers.

    1. Henrietta Lays Some Eggs ◆ 1977
    2. Henrietta, the Early Bird ◆ 1978
    3. Henrietta, Circus Star ◆ 1978
    4. Henrietta Goes to the Fair ◆ 1979
    5. Henrietta's Halloween ◆ 1980
    6. Merry Christmas, Henrietta ◆ 1980
    7. Henrietta's Fourth of July ◆ 1981
    8. Happy Birthday, Henrietta ◆ 1983

HENRY AND MUDGE

E Ryl

Rylant, Cynthia

SIMON & SCHUSTER

GRADES K–3

HUMOR | REAL LIFE

Mudge is a huge dog owned by Henry. The series takes them through the seasons, with special times for each one. Stories continue with their encounters with a fussy cousin named Annie, a straggly stray cat, and even all the relatives at a family reunion. Henry's mother and father are kind and understanding when owning a big dog like Mudge causes problems for Henry. Dealing with real-life fun and worries, these beginning readers are just right for students in early elementary school grades. There is a Henry and Mudge fan club for more fun.

    1. Henry and Mudge ◆ 1987
    2. Henry and Mudge in Puddle Trouble ◆ 1987
    3. Henry and Mudge in the Green Time ◆ 1987
    4. Henry and Mudge Under the Yellow Moon ◆ 1987
    5. Henry and Mudge in the Sparkle Days ◆ 1988
    6. Henry and Mudge and the Forever Sea ◆ 1989

7. Henry and Mudge Get the Cold Shivers ◆ 1989
8. Henry and Mudge and the Happy Cat ◆ 1990
9. Henry and Mudge and the Bedtime Thumps ◆ 1991
10. Henry and Mudge Take the Big Test ◆ 1991
11. Henry and Mudge and the Long Weekend ◆ 1992
12. Henry and Mudge and the Wild Wind ◆ 1993
13. Henry and Mudge and the Careful Cousin ◆ 1994
14. Henry and Mudge and the Best Day of All ◆ 1995
15. Henry and Mudge in the Family Trees ◆ 1997
16. Henry and Mudge and the Sneaky Crackers ◆ 1998
17. Henry and Mudge and the Starry Night ◆ 1998
18. Henry and Mudge and Annie's Good Move ◆ 1998
19. Henry and Mudge and Annie's Perfect Pet ◆ 1999

HENRY HUGGINS

Cleary, Beverly
MORROW
GRADES 1–4
HUMOR | REAL LIFE

Henry Huggins lives with his Mom and Dad and dog Ribsy on Klickitat Street, near Beezus and Ramona. His adventures parallel the Ramona books but are more typical of a boy's activities in the 1950s. Ribsy and Henry often get in and out of scrapes, such as when Ribsy steals a roast from a neighbor's barbecue. Henry's overwhelming desire is for a bike, and he engages in many money-making schemes to obtain it.

1. Henry Huggins ◆ 1950
2. Henry and Beezus ◆ 1952
3. Henry and Ribsy ◆ 1954
4. Henry and the Paper Route ◆ 1957
5. Henry and the Clubhouse ◆ 1962
6. Ribsy ◆ 1964

HENRY REED

Robertson, Keith
VIKING
GRADES 4–6
HUMOR | REAL LIFE

Henry Reed is a very mature 15-year-old who has traveled all over the world with his father, who is in the diplomatic service. Henry spends his summers with his aunt and uncle in Grover's Corners near Princeton,

New Jersey. The time is the 1950s and the series is in the form of a journal that Henry keeps. In the first book, he and Midge start a research service, getting into many funny situations. The series continues with a trip across the country by car and Henry's second summer with Midge, when they start a baby-sitting service.

1. Henry Reed, Inc. ◆ 1958
2. Henry Reed's Journey ◆ 1963
3. Henry Reed's Baby-Sitting Service ◆ 1966
4. Henry Reed's Big Show ◆ 1970
5. Henry Reed's Think Tank ◆ 1986

HENRY THE CAT

Calhoun, Mary
MORROW
GRADES K–2
ADVENTURE | ANIMAL FANTASY

Henry is most unusual. He is a very clever Siamese cat who likes to walk on his hind legs and he is also able to have exciting adventures wherever he happens to land. Henry shows up in unusual situations—a sailing excursion, skiing in the mountains, and a ballooning trip—all by chance. Henry gets upset when a new puppy steals the attention in *High-Wire Henry*. Short sentences and lots of action will hold the attention of readers. The illustrations add to the suspense and the humor, capturing the sense of adventure of Henry and his family.

1. Cross-Country Cat ◆ 1979
2. Hot-Air Henry ◆ 1981
3. High-Wire Henry ◆ 1991
4. Henry the Sailor Cat ◆ 1994

HENRY THE EXPLORER

Taylor, Mark
ATHENEUM
GRADES K–3
ADVENTURE | HUMOR

Henry and his dog, Laird Angus McAngus, read about exciting places and then set out to explore the countryside around their home, always sure to take flags with them to mark the way. They capture a tiger, save a forest from fire, and get lost in a snowstorm.

1. Henry the Explorer ◆ 1966

2. Henry the Castaway ◆ 1970
3. Henry Explores the Mountains ◆ 1975
4. Henry Explores the Jungle ◆ 1988

HERBIE JONES

Kline, Suzy

PUTNAM

GRADES 2–4

REAL LIFE

In Miss Pinkham's third-grade class, Herbie Jones and Raymond Martin are in the lowest reading group. Not only do they dislike being in this group, they dislike the group's name, the Apples. When Herbie starts to do well in spelling, he is moved out of the Apples, leaving his best friend behind. Although he can't get Raymond out of the low reading group, Herbie can help him get the group's name changed to the Spiders! The stories about Herbie and his friends feature events that will be familiar to many students: birthday parties, baseball games, spelling tests, and finding a stray dog. The friendships are realistic, even Herbie's friendship with the smartest girl in the class, Annabelle Louisa Hodgekiss. There is humor mixed in with the everyday concerns. *Herbie Jones Readers' Theater* is a companion book of excerpts arranged for student performance.

1. Herbie Jones ◆ 1985
2. What's the Matter with Herbie Jones? ◆ 1986
3. Herbie Jones and the Class Gift ◆ 1987
4. Herbie Jones and the Monster Ball ◆ 1988
5. Herbie Jones and Hamburger Head ◆ 1989
6. Herbie Jones and the Dark Attic ◆ 1992
7. Herbie Jones and the Birthday Showdown ◆ 1993

HERCULEAH JONES

Byars, Betsy

PENGUIN

GRADES 5–7

HUMOR | MYSTERY

Herculeah Jones is the daughter of a divorced police detective and a private investigator, so mystery solving comes naturally to her. Her friend Meat appreciates being allowed to help out and occasionally works on his own. In *Dead Letter*, Herculeah buys a coat at a thrift store and finds a note in its hem. A woman is trapped and someone is going to kill her. Meat and Herculeah trace the note to a wealthy older woman being cared for by her nephew. In and out of danger the whole time, they are eventually responsible for the culprit's arrest. Herculeah is proud of being strong, and her hair always stands on end when there is danger. Girls will appreciate tough, smart Herculeah, and the relationship between her and Meat provides some humor.

1. The Dark Stairs: A Herculeah Jones Mystery ◆ 1994
2. Tarot Says Beware: A Herculeah Jones Mystery ◆ 1995
3. Dead Letter: A Herculeah Jones Mystery ◆ 1996
4. Death's Door: A Herculeah Jones Mystery ◆ 1997
5. Disappearing Acts: A Herculeah Jones Mystery ◆ 1998

HERE COME THE BROWNIES

Various authors
PUTNAM
GRADES 1–3
REAL LIFE

The girls in 2-B are all in the same Brownie Girl Scout group. Each book describes a simple problem that is solved through the camaraderie and caring of the group. After she moves to town, Corrie joins the group and makes many new friends. Sarah learns to speak up and share her good ideas with her friends. Krissy S. finds a way to earn some money for a special event. At the end of each book, there is a section called Girl Scout Ways that suggests projects and activities—making a friendship bracelet or designing a card to share with friends in a home for the elderly.

1. Corrie's Secret Pal (O'Connor, Jane) ◆ 1993
2. Sarah's Incredible Idea (O'Connor, Jane) ◆ 1993
3. Make Up Your Mind, Marsha! (O'Connor, Jane) ◆ 1993
4. Amy's (Not So) Great Camp-Out (O'Connor, Jane) ◆ 1993
5. Think, Corrie Think! (O'Connor, Jane) ◆ 1994
6. Lauren and the New Baby (O'Connor, Jane) ◆ 1994
7. Take a Bow, Krissy! (Leonard, Marcia) ◆ 1994
8. Is That Really You, Amy? (Leonard, Marcia) ◆ 1994
9. Lights Out, Sarah! (Leonard, Marcia) ◆ 1995
10. Marsha's Unbearable Day (Leonard, Marcia) ◆ 1995
11. JoAnn and the Surprise Party (Leonard, Marcia) ◆ 1996
12. Krissy and the Big Snow (Leonard, Marcia) ◆ 1996

THE HIT AND RUN GANG

Kroll, Steven
AVON
GRADES 2–4
REAL LIFE | RECREATION

Each book features a different member of this small-town baseball team, the Raymondtown Rockets. Luke is in a hitting slump, Jenny muffs an easy fly ball, Brian's hitting streak comes to an end, Justin does not want to change his pitching style, Adam is benched, Andy plays hooky from a game, and Vicky loses her confidence. Baseball action mixes with believable friendships. Many of the books teach readers about being good sports and accepting victory and defeat.

1. New Kid in Town ◆ 1992
2. Playing Favorites ◆ 1992
3. The Slump ◆ 1992
4. The Streak ◆ 1992
5. Pitching Trouble ◆ 1994
6. You're Out! ◆ 1994
7. Second Chance ◆ 1994
8. Pride of the Rockets ◆ 1994

HOBIE HANSON

Gilson, Jamie
LOTHROP, LEE & SHEPARD
GRADES 4–6
HUMOR | REAL LIFE

Realistic dialogue and lots of action keep fans of Hobie Hanson coming back for more of this popular series. In *Thirteen Ways to Sink a Sub* Hobie organizes his classmates to make their substitute teacher cry. Other escapades feature Hobie and his friends on a camping trip, playing soccer, and attending school in a vacant store at the mall while the regular school is being repaired following a flood. Humorous situations with a good sense of fair play and a variety of interesting characters make this series a winner.

1. Thirteen Ways to Sink a Sub ◆ 1982
2. 4B Goes Wild ◆ 1983

3. Hobie Hanson, You're Weird ◆ 1987
4. Double Dog Dare ◆ 1988
5. Hobie Hanson, Greatest Hero of the Mall ◆ 1989
6. Sticks and Stones and Skeleton Bones ◆ 1991
7. Soccer Circus ◆ 1993

HOLIDAY FIVE

Cooper, Ilene
VIKING
GRADES 3–5
REAL LIFE

Five girls (Lia, Maddy, Jill, Erin, and Kathy) who meet at summer camp plan visits on holidays throughout the year and call themselves the Holiday Five. The stories focus on everyday concerns—being popular, getting along with your family, and developing a positive self-image. In one book, *Stupid Cupid*, Lia and Maddy become rivals for the attention of a boy; another focuses on a visit the five girls make to New York City. These books have realistic dialogue and events that many girls will find familiar.

1. Trick or Trouble? ◆ 1994
2. The Worst Noel ◆ 1994
3. Stupid Cupid ◆ 1995
4. No-Thanks Thanksgiving ◆ 1996
5. Star Spangled Summer ◆ 1996

HOLIDAY FRIENDS

Hermes, Patricia
SCHOLASTIC
GRADES 3–5
REAL LIFE

Many girls will identify with Katie Potts. Despite her best intentions, she seems to cause problems. At Christmas, she and her best friend Amelia have a fight. At Thanksgiving, Katie wants the lead in the play but perfect Tiffany already has the perfect costume. Other books feature Katie and her friends at other holidays. This series is fun reading for middle grade girls.

1. Turkey Trouble ◆ 1996
2. Christmas Magic ◆ 1996
3. My Secret Valentine ◆ 1996
4. Hoppy Easter ◆ 1998

THE HOME SCHOOL DETECTIVES

Bibee, John

INTERVARSITY PRESS

GRADES 4–6

MYSTERY | VALUES

Featuring a multiracial group of kids, these books describe their mystery adventures within the context of their home-schooling experiences. In cooperation with their church, the families support Christian values in their educational efforts. Beyond this context, the stories are filled with adventure as the characters stumble onto a mysterious cave, solve a series of thefts, and deal with a stolen treasure. Siblings Josh and Emily are tall, blond, and athletic. Becky and Billy are twins of African American heritage. Julie has a Mexican brother, Carlos, who was adopted by her father, Pastor Brown.

1. The Mystery of the Homeless Treasure ◆ 1994
2. The Mystery of the Missing Microchips ◆ 1995
3. The Mystery of the Mexican Graveyard ◆ 1995
4. The Mystery of the Campus Crook ◆ 1996
5. The Mystery of the Vanishing Cave ◆ 1996
6. The Mystery at the Broken Bridge ◆ 1997
7. The Mystery in Lost Canyon ◆ 1997
8. The Mystery of the Widow's Watch ◆ 1998

HOPPER

Pfister, Marcus

NORTH-SOUTH BOOKS

GRADES K–2

ANIMAL FANTASY

These are gentle stories about a rabbit and his Mama. Hopper looks for spring and makes friends with a squirrel who teaches him to climb a tree and a stag who helps him down. His mother teaches him to avoid enemies and find food, even in winter.

1. Hopper ◆ 1991
2. Hopper Hunts for Spring ◆ 1992
3. Hopper's Easter Surprise ◆ 1992
4. Hang On, Hopper! ◆ 1995
5. Hopper's Treetop Adventure ◆ 1997

HORRIBLE HARRY

Kline, Suzy
VIKING
GRADES 2–4
REAL LIFE

Ji Kli

Horrible Harry and the kids in Miss Mackle's Room 2B have many experiences that will be familiar to readers. Harry continues to have horrible ideas that turn out great. They put on a play, celebrate Christmas, care for an ant farm, fall "in love," and share secrets. Many of Harry's adventures involve Song Lee, a Korean girl, and Doug, Harry's friend. A sister series to Song Lee.

1. Horrible Harry in Room 2B ◆ 1988
2. Horrible Harry and the Ant Invasion ◆ 1989
3. Horrible Harry and the Green Slime ◆ 1989
4. Horrible Harry's Secret ◆ 1990
5. Horrible Harry and the Christmas Surprise ◆ 1991
6. Horrible Harry and the Kickball Wedding ◆ 1992
7. Horrible Harry and the Dungeon ◆ 1996
8. Horrible Harry and the Purple People ◆ 1997
9. Horrible Harry and the Drop of Doom ◆ 1998
10. Horrible Harry Moves Up to Third Grade ◆ 1998

HORSESHOES

Leitch, Patricia
HARPERCOLLINS
GRADES 5–7
REAL LIFE | RECREATION

Living in a manor in Scotland gives Sally Lorimer what she has always wanted: the chance to own a horse. After finding the right horse, Sally and her friend Thalia take riding lessons, participate in horse shows, and make the Pony Club team. In one book, Thalia is injured in a riding accident and Sally helps Thalia deal with her father's decision to take away her horse. Girls who enjoy the many horse and riding series set in America will like the Scottish setting and riding details in these books.

1. The Perfect Horse ◆ 1992
2. Jumping Lessons ◆ 1992
3. Cross-country Gallop ◆ 1996
4. Pony Club Rider ◆ 1996
5. Show Jumper Wanted ◆ 1997
6. Mystery Horse ◆ 1997

HOUDINI CLUB MAGIC MYSTERY

Adler, David A.

RANDOM HOUSE

GRADES 1–3

MYSTERY

Herman Foster has a nickname: Houdini. He has formed the Houdini Club so that he can perform magic tricks for his friends and then teach them how to do tricks, too. In these amusing mystery stories, Houdini and his cousin Janet Perry solve simple mysteries such as the disappearance and reappearance of the classroom hamster, a missing coat at the library, and a theft at the mall. At the end of each book, readers are shown how to do a magic trick. See how to make a torn dollar bill whole again or predict the star that will be randomly selected. Readers will enjoy the simple mysteries and the opportunity to learn magic.

1. Onion Sundaes ◆ 1994
2. Wacky Jacks ◆ 1994
3. Lucky Stars ◆ 1996
4. Magic Money ◆ 1997

HOUSE OF HORRORS

Various authors

HARPERTROPHY

GRADES 5–7

HORROR

What would you do if a ghost were stalking your brother? And then, what if your Aunt Wendy came to visit and took off her head? How about if your dog turned into an angry beast and brought home a gross claw that wasn't quite dead? These are just some of the problems faced by Sara and Michael Buckner in the House of Horrors series. There are oozing eggs and a scheming gargoyle. Readers who enjoy being scared and disgusted will want to read these creepy adventures.

1. My Brother, the Ghost (Weyn, Suzanne) ◆ 1994
2. Rest in Pieces (Weyn, Suzanne) ◆ 1994
3. Jeepers Creepers (Weyn, Suzanne) ◆ 1995
4. Aunt Weird (Lloyd, Alan) ◆ 1995
5. Knock, Knock . . . You're Dead (Stine, Megan) ◆ 1995
6. Night of the Gargoyle (Lloyd, Alan) ◆ 1995
7. Evil on Board (Moore, Leslie) ◆ 1995

HUGH PINE

van de Wetering, Janwillem

BANTAM

GRADES 4–6

ANIMAL FANTASY | HUMOR

Hugh Pine is the world's most intelligent porcupine. With his human friend Mr. McTosh, he cares for the animals in the countryside surrounding Sorry Bay and the little town of Rotworth. In subsequent books, they go on vacation, and Hugh tries to leave the others to live by himself, with amusing results.

1. Hugh Pine ◆ 1980
2. Hugh Pine and the Good Place ◆ 1986
3. Hugh Pine and Something Else ◆ 1989

HUMBUG

Balian, Lorna

ABINGDON PRESS

GRADES K–1

HUMOR

This whimsical series teases the reader into believing in the existence of Santa, witches, and the Easter Bunny. There are no connecting characters in the books, although the illustrations provide some continuity with familiar-looking characters. *Bah! Humbug?* and *Humbug Rabbit* try to create doubt about the identity of Santa Claus and the Easter Bunny, while *Humbug Witch* is a gentle reminder that dressing up as a witch does not guarantee your magic will work. The subtle humor will appeal to early readers and as a read-aloud.

1. Humbug Witch ◆ 1965
2. Humbug Rabbit ◆ 1974
3. Bah! Humbug? ◆ 1977
4. Humbug Potion ◆ 1984

IKE AND MAMA

Snyder, Carol
JEWISH PUBLICATION SOCIETY
GRADES 3–5
FAMILY LIFE | HISTORICAL

Ike is a Jewish boy living in New York City during the 1920s. His father has tuberculosis and is in the hospital for much of the series. The stories in this easy-chapter series center on Ike, his mother, and their close-knit neighborhood. Ike's mother is a woman of extraordinary wisdom and strength. In one book, she organizes the neighborhood to plan a wedding for a family that can't afford one. With humor and sympathy, Jewish ways and the sense of this time and place are woven into the stories.

1. Ike and Mama and the Once-a-Year Suit ◆ 1978
2. Ike and Mama and the Block Wedding ◆ 1979
3. Ike and Mama and the Once-in-a-Lifetime Movie ◆ 1981
4. Ike and Mama and the Trouble at School ◆ 1983

INCOGNITO MOSQUITO

Hass, E. A.
RANDOM HOUSE
GRADES 4–6
HUMOR | MYSTERY

Incognito Mosquito is an insect detective who describes his best cases in corny puns and silly twists on names. The first volume sets up his persona as he recounts five cases to a reporter whose job it is to interview the "famous" detective. Subsequent books offer other reasons for him to describe his exploits, including appearing on the TV talk show *Late Flight with David Litterbug*. Each case includes clues to help the reader guess how Incognito Mosquito figures out "who dunnit."

1. Incognito Mosquito, Private Insective ◆ 1982
2. Incognito Mosquito Flies Again ◆ 1985
3. Incognito Mosquito Takes to the Air ◆ 1986
4. Incognito Mosquito Makes History ◆ 1987

INDIAN IN THE CUPBOARD

Banks, Lynne Reid

DOUBLEDAY; AVON

GRADES 4–7

ADVENTURE | FANTASY

This series, also known as the Omri series, begins with *The Indian in the Cupboard*. Omri discovers that with the turn of a special key, he can bring plastic figures to life. An Indian, Little Bear, is the first figure. When Omri's best friend, Patrick, finds out, he brings Boone, his plastic cowboy, to life. The boys soon learn the consequences of using this magic to bring people across time and space. Each book in the series continues the adventures. A very brief retelling of previous events is included in the subsequent novels, which aids in comprehension. A movie version of the *Indian in the Cupboard* expanded the popularity of the books.

1. The Indian in the Cupboard ◆ 1981
2. The Return of the Indian ◆ 1986
3. The Secret of the Indian ◆ 1989
4. The Mystery of the Cupboard ◆ 1993
5. The Key to the Indian ◆ 1998

INTERNET DETECTIVES

Coleman, Michael

BANTAM

GRADES 4–6

ADVENTURE | MYSTERY

Using electronic mail and the Internet, three friends—Tamsyn Smith, Josh Allan, and Rob Zanelli—solve crimes around the world. Rob lives in Manor House in Portsmouth, England. After being paralyzed in a traffic accident, Rob is tutored at home and spends a lot of his time surfing the Net. Tamsyn and Josh attend Abbey School in Portsmouth. When Rob is in danger, his computer links to Tamsyn and Josh bring help. In later adventures, Rob attends Abbey School with his friends. The format of the series incorporates computer screens and messages into the narrative. The characters connect with others around the world to gather information and solve mysteries involving art theft, blackmail, and kidnapping as well as computer hacking and cyber-codes.

1. Net Bandits ◆ 1997
2. Escape Key ◆ 1997
3. Speed Surf ◆ 1997
4. Cyber Feud ◆ 1998
5. System Crash ◆ 1998

INVESTIGATORS OF THE UNKNOWN

Lisle, Janet Taylor
ORCHARD
GRADES 3–5
FAMILY LIFE | FANTASY

The Investigators of the Unknown form their group while trying to make contact with an invisible spirit who leaves letters filled with gold dust for Angela Harrell. Angela's friend Poco talks to animals, and her friend Georgina is as down-to-earth and practical as the other two are fanciful. Their investigations are always tinged with magical happenings that turn out to be grounded in reality, although a touch of magic or the unexplainable remains. In the second and third volumes, Angela is living with her father and brother in Mexico, and a fourth character—Walter, an orphan—is introduced. His story is featured in book three, where he begins to get ghostly messages from his dead mother. By the fourth book, Angela has returned from Mexico, acting strangely and reporting having been abducted by aliens.

1. The Gold Dust Letters ◆ 1994
2. Looking for Juliette ◆ 1994
3. A Message from the Match Girl ◆ 1995
4. Angela's Aliens ◆ 1996

INVISIBLE INC.

Levy, Elizabeth
SCHOLASTIC
GRADES 1–3
HUMOR | MYSTERY

Each member of Invisible Inc. contributes something special in this series: Chip is invisible; because of a hearing loss, Justin has learned to read lips; and Charlene is both very strong-willed and very brave. The simple mysteries in these books revolve around the three friends, their school, and their neighborhood. In one book, someone is stealing the snacks in the classroom; and in another, Justin's karate belt is stolen. With no element of real danger and a very accessible format, these books are just right for younger elementary school students. There are also many humorous moments, which often stem from Chip being invisible.

1. The Schoolyard Mystery ◆ 1994
2. The Mystery of the Missing Dog ◆ 1995
3. The Snack Attack Mystery ◆ 1996
4. The Creepy Computer Mystery ◆ 1996
5. The Karate Class Mystery ◆ 1996
6. Parents' Night Fright ◆ 1998

ISABELLE

Greene, Constance C.

VIKING

GRADES 3–6

HUMOR | REAL LIFE

Isabelle is a feisty ten-year-old who is well known for her ability to get in trouble. Throughout the series she tries to recruit other people to learn the art of itchiness, i.e., troublemaking, often with surprising results. Entertaining reading.

1. Isabelle the Itch ◆ 1973
2. Isabelle Shows Her Stuff ◆ 1984
3. Isabelle and Little Orphan Frannie ◆ 1988

ISLAND STALLION

Farley, Walter

RANDOM HOUSE

GRADES 4–6

ADVENTURE

Steve Duncan finds a wild red stallion on Azul Island in the Caribbean Sea. Naming the stallion Flame, Steve wants to train and race it, but first he must gain its trust. On the island, Flame battles with other stallions. With Steve, Flame competes against the best horses in the world. Horse-loving readers will appreciate the action-packed races and the many insights into horses and riding. Like Farley's Black Stallion series, this will appeal to readers who enjoy animal stories and adventure.

1. The Island Stallion ◆ 1948
2. The Island Stallion Races ◆ 1955
3. The Island Stallion's Courage ◆ 1956

JACK AND DANNY ONE

Slote, Alfred

HARPERCOLLINS

GRADES 2–4

ADVENTURE | SCIENCE FICTION

Jack Jameson gets a special present for his tenth birthday: a robot twin. Named Danny One, the robot will keep Jack company, play with him, and participate in many outer-space adventures. In *C.O.L.A.R.*, which stands for Community of Lost Atkins Robots, Jack and Danny One find a community of lost robots that were made by Dr. Atkins, who also made Danny. In another story, Jack travels alone to Alpha I and finds that his Aunt Katherine is behaving strangely and he must find out why. Each book is fast-paced and imaginative, involving futuristic scenarios and creative characters.

1. My Robot Buddy ◆ 1975
2. My Trip to Alpha 1 ◆ 1978
3. C.O.L.A.R. ◆ 1981
4. The Trouble on Janus ◆ 1985
5. Omega Station ◆ 1983

JAFTA

Lewin, Hugh
CAROLRHODA
GRADES K–3
FAMILY LIFE

Jafta lives with his mother and father in South Africa. His father works in the city, but Jafta receives plenty of love and attention from his mother and other adults in the village. One book shows preparations for a village wedding, and one is about Jafta waiting for his father's return from the city. All of the adults in Jafta's life, but especially his parents, are treated with the utmost respect and affection. Each page in this picture book series is illustrated in brown and black watercolors. Very simple text and large print make this accessible to beginning readers. Occasional Zulu words are explained in a note at the end.

1. Jafta ◆ 1981
2. Jafta's Father ◆ 1983
3. Jafta's Mother ◆ 1983
4. Jafta and the Wedding ◆ 1983
5. Jafta: The Journey ◆ 1984
6. Jafta: The Town ◆ 1984
7. Jafta: The Homecoming ◆ 1994

JAMAICA

Havill, Juanita
HOUGHTON MIFFLIN
GRADES K–2
FAMILY LIFE | REAL LIFE

Jamaica is an African American child living in a loving middle class family with her mother, father, and older brother. The series is about Jamaica's relationships with family and friends, and each book contains a very gentle lesson about getting along. In one, a small boy wants to play with her. At first, she rebuffs him; but as she considers how she felt when her brother wouldn't let her play, she builds a sand castle with him. It turns out so well that her brother wants to help. All the stories have this kind of wholesome, intelligent approach to getting along.

1. Jamaica's Find ◆ 1986
2. Jamaica Tag-Along ◆ 1989
3. Jamaica and Brianna ◆ 1993
4. Jamaica's Blue Marker ◆ 1996

JAMES STEVENSON'S AUTOBIOGRAPHICAL STORIES

Stevenson, James
GREENWILLOW
GRADES 1–3
REAL LIFE

With his series of autobiographical memoirs, James Stevenson gives readers a sense of family relationships. He creates intimacy and nostalgia with fond memories of his childhood summers on the beach with his grandparents in *July* and simple pleasures like burning leaves in *Fun/No Fun*. As his young daughter experiences events, Stevenson recalls them in *I Meant to Tell You*. Stevenson's watercolor illustrations are brief and faceless, allowing readers to fill in their own thoughts and memories. This is pleasurable reading for young and old.

1. When I Was Nine ◆ 1986
2. Higher on the Door ◆ 1987
3. July ◆ 1990
4. Don't You Know There's a War On? ◆ 1992
5. Fun/No Fun ◆ 1994
6. I Had a Lot of Wishes ◆ 1995
7. I Meant to Tell You ◆ 1996

JEFFREY'S GHOST

Adler, David A.
HENRY HOLT
GRADES 4–6
HUMOR | MYSTERY

Bradford was a boy of ten when he was killed by a horse in a barn. His ghost lived on in the barn, and when the barn was torn down, the ghost went to live in a nearby house. When Jeffrey moves into the house, he meets Bradford; and together with Jeffrey's friend Laura, they begin to solve problems. He helps a baseball team made up of kids that no other team wants and finds out who is cheating in the games at a fair. Bradford also causes problems for Jeffrey and Laura, being both invisible and mischievous, and this leads to some humorous situations.

1. Jeffrey's Ghost and the Leftover Baseball Team ◆ 1984
2. Jeffrey's Ghost and the Fifth Grade Dragon ◆ 1985
3. Jeffrey's Ghost and the Ziffel Fair Mystery ◆ 1987

JENNA V.

Hoehne, Marcia
CROSSWAY BOOKS
GRADES 4–6
FAMILY LIFE | VALUES

This series begins when Jenna is ten years old. As part of an active family, she sometimes struggles to find her place. When a foster child arrives, Jenna's feelings of isolation intensify. Her faith in God helps her realize the importance of giving love to others. In subsequent books, Jenna is still seeking to establish her identity, but she learns to value her own talents and reach out to others, including a young woman who is dying. Values like trust, honesty, and belief in God are an integral part of this series.

1. A Place of My Own ◆ 1993
2. A Pocket in My Heart ◆ 1994
3. The Fairy-Tale Friend ◆ 1994
4. Sunflower Girl ◆ 1995

JENNY AND THE CAT CLUB

Averill, Esther
HARPERCOLLINS
GRADES 3–6
ANIMAL FANTASY

Jenny is a shy little cat with a red scarf who lives with her friend Captain Tinker in New York City. She wants to join the Cat Club and spy on their meetings. Mr. President calls them to order, and each cat does something special. One cat plays a flute, and another dances. Jenny runs away because she can't do anything. Then the Captain makes four silver ice skates for her, and she learns to cut figure eights and flowers. Jenny becomes a member of the Cat Club, and the rest of the series is about her and all the other cats that live in the neighborhood. Some are tough, with no homes at all, while others live pampered lives and have to sneak away from overprotective owners. Delicate black-and-white drawings with occasional red or yellow splashes of color are on nearly every page.

1. The Cat Club; or, The Life and Times of Jenny Linsky ◆ 1944
2. The Adventures of Jack Ninepins ◆ 1944
3. The School for Cats ◆ 1947
4. Jenny's First Party ◆ 1948
5. Jenny's Moonlight Adventure ◆ 1949
6. When Jenny Lost Her Scarf ◆ 1951
7. Jenny's Adopted Brothers ◆ 1952
8. How the Brothers Joined the Cat Club ◆ 1953
9. Jenny's Birthday Book ◆ 1954
10. Jenny Goes to Sea ◆ 1957
11. Jenny's Bedside Book ◆ 1959
12. The Fire Cat ◆ 1961
13. The Hotel Cat ◆ 1969
14. Captains of the City Streets; a Story of the Cat Club ◆ 1972
15. Jenny and the Cat Club; a Collection of Favorite Stories About Jenny Linsky ◆ 1973

JENNY ARCHER

Conford, Ellen

LITTLE, BROWN

GRADES 2–4

HUMOR | REAL LIFE

Jenny Archer lives with her parents in a comfortable middle class neighborhood. This easy chapter book series is about her experiences as she enthusiastically throws herself into life. In one book, she is offered the chance to make a TV commercial. Her enthusiasm dims when she discovers that the commercial is for gerbil food. In other books, she writes her autobiography with some embellishments and learns first aid. Her parents and her friends Wilson and Beth provide unfailing understanding and support in all her endeavors.

1. A Job for Jenny Archer ◆ 1988
2. Case for Jenny Archer ◆ 1988
3. Jenny Archer, Author ◆ 1989
4. What's Cooking, Jenny Archer? ◆ 1989
5. Jenny Archer to the Rescue ◆ 1990
6. Can Do, Jenny Archer ◆ 1991
7. Nibble, Nibble, Jenny Archer ◆ 1993
8. Get the Picture, Jenny Archer? ◆ 1994

JENNY LINSKY *see* Jenny and the Cat Club

JEREMY BLUETT *see* Germy

JESSE BEAR

Carlstrom, Nancy White
SIMON & SCHUSTER
GRADES K–1
ANIMAL FANTASY

This picture book series stars a happy little bear named Jesse and his parents. They live in a cozy little house, which is illustrated in full color in great detail. Each book has a rhyming text that illustrates a concept. One shows counting, with a rhyme for bubbles, stars, Band-Aids, and other things that Jesse and his parents count. Birthdays, clothes, and getting wet are some of the other themes that are given this treatment. There are related and board books for younger children.

1. Jesse Bear, What Will You Wear? ◆ 1986
2. Better Not Get Wet, Jesse Bear ◆ 1988
3. It's About Time, Jesse Bear and Other Rhymes ◆ 1990
4. How Do You Say It Today, Jesse Bear? ◆ 1992
5. Happy Birthday, Jesse Bear ◆ 1994
6. Let's Count It Out, Jesse Bear ◆ 1996

JEWEL KINGDOM

Malcolm, Jahnna N.
SCHOLASTIC
GRADES 3–4
FANTASY

The Jewel Kingdom consists of White Winterland, Rushing River, Greenwood, Mysterious Forest, Blue Lake, Red Mountains, and Jewel Palace. The Jewel Princesses rule these lands and contend with wizards, dragons, and fantastic events. The plots are simple, and the reading level is accessible to middle grade readers. A jewel necklace is included with each book, which should attract many girls.

1. The Ruby Princess Runs Away ◆ 1997
2. The Sapphire Princess Meets the Monster ◆ 1997
3. The Emerald Princess Plays a Trick ◆ 1997
4. The Diamond Princess Saves the Day ◆ 1997

5. The Ruby Princess Sees a Ghost ◆ 1997
6. The Sapphire Princess Hunts for Treasure ◆ 1998
7. The Jewel Princess and the Missing Crown ◆ 1998
8. The Emerald Princess Finds a Fairy ◆ 1998
9. The Diamond Princess and the Magic Ball ◆ 1998
10. The Ruby Princess and the Baby Dragon ◆ 1998

JIMMY AND JANET

Cleary, Beverly
MORROW
GRADES K–2
FAMILY LIFE | HUMOR

These charming, old-fashioned family stories could have been taken from the author's own experiences with her twin children. Throughout the series, twins Jimmy and Janet remain four years old and become involved in simple plots in an ideal family setting. For example, in *The Growing-Up Feet*, the twins' feet are not quite ready for new shoes, so shiny red boots are substituted. Janet and Jimmy then wait impatiently for rain puddles until Dad provides a solution. Other titles deal with sibling rivalry, growing into big beds, and sharing. Full-color illustrations have updated these books, which were originally published in the 1960s.

1. The Real Hole ◆ 1960
2. Two Dog Biscuits ◆ 1961
3. Janet's Thingamajigs ◆ 1987
4. The Growing-Up Feet ◆ 1987

JIMMY'S BOA

Noble, Trinka Hakes
DIAL
GRADES K–2
HUMOR

What would happen if a student took his pet boa constrictor on a class field trip to a farm? Or to a birthday party at SeaLand? Jimmy takes his large, friendly boa to very inappropriate events, and the results are chaotic. Adding to the humor is the way the stories are presented, as Maggie describes events to her mother bit by bit. Steven Kellogg's illustrations are detailed and full of fun, capturing the frenzied activities of Jimmy and his boa.

1. The Day Jimmy's Boa Ate the Wash ◆ 1980
2. Jimmy's Boa Bounces Back ◆ 1984
3. Jimmy's Boa and the Big Splash Birthday Bash ◆ 1989

JOHNNY DIXON

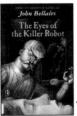

Bellairs, John, and Brad Strickland

DIAL

GRADES 5–8

FANTASY | MYSTERY

Johnny Dixon's mother is dead, and his dad is fighting in the Korean War. He lives with his grandparents across the street from the eccentric but kindly Professor Childermass. The two strike up a strange friendship; and together with Johnny's friend Fergie they solve mysteries involving ghosts, demon possession, and even time travel. Johnny is a small, almost timid boy who seems to be an unlikely candidate for such adventures. The professor is knowledgeable in many areas and sometimes unwillingly draws the boys into things. Fergie is a bit of a smart aleck, who adds some humor to the situations. Edward Gorey's black-and-white drawings add to the air of mystery. *The Drum, the Doll, and the Zombie* was completed by Strickland after Bellair's death. *The Hand of the Necromancer* and *The Bell, the Book, and the Spellbinder* are by Strickland.

1. The Curse of the Blue Figurine ◆ 1983
2. The Mummy, the Will, and the Crypt ◆ 1983
3. The Spell of the Sorcerer's Skull ◆ 1984
4. The Revenge of the Wizard's Ghost ◆ 1985
5. The Eyes of the Killer Robot ◆ 1986
6. The Trolley to Yesterday ◆ 1989
7. The Chessmen of Doom ◆ 1989
8. The Secret of the Underground Room ◆ 1990
9. The Drum, the Doll, and the Zombie ◆ 1994
10. The Hand of the Necromancer ◆ 1996
11. The Bell, the Book, and the Spellbinder ◆ 1997

JOHNNY LION

Hurd, Edith Thacher

HARPERCOLLINS

GRADES K–1

ANIMAL FANTASY | HUMOR

A little lion lives with his understanding mother and father in this first-reader series. He catches a bad cold and has to take medicine, which he thinks is making him have bad dreams. He learns to read, and his mother buys him a book about another lion, which he reads when his parents go out. Then he pretends that he is the lion in the book and jokingly tells his parents that he did the same things that Oliver P. Lion did.

1. Johnny Lion's Book ◆ 1965
2. Johnny Lion's Bad Day ◆ 1970
3. Johnny Lion's Rubber Boots ◆ 1972

JOHNNY MAY

Branscum, Robbie

HARPERCOLLINS

GRADES 4–6

FAMILY LIFE | HISTORICAL

Johnny May is an orphan who lives with and takes care of her grandparents in a poverty-stricken area of the Arkansas hills. This resourceful 11-year-old wonders in one book how she can provide a Christmas for herself and her grandparents. As the book opens, she comes upon a man she had admired shooting another man. As she and her friend Aron try to solve this mystery, Johnny deals with her feelings about violence in general, even as it relates to hunting animals. Other books in the series deal with her sort-of romance with Aron and a mix-up with a neighbor they think is a killer.

1. Johnny May ◆ 1975
2. The Adventures of Johnny May ◆ 1984
3. Johnny May Grows Up ◆ 1987

JOSEFINA *see* American Girls: Josefina

JOSHUA T. BATES

Shreve, Susan

KNOPF

GRADES 3–6

REAL LIFE

Just as school is going to begin, Joshua T. Bates finds out that he will be repeating the third grade. Even though everyone explains the situation very carefully and with sensitivity, he is dismayed to be "flunking." He works very hard and is promoted to the fourth grade in the middle of the school year. Once he is moved up, he worries about fitting in and must deal with a school bully. These situations will be familiar to many students, who will admire Joshua's efforts to solve his problems.

1. The Flunking of Joshua T. Bates ◆ 1984
2. Joshua T. Bates Takes Charge ◆ 1993
3. Joshua T. Bates in Trouble Again ◆ 1997

JOSIE SMITH

Nabb, Magdalen
MACMILLAN
GRADES 1–3
HUMOR | REAL LIFE

Josie lives with her mother in a lower middle class neighborhood in England. She is honest and independent, but she is always getting into trouble, even though she has the best of intentions. She feeds the neighbor's hens, befriends a girl from India, tries to buy a birthday present for her mother, and tries to help her mother paint a blackboard, all with humorous results. Eileen is her best friend, even though she is sometimes "horrible," and Gary Grimes is a low-keyed observer. Her mother is wise and understanding, saving the day when everyone is crying about their parts in the school play.

1. Josie Smith ◆ 1989
2. Josie Smith at the Seashore ◆ 1990
3. Josie Smith at School ◆ 1991
4. Josie Smith and Eileen ◆ 1992
5. Josie Smith's Christmas ◆ 1992
6. Josie Smith in Hospital ◆ 1993
7. Josie Smith at the Market ◆ 1995

JUDGE AND JURY

Banks, Jacqueline Turner
HOUGHTON MIFFLIN
GRADES 4–6
FAMILY LIFE | REAL LIFE

Judge and Jury Jenkins are twin brothers with very different personalities. Judge's dyslexia makes it difficult for him to do well at school. As sixth-graders at Plank Elementary School, the brothers and their friends work to help a student who needs a motorized wheelchair. Judge needs Jury's help to participate in the egg-drop contest for their science class. There are realistic events and dialogue in these novels, which feature African Americans as the main characters and deal with issues of diversity, including prejudice.

1. Project Wheels ◆ 1993
2. The New One ◆ 1994
3. Egg-Drop Blues ◆ 1995

JUDGE BENJAMIN

McInerney, Judith Whitelock

HOLIDAY HOUSE; POCKET BOOKS

GRADES 4–6

ANIMAL FANTASY | HUMOR

The narrator of this series is a huge St. Bernard who loves and protects his family through thick and thin—whether they appreciate him or not. Seth, Kathleen, and Ann Elizabeth look forward to staying with their grandmother while their parents are away, but Judge Benjamin feels that his territory is being invaded when the grandmother's dog comes along. With the children's parents away, the dogs form an uneasy partnership to solve problems. In other books in the series, Judge Benjamin stows away in the family's camper, finds a mate, and solves a mystery while snowbound in a cabin with his family.

1. Judge Benjamin: Superdog ◆ 1982
2. Judge Benjamin: The Superdog Secret ◆ 1983
3. Judge Benjamin: The Superdog Rescue ◆ 1984
4. Judge Benjamin: The Superdog Surprise ◆ 1985
5. Judge Benjamin: The Superdog Gift ◆ 1986

JULI SCOTT SUPER SLEUTH

Reece, Colleen L.

BARBOUR PUBLISHING

GRADES 5–8

MYSTERY | VALUES

Juli Scott imagines that she will be an author of Nancy Drew-style mysteries. Meanwhile, she solves some of her own mysteries, including the mysterious "death" of her own father. In *Mysterious Monday*, Juli's father, Gary, who is a policeman, loses his memory after an explosion. Trying to trick some drug dealers, the local police tell Juli and her mother, Anne, that Gary is dead. In other books, Juli tries to rescue her friend Shannon Riley from the influence of a spiritualist, and Juli and her boyfriend, Dave Gilmore, are in danger as witnesses to a robbery. Juli and her family incorporate Christian values into their daily lives and activities. Juli often writes in her journal, struggling with her conscience, beliefs, and spiritual questions.

1. Mysterious Monday ◆ 1997
2. Trouble on Tuesday ◆ 1997
3. Wednesday Witness ◆ 1998
4. Thursday Trials ◆ 1998
5. Friday Flight ◆ 1998
6. Saturday Scare ◆ 1998

JULIA REDFERN

Cameron, Eleanor

DUTTON

GRADES 4–6

FAMILY LIFE | HUMOR | REAL LIFE

Julia is a girl who loves to write, just like her father. He goes off to fight in World War I. He is killed, but Julia has a dream, just as he is dying, in which he asks her to tell her mother to be sure to go through his papers. There she finds a story that he wrote just before he went away, which eventually is accepted for publication. Starting when Julia is about four, the series follows her through high school as she writes about the people around her. First love, writing, and the love and support of her adored Uncle Hugh are the themes of the rest of the series.

1. A Room Made of Windows ◆ 1971
2. Julia and the Hand of God ◆ 1977
3. That Julia Redfern ◆ 1982
4. Julia's Magic ◆ 1984
5. The Private Worlds of Julia Redfern ◆ 1988

JULIAN AND HUEY

Cameron, Ann

FARRAR, STRAUS & GIROUX

GRADES 2–4

FAMILY LIFE

Julian is full of creative ideas for activities and projects, many of which involve his younger brother, Huey, and their friend Gloria. One time, the friends form the Crimebusters and notice that there are many mysterious circumstances around them. Another time, Julian tries to find out what his father is dreaming so that he can get his father the best birthday gift. Julian sometimes takes advantage of Huey's gullibility, but throughout the stories, there is a strong sense of family support and love.

1. The Stories Julian Tells ◆ 1981
2. More Stories Julian Tells ◆ 1986
3. Julian's Glorious Summer ◆ 1987
4. Julian, Secret Agent ◆ 1988
5. Julian, Dream Doctor ◆ 1990
6. The Stories Huey Tells ◆ 1995
7. More Stories Huey Tells ◆ 1997

JULIAN ESCOBÁR

O'Dell, Scott
HOUGHTON MIFFLIN
GRADES 5–8
HISTORICAL

Set in the 16th century, this series chronicles the adventures of Julian Escobár, a young seminarian from Spain who journeys to the Americas. He is captured by Mayan Indians and manages to convince them that he is Kukulcan, a god who had promised to return to them. He continues this charade in the second book when he leaves the Maya and encounters Cortez in the days when the Aztec king Moctezuma is conquered by a few hundred Spanish soldiers. In the third book, his fortunes change and he becomes a wanderer, but eventually he ends up with Francisco Pizarro in the land of the Incas.

1. The Captive ◆ 1979
2. The Feathered Serpent ◆ 1981
3. The Amethyst Ring ◆ 1983

JULIET *see* Girlhood Journeys: Juliet

JUNIE B. JONES

Ji Par

Park, Barbara
RANDOM HOUSE
GRADES 1–2
HUMOR | REAL LIFE

Junie B. Jones is a very strong-willed kindergarten student. She hides in the school building so she won't have to ride the bus, she learns about right and wrong when she loses her special new mittens, and she doesn't like her school picture. Throughout her adventures, Junie B. is helped by her teacher (whom she calls "Mrs."), her parents, and her grandparents. She speaks up for herself and for her friends, Grace and Lucille.

1. Junie B. Jones and the Stupid Smelly Bus ◆ 1992
2. Junie B. Jones and a Little Monkey Business ◆ 1993
3. Junie B. Jones and Her Big Fat Mouth ◆ 1993
4. Junie B. Jones and Some Sneaky Peeky Spying ◆ 1994
5. Junie B. Jones and the Yucky Blucky Fruitcake ◆ 1995
6. Junie B. Jones and That Meanie Jim's Birthday ◆ 1996
7. Junie B. Jones Loves Handsome Warren ◆ 1996
8. Junie B. Jones Has a Monster Under Her Bed ◆ 1997

9. Junie B. Jones Is Not a Crook ◆ 1997
10. Junie B. Jones Is a Party Animal ◆ 1997
11. Junie B. Jones Is a Beauty Shop Guy ◆ 1998
12. Junie B. Jones Smells Something Fishy ◆ 1998

JUNIOR GYMNASTS

Slater, Teddy

SCHOLASTIC

GRADES 3–5

REAL LIFE | RECREATION

A group of girls are on a local gymnastics team. Their goal is to be in the Olympics. When a new girl, Amanda Calloway, joins the team, there is some friction and jealousy. Dana Lewis had been looking forward to her first competition, thinking that she was the best member of the team. But Amanda is a great gymnast, too. This series emphasizes the training, effort, dedication, and energy that go into competitive gymnastics. There are also issues of competition and supporting teammates. An introduction by Olympic Gymnast Dominique Dawes stresses the importance of doing your best to fulfill your dreams.

1. Dana's Competition ◆ 1996
2. Katie's Big Move ◆ 1996
3. Amanda's Perfect Ten ◆ 1996
4. Dana's Best Friend ◆ 1996
5. Katie's Gold Medal ◆ 1996
6. Amanda's Unlucky Day ◆ 1997

JUNIOR JEDI KNIGHTS *see* Star Wars Junior Jedi Knights

JUST ME AND MY DAD

Gauthier, Bertrand

GARETH STEVENS

GRADES 1–3

FAMILY LIFE | REAL LIFE

Zachary and his dad, a single parent, are on their own. They have a lot of fun together in these simple, short tales for young readers. They go shopping, ice skating, and camping together. Zachary and his dad don't always get along; sometimes Zachary gets angry (but not for long). He even gets lost in one book. These are comforting stories that "only children" and children in single-parent households will relate to.

1. Zachary in I'm Zachary ◆ 1993
2. Zachary in the Championship ◆ 1993
3. Zachary in the Winner ◆ 1993
4. Zachary in the Present ◆ 1993
5. Zachary in the Wawabongbong ◆ 1993
6. Zachary in Camping Out ◆ 1993

JUSTICE TRILOGY

Hamilton, Virginia

GREENWILLOW

GRADES 5–8

FANTASY | SCIENCE FICTION

Justice and her two brothers discover that they are the first of a new race with extraordinary powers. Together with their friend Dorian, they form a unit that is able to travel into the distant future. Among the beings they find there is Duster, the leader of a group of young people. He is hindered, as is all of this world, by the evil Mal. When the Mal is defeated, all the friends they have made are free to be themselves. When Justice and her brothers return to their own time, they find that they have lost some of their powers but have gained maturity.

1. Justice and Her Brothers ◆ 1978
2. Dustland ◆ 1980
3. The Gathering ◆ 1981

KAI *see* Girlhood Journeys: Kai

KANE FAMILY

Caseley, Judith

GREENWILLOW

GRADES 3–4

FAMILY LIFE | REAL LIFE

This series explores such childhood experiences as starting school, feeling lonely, getting lost, confronting a school bully, and family relationships. Each title focuses on one of the Kane children with lots of interaction within the family. In *Dorothy's Darkest Days*, Dorothy must confront her feelings about a classmate who has died, particularly the fact that Dorothy did not like her. Harry is a busy, charming preschooler in *Hurricane Harry*.

In *Harry and Arney*, he must relinquish his role as the youngest child and accept a new baby in the family. Affectionate humor and an accessible reading level make this a good choice for middle elementary school.

1. Hurricane Harry ◆ 1991
2. Starring Dorothy Kane ◆ 1992
3. Chloe in the Know ◆ 1993
4. Harry and Arney ◆ 1994
5. Dorothy's Darkest Days ◆ 1997

KATE

Brisson, Pat
SIMON & SCHUSTER
GRADES 2–4
REAL LIFE

Kate, a young girl from New Jersey, travels across the country, writing letters to her best friend back home. At every stop she describes interesting things she sees, and the trials and tribulations of dealing with Brian, her pesky younger brother. In Baltimore, they go to the aquarium and he says they should have brought Kate's pet goldfish, because the sharks look hungry. In Washington, they visit the National Air and Space Museum, where Brian tells Kate she should be an astronaut, because she looks like something from outer space. The family makes a circle of the eastern states and comes back to New Jersey. In sequels, Kate goes to the West Coast, and then out West. Full-color illustrations on every page make this a fun way for younger students to study the states.

1. Your Best Friend, Kate ◆ 1989
2. Kate Heads West ◆ 1990
3. Kate on the Coast ◆ 1992

KATE

Chorao, Kay
DUTTON
GRADES K–2
ANIMAL FANTASY

Kate is a little elephant who lives with her parents and brother. There are some toddler books in this series with just a few words on each page, and there are picture books for a slightly older crowd. In *George Told Kate,* Kate's brother tells her all kinds of terrible things that are going to happen in one of the picture books. Full-color, full-page illustrations show all

Kate's imaginings, but the real thing turns out to be fine. In one of the small preschool books, *Kate's Box*, Kate doesn't want anything to do with a young cousin, until she finds a way to entertain him with her box.

1. Kate's Box ◆ 1982
2. Kate's Car ◆ 1982
3. Kate's Quilt ◆ 1982
4. Kate's Snowman ◆ 1982
5. George Told Kate ◆ 1987

KATE GORDON

Barron, T. A.
PUTNAM
GRADES 5–8
FANTASY

Kate Gordon, 13, and her 80-year-old grandfather, Dr. Miles Prancer, have a special bond and an ability to journey through time and space. Dr. Prancer is an astrophysicist working on saving the planet Earth and its solar system from total destruction. This fantasy (with elements of science fiction) is complete with conflicts between the forces of good and evil. As the fantasy progresses, there are links to Arthurian legends, which should appeal to many readers. Readers who enjoyed L'Engle's Time Fantasy Series will enjoy these adventures, which are somewhat technical and a little more scientific.

1. Heartlight ◆ 1990
2. The Ancient One ◆ 1992
3. The Merlin Effect ◆ 1994

KATIE

McDaniel, Becky Bring
CHILDREN'S PRESS
GRADES K–1
REAL LIFE

In a beginning-reader format with a controlled vocabulary, this series focuses on Katie, the youngest and smallest child in her family. Katie struggles to do things that her older siblings, Jenny and Kris, can already do. She is pleased with her accomplishments, like teaching the dog a trick and giving her mother flowers. Sometimes, her siblings are supportive, but other times they take advantage of her being the youngest. Young readers will empathize with the predicament of being little and wanting to do more things. The simple text will provide a satisfying reading experience for beginners.

1. Katie Did It ◆ 1983
2. Katie Couldn't ◆ 1985
3. Katie Can ◆ 1987

KATIE JOHN

Calhoun, Mary
HARPERCOLLINS
GRADES 4–8
FAMILY LIFE | REAL LIFE

Katie John's story begins when her parents inherit a huge, decrepit house in a small town. They decide to move there for the summer, but Katie is not happy about leaving her friends. Over the summer, she makes new friends and begins to appreciate the house and its family history. In the end, she convinces her parents to stay and make a living by renting out rooms. She agrees to help with all the work involved in such an endeavor. In subsequent books, she starts a "boy haters" club, but in junior high becomes a romantic after reading *Wuthering Heights* and begins to look for her Heathcliff.

1. Katie John ◆ 1960
2. Depend on Katie John ◆ 1961
3. Honestly, Katie John ◆ 1963
4. Katie John and Heathcliff ◆ 1980

KATIE MORAG

Hedderwick, Mairi
LITTLE, BROWN
GRADES 1–2
FAMILY LIFE

A new baby, a visit from mischievous cousins, and rivalry between Grannie Island and Grannie Mainland are some of the plots presented in this light-hearted series. Katie Morag lives in a tiny fishing village off the coast of Scotland. Whimsical details of the setting are captured in the humorous illustrations. Katie Morag is a young girl who gives early readers a glimpse of growing up in another country.

1. Katie Morag Delivers the Mail ◆ 1984
2. Katie Morag and the Two Grandmothers ◆ 1985

3. Katie Morag and the Tiresome Ted ◆ 1986
4. Katie Morag and the Big Boy Cousins ◆ 1987
5. Katie Morag and the Grand Concert ◆ 1988
6. Katie Morag and the New Pier ◆ 1994
7. Katie Morag and the Wedding ◆ 1996

KATIE POTTS *see* Holiday Friends

KEITH SHIPLEY

Gleitzman, Morris
HARCOURT
GRADES 4–7
FAMILY LIFE | REAL LIFE

Keith worries that his parents aren't happy running a fish-and-chips shop in dreary London, so he invents all kinds of schemes to cheer them up. After convincing his parents to move to sunnier Australia, Keith plans to seek a fortune for his family in the opal mines. When his parents separate, Keith suggests ways for both of them to become better-looking to attract new mates. Throughout the series, Keith's humorous adventures border on the absurd.

1. Misery Guts ◆ 1991
2. Worry Warts ◆ 1991
3. Puppy Fat ◆ 1994

KERBY MAXWELL BOOKS *see* Trick Books

KIDS IN MS. COLEMAN'S CLASS

Martin, Ann M.
SCHOLASTIC
GRADES 1–3
REAL LIFE

There are 16 kids in Ms. Coleman's second-grade class—six boys and ten girls. Each book involves these students in common classroom situations. In *Science Fair*, Bobby and his group are studying a mouse named Harriet. When Harriet goes missing, is the science project ruined? In *Snow War*, Ian Johnson loves to read. He even reads while his friends are building snow forts and throwing snowballs. But he stops reading when he realizes that his friends have started to get mean in their snow fights. Other books deal with being afraid of animals, enjoying a favorite author, being on summer vacation, and celebrating holidays. There is diversity in the class and a common theme is that the boys often feel outnumbered, which should appeal to many readers.

1. Teacher's Pet ◆ 1995
2. Author Day ◆ 1996
3. Class Play ◆ 1996
4. Second Grade Baby ◆ 1996
5. Snow War ◆ 1997
6. Twin Trouble ◆ 1997
7. Science Fair ◆ 1997
8. Summer School ◆ 1997
9. Halloween Parade ◆ 1997
10. Holiday Time ◆ 1997
11. Spelling Bee ◆ 1998
12. Baby Animal Zoo ◆ 1998

KIDS OF THE POLK STREET SCHOOL

Giff, Patricia Reilly
DELL
GRADES 1–3
HUMOR | REAL LIFE

A group of children learn to get along in the classroom in some very funny situations. The star of the series is Richard "Beast" Best, who is held back in the second grade and keeps getting in trouble. In the first book, he becomes interested in reading. Emily has trouble with reading, and one of the books deals with her experiences with the library summer reading game. Matthew is Beast's best friend, and when he moves away, one of the books follows him. Short sentences and paragraphs characterize this easy chapter series. The Kids of the Polk Street School Specials include special sections with activities and projects. Some even have travel information as the kids become interested in different topics and places. See also the New Kids at the Polk Street School.

1. The Beast in Ms. Rooney's Room ◆ 1984
2. Fish Face ◆ 1984
3. The Candy Corn Contest ◆ 1984
4. December Secrets ◆ 1984
5. In the Dinosaur's Paw ◆ 1985
6. The Valentine Star ◆ 1985
7. Lazy Lions, Lucky Lambs ◆ 1985
8. Snaggle Doodles ◆ 1985
9. Purple Climbing Days ◆ 1985
10. Say "Cheese" ◆ 1985
11. Sunny-Side Up ◆ 1986

12. Pickle Puss ◆ 1986
13. Beast and the Halloween Horror ◆ 1990
14. Emily Arrow Promises to Do Better This Year ◆ 1990
15. Monster Rabbit Runs Amuck! ◆ 1991
16. Wake Up, Emily, It's Mother's Day ◆ 1991

KIDS OF THE POLK STREET SCHOOL SPECIALS

1. Write Up a Storm with the Polk Street School ◆ 1993
2. Count Your Money with the Polk Street School ◆ 1994
3. The Postcard Pest ◆ 1994
4. Turkey Trouble ◆ 1994
5. Look Out, Washington D.C.! ◆ 1995
6. Green Thumbs, Everyone ◆ 1996
7. Pet Parade ◆ 1996
8. Next Stop, New York City! ◆ 1997
9. Oh Boy, Boston! ◆ 1997
10. Let's Go, Philadelphia! ◆ 1998

KIDS ON BUS 5

Leonard, Marcia
MINSTREL/POCKET BOOKS
GRADES 1–3
REAL LIFE

Natalie Adams and James Perry are in the third grade at Maple Street School. They are good friends and they enjoy school, except for riding the bus to get there. The bus driver, Mr. Balter, tries to keep control of things, but he yells so much the kids call him "Old Yeller." Natalie, James, and Natalie's little brother Cody must deal with bullies on the bus, a break-down, and wondering if someone on their route is a thief. When Mr. Balter is sick for a while, the kids find out that his substitutes bring different problems. Readers who ride the bus will recognize many of these situations and will be reassured by the satisfying solutions.

1. The Bad News Bully ◆ 1996
2. Wild Man at the Wheel ◆ 1996
3. Finders Keepers ◆ 1997
4. I Survived on Bus Five ◆ 1997

KING ARTHUR

Talbott, Hudson, reteller
MORROW
GRADES 3–5
FANTASY

This adaptation from the original Arthur story has the appeal of simpler language and vivid illustrations. The series is filled with the pageantry of medieval times. The tale begins in *The Sword in the Stone* when 16-year-old Arthur discovers that he has been chosen to be king of Britain. Sir Ector, his adoptive father, fully understands the truth when Arthur pulls the fabled sword from its stone and becomes the rightful king. Merlin, the ancient magician, becomes Arthur's guide in uniting the country. In other books, Arthur's feat becomes legendary, he establishes the model for chivalry, and he creates Camelot. The illustrations bring the adventures to life, especially for younger readers.

1. King Arthur: The Sword in the Stone ◆ 1991
2. King Arthur and the Round Table ◆ 1995
3. Excalibur ◆ 1996

KIRSTEN *see* American Girls: Kirsten

KITTY

Delton, Judy
HOUGHTON MIFFLIN
GRADES 3–6
HISTORICAL | REAL LIFE

Set in the 1930s, the first book in this series finds third-grader Kitty changing from one Catholic school to another. At her new school, she meets Margaret Mary, an A student, the oldest of many children, a great help to her mother, and a devout Catholic. She also meets Eileen, bored with school, a wealthy only child, and indifferent to the Church. The three girls form an unlikely friendship; and for the rest of the series, Kitty feels herself pulled between the other two. In fourth grade, they experience first love and explore an old house together. The series follows them up to high school, when Margaret Mary's behavior takes a surprising turn and they all discover boys.

1. Kitty in the Middle ◆ 1979
2. Kitty in the Summer ◆ 1980
3. Kitty in High School ◆ 1984
4. Kitty from the Start ◆ 1987

KOBIE ROBERTS

Ransom, Candice F.
SCHOLASTIC
GRADES 4–7
REAL LIFE

Kobie lives with her parents in the country. We first meet Kobie persuading her best friend, Gretchen, to help her build a roller coaster ride. She is ten at the time, and the series follows her until she is 15. The series deals in some depth with her maturing process as she learns to get along better with her mother, with Gretchen, and with the other children in her class. A good artist, but a poor student, she learns to make the most of her abilities and to see things from others' points of view.

1. Thirteen ◆ 1986
2. Fourteen and Holding ◆ 1987
3. Fifteen at Last ◆ 1987
4. Going on Twelve ◆ 1988
5. Almost Ten and a Half ◆ 1990

LADD FAMILY

Roddy, Lee
FOCUS ON THE FAMILY
GRADES 4–6
ADVENTURE | FAMILY LIFE | VALUES

This series features exotic locations as the Ladd family spends time in Hawaii and Alaska and goes on a cruise to Mexico. Josh Ladd, 12, and his friend Tank are featured in most of the stories, which include dealing with poachers, surviving a hurricane, adapting to the wilderness, recovering a stolen surfboard, and searching for treasure in shark-infested waters.

Occasionally, there is an element of mystery in these books, but the main emphasis is on values like friendship, honesty, trust, and obedience.

1. The Secret of the Shark Pit ◆ 1988
2. The Legend of Fire ◆ 1988
3. The Mystery of the Island Jungle ◆ 1989
4. The Secret of the Sunken Sub ◆ 1990
5. The Dangerous Canoe Race ◆ 1990
6. The Mystery of the Wild Surfer ◆ 1990
7. Peril at Pirate's Point ◆ 1992
8. Terror at Forbidden Falls ◆ 1993
9. Case of the Dangerous Cruise ◆ 1994
10. The Eye of the Hurricane ◆ 1994
11. The Night of the Vanishing Lights ◆ 1994
12. Panic in the Wild Waters ◆ 1995
13. Hunted in the Alaskan Wilderness ◆ 1996
14. Stranded on Terror Island ◆ 1997
15. Tracked by the Wolf Pack ◆ 1997

LASSIE

Bray, Marian, adapter
CHARIOT BOOKS
GRADES 4–8
REAL LIFE | VALUES

These books feature the familiar characters of Lassie and the Harmon family. Jimmy and Lassie are more than owner and pet; they are best friends. In one book, Lassie is lost and Jimmy is devastated. His father, Reverend Harmon, reminds Jimmy of his faith in God and helps him accept the circumstances and trust God's judgment. When Lassie returns, Jimmy and his family are thankful, knowing that their prayers have been answered. Lessons about honesty, hope, courage, and faith pervade these books, supporting the Christian values of the publishers, a division of Cook Communications Ministries.

1. Under the Big Top ◆ 1995
2. Treasure at Eagle Mountain ◆ 1995
3. To the Rescue ◆ 1995
4. Hayloft Hideout ◆ 1996
5. Danger at Echo Cliffs ◆ 1996

THE LAURA YEARS *see* Little House

LECHOW FAMILY

Benary-Isbert, Margot
HARCOURT
GRADES 5–8
FAMILY LIFE | HISTORICAL

Set in postwar Germany, *The Ark* begins the trilogy of the Lechow family. Mrs. Lechow is trying to keep her family alive while her husband is in a Russian prison camp. The family fortunately finds its way to Rowan Farm and makes a home in the Ark, an old railroad car on the farm. The story continues in *Rowan Farm* and *Castle on the Border*. The author was born in Germany, lived under Nazi rule, and arrived in the United States in 1957. The stories, translated from the German, are based on the author's childhood.

1. The Ark ◆ 1948
2. Rowan Farm ◆ 1949
3. Castle on the Border ◆ 1956

LEO AND EMILY

Brandenberg, Franz
GREENWILLOW
GRADES K–3
HUMOR | REAL LIFE

This is a charming series of beginning chapter books. Leo and Emily are best friends. They go on a hike and search for dragons, make their babysitter earn his money, and generally have a good time.

1. Leo and Emily ◆ 1981
2. Leo and Emily's Big Ideas ◆ 1982
3. Leo and Emily and the Dragon ◆ 1984
4. Leo and Emily's Zoo ◆ 1988

LEWIS BARNAVELT

Bellairs, John, and Brad Strickland
DIAL
GRADES 5–8
FANTASY

Lewis is a ten-year-old orphan who goes to live with his Uncle Jonathan in the small town of New Zebedee. His uncle is a kind old man who practices "white magic," and his neighbor and best friend is Mrs. Zimmerman, who is a good witch. Jonathan lives in a big old house that was previously owned by an evil man who practiced black magic. Lewis makes a new friend toward the end of the first book in the series: Rose Rita, who loves baseball and lives in a nearby mansion. Some of the books in the series concern Rose Rita and Mrs. Zimmerman as they fight black magic together. The first three books were written by Bellairs; the fourth and fifth were completed by Strickland after Bellairs's death; and the sixth and seventh were written by Strickland and are based on the characters of Bellairs.

1. The House with a Clock in Its Walls ◆ 1973
2. The Figure in the Shadows ◆ 1975
3. The Letter, the Witch, and the Ring ◆ 1976
4. The Ghost in the Mirror ◆ 1993
5. The Vengeance of the Witch-Finder ◆ 1993
6. The Doom of the Haunted Opera ◆ 1995
7. The Specter from the Magician's Museum ◆ 1998

LILA FENWICK

McMullan, Kate

DIAL

GRADES 4–6

FAMILY LIFE | HUMOR

Lila has "great ideas," whether it be finding the lost class guinea pig or taking a dare. Whatever she does is a real challenge for fifth-grade Lila in *The Great Ideas of Lila Fenwick*. In *Great Advice from Lila Fenwick*, Lila and her friend Rita join Lila's doctor father at a Boy Scout camp. Lila gets involved with a project in which each sixth-grader must take care of an egg as if it were a newborn in *The Great Eggspectations of Lila Fenwick*. These are warm and funny stories of growing up.

1. The Great Ideas of Lila Fenwick ◆ 1986
2. Great Advice from Lila Fenwick ◆ 1988
3. The Great Eggspectations of Lila Fenwick ◆ 1991

LILLY

Henkes, Kevin

GREENWILLOW

GRADES K–2

ANIMAL FANTASY | HUMOR

Best friends Chester and Wilson are dismayed when the flamboyant Lilly moves into their neighborhood. Lilly comes to their rescue, and the three mice become friends. In another story, Lilly looks forward to the arrival of her baby brother—until he actually gets there. Then she is not amused. At first, she is not a very good big sister; but when her cousin is disdainful of her brother Julius, Lilly rises to his defense. The third book shows Lilly at school. She loves her teacher, Mr. Slinger. After he takes away her special treasures (including her new purple plastic purse), her temper gets the better of her. This is a fun group of books with lively language and situations.

1. Chester's Way ◆ 1988
2. Julius, the Baby of the World ◆ 1990
3. Lilly's Purple Plastic Purse ◆ 1998

LINCOLN LIONS BAND

Giff, Patricia Reilly

DELL

GRADES 2–4

HUMOR

Chrissie, Willie, Kenny, and Michelle are part of a new "junior" band at school. Each experiences the trials and tribulations of elementary school life, such as a little fibbing, inability to keep a clean desk, a parent who isn't home enough, and the capacity to get into scrapes with one another. Each book features a different problem and resolves it realistically and with gentle humor. After the first book, the remaining volumes involve a season or a holiday.

1. Meet the Lincoln Lions Band ◆ 1992
2. Yankee Doodle Drumsticks ◆ 1992
3. The Jingle Bell Jam ◆ 1992
4. The Rootin' Tootin' Bugle Boy ◆ 1992
5. The Red, White, & Blue Valentine ◆ 1993
6. The Great Shamrock Disaster ◆ 1993

LIONEL

Krensky, Stephen

DIAL

GRADES 1–2

REAL LIFE

This is a series of short, episodic tales about young Lionel and his family and friends. Lionel has a new teacher, goes trick-or-treating, gets a shot from the doctor, and goes to his first sleepover. Gently comic illustrations enhance the good-natured text. Good for reading aloud or reading alone.

1. Lionel at Large ◆ 1986
2. Lionel in the Fall ◆ 1987
3. Lionel in the Spring ◆ 1990
4. Lionel and Louise ◆ 1992
5. Lionel in Winter ◆ 1994
6. Lionel and His Friends ◆ 1996
7. Lionel in the Summer ◆ 1998

LITTLE BEAR

Minarik, Else Holmelund
HarperCollins
Grades K–2
Animal Fantasy | Family Life

Each book in this series contains four vignettes about Little Bear, who acts much like a preschool child. In *Little Bear*, he persuades his mother to make him a winter outfit, makes himself some birthday soup, takes an imaginary trip to the moon, and goes happily to sleep when his mother tells him a story about Little Bear. In *Father Bear Comes Home*, Little Bear has the hiccups, looks for a mermaid, goes fishing, and welcomes Father home from the sea. Little Bear becomes friends with a little girl named Emily in *Little Bear's Friend*. This series was the first in the I Can Read series, published at a time when there was a lack of good easy-to-read children's books.

1. Little Bear ◆ 1957
2. Father Bear Comes Home ◆ 1959
3. Little Bear's Friend ◆ 1960
4. Little Bear's Visit ◆ 1961
5. A Kiss for Little Bear ◆ 1968

LITTLE BEAR BOOKS

Waddell, Martin
Candlewick
Grades K–1
Animal Fantasy

These are the picture book stories of two bears, Big Bear and Little Bear. In the first, Little Bear is afraid of the darkness inside and outside their cave, so Big Bear shows him the light he's missing. In the second, Little Bear is afraid of the noises he hears while on a walk. Once again, Big Bear reassures him. The third book is more about shared activities and learning to spend time alone. In each, the interaction between the two bears highlights a tender, caring relationship between a very young "child" and a patient, understanding "adult."

1. Can't You Sleep, Little Bear? ◆ 1992
2. Let's Go Home, Little Bear ◆ 1993
3. You and Me, Little Bear ◆ 1996

LITTLE BILL

Cosby, Bill
SCHOLASTIC
GRADES K–2
REAL LIFE

Comedian Bill Cosby has developed a series of fully illustrated easy readers that gently teach values to children and parents. Little Bill and his friends encounter a bully who makes a game of insults. Little Bill is advised to simply say "So?" and the strategy works by making the situation funny. When Little Bill develops a crush on a girl, he makes her a special valentine but then is afraid to give it to her. His friends try to make it easier for him, and he conquers his fear. The same group of friends learns that it is more fun to have imaginative play than to watch TV all the time. Each of the books begins with a note from psychiatrist Alvin F. Poussaint explaining the lesson to parents.

1. The Best Way to Play ◆ 1997
2. The Meanest Thing to Say ◆ 1997
3. The Treasure Hunt ◆ 1997
4. Super-Fine Valentine ◆ 1997
5. Money Troubles ◆ 1998
6. Shipwreck Saturday ◆ 1998

LITTLE BROWN BEAR

Lebrun, Claude
CHILDREN'S PRESS
GRADES K–1
ANIMAL FANTASY | FAMILY LIFE

This series, originally published in France, offers glimpses into everyday activities with which very young children will identify. Each story presents typical situations and problems. Small-format pages of brief text face full-color illustrations.

1. Little Brown Bear Gets Dressed ◆ 1979
2. Little Brown Bear Says No ◆ 1979
3. Little Brown Bear Takes a Bath ◆ 1979

4. Little Brown Bear Is Ill ◆ 1982
5. Little Brown Bear Wakes Up ◆ 1982
6. Little Brown Bear Wants a Kiss ◆ 1982
7. Little Brown Bear's Cold ◆ 1982
8. Little Brown Bear Is Cross ◆ 1982
9. Little Brown Bear's Story ◆ 1982
10. Little Brown Bear's Tricycle ◆ 1982
11. Little Brown Bear's Walk ◆ 1982
12. Little Brown Bear Won't Eat! ◆ 1982
13. Little Brown Bear's Bad Days ◆ 1983
14. Little Brown Bear's Breakfast Egg ◆ 1983
15. Little Brown Bear Can Cook! ◆ 1983
16. Little Brown Bear Is Big! ◆ 1983
17. Little Brown Bear's Playtime ◆ 1983
18. Little Brown Bear's Snowball ◆ 1983

LITTLE CHICK

Kwitz, Mary DeBall

HARPERTROPHY

GRADES K–2

ANIMAL FANTASY

This is a delightful beginning-to-read series about life on a farm. Little Chick runs away from Broody Hen when she doesn't want to take a nap and discovers the animals in a pond. As Little Chick waits for breakfast, she discovers what all the other animals eat. This series could be useful both as practice for beginning readers and as part of a discovery unit about life on a farm.

1. Little Chick's Story ◆ 1978
2. Little Chick's Big Day ◆ 1981
3. Little Chick's Breakfast ◆ 1983
4. Little Chick's Friend, Duckling ◆ 1992

LITTLE HOUSE

Wilder, Laura Ingalls

HARPERCOLLINS

GRADES 3–6

FAMILY LIFE | HISTORICAL

These are the original Little House books and are now also called The Laura Years. Nine stories narrate the life of the author and her family during the 1870s and 1880s. From Laura's childhood home in Wisconsin, the family moves west to Kansas, lives for a while in a dugout in Minnesota, and then moves to the Dakota Territory, where Laura lives until her marriage to Almanzo Wilder. The stories, narrated by Laura, are filled with humor and tenderness as this closely knit pioneer family overcomes adversity and hardship. This series has been extended and repackaged into other series (see following entries). In addition to the related series there are toddler board books, pioneer activity books, cookbooks, craft books, and other novelty books and items.

1. Little House in the Big Woods ◆ 1932
2. Farmer Boy ◆ 1933
3. Little House on the Prairie ◆ 1935
4. On the Banks of Plum Creek ◆ 1937
5. By the Shores of Silver Lake ◆ 1939
6. The Long Winter ◆ 1940
7. Little Town on the Prairie ◆ 1941
8. These Happy Golden Years ◆ 1943
9. The First Four Years ◆ 1971

LITTLE HOUSE: MY FIRST LITTLE HOUSE BOOKS

Wilder, Laura Ingalls

HARPERCOLLINS

GRADES K–2

FAMILY LIFE | HISTORICAL

The original Little House books are classics in children's literature. These picture books are adaptations of the original books and make some of the stories more accessible to younger readers. All of the familiar characters are here—Pa, Ma, Mary, Laura, and Carrie—and there is even a book that features Laura's future husband, Almanzo Wilder. Warm illustrations portray the loving family moments of these well-known stories.

1. Dance at Grandpa's ◆ 1994
2. Winter Days in the Big Woods ◆ 1994
3. Christmas in the Big Woods ◆ 1995
4. The Deer in the Wood ◆ 1995
5. Going to Town ◆ 1995
6. Bedtime for Laura ◆ 1996
7. Going West ◆ 1996
8. Summertime in the Big Woods ◆ 1996
9. Winter on the Farm ◆ 1996
10. County Fair ◆ 1997
11. Prairie Day ◆ 1997
12. A Little House Birthday ◆ 1997
13. My Little House 123 ◆ 1997

14. My Little House ABC ◆ 1997
15. A Farmer Boy Birthday ◆ 1998
16. A Little Prairie House ◆ 1998
17. My Little House Book of Animals ◆ 1998
18. My Little House Book of Family ◆ 1998
19. Sugar Snow ◆ 1998

LITTLE HOUSE: THE CAROLINE YEARS

Wilkes, Maria D.

HARPERCOLLINS

GRADES 3–6

FAMILY LIFE | HISTORICAL

This series features the early years of Caroline Quiner, who would grow up to marry Charles Ingalls and become the mother of Laura and her sisters. The family moved to towns and settlements in Wisconsin, experiencing the life on frontier outposts. *Little House in Brookfield* introduces us to Caroline and her family of five brothers and sisters. Her father was lost at sea the year before the book begins, and resourceful Caroline is busy helping her family cope with the loss. *Little Town at the Crossroads* tells more of Caroline's life in the growing town of Brookfield. This series provides background information about the years prior to the Little House books. It has also been called the Brookfield Years.

1. Little House in Brookfield ◆ 1996
2. Little Town at the Crossroads ◆ 1997
3. Little Clearing in the Woods ◆ 1998

LITTLE HOUSE: THE ROSE YEARS

MacBride, Roger Lea

HARPERCOLLINS

GRADES 3–6

FAMILY LIFE | HISTORICAL

Ji Mac

This continuation of the popular Little House series follows the childhood of Rose, the daughter of Laura and Almanzo Wilder. The early books describe the family's move from South Dakota to Missouri, where they buy the Rocky Ridge Farm and settle down to life in the Ozark Mountains. In later books, their quiet life is shattered by natural disasters that ultimately force them to leave their farm. Written by Rose Wilder's adopted grandson, this series maintains the warmth and charm of the Little

House series, reflecting a place and time that appeals to many young readers. This series has also been called the Rocky Ridge Years.

1. Little House on Rocky Ridge ◆ 1993
2. Little Farm in the Ozarks ◆ 1994
3. In the Land of the Big Red Apple ◆ 1995
4. On the Other Side of the Hill ◆ 1995
5. Little Town in the Ozarks ◆ 1996
6. New Dawn on Rocky Ridge ◆ 1997
7. On the Banks of the Bayou ◆ 1998

LITTLE HOUSE CHAPTER BOOKS

Wilder, Laura Ingalls

Ji Wil

HARPERCOLLINS

GRADES K–2

FAMILY LIFE | HISTORICAL

The books for this series are adapted from the original Little House books. They feature some of the more exciting and entertaining moments, like Laura's escapades with her dog, Jack, and the family's struggles after a prairie fire and a blizzard. The shorter chapters will be more accessible to younger readers who enjoy these high-spirited stories of pioneer life.

1. The Adventures of Laura and Jack ◆ 1997
2. Animal Adventures ◆ 1997
3. Pioneer Sisters ◆ 1997
4. School Days ◆ 1997
5. Farmer Boy Days ◆ 1998
6. Hard Times on the Prairie ◆ 1998
7. Laura & Nellie ◆ 1998
8. Little House Farm Days ◆ 1998

LITTLE MOUSE

Kraus, Robert

GREENWILLOW

GRADES K–1

ANIMAL FANTASY

Little Mouse is lonely because he thinks he is nobody's mouse in the first book of the series, *Whose Mouse Are You?* In the other stories, Little Mouse accepts a cat's invitation to come out and play, and then runs away from home to find a family who will pay more attention to him. Kraus's simple text and Jose Aruego and Ariane Dewey's bright, inventive illustrations combine to make this a winning series.

1. Whose Mouse Are You? ◆ 1970
2. Where Are You Going, Little Mouse? ◆ 1986
3. Come Out and Play, Little Mouse ◆ 1987

LITTLE POLAR BEAR

de Beer, Hans

NORTH-SOUTH BOOKS

GRADES K–3

ANIMAL FANTASY

EP DeB

Lars the Little Polar Bear lives at the North Pole, where he finds plenty to do. He is often alone, but sometimes encounters animal playmates, or the scientists at the nearby polar research station. Charming illustrations of Lars against white snow and a pink and blue sky make these engrossing books for beginning readers. There are related pop-up and specialty books.

1. Little Polar Bear ◆ 1987
2. Ahoy There, Little Polar Bear ◆ 1988
3. Little Polar Bear Finds a Friend ◆ 1990
4. Little Polar Bear and the Brave Little Hare ◆ 1992
5. Little Polar Bear, Take Me Home! ◆ 1996

LITTLE SOUP

Peck, Robert Newton

DELL

GRADES 2–3

HUMOR

In this series, Soup (who is the main character in another series) is much younger, but his antics with his friend Rob are just the same. The two manage to create problems at a Thanksgiving play and on a hayride. At Easter, they dye eggs—and a whole lot more. This is an easier series that sets the stage for the friendship between Soup and Rob that is more fully developed in the Soup series.

1. Little Soup's Hayride ◆ 1991
2. Little Soup's Birthday ◆ 1991
3. Little Soup's Turkey ◆ 1992
4. Little Soup's Bunny ◆ 1993

LITTLE TOOT

Gramatky, Hardie
PUTNAM
GRADES K–1
ADVENTURE | FANTASY | VALUES

Little Toot is introduced in the first book as a small tugboat who doesn't really want to do anything but play. Best of all, he loves to make huge figure eights, which get in the way of other tugboats. When he finally decides to get serious, the other boats don't believe him. Eventually, he saves an ocean liner and proves his worth. Subsequent stories find him in various exotic locales, with descriptions of famous landmarks. In each story, his resourcefulness is tested and he comes through to save the situation, often with the use of a figure eight. Little messages about the important things in life are woven through his thoughts. After the author's death, the last book was completed from unfinished sketches and drawings.

1. Little Toot ◆ 1939
2. Little Toot on the Thames ◆ 1964
3. Little Toot on the Grand Canal ◆ 1968
4. Little Toot on the Mississippi ◆ 1973
5. Little Toot Through the Golden Gate ◆ 1975
6. Little Toot & the Loch Ness Monster ◆ 1989

LITTLE WOMEN JOURNALS

Emerson, Charlotte
AVON
GRADES 4–6
FAMILY LIFE | HISTORICAL

These books, published in association with a series of dolls, extend the stories of Louisa May Alcott's *Little Women*. Each book features one of the March sisters. Amy faces a dilemma in an art contest. Beth tries to rescue a pony. Jo is tense about the publication of her first story. Meg is embarrassed when she is asked to the home of a wealthy family and is expected to help out with chores. Girls who have been reading the American Girls series may enjoy this similar series.

1. Amy's True Prize ◆ 1998
2. Beth's Snow Dancer ◆ 1998
3. Jo's Troubled Heart ◆ 1998
4. Meg's Dearest Wish ◆ 1998

LITTLE WOMEN PORTRAITS *see* Portraits of Little Women

THE LITTLES

Peterson, John

SCHOLASTIC

GRADES 2–4

FANTASY

The Little family lives in the walls of the home of Mr. and Mrs. George Bigg and their son, Henry. Mr. William T. Little, the father, is tall (for a Little) at six inches; and like all Littles, he looks just like a small person with a tail. In this series, the Little family has adventures involving their size and the secrecy of their existence. The first book, *The Littles*, describes what happens when the Bigg family goes on a three-month vacation and rents its home in the country to a couple from the city. Because the Newcombs are messy, mice come into the home and create a problem for the Littles. Later, they encounter a dangerous cat and must find a way to get rid of it. Lucy's bravery saves her father, brother Tom, and Uncle Pete. Other adventures include Uncle Nick Little in *The Littles and the Lost Children* and Cousin Dinky and Mr. Speck in *The Littles Take a Trip*. The humor and escapades in this book will attract many readers.

1. The Littles ◆ 1967
2. The Littles Take a Trip ◆ 1968
3. The Littles to the Rescue ◆ 1968
4. The Littles Have a Wedding ◆ 1971
5. The Littles Give a Party ◆ 1972
6. Tom Little's Great Halloween Scare ◆ 1975
7. The Littles and the Trash Tinies ◆ 1977
8. The Littles Go Exploring ◆ 1978
9. The Littles and the Big Storm ◆ 1979
10. The Littles and Their Friends ◆ 1981
11. The Littles Go to School ◆ 1983
12. The Littles and the Lost Children ◆ 1991
13. The Littles and the Terrible Tiny Kid ◆ 1993

LIZA, BILL, AND JED

Parish, Peggy

MACMILLAN

GRADES 2–5

ADVENTURE | MYSTERY

This mystery-adventure series features siblings Liza, Bill, and Jed Roberts, who always seem to find a mystery when visiting their grandparents. They are first introduced in *Key to the Treasure*, and the three young sleuths go on treasure hunts and solve mysteries involving ghosts and lost treasure in the next four books. Peggy Parish is also the author of the ever-popular Amelia Bedelia books.

1. Key to the Treasure ◆ 1966
2. Clues in the Woods ◆ 1968
3. Haunted House ◆ 1971
4. Pirate Island Adventure ◆ 1975
5. Hermit Dan ◆ 1977
6. The Ghosts of Cougar Island ◆ 1986

LIZZIE LOGAN

Spinelli, Eileen
SIMON & SCHUSTER
GRADES 2–4
FAMILY LIFE

Heather's first encounter in her new neighborhood is with bold, bossy Lizzie Logan. Lizzie scares Heather with gruesome stories and demands to be her friend. Lizzie and Heather do become friends, and together they battle school bullies, celebrate family events, and cope with growing up. In *Lizzie Logan Gets Married*, Lizzie's mom remarries, making Lizzie's wish for a real father come true. *Lizzie Logan, Second Banana* shows Lizzie's insecurity as she is about to become a big sister. Both Lizzie and Heather are sincere, likable, and funny in these real-life situations.

1. Lizzie Logan Wears Purple Sunglasses ◆ 1995
2. Lizzie Logan Gets Married ◆ 1997
3. Lizzie Logan, Second Banana ◆ 1998

LOGAN FAMILY

Taylor, Mildred D.
DIAL
GRADES 4–7
HISTORICAL | REAL LIFE

Cassie tells the story of the African American Logan family, living in Mississippi during the Great Depression. High taxes and the mortgage on their house have forced her father to take a job away from home on the railroad. Mrs. Logan works as a schoolteacher. Although poor, the Logans are economically self-sufficient, which makes them more fortunate than their neighbors, who are all in debt to the local store. When Mrs. Logan is fired for teaching black history and Mr. Logan loses his job when he is injured by some angry white men, the family lives in fear that they will lose their land. *Roll of Thunder, Hear My Cry* is a Newbery Award winner. *Song of the Trees* is written for younger readers. Members of the Logan family appear as peripheral characters in other books by this author.

1. Song of the Trees ◆ 1975
2. Roll of Thunder, Hear My Cry ◆ 1976
3. Let the Circle Be Unbroken ◆ 1981
4. The Road to Memphis ◆ 1990
5. The Well: David's Story ◆ 1995

THE LONELY DOLL

Wright, Dare
HOUGHTON MIFFLIN

GRADES K–2

FANTASY

From the first Lonely Doll book (published in 1957 and recently reissued) through the many sequels, readers have been enchanted. Illustrated with black-and-white photographs of Edith, a doll, in adventurous settings, the books blend fantasy and reality. Edith is lonely until she makes friends with the teddy bears who join in her outings. They meet horses and a duckling and go on a holiday. These books still have a loyal following of fans.

1. The Lonely Doll ◆ 1957
2. Holiday for Edith and the Bears ◆ 1958
3. The Lonely Doll Learns a Lesson ◆ 1961
4. Edith and Mr. Bear ◆ 1964
5. A Gift from the Lonely Doll ◆ 1966
6. Edith and Little Bear Lend a Hand ◆ 1972
7. Edith and Midnight ◆ 1978
8. Edith and the Duckling ◆ 1981

LONG POND

George, William T., and Lindsay Barrett George
GREENWILLOW

GRADES K–2

REAL LIFE

The main character in this series is really Long Pond, shown throughout the cycle of the seasons. Readers observe a wealth of animal residents and a few appreciative humans who fish and enjoy the landscape. Cutting a tree for Christmas becomes a nature trek for an observant father and son in

Christmas at Long Pond. Fishing at Long Pond is a memorable experience for Grandpa and Katie. The extremely detailed, almost photographic illustrations, coupled with a brief text, draw the reader into this celebration of nature. The first book, *Beaver at Long Pond*, was written by both William T. George and Lindsay Barrett George. The remaining books are written by William T. George. All the books are illustrated by Lindsay Barrett George.

1. Beaver at Long Pond ◆ 1988
2. Box Turtle at Long Pond ◆ 1989
3. Fishing at Long Pond ◆ 1991
4. Christmas at Long Pond ◆ 1992

THE LORD OF THE RINGS

Tolkien, J. R. R.
HOUGHTON MIFFLIN
GRADES 5–8
FANTASY

When Hobbit Bilbo Baggins is visited by Gandalf the wizard, he finds himself tricked into being part of a dangerous quest. Together, they seek to recover a stolen treasure hidden in Lonely Mountain, guarded by Smaug the Dragon. *The Hobbit* is the introduction to Middle Earth and the Lord of the Rings trilogy, in which Bilbo names his cousin, Frodo Baggins, his heir. Frodo embarks on a journey to destroy the Ring of Power, a ring that would enable evil Sauron to destroy all that is good in Middle Earth. It is up to Frodo and his servant, Sam, to carry the Ring to the one place it can be destroyed. Author Tolkien was an eminent philologist and an authority on myths and sagas.

1. The Fellowship of the Ring ◆ 1954
2. The Two Towers ◆ 1954
3. The Return of the King ◆ 1955

THE LOST YEARS OF MERLIN *see* Merlin

LOTTERY LUCK

Delton, Judy
HYPERION
GRADES 4–6
FAMILY LIFE

Daisy Green thinks her family is unusual. Her mother spends a lot of time gardening on the rooftop of their condo building while her father makes copper animals to decorate lawns (the copper alligators are the best sellers). Her brother, Delphie, is named after her mother's prize delphiniums. Money is often a problem until Daisy and her friend Lois find a way to buy some lottery tickets—and the Greens win! One book describes their efforts to cash in the tickets while other books have moments of risk as thieves seem to be after their winnings. Finally, the Greens move to St. Paul and Daisy is sad to be leaving Lois. All ends well when Lois and her family move to Minneapolis. These stories feature friendship and adventure and are accessible to middle grade readers.

1. Winning Ticket! ◆ 1995
2. Prize-Winning Private Eyes ◆ 1995
3. Ten's a Crowd! ◆ 1995
4. Moving Up ◆ 1995
5. Ship Ahoy ◆ 1995
6. Next Stop, The White House ◆ 1995
7. Royal Escapade ◆ 1995
8. Cabin Surprise ◆ 1995

LOUANNE PIG

Carlson, Nancy

CAROLRHODA

GRADES K–2

ANIMAL FANTASY | FAMILY LIFE

There is warmth, love, and fun in the stories about Louanne Pig. She is envious of her friend George's large family until she finds out that she has the talent to make a good master of ceremonies. She also realizes that looks can be deceiving as she gets to know the "witch lady." Carlson creates charming animal characters in both the text and the illustrations.

1. Louanne Pig in the Perfect Family ◆ 1986
2. Louanne Pig in Making the Team ◆ 1986
3. Louanne Pig in Witch Lady ◆ 1986
4. Louanne Pig in the Talent Show ◆ 1986
5. Louanne Pig in the Mysterious Valentine ◆ 1986

LOUDMOUTH GEORGE

Carlson, Nancy

CAROLRHODA

GRADES K–1

ANIMAL FANTASY | HUMOR

George is a rabbit whose outspoken attitudes and pushy nature have earned him the nickname Loudmouth. (Actually, he is referred to as

Loudmouth George in the titles, but in the text he is just George.) Younger readers will get the message in these mildly didactic books as George learns what it feels like to be picked on. When a family of pigs moves into the neighborhood, George must develop more tolerance for those who are different. In another book, George finds out that being a show-off can cause problems. In spite of his faults, George is a likable character who just needs to use more restraint and better judgment so he can get along with others. The situations will ring true to young children.

1. Loudmouth George and the Big Race ◆ 1983
2. Loudmouth George and the Cornet ◆ 1983
3. Loudmouth George and the Fishing Trip ◆ 1983
4. Loudmouth George and the New Neighbors ◆ 1983
5. Loudmouth George and the Sixth-Grade Bully ◆ 1985

LOUIE

Keats, Ezra Jack
GREENWILLOW/FOUR WINDS
GRADES K–1
FAMILY LIFE | REAL LIFE

Louie is a shy, withdrawn boy whose first friend is a puppet. In other books in the series, Louie moves into a new neighborhood, where he creates a shoebox diorama and makes an imaginary flight back to see some friends; Louie longs for a father and finds one in a junkman named Barney; and Louie has an imaginary visit to outer space in a rocket made of junkyard castoffs. Keats's colorful collages depict inner-city life.

1. Louie ◆ 1975
2. The Trip ◆ 1978
3. Louie's Search ◆ 1980

LUCAS COTT *see* Edison-Armstrong School

LUCKY

Duffey, Betsy
SIMON & SCHUSTER
GRADES 2–4
FAMILY LIFE | HUMOR

George has wanted a puppy for such a long time. Now he has Lucky, and he is finding out how hard it is to train and care for a dog. The first book, *A Boy in the Doghouse*, describes George's efforts to housebreak Lucky. Subsequent books focus on Lucky and baseball and Lucky being lost. Chapters alternate from George's point of view (e.g., "Why can't Lucky learn to come to me?") to Lucky's interpretation of events ("What does the boy mean by 'Come?'") This shift in perspective gives readers insight into the puppy and adds to the humor and interest.

1. A Boy in the Doghouse ◆ 1991
2. Lucky in Left Field ◆ 1992
3. Lucky on the Loose ◆ 1993
4. Lucky Christmas ◆ 1994

LUDELL

Wilkinson, Brenda

HARPERCOLLINS

GRADES 5–8

FAMILY LIFE | HISTORICAL

Ludell Wilson is an African American girl growing up in the rural town of Waycross, Georgia, in the mid-1950s. She is raised by her loving, protective, but strict grandmother because her mother is living in New York City. *Ludell* depicts three years in a segregated Southern school, her friends and family, and the people who affect her life. In *Ludell and Willie*, Ludell and her boyfriend are seniors in high school, frustrated by the standards of their small town. In *Ludell's New York Time*, Ludell moves to Harlem to plan her wedding. A strong portrait of growing up in the South in the 1950s and 1960s.

1. Ludell ◆ 1975
2. Ludell and Willie ◆ 1977
3. Ludell's New York Time ◆ 1980

LUNCHROOM

Hodgman, Ann

SPLASH/BERKLEY

GRADES 4–6

HUMOR

Hollis Elementary School may *seem* like any other school, but wait until you visit their new cafeteria. There are neon signs, an ornamental waterfall, vending machines, and a milkshake machine that will make 30 milkshakes at once. There is even a machine that makes 100 pizzas at once, although a programming error makes 1,000 pizzas. The cafeteria serves pizza every day until the freezer is finally empty. There are problems with cookies, french fries, and stew. The events are implausible, the adults are dim-witted, and the kids are lively.

1. Night of a Thousand Pizzas ◆ 1990
2. Frog Punch ◆ 1990
3. The Cookie Caper ◆ 1990
4. The French Fry Aliens ◆ 1990
5. Rubberband Stew ◆ 1990
6. The Flying Popcorn Experiment ◆ 1990
7. Invasion of the Fast Food ◆ 1990
8. Space Food ◆ 1990
9. Day of the Monster Plant ◆ 1991
10. Mutant Garbage ◆ 1991

LYLE

Waber, Bernard

HOUGHTON MIFFLIN

GRADES K–3

ANIMAL FANTASY | FAMILY LIFE

When the Primm family moves into the house on East 88th Street, they discover a performing crocodile, Lyle, in their bathtub. He had been left there by former resident Hector P. Valenti, star of stage and screen. It is not long before Lyle wins the hearts of the family, but Hector is always thinking of ways to lure Lyle away from the Primms. In other adventures, Lyle's mother, Felicity, becomes a permanent resident at the Primm household and a nurse to their new baby.

1. The House on East Eighty Eighth Street ◆ 1962
2. Lyle, Lyle, Crocodile ◆ 1965
3. Lyle and the Birthday Party ◆ 1966
4. Lovable Lyle ◆ 1969
5. Lyle Finds His Mother ◆ 1974
6. Funny, Funny Lyle ◆ 1987
7. Lyle at the Office ◆ 1994
8. Lyle at Christmas ◆ 1998

M AND M

Ross, Pat

VIKING

GRADES 1–3

HUMOR | MYSTERY

Mandy and Mimi are two little girls living in the same apartment building who have active imaginations that get them into adventures. In one book, they sneak into a museum early to see a mummy exhibit; a haunted house provides a way to scare a friend in another story. At Halloween, they see a shadow that appears to be a headless monster, but it turns out to be a new boy in the building carrying his football helmet. "Drops of blood" turn out to be red paint, and at a party they find out that some of their "creepy" neighbors are not so scary after all. Some of their escapades are less frightening, as when they baby-sit for a neighbor and find a way to make her badly behaved twins into perfect angels. In a story about learning to read, they take a list to the grocery store, with funny results. All of the books have short, easy-to-read chapters.

1. Meet M and M ◆ 1980
2. M and M and the Haunted House Game ◆ 1980
3. M and M and the Big Bag ◆ 1981
4. M and M and the Bad News Babies ◆ 1983
5. M and M and the Mummy Mess ◆ 1985
6. M and M and the Santa Secrets ◆ 1985
7. M and M and the Superchild Afternoon ◆ 1987
8. M and M and the Halloween Monster ◆ 1991

MCBROOM

Fleischman, Sid

LITTLE, BROWN; GREENWILLOW

GRADES 3–5

FANTASY | HUMOR

McBroom and his wife live with their 11 children on the prairie, and McBroom tells stories of their life there, exaggerated to the point of being tall tales. In his story of the Big Wind, he tells of fitting out his children with iron shoes to keep them from blowing away. He also tells about mosquitoes that grew so large that they used chicken wire for mosquito netting. But when he entered the World Champion's Liar's Contest, they disqualified him for telling the truth. These are short, easy books, illustrated on every page. Some of the titles are available with new illustrations.

1. McBroom Tells the Truth ◆ 1966
2. McBroom and the Big Wind ◆ 1967
3. McBroom's Ear ◆ 1969
4. McBroom's Ghost ◆ 1971
5. McBroom's Zoo ◆ 1972
6. McBroom the Rainmaker ◆ 1973
7. McBroom Tells a Lie ◆ 1976
8. McBroom and the Beanstalk ◆ 1978
9. McBroom and the Great Race ◆ 1980
10. McBroom's Almanac ◆ 1984
11. McBroom's Wonderful One-Acre Farm ◆ 1992

MACDONALD HALL *see* Bruno and Boots

McDuff

Wells, Rosemary
HYPERION
GRADES K–1
REAL LIFE

McDuff is a white Highland Terrier who escapes from the dog catcher and finds his way to a sympathetic couple, Fred and Lucy, who decide to keep him. His life is filled with the typical adventures of a lucky little dog, including chasing a rabbit and getting lost, coming to grips with a new baby, and learning that he is still loved. Rather more doglike than many anthropomorphic picture book characters, McDuff's problems are closer to those of dogs than of children, even when he encounters Santa Claus.

1. McDuff Moves In ◆ 1997
2. McDuff Comes Home ◆ 1997
3. McDuff and the Baby ◆ 1997
4. McDuff's New Friend ◆ 1998

McGee and Me!

Various authors
TYNDALE HOUSE
GRADES 4–6
FAMILY LIFE | VALUES

Nicholas Martin and his best friend, McGee—an animated character who talks to Nick—get involved in many familiar situations, including wanting to win the big baseball game and being a contestant on a TV game show. Throughout these books (from the Living Bible International), there are positive messages about family, values, and the importance of accepting God in everyday life. Concepts discussed include honesty, obedience, faith, jealousy, trusting God, and experiencing God's love. A McGee and Me video series is also available.

1. The Big Lie (Myers, Bill, and Ken Johnson) ◆ 1989
2. A Star in the Breaking (Myers, Bill, and Ken Johnson) ◆ 1989
3. The Not-So-Great Escape (Myers, Bill, and Ken Johnson) ◆ 1989
4. Skate Expectations (Myers, Bill, and Ken Johnson) ◆ 1989
5. Twister and Shout (Myers, Bill, and Ken Johnson) ◆ 1989
6. Back to the Drawing Board (Teske, Robert T.) ◆ 1990
7. Do the Bright Thing (Teske, Robert T.) ◆ 1990
8. Take Me Out of the Ball Game (Myers, Bill) ◆ 1990
9. 'Twas the Fight Before Christmas (Myers, Bill) ◆ 1990
10. In the Nick of Time (Myers, Bill, and Robert West) ◆ 1993

11. The Blunder Years (Myers, Bill, and Robert West) ◆ 1993
12. Beauty in the Least (Myers, Bill, and Robert West) ◆ 1993

McGurk

Hildick, E. W.
MacMillan
Grades 2–5
Humor | Mystery

Ten-year-old McGurk runs his detective organization with an iron fist, leading a team with different talents and abilities. The narrator, Joey, is good with words, and scientific expertise is provided by "Brains." Willie has a good nose, and Wanda likes high places and danger. In a typical story, an old lady asks the group to baby-sit her nephew. They indignantly tell her that the McGurk organization does not baby-sit. She admits that there is a case she wants them to solve. There seems to be a gigantic frog making noise in her house. Clever investigating leads the group to discover that her lonely nephew has been secretly harboring a pet frog, a species that makes a very loud noise. The humor here comes from the pint-size tyrant's control over his "officers" and their mishaps on the way to solving cases. McGurk's adventures take a fantastic turn in some of the books, which combine time travel and solving mysteries.

1. The Nose Knows ◆ 1973
2. Dolls in Danger (Deadline for McGurk) ◆ 1974
3. The Case of the Condemned Cat ◆ 1975
4. The Case of the Nervous Newsboy ◆ 1976
5. The Great Rabbit Robbery ◆ 1976
6. The Case of the Invisible Dog ◆ 1977
7. The Case of the Secret Scribbler ◆ 1978
8. The Case of the Phantom Frog ◆ 1979
9. The Case of the Treetop Treasure ◆ 1980
10. The Case of the Snowbound Spy ◆ 1980
11. The Case of the Bashful Bank Robber ◆ 1981
12. The Case of the Four Flying Fingers ◆ 1981
13. McGurk Gets Good and Mad ◆ 1982
14. The Case of the Felon's Fiddle ◆ 1982
15. The Case of the Slingshot Sniper ◆ 1983
16. The Case of the Vanishing Ventriloquist ◆ 1985
17. The Case of the Muttering Mummy ◆ 1986
18. The Case of the Wandering Weathervanes ◆ 1988
19. The Case of the Purloined Parrot ◆ 1990
20. The Case of the Dragon in Distress ◆ 1991
21. The Case of the Weeping Witch ◆ 1992
22. The Case of the Desperate Drummer ◆ 1993

23. The Case of the Fantastic Footprints ◆ 1994
24. The Case of the Absent Author ◆ 1995
25. The Case of the Wiggling Wig ◆ 1996

MADELINE

Bemelmans, Ludwig

VIKING

GRADES K–2

HUMOR

The classic picture book and its sequels tell of brave young Madeline, who lives in a boarding school in Paris with 11 other little girls and their teacher, Miss Clavel. Madeline is a brave little girl, and says "'pooh' to the tiger in the zoo." When she has her appendix out, she gets such nice presents and has such a great scar that all the other girls want to have theirs out too. Madeline, Miss Clavel, and the girls continue their adventures in many sequels. One tells of the Spanish ambassador's son, who is a "bad hat." In another, Madeline travels to London and goes on an adventure with a horse. The recent film version has sparked interest. *Madeline's Christmas* is the reprint of a *McCall's* magazine feature.

1. Madeline ◆ 1939
2. Madeline's Rescue ◆ 1953
3. Madeline and the Bad Hat ◆ 1956
4. Madeline and the Gypsies ◆ 1959
5. Madeline in London ◆ 1961
6. Madeline's Christmas ◆ 1985

MAGGIE MARMELSTEIN

Sharmat, Marjorie

HARPERCOLLINS

GRADES 4–6

HUMOR | REAL LIFE

Thad and Maggie are sometimes friends, sometimes rivals, sometimes enemies in typical and humorous upper-grade-school situations. In one book, Thad decides to run for class president. Maggie volunteers to be his campaign manager, but Thad refuses, infuriating Maggie to the point that she decides to run for president herself. She recruits Noah, the smartest boy in the class, to be her campaign manager, and it soon becomes apparent that he is much better qualified to be president than either Thad or Maggie. In another story, Maggie's mother talks Thad into helping her cook, and

Maggie catches him in an apron. Each story involves the complicated relationships among Thad, Maggie, Noah, and Maggie's shy friend Ellen.

1. Getting Something on Maggie Marmelstein ◆ 1971
2. Maggie Marmelstein for President ◆ 1975
3. Mysteriously Yours, Maggie Marmelstein ◆ 1982

MAGIC ATTIC CLUB

Various authors

MAGIC ATTIC PRESS (MILLBROOK)

GRADES 2–4

ADVENTURE | FANTASY

The Magic Attic Club begins when Heather Hardin, Alison McCann, Keisha Vance, and Megan Ryder find a golden key that unlocks a neighbor's attic. There they find a trunk filled with beautiful clothes and a magic mirror that transports them to unusual places in the past. Some of the adventures feature the group, including Rose Hopkins, who joins them later. Others feature individual girls. The girls represent diverse backgrounds (Keisha is African American; Rose has ancestors who were Cheyenne). Their adventures are exotic, often including special interests like ballet, dressage, gymnastics, cheerleading, and magic.

1. The Secret of the Attic (Sinykin, Sheri Cooper) ◆ 1995
2. Alison Goes for the Gold (Connor, Catherine) ◆ 1995
3. Alison on the Trail (Connor, Catherine) ◆ 1995
4. Cowgirl Megan (Magraw, Trisha) ◆ 1995
5. Heather at the Barre (Sinykin, Sheri Cooper) ◆ 1995
6. Heather, Belle of the Ball (Sinykin, Sheri Cooper) ◆ 1995
7. Keisha the Fairy Snow Queen (Reed, Teresa) ◆ 1995
8. Princess Megan (Magraw, Trisha) ◆ 1995
9. Three Cheers for Keisha (Reed, Teresa) ◆ 1995
10. Alison Saves the Wedding (Connor, Catherine) ◆ 1996
11. Alison Walks the Wire (Sinykin, Sheri Cooper) ◆ 1996
12. Downhill Megan (Magraw, Trisha) ◆ 1996
13. Heather Takes the Reins (Sinykin, Sheri Cooper) ◆ 1996
14. Keisha Leads the Way (Reed, Teresa) ◆ 1996
15. Keisha to the Rescue (Reed, Teresa) ◆ 1996
16. Megan's Masquerade (Magraw, Trisha) ◆ 1996
17. Viva Heather! (Sinykin, Sheri Cooper) ◆ 1996
18. Alison of Arabia (Alexander, Nina) ◆ 1997
19. Cheyenne Rose (Williams, Laura E.) ◆ 1997
20. Heather Goes to Hollywood (Sinykin, Sheri Cooper) ◆ 1997
21. Keisha's Maze Mystery (Benson, Lauren) ◆ 1997
22. Megan's Balancing Act (Korman, Susan) ◆ 1997

23. Rose Faces the Music (Alexander, Nina, and Laura E. Williams) ◆ 1997
24. Rose's Magic Touch (Alexander, Nina) ◆ 1997
25. Trapped Beyond the Magic Attic (Sinykin, Sheri Cooper) ◆ 1997
26. Alison Rides the Rapids (Alexander, Nina) ◆ 1998
27. Ghost of Camp Whispering Pines (Korman, Susan) ◆ 1998
28. Heather and the Pink Poodles (Engle, Marion) ◆ 1998
29. Island Rose (Williams, Laura E.) ◆ 1998
30. Keisha Discovers Harlem (Lewis, Zoe) ◆ 1998
31. Megan in Ancient Greece (Korman, Susan) ◆ 1998

MAGIC MOSCOW

Pinkwater, Daniel
FOUR WINDS
GRADES 3–4
FANTASY | HUMOR

An ice cream parlor in Hoboken, the Magic Moscow, is where this zany adventure series begins. The first title tells the adventure of Edward, grandson of a famous TV sled dog, and his owner, Steve Nicholson. Steve returns with his assistant Norman Bleistift who have an out-of-earth experience in *Slaves of Spiegel*. This is an easy-to-read series written with humor and creative dialogue. Each book has a different focus—dog story, ghost story, space travel. This series connects and is a companion to Pinkwater's Fat Men from Space books.

1. Magic Moscow ◆ 1980
2. Attila the Pun ◆ 1981
3. Slaves of Spiegel ◆ 1982

MAGIC MYSTERY

Levy, Elizabeth
SIMON & SCHUSTER
GRADES 1–3
MYSTERY

Kate wants to solve mysteries (and make money at the school Thanksgiving Fair), so she sits in a booth with a sign that reads "Mysteries Solved: No Job Too Small, Too Big, or Too Weird." Her friends think she is weird! She meets up with Max, a classmate who practices magic, and helps him find his missing bunny. They find that they like working together and go on to solve more simple mysteries. Max's magic becomes a focal point of every book, and the last chapter describes some of the magic tricks in the story. Readers will find it fun to read about these lively characters and then will like learning how to do tricks with cards, coins, misdirection, and ventriloquism.

1. The Case of the Gobbling Squash ◆ 1988
2. The Case of the Mind-Reading Mommies ◆ 1989
3. The Case of the Tattletale Heart ◆ 1990
4. The Case of the Dummy with Cold Eyes ◆ 1991

MAGIC SCHOOL BUS

Cole, Joanna

SCHOLASTIC

GRADES 1–4

ADVENTURE | FANTASY | HUMOR

Although these books are packed with information, the basic premise of the series is fantastic. Ms. Frizzle uses a magic school bus to take her class on incredible field trips. Arnold, Ralphie, Dorothy Ann, Phoebe, Carlos, Florrie, Shirley, Tim, and the other members of the class learn science on these wild rides. They go inside the body, out into space, into a beehive, and back to the time of dinosaurs. The journey is always educational, with information presented in the text and the illustrations. For example, student reports on lined notebook paper cover topics like "Why Do Bees Sting?" and "How to Feed Baby Bees." There are many jokes and humorous remarks that make this series a good combination of facts and fun. Many of the books are tie-ins to the PBS television series. There are activity books and Explorations books that guide students and teachers through science experiments.

1. The Magic School Bus at the Waterworks ◆ 1986
2. The Magic School Bus Inside the Earth ◆ 1987
3. The Magic School Bus Inside the Human Body ◆ 1989
4. The Magic School Bus Lost in the Solar System ◆ 1990
5. The Magic School Bus on the Ocean Floor ◆ 1992
6. The Magic School Bus in the Time of the Dinosaurs ◆ 1994
7. The Magic School Bus Inside a Hurricane ◆ 1995
8. The Magic School Bus Inside a Beehive ◆ 1996
9. The Magic School Bus and the Electric Field Trip ◆ 1997

MAGIC SCHOOL BUS TV TIE-IN BOOKS

1. The Magic School Bus Gets Baked in a Cake: A Book About Kitchen Chemistry ◆ 1995
2. The Magic School Bus Hops Home: A Book About Animal Habitats ◆ 1995
3. The Magic School Bus in the Haunted Museum: A Book About Sound ◆ 1995
4. The Magic School Bus Inside Ralphie: A Book About Germs ◆ 1995
5. The Magic School Bus Meets the Rot Squad: A Book About Decomposition ◆ 1995
6. The Magic School Bus Plants Seeds: A Book About How Living Things Grow ◆ 1995
7. The Magic School Bus All Dried Up: A Book About Deserts ◆ 1996
8. The Magic School Bus Blows Its Top: A Book About Volcanoes ◆ 1996
9. The Magic School Bus Butterfly and the Bog Beast: A Book About Butterfly Camouflage ◆ 1996
10. The Magic School Bus Gets Ants in Its Pants: A Book About Ants ◆ 1996
11. The Magic School Bus Gets Eaten: A Book About Food Chains ◆ 1996
12. The Magic School Bus Going Batty: A Book About Bats ◆ 1996
13. The Magic School Bus Out of This World: A Book About Space Rocks ◆ 1996
14. The Magic School Bus Wet All Over: A Book About the Water Cycle ◆ 1996
15. The Magic School Bus Gets Planted: A Book About Photosynthesis ◆ 1997
16. The Magic School Bus Goes Upstream: A Book About Salmon Migration ◆ 1997
17. The Magic School Bus Makes a Rainbow: A Book About Color ◆ 1997
18. The Magic School Bus Plays Ball: A Book About Forces ◆ 1997
19. The Magic School Bus Shows and Tells: A Book About Archaeology ◆ 1997
20. The Magic School Bus Takes Flight: A Book About Flight ◆ 1997
21. The Magic School Bus Ups and Downs: A Book About Floating and Sinking ◆ 1997
22. The Magic School Bus Gets Cold Feet: A Book About Warm- and Cold-Blooded Animals ◆ 1998
23. The Magic School Bus in a Pickle: A Book About Microbes ◆ 1998
24. The Magic School Bus in the Rainforest: A Book About Rainforest Ecology ◆ 1998
25. The Magic School Bus Spins a Web: A Book About Spiders ◆ 1998
26. The Magic School Bus in the Arctic: A Book About Heat ◆ 1998
27. The Magic School Bus Takes a Dive: A Book About Coral Reefs ◆ 1998

MAGIC SHOP

Coville, Bruce

HARCOURT

GRADES 3–6

FANTASY

Each of these stories centers on a new character in an entirely different setting. All of the central characters make a purchase at a magic shop that travels from town to town, owned by the mysterious Mr. Elives. Their encounters lead to adventures with talking toads, baby dragons, and ancient skulls. The stories generally teach a lesson, such as the importance of inner beauty over outer beauty.

1. Jeremy Thatcher, Dragon Hatcher ◆ 1991
2. Jennifer Murdley's Toad ◆ 1992
3. The Skull of Truth ◆ 1997

MAGIC TREE HOUSE

Ji Osb

Osborne, Mary Pope

RANDOM HOUSE

GRADES 2–4

FANTASY | MYSTERY

Jack and Annie discover a mysterious tree house in the woods near their home in Frog Creek, Pennsylvania. The tree house is filled with books that can trigger trips through time. In their first adventure, the two children accidentally travel to the time of the dinosaurs and must use their wits to return home. Later, they find out that the tree house belongs to Morgan le Fay, a librarian-magician from the time of King Arthur. She helps Jack and Annie become Master Librarians so that they can help her save stories from ancient libraries. The adventures take Jack and Annie to ancient Egypt, the Amazon River, the old West, the moon, a volcano, and ancient China. The fast-paced action and short sentences make this a good choice for reluctant readers and for students looking for beginning chapter books.

1. Dinosaurs Before Dark ◆ 1992
2. The Knight at Dawn ◆ 1993
3. Mummies in the Morning ◆ 1993
4. Pirates Past Noon ◆ 1994
5. Night of the Ninjas ◆ 1995
6. Afternoon on the Amazon ◆ 1995
7. Sunset of the Sabertooth ◆ 1996
8. Midnight on the Moon ◆ 1996

9. Dolphins at Daybreak ◆ 1997
10. Ghost Town at Sundown ◆ 1997
11. Lions at Lunchtime ◆ 1997
12. Polar Bears Past Bedtime ◆ 1997
13. Vacation Under the Volcano ◆ 1998
14. Day of the Dragon King ◆ 1998
15. Viking Ships at Sunrise ◆ 1998
16. Hour of the Olympics ◆ 1998
17. Tonight on the Titanic ◆ 1999

MAGICAL MYSTERY

Stanton, Mary
BERKLEY
GRADES 4–6
FANTASY | MYSTERY

In this series, Natalie Ross, 13, deals with the magical powers of her six-year-old brother Denny. One adventure features an unusual, bad-tempered aunt, whom Denny turns into a griffin. Natalie must find a way to undo the spell. Another book follows Natalie's interest in equestrian events; she even lets Denny use his magic to help her, which sets off a series of problems. In *Next Door Witch*, Natalie encourages Denny to use his powers to help undo the spells of Zeuxippe Smith. The magical elements will appeal to many readers.

1. My Aunt, the Monster ◆ 1997
2. White Magic ◆ 1997
3. Next Door Witch ◆ 1997

MAGICIAN TRILOGY

McGowen, Tom
PENGUIN
GRADES 4–7
SCIENCE FICTION

Far in the future, civilization has been destroyed by war, and the people look back at our era as the Age of Magic and call all our inventions "spells." People who seek after wisdom are called Sages, and they attempt to make sense of the ruins and find out what ancient objects were used for. The head of these Sages, Armindor, takes as an apprentice a boy named Tigg, who had been a pickpocket. Together, they travel to the Wild Lands and find a tape recorder with a tape in it that they believe will help them find the key to the ancient language. First, they must fight a terrible threat from intelligent ratlike creatures bent on taking over the human race. Together with Jilla, an orphan girl, and Reepah, a "grubber," they travel to the city of Ingarron and lead a successful attack.

1. The Magician's Apprentice ◆ 1987
2. The Magician's Company ◆ 1988
3. The Magician's Challenge ◆ 1989

MAISY THE MOUSE

Cousins, Lucy
CANDLEWICK
GRADES K–2
ANIMAL FANTASY

This is a series of lift-the-flap and pull-the-tab books. Children will enjoy playing with Maisy as they help her write a story, dance like a ballerina, paint pictures, and more. There are related board books.

1. Maisy Goes Swimming ◆ 1990
2. Maisy Goes to Bed ◆ 1990
3. Maisy Goes to School ◆ 1992
4. Maisy Goes to the Playground ◆ 1992
5. Maisy's ABC ◆ 1995
6. Maisy at the Farm ◆ 1998
7. Happy Birthday, Maisy ◆ 1998

MAIZON

Woodson, Jacqueline
DELACORTE
GRADES 6–8
FAMILY LIFE | REAL LIFE

Margaret and Maizon are best friends, but they are separated when Maizon leaves to attend a boarding school. At Blue Hill, Maizon adjusts to being one of only five African American students. She misses her grandmother and her friends. Returning home, she rebuilds her friendship with Margaret and makes some new friends. Maizon even meets her father, who left when she was a baby. This series follows a character from the end of her childhood into independence and young adulthood.

1. Last Summer with Maizon ◆ 1990
2. Maizon at Blue Hill ◆ 1992
3. Between Madison and Palmetto ◆ 1993

MALLOY GIRLS *see* Hatford Boys

MANDIE

Leppard, Lois Gladys
BETHANY HOUSE
GRADES 4–6
ADVENTURE I HISTORICAL I MYSTERY

Mandie Shaw and her friends get involved in exciting adventures around the turn of the 20th century. In one book, they find a treasure map that leads them to discover a hidden treasure and restore it to its rightful owner. In another book, Grandmother Taft takes Mandie to Washington, D.C., for the inauguration of President McKinley. Mandie's friends Sallie, Celia, and Joe often get entangled in the mysteries, and readers will travel around the world following the intrepid young teens. Companion books include *Mandie Diary*, *Mandie Datebook*, *Mandie and Joe's Christmas Surprise*, and *Mandie's Cookbook*.

1. Mandie and the Secret Tunnel ◆ 1983
2. Mandie and the Cherokee Legend ◆ 1983
3. Mandie and the Ghost Bandits ◆ 1984
4. Mandie and the Forbidden Attic ◆ 1985
5. Mandie and the Trunk's Secret ◆ 1985
6. Mandie and the Medicine Man ◆ 1986
7. Mandie and the Charleston Phantom ◆ 1986
8. Mandie and the Abandoned Mine ◆ 1987
9. Mandie and the Hidden Treasure ◆ 1987
10. Mandie and the Mysterious Bells ◆ 1988
11. Mandie and the Holiday Surprise ◆ 1988
12. Mandie and the Washington Nightmare ◆ 1989
13. Mandie and the Midnight Journey ◆ 1989
14. Mandie and the Shipboard Mystery ◆ 1990
15. Mandie and the Foreign Spies ◆ 1990
16. Mandie and the Silent Catacombs ◆ 1990
17. Mandie and the Singing Chalet ◆ 1991
18. Mandie and the Jumping Juniper ◆ 1991
19. Mandie and the Mysterious Fisherman ◆ 1992
20. Mandie and the Windmill's Message ◆ 1992
21. Mandie and the Fiery Rescue ◆ 1993
22. Mandie and the Angel's Secret ◆ 1993
23. Mandie and the Dangerous Imposter ◆ 1994
24. Mandie and the Invisible Troublemaker ◆ 1994
25. Mandie and Her Missing Kin ◆ 1995
26. Mandie and the Schoolhouse Secret ◆ 1996
27. Mandie and the Courtroom Battle ◆ 1996

28. Mandie and Jonathan's Predicament ◆ 1997
29. Mandie and the Unwanted Gift ◆ 1997

MARIE *see* Girlhood Journeys: Marie

MARTHA

Meddaugh, Susan

HOUGHTON MIFFLIN

GRADES K–2

ANIMAL FANTASY | HUMOR

Martha the dog can speak! After her family feeds her alphabet soup, the letters go to Martha's brain and she talks. Now she can tell her family when she wants to go out or come in, eat, or watch television. In fact, she talks so much that her family can't stand it. When Martha calls the police to report a robbery at their home, her family realizes that having a talking dog can be very helpful. Other books feature Martha talking on the telephone and the soup company changing the recipe for alphabet soup. This is a humorous, imaginative series with delightful illustrations that will attract young readers.

1. Martha Speaks ◆ 1992
2. Martha Calling ◆ 1994
3. Martha Blah Blah ◆ 1996
4. Martha Walks the Dog ◆ 1998

MARVIN REDPOST

Sachar, Louis

RANDOM HOUSE

GRADES 1–3

FAMILY LIFE | HUMOR

Marvin Redpost's active imagination often gets this nine-year-old boy into difficult situations. In the first book, Marvin is convinced that he is really descended from royalty because he is the only member of his family with red hair and blue eyes. His friends believe him, but Mr. and Mrs. Redpost react differently to this news. Marvin's adventures with his best friends, Stuart and Nick, involve growing up and assuming responsibility. This easy chapter series offers readers lots of dialogue as well as appealing humor.

1. Marvin Redpost: Kidnapped at Birth? ◆ 1992
2. Marvin Redpost: Is He a Girl? ◆ 1993

3. Marvin Redpost: Why Pick on Me? ◆ 1993
4. Marvin Redpost: Alone in His Teacher's House ◆ 1994

MARVIN THE MAGNIFICENT

Van Leeuwen, Jean
DIAL
GRADES 3–5
ANIMAL FANTASY

Merciless Marvin and his two fearless gang members, Raymond and Fats, are mice who live in a luxury dollhouse in Macy's toy department in New York City. In one adventure, Henry Simpson, a known mouse torturer, captures Fats, and Marvin and Raymond must rescue him. In another adventure, the mice are accidentally packaged and sent to a ten-year-old boy at a Vermont camp. This humorous, lively series is similar to Margery Sharp's Rescuers series.

1. The Great Cheese Conspiracy ◆ 1969
2. The Great Christmas Kidnapping Caper ◆ 1975
3. The Great Rescue Operation ◆ 1982
4. The Great Summer Camp Catastrophe ◆ 1992

MARY-KATE AND ASHLEY *see* The Adventures of Mary-Kate and Ashley

MARY MARONY

Kline, Suzy
PUTNAM
GRADES 2–4
REAL LIFE

Mary Marony is in the second grade. She likes her teacher, Mrs. Bird, and she likes her friend Elizabeth Conway. She does not like the way Marvin Higgins teases her. Mary stutters, often on the letter "m," but also with other letters and even more so when she is nervous. Her parents and her teacher are understanding and helpful, but there are so many times when a student is called upon to speak. For example, Mary's favorite author is coming to school, and she is chosen to speak in front of the school. Another time, Mary's teacher organizes a surprise for her students by hiding something in the wrappers of five chocolate bars. Marvin tries to spoil the fun for Mary, but she ends up winning a prize and feeling good about herself.

1. Mary Marony and the Snake ◆ 1992
2. Mary Marony, Mummy Girl ◆ 1994
3. Mary Marony and the Chocolate Surprise ◆ 1995
4. Mary Marony Hides Out ◆ 1996

MARY POPPINS

Travers, P. L.

HARCOURT

GRADES 4–7

FANTASY

A middle-class British family is having trouble finding a nanny for their difficult children, Jane and Michael. With a combination of magic, sternness, and real love for the children, Mary Poppins brings order to the household and delight into the lives of Jane and Michael. She leaves when the wind changes, but she returns twice, and other books in the series are to be imagined as happening during the times when she was there. In a typical story from the books, a starling speaks to the newborn twins and asks if they remember everything from before they were born. They assure him that they do, and he moans that they will forget, just as all before them have—all, that is, except Mary Poppins.

1. Mary Poppins ◆ 1934
2. Mary Poppins Comes Back ◆ 1935
3. Mary Poppins Opens the Door ◆ 1943
4. Mary Poppins in the Park ◆ 1945
5. Mary Poppins from A to Z ◆ 1963
6. Mary Poppins in the Kitchen ◆ 1975
7. Mary Poppins in Cherry Tree Lane ◆ 1982
8. Mary Poppins and the House Next Door ◆ 1989

MARY ROSE

Clifford, Eth

HOUGHTON MIFFLIN

GRADES 3–5

HUMOR | REAL LIFE

Mary Rose and Jo-Beth are sisters as different as night and day. Mary Rose, the older by three years, is practical, responsible, and dependable. Jo-Beth is a daydreamer who has a hard time with reality. Through a series of mishaps, they are stranded during a blizzard in an old house that has been turned into a library. They find an exhibit from the 1800s and dress up in old-fashioned clothes to hide from burglars. They find the librarian, who has tripped and fallen, and think of a way to help her save the old house. When their cousin Jeff runs away to an island, they follow him and manage to stop a pair of robbers before they can get away with stolen money. The intermediate reading level—with lots of humor, mystery, and excitement—will appeal to real-life and adventure fans.

1. Help, I'm a Prisoner in the Library! ◆ 1979
2. The Dastardly Murder of Dirty Pete ◆ 1981
3. Just Tell Me When We're Dead ◆ 1983
4. Scared Silly ◆ 1988
5. Never Hit a Ghost with a Baseball Bat ◆ 1993

MATCH WITS WITH SHERLOCK HOLMES

Shaw, Murray, adapter

CAROLRHODA

GRADES 4–8

MYSTERY

These adaptations of stories by Sir Arthur Conan Doyle explain the clues and allow readers to follow the logic of the stories and the solutions. A map of London shows the locations of the crimes. This format makes the stories of Sherlock Holmes accessible to a younger audience.

1. Volume 1: The Adventure of Black Peter; The Gloria Scott ◆ 1990
2. Volume 2: The Adventure of the Cardboard Box; A Scandal in Bohemia ◆ 1990
3. Volume 3: The Adventure of the Six Napoleons; The Blue Carbuncle ◆ 1990
4. Volume 4: The Adventure of the Copper Beeches; The Redheaded League ◆ 1990
5. Volume 5: The Adventure of the Speckled Band; The Sussex Vampire ◆ 1991
6. Volume 6: The Adventure of the Abbey Grange; The Boscombe Valley Mystery ◆ 1991
7. Volume 7: The Adventure of the Dancing Men; The Three Garridebs ◆ 1993
8. Volume 8: The Hound of the Baskervilles ◆ 1993

MATTHEW MARTIN

Danziger, Paula
DELACORTE
GRADES 4–5
FAMILY LIFE | HUMOR

Matthew Martin is a sixth-grader who always seems to be in trouble both at home and at school. He is saddled with an older sister, Amanda, who can make his life miserable or rescue him from disaster. With a loyal group of friends, Matthew's escapades range from mummifying one of his friends for an Egyptian project to earning money for a computer program. Matthew and his friends show some signs of maturity in *Not for a Billion Gazillion Dollars*. Written in a breezy style with puns and witty dialogue, this will appeal to readers looking for humor and may be a good choice for boys who are reluctant readers.

1. Everyone Else's Parents Said Yes ◆ 1989
2. Make Like a Tree and Leave ◆ 1990
3. Earth to Matthew ◆ 1991
4. Not for a Billion Gazillion Dollars ◆ 1992

MAX AND RUBY

Wells, Rosemary
DIAL
GRADES K–2
ANIMAL FANTASY | HUMOR

Ruby, the older of two little rabbits, thinks she knows everything, and she is eager to instruct her little brother, Max, in the ways of the world. Max is just as sure that she is wrong, and he is usually proved right in this picture book series. In a typical book, Ruby tells Max that whoever finds the most eggs on Easter morning gets the chocolate chicken. Max can't find any eggs, but he does find mud, acorns, ants, and a spoon and makes ant and acorn pancakes. Then he steals and eats the chocolate chicken, much to Ruby's dismay. But all is not lost—the Easter Bunny leaves another one. When their grandmother's birthday comes around, Max makes an earthworm cake for her. In another book, they learn about money by buying presents for their grandmother. There are many Max board books for toddlers.

1. Max's Christmas ◆ 1986
2. Max's Chocolate Chicken ◆ 1989
3. Max's Dragon Shirt ◆ 1991
4. Max and Ruby's First Greek Myth ◆ 1993
5. Max and Ruby's Midas ◆ 1995
6. Bunny Cakes ◆ 1997
7. Bunny Money ◆ 1997

MAX MALONE

Herman, Charlotte

HENRY HOLT

GRADES 2–5

HUMOR | REAL LIFE

Max Malone lives with his mother, father, and older sister Rosalie. His best friend, Gordy, lives close by; and the youngest kid in the neighborhood, Austin Healy, lives down the street. When we meet Max, he is annoyed at cereal companies because the things he sends for turn out to be junk. At the same time, he is planning to trade baseball cards with Austin and take advantage of his ignorance. By the end of the book, Max makes the connection and instead of taking advantage of Austin, helps him make a wise purchase at a garage sale. In a subsequent book, Max decides to make a million dollars, but while he and Gordy fumble around, Austin actually starts some businesses that make money. Austin and Max continue their relationship when Max fails to get a part in a commercial and decides instead to become Austin's manager.

1. Max Malone and the Great Cereal Rip-Off ◆ 1990
2. Max Malone Makes a Million ◆ 1991
3. Max Malone, Superstar ◆ 1992
4. Max Malone the Magnificent ◆ 1993

MAX THE DOG

Kalman, Maira
VIKING
GRADES K–2
ANIMAL FANTASY

Max the dog is a poet. While he wants to become famous as a poet, he also wants to achieve his success in Paris. With help from his owners and a few friends, Max actually heads for France and this wacky fantasy series begins. Written and illustrated with a rhythm that bounces off the pages, these books will have a great appeal for beginning readers.

1. Max Makes a Million ◆ 1990
2. Ooh La La: Max in Love ◆ 1991
3. Max in Hollywood, Baby ◆ 1992
4. Swami on Rye: Max in India ◆ 1995

MED CENTER

Hoh, Diane
SCHOLASTIC
GRADES 6–8
REAL LIFE

Abby and Susannah are best friends who love their work as volunteers at the large Medical Center in Grant, Massachusetts. The two girls come from very different backgrounds. Susannah is the descendent of the town's founders and lives in the most lavish house in town. Abby comes from a more middle-class family. Each book deals with a disaster that strikes the small town and the reactions of the girls, their families, and friends.

1. Virus ◆ 1996
2. Flood ◆ 1996
3. Fire ◆ 1996
4. Blast ◆ 1996
5. Blizzard ◆ 1997
6. Poison ◆ 1997

MEG MACKINTOSH: A SOLVE-IT-YOURSELF MYSTERY

Landon, Lucinda
SECRET PASSAGE PRESS
GRADES 1–3
MYSTERY

This series encourages the reader to work along with Meg Mackintosh to solve the mysteries that she has uncovered. In one book, Meg finds her grandfather's autographed baseball, which has been missing for more than 50 years. In another book, Meg and her friends visit a medieval castle, and Meg identifies the thief of a jeweled chalice. Many of the clues are linked to the illustrations, making this a fun book for readers. For example, in *Meg Mackintosh and the Mystery at the Medieval Castle*, studying the floor plan of the castle leads to solving the theft. The participation element as well as the brief chapters, simple sentences, and interrelationship between the text and illustrations make this a fine choice for reluctant readers and mystery fans.

1. Meg Mackintosh and the Case of the Missing Babe Ruth Baseball ◆ 1986
2. Meg Mackintosh and the Case of the Curious Whale Watch ◆ 1987
3. Meg Mackintosh and the Mystery at the Medieval Castle ◆ 1989
4. Meg Mackintosh and the Mystery at Camp Creepy ◆ 1990
5. Meg Mackintosh and the Mystery in the Locked Library ◆ 1993
6. Meg Mackintosh and the Mystery at the Soccer Match ◆ 1997

MEG MURRY *see* Time Fantasy Series

MELENDY FAMILY

Enright, Elizabeth
VIKING
GRADES 4–7
FAMILY LIFE | REAL LIFE

The Melendys are living in New York City just before the Second World War when they are introduced to the reader. Their mother is dead and their father is often away, so the children are looked after by Cuffy, their nurse-housekeeper-cook. They decide to pool their Saturday allowances and take turns having one terrific day out. In the next book, their father decides to move them all to the country and finds a remarkable house called the Four-Story Mistake. Here the children continue their adventures and pursue their various interests. Mona wants to be an actress, and after the children put on an informal show, a guest offers her a spot on a radio show. Rush is talented in music, and Oliver wants to study insects. Randy loves dancing and art, and all the children enjoy the outdoors. In *Then There Were Five*, the family adopts an orphan boy they have befriended.

1. The Saturdays ◆ 1941
2. The Four-Story Mistake ◆ 1942
3. Then There Were Five ◆ 1944
4. Spiderweb for Two ◆ 1951

MENNYMS

Waugh, Sylvia

GREENWILLOW

GRADES 5–8

FAMILY LIFE | FANTASY

This is a fantasy quintet set in England that older readers will enjoy. The Mennyms are a family of rag dolls that are able to quietly pass for human—that is to say, until various adventures happen to them. First, there is the Australian owner of the house who comes to pay a visit. Then they discover that they are in the care of an antiques dealer, who, it seems, will shortly discover their secret. Readers will want to read all five books in the series.

1. The Mennyms ◆ 1994
2. Mennyms in the Wilderness ◆ 1995
3. Mennyms Under Siege ◆ 1996
4. Mennyms Alone ◆ 1996
5. Mennyms Alive ◆ 1997

MERCER MAYER'S CRITTERS OF THE NIGHT

Farber, Erica, and J. R. Sansevere

RANDOM HOUSE

GRADES K–4

FANTASY | HUMOR

These books feature a variety of creepy characters in not very scary adventures. There are monsters, dragons, mummies, walking dead, vampires, werewolves, and zombies. Mercer Mayer's illustrations are colorful and add humor to the series, making it a good choice for younger audiences.

1. If You Dream a Dragon ◆ 1996
2. Kiss of the Mermaid ◆ 1996
3. No Howling in the House ◆ 1996

4. Pirate Soup ◆ 1996
5. Purple Pickle Juice ◆ 1996
6. The Goblin's Birthday Party ◆ 1996
7. The Headless Gargoyle ◆ 1996
8. The Vampire Brides ◆ 1996
9. Werewolves for Lunch ◆ 1996
10. Zombies Don't Do Windows ◆ 1996
11. To Catch a Little Fish ◆ 1996
12. Night of the Walking Dead, Part 1 ◆ 1997
13. Night of the Walking Dead, Part 2 ◆ 1997
14. Chomp Chomp ◆ 1998
15. Ooey Gooey ◆ 1998
16. Roast and Toast ◆ 1998
17. Zoom on My Broom ◆ 1998

MERLIN

Barron, T. A.

PUTNAM

GRADES 6–8

FANTASY

Using the well-known Arthurian legends about Merlin as a base, Barron speculates about the unknown details of the wizard's childhood. From when he is washed onto the shores of ancient Wales and raised by Branwen, to his journey to the isle of Fincayra and his challenge to solve the riddle of the Dance of the Giants, these books weave adventure and fantasy. Merlin encounters and battles mythic creatures— Balor the ogre and a sleeping dragon; he also grapples with his own evil, greed, and desires. This fantasy will connect with readers who have read Jane Yolen's Young Merlin books and who enjoy Arthurian legends.

1. The Lost Years of Merlin ◆ 1996
2. The Seven Songs of Merlin ◆ 1997
3. The Fires of Merlin ◆ 1998

MESSY BESSEY

McKissack, Patricia, and Fredrick McKissack

CHILDREN'S PRESS

GRADES K–1

HUMOR | REAL LIFE

Messy Bessey introduces young readers to Bessey, a girl with a very messy room, which she cleans by pushing everything into the closet. Of course, when she opens the closet, everything falls out, so she decides to give away the things she does not need. In a later book, Bessey cares for her garden. These books have a rhyming, predictable text that can be helpful to beginning readers.

1. Messy Bessey ◆ 1987
2. Messy Bessey's Closet ◆ 1989
3. Messy Bessey's Garden ◆ 1991
4. Messy Bessey's School Desk ◆ 1998

MICHELLE *see* Full House: Michelle

MIKE AND HARRY

Christopher, Matt

LITTLE, BROWN

GRADES 1–3

ANIMAL FANTASY I HUMOR

Harry is an Airedale that looks like any other dog. He is not! Harry can communicate with Mike telepathically. Together, they participate in sports activities, sometimes using their skill in unusual ways. In *The Dog That Stole Football Plays*, the two decide that they will not use Harry's ability to learn the other team's plays. Mike's team may win or lose, but they won't cheat. In a recent book, *The Dog That Called the Pitch*, Harry helps out the umpire after his glasses are broken. This has been a popular series since the first book in 1980. It is easy to read and lots of fun—a good choice for reluctant readers.

1. The Dog That Stole Football Plays ◆ 1980
2. The Dog That Called the Signals ◆ 1982
3. The Dog That Pitched a No-Hitter ◆ 1988
4. The Dog That Stole Home ◆ 1993
5. The Dog That Called the Pitch ◆ 1998

MIND OVER MATTER

Zach, Cheryl

AVON

GRADES 4–8

ADVENTURE I MYSTERY

Quinn McMann lives with his cousin Jamie Anderson and her mother, Maggie. Although they live in Los Angeles, Maggie's job as a television producer allows the group to travel for some of their adventures. The two 12-year-old cousins join forces to solve mysteries. Quinn has psychic powers, and Jamie is a genius and a computer whiz. These books combine supernatural elements with mysterious adventures. One book features a mummy that is stalking Quinn in his nightmares. When Quinn and Jamie get locked in a museum, they are able to find the hidden entrance to a vault filled with stolen treasures. In other books, they find out who is sabotaging a movie production, and Quinn answers the call of an ancient skull.

1. The Mummy's Footsteps ◆ 1997
2. The Phantom of the Roxy ◆ 1997
3. The Curse of the Idol's Eye ◆ 1997
4. The Gypsy's Warning ◆ 1997

MINDWARP

Archer, Chris

MINSTREL/POCKET BOOKS

GRADES 6–8

ADVENTURE I FANTASY I HORROR

A group of friends at Metier (Wisconsin) Junior High School seem to be the only ones who are aware that there are aliens among us. Ethan Rogers is kind of a geek until an alien force invades him. Ethan knows that something is wrong but he can't seem to convince anyone else in town, including his father, the police chief. Can Ethan save the town from the *Alien Terror*? Ashley Rose is the next victim of the aliens. They take over her body, giving her special powers. In another adventure, Ashley and her friends try to escape the aliens in a UFO only to enter a future world that is worse than their own. This series will interest the readers of Goosebumps and Ghosts of Fear Street.

1. Alien Terror ◆ 1997
2. Alien Blood ◆ 1997
3. Alien Scream ◆ 1997
4. Second Sight ◆ 1998
5. Shape-Shifter ◆ 1998
6. Aftershock ◆ 1998
7. Flash Forward ◆ 1998
8. Face the Fear ◆ 1998
9. Out of Time ◆ 1998
10. Meltdown ◆ 1999

MINERVA LOUISE

Stoeke, Janet Morgan

DUTTON

GRADES K–3

ANIMAL FANTASY | HUMOR

Minerva Louise is a lovable but silly chicken who lives on a farm. She is sure she has everything figured out: The playpen must be a rabbit hutch, the hose is a scarf that is way too big, and the bedspread is a meadow of flowers. Children will laugh as they read about her silly antics on and off the farm.

1. Minerva Louise ◆ 1988
2. Minerva Louise at School ◆ 1996
3. A Hat for Minerva Louise ◆ 1994
4. A Friend for Minerva Louise ◆ 1997

MISERY GUTS *see* Keith Shipley

MISHMASH

Cone, Molly

POCKET BOOKS

GRADES 3–4

FAMILY LIFE | HUMOR

Pete's parents have finally granted his wish for a dog. Mishmash is more than a large friendly mutt—he thinks he is a human. This leads to several wacky adventures solving mysteries, confronting a grocery store robot, and dealing with tests and substitute teachers. In *Mishmash and the Big Fat Problem*, Mishmash must lose extra doggy pounds with help from Pete and Wanda. There is plenty of humor and lively action along with positive family and school situations in this series.

1. Mishmash ◆ 1962
2. Mishmash and the Substitute Teacher ◆ 1963
3. Mishmash and the Sauerkraut Mystery ◆ 1965
4. Mishmash and Uncle Looey ◆ 1968
5. Mishmash and the Venus Flytrap ◆ 1976

6. Mishmash and the Robot ◆ 1981
7. Mishmash and the Big Fat Problem ◆ 1982

MISS BIANCA *see* The Rescuers

MISS FLORA MCFLIMSEY

Mariana
LOTHROP, LEE & SHEPARD
GRADES K–2
FANTASY

Miss Flora McFlimsey is a whimsical doll who lives with Diana and her sister Toto, but remembers a time long before when she was owned by a little girl with "red-topped shoes." The Christmas story recalls the time when she was forgotten and neglected in the attic and was restored by an angel and placed under the tree so that Diana and Toto would find her. Some of the other holiday stories are about Flora's life with the long-ago girl, the conceited PooKoo Cat, and other woodland friends. Easter finds her with Diana, recalling the story of the time when she won a prize for the bonnet that was given to her by Peterkins Rabbit. There is a book for most holidays, and all are illustrated throughout with nostalgic pastels.

1. Miss Flora McFlimsey's Christmas Eve ◆ 1949
2. Miss Flora McFlimsey's Easter Bonnet ◆ 1951
3. Miss Flora McFlimsey and the Baby New Year ◆ 1951
4. Miss Flora McFlimsey's Birthday ◆ 1952
5. Miss Flora McFlimsey and Little Laughing Water ◆ 1954
6. Miss Flora McFlimsey and the Little Red School House ◆ 1957
7. Miss Flora McFlimsey's Valentine ◆ 1962
8. Miss Flora McFlimsey's May Day ◆ 1969
9. Miss Flora McFlimsey's Halloween ◆ 1972

MISS KNOW IT ALL

York, Carol Beach
BANTAM
GRADES 2–4
FANTASY

The Good-Day Orphanage on Butterfield Square has 28 girls and a very good friend in Miss Know It All, a magical lady who does seem to know everything. Miss Plum and Miss Lavender try to run the orphanage with kindness and love, but it is Miss Know It All who steps in with her unique gifts when the girls have a problem. She sends tickets for everyone in the orphanage, even the cook, to go to the circus, and she helps out when the girls want to have their own circus. Her magic delights all the girls, especially her always-full box of chocolates.

1. Miss Know It All ◆ 1966
2. The Christmas Dolls ◆ 1967
3. The Good Day Mice ◆ 1968
4. Good Charlotte ◆ 1969
5. The Ten O'Clock Club ◆ 1970
6. Miss Know It All Returns ◆ 1972
7. Kate Be Late ◆ 1987
8. Miss Know It All and the Wishing Lamp ◆ 1987
9. Miss Know It All and the Three-Ring Circus ◆ 1988
10. Miss Know It All and the Secret House ◆ 1988
11. Miss Know It All and the Magic House ◆ 1988

MISS MALLARD

Quackenbush, Robert
PRENTICE-HALL

GRADES 2–4

ANIMAL FANTASY | HUMOR | MYSTERY

Miss Mallard, the globe-trotting "ducktective," recovers stolen art in Venice, rescues an abducted scientist in Rio, and uncovers a crooked archeologist's plans in Central America. On this particular trip, some of the travelers are afraid of a headless monster. Through clever reasoning, she proves that the monster is a sham created by an archeologist who is a rival of the expedition's leader.

1. Express Train to Trouble ◆ 1981
2. Cable Car to Catastrophe ◆ 1982
3. Dig to Disaster ◆ 1982
4. Gondola to Danger ◆ 1983
5. Stairway to Doom ◆ 1983
6. Rickshaw to Horror ◆ 1984
7. Taxi to Intrigue ◆ 1984
8. Stage Door to Terror ◆ 1985
9. Bicycle to Treachery ◆ 1985
10. Surfboard to Peril ◆ 1986
11. Texas Trail to Calamity ◆ 1986
12. Dog Sled to Dread ◆ 1987
13. Danger in Tibet ◆ 1989
14. Lost in the Amazon ◆ 1990
15. Evil Under the Sea ◆ 1992

MISS NELSON

Marshall, James
HOUGHTON MIFFLIN
GRADES K–3
HUMOR

When the kids in Miss Nelson's class begin to take advantage of her sweet nature, she decides to take some action. She becomes Miss Viola Swamp, the meanest substitute teacher in the world. A little dose of Miss Swamp is all it takes for the kids to appreciate Miss Nelson again and behave for her. The class impersonates Miss Nelson while she impersonates Miss Swamp in one book; and in another, Miss Swamp is brought in to whip the football team into shape. The illustrations are colorful and cartoony and the humor is satirical in this picture book series.

1. Miss Nelson Is Missing! ◆ 1977
2. Miss Nelson Is Back ◆ 1982
3. Miss Nelson Has a Field Day ◆ 1985

MISS PICKERELL

MacGregor, Ellen, and Dora Pantell
MCGRAW-HILL
GRADES 4–5
ADVENTURE

Miss Pickerell will take up a good cause in a flash, using all her wits and energy to cope with a strange earthquake, oil spills, or even to take an exciting voyage to a new place. Her adventures always include her very bright nephew, Euphus, who is very useful. The original stories, written by MacGregor in the 1950s, ceased at her death in 1954. The series continued ten years later written by Dora Pantell, who sent Miss Pickerell on to further action.

1. Miss Pickerell Goes to Mars ◆ 1951
2. Miss Pickerell and the Geiger Counter ◆ 1953
3. Miss Pickerell Goes Undersea ◆ 1953
4. Miss Pickerell Goes to the Arctic ◆ 1954
5. Miss Pickerell on the Moon ◆ 1965
6. Miss Pickerell Goes on a Dig ◆ 1966
7. Miss Pickerell Harvests the Sea ◆ 1968
8. Miss Pickerell and the Weather Satellite ◆ 1971
9. Miss Pickerell Meets Mr. H.U.M. ◆ 1974
10. Miss Pickerell Takes the Bull by the Horns ◆ 1976
11. Miss Pickerell to the Earthquake Rescue ◆ 1977

12. Miss Pickerell and the Supertanker ◆ 1978
13. Miss Pickerell Tackles the Energy Crisis ◆ 1980
14. Miss Pickerell on the Trail ◆ 1982
15. Miss Pickerell and the Blue Whales ◆ 1983
16. Miss Pickerell and the War of the Computers ◆ 1984
17. Miss Pickerell and the Lost World ◆ 1986

MISS SPIDER

Kirk, David

SCHOLASTIC

GRADES K–2

ANIMAL FANTASY

Miss Spider is 1 lonely spider, who wants to invite other bugs to tea; but counting from 2 beetles (Ike and May) to 9 moths, they say no. Finally, holding 10 cups of tea, Miss Spider aids a wet moth, who tells the others of her kindness. In other stories, Miss Spider marries Holley, and they go looking for the perfect car. The rhyming text and lush paintings capture the personalities of the many characters.

1. Miss Spider's Tea Party ◆ 1994
2. Miss Spider's Wedding ◆ 1995
3. Miss Spider's New Car ◆ 1997
4. Miss Spider's ABC ◆ 1998

MISTY SERIES *see* Chincoteague

MITZI

Williams, Barbara

DUTTON

GRADES 4–6

FAMILY LIFE | REAL LIFE

When Mitzi's mother remarries, her new husband moves in with his two sons, Frederick and little Darwin, and his mother, Nana Potts. While the newlyweds go on their honeymoon, Mitzi and her new brothers and grandmother have their own "honeymoon." Mitzi learns that her new stepbrothers are not so bad in the next two books; and in the last book, Mitzi decides that she wants to be a biologist. When she meets the elephant keeper at the zoo, she learns all about taking care of elephants and their different personalities. It turns out that she is a natural elephant person; and when one of them gets sick, it is Mitzi who saves the day.

1. Mitzi and the Terrible Tyrannosaurus Rex ◆ 1982
2. Mitzi's Honeymoon with Nana Potts ◆ 1983
3. Mitzi and Frederick the Great ◆ 1984
4. Mitzi and the Elephants ◆ 1985

MOESHA

Various authors
ARCHWAY
GRADES 6–8
REAL LIFE

Based on the television series starring teen star Brandy, these books feature Moesha Mitchell, a 15-year-old African American girl who experiences typical teen dilemmas. Her family consists of a younger brother, father, and a new stepmother (her mother died several years ago), and there are realistic moments involving family adjustments and concerns. Moesha's friends often come to her aid with guidance and support, but they also get involved in some minor scrapes and misunderstandings. With plots that are current, upbeat language, and a positive family model, this series provides solid reading that will be of special interest to girls.

1. Everybody Say Moesha! (Scott, Stefanie) ◆ 1997
2. Keeping It Real (Scott, Stefanie) ◆ 1997
3. Trippin' Out (Scott, Stefanie) ◆ 1997
4. Hollywood Hook-Up (Scott, Stefanie) ◆ 1998
5. What's Up, Brother (Reed, Teresa) ◆ 1998

THE MOFFATS

Estes, Eleanor
HARCOURT
GRADES 3–6
FAMILY LIFE

The Moffats are a warm, fun-loving family in New England who just manage to make ends meet. The books take place approximately 50 years ago in a small town and provide a good feel for that time period. Readers will find many humorous moments.

1. The Moffats ◆ 1941

2. The Middle Moffat ◆ 1943
3. Rufus M. ◆ 1943
4. The Moffat Museum ◆ 1983

MOLE AND TROLL

Johnston, Tony

BANTAM DOUBLEDAY DELL

GRADES K–3

ANIMAL FANTASY

Mole and Troll are two very good friends. As good friends do, they share their fears, have their quarrels, and generally have a good time.

1. The Adventures of Mole and Troll ◆ 1989
2. Happy Birthday, Mole and Troll ◆ 1989
3. Mole and Troll Trim the Tree ◆ 1989
4. Night Noises: And Other Mole and Troll Stories ◆ 1989

MOLESONS

Bos, Burny

NORTH-SOUTH BOOKS

GRADES K–2

ANIMAL FANTASY | FAMILY LIFE

Dug and Dusty Moleson are twin moles from a close, working-class mole family. Their parents, Molly and Morris (called Mud), are lots of fun and unpredictable. When Dug and Dusty decide to do the dishes in the backyard, their parents join in, instead of getting angry. Their mother even joins the twins in applying fake chicken pox so they can stay in bed all day. Grandma takes them for rides on her electric wheelchair. Often, the stories are about family projects or outings that go wrong, usually thanks to Mud's miscalculations.

1. Meet the Molesons ◆ 1994
2. More from the Molesons ◆ 1995
3. Leave It to the Molesons! ◆ 1995

MOLLY *see* American Girls: Molly

MOLLY

Chaikin, Miriam
HARPERCOLLINS
GRADES 4–7
FAMILY LIFE | HISTORICAL | REAL LIFE

A Jewish immigrant family living in Brooklyn during World War II struggles with staying true to its roots while at the same time becoming more
American. Molly has an older brother, Joey; a younger sister, Rebecca; and
Yaaki, the beautiful baby brother whom everyone adores. Molly's best
friend is Tsippi, but she has other friends at school with whom she quarrels and makes up, in typical schoolgirl fashion. One of them asks her to
go to a restaurant that is not kosher, and she sneaks out and goes, only to
get sick. As she talks to God about this (out of a special window that she
reserves for this purpose), she realizes she was wrong. The series follows her
to her upper elementary years, when many of her friends get their periods, causing her to feel left behind. Details of Jewish life are woven into all
of the books.

1. I Should Worry, I Should Care ◆ 1979
2. Finders Weepers ◆ 1980
3. Getting Even ◆ 1982
4. Lower! Higher! You're a Liar! ◆ 1984
5. Friends Forever ◆ 1988

MONSTER FAMILY see Very Worst Monster

MOOMINTROLL

Jansson, Tove
FARRAR, STRAUS & GIROUX
GRADES 4–7
FANTASY

From Scandinavia comes the story of beasties who inhabit the
Moominvalley. The black-and-white drawings show them as little hippo-
like creatures, but they have very human qualities. They are supposed to
sleep all winter and wake to adventures in the spring, but in one of the
books Moomintroll wakes up in January and finds all of his summer haunts
gone. Their stories are full of human-like foibles, slightly surreal happenings, and gentle satire.

1. Finn Family Moomintroll ◆ 1989
2. Comet in Moominland ◆ 1990
3. Moominsummer Madness ◆ 1991

4. Moominland Midwinter ◆ 1992
5. Moominpappa at Sea ◆ 1993
6. Moominpappa's Memoirs ◆ 1994
7. Tales from Moominvalley ◆ 1995

MOONBEAR

Asch, Frank

SIMON & SCHUSTER; SCHOLASTIC

GRADES K–2

ANIMAL FANTASY | FAMILY LIFE

Many of these books feature Bear's interest in the moon, while others include Bear's friend, Little Bird. Bear wants to dance with the moon. He searches for gold at the end of the rainbow and finds honey. He discovers a pet fish only to realize it is a pollywog (that becomes a frog). Like Asch's Bear stories, these are filled with gentle humor.

1. Moon Bear ◆ 1978
2. Happy Birthday, Moon ◆ 1982
3. Mooncake ◆ 1983
4. Moongame ◆ 1984
5. Skyfire ◆ 1984
6. Bear Shadow ◆ 1985
7. Bear's Bargain ◆ 1985
8. Goodbye House ◆ 1986
9. Moonbear's Pet ◆ 1987
10. Moondance ◆ 1993

MORRIS AND BORIS

Wiseman, Bernard

PUTNAM

GRADES K–2

ANIMAL FANTASY | HUMOR

Each book in this series builds on the literal-mindedness of Morris the Moose and the practical nature of Boris the Bear. At the circus, Morris rides "bear" back on Boris. When Morris has a cold, Boris wants to make him some tea, but Morris wonders about the other letters, like, *a, b, c.* There is a lot of fun in the situations and in the misunderstandings.

1. Morris the Moose ◆ 1959
2. Morris Is a Cowboy, a Policeman, and a Baby Sitter ◆ 1960
3. Morris Goes to School ◆ 1970
4. Morris and Boris ◆ 1974

5. Halloween with Morris and Boris ◆ 1975
6. Morris Has a Cold ◆ 1978
7. Morris Tells Boris Mother Moose Stories and Rhymes ◆ 1979
8. Christmas with Morris and Boris ◆ 1983
9. Morris Has a Birthday Party ◆ 1983
10. Morris and Boris at the Circus ◆ 1988

MOUSE AND MOLE

Cushman, Doug
SCIENTIFIC AMERICAN
GRADES K–3
ANIMAL FANTASY

This series shows two lovable creatures, Mouse and Mole, enjoying the outdoors. At the bottom of each page are simple scientific explanations of elements of the story: firefly light, seaweed, short winter nights, frost, and so on. Young scientists will enjoy the stories along with the information.

1. Mouse & Mole and the Year-Round Garden ◆ 1994
2. Mouse & Mole and the Christmas Walk ◆ 1994
3. Mouse & Mole and the All-Weather Train Ride ◆ 1995

MOUSEKIN

Miller, Edna
PRENTICE-HALL
GRADES K–2
REAL LIFE

Mousekin is a gentle white-footed mouse who lives in a lovely forest portrayed in watercolors on every page. People living on the edge of the forest sometimes touch the mouse's life, as when they leave a jack-o'-lantern into which Mousekin crawls. In the Christmas story, he is attracted to a house by its bright lights. Another book deals with dangers from predators, as Mousekin is pursued by an owl. Other animals in the forest hibernate, but Mousekin does not. One book portrays his winter adventures, while another tells of his mate and children. Accurate nature information combines with narrative in a unique way in this picture book series.

1. Mousekin's Golden House ◆ 1964
2. Mousekin's Christmas Eve ◆ 1965
3. Mousekin Finds a Friend ◆ 1967
4. Mousekin's Family ◆ 1969
5. Mousekin's Woodland Sleepers ◆ 1970

6. Mousekin's ABC ◆ 1972
7. Mousekin's Birth ◆ 1974
8. Mousekin's Woodland Birthday ◆ 1974
9. Mousekin Takes a Trip ◆ 1976
10. Mousekin's Close Call ◆ 1978
11. Mousekin's Fables ◆ 1982
12. Mousekin's Mystery ◆ 1983
13. Mousekin's Thanksgiving ◆ 1985
14. Mousekin's Easter Basket ◆ 1987
15. Mousekin's Frosty Friend ◆ 1990
16. Mousekin's Lost Woodland ◆ 1992

MR. AND MRS. PIG

Rayner, Mary

ATHENEUM; MACMILLAN

GRADES K–3

ANIMAL FANTASY | FAMILY LIFE | HUMOR

The first book of this series, *Mr. and Mrs. Pig's Evening Out*, shows readers how quickly the ten piglets use their wits to unmask the true identity of their baby-sitter. Clever Mrs. Wolf tries to steal the piglets in subsequent titles, but she is always foiled by the quick-thinking pigs. Mrs. Pig is also very good at being clever, particularly when the piglets want only ketchup—even for dessert. Full watercolor illustrations, satisfying solutions, and gentle humor in familiar family situations will engage young readers.

1. Mr. & Mrs. Pig's Evening Out ◆ 1976
2. Garth Pig and the Ice Cream Lady ◆ 1978
3. Mrs. Pig's Bulk Buy ◆ 1981
4. Mrs. Pig Gets Cross ◆ 1987
5. Garth Pig Steals the Show ◆ 1993

MR. PUTTER AND TABBY

Rylant, Cynthia

HARCOURT

GRADES K–3

HUMOR | REAL LIFE

In the first book, Mr. Putter is lonely and decides to get a cat. He goes to the pet store, but they have only kittens, so he goes to the shelter and finds an old cat. After a while, neither can remember what life was like without the other. Now Mr. Putter has someone with whom to share his English muffins, tea, and stories. Tabby likes to roll in his tulips, and each one knows what the other one is going to do. In subsequent books, they take care of the neighbor's dog and have other gentle adventures. Each book in this easy-reader series is divided into short chapters and illustrated in full color.

1. Mr. Putter and Tabby Pour the Tea ◆ 1994
2. Mr. Putter and Tabby Walk the Dog ◆ 1994
3. Mr. Putter and Tabby Bake the Cake ◆ 1994
4. Mr. Putter and Tabby Pick the Pears ◆ 1995
5. Mr. Putter and Tabby Row the Boat ◆ 1997
6. Mr. Putter and Tabby Fly the Plane ◆ 1997
7. Mr. Putter and Tabby Toot the Horn ◆ 1998
8. Mr. Putter and Tabby Take the Train ◆ 1998

MR. ROSE'S CLASS

Ziefert, Harriet
LITTLE, BROWN
GRADES K–3
REAL LIFE

In a simple and humorous way, Mr. Rose challenges his students to make scientific deductions with the materials that he gives them. For example, in *Egg-Drop Day* each student is challenged to discover a material to protect eggs from breaking when they are dropped. Everybody joins in the fun! In *Worm Day*, the students find out everything they can about worms. At the end of each book, there is an assignment from Mr. Rose that the reader can do at home.

1. Mystery Day ◆ 1988
2. Pet Day ◆ 1988
3. Trip Day ◆ 1988
4. Worm Day ◆ 1988
5. Egg-Drop Day ◆ 1989

MR. YOWDER

Rounds, Glenn
HOLIDAY HOUSE
GRADES 3–5
HISTORICAL | HUMOR

Mr. Yowder is a wandering sign painter in the old West. His adventures are of the tall-tale variety, told in laconic style and illustrated with humorous black-and-white drawings. In one book, he befriends a body-building bull snake. The snake becomes so big that Mr. Yowder rides him like a horse. Together, they hunt buffalo and put Buffalo Bill out of a job. In another story, he obtains an old lion who is worthless except for his roar. So Mr. Yowder decides to put his roar into capsules and sell it. Disaster strikes when a rainstorm releases all the roars too early. Another story tells how Mr. Yowder rigged up sails on prairie schooners, with predictable results.

1. Mr. Yowder and the Lion Roar Capsules ◆ 1976
2. Mr. Yowder and the Steamboat ◆ 1977
3. Mr. Yowder and the Giant Bullsnake ◆ 1978
4. Mr. Yowder, the Peripatetic Sign Painter ◆ 1980
5. Mr. Yowder and the Train Robbers ◆ 1981
6. Mr. Yowder and the Windwagon ◆ 1983

MRS. COVERLET

Nash, Mary
LITTLE, BROWN
GRADES 3–5
FAMILY LIFE | HUMOR

Usually, the three Persever children—Malcolm, Molly, and Toad (a nickname for Theobald)—are very well-behaved. Their housekeeper, Mrs. Coverlet, sees to that. But when their father goes to New Zealand and Mrs. Coverlet leaves to care for her grandchildren, the Persever household is topsy-turvy. This well-known, old-fashioned series is still a choice for readers. Like the Mary Poppins book, these books feature intrepid children inexplicably left on their own. Their humorous antics make for fun reading.

1. While Mrs. Coverlet Was Away ◆ 1958
2. Mrs. Coverlet's Magicians ◆ 1961
3. Mrs. Coverlet's Detectives ◆ 1965

MRS. FRISBY *see* The Rats of NIMH

MRS. GADDY

Gage, Wilson
GREENWILLOW
GRADES K–3
HUMOR

A wonderful, humorous series for beginning chapter readers. Whether it's outwitting a ghost, a fast-growing vine, or a greedy crow, Mrs. Gaddy always has a silly way of solving her problems so that everybody is happy.

1. Mrs. Gaddy and the Ghost ◆ 1979
2. The Crow and Mrs. Gaddy ◆ 1984
3. Mrs. Gaddy and the Fast-Growing Vine ◆ 1985
4. My Stars, It's Mrs. Gaddy ◆ 1991

MRS. PEPPERPOT

Prøysen, Alf

FARRAR, STRAUS & GIROUX

GRADES 2–5

FANTASY | HUMOR

Mr. and Mrs. Pepperpot live an ordinary, quiet life on a farm, except that every once in a while, with no warning and for no reason, Mrs. Pepperpot shrinks to the size of a pepperpot. When they go for an outing in their new car, Mr. Pepperpot unwittingly drops an ice cream cone on her. All is well when a little kitten licks her clean. In another story, she scares a bothersome moose while she is small and he never bothers her again. Some of the books in this series are quite a bit longer than the others.

1. Little Old Mrs. Pepperpot, and Other Stories ◆ 1960
2. Mrs. Pepperpot Again, and Other Stories ◆ 1960
3. Mrs. Pepperpot to the Rescue, and Other Stories ◆ 1963
4. Mrs. Pepperpot's Busy Day ◆ 1967
5. Mrs. Pepperpot in the Magic Wood, and Other Stories ◆ 1968
6. Mrs. Pepperpot's Year ◆ 1970
7. Mrs. Pepperpot's Outing, and Other Stories ◆ 1971
8. Mrs. Pepperpot Goes Berry Picking ◆ 1990
9. Mrs. Pepperpot and the Moose ◆ 1991

MRS. PIGGLE-WIGGLE

MacDonald, Betty

HarperCollins

GRADES 3–6

FANTASY | HUMOR

Generations of children have loved the Mrs. Piggle-Wiggle stories. She is a grandmotherly person whom every child wishes they knew. She lives in an upside-down house and was once married to a pirate, who left buried treasure in the yard. Parents love her for her magical (and very humorous) cures: for tattletales, for selfishness, and so on. Not only good chapter book choices, these also make fun read-alouds.

1. Mrs. Piggle-Wiggle ◆ 1947

2. Mrs. Piggle-Wiggle's Magic ◆ 1949
3. Mrs. Piggle-Wiggle's Farm ◆ 1954
4. Hello, Mrs. Piggle-Wiggle ◆ 1957

MRS. TOGGLE

Pulver, Robin

FOUR WINDS

GRADES K–3

HUMOR

Mrs. Toggle is a perfectly lovable teacher who enlists the help of her class when she has a problem. From being stuck inside her coat when the zipper won't work to losing her blue shoe during a game of kickball, her class is always able to help her out.

1. Mrs. Toggle's Zipper ◆ 1990
2. Mrs. Toggle and the Dinosaur ◆ 1991
3. Mrs. Toggle's Beautiful Blue Shoe ◆ 1994

MUD FLAT

Stevenson, James

GREENWILLOW

GRADES K–2

ANIMAL FANTASY | HUMOR

The community of Mud Flat is filled with many animals who enjoy activities like playing April Fool's Day jokes and organizing an Olympics. Different animals are featured in different books. In *Mud Flat April Fool*, Alice the mole teases Mr. Goodhue the bear. George the fox squirts Lila the dog with his squirting rose, although she is able to pay him back later. In *The Mud Flat Olympics*, Harold the owl is the judge of the Deepest Hole Contest (entered by three moles), and old Mr. Tokay wins the Smelliest Skunk Contest. These are funny books with a simple text and delightful illustrations. Most young readers will appreciate the sly humor and will find the short chapters very accessible.

1. The Mud Flat Olympics ◆ 1994
2. Yard Sale ◆ 1996
3. Heat Wave at Mud Flat ◆ 1997
4. The Mud Flat Mystery ◆ 1997
5. Mud Flat April Fool ◆ 1998

MURPHY FAMILY

McKenna, Colleen O'Shaughnessy
SCHOLASTIC
GRADES 4–6
FAMILY LIFE | HUMOR

This series begins when Collette is in third grade. She is the oldest of four children; and although she loves her younger brothers and sister, it bothers her that her mother is too busy tending to the other children to do things with her alone. Collette wishes that she were an only child and is surprised when her wish comes true. In other books, Collette goes to summer camp, she and her friends run a summer camp for kids in the neighborhood, her mother is expecting another child and has to stay off her feet, and Collette starts sixth grade in a new school on an island.

1. Too Many Murphys ◆ 1988
2. Fourth Grade Is a Jinx ◆ 1989
3. Fifth Grade, Here Comes Trouble ◆ 1989
4. Eenie, Meenie, Murphy, No ◆ 1990
5. Murphy's Island ◆ 1990
6. The Truth About Sixth Grade ◆ 1991
7. Mother Murphy ◆ 1992
8. Camp Murphy ◆ 1993

MUSHROOM PLANET *see* Tyco Bass

MY BABYSITTER

Hodgman, Ann
MINSTREL/POCKET BOOKS
GRADES 4–6
HORROR

When this series begins, Meg Swain is 11 and she resents having to be left with a babysitter. Her resentment turns to dismay when she begins to suspect that her weird babysitter, Vincent Graver, is really a vampire. Meg and her brother Trevor outwit the vampire and escape, only to encounter him again . . . and again . . . and again. In one book, Meg and her friend Kelly Pitts are old enough to be babysitters, but the baby they are watching seems very strange—he likes bats and hides from the sunshine. And what about Vodar, the exchange student in *My Babysitter Flies by Night*, with his pale skin and pointed teeth? This series could meet the needs of readers who have read Goosebumps and other eerie series.

1. My Babysitter Is a Vampire ◆ 1991

2. My Babysitter Has Fangs ◆ 1992
3. My Babysitter Bites Again ◆ 1993
4. My Babysitter Flies by Night ◆ 1994
5. My Babysitter Goes Bats ◆ 1994
6. My Babysitter Is a Movie Monster ◆ 1995

MY DOG

Adler, David A.

HOLIDAY HOUSE

GRADES 1–2

MYSTERY

Humorous, easy mysteries are solved with Jennie's observant eye and her big shaggy pet, simply called My Dog. In *My Dog and the Birthday Mystery*, Jennie's friends trick her into solving a mystery that is really a surprise birthday party. My Dog helps to solve the Green Sock and Knock-Knock mysteries with simple animal instincts. Easy sentence structure and humorous color illustrations make this series appealing to first readers.

1. My Dog and the Key Mystery ◆ 1982
2. My Dog and the Knock Knock Mystery ◆ 1985
3. My Dog and the Green Sock Mystery ◆ 1986
4. My Dog and the Birthday Mystery ◆ 1987

MY FATHER'S DRAGON *see* Dragon

MY FIRST LITTLE HOUSE BOOKS *see* Little
House: My First Little House Books

MY NAME IS AMERICA

Various authors

SCHOLASTIC

GRADES 4–6

HISTORICAL

This series is similar in format to the Dear America series, except that the fictional journal entries are written by boys. Written by different authors, including Jim Murphy, who has received a Newbery Honor medal, this series merges historical facts with personal reflections. One book examines the experiences of an orphan who became a spy for the colonists during the Revolutionary War. The Civil War is the setting for another book that describes the brutality and courage of people in this conflict. Lots of action, as well as personal insights, make this a good choice for upper elementary school readers.

1. The Journal of William Thomas Emerson: A Revolutionary War Patriot, Boston, Massachusetts, 1774 (Denenberg, Barry) ◆ 1998
2. The Journal of James Edmond Pease: A Civil War Union Soldier, Virginia, 1863 (Murphy, Jim) ◆ 1998

MY ROBOT BUDDY *see* Jack and Danny One

MY TEACHER

Coville, Bruce

MINSTREL/POCKET BOOKS

GRADES 4–6

ADVENTURE | SCIENCE FICTION

In the first book of this series, *My Teacher Is an Alien*, Peter Thompson and his friend Susan Simmons discover that aliens have invaded his sixth-grade class. It is Peter's mission to save the class. In succeeding adventures, the aliens attempt to attack and destroy the Earth. There is enough suspense in each title to sustain interest in this fast-paced adventure series.

1. My Teacher Is an Alien ◆ 1989
2. My Teacher Fried My Brains ◆ 1991
3. My Teacher Glows in the Dark ◆ 1991
4. My Teacher Flunked the Planet ◆ 1992

MY TEDDY BEAR

Jorvik, Irwin

GARETH STEVENS

GRADES K–2

FANTASY

This teddy bear is the old-fashioned type. In fact, he is an Edwardian teddy bear, and his nursery friends include a jack-in-the-box and other stuffed animals. He and his toy friends keep busy playing in the garden, reading books, having parties, and traveling to the seashore. In *My Teddy Bear at Work*, Teddy experiments with different careers before returning to his vocation of bear.

1. My Teddy Bear at Play ◆ 1996

2. My Teddy Bear at Work ◆ 1996
3. My Teddy Bear at Home ◆ 1996
4. My Teddy Bear on Vacation ◆ 1996

THE MYSTERY FILES OF SHELBY WOO

Various authors

MINSTREL/POCKET BOOKS

GRADES 4–6

MYSTERY

Shelby Woo has always dreamed of being a detective because her grandfather solved crimes for the San Francisco Police Department. Now she lives with him in Florida and works as an intern for Detective Whit Hineline of the Cocoa Beach Police Department. As a budding sleuth, she likes to take neglected investigations into her own hands. She solves cases with her friends Cindy and Noah, even though the police want her to stay out of the way. In the early books of this series, Shelby establishes her credentials as she works on such cases as a series of muggings at C.J.'s, a local eatery. In later books, Shelby has developed a more official role with the police department and works on cases like the disappearance of a comic book creator—right from her grandfather's bed-and-breakfast! Each book opens with a synopsis of the case file. Bold-faced text written in the first person provides Shelby's perspective. This series connects with the *Nickelodeon* TV programs.

1. A Slash in the Night (Goodman, Alan) ◆ 1997
2. Takeout Stakeout (Gallagher, Diana G.) ◆ 1997
3. Hot Rock (Peel, John) ◆ 1997
4. Rock 'n' Roll Robbery (Marano, Lydia C.) ◆ 1997
5. Cut and Run (Gallagher, Diana G.) ◆ 1998
6. House Arrest (Marano, Lydia C.) ◆ 1998
7. Comic Book Criminal (Dubowski, Cathy East, and Mark Dubowski) ◆ 1998
8. Copper Frame (Strickland, Brad, and Barbara Strickland) ◆ 1998

NANCY BRUCE

Lindquist, Jennie Dorothea

PETER SMITH

GRADES 4–6

FAMILY LIFE

Set in rural 20th century America, the Nancy Bruce books are delightful character-based novels. *The Golden Name Day* introduces readers to Nancy, who has come to live with her grandparents while her mother recovers from an illness. Nancy has a wonderful time learning Swedish customs; building friendships with her cousins, the Carlson girls; and basking in the love and warmth of her caring relatives. The other books in this series follow Nancy as she meets new friends and continues to delight in the world around her.

1. The Golden Name Day ◆ 1955
2. The Little Silver House ◆ 1959
3. The Crystal Tree ◆ 1966

NANCY DREW

Keene, Carolyn

SIMON & SCHUSTER

GRADES 4–7

MYSTERY

Nancy Drew is a teenage detective who solves crimes while her friends George and Bess tag along. In one book, Bess helps a wedding consultant who works out of an old mansion on the outskirts of River Heights. During a busy week in June, she asks George and Nancy to help out. As the first wedding begins, it seems that someone is trying to sabotage it. Nancy suspects a cousin of the bride; but when a second wedding is sabotaged, suspicion shifts to the sister of the wedding manager. The history of the old house eventually helps solve the mystery. Throughout the series, Nancy is thorough, methodical, and undistracted. Bess and George provide contrast, Bess being a food-loving flirt and George serious and athletic.

1. The Secret of the Old Clock ◆ 1930
2. The Hidden Staircase ◆ 1930
3. The Bungalow Mystery ◆ 1930
4. The Mystery at Lilac Inn ◆ 1930
5. The Secret of Shadow Ranch ◆ 1930
6. The Secret of Red Gate Farm ◆ 1931
7. The Clue in the Diary ◆ 1932
8. Nancy's Mysterious Letter ◆ 1932
9. The Sign of the Twisted Candles ◆ 1933
10. The Password to Larkspur Lane ◆ 1933
11. The Clue of the Broken Locket ◆ 1934
12. The Message in the Hollow Oak ◆ 1935
13. The Mystery of the Ivory Charm ◆ 1936
14. The Whispering Statue ◆ 1937
15. The Haunted Bridge ◆ 1937
16. The Clue of the Tapping Heels ◆ 1939
17. The Mystery of the Brass-Bound Trunk ◆ 1940

18. The Mystery of the Moss-Covered Mansion ◆ 1941
19. The Quest of the Missing Map ◆ 1942
20. The Clue in the Jewel Box ◆ 1943
21. The Secret in the Old Attic ◆ 1944
22. The Clue in the Crumbling Wall ◆ 1945
23. The Mystery of the Tolling Bell ◆ 1946
24. The Clue in the Old Album ◆ 1947
25. The Ghost of Blackwood Hall ◆ 1948
26. The Clue of the Leaning Chimney ◆ 1949
27. The Secret of the Wooden Lady ◆ 1950
28. The Clue of the Black Keys ◆ 1951
29. The Mystery at the Ski Jump ◆ 1952
30. The Clue of the Velvet Mask ◆ 1953
31. The Ringmaster's Secret ◆ 1953
32. The Scarlet Slipper Mystery ◆ 1954
33. The Witch Tree Symbol ◆ 1955
34. The Hidden Window Mystery ◆ 1956
35. The Haunted Showboat ◆ 1957
36. The Secret of the Golden Pavilion ◆ 1959
37. The Clue in the Old Stagecoach ◆ 1960
38. The Mystery of the Fire Dragon ◆ 1961
39. The Clue of the Dancing Puppet ◆ 1962
40. The Moonstone Castle Mystery ◆ 1963
41. The Clue of the Whistling Bagpipes ◆ 1964
42. The Phantom of Pine Hill ◆ 1965
43. The Mystery of the 99 Steps ◆ 1966
44. The Clue in the Crossword Cypher ◆ 1967
45. The Spider Sapphire Mystery ◆ 1968
46. The Invisible Intruder ◆ 1969
47. The Mysterious Mannequin ◆ 1970
48. The Crooked Bannister ◆ 1971
49. The Secret of Mirror Bay ◆ 1972
50. The Double Jinx Mystery ◆ 1974
51. The Mystery of the Glowing Eye ◆ 1974
52. The Secret of the Forgotten City ◆ 1975
53. The Sky Phantom ◆ 1976
54. Strange Message in the Parchment ◆ 1977
55. Mystery of Crocodile Island ◆ 1978
56. The Thirteenth Pearl ◆ 1979
57. Triple Hoax ◆ 1979
58. The Flying Saucer Mystery ◆ 1980
59. The Secret in the Old Lace ◆ 1980
60. The Greek Symbol Mystery ◆ 1981
61. The Swami's Ring ◆ 1981
62. The Kachina Doll Mystery ◆ 1981
63. The Twin Dilemma ◆ 1981
64. Captive Witness ◆ 1981
65. Mystery of the Winged Lion ◆ 1982

66. Race Against Time ◆ 1982
67. The Sinister Omen ◆ 1982
68. The Elusive Heiress ◆ 1982
69. Clue in the Ancient Disguise ◆ 1982
70. The Broken Anchor ◆ 1983
71. The Silver Cobweb ◆ 1983
72. The Haunted Carousel ◆ 1983
73. Enemy Match ◆ 1984
74. The Mysterious Image ◆ 1984
75. The Emerald-Eyed Cat ◆ 1984
76. The Eskimo's Secret ◆ 1985
77. The Bluebeard Room ◆ 1985
78. The Phantom of Venice ◆ 1985
79. The Double Horror of Fenley Place ◆ 1987
80. The Case of the Disappearing Diamonds ◆ 1987
81. Mardi Gras Mystery ◆ 1988
82. The Clue in the Camera ◆ 1988
83. The Case of the Vanishing Veil ◆ 1988
84. The Joker's Revenge ◆ 1988
85. The Secret of Shady Glen ◆ 1988
86. The Mystery of Misty Canyon ◆ 1988
87. The Case of the Rising Stars ◆ 1988
88. The Search for Cindy Austin ◆ 1988
89. The Case of the Disappearing Deejay ◆ 1989
90. The Puzzle at Pineview School ◆ 1989
91. The Girl Who Couldn't Remember ◆ 1989
92. The Ghost of Craven Cove ◆ 1989
93. The Case of the Safecracker's Secret ◆ 1990
94. The Picture-Perfect Mystery ◆ 1990
95. The Silent Suspect ◆ 1990
96. The Case of the Photo Finish ◆ 1990
97. The Mystery at Magnolia Mansion ◆ 1990
98. The Haunting of Horse Island ◆ 1990
99. The Secret at Seven Rocks ◆ 1991
100. A Secret in Time: Nancy Drew's 100th Anniversary Edition ◆ 1991
101. The Mystery of the Missing Millionaires ◆ 1991
102. The Secret in the Dark ◆ 1991
103. The Stranger in the Shadows ◆ 1991
104. The Mystery of the Jade Tiger ◆ 1991
105. The Clue in the Antique Trunk ◆ 1992
106. The Case of the Artful Crime ◆ 1992
107. The Legend of Miner's Creek ◆ 1992
108. The Secret of the Tibetan Treasure ◆ 1992
109. The Mystery of the Masked Rider ◆ 1992
110. The Nutcracker Ballet Mystery ◆ 1992
111. The Secret at Solitaire ◆ 1993
112. Crime in the Queen's Court ◆ 1993

113. The Secret Lost at Sea ◆ 1993
114. The Search for the Silver Persian ◆ 1993
115. The Suspect in the Smoke ◆ 1993
116. The Case of the Twin Teddy Bears ◆ 1993
117. Mystery on the Menu ◆ 1993
118. Trouble at Lake Tahoe ◆ 1994
119. The Mystery of the Missing Mascot ◆ 1994
120. The Case of the Floating Crime ◆ 1994
121. The Fortune-Teller's Secret ◆ 1994
122. The Message in the Haunted Mansion ◆ 1994
123. The Clue on the Silver Screen ◆ 1995
124. The Secret of the Scarlet Hand ◆ 1995
125. The Teen Model Mystery ◆ 1995
126. The Riddle in the Rare Book ◆ 1995
127. The Case of the Dangerous Solution ◆ 1995
128. The Treasure in the Royal Tower ◆ 1995
129. The Baby-Sitter Burglaries ◆ 1996
130. The Sign of the Falcon ◆ 1996
131. The Hidden Inheritance ◆ 1996
132. The Fox Hunt Mystery ◆ 1996
133. The Mystery at the Crystal Palace ◆ 1996
134. The Secret of the Forgotten Cave ◆ 1996
135. The Riddle of the Ruby Gazelle ◆ 1997
136. The Wedding Day Mystery ◆ 1997
137. In Search of the Black Rose ◆ 1997
138. Legend of the Lost Gold ◆ 1997
139. The Secret of Candlelight Inn ◆ 1997
140. The Door-to-Door Deception ◆ 1997
141. The Wild Cat Crime ◆ 1997
142. The Case of Capital Intrigue ◆ 1998
143. Mystery on Maui ◆ 1998
144. The E-Mail Mystery ◆ 1998
145. The Missing Horse Mystery ◆ 1998

NANCY DREW FILES

Keene, Carolyn
ARCHWAY
GRADES 6–8
MYSTERY

In the Nancy Drew Files, geared more for older readers, Nancy remains the same gutsy, smart, accomplished sleuth she has always been. In this series, Nancy goes undercover at a high school, solves a rock 'n' roll mystery, and travels to exotic places, such as a ski resort and Fort Lauderdale during spring break. A new character in this series is Brenda Carlton, an aspiring investigative reporter who thinks she can outsmart Nancy and has the habit of messing up her investigations.

1. Secrets Can Kill ◆ 1986
2. Deadly Intent ◆ 1986
3. Murder on Ice ◆ 1986
4. Smile and Say Murder ◆ 1986
5. Hit and Run Holiday ◆ 1986
6. White Water Terror ◆ 1987
7. Deadly Doubles ◆ 1987
8. Two Points for Murder ◆ 1987
9. False Moves ◆ 1987
10. Buried Secrets ◆ 1987
11. Heart of Danger ◆ 1987
12. Fatal Ransom ◆ 1987
13. Wings of Fear ◆ 1987
14. This Side of Evil ◆ 1987
15. Trial by Fire ◆ 1987
16. Never Say Die ◆ 1987
17. Stay Tuned for Danger ◆ 1987
18. Circle of Evil ◆ 1987
19. Sisters in Crime ◆ 1988
20. Very Deadly Yours ◆ 1988
21. Recipe for Murder ◆ 1988
22. Fatal Attraction ◆ 1988
23. Sinister Parade ◆ 1988
24. Till Death Do Us Part ◆ 1988
25. Rich and Dangerous ◆ 1988
26. Playing with Fire ◆ 1988
27. Most Likely to Die ◆ 1988
28. The Black Widow ◆ 1988
29. Pure Poison ◆ 1988
30. Death by Design ◆ 1988
31. Trouble in Tahiti ◆ 1989
32. High Marks for Malice ◆ 1989
33. Danger in Disguise ◆ 1989
34. Vanishing Act ◆ 1989
35. Bad Medicine ◆ 1989
36. Over the Edge ◆ 1989
37. Last Dance ◆ 1989
38. The Final Scene ◆ 1989
39. The Suspect Next Door ◆ 1989
40. Shadow of a Doubt ◆ 1989
41. Something to Hide ◆ 1989
42. The Wrong Chemistry ◆ 1989
43. False Impressions ◆ 1990
44. Scent of Danger ◆ 1990
45. Out of Bounds ◆ 1990

46. Win, Place or Die ◆ 1990
47. Flirting with Danger ◆ 1990
48. A Date with Deception ◆ 1990
49. Portrait in Crime ◆ 1990
50. Deep Secrets ◆ 1990
51. A Model Crime ◆ 1990
52. Danger for Hire ◆ 1990
53. Trail of Lies ◆ 1990
54. Cold as Ice ◆ 1990
55. Don't Look Twice ◆ 1991
56. Make No Mistake ◆ 1991
57. Into Thin Air ◆ 1991
58. Hot Pursuit ◆ 1991
59. High Risk ◆ 1991
60. Poison Pen ◆ 1991
61. Sweet Revenge ◆ 1991
62. Easy Marks ◆ 1991
63. Mixed Signals ◆ 1991
64. The Wrong Track ◆ 1991
65. Final Notes ◆ 1991
66. Tall, Dark and Deadly ◆ 1991
67. Nobody's Business ◆ 1992
68. Crosscurrents ◆ 1992
69. Running Scared ◆ 1992
70. Cutting Edge ◆ 1992
71. Hot Tracks ◆ 1992
72. Swiss Secrets ◆ 1992
73. Rendezvous in Rome ◆ 1992
74. Greek Odyssey ◆ 1992
75. A Talent for Murder ◆ 1992
76. The Perfect Plot ◆ 1992
77. Danger on Parade ◆ 1992
78. Update on Crime ◆ 1992
79. No Laughing Matter ◆ 1993
80. Power of Suggestion ◆ 1993
81. Making Waves ◆ 1993
82. Dangerous Relations ◆ 1993
83. Diamond Deceit ◆ 1993
84. Choosing Sides ◆ 1993
85. Sea of Suspicion ◆ 1993
86. Let's Talk Terror ◆ 1993
87. Moving Target ◆ 1993
88. False Pretenses ◆ 1993
89. Designs in Crime ◆ 1993
90. Stage Fright ◆ 1993
91. If Looks Could Kill ◆ 1994
92. My Deadly Valentine ◆ 1994
93. Hotline to Danger ◆ 1994

94. Illusions of Evil ◆ 1994
95. An Instinct for Trouble ◆ 1994
96. The Runaway Bride ◆ 1994
97. Squeeze Play ◆ 1994
98. Island of Secrets ◆ 1994
99. The Cheating Heart ◆ 1994
100. Dance Till You Die ◆ 1994
101. The Picture of Guilt ◆ 1994
102. Counterfeit Christmas ◆ 1994
103. Heart of Ice ◆ 1995
104. Kiss and Tell ◆ 1995
105. Stolen Affections ◆ 1995
106. Flying Too High ◆ 1995
107. Anything for Love ◆ 1995
108. Captive Heart ◆ 1995
109. Love Notes ◆ 1995
110. Hidden Meanings ◆ 1995
111. The Stolen Kiss ◆ 1995
112. For Love or Money ◆ 1995
113. Wicked Ways ◆ 1996
114. Rehearsing for Romance ◆ 1996
115. Running into Trouble ◆ 1996
116. Under His Spell ◆ 1996
117. Skipping a Beat ◆ 1996
118. Betrayed By Love ◆ 1996
119. Against the Rules ◆ 1997
120. Dangerous Loves ◆ 1997
121. Natural Enemies ◆ 1997
122. Strange Memories ◆ 1997
123. Wicked for the Weekend ◆ 1997
124. Crime at the Ch@t Café ◆ 1997

NANCY DREW NOTEBOOKS

Keene, Carolyn
SIMON & SCHUSTER
GRADES 2–4
MYSTERY

In this Nancy Drew spin-off for younger readers, Nancy and her friends, the cousins George and Bess, are in third grade and already solving mysteries. In *The Funny Face Fight*, there is a class election coming up and Nancy and Bess end up on one girl's side while George is on another's. Someone starts to put mustaches on campaign posters, and accusations fly on both sides. Nancy writes down all the clues in her notebook and eventually finds the culprit. Broken friendships are mended, and apologies are made. In other books, Nancy solves mysteries that come up as the girls are trick-or-treating, on a skiing trip, or having a slumber party.

1. The Slumber Party Secret ◆ 1994
2. The Lost Locket ◆ 1994
3. The Secret Santa ◆ 1994
4. Bad Day for Ballet ◆ 1995
5. The Soccer Shoe Clue ◆ 1995
6. The Ice Cream Scoop ◆ 1995
7. Trouble at Camp Treehouse ◆ 1995
8. The Best Detective ◆ 1995
9. The Thanksgiving Surprise ◆ 1995
10. Not Nice on Ice ◆ 1995
11. The Pen Pal Puzzle ◆ 1996
12. The Puppy Problem ◆ 1996
13. The Wedding Gift Goof ◆ 1996
14. The Funny Face Fight ◆ 1996
15. The Crazy Key Clue ◆ 1996
16. The Ski Slope Mystery ◆ 1997
17. Whose Pet Is Best? ◆ 1997
18. The Stolen Unicorn ◆ 1997
19. The Lemonade Raid ◆ 1997
20. Hannah's Secret ◆ 1997
21. Princess on Parade ◆ 1997
22. The Clue in the Glue ◆ 1998
23. Alien in the Classroom ◆ 1998
24. The Hidden Treasures ◆ 1998
25. Dare at the Fair ◆ 1998
26. The Lucky Horseshoes ◆ 1998
27. Trouble Takes the Cake ◆ 1998
28. Thrill on the Hill ◆ 1999

NARNIA *see* Chronicles of Narnia

NASCAR POLE POSITION ADVENTURES

Calhoun, T. B.
HARPERENTERTAINMENT
GRADES 5–8
REAL LIFE | RECREATION

This new series should appeal to stock-car racing enthusiasts. Kin Travis is fifteen. Along with his sister Laura and his brother Laptop, Kin is involved in adventures involving cars, mysteries, and high-speed action. Throughout the books there is information about stock cars and NASCAR racing events. The Travis kids are helped by their grandfather, Hotshoe Hunter, a famous stock-car racer. His knowledge about racing and his connections with other racers give Kin and his siblings an up-close look at these exciting events.

1. Rolling Thunder ◆ 1998
2. In the Groove ◆ 1998
3. Race Ready ◆ 1998
4. Speed Demon ◆ 1999

NATE THE GREAT

Sharmat, Marjorie Weinman

DELACORTE; BANTAM DOUBLEDAY DELL

GRADES 1–3

HUMOR | MYSTERY

Nate the Great solves mysteries around the neighborhood with his loyal dog Sludge. An avid pancake lover and deep thinker, Nate leads the reader through each step in solving a mystery. Written in the first person, this series has an easy format with simple sentences for young readers. However, these simple sentences relate Nate's intricate thought processes and wry observations.

1. Nate the Great ◆ 1972
2. Nate the Great Goes Undercover ◆ 1974
3. Nate the Great and the Lost List ◆ 1975
4. Nate the Great and the Phony Clue ◆ 1977
5. Nate the Great and the Sticky Case ◆ 1978
6. Nate the Great and the Missing Key ◆ 1981
7. Nate the Great and the Snowy Trail ◆ 1982
8. Nate the Great and the Fishy Prize ◆ 1985
9. Nate the Great Stalks Stupidweed ◆ 1986
10. Nate the Great and the Boring Beach Bag ◆ 1987
11. Nate the Great Goes Down in the Dumps ◆ 1989
12. Nate the Great and the Halloween Hunt ◆ 1989
13. Nate the Great and the Musical Note ◆ 1990
14. Nate the Great and the Stolen Base ◆ 1992
15. Nate the Great and the Pillowcase ◆ 1993
16. Nate the Great and the Mushy Valentine ◆ 1994
17. Nate the Great and the Tardy Tortoise ◆ 1995
18. Nate the Great and the Crunchy Christmas ◆ 1996
19. Nate the Great Saves the King of Sweden ◆ 1997
20. Nate the Great and Me: The Case of the Fleeing Fang ◆ 1998

NED

Zinnemann-Hope, Pam

SIMON & SCHUSTER

GRADES K–1

FAMILY LIFE | REAL LIFE

Ned is full of energy and laughter. This series describes Ned in everyday situations, such as wanting to play and not wanting to go to sleep. Colorful illustrations capture children's attention, and the simple text appeals to beginning readers. Word recognition and comprehension are reinforced through the repetition of simple words.

1. Time for Bed, Ned ◆ 1987
2. Let's Go Shopping, Ned ◆ 1987
3. Find Your Coat, Ned ◆ 1988
4. Let's Play Ball, Ned ◆ 1988

NEPTUNE ADVENTURES

Saunders, Susan

AVON

GRADES 4–7

ADVENTURE | REAL LIFE

Dana Chapin and her cousin Tyler participate in Project Neptune, a resource designed to protect sea life from threats by environmental disasters. They also deal with the behavior of people whose greed or lack of knowledge puts sea creatures at risk. The two cousins help clean up after an oil spill; they come to the aid of a school of pilot whales; they protect a dolphin that has been released into the ocean. This series will appeal to readers who like to see characters like themselves taking action to help others and change the world.

1. Danger on Crab Island ◆ 1998
2. Disaster at Parson's Point ◆ 1998
3. The Dolphin Trap ◆ 1998
4. Stranding on Cedar Point ◆ 1998
5. Hurricane Rescue ◆ 1998
6. Red Tide Alert ◆ 1998

NEVER SINK NINE

Davis, Gibbs
BANTAM DOUBLEDAY DELL
GRADES 3–4
REAL LIFE | RECREATION

The Never Sink Nine series is centered around a group of baseball-loving kids. After Walter fails to make the fourth-grade team, he decides to create his own team. Walter's grandfather, who used to play in the minors, is their coach. The children learn to cooperate and begin to understand each other as the team competes. For example, Walter realizes that Melissa's collection of plastic horses is as important to her as his special socks are to him. Each book in the series contains an entire game.

1. Lucky Socks ◆ 1991
2. Major-League Melissa ◆ 1991
3. Slugger Mike ◆ 1991
4. Pete the Magnificent ◆ 1991
5. Tony's Double Play ◆ 1992
6. Christy's Magic Glove ◆ 1992
7. Olympics Otis ◆ 1993
8. Katie Kicks Off ◆ 1994
9. Diamond Park Dinosaur ◆ 1994
10. Pinheads, Unite! ◆ 1994

THE NEW BOBBSEY TWINS *see* Bobbsey Twins: The New Bobbsey Twins

NEW EDEN

Roos, Stephen
DELACORTE
GRADES 4–6
FAMILY LIFE | HUMOR

This series delves into the lives of middle school kids who live in the town of New Eden. Worries about friendship, fitting in, and dealing with siblings are the topics of these books. For example, a boy must decide how to hide the fact that he can't play baseball. In another book, a young girl plots revenge when her older sister no longer wants to spend a lot of time with her. These issues are presented with humor and sensitivity.

1. My Horrible Secret ◆ 1983

2. The Terrible Truth ◆ 1983
3. My Secret Admirer ◆ 1984

NEW KIDS AT THE POLK STREET SCHOOL

Giff, Patricia Reilly

DELL YEARLING

GRADES 1–3

REAL LIFE

Stacy Arrow is Emily Arrow's little sister. Emily is one of the featured characters in Ms. Rooney's second-grade class at Polk Street School (from the Kids of the Polk Street School series). This New Kids series looks at the antics of younger children—Stacy and her friends—as they adjust to being in kindergarten with their teacher, Mrs. Zachary. Issues like taking turns, saying kind things, being a good listener, and sharing are presented. In one book, the students make an About Me box; in another, Stacy cooperates to make stone soup. Although Stacy is the focus of the books, her friends Jiwon (a Korean American child) and Eddie are also featured. Readers looking for slightly longer chapter books with familiar situations will relate to these simple stories.

1. Watch Out! Man-Eating Snake ◆ 1988
2. Fancy Feet ◆ 1988
3. All About Stacy ◆ 1988
4. B-e-s-t Friends ◆ 1988
5. Spectacular Stone Soup ◆ 1988
6. Stacy Says Good-bye ◆ 1989

NICE MICE

Craig, Janet

TROLL

GRADES K–1

ANIMAL FANTASY | HUMOR

Humorous mice characters introduce seasonal activities in these cute books. Max and Maggie do spring cleaning, enjoy the clouds, pick a pumpkin, and make a special snowman in these simple stories.

1. Max and Maggie in Autumn ◆ 1994
2. Max and Maggie in Spring ◆ 1994
3. Max and Maggie in Summer ◆ 1994
4. Max and Maggie in Winter ◆ 1994

NICKI HOLLAND

Hunt, Angela Elwell

THOMAS NELSON

GRADES 5–6

MYSTERY

Nicki Holland and her best friends—Laura, Kim, Christine, and Meredith—solve mysteries together in this series. Sometimes the setting is at school, as in *The Case of the Terrified Track Star*, and sometimes they must save themselves from danger, as in *The Case of the Counterfeit Cash*. Regardless of where the puzzle begins, Nicki's resourceful and courageous actions always aid in solving the mystery.

1. The Case of the Mystery Mark ◆ 1991
2. The Case of the Phantom Friend ◆ 1991
3. The Case of the Teenager Terminator ◆ 1991
4. The Case of the Terrified Track Star ◆ 1992
5. The Case of the Counterfeit Cash ◆ 1992
6. The Case of the Haunting of Lowell Lanes ◆ 1992
7. The Case of the Birthday Bracelet ◆ 1993
8. The Secret of Cravenhill Castle ◆ 1993
9. The Riddle of Baby Rosalind ◆ 1993

NIGHTMARE HALL

Hoh, Diane

SCHOLASTIC

GRADES 6–8

HORROR | MYSTERY

The Nightmare Hall series takes place in a dormitory where evil seems to lurk. A girl is found hanged in her bedroom, and her spirit tries to help incoming students find the truth about her murder. Jessica Vogt leads the group in discovering the clues. As the first novel ends, there is a sense of relief but not complete peace. This sets the mood for the sequels.

1. The Silent Scream ◆ 1993
2. The Roommate ◆ 1993
3. Deadly Attraction ◆ 1993
4. The Wish ◆ 1993
5. The Scream Team ◆ 1993
6. Guilty ◆ 1993

7. Pretty Please ◆ 1994
8. The Experiment ◆ 1994
9. The Night Walker ◆ 1994
10. Sorority Sister ◆ 1994
11. Last Date ◆ 1994
12. The Whisperer ◆ 1994
13. Monster ◆ 1994
14. The Initiation ◆ 1994
15. Truth or Die ◆ 1994
16. Book of Horrors ◆ 1994
17. Last Breath ◆ 1994
18. Win, Lose, or Die ◆ 1994
19. The Coffin ◆ 1995
20. Deadly Visions ◆ 1995
21. Student Body ◆ 1995
22. The Vampire's Kiss ◆ 1995
23. Dark Moon ◆ 1995
24. The Biker ◆ 1995
25. Captives ◆ 1995
26. Revenge ◆ 1995
27. Kidnapped ◆ 1995
28. The Dummy ◆ 1995
29. The Voice in the Mirror ◆ 1995

NOAH

Topek, Susan Remick
KAR-BEN COPIES
GRADES K–1
FAMILY LIFE

Noah is a likable young boy. His concerns are common, such as not knowing what kind of costume to wear for a holiday and worrying about disliking a certain Passover food. His classmates and teacher help him to feel comfortable and decide what to do. This series is easy to read and has friendly, bright illustrations.

1. A Holiday for Noah ◆ 1990
2. A Turn for Noah ◆ 1992
3. A Taste for Noah ◆ 1993
4. A Costume for Noah ◆ 1995

NOMES *see* Bromeliad

NORA

Ichikawa, Satomi

PHILOMEL

GRADES 1–3

ADVENTURE | FANTASY

Author/illustrator Satomi Ichikawa invites readers into Nora's whimsical world in this enchanting series. Nora—with her dog, stuffed bear, and doll as faithful companions—turns any situation into an adventure. For example, a day spent inside with a cold turns exciting when friendly rose people appear and entertain her.

1. Nora's Castle ◆ 1986
2. Nora's Stars ◆ 1989
3. Nora's Duck ◆ 1991
4. Nora's Roses ◆ 1993
5. Nora's Surprise ◆ 1994

NORA AND TEDDY

Hurwitz, Johanna

PUFFIN

GRADES 3–4

FAMILY LIFE

This character-based series focuses on Nora's observations and reactions to life and the people around her. Nora and Teddy find ample situations and people to observe in their apartment building. They discover that some people don't appreciate their insights. Curious, outgoing, and imaginative Nora invites readers to share in her and Teddy's daily life. Each chapter is a new day for Nora and Teddy, which makes these books excellent for reading aloud. Nora and Teddy are friends with Russell and Elisa, who each have their own series of books.

1. Busybody Nora ◆ 1976
2. Nora and Mrs. Mind-Your-Own-Business ◆ 1977
3. New Neighbors for Nora ◆ 1979
4. Superduper Teddy ◆ 1980

NORBY

Asimov, Janet, and Isaac Asimov
WALKER PUBLISHING
GRADES 5–7
ADVENTURE | SCIENCE FICTION

Jeff Wells is a student at the Space Academy. He buys Norby as a teaching robot, but he soon discovers that Norby is unique. Norby has many useful abilities because he was fashioned from salvaged spaceship parts. In each novel, Jeff and Norby become involved in intergalactic intrigue. Often they must help Jeff's older, but not wiser, brother Fargo and save the galaxy. Science fiction, humor, and believable characters work well together in this entertaining series.

1. Norby, the Mixed-Up Robot ◆ 1983
2. Norby's Other Secret ◆ 1984
3. Norby and the Lost Princess ◆ 1985
4. Norby and the Invaders ◆ 1985
5. Norby and the Queen's Necklace ◆ 1986
6. Norby Finds a Villain ◆ 1987
7. Norby Down to Earth ◆ 1989
8. Norby and Yobo's Great Adventure ◆ 1989
9. Norby and the Oldest Dragon ◆ 1990
10. Norby and the Court Jester ◆ 1991
11. Norby and the Terrified Taxi ◆ 1997

NUTTY NUTSELL

Hughes, Dean
ATHENEUM
GRADES 4–6
HUMOR | REAL LIFE

"Nutty" Nutsell is a typical suburban fifth-grade boy when he is introduced in the first book of this series. However, when he meets William Bilks, Boy Genius, his life changes. Everyday situations are transformed into adventures as William challenges Nutty to try new things and stretch his mind to accomplish more. Each book of the series develops the strong bond of friendship between Nutty and William. Together they take on the challenges of their school and begin to understand life.

1. Nutty for President ◆ 1981
2. Nutty and the Case of the Mastermind Thief ◆ 1985
3. Nutty and the Case of the Ski-Slope Spy ◆ 1985
4. Nutty Can't Miss ◆ 1987
5. Nutty Knows All ◆ 1988
6. Nutty, the Movie Star ◆ 1989
7. Nutty's Ghost ◆ 1993
8. Re-elect Nutty! ◆ 1995

OBADIAH STARBUCK

Turkle, Brinton
VIKING
GRADES 2–3
FAMILY LIFE | HISTORICAL

Obadiah Starbuck is an energetic, irrepressible Quaker boy who lives in early-19th-century Nantucket. In one book, his parents admonish him for telling wildly exaggerated tales. In another, he decides that the wild life of a pirate is not what he wants. Whatever the situation, Obadiah and his family are quite likable, and the warm illustrations add to the cozy family atmosphere of this bygone time.

1. Obadiah the Bold ◆ 1965
2. Thy Friend, Obadiah ◆ 1969
3. The Adventures of Obadiah ◆ 1972
4. Rachel and Obadiah ◆ 1978

OLD BEAR STORIES

Hissey, Jane
PHILOMEL
GRADES K–2
FANTASY

Have you ever wondered what toys do when kids aren't around? In this series, they have adventures of their own. Teddy bears and other stuffed animals play games, have parties, and travel to the beach. The books are divided into individual stories, with poems interspersed. There are related board books.

1. Old Bear ◆ 1986

2. Old Bear Tales ◆ 1988
3. Little Bear Lost ◆ 1989
4. Little Bear's Trousers ◆ 1990

OLD TURTLE

Kessler, Leonard
GREENWILLOW
GRADES K–3
ANIMAL FANTASY | HUMOR

These are lovable stories about Old Turtle and his various animal friends, for students just beginning to read alone. They learn good sportsmanship when they play soccer and other games, write riddle and joke books, and generally have a good time.

1. Old Turtle's Baseball Stories ◆ 1982
2. Old Turtle's Winter Games ◆ 1983
3. Old Turtle's Soccer Team ◆ 1988

OLD WITCH

DeLage, Ida
GARRARD
GRADES K–2
FANTASY | HUMOR

Students just beginning to read alone will enjoy these humorous stories about the Old Witch and how she solves her problems by tricking people.

1. The Farmer and the Witch ◆ 1966
2. Weeny Witch ◆ 1968
3. The Old Witch Goes to the Ball ◆ 1969
4. The Old Witch and the Snores ◆ 1970
5. What Does a Witch Need? ◆ 1971
6. Beware! Beware! A Witch Won't Share ◆ 1972
7. The Old Witch and the Wizard ◆ 1974
8. The Old Witch's Party ◆ 1976
9. The Old Witch and the Ghost Parade ◆ 1978
10. The Old Witch and Her Magic Basket ◆ 1978
11. The Old Witch and the Dragon ◆ 1979
12. The Old Witch Finds a New House ◆ 1979
13. The Old Witch Gets a Surprise ◆ 1981
14. The Old Witch and the Crows ◆ 1983

OLGA DA POLGA

Bond, Michael
MACMILLAN
GRADES 3–5
ANIMAL FANTASY | HUMOR

Olga da Polga is a resourceful and imaginative guinea pig who goes to live with kind and loving humans who build her a wonderful home and take good care of her. Full of exaggerated tales of her life, she finds an appreciative audience in Noel, the cat; Fangio, the hedgehog; and other animal friends. Various adventures include an escape into the neighborhood, a visit from Santa, and another more-ominous visit from the dreaded Surrey Puma. Olga's tall tales often get her in trouble, but she is seldom abashed for long.

1. The Tales of Olga da Polga ◆ 1971
2. Olga Meets Her Match ◆ 1973
3. Olga Carries On ◆ 1977
4. Olga Takes Charge ◆ 1982

OLIVER AND AMANDA PIG

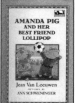

Van Leeuwen, Jean
DIAL; PUFFIN
GRADES K–2
ANIMAL FANTASY | FAMILY LIFE

Oliver Pig and his little sister Amanda have experiences that many siblings will identify with in this Puffin Easy-to-Read series. Though Oliver can be bossy and Amanda can be a pest, in the end they always learn to get along. Their adventures include celebrating holidays and going to school.

1. Tales of Oliver Pig ◆ 1979
2. More Tales of Oliver Pig ◆ 1981
3. Amanda Pig and Her Big Brother Oliver ◆ 1982
4. Tales of Amanda Pig ◆ 1983
5. More Tales of Amanda Pig ◆ 1985
6. Oliver, Amanda, and Grandmother Pig ◆ 1987
7. Oliver and Amanda's Christmas ◆ 1989
8. Oliver Pig at School ◆ 1990
9. Amanda Pig on Her Own ◆ 1991
10. Oliver and Amanda's Halloween ◆ 1992
11. Oliver and Amanda and the Big Snow ◆ 1995

12. Amanda Pig, School Girl ◆ 1997
13. Amanda Pig and Her Best Friend Lollipop ◆ 1998

OMRI *see* Indian in the Cupboard

THE ONCE AND FUTURE KING

White, Terence Hanbury
PUTNAM
GRADES 7–8
ADVENTURE | HISTORICAL

This classic series tells the entire glorious and tragic Arthurian legend. The first novel relates Arthur's life growing up with Kay, his older brother; Sir Ector, his father; and Merlyn, his tutor. The subsequent novels continue to unfold Arthur's life as he discovers that he is King and forms the Knights of the Round Table. Battles for power are fought and won, but Arthur's personal life unravels because of Sir Lancelot and Guinevere. This series is not merely a retelling, for T. H. White incorporates humor and fresh insights into the characters as real people with real problems. *The Book of Merlyn* was published separately in 1977, as a final chapter in the story.

1. The Sword in the Stone ◆ 1938
2. The Queen of Air and Darkness ◆ 1939
3. The Ill-Made Knight ◆ 1940
4. The Candle in the Wind ◆ 1958
5. The Book of Merlyn ◆ 1977

ONCE UPON AMERICA

Various authors
VIKING; PUFFIN
GRADES 3–6
HISTORICAL

This historical-fiction series is written by several authors, including Zibby Oneal, Kathleen V. Kudlinski, and Barthe deClements. Each book uses fictional characters to relate dramatic events from American history. Events such as the bombing of Pearl Harbor, the Alaskan Gold Rush, the Johnstown Flood, and the polio epidemic are brought to life through the eyes of people who were touched by them. This series would be a good one to share with readers of the American Girl, Girlhood Diaries, and Dear America series.

1. Hannah's Fancy Notions: A Story of Industrial New England (Ross, Pat) ◆ 1988
2. Hero Over Here: A Story of World War I (Kudlinski, Kathleen V.) ◆ 1990
3. A Long Way to Go: A Story of Women's Right to Vote (Oneal, Zibby) ◆ 1990
4. The Day It Rained Forever: A Story of the Johnstown Flood (Gross, Virginia T.) ◆ 1991
5. The Bite of the Gold Bug: A Story of the Alaskan Gold Rush (deClements, Barthe) ◆ 1992
6. Child Star: When Talkies Came to Hollywood (Weaver, Lydia) ◆ 1992
7. Fire! The Beginnings of the Labor Movement (Goldin, Barbara Diamond) ◆ 1992
8. It's Only Goodbye: An Immigrant Story (Gross, Virginia T.) ◆ 1992
9. Close to Home: A Story of the Polio Epidemic (Weaver, Lydia) ◆ 1993
10. Earthquake! A Story of Old San Francisco (Kudlinski, Kathleen V.) ◆ 1993
11. Hard Times: A Story of the Great Depression (Antle, Nancy) ◆ 1993
12. Night Bird: A Story of the Seminole Indians (Kudlinski, Kathleen V.) ◆ 1993
13. Pearl Harbor Is Burning! A Story of World War II (Kudlinski, Kathleen V.) ◆ 1993
14. Facing West: A Story of the Oregon Trail (Kudlinski, Kathleen V.) ◆ 1994
15. Lone Star: A Story of the Texas Rangers (Kudlinski, Kathleen V.) ◆ 1994
16. Red Means Good Fortune: A Story of San Francisco's Chinatown (Goldin, Barbara Diamond) ◆ 1996

ORP

Kline, Suzy

PUTNAM

GRADES 4–6

HUMOR | REAL LIFE

Orp (Orville Rudemeyer Pygenski, Jr.) and his best friend, Derrick, are inseparable. When Derrick asks Orp to try out for the basketball team with him, Orp agrees—although he's not sure that he'll make it. Orp is a likable character whose experiences are common to junior high kids. He is loyal to his friends and is annoyed by his younger sister Chloe. Whether he's forming the I Hate My Name Club or the F.B.I. (Famous Bathtub Investigators), Orp turns everyday happenings into events.

1. Orp ◆ 1989

2. Orp and the Chop Suey Burgers ◆ 1990
3. Orp Goes to the Hoop ◆ 1991
4. Who's Orp's Girlfriend? ◆ 1993
5. Orp and the FBI ◆ 1995

ORPHAN TRAIN ADVENTURES

Nixon, Joan Lowery

DELACORTE

GRADES 5–8

FAMILY LIFE | HISTORICAL

Originally published as a quartet of books, this series has been extended to relate more adventures of the Kelly children. The first book, *A Family Apart*, sets the stage for the series, which takes place in the mid-1800s. When their mother can no longer support them, the six Kelly children are sent from New York City to Missouri on an orphan train. They are placed with different farm families across the Great Plains. The series describes their experiences from the oldest, Frances Mary Kelly, to the youngest, Peaty. In *Caught in the Act*, Michael Patrick Kelly faces cruelty and a harsh life on a Missouri farm and, in a later book, becomes a Union soldier. Though orphan trains did exist, the characters and plots in this series are fictional.

1. A Family Apart ◆ 1987
2. Caught in the Act ◆ 1988
3. In the Face of Danger ◆ 1988
4. A Place to Belong ◆ 1989
5. A Dangerous Promise ◆ 1994
6. Keeping Secrets ◆ 1995
7. Circle of Love ◆ 1997

ORPHAN TRAIN CHILDREN

Nixon, Joan Lowery

DELACORTE

GRADES 3–5

HISTORICAL

In the Orphan Train Adventures, Joan Lowery Nixon focused on the six children in the Kelly family. In the Orphan Train Children series, each book describes the circumstances of an individual child. There is no connection among the children other than their participation on the orphan trains. In *Aggie's Home*, Agatha Mae Vaughn gets a fresh start with the

Bradons but there are adjustments along with the opportunities. David Howard, 11, arrives on a farm in Missouri knowing nothing about rural life and is aided by Amos, an ex-slave, in *David's Search*. Historical information, including documents and maps, follow each story.

1. Lucy's Wish ◆ 1998
2. Will's Choice ◆ 1998
3. Aggie's Home ◆ 1998
4. David's Search ◆ 1998

ORPHELINES

Carlson, Natalie Savage
BANTAM DOUBLEDAY DELL
GRADES 3–4
FAMILY LIFE

The Orphelines series takes its name from the French word for girl orphans. Josine is the youngest of the 20 girls; Brigitte is known as the happiest. Madame Flattot takes care of them all and calls them her family. The girls consider the boys from the orphanage their brothers. This large family has many exciting times together. In one book, Josine finds a foundling baby boy whom they all want to adopt. Another time, they search for a grandmother to make their family complete. Their high spirits and imaginations sometimes get them into trouble, but matters are always resolved in a loving manner.

1. The Happy Orpheline ◆ 1957
2. A Brother for the Orphelines ◆ 1959
3. A Pet for the Orphelines ◆ 1962
4. The Orphelines in the Enchanted Castle ◆ 1964
5. A Grandmother for the Orphelines ◆ 1980

OSCAR J. NOODLEMAN

Manes, Stephen
DUTTON
GRADES 3–5
HUMOR | SCIENCE FICTION

Oscar J. Noodleman has some of the world's strangest adventures in this series. It's not clear whether his world is the present or the future—it's more like a parallel universe. In one book, he has his own television network; in another, he eats his way across the United States with a crazy second cousin. These silly books are sure to tempt reluctant readers.

1. That Game from Outer Space ◆ 1983
2. Oscar J. Noodleman Television Network ◆ 1984
3. Chicken Trek ◆ 1987

OTTO

Pène Du Bois, William
VIKING
GRADES 1–3
FANTASY

Otto is a world-famous giant dog. He has performed many heroic deeds that have earned him medals, such as catching some very bad men in Texas. Although Otto seems to be simply acting as any dog would, he is always in the right place at the right time. Otto and his master Duke sometimes find it difficult to relax because they are recognized wherever they go. Nevertheless, they enjoy helping the people they meet.

1. Giant Otto ◆ 1936
2. Otto at Sea ◆ 1936
3. Otto in Texas ◆ 1959
4. Otto in Africa ◆ 1961
5. Otto and the Magic Potatoes ◆ 1970

OUR SECRET GANG

Gilligan, Shannon
BANTAM
GRADES 4–6
MYSTERY

Four friends feel isolated by individual problems. When Davey finds Jeanine crying, they decide to open up to each other, sharing their secret worries. Two other sixth-grade friends, Nancy and Jason, also end up telling their concerns and the friends form "Our Secret Gang." Having good friends that you can trust with your secrets is a relief for each student. Now, they can put their energy toward solving mysteries—like finding the missing hands from the clock tower at the museum. At the end of each book, a crime scene technique is explained, such as taking fingerprints and writing with invisible ink.

1. The Clue in the Clock Tower ◆ 1991
2. The Haunted Swamp ◆ 1991
3. The Case of the Missing Formula ◆ 1991
4. The Locker Thief ◆ 1991

5. Science-lab Sabotage ◆ 1991
6. There's a Body in the Brontosaurus Room! ◆ 1992

OUTER BANKS TRILOGY

Taylor, Theodore
DOUBLEDAY
GRADES 5–8
ADVENTURE | HISTORICAL

This adventure trilogy is by the author of *The Cay*. Teetoncey is a frail young girl whom Ben helps rescue from a shipwreck, but many mysteries surround her. Later, as he searches for his brother, he discovers that their fates are more closely entwined than he first thought.

1. Teetoncey ◆ 1974
2. Teetoncey and Ben O'Neal ◆ 1975
3. The Odyssey of Ben O'Neal ◆ 1977

THE OUTER LIMITS

Peel, John
TOR BOOK
GRADES 6–8
FANTASY | HORROR

The books in this series feature different characters in fantastic, even bizarre, situations. In *The Zanti Misfits*, the Zanti have sent their problem creatures to Earth, putting human society in danger of destruction. Deciding what to do with these dangerous misfits is a dilemma—the misfits may destroy Earth, but killing them may bring the wrath of the Zanti. Another book features a character with telekinetic powers, and still another deals with the planet Tarnish, which is ruled by children. Recommend this series to readers who like unusual creatures and surprising plot twists.

1. The Zanti Misfits ◆ 1997
2. The Choice ◆ 1997
3. The Time Shifter ◆ 1997
4. The Lost ◆ 1997
5. The Invaders ◆ 1998
6. The Innocent ◆ 1998

Oz

Baum, Lyman Frank

MORROW; GREENWILLOW

GRADES 5–8

FANTASY

The popular *Wizard of Oz* was only the first of a great many adventures about the land of Oz, which were continued by others after Baum's death. Dorothy returns many times and fights villains; and other children, such as Peter and Betsy Bobbins, find their way to the magical land. The Tin Man and Scarecrow are involved in various battles for the control of Oz, but Ozma of Oz is the rightful ruler. All the books share a rich and detailed fantasy laced with satire. The first fifteen books were written by L. Frank Baum. Other authors have extended the series. Greenwillow has reissued many of these titles in its Books of Wonder series.

ORIGINAL OZ BOOKS

1. The Wonderful Wizard of Oz ◆ 1900
2. The New Wizard of Oz ◆ 1903
3. The Marvelous Land of Oz ◆ 1904
4. Ozma of Oz ◆ 1907
5. Dorothy and the Wizard of Oz ◆ 1908
6. The Road to Oz ◆ 1909
7. The Emerald City of Oz ◆ 1910
8. The Patchwork Girl of Oz ◆ 1913
9. Tik-Tok of Oz ◆ 1914
10. The Scarecrow of Oz ◆ 1915
11. Rinkitink in Oz ◆ 1916
12. The Lost Princess of Oz ◆ 1917
13. The Tin Woodman of Oz ◆ 1918
14. The Magic of Oz ◆ 1919
15. Glinda of Oz ◆ 1920

OZ CONTINUED

1. The Royal Book of Oz (Thompson, Ruth Plumly) ◆ 1921
2. The Cowardly Lion of Oz (Thompson, Ruth Plumly) ◆ 1923
3. Grampa in Oz (Thompson, Ruth Plumly) ◆ 1924
4. The Lost King of Oz (Thompson, Ruth Plumly) ◆ 1925
5. The Hungry Tiger in Oz (Thompson, Ruth Plumly) ◆ 1926
6. The Gnome King of Oz (Thompson, Ruth Plumly) ◆ 1927
7. The Giant Horse of Oz (Thompson, Ruth Plumly) ◆ 1928
8. Jack Pumpkinhead of Oz (Thompson, Ruth Plumly) ◆ 1929

9. The Yellow Knight of Oz (Thompson, Ruth Plumly) ◆ 1930
10. The Pirates in Oz (Thompson, Ruth Plumly) ◆ 1931
11. Purple Prince of Oz (Thompson, Ruth Plumly) ◆ 1932
12. Ojo in Oz (Thompson, Ruth Plumly) ◆ 1933
13. Speedy in Oz (Thompson, Ruth Plumly) ◆ 1934
14. Wishing Horse of Oz (Thompson, Ruth Plumly) ◆ 1935
15. Captain Salt in Oz (Thompson, Ruth Plumly) ◆ 1936
16. Kabumpo in Oz (Thompson, Ruth Plumly) ◆ 1936
17. Handy Mandy in Oz (Thompson, Ruth Plumly) ◆ 1937
18. The Silver Princess in Oz (Thompson, Ruth Plumly) ◆ 1938
19. Ozoplaning with the Wizard of Oz (Thompson, Ruth Plumly) ◆ 1939
20. The Wonder City of Oz (Neill, John Rea) ◆ 1940
21. The Scalawagons of Oz (Neill, John Rea) ◆ 1941
22. Lucky Bucky in Oz (Neill, John Rea) ◆ 1942
23. The Magical Mimics in Oz (Snow, Jack) ◆ 1946
24. The Shaggy Man of Oz (Snow, Jack) ◆ 1949
25. Hidden Valley of Oz (Cosgrove, Rachel) ◆ 1951
26. Merry Go Round in Oz (McGraw, Eloise Jervis) ◆ 1963
27. Yankee in Oz (Thompson, Ruth Plumly) ◆ 1972
28. Autocrats of Oz (Suter, Jon Michael) ◆ 1976
29. Enchanted Island of Oz (Thompson, Ruth Plumly) ◆ 1976
30. Orange Knight of Oz (Suter, Jon Michael) ◆ 1976
31. Forbidden Fountain of Oz (McGraw, Eloise Jervis) ◆ 1980
32. Barnstormer in Oz (Farmer, Philip Jose) ◆ 1982
33. Return to Oz (Vinge, Joan Dennison) ◆ 1982
34. Dorothy and the Magic Belt (Saunders, Susan) ◆ 1985
35. Mister Tinker of Oz (Howe, James) ◆ 1985
36. Dorothy of Oz (Baum, Roger S.) ◆ 1989
37. Rewolf of Oz (Baum, Roger S.) ◆ 1990
38. How the Wizard Came to Oz (Abbott, Donald) ◆ 1991
39. SillyOZbuls of Oz (Baum, Roger S.) ◆ 1991
40. The Nome King's Shadow in Oz (Sprague, Gilbert M.) ◆ 1992
41. The SillyOZbul of Oz and the Magic Merry-Go-Round (Baum, Roger S.) ◆ 1992
42. The SillyOZbul of Oz & Toto (Baum, Roger S.) ◆ 1992
43. The Blue Witch of Oz (Shanower, Eric) ◆ 1993
44. The Enchanted Apples of Oz (Shanower, Eric) ◆ 1993
45. The Forgotten Forest of Oz (Shanower, Eric) ◆ 1993
46. The Giant Garden of Oz (Shanower, Eric) ◆ 1993
47. The Magic Chest of Oz (Abbott, Donald) ◆ 1993
48. The Patchwork Bride of Oz (Sprague, Gilbert M.) ◆ 1993
49. Queen Ann in Oz (Carlson, Karyl, and Eric Gjovaag) ◆ 1993
50. Father Goose in Oz (Abbott, Donald) ◆ 1994
51. Christmas in Oz (Hess, Robin) ◆ 1995
52. The Glass Cat of Oz (Hulan, David) ◆ 1995
53. The Magic Dishpan of Oz (Freedman, Jeff) ◆ 1995
54. Masquerade in Oz (Campbell, Bill, and Irwin Terry) ◆ 1995
55. The Runaway in Oz (Neill, John R.) ◆ 1995

56. The Speckled Rose of Oz (Abbott, Donald) ◆ 1995
57. How the Wizard Saved Oz (Abbott, Donald) ◆ 1996
58. The Lavender Bear of Oz (Campbell, Bill) ◆ 1998

P.J. FUNNYBUNNY

Sadler, Marilyn
RANDOM HOUSE
GRADES K–1
ANIMAL FANTASY | HUMOR

P.J. Funnybunny doesn't mean to be bad, but he is always getting into trouble with his family. When his cousin comes over to play, he is even worse than P.J. and all the Funnybunnys are glad to see him go. The whole family pitches in to help P.J. win the Great Turtle Creek Tricycle Race, even though he takes the first turn too fast and falls down. When he goes camping with his friends, he refuses to take his sister along. She and her friend come anyway, but ghosts scare them all home. Extra-large text and short sentences will appeal to beginning readers. There are skills books featuring P.J. Funnybunny.

1. It's Not Easy Being a Bunny ◆ 1983
2. P.J. The Spoiled Bunny ◆ 1986
3. P.J. Funnybunny in the Great Tricycle Race ◆ 1988
4. P.J. Funnybunny in the Perfect Hiding Place ◆ 1988
5. P.J. Funnybunny Camps Out ◆ 1994
6. P.J. Funnybunny and His Very Cool Birthday Party ◆ 1996
7. Honey Bunny Funnybunny ◆ 1997

PADDINGTON

Bond, Michael
HOUGHTON MIFFLIN
GRADES 2–5
ANIMAL FANTASY | HUMOR

After Mr. and Mrs. Brown see Paddington at the train station with a note that states, "Please look after this bear. Thank you," their lives are never the same. The Brown children, Jonathan and Judy, are delighted when Paddington arrives. He nearly floods the house when he takes his first bath. When asked to usher at a wedding, he gets the ring stuck on his paw. Paddington, a gentle, well-meaning bear, unwittingly causes havoc wherever he goes. There are related groups of picture books and activity books for very young children.

1. A Bear Called Paddington ◆ 1958
2. More About Paddington ◆ 1959
3. Paddington Helps Out ◆ 1960
4. Paddington Abroad ◆ 1961
5. Paddington at Large ◆ 1962
6. Paddington Marches On ◆ 1964
7. Paddington at Work ◆ 1966
8. Paddington Goes to Town ◆ 1968
9. Paddington Takes the Air ◆ 1970
10. Paddington on Top ◆ 1974
11. Paddington on Stage ◆ 1977
12. Paddington Takes the Test ◆ 1979

PADDY PORK

Goodall, John Strickland

ATHENEUM

GRADES K–3

ANIMAL FANTASY

Paddy is a sophisticated, helpful pig whose adventures are portrayed without words in detailed drawings. He goes to Monte Carlo, tries to rescue a young pig's lost kite, and ends up on top of a car headed for the Swiss Alps. Later, the dauntless pig pursues a robber over land and sea and finally gets his man. When he tries to do odd jobs, he gets into one disaster after another; but finally he finds a missing child, to the delight of all the animals in town. Turn-of-the-century Old-World costumes and scenery surround the courtly pig and provide entertainment for young and old.

1. The Adventures of Paddy Pork ◆ 1968
2. The Ballooning Adventures of Paddy Pork ◆ 1969
3. Paddy's Evening Out ◆ 1973
4. Paddy Pork's Holiday ◆ 1976
5. Paddy's New Hat ◆ 1980
6. Paddy Goes Traveling ◆ 1982
7. Paddy Pork, Odd Jobs ◆ 1983
8. Paddy Under Water ◆ 1984
9. Paddy to the Rescue ◆ 1986

PASSPORT

Various authors

BANTAM

GRADES 4–8

ADVENTURE | REAL LIFE

Intrigue, suspense, adventure, mystery—these are all elements of the Passport Choose Your Own Adventure series. Exotic locations around the world provide the settings for these books, which allow readers to select the direction of the plot. Many reluctant readers are attracted to these books, which combine excitement and reader participation.

1. Tour de France (Beckett, James) ◆ 1992
2. Forgotten Days (Mueller, Kate) ◆ 1992
3. On Tour (McMurtry, Ken) ◆ 1992
4. Path of the Crusaders (McMurtry, Ken) ◆ 1992
5. Mystery on the Trans-Siberian Express (McMurtry, Ken) ◆ 1992
6. Manhunt (McMurtry, Ken) ◆ 1992

PATRICK'S PALS

Armstrong, Robb
HarperCollins
Grades 3–6
Recreation

This fiction series features three real NBA players—Patrick Ewing, Dikembe Mutombo, and Alonzo Mourning—in stories that portray them as school-aged friends who love basketball. There is lots of basketball action, but there are also themes about teamwork, fair play, and the importance of an education. In one book, the friends are in a Thanksgiving play, but their math grades are suffering. Their math teacher gives them an ultimatum: better grades or no play . . . and no basketball, either. Patrick's friend Ronnie Miller (who is a fictional character) devises a plan to cheat, prompting Patrick to make a choice. Many reluctant readers will be attracted by the high-profile NBA stars.

1. Runnin' with the Big Dawgs ◆ 1998
2. In Your Face! ◆ 1998
3. Got Game? ◆ 1998
4. Stuffin' It ◆ 1998
5. Schoolin' ◆ 1998

PAXTON CHEERLEADERS

Hall, Katy
Minstrel/Pocket Books
Grades 6–8
Real Life | Recreation

Patti wants to be one of the Paxton cheerleaders. She has been practicing with her friend, Tara, for the tryouts, but Tara can't do all the moves. Will Patti stick with her friend or find a way to get on the team on her own? This is the sort of dilemma in this series. Lauren and Cassie have to deal with not always being the best while Patti has to resist being influenced by a new girl. School concerns, worries about boys, and team spirit are issues that will appeal to young teen readers.

1. Go for It, Patti! ◆ 1994
2. Three Cheers for You, Cassie! ◆ 1994
3. Winning Isn't Everything, Lauren! ◆ 1994
4. We're in This Together, Patti! ◆ 1995
5. Nobody's Perfect, Cassie! ◆ 1995
6. We Did It, Tara! ◆ 1995

PEACH STREET MUDDERS

Christopher, Matt

LITTLE, BROWN

GRADES 2–4

REAL LIFE | RECREATION

Readers who are a bit too young for some of Matt Christopher's longer sports stories will find something on their level in his Peach Street Mudders series. Nicky is going after a league record for RBIs and is very superstitious about it. He goes through pre-batting rituals and doesn't want anyone to mention the record. The holder of the record tries a little sabotage to keep it, but the effort is thwarted. Turtleneck, after being hit by a ball, becomes afraid, until a blind neighbor helps him to overcome his fears. There is enough baseball action and lingo here to satisfy die-hard fans and enough of a story to appeal to all.

1. The Hit-Away Kid ◆ 1988
2. The Spy on Third Base ◆ 1988
3. Centerfield Ballhawk ◆ 1992
4. Man Out at First ◆ 1993
5. Zero's Slider ◆ 1994
6. All-Star Fever ◆ 1995
7. Shadow Over Second ◆ 1996
8. Baseball Turnaround ◆ 1997
9. Stranger in Right Field ◆ 1997
10. The Catcher's Mask ◆ 1998

PEANUT BUTTER AND JELLY

Haas, Dorothy

SCHOLASTIC

GRADES 2–4

REAL LIFE

After the death of her father, Polly Butterman and her family move to a new town. While living with Grandpa in Evanston, Illinois, Polly gets a new puppy, but she struggles to adjust to being the new kid. Nicknamed Peanut, lively Polly meets Jillian "Jilly" Matthews, who is quiet. The two girls become friends and enjoy working on school projects and solving neighborhood problems. Many readers will relate to the common concerns, like the time that Peanut's best friend from Minneapolis—Regan—comes to visit her in Evanston. How can you have two best friends? The books in this series have been especially popular with middle grade girls.

1. New Friends ◆ 1988
2. Peanut and Jilly Forever ◆ 1988
3. The Haunted House ◆ 1988
4. Trouble at Alcott School ◆ 1989
5. Not Starring Jilly! ◆ 1989
6. Peanut in Charge ◆ 1989
7. The Friendship Test ◆ 1990
8. Two Friends Too Many ◆ 1990
9. Alcott Library Is Falling Down ◆ 1991

PEE WEE SCOUTS

Delton, Judy

BANTAM

GRADES 2–4

REAL LIFE

The Pee Wee Scouts meet in Mrs. Peter's basement after school, and they love getting badges. They are a group of normal-acting kids, including rude boys and the girls they annoy. Molly is the point-of-view character, but there are 13 scouts altogether. Each book in the series is about another badge that the scouts earn and their different reactions to it. A hobby badge is announced, and Molly can't think of anything to do, while most of the others have good ideas. Getting library cards doesn't sound like fun at first, but they all learn to enjoy reading more and Molly helps Tim, who is having trouble reading. The Pee Wee song and a Pee Wee badge to cut out are included in each title.

1. Cookies and Crutches ◆ 1988
2. Camp Ghost-Away ◆ 1988
3. Lucky Dog Days ◆ 1988
4. Blue Skies, French Fries ◆ 1988
5. Grumpy Pumkins ◆ 1988
6. Peanut-Butter Pilgrims ◆ 1988
7. A Pee Wee Christmas ◆ 1988
8. That Mushy Stuff ◆ 1989
9. Spring Sprouts ◆ 1989
10. Pooped Troop ◆ 1989
11. The Pee Wee Jubilee ◆ 1989

12. Bad, Bad Bunnies ◆ 1990
13. Rosy Noses, Freezing Toes ◆ 1990
14. Sonny's Secret ◆ 1991
15. Sky Babies ◆ 1991
16. Trash Bash ◆ 1992
17. Pee Wees on Parade ◆ 1992
18. Lights, Action, Land-ho! ◆ 1992
19. Piles of Pets ◆ 1993
20. Fishy Wishes ◆ 1993
21. Pee Wees on Skis ◆ 1993
22. Greedy Groundhogs ◆ 1994
23. All Dads on Deck ◆ 1994
24. Tricks and Treats ◆ 1994
25. Pee Wees on First ◆ 1995
26. Super Duper Pee Wee! ◆ 1995
27. Teeny Weeny Zucchinis ◆ 1995
28. Eggs With Legs ◆ 1996
29. Pee Wee Pool Party ◆ 1996
30. Bookworm Buddies ◆ 1996
31. Moans and Groans and Dinosaur Bones ◆ 1997
32. Stage Frightened ◆ 1997
33. Halloween Helpers ◆ 1997
34. Planet Pee Wee ◆ 1998
35. Pedal Power ◆ 1998
36. Computer Clues ◆ 1998
37. Wild, Wild West ◆ 1999

PENGUIN PETE

Pfister, Marcus

NORTH-SOUTH BOOKS

GRADES K–2

ANIMAL FANTASY

Pete is a penguin who lives in an icy land. One adventure features Pete and his young son, Little Tim. Papa Pete shows Little Tim around the frozen landscape and when he is tired carries him home to Mother Pat. Another book finds Pete on an abandoned ship with a young mouse named Horatio. Pete finds it difficult to do the tasks on the ship, but he saves the day when his help is needed out at sea. This series features animal families and friends in sweet and humorous situations.

1. Penguin Pete ◆ 1987
2. Penguin Pete's New Friends ◆ 1988
3. Penguin Pete and Pat ◆ 1989

4. Penguin Pete, Ahoy! ◆ 1993
5. Penguin Pete and Little Tim ◆ 1994

PENNY

Haywood, Carolyn
HARCOURT
GRADES 2–4
FAMILY LIFE

A little boy with hair the color of a new penny is adopted and called Penny by his adoptive parents. When he is older, his neighbor Patsy tells him during a quarrel that he is not really his Mommy and Daddy's boy. His mother explains that he is theirs because they chose him, so he decides he will adopt a kitten the same way. He meets Peter, a boy from an orphanage, who helps him learn to play baseball. Penny asks his parents if they will adopt Peter, too. They finally agree, and the two boys continue their adventures together. Their father rents a cabin in the woods that the boys long to own, and they fish and explore a stream. Patsy joins the boys occasionally, and one chapter is about her huge dog, Tootsie. Gentle tales set in the 1950s will show young readers a simpler time.

1. Here's Penny ◆ 1944
2. Penny and Peter ◆ 1946
3. Penny Goes to Camp ◆ 1948

PENROD

Christian, Mary Blount
MACMILLAN
GRADES K–2
ANIMAL FANTASY

A little porcupine named Penrod always manages to hoodwink his best friend Griswold, a bear. Amusing, detailed, full-color illustrations accompany the short chapter stories. Griswold persuades Penrod that he needs glasses, but the only reason he can't see is that his hair is too long. Later, Penrod lets Griswold know that he is having a party but that Griswold is not invited. Griswold's reaction is "GRR" when he finds out the party is a surprise for him.

1. Penrod's Pants ◆ 1986
2. Penrod Again ◆ 1987
3. Penrod's Party ◆ 1990
4. Penrod's Picture ◆ 1991

PET LOVERS CLUB

Roos, Stephen
DELACORTE
GRADES 3–5
REAL LIFE

The Pet Lovers Club has 12 members. Each book in this series features one of the members and a problem with a pet. They also correlate with a holiday. For Halloween, the Pet Lovers plan a party, and one member, Bernie, tries to find a way to keep a stray dog. An Easter story focuses on Erin's rabbit. The Christmas story looks at Lem, who wants his own pet so much that he makes up a story about getting a crocodile. The club has fund-raising events for animal shelters that might provide readers with ideas for their own service projects. Betsy Duffey's Pet Patrol series would complement these books.

1. Love Me, Love My Werewolf ◆ 1991
2. Crocodile Christmas ◆ 1992
3. The Cottontail Caper ◆ 1992

PET PATROL

Duffey, Betsy
PUFFIN
GRADES 2–4
REAL LIFE

Evie and Megan love animals. In fact, they have formed their own Pet Patrol to look out for lost or needy animals. Of course, they face many problems when they find them. In one book the girls try to care for four puppies; in another book, they try to find the owners of some abandoned pets. In *Wild Things*, they even solve a minor mystery over why the trash cans are being raided. These are easy-to-read books that will connect with readers who enjoy humorous stories and pets.

1. Puppy Love ◆ 1992
2. Wild Things ◆ 1993
3. Throw-Away Pets ◆ 1993

PETER

Keats, Ezra Jack

VIKING

GRADES K–2

REAL LIFE

In *The Snowy Day* (which won the Caldecott Medal), Peter is a young boy out on his own in the snow. Each succeeding book follows Peter on a new adventure as he grows older. In one book, he is apprehensive about the arrival of a new sibling. In another, he worries about what his friends will say after he invites a girl to his birthday party. Peter enjoys everyday activities like learning to whistle for his dog, Willie, and playing with friends. When Peter is older, his young friend Archie becomes the focus of some stories—when the boys participate in a pet show and when they find a pair of goggles. This is a very popular series with African American characters and an urban setting.

1. The Snowy Day ◆ 1962
2. Whistle for Willie ◆ 1964
3. Peter's Chair ◆ 1967
4. A Letter to Amy ◆ 1968
5. Goggles ◆ 1969
6. Hi, Cat! ◆ 1970
7. Pet Show ◆ 1972

PETSITTERS CLUB

Krailing, Tessa

BARRON'S

GRADES 2–4

REAL LIFE

Sam (Samantha) got the idea for the Petsitters Club while she was weeding Mrs. Bratby's garden. She and her friends Jovan, Matthew, and Katie were always looking for community service projects that would be acceptable to Mr. Grantham, the principal of their school. Watching a goat, worrying about a snake, even supervising a guess-the-weight contest for Scruncher the pig keep the friends busy. Originally published in Great

Britain, the setting is not clearly defined. This is a good choice for middle grade readers and pet enthusiasts.

1. Jilly the Kid ◆ 1998
2. The Cat Burglar ◆ 1998
3. Donkey Rescue ◆ 1998
4. Snake Alarm! ◆ 1998
5. Scruncher Goes Wandering ◆ 1998
6. Trixie and the Cyber Pet ◆ 1998

PETUNIA

Duvoisin, Roger

KNOPF

GRADES K–2

ANIMAL FANTASY | HUMOR

Petunia, a silly goose, finds a book and remembers hearing the farmer say that books will make one wise. Thinking she can lose her reputation for silliness and become wise, she starts to carry the book around. Noisy the dog, Clover the cow, and the other animals begin to think she is wise and go along with her in all sorts of silly solutions to their problems. Other barnyard adventures include being wooed by an amorous raccoon and having a song written just for her by the farmer's wife. A funny, classic picture book series that makes a good family read-aloud.

1. Petunia ◆ 1950
2. Petunia and the Song ◆ 1951
3. Petunia's Christmas ◆ 1952
4. Petunia Takes a Trip ◆ 1953
5. Petunia, Beware! ◆ 1958
6. Our Veronica Goes to Petunia's Farm ◆ 1962
7. Petunia, I Love You ◆ 1965
8. Petunia's Treasure ◆ 1975

PHANTOM RIDER

Simner, Janni Lee

SCHOLASTIC

GRADES 4–6

FANTASY

Callie Fern is struggling to adjust to her new home in Arizona. One night, she looks out her window and sees a beautiful silvery horse that turns out to be a ghost. Only Callie can see the ghost horse, Star, who comes to her aid in many ways and eases her loneliness. When Callie does make friends, Amy and Melissa, and the girls are stranded on a rugged trail, Star comes to their rescue. In one book, Callie and Star are both affected by a strange, numbing cold and they must join their powers to escape it. Merging ghosts and the supernatural with the ever-popular horse stories will make this attractive to many readers.

1. Ghost Horse ◆ 1996
2. The Haunted Trail ◆ 1996
3. Ghost Vision ◆ 1996

PIG PIG

McPhail, David

DUTTON

GRADES K–2

ANIMAL FANTASY | HUMOR

Pig Pig doesn't want to grow up. He insists on wearing his old baby clothes and riding in a too-small stroller. Then one day he is caught in an emergency with a real baby and decides to grow up fast. In *Pig Pig Rides*, he tells his mother at breakfast about all the adventures he is going to have on trains, planes, and motorcycles, and she wants to know if he'll be home for dinner. Adults will enjoy the absurd humor and full-color illustrations of this read-aloud series.

1. Pig Pig Grows Up ◆ 1980
2. Pig Pig Rides ◆ 1982
3. Pig Pig Goes to Camp ◆ 1983
4. Pig Pig and the Magic Photo Album ◆ 1986
5. Pig Pig Gets a Job ◆ 1990

PIGANEERS

Salmon, Michael

SIMON & SCHUSTER

GRADES K–2

ANIMAL FANTASY | HUMOR

Climb aboard the *Hogwash* for fun and adventure. Captain Porker runs a shipshape ship—except when the crew plays a prank and hides his treasure. The crew acts up again when they have to let a woman on the ship—but no one will say no to Big Boar's mom! What do "piganeers" do when they are bored? How about putting on a talent show? The fourth book,

Peg Leg Pete and the Mermaid, shows the piganeers at their best as they come to the aid of a mermaid. Cartoon-style illustrations add to the fun of this silly series.

1. Who Stole Captain Porker's Treasure? ◆ 1998
2. Big Boar's Mom Comes to Stay ◆ 1998
3. Talent Night Aboard the Hogwash ◆ 1998
4. Peg Leg Pete and the Mermaid ◆ 1998

PIGGINS

Yolen, Jane
HARCOURT
GRADES K–3
ANIMAL FANTASY | MYSTERY

Piggins, the butler at the home of Mr. and Mrs. Reynard at 47 The Meadows, is a sophisticated and handsome pig. A veteran of the Boar Wars, he solves mysteries and is a favorite of the Reynard children, Rexy and Trixy. When they are in a royal wedding, Rexy is accused of stealing the wedding ring. Piggins is called in, concludes that the ring was a fake, and points the police to the real thief. On a picnic by the river, the children concoct their own mystery for him to solve—a birthday surprise. Detailed full-color illustrations portray a wealthy turn-of-the-century animal world.

1. Piggins ◆ 1988
2. Picnic with Piggins ◆ 1988
3. Piggins and the Royal Wedding ◆ 1989

PIGS

Dubanevich, Arlene
FRANKLIN WATTS
GRADES K–2
ANIMAL FANTASY | HUMOR

Cartoonlike adventures of a large family of pig brothers and sisters feature zany action on every page. Pete is in charge when they go to the circus because their Mom gave him the money. Piggles, the baby, doesn't want to give her hat up at the hat check—and that's just the beginning of Pete's troubles with her. Chasing her balloon, she breaks up a team of pig acrobats and distracts a juggler who is trying to set the record for the most peanut butter sandwiches juggled. The whole circus joins in to rescue her when she chases the balloon up a tower. Other books find the pigs celebrating Christmas and playing hide-and-seek.

1. Pigs in Hiding ◆ 1983
2. Pig William ◆ 1985
3. Pigs at Christmas ◆ 1986
4. The Piggest Show on Earth ◆ 1988

PIGS

Geisert, Arthur

HOUGHTON MIFFLIN

GRADES K–1

ANIMAL FANTASY

These adventures of a pig family use just one word: *oink*. Mama Pig shows her piglets around the farm until she goes to sleep, when they decide to go out on their own. In the next book, the piglets get into a field of corn and Mama comes roaring after them. They escape to the river and enjoy the corn. In *Pigs from 1 to 10*, the piglets are determined to find a "lost place with stone configurations." The configurations are the numbers 1 to 9, which also are hidden in each picture. Black-and-white drawings accompany the minimal text.

1. Pigs from A to Z ◆ 1986
2. Oink ◆ 1991
3. Pigs from 1 to 10 ◆ 1992
4. Oink Oink ◆ 1993

PINKERTON

Kellogg, Steven

DIAL

GRADES K–2

FAMILY LIFE | HUMOR

Pinkerton is a Great Dane whose size and enthusiasm create many predicaments for the little girl and her family who own him. In various books, Pinkerton is taken to obedience school, he and his family befriend a cat named Rose, he meets up with hunters searching for a fox, and he visits the Natural History Museum. Each situation offers a great opportunity for zany adventures. Kellogg's illustrations are great, filled with action and fun. Young readers will enjoy Pinkerton's antics and want to read more.

1. Pinkerton, Behave! ◆ 1979
2. A Rose for Pinkerton ◆ 1981
3. Tallyho, Pinkerton ◆ 1983
4. Prehistoric Pinkerton ◆ 1987

PINKY AND REX

Howe, James

SIMON & SCHUSTER

GRADES 1–3

REAL LIFE

Pinky loves the color pink and stuffed animals. His friend Rex lives across the street, and she loves dinosaurs. They do everything together, including coping with Pinky's little sister Amanda. When they all go to the museum together, they see a pink dinosaur in the gift shop, but no one has enough money for it. They solve the problem by putting all their money together and sharing it. As the series continues, Pinky and Rex have a play wedding and compete in a school spelling bee.

1. Pinky and Rex ◆ 1990
2. Pinky and Rex Get Married ◆ 1990
3. Pinky and Rex and the Spelling Bee ◆ 1991
4. Pinky and Rex and the Mean Old Witch ◆ 1991
5. Pinky and Rex Go to Camp ◆ 1992
6. Pinky and Rex and the New Baby ◆ 1993
7. Pinky and Rex and the Double-Dad Weekend ◆ 1995
8. Pinky and Rex and the Bully ◆ 1996
9. Pinky and Rex and the New Neighbors ◆ 1997
10. Pinky and Rex and the Perfect Pumpkin ◆ 1998
11. Pinky and Rex and the School Play ◆ 1998

PIPPA MOUSE

Boegehold, Betty

RANDOM HOUSE

GRADES 1–3

ANIMAL FANTASY

A little mouse and her mother live in a snug mouse hole in the forest. One day it starts to rain, but their house has no door. So Pippa takes a hammer and some wood and makes one. Mother is delighted and tells her a story by the fire. Pippa goes to visit other animals in the forest, and tries out their homes. In the end she decides she likes her own cozy home the best. Little black-and-white illustrations show Pippa and her parents and the other animals in the forest.

1. Pippa Mouse ◆ 1973
2. Here's Pippa Again! ◆ 1975
3. Pippa Pops Out! ◆ 1979

4. Hurray for Pippa! ◆ 1980
5. Pippa's Mouse House ◆ 1998

PIPPI LONGSTOCKING

Lindgren, Astrid
PUFFIN
GRADES 3–5
HUMOR

Pippi (her full name is Pippilotta Delicatessa Windowshade Mackrelmint Efraim's Daughter Longstocking) lives alone in her house Villa Villekulla, with only her horse and her monkey, Mr. Nilsson, for company. Not only that, she's rich as a troll (as she puts it), thanks to the suitcase of gold pieces her father left for her before he disappeared at sea. No wonder Tommy and Annika—who live next door in an ordinary house with an ordinary father and mother—love to play with her! These stories are translated from the Swedish and have become popular all over the world. *Pippi Goes to School* (Viking 1998), illustrated by Michael Chesworth, is part of the new Pippi Longstocking Storybook series that excerpts vignettes from the original Pippi books and makes these stories more accessible to a younger audience of readers.

1. Pippi Longstocking ◆ 1945
2. Pippi Goes on Board ◆ 1946
3. Pippi in the South Seas ◆ 1948

PIT DRAGON TRILOGY

Yolen, Jane
HARCOURT
GRADES 6–8
ADVENTURE | FANTASY

On a distant planet, a thousand years in the future, fighting pit dragons provide the basis for a people's way of life. Jakkin Stewart gains his freedom by training his dragon, Heart's Blood, to victory in the pits. Along the way, he gains the respect and love of Akki and crusades for the destiny of his planet, Austar IV.

1. Dragon's Blood ◆ 1982
2. Heart's Blood ◆ 1984
3. A Sending of Dragons ◆ 1987

THE PLANT THAT ATE DIRTY SOCKS

McArthur, Nancy

AVON

GRADES 4–7

HUMOR | SCIENCE FICTION

When the dirty socks in Michael and Norman's room start to disappear, the boys discover that they are being eaten by two strange plants in their room. The plants were grown from some mysterious beans that arrived in the mail. The plants grow and develop distinct personalities, so the brothers name them Stanley and Fluffy and they all become friends. Biological experts analyze the plants, the parents want to get rid of them, and the plants have children, some of which turn out to be not friendly at all. Other situations involve the boys' efforts to make sure the plants' unique qualities don't become public. The humor of the series comes from the relationship between the odd-couple brothers, with neat-freak Norman trying to keep Michael's mess on his side of the room.

1. The Plant That Ate Dirty Socks ◆ 1988
2. The Return of the Plant That Ate Dirty Socks ◆ 1990
3. The Escape of the Plant That Ate Dirty Socks ◆ 1992
4. The Secret of the Plant That Ate Dirty Socks ◆ 1993
5. More Adventures of the Plant That Ate Dirty Socks ◆ 1994
6. The Plant That Ate Dirty Socks Goes Up in Space ◆ 1995
7. The Mystery of the Plant That Ate Dirty Socks ◆ 1996
8. The Plant That Ate Dirty Socks Gets a Girlfriend ◆ 1997
9. The Plant That Ate Dirty Socks Goes Hollywood ◆ 1999

PLEASANT FIELDMOUSE

Wahl, Jan

HARPERCOLLINS

GRADES 2–4

ANIMAL FANTASY

Pleasant Fieldmouse wants to be a fireman. He has thought it over and decided that he wants to serve his woodland community. Haunted Beaver, who always has a bee following him, doesn't know about any fires, and neither does Worry-Wind Hedgehog, who is too worried about the fox catching her to care much anyway. When he finally sees a fire, it turns out to be a cloud of grasshoppers, which he scares away, thereby earning a reputation as a firefighter. This series will appeal to children who liked Lobel's Frog and Toad series and are ready for something just a little harder.

1. Pleasant Fieldmouse ◆ 1964

2. Pleasant Fieldmouse's Halloween Party ◆ 1974
3. Pleasant Fieldmouse's Valentine Trick ◆ 1977
4. The Pleasant Fieldmouse Storybook ◆ 1977

POLK STREET SCHOOL *see* Kids of the Polk Street School *and* New Kids at the Polk Street School

POLKA DOT PRIVATE EYE

Giff, Patricia Reilly
DELL
GRADES 1–3
MYSTERY

Dawn Bosco, the Polka Dot Detective, is one of the Polk Street School kids. She has a detective box that includes a book called *The Polka Dot Private Eye*, a wig, and a big polka-dot detective hat. Her grandmother, Noni, takes Dawn and her friends Jill and Jason to the beach for the day, and they encounter a teenage girl who has lost her necklace. Dawn takes the case and runs through several suspects before the necklace is found in her own box, where the girl dropped it accidentally. Jason is always glad to help Dawn on a case, but Jill is a terrible detective. Easy clues and Giff's characteristic short paragraphs make a nice introduction to mysteries.

1. The Mystery of the Blue Ring ◆ 1987
2. The Riddle of the Red Purse ◆ 1987
3. The Secret at the Polk Street School ◆ 1987
4. The Powder Puff Puzzle ◆ 1987
5. The Case of the Cool-Itch Kid ◆ 1989
6. Garbage Juice for Breakfast ◆ 1989
7. The Trail of the Screaming Teenager ◆ 1990
8. The Clue at the Zoo ◆ 1990

PONY PALS

Betancourt, Jeanne
SCHOLASTIC
GRADES 3–5
REAL LIFE | RECREATION

Pam Crandal is one of the featured characters in the Pony Pals series. Her father is a veterinarian and her mother is a riding teacher, so Pam is used to being around animals. There is a trail behind her family's land that leads to Anna Harley's house, where Anna and her friend Lulu Sanders keep their horses. The three friends call themselves the Pony Pals, and these stories revolve around their problems with ponies and with friends. In one book, Pam's pony is sick and the girls try to find out why. In another book, new neighbors block the Pony Pal Trail, and the girls worry about how they will get together. The cover art shows Pam as an African American girl, which may expand the appeal of this series. Pony Tails is a series similar to this one. The Pony Pals Super Specials are also listed below.

1. I Want a Pony ◆ 1994
2. A Pony for Keeps ◆ 1995
3. A Pony in Trouble ◆ 1995
4. Give Me Back My Pony ◆ 1995
5. Pony to the Rescue ◆ 1995
6. Too Many Ponies ◆ 1995
7. Runaway Pony ◆ 1995
8. Good-bye Pony ◆ 1996
9. The Wild Pony ◆ 1996
10. Don't Hurt My Pony ◆ 1996
11. Circus Pony ◆ 1996
12. Keep Out, Pony! ◆ 1996
13. The Girl Who Hated Ponies ◆ 1997
14. Pony-Sitters ◆ 1997
15. The Blind Pony ◆ 1997
16. The Missing Pony Pal ◆ 1997
17. Detective Pony ◆ 1998

SUPER SPECIALS

1. The Baby Pony ◆ 1996
2. The Story of Our Ponies ◆ 1997
3. The Ghost Pony ◆ 1998

PONY TAILS

Bryant, Bonnie
BANTAM SKYLARK
GRADES 3–5
REAL LIFE | RECREATION

Jasmine, Corey, and May are best friends who take riding lessons at the Pony Club. These books include details about riding that will appeal to younger horse enthusiasts. Girls will also relate to the problems among the three friends, such as when Corey is chosen to participate in the Starlight Ride and Jasmine is not. In *May's Runaway Ride*, May has such a difficult time that her friends think she has run away. Girls who read these books may enjoy Jeanne Betancourt's series Pony Pals and then move on to Bonnie Bryant's series about older girls, The Saddle Club.

1. Pony Crazy ◆ 1995
2. May's Riding Lesson ◆ 1995
3. Corey's Pony Is Missing ◆ 1995
4. Jasmine's Christmas Ride ◆ 1995
5. May Takes the Lead ◆ 1996
6. Corey in the Saddle ◆ 1996
7. Jasmine Trots Ahead ◆ 1996
8. May Rides a New Pony ◆ 1996
9. Corey and the Spooky Pony ◆ 1996
10. Jasmine Helps a Foal ◆ 1996
11. May Goes to England ◆ 1997
12. Corey's Secret Friend ◆ 1997
13. Jasmine's First Horse Show ◆ 1997
14. May's Runaway Ride ◆ 1997
15. Corey's Christmas Wish ◆ 1997
16. Jasmine and the Jumping Pony ◆ 1998

POPPLETON

Rylant, Cynthia

SCHOLASTIC

GRADES K–3

ANIMAL FANTASY | HUMOR

Poppleton the Pig and his friends Cherry Sue the Llama and Hudson the Mouse are good friends who help each other out and share good times together. When Poppleton and Cherry Sue first meet, she thinks she needs to invite him over every day, but he would rather be alone sometimes. Finally, he gets frustrated and sprays her with a hose. She confesses that she likes to be alone sometimes, too, and they become friends. When Poppleton and Hudson go to the beach together, the best part is when they tell Cherry Sue all about it.

1. Poppleton ◆ 1997
2. Poppleton and Friends ◆ 1997
3. Poppleton Everyday ◆ 1998
4. Poppleton Forever ◆ 1998

PORTRAITS OF LITTLE WOMEN

Pfeffer, Susan Beth

DELACORTE

GRADES 4–6

FAMILY LIFE | HISTORICAL

Featuring the characters from Louisa May Alcott's *Little Women*, these are original stories. Each of the March sisters is true to her original personality: Jo is feisty, Beth is sensitive. The books give a sense of the era with encounters with immigrants and details about life in the mid 1800s. There is a strong sense of family in these stories. Sometimes, the loyalty of the girls is tested, like when Jo is invited to a picnic but Beth is not. The original *Little Women* is still very popular with girls, and this series will extend the interest and be accessible to a wider audience of readers.

1. Amy's Story ◆ 1997
2. Beth's Story ◆ 1997
3. Jo's Story ◆ 1997
4. Meg's Story ◆ 1997
5. Amy Makes a Friend ◆ 1998
6. Beth Makes a Friend ◆ 1998
7. Christmas Dreams: Four Stories ◆ 1998
8. Jo Makes a Friend ◆ 1998
9. Meg Makes a Friend ◆ 1998

POSSUM FAMILY

Conford, Ellen

LITTLE, BROWN

GRADES K–2

ANIMAL FANTASY | HUMOR

The three young possums in the family are each featured in one of the books in this series. Geraldine's story (*Just the Thing for Geraldine*) describes her efforts to find something that she can do well. She goes to schools for ballet, weaving, and sculpture before she realizes that she is already a great juggler and can give lessons. Eugene is afraid of the dark but, with Geraldine's help, becomes *Eugene the Brave*. In *Impossible, Possum*, Randolph cannot hang by his tail, but Geraldine tricks him into developing confidence. The books are humorous and focus on everyday worries of young children, such as being special and being afraid.

1. Impossible, Possum ◆ 1971
2. Just the Thing for Geraldine ◆ 1974
3. Eugene the Brave ◆ 1978

POSY BATES

Cresswell, Helen

MACMILLAN

GRADES 3–5

FAMILY LIFE | HUMOR

Posy Bates lives with her Mom, whom everyone calls Daff; her Dad, George; and her older sister, Pippa, and baby Fred. She occasionally aligns with Pippa, who wants to get her ears pierced. Her project for Fred is to make him a genius. To accomplish this, she talks to him about animals, her favorite subject. The short chapters are full of her funny antics as Posy tries to keep a hedgehog and plots to keep a stray dog that appears. Her neighbor Sam is her sometimes willing accomplice.

1. Meet Posy Bates ◆ 1990
2. Posy Bates, Again! ◆ 1991
3. Posy Bates and the Bag Lady ◆ 1993

PRESTON

McNaughton, Colin

HARCOURT

GRADES K–1

ANIMAL FANTASY | HUMOR

Preston, a young pig, blithely and unknowingly avoids the cunning and hungry, big, bad wolf in this series. The wolf slips, trips, and crushes himself trying to get Preston. Each comical book in the series has eye-catching illustrations that add to the humor. The large print aids in easy reading.

1. Suddenly! ◆ 1995
2. Boo! ◆ 1996
3. Oops! ◆ 1997
4. Preston's Goal! ◆ 1998

PRINCE TRILOGY *see* Sword of the Spirits

PRIVATE EYES CLUB

Bonsall, Crosby

HARPERCOLLINS

GRADES K–3

MYSTERY

In this beginning-to-read series, Wizard has decided to become a private eye along with his friends Skinny and Tubby. Snitch, Wizard's little brother, is always around as they solve various cases: who stole Snitch's cat, who took Mrs. Meech's pie, and so on. Readers will want to continue reading to learn the outcome of each mystery.

1. The Case of the Hungry Stranger ◆ 1963
2. The Case of the Cat's Meow ◆ 1965
3. The Case of the Dumb Bells ◆ 1966
4. The Case of the Scaredy Cats ◆ 1971
5. The Case of the Double Cross ◆ 1980

PROFESSOR XARGLE

Willis, Jean

DUTTON

GRADES K–3

HUMOR | SCIENCE FICTION

Professor Xargle, an alien, is constantly teaching his young alien students about Earth and the humans who inhabit it. With much tongue-in-cheek humor, he explores the silly things that humans do: in different kinds of weather, with their relatives, with their pets, and so on. Young readers will enjoy the silly stories and illustrations.

1. Earthlets, As Explained by Professor Xargle ◆ 1989
2. Earth Hounds, As Explained by Professor Xargle ◆ 1990
3. Earth Tigerlets, As Explained by Professor Xargle ◆ 1991
4. Earth Mobiles, As Explained by Professor Xargle ◆ 1992
5. Earth Weather, As Explained by Professor Xargle ◆ 1993
6. Relativity, As Explained by Professor Xargle ◆ 1994

PRYDAIN CHRONICLES

Alexander, Lloyd

DELL

GRADES 5–8

FANTASY

Taran, a foundling who has no known parents, is Assistant Pig-Keeper for Hen Wen, an oracular pig who is kept in a safe, quiet place by Dallben the wizard. The country is Prydain, a fantasy land loosely based on Welsh legends. Taran dreams of adventure and longs to serve with Gwydion, a warrior of the House of Don. When Hen Wen runs away, Taran gives chase and runs into the warrior's life of which he dreamed. He meets a young enchantress named Eilonwy, and the two of them and many other friends fight against the Death Lord, who would enslave the whole land. They are finally victorious, and the House of Don decides to go to a perfect land. When Taran is invited to go with them, he decides instead to stay and take his rightful place as High King of Prydain. The *High King* won the Newbery Award. A volume of short stories about Prydain, *The Foundling, and other Tales of Prydain* was published in 1973.

1. The Book of Three ◆ 1964
2. The Black Cauldron ◆ 1965
3. The Castle of Llyr ◆ 1966
4. Taran Wanderer ◆ 1967
5. The High King ◆ 1968

RAINBOW FISH

Pfister, Marcus

NORTH-SOUTH BOOKS

GRADES K–2

ANIMAL FANTASY

Rainbow Fish is the most beautiful fish in the ocean. He has silvery scales that make him different from all the other fish. When a little fish asks him for one, he refuses because he is selfish and vain. The other fish refuse to have anything to do with him, and he becomes lonely until he talks to a wise octopus who advises him to give away his scales. When he gives away just one to the little blue fish, it makes him so happy that he decides to give away the others until he is left with just one. Two more stories in the series find Rainbow Fish helping everyone learn to get along.

1. The Rainbow Fish ◆ 1992
2. Rainbow Fish to the Rescue! ◆ 1995
3. Rainbow Fish and the Big Blue Whale ◆ 1998

RALPH S. MOUSE

Cleary, Beverly

MORROW

GRADES 2–4

ANIMAL FANTASY | HUMOR

In the first book, *The Mouse and the Motorcycle*, a small brown mouse named Ralph discovers his motoring skills when he experiments with a toy motorcycle that belongs to a young guest staying in the hotel where Ralph lives. His daredevil antics get Ralph into many tricky situations and even take him on an adventure to a summer camp in *Runaway Ralph*. In *Ralph S. Mouse*, the inquisitive mouse must demonstrate how smart he is and ends up having some wild adventures at school. The great success of this series lies in Beverly Cleary's ability to view the harsh and humorous aspects of the human world from the perspective of a mouse.

1. The Mouse and the Motorcycle ◆ 1965
2. Runaway Ralph ◆ 1970
3. Ralph S. Mouse ◆ 1982

RAMONA QUIMBY

Cleary, Beverly

MORROW

GRADES 2–4

FAMILY LIFE | HUMOR

First introduced as Beezus's pesky kid sister in the Henry Huggins series, Ramona inspired a successful series all her own and quickly became a favorite for young readers. The series follows Ramona from kindergarten through the fourth grade as she encounters many of childhood's challenging situations—a strict teacher, a bossy big sister, a working mother, and a temporarily out-of-work father—and gets involved in some hilarious escapades. Young readers will relate to Ramona as she tries very hard to behave but sometimes just can't help acting up. Through it all, Ramona faces life with tenacity, spunk, and a wild imagination.

1. Beezus and Ramona ◆ 1955
2. Ramona the Pest ◆ 1968
3. Ramona the Brave ◆ 1975
4. Ramona and Her Father ◆ 1977
5. Ramona and Her Mother ◆ 1979
6. Ramona Quimby, Age 8 ◆ 1981
7. Ramona, Forever ◆ 1984

THE RATS OF NIMH

O'Brien, Robert C., and Jane Leslie Conly

ATHENEUM; HARPERCOLLINS

GRADES 3–6

ANIMAL FANTASY

A delightful science fiction trilogy for intermediate readers. A group of rats have built an intelligent community in Thorn Valley after they escaped from a laboratory where they were test subjects. In the first book of the trilogy, Mrs. Frisby goes to these rats for advice because of their intelligence and wisdom. Many adventures ensue. In the second book, Mrs. Frisby's son Timothy meets up with Racso, and together they are able to save Thorn Valley from destruction. Finally, in the third book, the rat community helps two children who are lost, but then they must take the risk of being discovered. *Mrs. Frisby and the Rats of NIMH* won the Newbery Medal. O'Brien's daughter, Jane Leslie Conly, continued the series, writing the two sequels.

1. Mrs. Frisby and the Rats of NIMH ◆ 1971
2. Racso and the Rats of NIMH ◆ 1988
3. R-T, Margaret and the Rats of NIMH ◆ 1990

RED

Kjelgaard, Jim
HOLIDAY HOUSE
GRADES 4–6
ADVENTURE

The adventures of a young boy and his lovable Irish setter form the basis for this series. Together, they survive the rugged Wintupi wilderness. Other stories are about Big Red's offspring. This series will appeal to dog lovers and fans of *Old Yeller*.

1. Big Red ◆ 1945
2. Irish Red, Son of Big Red ◆ 1951
3. Outlaw Red, Son of Big Red ◆ 1953

REDWALL

Jacques, Brian
PHILOMEL
GRADES 4–8
ADVENTURE | ANIMAL FANTASY

Redwall Abbey is the focal point for the mice and other creatures who live in Mossflower Woods. In the first book, *Redwall*, an army of rats tries to conquer the abbey, and the defending mice must find the lost sword of Martin the Warrior to save themselves and their beloved abbey. Subsequent titles introduce a changing cast of heroes, heroines, and evildoers who interact in an epic saga full of conspiracies, adventures, and heroics. *The Great Redwall Feast* is a colorfully illustrated companion book directed toward a younger audience about the secret preparations by the Redwall creatures for a feast in honor of the Abbott.

1. Redwall ◆ 1986
2. Mossflower ◆ 1988
3. Mattimeo ◆ 1989
4. Mariel of Redwall ◆ 1991
5. Salamandastron ◆ 1992
6. Martin the Warrior ◆ 1993
7. The Bellmaker ◆ 1994
8. Outcast of Redwall ◆ 1995
9. Pearls of Lutra ◆ 1996
10. The Long Patrol ◆ 1998
11. Marlfox ◆ 1999

REEL KIDS ADVENTURES

Gustaveson, Dave
YOUTH WITH A MISSION PUBLISHING
GRADES 5–7
ADVENTURE | VALUES

Jeff Caldwell, 15, is interested in the Media Club at his new high school. The club has a mission—to spread a Christian message to other kids at home and around the world. In order to travel with the club, Jeff's parents insist that his 13-year-old sister Mindy be included. This causes some tension for Jeff as well as some scary moments that result from Mindy's impetuous actions. Quickly paced with lots of dialogue, this will appeal to readers who like action and discussions of values.

1. The Missing Video ◆ 1993
2. Mystery at Smokey Mountain ◆ 1994
3. The Stolen Necklace ◆ 1994
4. The Mysterious Case ◆ 1995
5. The Amazon Stranger ◆ 1995
6. The Dangerous Voyage ◆ 1995
7. The Lost Diary ◆ 1996
8. The Forbidden Road ◆ 1996
9. The Danger Zone ◆ 1997

THE RESCUERS

Sharp, Margery
LITTLE, BROWN
GRADES 4–7
ADVENTURE | ANIMAL FANTASY

A lovely white mouse enjoys a special relationship with an ambassador's son, living in the embassy in great luxury. She is also Madam President of the Mouse Prisoners Aid Society, which was founded with the intent of cheering up prisoners but ends up rescuing them. Miss Bianca is a well-brought-up mouse with exquisite manners, and Bernard is a brave but rough-around-the-edges companion. Together, with the help of the other mice in the society, they embark on one daring rescue after another. They travel to the Orient and the Antarctic and even to the Salt Mines. Their most frightening rescue, however, is one they perform right in their own embassy when the ambassador's niece is put under a spell by an evil doll.

1. The Rescuers ◆ 1959
2. Miss Bianca ◆ 1962
3. The Turret ◆ 1963
4. Miss Bianca in the Salt Mines ◆ 1966
5. Miss Bianca in the Orient ◆ 1970
6. Miss Bianca in the Antarctic ◆ 1971
7. Miss Bianca and the Bridesmaid ◆ 1972
8. Bernard the Brave ◆ 1977
9. Bernard into Battle ◆ 1978

REX AND LILLY

Brown, Laurie Krasny

LITTLE, BROWN

GRADES K–2

ANIMAL FANTASY | FAMILY LIFE

Rex and Lilly are brother and sister dinosaurs. Each title has three stories about the siblings and their everyday experiences. Children can read about Rex and Lilly doing tricks in the pool, going to dance class, keeping themselves busy on rainy days, celebrating their mother's birthday, cleaning their house, and getting a new pet.

1. Rex and Lilly Family Time ◆ 1995
2. Rex and Lilly Play Time ◆ 1995
3. Rex and Lilly Schooltime ◆ 1997

RIDING ACADEMY

Hart, Alison

RANDOM HOUSE

GRADES 4–6

REAL LIFE | RECREATION

Mary Beth, Andie, Jina, and Lauren are roommates at Foxhall Academy, a girls prep school. Despite their different backgrounds and personalities, the four girls find a common bond in their love for horses. Luckily for them the school offers an excellent riding program that helps the girls learn about competition, friendship, sharing, failure, and growing up. *Haunted Horseback Holiday* is Riding Academy Super Special (1996).

1. A Horse for Mary Beth ◆ 1994
2. Andie Out of Control ◆ 1994
3. Jina Rides to Win ◆ 1994
4. Lessons for Lauren ◆ 1994
5. Mary Beth's Haunted Ride ◆ 1994
6. Andie Shows Off ◆ 1994
7. Jina's Pain-in-the-Neck Pony ◆ 1995
8. The Craziest Horse Show Ever ◆ 1995
9. Andie's Risky Business ◆ 1995
10. Trouble at Foxhall ◆ 1995
11. Foxhunt ◆ 1995
12. Lauren Rides to the Rescue ◆ 1995
13. Rivals in the Ring ◆ 1996
14. Million-Dollar Mare ◆ 1998

RINALDO

Scheffler, Ursel

NORTH-SOUTH BOOKS

GRADES 2–4

ANIMAL FANTASY | HUMOR

Rinaldo is a sly fox—in fact, he's a con man who spends most of his time avoiding the police and running from the poor souls (chickens, moles, cats, and other animals) he's swindled. Young readers (and listeners) will enjoy the stories of this wily adventurer, although the plot lines are sophisticated tales in the tradition of adult action-adventure novels.

1. Rinaldo, the Sly Fox ◆ 1992
2. The Return of Rinaldo, the Sly Fox ◆ 1993
3. Rinaldo on the Run ◆ 1995

RINKO

Uchida, Yoshiko

ATHENEUM

GRADES 4–6

FAMILY LIFE | HISTORICAL

Rinko and her family live in California during the Depression. They maintain their connection to their relatives in Japan even as they try to adjust to life in the United States. Some of the events in the book revolve around visits from Japanese family and friends; others deal with the clash between the two cultures. Rinko is much more Americanized than her parents. These books provide information about the immigrant experience along with cultural details and historical information about the Depression.

1. A Jar of Dreams ◆ 1981
2. The Best Bad Thing ◆ 1983
3. The Happiest Ending ◆ 1985

ROBERTS FAMILY *see* Liza, Bill, and Jed

THE ROCKY RIDGE YEARS *see* Little House: The Rose Years

RONALD MORGAN

Giff, Patricia Reilly

VIKING KESTREL

GRADES K–3

HUMOR | REAL LIFE

Ronald Morgan is a second-grader who can't do anything right. However, with the support of his friends, Rosemary and Michael, and his teacher, Miss Farley, Ronald keeps trying until he experiences success. Young readers will recognize their own frustrations and relate to Ronald's feeling of pride when he achieves success.

1. Today Was a Terrible Day ◆ 1980
2. The Almost Awful Play ◆ 1984
3. Watch Out, Ronald Morgan! ◆ 1985
4. Happy Birthday, Ronald Morgan ◆ 1986
5. Ronald Morgan Goes to Bat ◆ 1988
6. Ronald Morgan Goes to Camp ◆ 1995
7. Good Luck, Ronald Morgan ◆ 1996

ROOMMATES

Galbraith, Kathryn O.

SIMON & SCHUSTER

GRADES 1–3

FAMILY LIFE

These early chapter books are warm and funny. Mimi and Beth are sisters. They first become roommates when their mom is going to have another baby. Even though they are very different people, they discover that being roommates can be lots of fun. As the series continues, they experience the arrival of a new baby in the house and go to camp together as roommates.

1. Roommates ◆ 1990
2. Roommates and Rachel ◆ 1991
3. Roommates Again ◆ 1994

ROSA TRILOGY

Williams, Vera B.

MULBERRY BOOKS

GRADES K–3

FAMILY LIFE

A charming picture book trilogy about a small Hispanic family working together in the big city. The first title, *A Chair for My Mother*, was a Caldecott Honor book. Rosa's family has a big jar in which they put spare change, saving for special things: first a big chair for her mother after they lose everything in a fire; then an accordion for Rosa's birthday. The family pulls together once more in the last book when Rosa's grandmother is sick and Rosa and her friends play music to raise money.

1. A Chair for My Mother ◆ 1982
2. Something Special for Me ◆ 1983
3. Music, Music for Everyone ◆ 1984

THE ROSE YEARS *see* Little House: The Rose Years

ROSY COLE

Greenwald, Sheila

LITTLE, BROWN

GRADES 3–5

FAMILY LIFE | HUMOR

Artistic Rosy Cole lives in Manhattan with her parents, her sisters, and her cat. This series chronicles her adventures with best friend Hermione Wong and other friends from her all-female private school. Over the course of the series, Rosy learns to accept herself and appreciate her talent for art. Rosy's observations about life and her efforts to succeed are often hilarious. Along with the funny stories is a fascinating look at life in New York.

1. Give Us a Great Big Smile, Rosy Cole ◆ 1981

2. Valentine Rosy ◆ 1984
3. Rosy Cole's Great American Guilt Club ◆ 1985
4. Write on, Rosy! ◆ 1988
5. Rosy's Romance ◆ 1989
6. Here's Hermione ◆ 1991
7. Rosy Cole Discovers America! ◆ 1992
8. She Walks in Beauty ◆ 1992
9. She Grows and Graduates ◆ 1997

ROTTEN RALPH

Gantos, Jack
HOUGHTON MIFFLIN
GRADES K–1
ANIMAL FANTASY | HUMOR

Rotten Ralph is a cat who deserves his name because his behavior is awful. His owner, Sarah, hopes he will reform, but he never does. He even misbehaves at his own birthday party. There are titles for Halloween, Valentine's Day, and Christmas and a book in which Ralph goes to school. Children enjoy Ralph's schemes and delight in his audacity.

1. Rotten Ralph ◆ 1976
2. Worse than Rotten Ralph ◆ 1978
3. Rotten Ralph's Rotten Christmas ◆ 1984
4. Rotten Ralph's Rotten Romance ◆ 1984
5. Rotten Ralph's Trick or Treat ◆ 1986
6. Rotten Ralph's Show and Tell ◆ 1989
7. Happy Birthday, Rotten Ralph ◆ 1990
8. Not So Rotten Ralph ◆ 1994
9. Back to School for Rotten Ralph ◆ 1998

RUSSELL

Hurwitz, Johanna
MORROW
GRADES 1–3
FAMILY LIFE | HUMOR

First introduced as a neighbor in the Nora and Teddy series by the same author, Russell inspired a series of his own. In the first stories, Russell is a rambunctious little boy who throws temper tantrums when things don't go his way. As he grows older, however, he learns to control his temper and even to appreciate his little sister, Elisa.

Children will be able to relate to the emotional ups and downs Russell experiences in everyday life. Russell's sister Elisa has a spinoff series of her own.

1. Rip-Roaring Russell ◆ 1983
2. Russell Rides Again ◆ 1985
3. Russell Sprouts ◆ 1987
4. Russell and Elisa ◆ 1989

SABRINA THE TEENAGE WITCH

Various authors

SIMON & SCHUSTER

GRADES 2–4

FANTASY | HUMOR

This series features Sabrina, her aunts Hilda and Zelda, and her cat, Salem. All of them have magical powers. The circumstances involve a lot of humor as the witches try to live in human society. This group of books is based on the popular television show. There is also a series of episode storybooks based on individual episodes and including photographs from the production.

1. Sabrina, the Teenage Witch (Weiss, David Cody, and Bobbi J. G. Weiss) ◆ 1997
2. Showdown at the Mall (Gallagher, Diana G.) ◆ 1997
3. Good Switch, Bad Switch (Weiss, David Cody, and Bobbi J. G. Weiss) ◆ 1997
4. Halloween Havoc (Gallagher, Diana G.) ◆ 1997
5. Santa's Little Helper (Dubowski, Cathy East) ◆ 1997
6. Ben There, Done That (Locke, Joseph) ◆ 1998
7. All You Need Is a Love Spell (Reisfeld, Randi) ◆ 1998
8. Salem on Trial (Weiss, Bobbi J. G., and David Cody Weiss) ◆ 1998
9. A Dog's Life (Dubowski, Cathy East) ◆ 1998
10. Lotsa Luck (Gallagher, Diana G.) ◆ 1998
11. Prisoner of Cabin 13 (Vornholt, John) ◆ 1998
12. All That Glitters (Garton, Ray) ◆ 1998
13. Go Fetch! (Weiss, David Cody, and Bobbi J. G. Weiss) ◆ 1998
14. Spying Eyes (Holder, Nancy) ◆ 1998
15. Harvest Moon (Odom, Mel) ◆ 1998
16. Now You See Her, Now You Don't (Gallagher, Diana G.) ◆ 1998

THE SADDLE CLUB

Bryant, Bonnie

BANTAM DOUBLEDAY DELL

GRADES 4–6

REAL LIFE | RECREATION

Stevie, Lisa, and Carole, young riders at the Pine Hollow stables, make up the Saddle Club. Competition and outsiders (occasionally boys) challenge their friendship, but the girls always manage to stay together. Carole is horse-crazy. The rest of her life is disorganized; but when she is around horses, she becomes focused. Stevie is a practical joker, always looking for fun and coming up with new schemes. Lisa is quiet and serious, a good student, plagued by a pushy mother. The girls encounter snobby rich girls who don't want to take good care of horses and, at other times, excellent riders whom they admire. Their love for horses takes them to a dude ranch, to horse shows and competitions, and to riding camps and rodeos. More than 80 books will keep horse lovers busy.

1. Horse Crazy ◆ 1988
2. Horse Shy ◆ 1988
3. Horse Sense ◆ 1989
4. Horse Power ◆ 1989
5. Trail Mates ◆ 1989
6. Dude Ranch ◆ 1989
7. Horse Play ◆ 1989
8. Horse Show ◆ 1989
9. Hoof Beat ◆ 1990
10. Riding Camp ◆ 1990
11. Horse Wise ◆ 1990
12. Rodeo Rider ◆ 1990
13. Starlight Christmas ◆ 1990
14. Sea Horse ◆ 1991
15. Team Play ◆ 1991
16. Horse Games ◆ 1991
17. Horsenapped ◆ 1991
18. Pack Trip ◆ 1991
19. Star Rider ◆ 1991
20. Snow Ride ◆ 1992
21. Racehorse ◆ 1992

22. Fox Hunt ◆ 1992
23. Horse Trouble ◆ 1992
24. Ghost Rider ◆ 1992
25. Show Horse ◆ 1992
26. Beach Ride ◆ 1993
27. Bridle Path ◆ 1993
28. Stable Manners ◆ 1993
29. Ranch Hands ◆ 1993
30. Autumn Trail ◆ 1993
31. Hayride ◆ 1993
32. Chocolate Horse ◆ 1994
33. High Horse ◆ 1994
34. Hay Fever ◆ 1994
35. Horse Tale ◆ 1994
36. Riding Lesson ◆ 1994
37. Stage Coach ◆ 1994
38. Horse Trade ◆ 1994
39. Purebred ◆ 1994
40. Gift Horse ◆ 1994
41. Stable Witch ◆ 1995
42. Saddlebags ◆ 1995
43. Photo Finish ◆ 1995
44. Horseshoe ◆ 1995
45. Stable Groom ◆ 1995
46. Flying Horse ◆ 1995
47. Horse Magic ◆ 1995
48. Mystery Ride ◆ 1995
49. Stable Farewell ◆ 1995
50. Yankee Swap ◆ 1996
51. Pleasure Horse ◆ 1996
52. Riding Class ◆ 1996
53. Horse-Sitters ◆ 1996
54. Gold Medal Rider ◆ 1996
55. Gold Medal Horse ◆ 1996
56. Cutting Horse ◆ 1996
57. Tight Rein ◆ 1996
58. Wild Horses ◆ 1996
59. Phantom Horse ◆ 1996
60. Hobbyhorse ◆ 1996
61. Broken Horse ◆ 1996
62. Horse Blues ◆ 1997
63. Stable Hearts ◆ 1997
64. Horse Capades ◆ 1997
65. Silver Stirrups ◆ 1997
66. Saddle Sore ◆ 1997
67. Summer Horse ◆ 1997
68. Summer Rider ◆ 1997

69. Endurance Ride ◆ 1997
70. Horse Race ◆ 1997
71. Horse Talk ◆ 1997
72. Holiday Horse ◆ 1997
73. Horse Guest ◆ 1998
74. Horse Whispers ◆ 1998
75. Painted Horse ◆ 1998
76. Horse Care ◆ 1998
77. Rocking Horse ◆ 1998
78. Horseflies ◆ 1998
79. English Horse ◆ 1998
80. English Rider ◆ 1998
81. Wagon Trail ◆ 1998
82. Quarter Horse ◆ 1998
83. Horse Thief ◆ 1998
84. Schooling Horse ◆ 1998
85. Horse Fever ◆ 1998

SADDLE CLUB SUPER EDITIONS

1. A Summer Without Horses ◆ 1994
2. The Secret of the Stallion ◆ 1995
3. Western Star ◆ 1996
4. Dream Horse ◆ 1996
5. Before They Rode Horses ◆ 1997
6. Nightmare ◆ 1997
7. Christmas Treasure ◆ 1998
8. Horse Fever ◆ 1998

SALTY

Rand, Gloria
HENRY HOLT
GRADES K–2
ADVENTURE | REAL LIFE

Salty the dog and his master, Zack, own a sailboat. They share many adventures, from actually building the sailboat to sailing to Alaska and Hawaii. The illustrations are not only attractive but do a nice job of illustrating the various parts of sailboats and the process of sailing.

1. Salty Dog ◆ 1989
2. Salty Sails North ◆ 1990
3. Salty Takes Off ◆ 1991
4. Aloha, Salty! ◆ 1996

SAM AND DAVE MYSTERIES

Singer, Marilyn
HARPERCOLLINS
GRADES 3–5
MYSTERY

Sam and Dave Bean are mystery-solving twins who are different in more ways than they are alike. Dave is student council president, and Sam is into sports. In one book, the boys read about a hoax contest and try to think of a good one. Meanwhile, their friend Weezie shows up with a female exchange student who soon is a suspect in a series of robberies and the brothers work to clear up the confusion. In other books, they find their friend Rita's missing brother and solve a mystery involving forged lottery tickets. Different illustrators give each book a very different look, but the length of each is about the same.

1. Leroy Is Missing ◆ 1984
2. The Case of the Sabotaged School Play ◆ 1984
3. A Clue in Code ◆ 1985
4. The Case of the Cackling Car ◆ 1985
5. The Case of the Fixed Election ◆ 1989
6. The Hoax on You ◆ 1989

SAM AND ROBERT

Levy, Elizabeth
HARPERCOLLINS
GRADES 2–4
HUMOR | MYSTERY

Sam and Robert live with their mother on the 19th floor of an apartment building. Both boys are fascinated with the supernatural and monsters, and Robert sleeps with a Dracula doll. In one of the books, an unpleasant man named Mr. Frank moves in, and the boys become convinced that he is the real Frankenstein. They begin investigating and find more similarities between the two. Other books in the series find the boys fascinated with Dracula and other monsters and wondering if people in their everyday lives are the real thing. Children who enjoy the Adventures of the Bailey School Kids will enjoy this series.

1. Frankenstein Moved In on the Fourth Floor ◆ 1979
2. Dracula Is a Pain in the Neck ◆ 1983
3. Gorgonzola Zombies in the Park ◆ 1993
4. Wolfman Sam ◆ 1996

SAM KRUPNIK

Lowry, Lois
HOUGHTON MIFFLIN
GRADES 3–5
FAMILY LIFE | HUMOR

Anastasia Krupnik's little brother Sam has his own group of books. As a toddler, Sam is a handful. He flushes Anastasia's goldfish and adjusts to nursery school. He tries to find the very best birthday present for his mother. And he decides to run away. Sam is a lively, irrepressible little boy whose activities are filled with gentle humor.

1. All About Sam ◆ 1988
2. Attaboy, Sam! ◆ 1992
3. See You Around, Sam! ◆ 1996

SAM SNOUT *see* Super Snoop Sam Snout

SAMANTHA *see* American Girls: Samantha

SAVED BY THE BELL

Cruise, Beth
ALADDIN
GRADES 6–8
ADVENTURE

Different characters appear in the books in this series, which is linked to the television program of the same name. In fact, there are three parts to these books. There is a group of books that includes many of the original characters of the television show. Then there is a group of books featuring new classmates. The focus throughout the books is on conflicts that will be familiar to teens—dating, grades, responsibilities, romance, and even social and political issues. These books will appeal especially to teen-age girls. *Shiloh* won the Newbery Award.

1. Bayside Madness ◆ 1992
2. Zack Strikes Back ◆ 1992
3. California Scheming ◆ 1992
4. Girls' Night Out ◆ 1992
5. Zack's Last Scam ◆ 1992
6. Class Trip Chaos ◆ 1992
7. That Old Zack Magic ◆ 1993
8. Impeach Screech! ◆ 1993

9. One Wild Weekend ◆ 1993
10. Kelly's Hero ◆ 1993
11. Don't Tell a Soul ◆ 1994
12. Computer Confusion ◆ 1994
13. Silver Spurs ◆ 1994
14. Best Friend's Girl ◆ 1994
15. Zack in Action ◆ 1994
16. Operation: Clean Sweep ◆ 1994
17. Scene One, Take Two ◆ 1995
18. Fireside Manners ◆ 1995
19. Picture Perfect ◆ 1995
20. Surf's Up ◆ 1995
21. Screech in Love ◆ 1995
22. Ex-Zack-Ly ◆ 1995

SAVED BY THE BELL: THE NEW CLASS

1. Trouble Ahead ◆ 1994
2. Spilling the Beans ◆ 1994
3. Going, Going, Gone! ◆ 1995
4. Breaking the Rules ◆ 1994
5. Spreading the Word ◆ 1995
6. Lights, Camera, Action! ◆ 1995
7. May the Best Team Win ◆ 1995
8. It's the Thought That Counts ◆ 1995
9. Finders, Keepers ◆ 1995
10. Franken-Bobby! ◆ 1995

SCAREDY CATS

Stanley, George Edward
SIMON & SCHUSTER
GRADES 1–3
HUMOR

Mrs. O'Dell's students finds themselves in a horrifying situation that turns out to be humorous in *Mrs. O'Dell's Third-Grade Class Is Shrinking*. She does an experiment shrinking plants and ends up shrinking the entire class. They don doll costumes and carry on with their day, which includes battling vicious squirrels, but they are perfectly all right when their parents come to pick them up at three o'clock. Earlier books in this easy chapter book series have different characters but the same blend of scariness, humor, and everyday life.

1. Bugs for Breakfast ◆ 1996
2. The Day the Ants Got Really Mad ◆ 1996
3. There's a Shark in the Swimming Pool ◆ 1996
4. Mrs. O'Dell's Third-Grade Class Is Shrinking ◆ 1996

5. Who Invited Aliens to My Slumber Party? ◆ 1997
6. The New Kid in School Is a Vampire Bat ◆ 1997
7. A Werewolf Followed Me Home ◆ 1997
8. The Vampire Kittens of Count Dracula ◆ 1997
9. Don't Look a Ghost Horse in the Mouth ◆ 1997

SCRAPPER JOHN

Bagdon, Paul
AVON
GRADES 4–7
ADVENTURE | HISTORICAL

Scrapper John lives in the Montana Rockies with his half-wolf dog, Musket. His father has been killed by a one-eyed grizzly bear, but he has a good friend, Seeks the Far Sky, a Native American boy his age. Together, they have adventures involving wild horses, wagon trains, and survival in the wilderness. In a typical book, a wagon train is headed for sacred Native American ground, and the stubborn leader refuses to turn back, even though John and his friends warn him that it means a battle. Seeks the Far Sky and John find themselves on opposite sides as both try to find a way to avoid bloodshed.

1. Valley of the Spotted Horse ◆ 1992
2. Showdown at Burnt Rock ◆ 1992
3. Rendezvous at Skull Mountain ◆ 1992

SEASONAL ADVENTURES

Hurwitz, Johanna
MORROW
GRADES 4–6
HUMOR | REAL LIFE

In *The Hot and Cold Summer*, Rory and Derek are dismayed to learn that they are expected to entertain a girl named Bolivia over their much-awaited summer vacation. Although they initially put much effort into avoiding Bolivia, her personality eventually wins the boys over and the children learn to enjoy each other's company and work out the intricacies of a triangular friendship. Things work out so well that the threesome reunites for subsequent vacations.

1. The Hot and Cold Summer ◆ 1984
2. The Cold and Hot Winter ◆ 1988
3. The Up and Down Spring ◆ 1993
4. The Down and Up Fall ◆ 1996

SEASONS WITH GRANDMA

Moore, Elaine

LOTHROP, LEE & SHEPARD

GRADES K–3

FAMILY LIFE

This quartet of stories follows young Kim on her visits to her grandmother's farm. Each visit is at a different time of year, and Kim learns about the characteristics of each season through the changes in nature and the activities she and her grandmother engage in. Together, they explore the countryside, do chores around the farm, plant a garden, carve pumpkins, and fly kites, all the while strengthening the bond between them. The endearing relationship between Kim and her grandmother provides the basis of these stories and reflects a child's warm memories of a loving grandparent.

1. Grandma's House ◆ 1985
2. Grandma's Promise ◆ 1988
3. Grandma's Garden ◆ 1994
4. Grandma's Smile ◆ 1995

SEBASTIAN BARTH

Howe, James

AVON

GRADES 5–7

MYSTERY

Sebastian Barth lives in rural Connecticut, where he has a weekly radio show. He becomes involved in mystery-solving as he looks for scoops for the show. He is friends with Alex, the police chief, who helps him out. In *Dew Drop Dead*, he and his friends Corrie and David befriend a homeless man when Corrie's father, a minister, begins a ministry to the homeless. At the same time, the children find a body in an abandoned inn. Clues seem to point to the homeless man, but police work determines that the man died of exposure and the confused homeless man hid the body. Other mysteries are about a poisoning in the school cafeteria and a famous actress in danger.

1. What Eric Knew ◆ 1985
2. Stage Fright ◆ 1986
3. Eat Your Poison, Dear ◆ 1986
4. Dew Drop Dead ◆ 1990

SEBASTIAN (SUPER SLEUTH)

Christian, Mary Blount
MACMILLAN
GRADES 3–5
ANIMAL FANTASY | MYSTERY

Sebastian is a lovable sheepdog who loves to dress up in human clothes and help his owner, Detective John Quincy Jones, solve puzzling crimes. Each title is devoted to a different mystery and illustrated with wonderfully detailed drawings.

1. Sebastian (Super Sleuth) ◆ 1974
2. Sebastian (Super Sleuth) and the Hair of the Dog Mystery ◆ 1983
3. Sebastian (Super Sleuth) and the Crummy Yummies Caper ◆ 1983
4. Sebastian (Super Sleuth) and the Bone to Pick Mystery ◆ 1983
5. Sebastian (Super Sleuth) and the Santa Claus Caper ◆ 1984
6. Sebastian (Super Sleuth) and the Secret of the Skewered Skier ◆ 1984
7. Sebastian (Super Sleuth) and the Clumsy Cowboy ◆ 1985
8. Sebastian (Super Sleuth) and the Purloined Sirloin ◆ 1986
9. Sebastian (Super Sleuth) and the Stars-in-His-Eyes Mystery ◆ 1987
10. Sebastian (Super Sleuth) and the Egyptian Connection ◆ 1988
11. Sebastian (Super Sleuth) and the Time Capsule Caper ◆ 1989
12. Sebastian (Super Sleuth) and the Baffling Bigfoot ◆ 1990
13. Sebastian (Super Sleuth) and the Mystery Patient ◆ 1991
14. Sebastian (Super Sleuth) and the Impossible Crime ◆ 1992
15. Sebastian (Super Sleuth) and the Copycat Crime ◆ 1993
16. Sebastian (Super Sleuth) and the Flying Elephant ◆ 1994

THE SECRET SEVEN

Blyton, Enid
CHIVERS NORTH AMERICA (LARGE PRINT)
GRADES 4–6
ADVENTURE | MYSTERY

Peter, Janet, Colin, Barbara, George, Jack, and Pam are the official members of the Secret Seven Society. Passwords, badges, and codes are part of membership in the society, which meets in Peter and Janet's garden shed. Jack's little sister Susie—not a member of the society—repeatedly tries to foil their plans. Scamper the dog is extremely useful because of his ability to sense danger and sniff out the bad guys. This series, like Blyton's Famous Five, was extremely popular in Great Britain, and Blyton has some loyal fans in the United States.

1. The Secret Seven ◆ 1949
2. Secret Seven Adventure ◆ 1950
3. Well Done, Secret Seven ◆ 1951
4. Secret Seven on the Trail ◆ 1952
5. Go Ahead, Secret Seven ◆ 1953
6. Good Work, Secret Seven ◆ 1954
7. Secret Seven Win Through ◆ 1955
8. Three Cheers, Secret Seven ◆ 1956
9. Secret Seven Mystery ◆ 1957
10. Puzzle for the Secret Seven ◆ 1958
11. Secret Seven Fireworks ◆ 1959
12. Good Old Secret Seven ◆ 1960
13. Shock for the Secret Seven ◆ 1961
14. Look Out Secret Seven ◆ 1962
15. Fun for the Secret Seven ◆ 1963

THE SECRET WORLD OF ALEX MACK

Various authors

MINSTREL/POCKET BOOKS

GRADES 5–8

ADVENTURE | FANTASY

Alex Mack was just an ordinary teenager until she was drenched by a strange chemical. Now she can move objects with her mind and change shapes by morphing into a liquid form. Alex and her friends Ray Alvarado, Robyn Russo, and Nicole Wilson and her boyfriend, Hunter Reeves, get involved in adventures such as capturing a pet-napping ring. Alex also has to worry about keeping her special powers a secret, especially when she gets sick on a trip to New York City and can't control her ability to become liquid. This series features the characters from the popular *Nickelodeon* TV program. Readers who enjoy the show will like seeing these familiar characters in this adventure series.

1. Alex, You're Glowing! (Gallagher, Diana G.) ◆ 1995
2. Bet You Can't! (Gallagher, Diana G.) ◆ 1995
3. Bad News Babysitting! (Lipman, Ken) ◆ 1995
4. Witch Hunt! (Gallagher, Diana G.) ◆ 1995
5. Mistaken Identity! (Gallagher, Diana G.) ◆ 1996
6. Cleanup Catastrophe! (Dubowski, Cathy East) ◆ 1996
7. Take a Hike! (Dubowski, Cathy East) ◆ 1996
8. Go for the Gold! (Gallagher, Diana G.) ◆ 1996
9. Poison in Paradise! (Gallagher, Diana G.) ◆ 1996
10. Zappy Holidays! (Super Edition) (Gallagher, Diana G.) ◆ 1996

11. Junkyard Jitters! (Barnes-Svarney, Patricia) ◆ 1997
12. Frozen Stiff! (Gallagher, Diana G.) ◆ 1997
13. I Spy! (Peel, John) ◆ 1997
14. High Flyer! (Barnes-Svarney, Patricia) ◆ 1997
15. Milady Alex! (Gallagher, Diana G.) ◆ 1997
16. Father-Daughter Disaster! (Emery, Clayton) ◆ 1997
17. Bonjour, Alex! (Dubowski, Cathy East) ◆ 1997
18. Close Encounters! (Weiss, David Cody, and Bobbi J. G. Weiss) ◆ 1997
19. Hocus Pocus! (Locke, Joseph) ◆ 1997
20. Halloween Invaders! (Vornholt, John) ◆ 1997
21. Truth Trap! (Dubowski, Cathy East) ◆ 1997
22. New Year's Revolution! (Gallagher, Diana G.) ◆ 1997
23. Lost in Vegas! (Peel, John) ◆ 1998
24. Computer Crunch! (Barnes-Svarney, Patricia) ◆ 1998
25. In Hot Pursuit! (Odom, Mel) ◆ 1998
26. Canine Caper! (Gallagher, Diana G.) ◆ 1998
27. Civil War in Paradise! (Stone, Bonnie D.) ◆ 1998
28. Pool Party Panic! (Mitchell, V. E.) ◆ 1998
29. Sink or Swim! (Dubowski, Cathy East) ◆ 1998
30. Gold Rush Fever! (Gallagher, Diana G.) ◆ 1998
31. New York Nightmare! (Pass, Erica) ◆ 1998
32. Haunted House Hijinks! (Vornholt, John) ◆ 1998
33. Lights Camera Action (Garton, Ray) ◆ 1998

SHAGGY DOG

Charles, Donald
CHILDREN'S PRESS
GRADES K–2
ANIMAL FANTASY

This series is intended for beginning readers, with spare text and amusing illustrations. At the end of each story, the reader is invited to answer a question that correlates with the story, such as sharing a tall tale of his or her own. Young readers will relate to the familiar experience of celebrating a birthday or enjoying Halloween.

1. Shaggy Dog's Animal Alphabet ◆ 1979
2. Shaggy Dog's Tall Tale ◆ 1980
3. Shaggy Dog's Halloween ◆ 1984
4. Shaggy Dog's Birthday ◆ 1986

SHANNON *see* Girlhood Journeys: Shannon

SHEEP

Shaw, Nancy
HOUGHTON MIFFLIN
GRADES K–3
ANIMAL FANTASY | HUMOR

A zany group of sheep has adventures on a ship, in a Jeep, and in a shop. Every time, they have a silly disaster that turns out all right in the end. On the ship, they "read a map" but "begin to nap," which results in a shipwreck. They make a raft, and it drifts as the storm lifts. "Land Ho. Not far to go." When they go for a ride in a Jeep, they get stuck in the mud. Some friendly pigs pull them out, but then the driver sheep forgets to steer and they crash into a tree. The sentences all rhyme and are often just two words.

1. Sheep in a Jeep ◆ 1986
2. Sheep on a Ship ◆ 1989
3. Sheep in a Shop ◆ 1991
4. Sheep Out to Eat ◆ 1992
5. Sheep Take a Hike ◆ 1994
6. Sheep Trick or Treat ◆ 1997

SHERLOCK CHICK

Quackenbush, Robert
PARENTS MAGAZINE PRESS
GRADES K–3
ANIMAL FANTASY | MYSTERY

Sherlock Chick, the famous detective, was born with a detective's hat, and his mother, Emma Hen, knew right then that he was special. In a typical book, a giant box is delivered to the farmer and Sherlock and his friends wonder what it could be. Out comes a giant egg, which Emma Hen decides to try to hatch. Meanwhile, Sherlock looks at the box for clues and reads the return address to discover that the box is from Africa. Stamps on the box show different animals, but one is torn and only says "ich." When the egg hatches, she remembers that "ich" is the last part of *ostrich*. Notes to parents at the end show how to use Sherlock to help students learn important concepts and to interact with the book.

1. Sherlock Chick's First Case ◆ 1986
2. Sherlock Chick and the Peekaboo Mystery ◆ 1987
3. Sherlock Chick and the Giant Egg Mystery ◆ 1988
4. Sherlock Chick and the Case of the Night Noises ◆ 1990

SHILOH

Naylor, Phyllis Reynolds
SIMON & SCHUSTER
GRADES 3–6
REAL LIFE

A touching dog story that deals with larger issues of prejudice and abuse. Marty makes friends with a beagle named Shiloh, only to discover that the dog is being abused. Readers are faced with the problem of what Marty should do, because the dog is not his. As the trilogy proceeds, Marty is forced to deal with Judd, the man who abuses Shiloh and his other dogs, and finally must decide whether he believes that Judd can change. Shiloh won the Newbery Award.

1. Shiloh ◆ 1991
2. Shiloh Season ◆ 1996
3. Saving Shiloh ◆ 1997

SHORT STIRRUP CLUB

Estes, Allison
POCKET BOOKS
GRADES 4–6
REAL LIFE | RECREATION

Five friends share adventures at the Thistle Ridge Farm, a stable owned by Olympic rider Sharon Wyndham. Megan and Max Morrison are twins who enjoy riding and competing. Amanda Sloane's mother is interested in riding, and she is pushing Amanda into training. Amanda dislikes her lessons and horse shows, but she wants to please her well-to-do parents. Chloe Goodman must do chores at the farm in order to keep her horse there, while Keith Hill, whose parents are Mexican and Native American, enjoys riding as an extension of his heritage. The plots are related to horse shows for younger riders: Short Stirrup is a division for riders 12 and under. The characters overcome fears, deal with jealousy, and participate in competitions, which will appeal to the many horse aficionados.

1. Blue Ribbon Friends ◆ 1996
2. Ghost of Thistle Ridge ◆ 1996
3. The Great Gymkhana Gamble ◆ 1996
4. Winner's Circle ◆ 1996
5. Gold Medal Mystery ◆ 1996
6. Friends to the Finish ◆ 1996
7. Legend of the Zuni Stallion ◆ 1996
8. Victory Ride ◆ 1997

9. Playing for Keeps ◆ 1997
10. Pony Express ◆ 1997

SIERRA JENSEN

Gunn, Robin Jones
FOCUS ON THE FAMILY, BETHANY HOUSE
GRADES 6–8
FAMILY LIFE | VALUES

Sierra lives with her sister Tawni, two younger brothers, and their parents and grandmother. Theirs is an upper-middle-class lifestyle, and Sierra is a casual teenager with a natural approach to life. This puts her in conflict with Tawni, whom Sierra believes always acts like she is on display. On a mission trip to England, Sierra makes friends with some older teens and meets a boy whom she seems to connect with. He is much older but she eventually dates him.

1. Only You—Sierra ◆ 1995
2. In Your Dreams ◆ 1996
3. Don't You Wish ◆ 1996
4. Close Your Eyes ◆ 1996
5. Without a Doubt ◆ 1997
6. With This Ring ◆ 1997
7. Open Your Heart ◆ 1997
8. Time Will Tell ◆ 1998
9. Now Picture This ◆ 1998
10. Hold on Tight ◆ 1998

SILLY TILLY

Hoban, Lillian
HARPERCOLLINS
GRADES K–2
ANIMAL FANTASY

Silly Tilly the mole is forgetful and easily distracted, but she is lovable. Mr. Bunny and her animal friends are always getting her out of silly scrapes and end up having fun in the process. These I Can Read books will be fun for children who are starting to have success reading by themselves. They are also enjoyable read-alouds for holiday groups of young children, who will have to listen closely to see what Silly Tilly is forgetting.

1. Silly Tilly and the Easter Bunny ◆ 1987
2. Silly Tilly's Thanksgiving Dinner ◆ 1990
3. Silly Tilly's Valentine ◆ 1997

SILVER BLADES

Lowell, Melissa

BANTAM

GRADES 4–7

REAL LIFE | RECREATION

Four girls who dream of going to the Olympics practice and compete at an exclusive skating club, the Silver Blades. The series starts with Nikki's arrival in Seneca Hills. She meets Jill, Tori, and Danielle and begins to practice for her Silver Blades tryout. She also meets other girls from school, is invited to join in their activities, and becomes interested in a handsome hockey player. In the end, she realizes that skating is really what she wants to do most. Each of the four girls star in subsequent books. Tori deals with her demanding mother, Jill moves to Colorado, and Danielle lands a starring role in an ice show. Lots of skating technicalities are a natural part of the stories.

In the Olympic trilogy, Silver Blades Gold Medal Dreams, Tori overcomes the odds and gets the chance to compete in the Winter Games.

1. Breaking the Ice ◆ 1993
2. In the Spotlight ◆ 1993
3. The Competition ◆ 1994
4. Going for the Gold ◆ 1994
5. The Perfect Pair ◆ 1994
6. Skating Camp ◆ 1994
7. The Ice Princess ◆ 1995
8. Rumors at the Rink ◆ 1995
9. Spring Break ◆ 1995
10. Center Ice ◆ 1995
11. A Surprise Twist ◆ 1995
12. The Winning Spirit ◆ 1995
13. The Big Audition ◆ 1995
14. Nutcracker on Ice ◆ 1995
15. A New Move ◆ 1996
16. Ice Magic ◆ 1996
17. A Leap Ahead ◆ 1996
18. More Than Friends ◆ 1996
19. Natalia Comes to America ◆ 1997
20. The One Way to Win ◆ 1997
21. Rival Roommates ◆ 1997

22. Double Dare ◆ 1998
23. Wanted: One Perfect Boy ◆ 1998

SILVER BLADES GOLD MEDAL DREAMS

1. On the Edge ◆ 1997
2. Now or Never ◆ 1997
3. Chance of a Lifetime ◆ 1998

SILVER BLADES FIGURE EIGHTS

Older, Effin

BANTAM

GRADES 2–4

REAL LIFE | RECREATION

Randi Wong is the younger sister of Jill Wong of the Silver Blades figure-skating club. Every day, she goes to the rink with Jill, but she is not allowed to take lessons because her family has a rule that each child must have a different activity. Randi's activity is supposed to be the violin, but she wants to quit and take skating lessons instead. When she signs up for skating lessons without permission, Jill intercedes with her parents and they let Randi join the newly formed group—the Silver Blades Figure Eights—which includes her friends Woody and Anna. The rest of the series is about Randi and her friends and their adventures on and off the ice. Silver Blades Figure Eights Super Editions include *Double Birthday Trouble* (1996) and *Randi Goes for the Gold* (1998).

1. Ice Dreams ◆ 1996
2. Star for a Day ◆ 1996
3. The Best Ice Show Ever! ◆ 1996
4. Bossy Anna ◆ 1996
5. Special Delivery Mess ◆ 1997
6. Randi's Missing Skates ◆ 1997
7. My Worst Friend, Woody ◆ 1997
8. Randi's Pet Surprise ◆ 1997

SILVER CREEK RIDERS

Kincaid, Beth

JOVE BOOKS

GRADES 6–8

REAL LIFE | RECREATION

Four friends—Melissa, Jenna, Katie, and Sharon—all love horses. After they meet at the Silver Creek riding camp, they find ways to keep in touch and help each other. At camp, they help Melissa as she learns to deal with a tragic accident and her fear of riding again. In another book, Katie meets Matt and it looks like love—except that Katie is attracted to Matt's horse (at first). During the Autumn Horse Show, Melissa helps a horse that is being mistreated. The audience for these books is primarily horse-crazy girls, who will also enjoy the Saddle Club books.

1. Back in the Saddle ◆ 1994
2. True Romance ◆ 1994
3. Winning ◆ 1995

SIMON

Tibo, Gilles
TUNDRA
GRADES K–3
FANTASY

Very simple stories of a boy interacting with nature characterize this picture book series. Simon wants to fly like the wind in the autumn story, and a friendly scarecrow tells him that it must be easy because birds do it. He asks the birds, but they just fly away. The sun says it must be easy because the clouds do it; but when he climbs a mountain to talk to the clouds, they turn to rain. Finally, Simon decides he can fly a kite—so that is what he and his friend Marlene do. A full-page illustration in muted tones appears with each page of text as Simon explores all the seasons.

1. Simon and the Snowflakes ◆ 1988
2. Simon and the Wind ◆ 1989
3. Simon Welcomes Spring ◆ 1990
4. Simon in Summer ◆ 1991
5. Simon and His Boxes ◆ 1992
6. Simon in the Moonlight ◆ 1993
7. Simon Finds a Feather ◆ 1994
8. Simon Makes Music ◆ 1995
9. Simon Finds a Treasure ◆ 1996
10. Simon at the Circus ◆ 1997

SISTER SISTER

Quin-Harkin, Janet
POCKET BOOKS
GRADES 4–6
FAMILY LIFE | REAL LIFE

Fans of the popular TV show *Sister Sister* will enjoy these light-hearted books about the adventures of twin sisters Tia and Tamera. Tia and her single mother, Lisa Landry, have moved in with Tia's sister Tamera and Tamera's father, Ray Campbell. (How the twins were split up and how they came to be living with Lisa and Ray is part of the story.) Their home situation causes some confusion, particularly in regard to decisions about child rearing. The adventures in this series primarily focus on the daily lives of the girls, including their interest in boys, projects at school, clubs, tests, and summer jobs. These are enjoyable books, and students will find it fun to read about familiar TV characters.

1. Cool in School ◆ 1996
2. You Read My Mind ◆ 1996
3. One Crazy Christmas ◆ 1996
4. Homegirl on the Range ◆ 1997
5. All Rapped Up ◆ 1997
6. Star Quality ◆ 1997
7. He's All That ◆ 1997
8. Summer Daze ◆ 1997

SISTERS

Kaye, Marilyn
HARCOURT
GRADES 6–8
REAL LIFE | FAMILY LIFE

Each book in this series is devoted to one of the four Gray sisters, each of whom has a very distinct personality. Lydia, the baby of the family, is a dreamer and content with being a child; Daphne is the sensitive poet; Cassie is the self-centered beauty; and Lydia, the eldest at 14, is a leader who is always taking on important causes. Readers may find that they relate strongly to one of the sisters or maybe to individual qualities of each girl. Although the individual stories stand on their own, the series provides the reader with a stronger sense of the individual personalities that make up a family.

1. Phoebe ◆ 1987
2. Daphne ◆ 1987
3. Cassie ◆ 1987
4. Lydia ◆ 1987
5. A Friend Like Phoebe ◆ 1989

SITTING PRETTY

Weyn, Suzanne
TROLL
GRADES 4–7
REAL LIFE

Three 14-year-old girls are employed by a posh hotel to baby-sit the children of the rich and famous patrons. Their boss, Mr. Parker, is strict and demanding, and the girls frequently have run-ins with him. Of the three girls, Sam is the responsible one, and Lisa and Chris are more boy crazy and fun-loving. In addition to the situations arising from their baby-sitting jobs, the girls are involved with boys and the everyday problems of friendship and families. Some of the situations involve the tension between their middle class backgrounds and the wealthy lifestyles of the Palm Pavilion customers.

1. Checking In ◆ 1991
2. True Blue ◆ 1991
3. Liza's Lucky Break ◆ 1991
4. A Chance for Chris ◆ 1991
5. Boy Trouble ◆ 1991
6. Star Magic ◆ 1991

THE SKINNER FAMILY *see* The Great Skinner

SLEEPOVER FRIENDS

Saunders, Susan
SCHOLASTIC
GRADES 3–5
REAL LIFE

Kate Beekman and Lauren Hunter have been friends since they were very young, and they have enjoyed regular sleep-over parties. In fourth grade, Stephanie Green moved to their neighborhood; and in fifth grade, Patti Jenkins joined the group. Now they spend a lot of time together, including Friday sleep-overs. Their adventures involve fairly standard school and friendship activities: problems with boys, worries about arguing parents, and jealousy over performing in the school play and a rock video. Girls enjoy this series because of the familiar situations and enduring friendships.

1. Patti's Luck ◆ 1987
2. Starring Stephanie ◆ 1987
3. Kate's Surprise ◆ 1987
4. Patti's New Look ◆ 1988
5. Lauren's Big Mix-Up ◆ 1988
6. Kate's Camp-Out ◆ 1988
7. Stephanie Strikes Back ◆ 1988
8. Lauren's Treasure ◆ 1988
9. No More Sleepovers Patti? ◆ 1988
10. Lauren's Sleepover Exchange ◆ 1989
11. Stephanie's Family Secret ◆ 1989
12. Kate's Sleepover Disaster ◆ 1989
13. Patti's Secret Wish ◆ 1989
14. Lauren Takes Charge ◆ 1989
15. Stephanie's Big Story ◆ 1989
16. Kate's Crush ◆ 1989
17. Patti Gets Even ◆ 1989
18. Stephanie and the Magician ◆ 1989
19. The Great Kate ◆ 1990
20. Lauren in the Middle ◆ 1990
21. Starstruck Stephanie ◆ 1990
22. The Trouble with Patti ◆ 1990
23. Kate's Surprise Visitor ◆ 1990
24. Lauren's New Friend ◆ 1990
25. Stephanie and the Wedding ◆ 1990
26. The New Kate ◆ 1990
27. Lauren's New Address ◆ 1990
28. Kate the Boss ◆ 1990
29. Lauren's Afterschool Job ◆ 1990
30. A Valentine for Patti ◆ 1991
31. Lauren's Double Disaster ◆ 1991
32. Kate the Winner! ◆ 1991
33. The New Stephanie ◆ 1991

SLIMEBALLS

Gross, U. B.
RANDOM HOUSE
GRADES 5–7
HUMOR

Two of the books in this series feature Gus, his friend Polly, and the class dullard Ray. Gus plans to win the science fair with his collection of unusual molds. This series is filled with gross humor and weird characters. A wacko school nurse is fired and returns in another book as a crazed bus driver. The characters often behave in ways that will appeal to the middle school sense of humor—food fights, slime attacks, and rodents that take over a home.

1. Fun Gus & Polly Pus ◆ 1996
2. Fun Gus Slimes the Bus ◆ 1997
3. The Slithers Buy a Boa ◆ 1997

SNAIL

Stadler, John

HARPERCOLLINS

GRADES K–3

ANIMAL FANTASY

Silly, slow-moving Snail is often late—not because he's slow, but because of the amazing things that happen to him. Of course, no one ever believes him. Simple text and humorous illustrations make this an enjoyable series for beginning readers.

1. The Adventures of Snail at School ◆ 1993
2. Hooray for Snail ◆ 1984
3. Snail Saves the Day ◆ 1985

SNARVEY GOOPER *see* Funny Firsts

SNOWY DAY *see* Peter

SOCCER STARS

Costello, Emily

BANTAM DOUBLEDAY DELL

GRADES 3–6

REAL LIFE | RECREATION

Serious soccer players will enjoy this series, packed full of game action. Off the field, the Soccer Stars (Rose, Jordan, Geena, Tess, Tameka, Lacey, Fiona, Yaz, and Nicole) are best friends; on the field, they're teammates and sometimes rivals. Endorsed by the American Youth Soccer Organization, with soccer tips at the back of each book, this is a series for girls who love soccer.

1. Foul Play ◆ 1998
2. On the Sidelines ◆ 1998
3. Against the Rules ◆ 1998

4. Best Friend Face-Off ◆ 1998
5. Lottery Blues ◆ 1998
6. Tournament Trouble ◆ 1998

SOMETHING QUEER

Levy, Elizabeth
HYPERION
GRADES 3–5
MYSTERY

Jill and Gwen are in a rock-and-roll band in *Something Queer in Rock 'n' Roll*. Gwen is fond of using disguises and always taps her braces and announces that she thinks "something queer" is going on. Their dog Fletcher is an important part of their act, howling along with them whenever they offer him pizza. The effect is so good that the band becomes a finalist in a contest, but their rivals capture Fletcher and force him to eat pizza until he is sick of it. All ends happily when Gwen discovers clues to solve the mystery and their rivals are disqualified. In another book, the girls have a lemonade stand that someone is trying to sabotage. All the books follow the same format, with easy-to-solve mysteries and plenty of humor.

1. Something Queer Is Going On ◆ 1973
2. Something Queer at the Ballpark ◆ 1975
3. Something Queer at the Library ◆ 1977
4. Something Queer on Vacation ◆ 1980
5. Something Queer at the Haunted School ◆ 1982
6. Something Queer at the Lemonade Stand ◆ 1982
7. Something Queer in Rock 'n' Roll ◆ 1987
8. Something Queer at the Birthday Party ◆ 1989
9. Something Queer in Outer Space ◆ 1993
10. Something Queer in the Cafeteria ◆ 1994
11. Something Queer at the Scary Movie ◆ 1995
12. Something Queer in the Wild West ◆ 1997

SONG LEE

Kline, Suzy
VIKING
GRADES 2–4
HUMOR | REAL LIFE

Doug, the young narrator of this easy-reader series, relates the doings of his second-grade class. In *Song Lee and the Hamster Hunt*, Song brings her pet hamster to school and it escapes. The class makes posters to alert everyone in the school to watch for him. The janitor finally finds the hamster and brings him back. Another book finds the kids on a field trip and Song Lee makes friends with the class tattle-tale, Sidney. During the trip, due to Song's peacemaking efforts, Sidney learns not to tattle. The Horrible Harry series by the same author features the same characters and is also narrated by Doug, Harry's best friend.

1. Song Lee in Room 2B ◆ 1993
2. Song Lee and the Hamster Hunt ◆ 1994
3. Song Lee and the Leech Man ◆ 1995

SONIC THE HEDGEHOG

Teitelbaum, Michael

TROLL

GRADES 2–3

SCIENCE FICTION

Sonic is a blue hedgehog who travels the galaxy battling evil robots controlled by Dr. Robotnik. In one book, the robots want to do away with having fun; in another, Dr. Robotnik has the secret list that could lead to the destruction of the freedom fighters. These books are easy to read, with lots of action. Sonic behaves like a superhero as he faces dangers throughout the galaxy.

1. Sonic the Hedgehog ◆ 1993
2. Sonic the Hedgehog: Fortress of Fear ◆ 1994
3. Sonic the Hedgehog: Robotnik's Revenge ◆ 1994
4. Sonic the Hedgehog: Friend or Foe? ◆ 1995

SOOKAN BAK

Choi, Sook Nyul

HOUGHTON MIFFLIN

GRADES 5–8

FAMILY LIFE | HISTORICAL

In the first book of this trilogy, *Year of Impossible Goodbyes*, Sookan Bak is ten. It is the 1940s, and she and her family are enduring the occupation of their homeland in northern Korea. When the country is divided at the end of the war, the family emigrates to the south, hoping for a better life. *Echoes of the White Giraffe* describes Sookan's life in Pusan and her growing friendship with Junho, a boy she knows from the church choir. In the final book, *Gathering of Pearls*, Sookan is in college in the United States, where she is challenged by a new language, a different culture, and the death of her mother.

1. Year of Impossible Goodbyes ◆ 1991
2. Echoes of the White Giraffe ◆ 1993
3. Gathering of Pearls ◆ 1994

SOPHIE

King-Smith, Dick

CANDLEWICK

GRADES 3–5

FAMILY LIFE | HUMOR

Sophie is a persistent little girl who is determined that one day she will be a farmer. Through all six books in this series, she saves her farm money and practices on everything from wood lice to cats. Her great-aunt Alice lives in Scotland and encourages Sophie's independence and zeal to become a farmer. Her twin brothers, Matthew and Mark, are fond of twirling a pointed finger at their heads to indicate what they think of Sophie, but readers will be charmed by her droll approach to life and friendships. Her growth is chronicled throughout the series, and eventually she and her family inherit Aunt Alice's farm and move to Scotland, where Sophie is given Lucky, a pony.

1. Sophie's Snail ◆ 1989
2. Sophie's Tom ◆ 1992
3. Sophie Hits Six ◆ 1993
4. Sophie in the Saddle ◆ 1994
5. Sophie Is Seven ◆ 1995
6. Sophie's Lucky ◆ 1996

SOUP

Peck, Robert Newton

KNOPF

GRADES 3–5

ADVENTURE | HUMOR

Soup and Rob are always getting into mischievous trouble that usually ends up involving the entire community. Young readers will enjoy the hilarious escapades of these two pals growing up in rural Vermont, where the author (*A Day No Pigs Would Die*) grew up. A couple of ABC Afterschool Specials were based on two of the series titles: *Soup and Me* and *Soup for President*. The Little Soup series features the boys when they are younger.

1. Soup ◆ 1974

2. Soup and Me ◆ 1975
3. Soup for President ◆ 1978
4. Soup's Drum ◆ 1980
5. Soup on Wheels ◆ 1981
6. Soup in the Saddle ◆ 1983
7. Soup's Goat ◆ 1984
8. Soup on Ice ◆ 1985
9. Soup on Fire ◆ 1987
10. Soup's Uncle ◆ 1988
11. Soup's Hoop ◆ 1989
12. Soup in Love ◆ 1992
13. Soup Ahoy ◆ 1994
14. Soup 1776 ◆ 1995

SPACE ABOVE AND BEYOND

Various authors
HARPERCOLLINS
GRADES 5–8
SCIENCE FICTION

In 2063, an Earth space station has been destroyed by aliens and now Earth is in danger. Lieutenants Vansen, West, and Hawke are thrown together to accomplish a dangerous mission and face the Artificial Intelligence (AI) creatures. There are encounters on Mars, a mutiny in space, and an electromagnetic lightning storm. Fans of Star Trek and Deep Space Nine will enjoy these books.

1. The Aliens Approach (Royce, Easton) ◆ 1996
2. Dark Side of the Sun (Anastasio, Dina) ◆ 1996
3. Mutiny (Royce, Easton) ◆ 1996
4. The Enemy (Anastasio, Dina) ◆ 1996
5. Demolition Winter (Telep, Peter) ◆ 1997

SPACE BRAT

Coville, Bruce
POCKET BOOKS
GRADES 3–5
HUMOR I SCIENCE FICTION

Blork the Space Brat throws the biggest tantrums on the planet Splat. Things began to go wrong for him when a piece of shell got stuck on his ear when he hatched and he was labeled a brat. When the Big Pest Squad starts to take away Lunk, his poodnoobie, he grabs one of their spaceships and goes to the land of the Things. The Things are huge, harmless creatures that are slaves to the evil tyrant Squat. Blork outwits Squat and sets the Things free and in the process learns how not to be a brat. He gains an evil twin and is kidnapped by Squat in the sequels, which are filled with the same zany humor.

1. Space Brat ◆ 1992
2. Blork's Evil Twin ◆ 1993
3. The Wrath of Squat ◆ 1994
4. The Planet of the Dips ◆ 1995
5. The Saber-Toothed Poodnoobie ◆ 1997

SPACE DOG

Standiford, Natalie
RANDOM HOUSE
GRADES 1–3
HUMOR | SCIENCE FICTION

Space Dog is from the planet Queekrg. His spaceship crashes in Roy's backyard, which works out fine because Roy has been wanting a dog to protect him from a bully. Space Dog understands the problem because he volunteered to come to Earth to get away from a bully. He looks exactly like an Earth dog; and when he is with people, he acts like one, so he can keep his mission secret. Only when he and Ray are alone does he read, write, talk, and walk on two legs. While he is stuck on Earth, he does a study of humans. Alice, Roy's friend, has a poodle named Blanche who likes Space Dog, but he thinks she is dumb, possibly because she's not allowed to go to school.

1. Space Dog and Roy ◆ 1990
2. Space Dog and the Pet Show ◆ 1990
3. Space Dog in Trouble ◆ 1991
4. Space Dog, the Hero ◆ 1991

SPACE SHIP UNDER THE APPLE TREE

Slobodkin, Louis
MACMILLAN
GRADES 3–5
SCIENCE FICTION

Eddie Blow visits his grandmother on her farm during the summer months. One summer, he meets a little man who is visiting from the planet Martinea. Marty, as he comes to be called, is short enough for Eddie's grandmother to think he is another boy, but he has powers of speed and levitation that depend on his planet's special tools. His mission is scientific: to learn about the United States. He and Eddie have many old-fashioned adventures together, with Eddie constantly having to bail Marty out of tight spots. In subsequent books, the two meet again, once in Central Park near Eddie's home. Their adventures take them to other planets as well, sometimes with Willie, a friend of Eddie's.

1. The Space Ship Under the Apple Tree ◆ 1952
2. The Space Ship Returns to the Apple Tree ◆ 1958
3. The Three-Seated Space Ship ◆ 1962
4. Round Trip Space Ship ◆ 1968
5. The Space Ship in the Park ◆ 1972

SPENCER'S ADVENTURES

Hogg, Gary
SCHOLASTIC
GRADES 1–3
HUMOR

Wherever there is Spencer, there is trouble, and it usually involves zany schemes and slimy situations. Like Dennis the Menace, Spencer wreaks havoc throughout his neighborhood. Readers who laugh at humor involving garbage, toilet paper, and slime will find this great fun.

1. Stop That Eyeball! ◆ 1997
2. Garbage Snooper Surprise ◆ 1997
3. Hair in the Air ◆ 1997
4. The Great Toilet Paper Caper ◆ 1997
5. Don't Bake That Snake ◆ 1997
6. Let Go of That Toe! ◆ 1998

SPIDER

Kraus, Robert
SCHOLASTIC
GRADES K–2
ANIMAL FANTASY

Lovable Spider and his good friends Fly and Ladybug have adventures as they save the day. The holiday connection appeals to many children.

1. The Trouble with Spider ◆ 1962

2. How Spider Saved Christmas ◆ 1970
3. How Spider Saved Halloween ◆ 1973
4. How Spider Saved Turkey ◆ 1981
5. How Spider Saved Valentine's Day ◆ 1985
6. Spider's First Day at School ◆ 1987
7. How Spider Saved Easter ◆ 1988
8. How Spider Saved the Baseball Game ◆ 1989
9. How Spider Saved Santa Bug ◆ 1989
10. Spider's Baby-Sitting Job ◆ 1990
11. How Spider Saved Thanksgiving ◆ 1991
12. How Spider Saved the Flea Circus ◆ 1991
13. How Spider Stopped the Litterbugs ◆ 1991
14. Dance, Spider, Dance! ◆ 1993

SPINETINGLERS

Coffin, M. T.

AVON

GRADES 6–8

HORROR

Suppose you went to class and your teacher was a bug. When you tried to tell others about it, you realized that there were bugs everywhere. In fact, everyone in town is a bug. This is just one weird scenario in the Spinetingler series. There are spooky libraries (*Check It Out—and Die!*), scary schools (*Don't Go to the Principal's Office*), and spooky T.V. (*The Monster Channel*). Bizarre creatures, zombie dogs, cursed cheerleaders, lizard people, and freaks inhabit the books, which also include cliff-hanging plot twists and breathtaking encounters. There are also humorous moments, which you would expect from an author named M.T. Coffin who claims to live in Tombstone with children named Phillip A. Coffin and Carrie A. Coffin. Fans of Goosebumps will take to these books.

1. The Substitute Creature ◆ 1995
2. Billy Baker's Dog Won't Stay Buried ◆ 1995
3. My Teacher's a Bug ◆ 1995
4. Where Have All the Parents Gone? ◆ 1995
5. Check It Out—and Die! ◆ 1995
6. Simon Says, "Croak!" ◆ 1995
7. Snow Day ◆ 1996
8. Don't Go to the Principal's Office ◆ 1996
9. Step on a Crack ◆ 1996
10. The Dead Kid Did It ◆ 1996
11. Fly by Night ◆ 1996

12. Killer Computer ◆ 1996
13. Pet Store ◆ 1996
14. Blood Red Eightball ◆ 1996
15. Escape from the Haunted Mountain ◆ 1996
16. We Wish You a Scary Christmas ◆ 1996
17. The Monster Channel ◆ 1997
18. Mirror, Mirror ◆ 1997
19. Boogey's Back for Blood ◆ 1997
20. Lights, Camera, Die! ◆ 1997
21. Camp Crocodile ◆ 1997
22. Student Exchange ◆ 1997
23. Gimme Back My Brain ◆ 1997
24. Your Turn—to Scream! ◆ 1997
25. The Curse of the Cheerleaders ◆ 1997
26. Wear and Scare ◆ 1997
27. Lizard People ◆ 1997
28. Circus F.R.E.A.K.S. ◆ 1997
29. My Dentist Is a Vampire ◆ 1998
30. Saber-Toothed Tiger ◆ 1998

SPIRIT FLYER

Bibee, John
INTERVARSITY PRESS
GRADES 4–6
FANTASY

In the first book of this series, *The Magic Bicycle*, John Kramer's bike is run over by a car, so he fixes up an old Spirit Flyer bicycle he finds at the dump. He soon discovers that it is no ordinary bike—for one thing, it flies, and also, the people at Goliath Industries seem awfully eager to take it away from John. The stories become more fantastic as John and other Centerville children enter the Deeper World, fight off a giant snake, break the Order of the Chains, and have other adventures while riding Spirit Flyer.

1. The Magic Bicycle ◆ 1983
2. The Toy Campaign ◆ 1987
3. The Only Game in Town ◆ 1988
4. Bicycle Hills ◆ 1989
5. The Last Christmas ◆ 1990
6. The Runaway Parents ◆ 1991
7. The Perfect Star ◆ 1992
8. The Journey of Wishes ◆ 1993

SPOOKSVILLE

Pike, Christopher

POCKET BOOKS

GRADES 5–8

HORROR

Springville seems like an ordinary town, but a closer look reveals strange things going on. Cindy Mackey finds this out when her brother Neil is kidnapped by a ghost. Adam Freeman knows things are different. One of his best friends is Watch, a creature who has returned from the dead. Cindy, Adam, Watch, and their friends Sally Wilcox and Bryce Poole confront howling ghosts, aliens, witches, wicked cats, killer crabs, vampires, and other demons as they try to survive in a very strange town. This series will be a hit with readers who enjoy Goosebumps and Buffy the Vampire Slayer.

1. The Secret Path ◆ 1995
2. The Howling Ghost ◆ 1995
3. The Haunted Cave ◆ 1995
4. Aliens in the Sky ◆ 1996
5. The Cold People ◆ 1996
6. The Witch's Revenge ◆ 1996
7. The Dark Corner ◆ 1996
8. The Little People ◆ 1996
9. The Wishing Stone ◆ 1996
10. The Wicked Cat ◆ 1996
11. The Deadly Past ◆ 1996
12. The Hidden Beast ◆ 1996
13. The Creature in the Teacher ◆ 1996
14. The Evil House ◆ 1997
15. Invasion of the No-Ones ◆ 1997
16. Time Terror ◆ 1997
17. The Thing in the Closet ◆ 1997
18. Attack of the Killer Crabs ◆ 1997
19. Night of the Vampire ◆ 1997
20. The Dangerous Quest ◆ 1998
21. The Living Dead ◆ 1998
22. The Creepy Creature ◆ 1998

SPOOKY THE CAT

Carlson, Natalie Savage

LOTHROP, LEE & SHEPARD

GRADES K–2

ANIMAL FANTASY

Spooky is a big black cat with big green eyes, who used to belong to a witch down the road and now belongs to the Bascomb family. But the witch is never out of his life. In the first book, Spooky rescues Snowball, a ghost cat who lives with the witch but who comes to live with the Bascombs when she becomes real. In each of the following books, Spooky confronts and outwits the witch or her cohorts with the Bascombs none the wiser.

1. Spooky Night ◆ 1982
2. Spooky and the Ghost Cat ◆ 1985
3. Spooky and the Wizard's Bats ◆ 1986
4. Spooky and the Bad Luck Raven ◆ 1988
5. Spooky and the Witch's Goat ◆ 1989

SPORTS MYSTERIES

Edwards, T. J.

SCHOLASTIC

GRADES 4–6

MYSTERY

Many readers are interested in books about sports. Combine that with an element of mystery and you have a series of books that should reach a wide audience. Corey, Jack Bryan, and Sam are some of the key players on several sports teams. In one book, an autographed football is missing and Jack is the prime suspect. In another book, there may be a ghost looking for a stolen treasure—and he seems to be haunting the soccer field. Lara, a lively, sports-minded girl, sometimes helps with the mysteries, too, which may broaden the appeal of these books.

1. The Case of the Missing Pitcher ◆ 1995
2. The Haunted Soccer Field ◆ 1995
3. The Mystery of the Stolen Football ◆ 1995
4. The Case of the Basketball Video ◆ 1995

SPOT

Hill, Eric

PUTNAM

GRADES K–1

ANIMAL FANTASY

A little yellow dog with brown spots lives with his loving mother and father in this series for young readers. In *Where's Spot?*, his mother looks everywhere for him, but only finds various jungle animals until she looks in a little basket. In another book, Spot gets a little sister, and his friends come over to see her. There are several different formats: some lift-the-flaps, some coloring books, and some board books. There is also a popular video series.

1. Where's Spot ◆ 1980
2. Spot's First Walk ◆ 1981
3. Spot's Birthday Party ◆ 1982
4. Spot's Busy Year ◆ 1983
5. Spot's First Christmas ◆ 1983
6. Spot Learns to Count ◆ 1983
7. Spot Tells the Time ◆ 1983
8. Spot's Alphabet ◆ 1983
9. Sweet Dreams, Spot ◆ 1984
10. Spot's Friends ◆ 1984
11. Spot's Toys ◆ 1984
12. Here's Spot ◆ 1984
13. Spot Goes Splash! ◆ 1984
14. Spot Goes to School ◆ 1984
15. Spot on the Farm ◆ 1985
16. Spot Goes to the Beach ◆ 1985
17. Spot at Play ◆ 1985
18. Spot at the Fair ◆ 1985
19. Spot Goes to the Circus ◆ 1986
20. Spot's First Words ◆ 1986
21. Spot's Doghouse ◆ 1986
22. Spot Looks at Colors ◆ 1986
23. Spot Looks at Shapes ◆ 1986
24. Spot Goes to the Farm ◆ 1987
25. Spot's First Picnic ◆ 1987
26. Spot Visits the Hospital ◆ 1987
27. Spot's Big Book of Words ◆ 1988

28. Spot's First Easter ◆ 1988
29. Spot Counts from One to Ten ◆ 1989
30. Spot Looks at Opposites ◆ 1989
31. Spot Looks at the Weather ◆ 1989
32. Spot's Baby Sister ◆ 1989
33. Spot Sleeps Over ◆ 1990
34. Spot Goes to the Park ◆ 1991
35. Spot in the Garden ◆ 1991
36. Spot's Toy Box ◆ 1991
37. Spot at Home ◆ 1991
38. Spot's Walk in the Woods ◆ 1992
39. Spot Goes to a Party ◆ 1993
40. Spot's Big Book of Colors, Shapes, and Numbers ◆ 1994
41. Spot Bakes a Cake ◆ 1994
42. Spot's Magical Christmas ◆ 1995
43. Spot Visits His Grandparents ◆ 1996
44. Spot and Friends Dress Up ◆ 1996
45. Spot and Friends Play ◆ 1996
46. Spot's Touch and Feel Day ◆ 1997
47. Spot's Favorite Words ◆ 1997
48. Spot's Favorite Numbers ◆ 1997
49. Spot's Favorite Colors ◆ 1997
50. Spot's Favorite Baby Animals ◆ 1997
51. Spot Joins the Parade ◆ 1998

STANLEY

Brown, Jeff

HARPERCOLLINS

GRADES K–3

FAMILY LIFE | HUMOR

Readers will giggle at the silly adventures that Stanley has as a result of all the strange things that happen to him. On the night after a bad storm his family discovers he is still there but invisible. Or there's the time the bulletin board falls and flattens him. Luckily, his brother figures out how to blow him back up.

1. Flat Stanley ◆ 1964
2. Invisible Stanley ◆ 1996
3. Stanley and the Magic Lamp ◆ 1996

STAR TREK: DEEP SPACE NINE

Various authors

POCKET BOOKS

GRADES 4–8

ADVENTURE | SCIENCE FICTION

Fans of the TV series *Deep Space Nine* will enjoy reading adventures featuring their favorite characters. Young Jake Sisko and his Ferengi friend Nog are involved in time travel, attending Starfleet Academy's summer space camp, and even a field trip through the Worm Hole. They meet unusual creatures and are often in situations that threaten the future of the world. Jake's father, Commander Benjamin Sisko, supervises the Deep Space Nine space station with the assistance of security officer Odo and first officer Major Kira Nerys. Other characters from the show, including Miles and Keiko O'Brien and the Ferengi businessman Quark, appear in the books. There is lots of action and imaginative situations that should attract science fiction fans.

1. The Star Ghost (Strickland, Brad) ◆ 1994
2. Stowaways (Strickland, Brad) ◆ 1994
3. Prisoners of Peace (Peel, John) ◆ 1994
4. The Pet (Gilden, Mel, and Ted Pedersen) ◆ 1994
5. Arcade (Gallagher, Diana G.) ◆ 1995
6. Field Trip (Peel, John) ◆ 1995
7. Gypsy World (Pedersen, Ted, and John Peel) ◆ 1996
8. Highest Score (Antilles, Kem) ◆ 1996
9. Cardassian Imps (Gilden, Mel) ◆ 1997
10. Space Camp (Pedersen, Ted, and John Peel) ◆ 1997
11. Day of Honor: Honor Bound (Gallagher, Diana G.) ◆ 1997
12. Trapped in Time (Pedersen, Ted) ◆ 1998

STAR TREK: STARFLEET ACADEMY

Various authors

POCKET BOOKS

GRADES 4–8

ADVENTURE | SCIENCE FICTION

Many fans of science fiction series want to know everything about the characters. These fans are often so enthralled with the series that publishers and media producers provide numerous spin-offs and related activities (e.g., computer games, Web sites, conventions). *Star Trek* fans are among the most loyal and intense. The ongoing popularity of the TV series, along with every related item, is a testament to that. This series examines the early lives and training of key characters: James T. Kirk, Spock, and Leonard McCoy. Their adventures at the Starfleet Academy include escaping from space pirates and saving earthquake victims on the planet Playamar. Fans will especially enjoy *Crisis on Vulcan*, in which Spock meets young Christopher Pike (who was the captain in the *Star Trek* pilot program).

1. Crisis on Vulcan (Strickland, Brad, and Barbara Strickland) ◆ 1996
2. Aftershock (Vornholt, John) ◆ 1996
3. Cadet Kirk (Carey, Diane L.) ◆ 1996

STAR TREK: THE NEXT GENERATION: STARFLEET ACADEMY

Various authors

POCKET BOOKS

GRADES 4–8

ADVENTURE | SCIENCE FICTION

Focusing on the early years of the crew of the *U.S.S. Enterprise*, this series features the Starfleet Academy training experiences of familiar characters including Picard, Worf, Geordi, and Data. In *Deceptions*, Data participates in a research investigation of ancient ruins on the planet Arunu. When the communications system is sabotaged, Data must use his powers as an android to rescue his friends. In *Survival*, Worf and several Starfleet cadets work with a group of Klingon cadets to escape from the evil of an alien force. This series will interest fans of the TV programs and movies as well as readers who like fast-paced adventures.

1. Worf's First Adventure (David, Peter) ◆ 1993
2. Line of Fire (David, Peter) ◆ 1993
3. Survival (David, Peter) ◆ 1993
4. Capture the Flag (Vornholt, John) ◆ 1994
5. Atlantis Station (Mitchell, V. E.) ◆ 1994
6. Mystery of the Missing Crew (Friedman, Michael J.) ◆ 1995
7. Secret of the Lizard People (Friedman, Michael J.) ◆ 1995
8. Starfall (Strickland, Brad, and Barbara Strickland) ◆ 1995
9. Nova Command (Strickland, Brad, and Barbara Strickland) ◆ 1995
10. Loyalties (Barnes-Svarney, Patricia) ◆ 1996
11. Crossfire (Vornholt, John) ◆ 1996
12. Breakaway (Weiss, Bobbi J. G., and David Cody Weiss) ◆ 1997
13. The Haunted Starship (Ferguson, Brad, and Kathi Ferguson) ◆ 1997
14. Deceptions (Weiss, Bobbi J. G., and David Cody Weiss) ◆ 1998

STAR TREK: VOYAGER: STARFLEET ACADEMY

Various authors

POCKET BOOKS

GRADES 4–8

ADVENTURE | SCIENCE FICTION

The *Voyager* series (on TV and in these books) revolves around Kathryn Janeway, daughter of Vice Admiral Edward Janeway. At the Starfleet Academy, Kathryn wants to step out from the shadow of her successful father and establish her own credentials. These adventures put her in situations involving alien animals and an outer-space quarantine that could prove deadly. There is lots of action in these books, which should appeal to fans of the show and of science fiction. The creatures and outer-space setting may attract reluctant readers.

1. Lifeline (Weiss, Bobbi J. G., and David C. Weiss) ◆ 1997
2. The Chance Factor (Gallagher, Diana G., and Martin R. Burke) ◆ 1997
3. Quarantine (Barnes-Svarney, Patricia) ◆ 1997

STAR WARS GALAXY OF FEAR

Whitman, John

BANTAM

GRADES 4–8

ADVENTURE | SCIENCE FICTION

Tash Arranda, 13, and her brother Zak, 12, travel through space encountering strange creatures and circumstances that threaten the security of space communities. In *Spore*, the two children and their Uncle Hoole visit a mining community that has released an ancient, evil force. *Clones* features a visit to a remote planet that is inhabited by familiar characters who turn out to be clones. Readers who enjoy *Star Wars* will enjoy these adventures, many of which include appearances by characters from the movies, such as Luke Skywalker and Darth Vader. These are exciting adventures with gruesome creatures that link the horror genre to science fiction.

1. Eaten Alive ◆ 1997
2. City of the Dead ◆ 1997
3. Planet Plague ◆ 1997
4. The Nightmare Machine ◆ 1997
5. Ghost of the Jedi ◆ 1997
6. Army of Terror ◆ 1997

7. The Brain Spiders ◆ 1997
8. The Swarm ◆ 1998
9. Spore ◆ 1998
10. The Doomsday Ship ◆ 1998
11. Clones ◆ 1998
12. The Hunger ◆ 1998

STAR WARS JUNIOR JEDI KNIGHTS

Various authors
BERKLEY

GRADES 4–6

ADVENTURE | SCIENCE FICTION

Anakin Solo is the youngest son of Leia Organa Solo and Han Solo. In this series, Anakin attends Luke Skywalker's Jedi Academy, where he makes friends with a child of the Sand People named Tahiri. The friends go through a rigorous training program and become involved in many exciting adventures. In one book, they search the abandoned fortress of Darth Vader for Obi-Wan Kenobi's lightsaber. In another, they travel to the distant moon of Yavin 8 and try to break the curse of the Golden Globe. Readers who enjoy science fiction, especially those who like the *Star Wars* films, will be attracted to this series. The familiar characters and exciting situations should appeal to reluctant readers.

1. The Golden Globe (Richardson, Nancy) ◆ 1995
2. Lyric's World (Richardson, Nancy) ◆ 1996
3. Promises (Richardson, Nancy) ◆ 1996
4. Anakin's Quest (Moesta, Rebecca) ◆ 1997
5. Vader's Fortress (Moesta, Rebecca) ◆ 1997
6. Kenobi's Blade (Moesta, Rebecca) ◆ 1997

STAR WARS YOUNG JEDI KNIGHTS

Anderson, Kevin J., and Rebecca Moesta
BERKLEY

GRADES 4–6

ADVENTURE | SCIENCE FICTION

Jacen and Jaina are the twins of Han Solo and Princess Leia. They are the future of the New Republic and are being trained in the powers of the Force. In one book, the twins help Anja Gallandro, who had planned to destroy their family but has become their friend. In another, Lando Calrissian takes the twins and Anja on a vacation that turns deadly. Encounters with the Dark Side and adventures across the galaxy should attract fans of Star Wars and science fiction.

1. Heirs of the Force ◆ 1995
2. Shadow Academy ◆ 1995
3. The Lost Ones ◆ 1995
4. Lightsabers ◆ 1996
5. Darkest Knight ◆ 1996
6. Jedi Under Siege ◆ 1997
7. Shards of Alderaan ◆ 1997
8. Diversity Alliance ◆ 1997
9. Delusions of Grandeur ◆ 1997
10. Jedi Bounty ◆ 1997
11. The Emperor's Plague ◆ 1998
12. Return to Ord Mantell ◆ 1998
13. Trouble on Cloud City ◆ 1998
14. Crisis at Crystal Reef ◆ 1998

STARBUCK FAMILY ADVENTURES

Lasky, Kathryn

HARCOURT

GRADES 4–7

MYSTERY

The Starbuck family includes two sets of twins: Liberty and July, and Charly and Molly. All of the twins can communicate with each other through mental telepathy, a power that they use to solve mysteries. Liberty and July, the older twins, receive telepathic messages that set them off on a series of adventures, from a Sherlock Holmes–inspired mystery in London to an investigation alongside Native Americans in New Mexico.

1. Double Trouble Squared ◆ 1991
2. Shadows in the Water ◆ 1992
3. A Voice in the Wind ◆ 1993

STARS

Various authors

KNOPF

GRADES 4–7

REAL LIFE

Five fifth-graders move to the Sugar Trees Acres development one summer and begin school at River Grove elementary school in the fall. Because their school bus has a sign that says, "Sugar Trees Acres Route," they call themselves the Stars. Holly Hudnut, rich and pretty, is the self-styled queen of the fifth grade and the president of their rival group, the Clovers. Each Star is different. Karen concentrates on getting good grades, while Jan is good at cooking. Sara and Beth are twins with very different personalities, and Amy is the flamboyant, stylish member of the group. The series takes them all through the normal activities of fifth-graders, with the two groups of girls in constant competition.

1. The Holly Hudnut Admiration Society (Norby, Lisa) ◆ 1989
2. Rent-a-Star (Saunders, Susan) ◆ 1989
3. Crazy Campout (Norby, Lisa) ◆ 1989
4. Twin Trouble (Saunders, Susan) ◆ 1989
5. Star Reporter (Norby, Lisa) ◆ 1989
6. The Goofy Gamble (Douglas, Anna Joe) ◆ 1989

STARSHINE!

Schwartz, Ellen

POLESTAR

GRADES 4–6

FAMILY LIFE

Starshine Bliss Shapiro hates her name and loves spiders. She lives with her parents and little sister Peggy in Vancouver, British Columbia. Her parents are very relaxed and artistic and Star has a lot of freedom to be with her friends. In the first book, she organizes a play around the story of Arachne. The second book features her adventures at summer camp, including her discovery of a rare fanged vampire spider. In the third book, Star is selected to be in a commercial only to be upstaged by her little sister. Starshine is a believable character whose emotions will mirror those of many girls who will be reading this series.

1. Starshine! ◆ 1987
2. Starshine at Camp Crescent Moon ◆ 1994
3. Starshine on TV ◆ 1996

STEPHANIE *see* Full House: Club Stephanie *and* Full House: Stephanie

STERLING FAMILY

Johnston, Norma

ATHENEUM

GRADES 6–8

FAMILY LIFE | HISTORICAL

These tales about the Sterlings and the Albrights are based on stories the author heard, while growing up in New Jersey, about her relatives living in Yonkers and the Bronx at the turn of the century. The first four books center on teenager Tish Sterling and the problems she and her family are coping with: Her mother is having yet another baby, her older sister marries a man with a child from a previous marriage, her grandfather dies, and the family business is in trouble. The last two books center on a child of the next generation, Saranne Albright, who experiences problems similar to her Aunt Tish's and is particularly distracted by the antics of her troubled friend Paul Hodge. The thoughtful perspectives presented by the two girls help readers to recognize similarities between their own situations and those of girls who grew up in the early part of this century.

1. The Keeping Days ◆ 1973
2. Glory in the Flower ◆ 1974
3. A Mustard Seed of Magic ◆ 1977
4. The Sanctuary Tree ◆ 1977
5. A Nice Girl Like You ◆ 1980
6. Myself and I ◆ 1981

STEVIE DIAMOND MYSTERIES

Bailey, Linda
WHITMAN
GRADES 4–6
MYSTERY

Stevie (formerly known as Stephanie) is a big fan of Nancy Drew, Hercule Poirot, and any mystery book she can get her hands on. So when mysterious things happen, she remembers how her detective heroes solve cases and uses their techniques to her advantage. She is aided in her sleuthing by a nerdy kid named Jesse, who lives in her building and who sometimes helps and sometimes hinders her investigations. Together, they form the Diamond and Kulnicki Detective Agency . . . No Mystery Too Tough For Us. In each volume of the series, they solve real mysteries while trying unsuccessfully to stay out of trouble themselves.

1. How Come the Best Clues Are Always in the Garbage? ◆ 1992
2. How Can I Be a Detective If I Have to Baby-Sit? ◆ 1993
3. Who's Got Gertie and How Can We Get Her Back? ◆ 1996
4. How Can a Frozen Detective Stay Hot on the Trail? ◆ 1996
5. What's a Daring Detective Like Me Doing in the Doghouse? ◆ 1997

STONE BOOK QUARTET

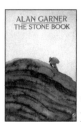

Garner, Alan

DELL

GRADES 3–5

FAMILY LIFE | HISTORICAL

This quartet is written in a rich prose combining modern English with the old northwest Mercian spoken pattern. The stories trace four generations of an English family of craftsmen from the Victorian era through World War II. Each book focuses on a different child—Mary, Joseph, Robert, and William—who learns about a family craft and, in doing so, learns about the family ancestry and gains a deeper connection to both the past and the present. Directed toward a young audience, the subject and fairly dark style of these books encourage readers to think about some very real issues, such as identity, courage, poverty, love, death, and the nature of the world around them.

1. The Stone Book ◆ 1976
2. Tom Fobble's Day ◆ 1977
3. Granny Reardun ◆ 1977
4. Aimer Gate ◆ 1978

STRANGE MATTER

Engle, Marty, and Johnny Ray Barnes, Jr.

GARETH STEVENS

GRADES 4–6

HORROR

These scary tales are labeled "Brave Readers Only" to keep the faint-hearted at bay. Realistic stories of terror at school, at home, and at camp make entertaining reads. Danger usually arises when someone breaks a rule or takes a dare, but all the stories have safe resolutions.

1. No Substitutions ◆ 1995
2. The Midnight Game ◆ 1995
3. Driven to Death ◆ 1995
4. A Place to Hide ◆ 1995

5. Last One In . . . ◆ 1995
6. Bad Circuits ◆ 1995
7. Fly the Unfriendly Skies ◆ 1995
8. Frozen Dinners ◆ 1995
9. Deadly Delivery ◆ 1995
10. Knightmare ◆ 1996
11. Something Rotten ◆ 1996
12. Dead on Its Tracks ◆ 1996
13. Toy Trouble ◆ 1996
14. The Plant People ◆ 1996
15. Creature Features ◆ 1996
16. Weird, Weird West ◆ 1996
17. Tune into Terror ◆ 1996
18. The Fairfield Triangle ◆ 1996
19. Big Foot, Big Trouble ◆ 1996
20. Doorway to Doom ◆ 1996
21. Under Wraps ◆ 1996
22. Dangerous Waters ◆ 1996
23. Second Sighting ◆ 1996
24. Nightcrawlers ◆ 1997
25. Splitting Image ◆ 1997
26. Headless Rider of Carson Creek ◆ 1997
27. Primeval ◆ 1997
28. Off-Worlder ◆ 1997
29. Shadow Chaser ◆ 1997
30. Escape from Planet Earth ◆ 1997
31. Rilo Buro's Summer Vacation ◆ 1997
32. Probe ◆ 1997
33. Fathom ◆ 1997
34. From the Ashes ◆ 1997

THE STUPIDS

Allard, Harry

HOUGHTON MIFFLIN

GRADES K–2

FAMILY LIFE | HUMOR

The Stupids are undoubtedly the stupidest family on earth. This humorous series tells of the silly misadventures of Mr. Stanley Q. Stupid, his wife, and their two children, Buster and Petunia, whose backward approach to everything creates confusion in the family's everyday activities. Only their pets, Kitty the dog and Xylophone the Cat, seem the least bit aware of the absurdity of it all. The hilarious antics described in the stories are accented by silly details in the illustrations. A careful observer will notice that the Stupids keep jam and tuna on their bathroom shelf, their hanging picture of Lake Stupid shows a bucket of water, and Mr. Stupid brushes his teeth with anchovy toothpaste!

1. The Stupids Step Out ◆ 1974
2. The Stupids Have a Ball ◆ 1978
3. The Stupids Die ◆ 1981
4. The Stupids Take Off ◆ 1989

SUGAR CREEK GANG

Hutchens, Paul
MOODY PRESS
GRADES 4–7
ADVENTURE | VALUES

A group of young boys living in rural Indiana in the 1950s have adventures of every kind, solving mysteries, getting in and out of danger, and learning about Christian life. The narrator, Bill, is an average red-headed boy who observes his friends and the world around him and passes on what he has learned to the reader. Poetry is barrel-shaped and always quoting lines of verse. Circus is the acrobat of the group, and Big Jim is a little older and considered the leader. Some of the boys' parents are Christians and good role models, and some are led to faith in Christ as the series progresses. This is one of the oldest and longest Christian series. The titles listed below are of the original editions; many books have been reissued with new titles.

1. Sugar Creek Gang ◆ 1939
2. Further Adventures of the Sugar Creek Gang ◆ 1940
3. We Killed a Bear ◆ 1940
4. Sugar Creek Goes Camping ◆ 1941
5. Sugar Creek in Chicago ◆ 1941
6. Sugar Creek Gang in School ◆ 1942
7. Mystery at Sugar Creek ◆ 1943
8. Sugar Creek Gang Flies to Cuba ◆ 1944
9. New Sugar Creek Gang Mystery ◆ 1946
10. One Stormy Day at Sugar Creek ◆ 1946
11. Shenanigans at Sugar Creek ◆ 1947
12. Sugar Creek Gang Goes North ◆ 1947
13. Adventure in an Indian Cemetery ◆ 1947
14. Sugar Creek Gang Digs for Treasure ◆ 1948
15. North Woods Manhunt ◆ 1948
16. Haunted House at Sugar Creek ◆ 1949
17. Lost in a Sugar Creek Blizzard ◆ 1950
18. Sugar Creek Gang on the Mexican Border ◆ 1950
19. Green Tent Mystery at Sugar Creek ◆ 1950

20. Ten Thousand Minutes at Sugar Creek ◆ 1952
21. Blue Cow at Sugar Creek ◆ 1953
22. Trapline Thief at Sugar Creek ◆ 1953
23. Watermelon Mystery at Sugar Creek ◆ 1953
24. Sugar Creek Gang at Snow Goose Lodge ◆ 1957
25. Sugar Creek Gang Goes Western ◆ 1957
26. Old Stranger's Secret at Sugar Creek ◆ 1957
27. Wild Horse Canyon Mystery ◆ 1959
28. Howling Dog in Sugar Creek ◆ 1960
29. We Killed a Wildcat at Sugar Creek ◆ 1966
30. Brown Box Mystery at Sugar Creek ◆ 1970
31. White Boat Rescue at Sugar Creek ◆ 1970
32. Worm Turns at Sugar Creek ◆ 1972
33. Sleeping Beauty at Sugar Creek ◆ 1972
34. Down in Sugar Creek Chimney ◆ 1973
35. Runaway Mystery at Sugar Creek ◆ 1973

SUPER HOOPS

Herman, Hank

BANTAM

GRADES 4–6

REAL LIFE | RECREATION

With lots of basketball action, this series is sure to appeal to sports fans. The Branford Bulls are a team of elementary school boys that includes Will Hopwood, Derek Roberts, Travis Barnes, and others. They are coached by two teenagers from the high school team: Nate Bowman and Will's brother, Jim. Having your brother for a coach can be a problem, especially when you are the star center. Along with court activities, there are problems with ego, sportsmanship, and teamwork that are resolved. There is even a player named Michael Jordan, although he is not the NBA superstar. As the publisher notes, this is "A slammin', jammin', in-your-face action series!"

1. Crashing the Boards ◆ 1996
2. In Your Face! ◆ 1996
3. Trash Talk ◆ 1996
4. Monster Jam ◆ 1996
5. One on One (Weiss, Dan) ◆ 1996
6. Show Time! (Weiss, Dan) ◆ 1996
7. Slam Dunk! ◆ 1996
8. Ball Hog (Herman, Hank) ◆ 1996
9. Hang Time (Herman, Hank) ◆ 1997
10. Foul! (Herman, Hank) ◆ 1997
11. Above the Rim (Herman, Hank) ◆ 1997

12. In the Zone ◆ 1997
13. Out of Bounds! ◆ 1997
14. Who's the Man? ◆ 1997
15. Rebound! ◆ 1998

SUPER SNOOP SAM SNOUT

LeMieux, Anne

AVON CAMELOT

GRADES 1–3

MYSTERY

Like Nate the Great, Sam Snout is a young detective solving neighbor-hood mysteries. When Sam's friend Tommy can't find his rare marble, Sam is on the case. Sam also looks into problems involving Heather's yogurt and a missing snowman. These easy-to-read books also have hidden clues on the covers, which should attract young readers.

1. The Case of the Stolen Snowman ◆ 1994
2. The Case of the Missing Marble ◆ 1994
3. The Case of the Yogurt-Poker ◆ 1994

SURVIVAL!

Duey, Kathleen, and Karen A. Bale

ALADDIN

GRADES 5–8

ADVENTURE | HISTORICAL

The sinking of the *Titanic*, the San Francisco earthquake, the Colorado blizzard—imagine that you are there. The Survival! series places young characters in the middle of exciting, even dangerous situations. In 1850, twins Jess and Will find themselves stranded in Death Valley. In 1871, the Chicago Fire places Nate Cooper and Julie Flynn in great danger from the chaotic crowds and the spreading inferno. Dramatic events are woven into the historical context of these real events, which should attract readers who want stories with adventure and coura-geous characters.

1. Titanic: April 14, 1912 ◆ 1998
2. Earthquake: San Francisco, 1906 ◆ 1998
3. Blizzard: Estes Park, Colorado, 1886 ◆ 1998
4. Fire: Chicago, 1871 ◆ 1998
5. Flood: Mississippi, 1927 ◆ 1998

    6. Stranded: Death Valley, Circa 1850 ◆ 1998
    7. Cave In: Pennsylvania, 1880s ◆ 1998

SUSANNAH

Elmore, Patricia
DUTTON
GRADES 4–6
MYSTERY | REAL LIFE

Susannah Higgins has a detective agency with her friend Lucy. The two African American girls investigate neighborhood mysteries, including a problem with tampered Halloween treats and two fires. They also look through the antique collection of Mr. Withers following his death. These books involve readers in mysterious, slightly dangerous situations that reach satisfying conclusions.

    1. Susannah and the Blue House Mystery ◆ 1980
    2. Susannah and the Poison Green Halloween ◆ 1982
    3. Susannah and the Purple Mongoose Mystery ◆ 1992

SWALLOWS AND AMAZONS

Ransome, Arthur
GODINE
GRADES 6–8
ADVENTURE

The first volume in this series introduces readers to an imaginative group of children. John, Susan, Titty, and Roger Walker are allowed to sail their small boat *Swallow* to an island and camp there without their parents. They meet up with Nancy and Peggy Blackett, who also enjoy a large amount of freedom in their boat *Amazon*. The six youngsters become embroiled in an adventure involving a stolen book. They finally solve the crime and move onto similar nautical adventures in subsequent novels.

    1. Swallows and Amazons ◆ 1930
    2. Swallowdale ◆ 1931
    3. Peter Duck ◆ 1932
    4. Winter Holiday ◆ 1933
    5. Coot Club ◆ 1934
    6. Pigeon Post ◆ 1936
    7. We Didn't Mean to Go to Sea ◆ 1937
    8. Secret Water ◆ 1939
    9. The Big Six ◆ 1940

10. Missee Lee ◆ 1941
11. The Picts and the Martyrs ◆ 1943
12. Great Northern? ◆ 1947

SWEET VALLEY HIGH

Pascal, Francine, creator

BANTAM

GRADES 6–8

REAL LIFE

This series of more than 140 titles follows the lives of popular identical twins Jessica and Elizabeth Wakefield. Their exploits at Sweet Valley High School in California include falling in and out of love, making and losing friends, traveling, modeling, having fun, and sometimes finding themselves in dangerous situations.

1. Double Love ◆ 1983
2. Secrets ◆ 1983
3. Playing with Fire ◆ 1983
4. Power Play ◆ 1983
5. All Night Long ◆ 1984
6. Dangerous Love ◆ 1984
7. Dear Sister ◆ 1984
8. Heartbreaker ◆ 1984
9. Racing Hearts ◆ 1984
10. The Wrong Kind of Girl ◆ 1984
11. Too Good to Be True ◆ 1984
12. When Love Dies ◆ 1984
13. Kidnapped! ◆ 1984
14. Deceptions ◆ 1984
15. Promises ◆ 1984
16. Rags to Riches ◆ 1985
17. Love Letters ◆ 1985
18. Head over Heels ◆ 1985
19. Showdown ◆ 1985
20. Crash Landing! ◆ 1985
21. Runaway ◆ 1985
22. Too Much in Love ◆ 1985
23. Say Goodbye ◆ 1985
24. Memories ◆ 1985
25. Nowhere to Run ◆ 1986
26. Hostage! ◆ 1986
27. Lovestruck ◆ 1986
28. Alone in the Crowd ◆ 1986
29. Bitter Rivals ◆ 1986

30. Jealous Lies ◆ 1986
31. Taking Sides ◆ 1986
32. The New Jessica ◆ 1986
33. Starting Over ◆ 1987
34. Forbidden Love ◆ 1987
35. Out of Control ◆ 1987
36. Last Chance ◆ 1987
37. Rumors ◆ 1987
38. Leaving Home ◆ 1987
39. Secret Admirer ◆ 1987
40. On the Edge ◆ 1987
41. Outcast ◆ 1987
42. Caught in the Middle ◆ 1988
43. Hard Choices ◆ 1988
44. Pretenses ◆ 1988
45. Family Secrets ◆ 1988
46. Decisions ◆ 1988
47. Troublemaker ◆ 1988
48. Slam Book Fever ◆ 1988
49. Playing for Keeps ◆ 1988
50. Out of Reach ◆ 1988
51. Against the Odds ◆ 1988
52. White Lies ◆ 1989
53. Second Chance ◆ 1989
54. Two-Boy Weekend ◆ 1989
55. Perfect Shot ◆ 1989
56. Lost at Sea ◆ 1989
57. Teacher Crush ◆ 1989
58. Broken-Hearted ◆ 1989
59. In Love Again ◆ 1989
60. That Fatal Night ◆ 1989
61. Boy Trouble ◆ 1990
62. Who's Who ◆ 1990
63. New Elizabeth ◆ 1990
64. Ghost of Tricia Martin ◆ 1990
65. Trouble at Home ◆ 1990
66. Who's to Blame? ◆ 1990
67. Parent Plot ◆ 1990
68. Love Bet ◆ 1990
69. Friend Against Friend ◆ 1990
70. Ms. Quarterback ◆ 1990
71. Starring Jessica! ◆ 1991
72. Rock Star's Girl ◆ 1991
73. Regina's Legacy ◆ 1991
74. Perfect Girl ◆ 1991
75. Amy's True Love ◆ 1991
76. Miss Teen Sweet Valley ◆ 1991
77. Cheating to Win ◆ 1991

78. Dating Game ◆ 1991
79. Long-Lost Brother ◆ 1991
80. The Girl They Both Loved ◆ 1991
81. Rosa's Lie ◆ 1992
82. Kidnapped by a Cult ◆ 1992
83. Steven's Bride ◆ 1992
84. Stolen Diary ◆ 1992
85. Soap Star ◆ 1992
86. Jessica Against Bruce ◆ 1992
87. My Best Friend's Boyfriend ◆ 1993
88. Love Letters for Sale ◆ 1993
89. Elizabeth Betrayed ◆ 1993
90. Don't Go Home with John ◆ 1993
91. In Love with a Prince ◆ 1993
92. She's Not What She Seems ◆ 1993
93. Stepsisters ◆ 1993
94. Are We in Love? ◆ 1993
95. The Morning After ◆ 1993
96. The Arrest ◆ 1993
97. The Verdict ◆ 1993
98. Wedding ◆ 1993
99. Beware the Babysitter ◆ 1993
100. The Evil Twin ◆ 1993
101. Boyfriend War ◆ 1994
102. Almost Married ◆ 1994
103. Operation Love Match ◆ 1994
104. Love and Death in London ◆ 1994
105. Date with a Werewolf ◆ 1994
106. Beware the Wolfman ◆ 1994
107. Jessica's Secret Love ◆ 1994
108. Left at the Altar ◆ 1994
109. Double-Crossed ◆ 1994
110. Death Threat ◆ 1994
111. Deadly Christmas ◆ 1994
112. Jessica Quits the Squad ◆ 1995
113. The Pom-Pom Wars ◆ 1995
114. "V" for Victory ◆ 1995
115. The Treasure of Death Valley ◆ 1995
116. Nightmare in Death Valley ◆ 1995
117. Jessica the Genius ◆ 1996
118. College Weekend ◆ 1996
119. Jessica's Older Guy ◆ 1996
120. In Love with the Enemy ◆ 1996
121. The High School War ◆ 1996
122. A Kiss Before Dying ◆ 1996
123. Elizabeth's Rival ◆ 1996
124. Meet Me at Midnight ◆ 1996
125. Camp Killer ◆ 1996

126. Tall, Dark, and Deadly ◆ 1996
127. Dance of Death ◆ 1996
128. Kiss of a Killer ◆ 1996
129. Cover Girls ◆ 1997
130. Model Flirt ◆ 1997
131. Fashion Victim ◆ 1997
132. Once Upon a Time ◆ 1997
133. To Catch a Thief ◆ 1997
134. Happily Ever After ◆ 1997
135. Lila's New Flame ◆ 1997
136. Too Hot to Handle ◆ 1997
137. Fight Fire with Fire ◆ 1997
138. What Jessica Wants ◆ 1998
139. Elizabeth Is Mine ◆ 1998
140. Please Forgive Me ◆ 1998
141. A Picture-Perfect Prom ◆ 1998
142. The Big Night ◆ 1998
143. Party Weekend! ◆ 1998

SWEET VALLEY HIGH MAGNA EDITIONS

1. The Wakefields of Sweet Valley ◆ 1991
2. The Wakefield Legacy: The Untold Story ◆ 1992
3. A Night to Remember ◆ 1993
4. The Evil Twin ◆ 1993
5. Elizabeth's Secret Diary ◆ 1994
6. Jessica's Secret Diary ◆ 1994
7. Return of the Evil Twin ◆ 1995
8. Elizabeth's Secret Diary Volume II ◆ 1996
9. Jessica's Secret Diary Volume II ◆ 1996
10. The Fowlers of Sweet Valley ◆ 1996
11. The Patmans of Sweet Valley ◆ 1997
12. Elizabeth's Secret Diary Volume III ◆ 1997
13. Jessica's Secret Diary Volume III ◆ 1997

SWEET VALLEY HIGH SUPER EDITIONS

1. Perfect Summer ◆ 1985
2. Special Christmas ◆ 1985
3. Spring Break ◆ 1986
4. Malibu Summer ◆ 1986
5. Winter Carnival ◆ 1986
6. Spring Fever ◆ 1987
7. Falling for Lucas ◆ 1996
8. Jessica Takes Manhattan ◆ 1997

SWEET VALLEY HIGH SUPER STARS

1. Lila's Story ◆ 1989
2. Bruce's Story ◆ 1990

3. Enid's Story ◆ 1990
4. Olivia's Story ◆ 1991
5. Todd's Story ◆ 1992

SWEET VALLEY HIGH SUPER THRILLERS

1. Double Jeopardy ◆ 1987
2. On the Run ◆ 1988
3. No Place to Hide ◆ 1988
4. Deadly Summer ◆ 1989
5. Murder on the Line ◆ 1992
6. Beware the Wolfman ◆ 1994
7. A Deadly Christmas ◆ 1994
8. Murder in Paradise ◆ 1995
9. A Stranger in the House ◆ 1995
10. A Killer on Board ◆ 1995
11. "R" for Revenge ◆ 1997

SWEET VALLEY KIDS

Francine Pascal, creator

BANTAM

GRADES 3–5

REAL LIFE

In this spin-off of the popular Sweet Valley Twins series, Jessica and Elizabeth are seven and in second grade. Jessica already likes clothes and doesn't like school, whereas Elizabeth is just the opposite. The stories deal with family, friends, and school, as in Sweet Valley Twins, except that the girls are younger and haven't yet discovered boys. In a typical book, one of their friends has a visiting cousin who tries to impress others by lying and causing trouble. All is forgiven when the girl says she was just trying to make friends, and the twins and their friends explain that lying is not the way to do it.

1. Surprise! Surprise! ◆ 1989
2. Runaway Hamster ◆ 1989
3. The Twins' Mystery Teacher ◆ 1989
4. Elizabeth's Valentine ◆ 1990
5. Jessica's Cat Trick ◆ 1990
6. Lila's Secret ◆ 1990
7. Jessica's Big Mistake ◆ 1990
8. Jessica's Zoo Adventure ◆ 1990
9. Elizabeth's Super-Selling Lemonade ◆ 1990
10. The Twins and the Wild West ◆ 1990
11. Crybaby Lois ◆ 1990
12. Sweet Valley Trick or Treat ◆ 1990

13. Starring Winston ◆ 1990
14. Jessica the Babysitter ◆ 1991
15. Fearless Elizabeth ◆ 1991
16. Jessica the TV Star ◆ 1991
17. Carolyn's Mystery Dolls ◆ 1991
18. Bossy Steven ◆ 1991
19. Jessica and the Jumbo Fish ◆ 1991
20. Twins Go to the Hospital ◆ 1991
21. Jessica and the Spelling Bee Surprise ◆ 1991
22. Sweet Valley Slumber Party ◆ 1991
23. Lila's Haunted House Party ◆ 1991
24. Cousin Kelly's Family Secret ◆ 1991
25. Left-Out Elizabeth ◆ 1991
26. Jessica's Snobby Club ◆ 1991
27. The Sweet Valley Clean-Up Team ◆ 1992
28. Elizabeth Meets Her Hero ◆ 1992
29. Andy and the Alien ◆ 1992
30. Jessica's Unburied Treasure ◆ 1992
31. Elizabeth and Jessica Run Away ◆ 1992
32. Left Back ◆ 1992
33. Caroline's Halloween Spell ◆ 1992
34. Best Thanksgiving Ever ◆ 1992
35. Elizabeth's Broken Arm ◆ 1992
36. Elizabeth's Video Fever ◆ 1993
37. Big Race ◆ 1993
38. Good-Bye, Eva? ◆ 1993
39. Ellen Is Home Alone ◆ 1993
40. Robin in the Middle ◆ 1993
41. Missing Tea Set ◆ 1993
42. Jessica's Monster Nightmare ◆ 1993
43. Jessica Gets Spooked ◆ 1993
44. Twins Big Pow-Wow ◆ 1993
45. Elizabeth's Piano Lessons ◆ 1994
46. Get the Teacher ◆ 1994
47. Elizabeth the Tattletale ◆ 1994
48. Lila's April Fool ◆ 1994
49. Jessica's Mermaid ◆ 1994
50. Steven's Twin ◆ 1994
51. Lois and the Sleepover ◆ 1994
52. Julie the Karate Kid ◆ 1994
53. Magic Puppets ◆ 1994
54. Star of the Parade ◆ 1994
55. Jessica and Elizabeth Show ◆ 1995
56. Jessica Plays Cupid ◆ 1995
57. No Girls Allowed ◆ 1995
58. Lila's Birthday Bash ◆ 1995
59. Jessica Plus Jessica Equals Trouble ◆ 1995
60. Amazing Jessica ◆ 1995

61. Scaredy-Cat Elizabeth ◆ 1995
62. Halloween War ◆ 1995
63. Lila's Christmas Angel ◆ 1995
64. Elizabeth's Horseback Adventure ◆ 1996
65. Steven's Big Crush ◆ 1996
66. And the Winner Is . . . Jessica Wakefield! ◆ 1996
67. Secret of Fantasy Forest ◆ 1996
68. A Roller Coaster for the Twins! ◆ 1996
69. Class Picture Day! ◆ 1997
70. Good-Bye, Mrs. Otis ◆ 1997
71. Jessica's Secret Friend ◆ 1997
72. The Macaroni Mess ◆ 1997
73. The Witch in the Pumpkin Patch ◆ 1997
74. Sweet Valley Blizzard! ◆ 1998
75. Little Drummer Girls ◆ 1998
76. Danger: Twins at Work! ◆ 1998

SWEET VALLEY TWINS

Pascal, Francine, creator

BANTAM

GRADES 6–8

REAL LIFE

Jessica and Elizabeth Wakefield are identical twins who, though close and usually supportive of each other, are also individuals with their own friends, interests, and abilities. In the first title of this popular paperback series, the twins start middle school. Each of the more than 100 subsequent titles deals with typical situations and predicaments that young teens may encounter in school and at home. Occasional titles, such as *Cammi's Crush*, feature students at Sweet Valley Middle School who are friends of Jessica and Elizabeth.

1. Best Friends ◆ 1986
2. Teacher's Pet ◆ 1986
3. Haunted House ◆ 1986
4. Choosing Sides ◆ 1986
5. Sneaking Out ◆ 1987
6. New Girl ◆ 1987
7. Three's a Crowd ◆ 1987
8. First Place ◆ 1987
9. Against the Rules ◆ 1987
10. One of the Gang ◆ 1987
11. Buried Treasure ◆ 1987
12. Keeping Secrets ◆ 1987
13. Stretching the Truth ◆ 1987

14. Tug of War ◆ 1987
15. Older Boy ◆ 1988
16. Second Best ◆ 1988
17. Boys Against Girls ◆ 1988
18. Center of Attention ◆ 1988
19. Bully ◆ 1988
20. Playing Hooky ◆ 1988
21. Left Behind ◆ 1988
22. Out of Place ◆ 1988
23. Claim to Fame ◆ 1988
24. Jumping to Conclusions ◆ 1988
25. Standing Out ◆ 1989
26. Taking Charge ◆ 1989
27. Teamwork ◆ 1989
28. April Fool! ◆ 1989
29. Jessica and the Brat Attack ◆ 1989
30. Princess Elizabeth ◆ 1989
31. Jessica's Bad Idea ◆ 1989
32. Jessica on Stage ◆ 1989
33. Elizabeth's New Hero ◆ 1989
34. Jessica the Rock Star ◆ 1989
35. Amy's Pen Pal ◆ 1990
36. Mary Is Missing ◆ 1990
37. War Between the Twins ◆ 1990
38. Lois Strikes Back ◆ 1990
39. Jessica and the Money Mix-Up ◆ 1990
40. Danny Means Trouble ◆ 1990
41. Twins Get Caught ◆ 1990
42. Jessica's Secret ◆ 1990
43. Elizabeth's First Kiss ◆ 1990
44. Amy Moves In ◆ 1991
45. Lucy Takes the Reins ◆ 1991
46. Mademoiselle Jessica ◆ 1991
47. Jessica's New Look ◆ 1991
48. Mansy Miller Fights Back ◆ 1991
49. Twins' Little Sister ◆ 1991
50. Jessica and the Secret Star ◆ 1991
51. Elizabeth the Impossible ◆ 1991
52. Booster Boycott ◆ 1991
53. Slime that Ate Sweet Valley ◆ 1991
54. Big Party Weekend ◆ 1991
55. Brooke and Her Rock Star Mom ◆ 1991
56. The Wakefields Strike It Rich ◆ 1991
57. Steven's in Love ◆ 1992
58. Elizabeth and the Orphans ◆ 1992
59. Barnyard Battle ◆ 1992
60. Ciao, Sweet Valley ◆ 1992
61. Jessica the Nerd ◆ 1992
62. Sarah's Dad and Sophia's Mom ◆ 1992

63. Poor Lila ◆ 1992
64. Charm School Mystery ◆ 1992
65. Patty's Last Dance ◆ 1993
66. Great Boyfriend Switch ◆ 1993
67. Jessica the Thief ◆ 1993
68. Middle School Gets Married ◆ 1993
69. Won't Someone Help Anna ◆ 1993
70. Psychic Sisters ◆ 1993
71. Jessica Saves the Trees ◆ 1993
72. Love Potion ◆ 1993
73. Lila's Music Video ◆ 1993
74. Elizabeth the Hero ◆ 1993
75. Jessica and the Earthquake ◆ 1994
76. Yours for a Day ◆ 1994
77. Todd Runs Away ◆ 1994
78. Steven and the Zombie ◆ 1994
79. Jessica's Blind Date ◆ 1994
80. Gossip War ◆ 1994
81. Robbery at the Mall ◆ 1994
82. Steven's Enemy ◆ 1994
83. Amy's Secret Sister ◆ 1994
84. Romeo and Two Juliets ◆ 1995
85. Elizabeth the Seventh Grader ◆ 1995
86. It Can't Happen Here ◆ 1995
87. Mother-Daughter Switch ◆ 1995
88. Steven Gets Even ◆ 1995
89. Jessica's Cookie Disaster ◆ 1995
90. Cousin War ◆ 1996
91. Deadly Voyage ◆ 1996
92. Escape from Terror Island ◆ 1996
93. Incredible Madame Jessica ◆ 1996
94. Don't Talk to Brian ◆ 1996
95. Battle of the Cheerleaders ◆ 1996
96. Elizabeth the Spy ◆ 1996
97. Too Scared to Sleep ◆ 1996
98. Beast Is Watching You ◆ 1996
99. Beast Must Die ◆ 1996
100. If I Die Before I Wake ◆ 1996
101. Twins in Love ◆ 1996
102. Mysterious Doctor Q ◆ 1996
103. Elizabeth Solves It All ◆ 1996
104. Big Brother's in Love Again ◆ 1997
105. Jessica's Lucky Millions ◆ 1997
106. Breakfast of Enemies ◆ 1997
107. The Twins Hit Hollywood ◆ 1997
108. Cammi's Crush ◆ 1997
109. Don't Go in the Basement ◆ 1997
110. Pumpkin Fever ◆ 1997
111. Sisters at War ◆ 1997

112. If Looks Could Kill ◆ 1997
113. The Boyfriend Game ◆ 1998
114. The Boyfriend Mess ◆ 1998
115. Happy Mother's Day, Lila ◆ 1998
116. Jessica Takes Charge ◆ 1998
117. Down with Queen Janet! ◆ 1998
118. No Escape! ◆ 1998

SWEET VALLEY TWINS SUPER EDITION

Pascal, Francine, creator

BANTAM

GRADES 6–8

REAL LIFE

This paperback series is a spin-off of the *Sweet Valley Twins and Friends* series; but in this series, identical twins Jessica and Elizabeth Wakefield venture away from their home turf, Sweet Valley Middle School, and become involved with extracurricular activities, such as volunteering at the zoo, going on a camping trip, and taking a vacation trip to Paris.

1. The Class Trip ◆ 1988
2. Holiday Mischief ◆ 1988
3. The Big Camp Secret ◆ 1989
4. The Unicorns Go Hawaiian ◆ 1991
5. Lila's Secret Valentine ◆ 1995
6. The Twins Take Paris ◆ 1996
7. Jessica's Animal Instincts ◆ 1996
8. Jessica's First Kiss ◆ 1997
9. The Twins Go to College ◆ 1997
10. The Year Without Christmas ◆ 1997
11. Jessica's No Angel ◆ 1998
12. Goodbye, Middle School ◆ 1998

SWEET VALLEY UNIVERSITY

Pascal, Francine, creator

BANTAM

GRADES 7–8

REAL life

Twins Jessica and Elizabeth Wakefield of the Sweet Valley series are off to college in this series. As they get older, they are involved in more grown-up relationships and adventures, and even face life-and-death situations. Fans of the other Sweet Valley series will enjoy following the collegiate exploits of Jessica and Elizabeth.

1. College Girls ◆ 1993
2. Love, Lies, and Jessica Wakefield ◆ 1993
3. What Your Parents Don't Know ◆ 1994
4. Anything for Love ◆ 1994
5. Married Woman ◆ 1994
6. Love of Her Life ◆ 1994
7. Good-Bye to Love ◆ 1994
8. Home for Christmas ◆ 1994
9. Sorority Scandal ◆ 1995
10. No Means No ◆ 1995
11. Take Back the Night ◆ 1995
12. College Cruise ◆ 1995
13. SS Heartbreak ◆ 1995
14. Shipboard Wedding ◆ 1995
15. Behind Closed Doors ◆ 1995
16. The Other Woman ◆ 1995
17. Deadly Attraction ◆ 1995
18. Billie's Secret ◆ 1996
19. Broken Promises, Shattered Dreams ◆ 1996
20. Here Comes the Bride ◆ 1996
21. For the Love of Ryan ◆ 1996
22. Elizabeth's Summer Love ◆ 1996
23. Sweet Kiss of Summer ◆ 1996
24. His Secret Past ◆ 1996
25. Busted! ◆ 1996
26. The Trial of Jessica Wakefield ◆ 1996
27. Elizabeth and Todd Forever ◆ 1997
28. Elizabeth's Heartbreak ◆ 1997
29. One Last Kiss ◆ 1997
30. Beauty and the Beach ◆ 1997
31. The Truth About Ryan ◆ 1997
32. The Boys of Summer ◆ 1997
33. Out of the Picture ◆ 1997
34. Spy Girl ◆ 1997
35. Undercover Angels ◆ 1997
36. Have You Heard About Elizabeth ◆ 1997
37. Breaking Away ◆ 1998
38. Good-Bye, Elizabeth ◆ 1998
39. Elizabeth ♥ New York ◆ 1998
40. Private Jessica ◆ 1998
41. Escape to New York ◆ 1998
42. Sneaking In ◆ 1998
43. The Price of Love ◆ 1998
44. Love Me Always ◆ 1998

SWEET VALLEY UNIVERSITY THRILLER EDITIONS

Pascal, Francine, creator
BANTAM
GRADES 7–8
HORROR | REAL LIFE

Companions to the Sweet Valley High University series, these mystery-thriller books are page-turners, with Sweet Valley University students investigating murders, being threatened by stalkers, and foiling other evil plots.

1. Wanted for Murder ◆ 1995
2. He's Watching You ◆ 1995
3. Kiss of the Vampire ◆ 1995
4. The House of Death ◆ 1995
5. Running for Her Life ◆ 1996
6. The Roommate ◆ 1996
7. What Winston Saw ◆ 1997
8. Dead Before Dawn ◆ 1997
9. Killer at Sea ◆ 1997
10. Channel X ◆ 1997
11. Love and Murder ◆ 1998
12. Don't Answer the Phone ◆ 1998
13. CyberStalker: The Return of William White, Part 1 ◆ 1998

SWORD OF THE SPIRITS

Christopher, John
ALADDIN
GRADES 5–8
ADVENTURE | SCIENCE FICTION

Post-apocalyptic England is the setting of this trilogy. It is a world of warriors, dwarfs, mutants, and seers. Luke Perry, the future ruler, is thrown into chaos as he finds out that his world is not as it seems. He must hide after his father is murdered and his half-brother takes the throne. Continuous action, drama, and intrigue create a satisfying read for fans of science fiction.

1. The Prince in Waiting ◆ 1970
2. Beyond the Burning Lands ◆ 1971
3. The Sword of the Spirits ◆ 1972

TACKY THE PENGUIN

Lester, Helen

HOUGHTON MIFFLIN

GRADES K–2

ANIMAL FANTASY

Tacky the penguin is a lively, enthusiastic character whose unusual behavior often annoys his friends. *Three Cheers for Tacky* focuses on the Penguin Cheering Contest, which provides a perfect opportunity to showcase Tacky's individuality. Just when it looks as if Tacky will spoil everything, his energy and spirit bring success. In *Tacky in Trouble*, Tacky travels to a tropical island, an unusual spot for a penguin! Young readers will find it satisfying that Tacky is different but still accepted and appreciated.

1. Tacky the Penguin ◆ 1988
2. Three Cheers for Tacky ◆ 1994
3. Tacky in Trouble ◆ 1998

TAFFY SINCLAIR

Haynes, Betsy

BANTAM SKYLARK

GRADES 4–6

REAL LIFE

Taffy Sinclair has various adventures in this series: getting a role in a real TV soap opera, modeling, and, best of all, keeping ahead of the Fabulous Five, a club created by five girls specifically to get Taffy. The Fabulous Five has its own series.

1. The Against Taffy Sinclair Club ◆ 1976
2. Taffy Sinclair Strikes Again ◆ 1984
3. Taffy Sinclair, Queen of the Soaps ◆ 1985
4. Taffy Sinclair and the Romance Machine Disaster ◆ 1987
5. Blackmailed by Taffy Sinclair ◆ 1987
6. Taffy Sinclair, Baby Ashley, and Me ◆ 1988
7. Taffy Sinclair and the Secret Admirer Epidemic ◆ 1988
8. The Truth About Taffy Sinclair ◆ 1988
9. Taffy Sinclair and the Melanie Makeover ◆ 1988
10. Taffy Sinclair Goes to Hollywood ◆ 1990
11. Nobody Likes Taffy Sinclair ◆ 1991

TALES FROM THE ODYSSEY

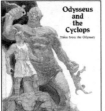

Richardson, I. M., adapter

TROLL

GRADES 5–8

FANTASY

In this series of stories from *The Odyssey*, Odysseus relates his adventures to various listeners. Some of these include the land of the Lotus Eaters and the Cyclops, as well as the Island of the Winds and man-eating giants. This will be a hit with mythology fans.

1. The Voyage of Odysseus ◆ 1984
2. Odysseus and the Cyclops ◆ 1984
3. Odysseus and the Giants ◆ 1984
4. Odysseus and the Great Challenge ◆ 1984
5. Odysseus and the Magic of Circe ◆ 1984
6. The Return of Odysseus ◆ 1984

TALES FROM THE SANDLOT

Gutman, Dan

SCHOLASTIC

GRADES 4–6

FANTASY | HUMOR | RECREATION

Each book in this series features a different character who experiences a weird encounter. In one book, Jake Miller is able to read minds. His special ability, which appears after he is hit by a pitch, lets him know the strategies of the other teams—which puts him in danger. Lee Madigan, left fielder, doesn't think there are any monsters in Oregon, until he meets Bigfoot. And Rob Newton is a pitcher who has an out-of-body experience. Connecting sports with weird events will expand the appeal of this series.

1. The Shortstop Who Knew Too Much ◆ 1997
2. The Green Monster in Left Field ◆ 1997
3. The Catcher Who Shocked the World ◆ 1997
4. The Pitcher Who Went Out of His Mind ◆ 1997

TALES FROM THIRD GRADE

Ransom, Candice F.
TROLL
GRADES 2–4
HUMOR | REAL LIFE

Third-grader Amber Cantrell has a great imagination, and it sometime causes her problems. She and her friend Delight Wakefield experience events that will be familiar to many elementary school children. For example, Amber is jealous that Delight is so good at gymnastics, but she appreciates her friend when she needs help finding a lost toy. The girls also have problems when David gives them both attention. Whom does he really like? Can the girls' friendship survive their jealousy? Match this up with the readers of Baby-sitters Club books.

1. Who Needs Third Grade? ◆ 1993
2. Third Grade Detectives ◆ 1994
3. Third Grade Stars ◆ 1994
4. Why Are Boys So Weird? ◆ 1994

TALES OF COVEN TREE *see* Coven Tree

TALES OF GOM IN THE LEGENDS OF ULM

Chetwin, Grace
LOTHROP, LEE & SHEPARD; BRADBURY BOOKS
GRADES 6–8
FANTASY

Fantasy lovers will enjoy this series full of mountain lore, wizardry, and adventure. Gom, a mountain boy growing up in the land of Ulm, has many unusual talents. In the first book, his mother has disappeared, leaving a mysterious stone rune with Gom. This leads to his first great challenge. In the second book, he tries to return the rune to his mother while being pursued by evil forces that also want it. In the third book, he finds his mother and begins to learn about wizardry and other worlds.

1. Gom on Windy Mountain ◆ 1986
2. The Riddle and the Rune ◆ 1987
3. The Crystal Stair ◆ 1988
4. The Starstone ◆ 1989

TALES OF TROTTER STREET

Hughes, Shirley

LOTHROP, LEE & SHEPARD

GRADES K–2

FAMILY LIFE

These are heartwarming tales of life in an urban neighborhood. *Wheels* has a little boy yearning for a bicycle that his mother cannot afford, but the best birthday surprise of all is the go-cart that his older brother makes for him. In *Angel Mae*, a little girl gets a new baby in her house for Christmas and appears in the Christmas play.

1. Angel Mae: A Tale of Trotter Street ◆ 1989
2. The Big Concrete Lorry: A Tale of Trotter Street ◆ 1990
3. The Snow Lady: A Tale of Trotter Street ◆ 1990
4. Wheels: A Tale of Trotter Street ◆ 1991

TANYA

Gauch, Patricia Lee

PUTNAM

GRADES K–3

REAL LIFE

Tanya is a little girl who loves to dance. Her older sister has already been taking dance lessons, and Tanya wants nothing more than to dance like all the students in the class. However, her attempts are sometimes less than perfect. A gentle series about the delights of dancing.

1. Dance, Tanya ◆ 1989
2. Bravo, Tanya! ◆ 1992
3. Tanya and Emily in a Dance for Two ◆ 1994
4. Tanya Steps Out ◆ 1996
5. Tanya and the Magic Wardrobe ◆ 1997

TEDDY BEARS

Gretz, Susanna

FOUR WINDS

GRADES K–3

FANTASY

The teddy bears, their dog Fred, and sometimes their Uncle Jerome share various adventures: They stay indoors and plan a trip to the moon; one of them gets a cold and the rest of the bears figure out how to make him better; on a train trip, they discover that the white bears they are so afraid of are actually very friendly. Gretz's amusing illustrations contain lots for young readers to look at, and the stories are heartwarming.

1. Teddy Bears' Moving Day ◆ 1981
2. Teddy Bears Go Shopping ◆ 1982
3. Teddy Bears Cure a Cold ◆ 1984
4. Teddy Bears ABC ◆ 1986
5. Teddy Bears 1 to 10 ◆ 1986
6. Teddy Bears Stay Indoors ◆ 1987
7. Teddy Bears Take the Train ◆ 1987
8. Teddy Bears at the Seaside ◆ 1989

TEENY WITCH

Matthews, Liz

TROLL

GRADES K–2

FANTASY

Teeny Witch and her three aunts—Vicky, Icky, and Ticky—have various amusing adventures, all with surprise endings. In *Teeny Witch and the Tricky Easter Bunny*, Teeny tries to catch the magical Easter Bunny she keeps seeing all over town, only to discover it is really a whole class of children dressed up for an Easter play. In *Teeny Witch and the Perfect Valentine*, Teeny tries to save her money to buy boxes of candy from the store, but somebody else keeps buying them. In the end, she discovers her three aunts were buying them for her. Young listeners will enjoy these silly read-alouds about Teeny and her three aunts.

1. Teeny Witch and Christmas Magic ◆ 1991
2. Teeny Witch and the Perfect Valentine ◆ 1991

3. Teeny Witch and the Terrible Twins ◆ 1991
4. Teeny Witch and the Tricky Easter Bunny ◆ 1991
5. Teeny Witch Goes on Vacation ◆ 1991
6. Teeny Witch Goes to School ◆ 1991
7. Teeny Witch Goes to the Library ◆ 1991
8. Teeny Witch and the Great Halloween Ride ◆ 1991

TEN COMMANDMENTS MYSTERIES

Murphy, Elspeth Campbell

CHARIOT BOOKS

GRADES 3–5

MYSTERY | VALUES

Three cousins—Timothy, Titus, and Sarah-Jane—solve mysteries in this Christian series. Each mystery centers on one of the Ten Commandments and explores a Christian theme. For example, *The Mystery of the Vanishing Present* centers on the commandment to remember the Sabbath by keeping it holy. The Christian theme is reverence. The T.C.D.C. (Three Cousins Detective Club) has to solve the mystery of a painting called *Sabbath Day*: who painted it, who left it for their grandfather, and who mysteriously took it. These entertaining mysteries, while centered on religious themes, are not too didactic. The cousins also appear in the Three Cousins Detective Club series.

1. The Mystery of the Vanishing Present ◆ 1988
2. The Mystery of the Laughing Cat ◆ 1988
3. The Mystery of the Messed-Up Wedding ◆ 1988
4. The Mystery of the Gravestone Riddle ◆ 1988
5. The Mystery of the Carousel Horse ◆ 1988
6. The Mystery of the Silver Dolphin ◆ 1988
7. The Mystery of the Tattletale Parrot ◆ 1988
8. The Mystery of the Second Map ◆ 1988
9. The Mystery of the Double Trouble ◆ 1988
10. The Mystery of the Silent Idol ◆ 1988

THE THIRTEEN MOONS

George, Jean Craighead

HARPERCOLLINS

GRADES 3–6

REAL LIFE

This is a wonderful series, full of the amazing ways that animals adapt to their surroundings. George, well known for her writing on the environment, has taken each of the 13 lunar months and highlighted one North American animal and how it adapts during that season in its native habitat. A wide variety of animals (alligators, wolves, mountain lions, etc.) and habitats (swamps, arctic tundras, deserts, etc.) are covered. Readers will enjoy the intricate illustrations and fascinating facts about North American animals and habitats.

1. The Moon of the Owls ◆ 1967
2. The Moon of the Bears ◆ 1967
3. The Moon of the Salamanders ◆ 1967
4. The Moon of the Chickarees ◆ 1968
5. The Moon of the Monarch Butterflies ◆ 1968
6. The Moon of the Fox Pups ◆ 1968
7. The Moon of the Wild Pigs ◆ 1968
8. The Moon of the Mountain Lions ◆ 1968
9. The Moon of the Deer ◆ 1969
10. The Moon of the Alligators ◆ 1969
11. The Moon of the Gray Wolves ◆ 1969
12. The Moon of the Winter Bird ◆ 1969
13. The Moon of the Moles ◆ 1969

39 KIDS ON THE BLOCK

Marzollo, Jean
SCHOLASTIC
GRADES 1–3
REAL LIFE

On Baldwin Street, there are 39 kids. Some live in apartments; others live in houses near a restaurant; and many attend the Appleville School. At the beginning of the books, there is a list of the kids who are featured. These are enjoyable stories about friends.

1. The Green Ghost of Appleville ◆ 1989
2. The Best Present Ever ◆ 1989
3. The Best Friends Club ◆ 1990
4. Roses Are Pink and You Stink! ◆ 1990
5. Chicken Pox Strikes Again ◆ 1990
6. My Sister the Blabbermouth ◆ 1990

THOMAS AND GRANDFATHER

Stolz, Mary
HARPERCOLLINS
GRADES 3–6
FAMILY LIFE

Thomas and his grandfather share many heartwarming moments in this series: fishing, having relatives come to visit, being brave during storms, and more. African heritage and bits of black history of the United States (such as the Negro Baseball League) are interwoven in these simple stories.

1. Storm in the Night ◆ 1988
2. Go Fish ◆ 1991
3. Stealing Home ◆ 1992
4. Coco Grimes ◆ 1994

THOROUGHBRED

Campbell, Joanna, creator

HARPERTROPHY

GRADES 3–7

REAL LIFE | RECREATION

Eighteen-year-old jockey Samantha McLean and her middle school-aged adopted sister live at Whitebrook, a thoroughbred breeding and training farm in Kentucky. In addition to typical problems with school, friends, boyfriends, and parents, the girls handle the pressures of riding and racing. Girls who like horses will enjoy this series about what it's like to live on a horse farm.

1. A Horse Called Wonder ◆ 1991
2. Wonder's Promise ◆ 1991
3. Wonder's First Race ◆ 1991
4. Wonder's Victory ◆ 1991
5. Ashleigh's Dream ◆ 1993
6. Wonder's Yearling ◆ 1993
7. Samantha's Pride ◆ 1993
8. Sierra's Steeplechase ◆ 1993
9. Pride's Challenge ◆ 1994
10. Pride's Last Race ◆ 1994
11. Wonder's Sister ◆ 1994
12. Shining's Orphan ◆ 1994
13. Cindy's Runaway Colt ◆ 1995
14. Cindy's Glory ◆ 1995
15. Glory's Triumph ◆ 1995
16. Glory in Danger ◆ 1996
17. Ashleigh's Farewell ◆ 1996
18. Glory's Rival ◆ 1997
19. Cindy's Heartbreak ◆ 1997
20. Champion's Spirit ◆ 1997
21. Wonder's Champion ◆ 1997
22. Arabian Challenge ◆ 1997
23. Cindy's Honor ◆ 1997
24. The Horse of Her Dreams ◆ 1997
25. Melanie's Treasure ◆ 1998

26. Sterling's Second Chance ◆ 1998
27. Christina's Courage ◆ 1998
28. Camp Saddlebrook ◆ 1998
29. Melanie's Last Ride ◆ 1998
30. Dylan's Choice ◆ 1998
31. A Home for Melanie ◆ 1998
32. Cassidy's Secret ◆ 1999

THOROUGHBRED SUPER EDITIONS

1. Ashleigh's Christmas Miracle (Campbell, Joanna) ◆ 1994
2. Ashleigh's Diary (Campbell, Joanna) ◆ 1995
3. Ashleigh's Hope (Campbell, Joanna) ◆ 1996
4. Samantha's Journey (Campbell, Joanna, and Karen Bentley) ◆ 1998

THREE COUSINS DETECTIVE CLUB

Murphy, Elspeth Campbell

BETHANY HOUSE

GRADES 2–4

MYSTERY | VALUES

Three cousins—Sarah-Jane, Timothy, and Titus—have formed the T.C.D.C. (Three Cousins Detective Club). In each of the books in this enjoyable series, they come across a different mystery to solve. In *The Mystery of the Haunted Lighthouse*, they discover who is trying to scare their uncle away from purchasing an old lighthouse. In *The Mystery of the Silent Nightingale*, they discover the mystery behind an old silver locket. In another book, the cousins must find a missing four-year-old named Patience. After they find her, they must unravel her unusual story about dancing angels. Each book centers around a religious theme such as joy, self-control, or patience. The cousins also appear in the Ten Commandments Mysteries.

1. The Mystery of the White Elephant ◆ 1994
2. The Mystery of the Silent Nightingale ◆ 1994
3. The Mystery of the Wrong Dog ◆ 1994
4. The Mystery of the Dancing Angels ◆ 1995
5. The Mystery of the Hobo's Message ◆ 1995
6. The Mystery of the Magi's Treasure ◆ 1995
7. The Mystery of the Haunted Lighthouse ◆ 1995
8. The Mystery of the Dolphin Detective ◆ 1995
9. The Mystery of the Eagle Feather ◆ 1995
10. The Mystery of the Silly Goose ◆ 1996
11. The Mystery of the Copycat Clown ◆ 1996
12. The Mystery of the Honeybees' Secret ◆ 1996
13. The Mystery of the Gingerbread House ◆ 1997

14. The Mystery of the Zoo Camp ◆ 1997
15. The Mystery of the Goldfish Pond ◆ 1997
16. The Mystery of the Traveling Button ◆ 1997
17. The Mystery of the Birthday Party ◆ 1997
18. The Mystery of the Lost Island ◆ 1997
19. The Mystery of the Wedding Cake ◆ 1998
20. The Mystery of the Sand Castle ◆ 1998
21. The Mystery of the Sock Monkeys ◆ 1998
22. The Mystery of the African Gray ◆ 1998

THREE INVESTIGATORS

Various authors

RANDOM HOUSE

GRADES 5–7

ADVENTURE | MYSTERY

Jupiter Jones and his friends Pete and Bob form the Three Investigators and operate out of a secret office in the junkyard owned by Jupiter's aunt and uncle. Jupiter is a young Sherlock Holmes, never missing anything and coming to conclusions that astonish his friends and nearly always turn out to be right. The mysteries are fairly complicated, and the solutions depend on historic or scientific knowledge. Jupiter, as the First Investigator, supplies the brains, and Pete, stronger and more athletic, is the Second Investigator. Bob is in charge of research and records. Boys who like the Hardy Boys will find more depth and realism in the Three Investigators.

1. The Secret of Terror Castle (Arthur, Robert) ◆ 1964
2. The Mystery of the Stuttering Parrot (Arthur, Robert) ◆ 1964
3. The Mystery of the Whispering Mummy (Arthur, Robert) ◆ 1965
4. The Mystery of the Green Ghost (Arthur, Robert) ◆ 1965
5. The Mystery of the Vanishing Treasure (Arthur, Robert) ◆ 1966
6. The Secret of Skeleton Island (Arthur, Robert) ◆ 1966
7. The Mystery of the Fiery Eye (Arthur, Robert) ◆ 1967
8. The Mystery of the Silver Spider (Arthur, Robert) ◆ 1967
9. The Mystery of the Screaming Clock (Arthur, Robert) ◆ 1968
10. The Mystery of the Moaning Cave (Arden, William) ◆ 1968
11. The Mystery of the Talking Skull (Arthur, Robert) ◆ 1969
12. The Mystery of the Laughing Shadow (Arden, William) ◆ 1969
13. The Secret of the Crooked Cat (Arden, William) ◆ 1970
14. The Mystery of the Coughing Dragon (West, Nick) ◆ 1970

15. The Mystery of the Flaming Footprints (Carey, M.V.) ◆ 1971
16. The Mystery of the Nervous Lion (West, Nick) ◆ 1971
17. The Mystery of the Singing Serpent (Carey, M.V.) ◆ 1972
18. The Mystery of the Shrinking House (Arden, William) ◆ 1972
19. The Secret of Phantom Lake (Arden, William) ◆ 1973
20. The Mystery of Monster Mountain (Carey, M.V.) ◆ 1973
21. The Secret of the Haunted Mirror (Carey, M.V.) ◆ 1974
22. The Mystery of the Dead Man's Riddle (Arden, William) ◆ 1974
23. The Mystery of the Invisible Dog (Carey, M.V.) ◆ 1975
24. The Mystery of Death Trap Mine (Carey, M.V.) ◆ 1976
25. The Mystery of the Dancing Devil (Arden, William) ◆ 1976
26. The Mystery of the Headless Horse (Arden, William) ◆ 1977
27. The Mystery of the Magic Circle (Carey, M.V.) ◆ 1978
28. The Mystery of the Deadly Double (Arden, William) ◆ 1978
29. The Mystery of the Sinister Scarecrow (Carey, M.V.) ◆ 1979
30. The Secret of Shark Reef (Arden, William) ◆ 1979
31. The Mystery of the Scar-Faced Beggar (Carey, M.V.) ◆ 1981
32. The Mystery of the Blazing Cliffs (Carey, M.V.) ◆ 1981
33. The Mystery of the Purple Pirate (Arden, William) ◆ 1982
34. The Mystery of the Wandering Caveman (Carey, M.V.) ◆ 1982
35. The Mystery of the Kidnapped Whale (Brandel, Marc) ◆ 1983
36. The Mystery of the Missing Mermaid (Carey, M.V.) ◆ 1983
37. The Mystery of the Two-Toed Pigeon (Brandel, Marc) ◆ 1984
38. The Mystery of the Smashing Glass (Arden, William) ◆ 1984
39. The Mystery of the Trail of Terror (Carey, M.V.) ◆ 1984
40. The Mystery of the Rogues' Reunion (Brandel, Marc) ◆ 1985
41. The Mystery of the Creep-Show Crooks (Carey, M.V.) ◆ 1985
42. The Mystery of Wreckers' Rock (Arden, William) ◆ 1986
43. The Mystery of the Cranky Collector (Carey, M.V.) ◆ 1986
44. The Case of the Savage Statue (Carey, M.V.) ◆ 1987

THREE INVESTIGATORS CRIMEBUSTERS

1. Hot Wheels (Arden, William) ◆ 1989
2. Murder to Go (Stine, Megan, and H. William Stine) ◆ 1989
3. Rough Stuff (Stone, G. H.) ◆ 1989
4. Funny Business (McCay, William) ◆ 1989
5. An Ear for Danger (Brandel, Marc) ◆ 1989
6. Thriller Diller (Stine, Megan, and H. William Stine) ◆ 1989
7. Reel Trouble (Stone, G. H.) ◆ 1989
8. Shoot the Works (McCay, William) ◆ 1990
9. Foul Play (Lerangis, Peter) ◆ 1990
10. Long Shot (Stine, Megan, and H. William Stine) ◆ 1990
11. Fatal Error (Stone, G. H.) ◆ 1990

TILLERMAN CYCLE

Voigt, Cynthia
ATHENEUM

GRADES 5–8

FAMILY LIFE

Two of the books in this outstanding series have won awards: *Dicey's Song*, a Newbery, and *A Solitary Blue*, a Newbery Honor. In *Homecoming*, the four Tillerman children are abandoned by their mother, and it is up to 13-year-old Dicey to get them safely to their grandmother's house, far away on Chesapeake Bay. *Dicey's Song* continues the story, with their adjustment to living with Gram. The rest of the titles are continuations of the story and companion titles about other people with whom the Tillermans come in contact.

1. Homecoming ◆ 1981
2. Dicey's Song ◆ 1982
3. A Solitary Blue ◆ 1983
4. The Runner ◆ 1985
5. Come a Stranger ◆ 1986
6. Sons from Afar ◆ 1987
7. Seventeen Against the Dealer ◆ 1989

TIME FANTASY SERIES

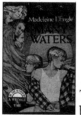

L'Engle, Madeleine
FARRAR, STRAUS & GIROUX; DELL

GRADES 4–8

ADVENTURE I FANTASY

The four books in this fantasy series feature different members of the Murry family in the classic struggle between good and evil in the universe. *A Wrinkle in Time*, which won the Newbery Award, chronicles Meg Murry's efforts to find her father, overcome the forces of darkness that are threatening the Earth, and recognize her own limitations and strengths. In doing these things, Meg, her brother Charles Wallace, and a friend, Calvin, travel through space and time to rescue Mr. Murry from the evil It. Later books focus on different members of the family as the struggle continues. Readers will be challenged by the intricate plot devices, including time travel and elements of classic literary tales. In all the books, there are complex issues of values, beliefs, and a connection with spiritual powers in the battle against cruelty, injustice, and intolerance.

1. A Wrinkle in Time ◆ 1962
2. A Wind in the Door ◆ 1973

3. A Swiftly Tilting Planet ◆ 1978
4. Many Waters ◆ 1986

TIME SURFERS

Abbott, Tony

BANTAM DOUBLEDAY DELL

GRADES 4–6

ADVENTURE | FANTASY

Since Ned Banks and his family moved to Lakewood, Ohio, strange things have been happening. Ned has become a Time Surfer, moving through time, making friends, and encountering strange creatures. In one book, Ned and his friend Ernie Somers must undo the work of Vorg, the evil master of time. In another book, Ned and Julie Tate must recover the stolen space shuttle and rescue Julie's father, Dr. Tate, a famous space scientist. There is plenty of action and enough weird creatures to interest fans of futuristic fantasies.

1. Space Bingo ◆ 1996
2. Orbit Wipeout! ◆ 1996
3. Mondo Meltdown ◆ 1996
4. Into the Zonk Zone! ◆ 1996
5. Splash Crash! ◆ 1997
6. Zero Hour ◆ 1997
7. Shock Wave ◆ 1997
8. Doom Star ◆ 1997

TIME TRILOGY

Anderson, Margaret J.

KNOPF

GRADES 5–8

FANTASY

In this science fantasy trilogy, Jennifer and Robert discover that they can slip through the Circle of Stones and travel through time to the year 2179. There they come upon a peaceful society trying to protect itself from a barbaric mechanized society. As the trilogy progresses, these people who refuse to meet violence with violence struggle to protect their community.

1. In the Keep of Time ◆ 1977
2. In the Circle of Time ◆ 1979
3. The Mists of Time ◆ 1984

TIME WARP TRIO

Scieszka, Jon

VIKING; PUFFIN

GRADES 3–6

HUMOR | SCIENCE FICTION

Joe's uncle gives him a book for his birthday that is really a time machine. It envelops Joe and his friends Sam and Fred in a green fog, twists them out of shape, and lands them in any time they ask for. The book is always present somewhere in the time they are in, and they must find it before they can go home. Slapstick humor combines with historical information supplied by Sam, the brains of the group. Lane Smith's drawings capture the hapless trio's expressions of disgust at the situations they find themselves in as they travel to the Middle Ages, Ancient Egypt, and the American West. A highly entertaining series. The humor and length of the books are perfect for intermediate readers.

1. Knights of the Kitchen Table ◆ 1991
2. The Not-So-Jolly Roger ◆ 1991
3. The Good, the Bad and the Goofy ◆ 1992
4. Your Mother Was a Neanderthal ◆ 1993
5. 2095 ◆ 1995
6. Tut Tut ◆ 1996
7. Summer Reading Is Killing Me ◆ 1998

TITCH

Hutchins, Pat

GREENWILLOW

GRADES K–2

FAMILY LIFE

Titch is the youngest in his family. This loving series chronicles the typical life of a youngest child: getting hand-me-down clothes, cleaning his room, feeling small, and playing with friends. The illustrations are delightful.

1. Titch ◆ 1972
2. You'll Soon Grow into Them, Titch ◆ 1983
3. Tidy Titch ◆ 1991
4. Titch and Daisy ◆ 1996

TOBIAS

Hertz, Ole

CAROLRHODA

GRADES K–3

REAL LIFE

The Tobias books are about a Greenlandic boy who lives with his family in a small settlement. Readers will get a feel for the different ways that families live and work in this country. This simple series takes readers through different times of the year in Greenland and includes many explanations, pictures, and diagrams of the village and lifestyle of the people.

1. Tobias Goes Seal Hunting ◆ 1984
2. Tobias Has a Birthday ◆ 1984
3. Tobias Goes Ice Fishing ◆ 1984
4. Tobias Catches Trout ◆ 1984

TOM AND PIPPO

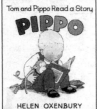

Oxenbury, Helen

CANDLEWICK

GRADES K–1

FAMILY LIFE

A very small boy and his little toy monkey have small adventures that prove Tom's loyalty to his stuffed friend, Pippo. Pippo plays in the mud, gets dirty, and has to go in the washing machine. Tom hugs him because he's afraid he'll never see him again. As all young children do, Tom yearns to do everything that older people do. When his father gets tired of reading books, Tom reads to Pippo. Tom and Pippo go to the beach with Tom's father, who insists that Tom wear a hat. Tom says that Pippo needs to wear a hat, too, and makes him one out of newspaper. Each book in this series has minimal text with a black-and-white drawing on one side of a spread and a charming full-color illustration on the other.

1. Tom and Pippo Go Shopping ◆ 1988
2. Tom and Pippo's Day ◆ 1988
3. Tom and Pippo in the Garden ◆ 1988
4. Tom and Pippo Go for a Walk ◆ 1988

5. Tom and Pippo Make a Mess ◆ 1988
6. Tom and Pippo Read a Story ◆ 1988
7. Tom and Pippo See the Moon ◆ 1988
8. Tom and Pippo and the Washing Machine ◆ 1988
9. Pippo Gets Lost ◆ 1989
10. Tom and Pippo and the Dog ◆ 1989
11. Tom and Pippo in the Snow ◆ 1989
12. Tom and Pippo Make a Friend ◆ 1989
13. Tom and Pippo on the Beach ◆ 1993
14. Tom and Pippo and the Bicycle ◆ 1994

TOM SWIFT

Appleton, Victor

ARCHWAY/POCKET BOOKS

GRADES 7–8

ADVENTURE | FANTASY

Mutant sea creatures, a cyborg kick boxer, and microbots are just some of the creatures that this updated Tom Swift and his friends battle to protect our world. In *Mutant Beach*, Tom faces a giant squid and a 50-foot shark, which could be the result of his research into growth hormones. Tom battles those who are out to blame him while he tries to find out who is really responsible. *Fire Biker* features Tom and his sister Sandra. They have invented a jet-powered cycle and a suit that makes the wearer invisible, but their inventions have been stolen and now the whole world is in danger. These are action-packed books with the kinds of creatures and suspense that will attract the readers of R. L. Stine's series, as well as readers who like the adventure of *Star Trek* and *Star Wars*.

1. The Black Dragon ◆ 1991
2. The Negative Zone ◆ 1991
3. Cyborg Kickboxer ◆ 1991
4. The DNA Disaster ◆ 1991
5. Monster Machine ◆ 1991
6. Aquatech Warriors ◆ 1991
7. Moonstalker ◆ 1992
8. The Microbots ◆ 1992
9. Fire Biker ◆ 1992
10. Mind Games ◆ 1992
11. Mutant Beach ◆ 1992

TRAILBLAZERS

Jackson, Dave, and Neta Jackson

BETHANY HOUSE

GRADES 4–7

HISTORICAL | VALUES

Christian heroes from every era of American history are featured in stories based on their lives. Each book focuses on an ordinary child whose life has been changed. A young slave girl is helped to escape by Harriet Tubman after hearing stories about this Moses who helped her people by following the Northern Star. A young orphan boy meets Peter Cartwright, one of the circuit-riding preachers, and is helped to find his mother, who was taken away by Indians. Celeste Key is a turn-of-the-century child whose family is harassed by the Ku Klux Klan. They move to Florida, and Celeste enters a school started by Mary McLeod Bethune. Each story is followed by information about the historical figure featured.

1. Kidnapped by River Rats: William & Catherine Booth ◆ 1991
2. The Queen's Smuggler: William Tyndale ◆ 1991
3. Spy for the Night Riders: Martin Luther ◆ 1992
4. The Hidden Jewel: Amy Carmichael ◆ 1992
5. Escape from the Slave Traders: David Livingston ◆ 1992
6. The Chimney Sweep's Ransom: John Wesley ◆ 1992
7. Imprisoned in the Golden City: Adoniram & Ann Judson ◆ 1993
8. The Bandit of Ashley Downs: George Mueller ◆ 1993
9. Shanghaied to China: Hudson Taylor ◆ 1993
10. Listen to the Whippoorwill: Harriet Tubman ◆ 1993
11. Attack in the Rye Grass: Narcissa & Marcus Whitman ◆ 1994
12. Trial by Poison: Mary Slessor ◆ 1994
13. Flight of the Fugitives: Gladys Aylward ◆ 1994
14. The Betrayer's Fortune: Menno Simons ◆ 1994
15. Danger on the Flying Trapeze: Dwight L. Moody ◆ 1995
16. Abandoned on the Wild Frontier: Peter Cartwright ◆ 1995
17. The Runaway's Revenge: John Newton ◆ 1995
18. Thieves of Tyburn Square: Elizabeth Fry ◆ 1995
19. The Warrior's Challenge: David Zeisberger ◆ 1996
20. Quest for the Lost Prince: Samuel Morris ◆ 1996
21. Traitor in the Tower: John Bunyan ◆ 1996
22. The Drummer Boy's Battle: Florence Nightingale ◆ 1996
23. Defeat of the Ghost Riders: Mary Bethune ◆ 1997
24. The Fate of the Yellow Woodbee: Nate Saint ◆ 1997

25. The Mayflower Secret: Governor William Bradford ◆ 1998
26. The Gold Miner's Rescue: Sheldon Jackson ◆ 1998
27. Assassins in the Cathedral: Festo Kivengere ◆ 1999
28. Mask of the Wolf Boy: Jonathan and Rosalind Goforth ◆ 1999

TREEHORN

Heide, Florence Parry

HOLIDAY HOUSE; DELL

GRADES 3–7

FANTASY | HUMOR

Treehorn has all kinds of mysterious adventures while his parents remain completely oblivious. His mother is concerned only with luncheons and decorating, his father with work and the money his mother is spending. Meanwhile, young Treehorn is shrinking, finding a money tree, and meeting a genie. A black-and-white drawing facing each page of text emphasizes the bland reactions of Treehorn and his parents to the fantastic things that happen to the boy. Adults will appreciate the humor as much as children will, making this great for family read-alouds.

1. The Shrinking of Treehorn ◆ 1971
2. Treehorn's Treasure ◆ 1981
3. Treehorn's Wish ◆ 1984
4. Treehorn Times Three ◆ 1991

TRICK BOOKS

Corbett, Scott

LITTLE, BROWN

GRADES 3–6

HUMOR

Kerby Maxwell, his dog Waldo, and his friend Fenton are always getting mixed up in strange situations. A dangerous chemistry set, a trip around the haunted house on Hangman's Knob, and a disappearing dog are just a few of the amazing things readers will find out about in this entertaining and humorous series.

1. The Lemonade Trick ◆ 1960
2. The Mailbox Trick ◆ 1961
3. The Disappearing Dog Trick ◆ 1963
4. The Limerick Trick ◆ 1964
5. The Baseball Trick ◆ 1965
6. The Turnabout Trick ◆ 1967

7. The Hairy Horror Trick ◆ 1969
8. The Hateful Plateful Trick ◆ 1971
9. The Home Run Trick ◆ 1973
10. The Hockey Trick ◆ 1974
11. The Black Mask Trick ◆ 1976
12. The Hangman's Ghost Trick ◆ 1977

TRIG

Peck, Robert Newton

LITTLE, BROWN

GRADES 3–5

HUMOR | REAL LIFE

Elizabeth Trigman's life is completely changed when her Uncle Fred gives her a genuine Melvin Purvis Official Junior G-Man Machine Gun. Bud and Skip, two older boys who would never let her play with them, join her gang and begin to call her Trig. Together, they get in and out of funny situations in their little Vermont town. Trig is completely baffled by the adult world, and much of the humor in the series comes from her misunderstandings and from the town itself. Fans of the Peck's Soup books will enjoy this series.

1. Trig ◆ 1977
2. Trig Sees Red ◆ 1978
3. Trig Goes Ape ◆ 1980
4. Trig or Treat ◆ 1982

TRIPLET TROUBLE

Dadey, Debbie, and Marcia Thornton Jones

SCHOLASTIC

GRADES K–3

REAL LIFE

Sam lives four doors down from the Tucker triplets. Alex is his best friend, and she is fun to be with, but sometimes her ideas get everyone in trouble. Ashley is quiet, and Adam is very smart. Sometimes they quarrel, and Sam is caught in the middle. When their second-grade class is promised a pizza party for good behavior, everyone in the class blames Alex for spoiling it by being noisy. She wants to have a cookie-making contest and ends up making an awful mess. Short, easy chapters and everyday situations make this series accessible to young readers.

1. Triplet Trouble and the Talent Show Mess ◆ 1995

2. Triplet Trouble and the Runaway Reindeer ◆ 1995
3. Triplet Trouble and the Red Heart Race ◆ 1996
4. Triplet Trouble and the Field Day Disaster ◆ 1996
5. Triplet Trouble and the Cookie Contest ◆ 1996
6. Triplet Trouble and the Pizza Party ◆ 1996
7. Triplet Trouble and the Bicycle Race ◆ 1997
8. Triplet Trouble and the Class Trip ◆ 1997

TRIPODS

Christopher, John
MACMILLAN
GRADES 5–8
SCIENCE FICTION

Aliens have taken over the Earth, and every Earth boy receives a cap at age 13 so the aliens can control his thoughts. The aliens take the form of huge metal tripods, and no one knows if that is their real form or if they are just machines that aliens use. Will, Henry, and Jean Paul escape to the White Mountains and find a colony of free men. Jean Paul, Will, and a German boy named Fritz are sent on a mission to the city of the aliens to learn their ways, and Will barely escapes with his life. The aliens are completely defeated as a result of what Fritz and Will are able to learn. *When the Tripods Came* is the prequel to the series, and readers may want to read it first.

1. The White Mountains ◆ 1967
2. The City of Gold and Lead ◆ 1967
3. The Pool of Fire ◆ 1968
4. When the Tripods Came ◆ 1988

THE TUCKET ADVENTURES

Paulsen, Gary
DELACORTE
GRADES 5–8
ADVENTURE | HISTORICAL

Francis Tucket is 14 when this series begins. While heading west on the Oregon Trail, Francis is separated from his family and captured by Pawnees. He is aided by Mr. Grimes, who teaches him survival skills but also gives him a look at the violent ways of a frontiersman. Francis leaves Mr. Grimes and searches for his family only to encounter more ruthless outlaws. This is a gritty series that does not romanticize the difficulties of life on the frontier. With lots of action, this should appeal to boys and perhaps to reluctant readers.

1. Mr. Tucket ◆ 1994
2. Call Me Francis Tucket ◆ 1995
3. Tucket's Ride ◆ 1997

TWELVE CANDLES CLUB

Schulte, Elaine L.

BETHANY HOUSE

GRADES 4–6

REAL LIFE | VALUES

Four friends—Jess McColl, Becky Hamilton, Cara Hernandez, and Tricia Bennett—have formed a club. All four girls are 12 years old, so they are the Twelve Candles Club. Their activities include doing chores, such as baby-sitting, light housekeeping, and helping at parties. They become involved in different situations, such as a drug-smuggling mystery and the theft of some art work; and some of the books feature exotic locations, like a trip to Israel and a Caribbean cruise. The girls also deal with everyday concerns such as the arrival of new girls (including an African American girl and a girl whose heritage is Chinese) and changing family situations. These books often place the girls in situations where their faith is tested and their Christian values influence their decisions.

1. Becky's Brainstorm ◆ 1992
2. Jess and the Fireplug Caper ◆ 1992
3. Cara's Beach Party Disaster ◆ 1993
4. Tricia's Got T-R-O-U-B-L-E! ◆ 1993
5. Melanie and the Modeling Mess ◆ 1994
6. Bridesmaid Blues for Becky ◆ 1994
7. Double Trouble for Jess McColl! ◆ 1995
8. Cara and the Terrible Teeners ◆ 1995
9. Tricia and the Money Mystery ◆ 1996
10. Melanie and the Cruise Caper ◆ 1996
11. Lily Vanessa and the Pet Panic ◆ 1996
12. Becky's Secret Surprise ◆ 1997

TYCO BASS

Cameron, Eleanor

LITTLE, BROWN

GRADES 4–7

SCIENCE FICTION

David answers a mysterious ad for a boy to build a spaceship. The ad was placed by Tyco Bass, a kind and scholarly person from a small planet near Earth. He senses that his people are in some kind of trouble and that David and Chuck can somehow help out, so he tells them to ask their parents if they can go on a trip to the planet. The boys are amazed when their parents agree. They solve the problem of the gentle mushroom people with the help of a chicken that they bring along. More comings and goings between Earth and the mushroom people, as well as the efforts of the boys to keep the planet a secret, keep the series going.

1. The Wonderful Flight to the Mushroom Planet ◆ 1954
2. Stowaway to the Mushroom Planet ◆ 1956
3. Mr. Bass's Planetoid ◆ 1958
4. A Mystery for Mr. Bass ◆ 1960
5. Time and Mr. Bass ◆ 1967

TYRONE

Wilhelm, Hans

SCHOLASTIC

GRADES K–2

HUMOR

Tyrone is a bully who enjoys causing trouble. Of course, being a dinosaur, Tyrone faces a lot of competition from other pushy dinosaurs, and he usually gets his come-uppance. When Tyrone cheats, he still loses. When Tyrone is horrible, he is punished. This series would be a good choice for discussing bad behaviors and learning to get along.

1. Tyrone, the Horrible ◆ 1988
2. Tyrone, the Double Dirty Rotten Cheater ◆ 1991
3. Tyrone and the Swamp Gang ◆ 1995

UNICORN CLUB

Pascal, Francine, creator

BANTAM

GRADES 4–6

REAL LIFE

The Unicorn Club is a group of friends who attend Sweet Valley Middle School. Lila Fowler, Mandy Miller, Ellen Riteman, Kimberly Haver, and Jessica Wakefield are the main members. They worry about clothes, boys, school, and snacks. Their club is more an extension of their friendship than an official organization. As with any group of friends, there are disagreements. In *Mandy in the Middle*, the Unicorns are on the outs with a rival group called the Angels. Mandy is in the Unicorns but has friends in the Angels. She must decide if it is more important to follow the unfair demands of a group or to make her own choices. Other books feature the Unicorns participating in school events, worrying about boyfriends, and going on a Caribbean cruise. These are like the Sweet Valley High books but for a younger audience.

1. Save the Unicorns! ◆ 1994
2. Maria's Movie Comeback ◆ 1994
3. The Best Friend Game ◆ 1994
4. Lila's Little Sister ◆ 1994
5. Unicorns in Love ◆ 1995
6. The Unicorns at War ◆ 1995
7. Too Close for Comfort ◆ 1995
8. Kimberly Rides Again ◆ 1995
9. Ellen's Family Secret ◆ 1996
10. Mandy in the Middle ◆ 1996
11. Angels Keep Out ◆ 1996
12. Five Girls and a Baby ◆ 1996
13. Who Will Be Miss Unicorn Club? ◆ 1996
14. Lila on the Loose ◆ 1996
15. Too Cool for the Unicorns ◆ 1997
16. Bon Voyage, Unicorns! ◆ 1997
17. Boyfriends for Everyone ◆ 1997
18. Rachel's In, Lila's Out ◆ 1997
19. The Most Beautiful Girl in the World ◆ 1997
20. In Love with Mandy ◆ 1997
21. Snow Bunnies ◆ 1997
22. Jessica's Dream Date ◆ 1998
23. Trapped in the Mall ◆ 1998

VAMPIRE PROMISE

Cooney, Caroline B.
SCHOLASTIC
GRADES 6–8
HORROR

Six teenagers decide to have a party in an old abandoned house and encounter a hungry vampire. He tells them that one of them is going to be his victim and they need to decide which one it will be. After some failed escape attempts, and encounters with various people who stumble on the scene, they all escape, only to encounter the monster again.

1. The Cheerleader ◆ 1991
2. The Return of the Vampire ◆ 1992
3. The Vampire Promise ◆ 1993

VERONICA

Robinson, Nancy K.
SCHOLASTIC
GRADES 3–6
HUMOR

Readers will have great fun reading about Veronica's exploits. Though she doesn't quite lie, Veronica's exaggerations often get her into trouble. For instance, there's the time she hints that she is an extremely gifted chess player when she meets an international chess champion. Or the Groundhog Salad she makes for her first luncheon party. These are entertaining reads for this age group.

1. Veronica the Show-Off ◆ 1984
2. Veronica Knows Best ◆ 1987
3. Veronica Meets Her Match ◆ 1990
4. Countess Veronica ◆ 1994

VERY WORST MONSTER

Hutchins, Pat
GREENWILLOW
GRADES K–2
FAMILY LIFE | FANTASY | HUMOR

Hazel Monster must accept a new baby into her family. At first, she resents the way her parents dote on Billy, but she finds a way to gain their attention by being *The Very Worst Monster*. Subsequent adventures show Billy as a toddler, wreaking havoc on the house. He pesters Hazel and acts up in nursery school, earning stars for his bad behavior. The colorful illustrations capture the monstrous antics and add to the humor.

1. The Very Worst Monster ◆ 1985
2. Where's the Baby? ◆ 1988
3. Silly Billy ◆ 1992
4. Three-Star Billy ◆ 1994

VESPER HOLLY

Alexander, Lloyd
DUTTON
GRADES 5–7
ADVENTURE | HUMOR

Vesper is the teenage daughter of a deceased famous scholar and adventurer. Her father's best friend, Brinnie, and his wife, Mary, have become Vesper's guardians, and together they travel the world from one adventure to another. The evil Dr. Helvitius is their arch enemy, always coming up with some evil scheme against innocent people. In Central America, he is building a canal that will ruin the land of the Indian people. In Europe, he is planning for a small country to be annexed by its neighbors. Vesper and Brinnie are always one step ahead of him, with the help of various friends they collect along the way. Brinnie's pompous behavior supplies humor, while Vesper is an exciting heroine.

1. The Illyrian Adventure ◆ 1986
2. The El Dorado Adventure ◆ 1987
3. The Drackenberg Adventure ◆ 1988
4. The Jedera Adventure ◆ 1989
5. The Philadelphia Adventure ◆ 1990

VICKY AUSTIN

L'Engle, Madeleine
FARRAR, STRAUS & GIROUX; BANTAM DOUBLEDAY DELL
GRADES 4–7
FAMILY LIFE | MYSTERY | REAL LIFE

In *Meet the Austins*, Vicky is 12 and her family is faced with taking in a spoiled orphan girl. The father, a country doctor, is offered a position in New York, where they become involved in an international plot. On a cross-country camping trip, they meet a spoiled rich boy who takes a liking to Vicky. The Austins spend summers on an island off the East Coast in their grandfather's house. Here Vicky befriends a boy who is doing research on dolphins and discovers that she has a real affinity for the animals. This series tackles issues of life and death, faith and cynicism, and shows a loving family dealing intelligently with problems. A simple Christmas story, *The Twenty-Four Days Before Christmas* (1964), is a prequel written on a much easier level than the rest of the series.

1. Meet the Austins ◆ 1960
2. The Moon by Night ◆ 1963
3. The Young Unicorns ◆ 1968
4. A Ring of Endless Light ◆ 1980
5. Troubling a Star ◆ 1994

VISITORS

Philbrick, Rodman, and Lynn Harnett
SCHOLASTIC
GRADES 5–8
ADVENTURE | FANTASY

Aliens have taken over the adults in the town of Harley Hills. Twins Nick and Jessie and Nick's best friend, Frasier, are trying to avoid the power of the aliens and rescue their town. The elements of suspense and danger will make this attractive to reluctant readers. This series capitalizes on the popularity of books about aliens and books in which the teenage characters are responsible for coping with the crisis.

1. Strange Invaders ◆ 1997
2. Things ◆ 1997
3. Brain Stealers ◆ 1997

VOYAGE TO THE BUNNY PLANET

Wells, Rosemary
DIAL
GRADES K–2
ANIMAL FANTASY

Visiting the Bunny Planet provides a remedy for some very bad days. Robert has a terrible visit to his relative. Claire has a bad day at school. Nothing goes right for Felix. Each bunny receives warmth and love from the Bunny Queen Janet in these reassuring stories.

1. First Tomato: A Voyage to the Bunny Planet ◆ 1992

2. The Island Light: A Voyage to the Bunny Planet ◆ 1992
3. Moss Pillows: A Voyage to the Bunny Planet ◆ 1992

WARTON AND MORTON

Erickson, Russell E.

LOTHROP, LEE & SHEPARD

GRADES 2–4

ANIMAL FANTASY

Toad brothers Warton and Morton live happily together in a little hole under a stump. Morton loves to cook and is very good at it. Warton prefers to clean. On a beautiful day when Warton has just finished his spring cleaning, he persuades the less adventurous Morton to go on a camping trip. They are separated by a flash flood; and as Warton is looking for Morton, he joins a group of muskrats. Meanwhile, Morton has joined the beavers, who are the muskrats' sworn enemies. When they meet, the toads clear up the misunderstandings between the two. Other adventures with the toads and their neighbors continue the series.

1. A Toad for Tuesday ◆ 1974
2. Warton and Morton ◆ 1976
3. Warton's Christmas Eve Adventure ◆ 1977
4. Warton and the King of the Skies ◆ 1978
5. Warton and the Traders ◆ 1979
6. Warton and the Castaways ◆ 1982
7. Warton and the Contest ◆ 1986

WAYSIDE SCHOOL

Sachar, Louis

MORROW

GRADES 3–6

FANTASY | HUMOR

When Wayside School was constructed, the builders made a mistake and built it 30 stories straight up instead of 30 rooms on one level. That's why the school is so strange, as the two- or three-page stories in each book attest. Mrs. Gorf is the meanest teacher in the school. She turns all the children into apples until they figure out the trick. Then they turn her into an apple. The children on the 30th floor get Mrs. Jewls for a teacher, and she is terribly nice. The rest of the Sideways Stories are about her funny, bizarre interactions with her class. The same format of very short stories is used throughout, except for the arithmetic books.

1. Sideways Stories from Wayside School ◆ 1985
2. Sideways Arithmetic from Wayside School ◆ 1989
3. Wayside School Is Falling Down ◆ 1990
4. More Sideways Arithmetic from Wayside School ◆ 1994
5. Wayside School Gets a Little Stranger ◆ 1995

Webster and Arnold

Roche, P. K.

Viking Kestrel

Grades k–3

Animal Fantasy

Another endearing beginning chapter book series. Webster and Arnold, two brothers, are mice who have various innocent adventures: fighting off dinosaurs, taking a (pretend) train to Africa, and so on. Somehow they always manage to save the day.

1. Goodbye, Arnold! ◆ 1979
2. Webster and Arnold and the Giant Box ◆ 1980
3. Webster and Arnold Go Camping ◆ 1988

The Weebie Zone

Spinner, Stephanie, and Ellen Weiss

HarperCollins

Grades 3–5

Fantasy | Humor

After being bitten by his gerbil Weebie, Garth finds that he can understand animals. Of course, Weebie has lots to tell him, and so do other pets. His aunt's dog, Elvis, wants to sing; a bunny is upset and runs away; a talking bird helps with a mean substitute teacher. In one book, Weebie is lost in Texas and must find his own way back to Garth. This is a fun series that will appeal to readers who like silly characters in incongruous situations.

1. Gerbilitis ◆ 1996
2. Sing, Elvis, Sing ◆ 1996
3. Born to Be Wild ◆ 1997
4. Bright Lights, Little Gerbil ◆ 1997
5. The Bird Is the Word ◆ 1997
6. We're Off to See the Lizard ◆ 1998

THE WEIRD ZONE

Abbott, Tony
SCHOLASTIC
GRADES 3–5
HUMOR

What makes Grover's Mill the Weird Zone? For one thing, there is a secret U.F.O. government test base there—not to mention a dinosaur graveyard and the Humongous Horror Movie Studios. These three elements make for some weird happenings. Liz Duffey, Mike Mazur, Jeff Ryan, Holly Vickers, and Sean Vickers attend W. Reid Elementary School, where they discover a beast beneath the cafeteria and conduct unusual science projects. They encounter alien mole invaders and commandos from Mars. Mixed in with the traditional horror elements are moments of humor as the kids also cope with strange adults like Principal Bell and his assistant, Miss Lieberman. This is a fun series for upper elementary school readers.

1. Zombie Surf Commandos from Mars! ◆ 1996
2. The Incredible Shrinking Kid! ◆ 1996
3. The Beast from Beneath the Cafeteria! ◆ 1996
4. Attack of the Alien Mole Invaders! ◆ 1996
5. The Brain That Wouldn't Obey! ◆ 1997
6. Gigantopus from Planet X! ◆ 1997
7. Cosmic Boy Versus Mezmo Head ◆ 1997
8. Revenge of the Tiki Men! ◆ 1997

WEREWOLF CHRONICLES

Philbrick, Rodman, and Lynn Harnett
SCHOLASTIC
GRADES 5–8
HORROR

Fox Hollow looks like an ordinary town, but there is something very frightening in the woods. Only the wolf-boy knows the secret, and only he can save the town. The wolf-boy, who is later called Gruff, was raised by wolves, who protected him and fed him after he was abandoned. Now a danger has entered the woods: the werewolves. They want Gruff to join them; and even though he tries to resist, their powers are beginning to affect him. His efforts to keep Fox Hollow from the werewolves put him into even more danger. Gruff may be able to save the town only by becoming a werewolf himself.

1. Night Creature ◆ 1996
2. Children of the Wolf ◆ 1996
3. The Wereing ◆ 1996

Westmark

Alexander, Lloyd
Bantam Doubleday Dell
Grades 5–7
Adventure | Fantasy

This series is set in a world much like our own in the late Renaissance. Theo is a printer's helper who is embroiled in a revolt against a corrupt government. When his master is killed, he falls in with the scheming Count and with Mickle, a poor girl with an amazing talent for ventriloquism. They meet up with a group of revolutionaries led by the charismatic Florian, who wants to do away with the monarchy altogether. Mickle and Theo fall in love, and she is revealed to be the king's long-lost daughter. She and Theo plan to marry, and the next two books in this trilogy concern their struggles against enemies in and out of Westmark.

1. Westmark ◆ 1981
2. The Kestrel ◆ 1982
3. The Beggar Queen ◆ 1984

What Ate Who

Marney, Dean
Scholastic
Grades 3–6
Fantasy | Humor

This humorous series centers around two different families. Similar to an earlier book, *The Computer That Ate My Brother* (1985), this series features Elizabeth and her family who are traumatized by such silly things as jack-o'-lanterns, turkeys, and Christmas trees.

1. The Christmas Tree That Ate My Mother ◆ 1992
2. The Jack-o'-Lantern That Ate My Brother ◆ 1994
3. The Turkey That Ate My Father ◆ 1995
4. The Easter Bunny That Ate My Sister ◆ 1996
5. The Valentine That Ate My Teacher ◆ 1998

THE WILD BABY

Lindgren, Barbo
GREENWILLOW
GRADES K–2
FANTASY | HUMOR

Adults and children alike will chuckle at wild Baby Ben as he gets into trouble and does not listen to his mother. Readers will smile as Baby Ben sails into a whale's mouth, scares off a wolf, and has various incredible adventures, all told in rhyme.

1. The Wild Baby ◆ 1981
2. The Wild Baby Goes to Sea ◆ 1983
3. The Wild Baby Gets a Puppy ◆ 1988

WILLY

Browne, Anthony
CANDLEWICK
GRADES K–2
ANIMAL FANTASY

A quiet, mild-mannered chimpanzee named Willy is featured in this series of picture books. Willy likes to read, daydream, and go to movies with his friend Milly. He is scorned and laughed at by the neighborhood chimps until he knocks out the neighborhood bully by accident. He longs to play soccer but isn't any good until a wizard gives him some magic shoes. In another book, Willy daydreams about being a movie star and a rock singer. The minimal text and very large type contrast with the sophisticated and detailed paintings on each page, providing appeal to all ages.

1. Willy the Wimp ◆ 1985
2. Willy the Champ ◆ 1986
3. Willy and Hugh ◆ 1991
4. Willy the Wizard ◆ 1996
5. Willy the Dreamer ◆ 1998

WILLY FREEMAN *see* The Arabus Family Saga

WINDS OF LIGHT

Brouwer, Sigmund
VICTOR BOOKS
GRADES 6–8
FANTASY | HISTORICAL | VALUES

As an orphan in the 1300s, Thomas must search for his rightful place. Leaving the monks who raised him, Thomas struggles to regain Magnus, an English manor that has been taken from its owners. He encounters a dangerous conspiracy, and he comes to realize that it is God's power, not his own anger and violence, that will restore the manor. Thomas's efforts are aided by Katherine, who loves him, and by Sir William, who has escaped the brutality of the conquest of Magnus. Once established as Thomas of Magnus, there are other tests of Thomas's faith. Evil within the leadership of the church threatens Thomas. He is enticed by a group of sorcerers to abandon his faith and enter their false world. The drama of this historical fiction series is supported by the dedication to Christian values.

1. Wings of an Angel ◆ 1992
2. Barbarians from the Isle ◆ 1992
3. Legend of Burning Water ◆ 1992
4. The Forsaken Crusade ◆ 1992
5. A City of Dreams ◆ 1993
6. Merlin's Destiny ◆ 1993
7. The Jester's Quest ◆ 1994
8. Dance of Darkness ◆ 1997

WINNIE THE POOH FIRST READERS

Gaines, Isabel
DISNEY PRESS
GRADES K–2
ANIMAL FANTASY | HUMOR

This series adapts some of the familiar stories (including when Pooh eats too much honey and gets stuck in Rabbit's door) and also creates new adventures in a format that is designed for beginning readers. The familiar characters—Winnie the Pooh, Christopher, Tigger, Eeyore, and others—will attract young children who are familiar with the Disney videos and could be an incentive for beginning readers.

1. Pooh Gets Stuck ◆ 1998
2. Pooh's Honey Tree ◆ 1998
3. Pooh's Pumpkin ◆ 1998
4. Rabbit Gets Lost ◆ 1998

5. Bounce, Tigger, Bounce ◆ 1998
6. Happy Birthday, Eeyore! ◆ 1998

WISCONSIN FARM

Pellowski, Anne
PHILOMEL
GRADES 3–6
FAMILY LIFE | HISTORICAL

This is a loving family story tracing four generations of a Polish American clan on a Wisconsin farm. A fascinating chronicle of the changes in both social customs and farming technology over the years, this series also portrays the strong values and traditions that are passed on in this family. The series contains many enjoyable stories, such as the day the pigs got tipsy from fermented blackberry preserves.

1. Willow Wind Farm: Betsy's Story ◆ 1981
2. Stairstep Farm: Anna Rose's Story ◆ 1981
3. First Farm in the Valley: Anna's Story ◆ 1982
4. Winding Valley Farm: Annie's Story ◆ 1982
5. Betsy's Up-and-Down Year ◆ 1983

WISHBONE ADVENTURES

Various authors
BIG RED CHAIR BOOKS/LYRICK PUBLISHING
GRADES 3–4
ADVENTURE

Cleverly retold traditional stories are given a fresh look for elementary readers by using a very smart dog named Wishbone who has a nose for adventure. Wishbone and his human friends—Joe Talbot, Samantha Kepler, and David Barnes—lead readers through action-packed plots retaining basic elements of the original stories. All the books in the series have been renamed. "The Three Musketeers" becomes "Muttketeer!" and "A Tale of Two Cities" is "A Tale of Two Sitters." Fun reading and very accessible to children who might not consider the original titles until high school.

1. Be a Wolf! (Strickland, Brad) ◆ 1997
2. Salty Dog (Strickland, Brad) ◆ 1997
3. The Prince and the Pooch (Leavitt, Caroline) ◆ 1997
4. Robinhound Crusoe (Leavitt, Caroline) ◆ 1997
5. The Hunchdog of Notre Dame (Friedman, Michael J.) ◆ 1997

6. Digging Up the Past (Sathre, Vivian) ◆ 1997
7. The Mutt in the Iron Muzzle (Friedman, Michael J.) ◆ 1997
8. Muttketeer! (Crider, Bill) ◆ 1997
9. A Tale of Two Sitters (Barkan, Joanne) ◆ 1998
10. Moby Dog (Steele, Alexander) ◆ 1998
11. The Pawloined Paper (Litowinsky, Olga) ◆ 1998
12. Dog Overboard! (Sathre, Vivian) ◆ 1998
13. Homer Sweet Homer (Jablonski, Carla) ◆ 1998
14. A Dog at the Round Table (Barkan, Joanne) ◆ 1998
15. Dr. Jekyll and Mr. Dog (Butcher, Nancy) ◆ 1998

WISHBONE CLASSICS

Various authors

HARPERCOLLINS

GRADES 3–5

ADVENTURE

The main narrator of these retold classics is a personable dog, Wishbone, who guides readers to better understand the characters and their actions. The stories range from *Don Quixote* to *Ivanhoe* to *The Red Badge of Courage*. Brief information is given about the author, main characters, era, and events so that readers obtain a sense of each classic tale. The character of Wishbone is popular from the TV programs (and other books), but the Wishbone Classics series does not feature Wishbone as a character but rather as the reader's guide to understanding these well-known stories.

1. Don Quixote ◆ 1996
2. The Odyssey ◆ 1996
3. Romeo and Juliet ◆ 1996
4. Joan of Arc ◆ 1996
5. Oliver Twist ◆ 1996
6. The Adventures of Robin Hood ◆ 1996
7. Frankenstein ◆ 1996
8. The Strange Case of Dr. Jekyll and Mr. Hyde ◆ 1996
9. A Journey to the Center of the Earth ◆ 1996
10. The Red Badge of Courage ◆ 1996
11. The Adventures of Tom Sawyer ◆ 1996
12. Ivanhoe ◆ 1997

WISHBONE MYSTERIES

Various authors

BIG RED CHAIR BOOKS/LYRICK PUBLISHING

GRADES 4–5

MYSTERY

The characters from the popular books and TV programs are back in this series of mysteries. Wishbone's friends are now older and are involved in explaining hauntings, finding missing mascots, and recovering stolen goods. The friends—Joe, Samantha, and David—are all successful sleuths, with the expert assistance of Wishbone the dog, who has a great nose for mystery and adventure.

1. The Treasure of Skeleton Reef (Strickland, Brad, and Thomas Fuller) ◆ 1997
2. The Haunted Clubhouse (Leavitt, Caroline) ◆ 1997
3. The Riddle of the Wayward Books (Strickland, Brad, and Thomas Fuller) ◆ 1997
4. Tale of the Missing Mascot (Steele, Alexander) ◆ 1998
5. The Stolen Trophy (Friedman, Michael J.) ◆ 1998
6. The Maltese Dog (Capeci, Anne) ◆ 1998
7. Drive-In of Doom (Strickland, Brad, and Thomas Fuller) ◆ 1998
8. Key to the Golden Dog (Capeci, Anne) ◆ 1998
9. Case of the On-Line Alien (Steele, Alexander) ◆ 1998
10. The Disappearing Dinosaurs (Strickland, Brad, and Thomas Fuller) ◆ 1998
11. Lights! Cameras! Action Dog! (Butcher, Nancy) ◆ 1998
12. Forgotten Heroes (Steele, Anthony) ◆ 1998
13. Case of the Unsolved Case (Steele, Alexander) ◆ 1998
14. Disoriented Express (Strickland, Brad) ◆ 1998

WITCH

Bridwell, Norman

SCHOLASTIC

GRADES K–3

FANTASY | HUMOR

This series will be fun for beginning readers. Two children live next door to a witch, who, of course, is a nice, helpful witch. She takes them to school when they are late, finds Santa Claus when he is missing, and has other adventures with the children as she tries to help them out. Many humorous moments make for pleasant reading.

1. The Witch Next Door ◆ 1966
2. The Witch's Christmas ◆ 1972
3. The Witch's Vacation ◆ 1975
4. The Witch Grows Up ◆ 1980
5. The Witch Goes to School ◆ 1992

WITCH

Naylor, Phyllis Reynolds
DELACORTE
GRADES 5–7
HORROR

Lynn is convinced that her neighbor, Mrs. Tuggle, is a witch; but when she and her best friend, Mouse, try to convince people, no one will listen. Readers will want to keep turning the pages in this suspenseful series as Mrs. Tuggle is overcome, only to return in another form and another way.

1. Witch's Sister ◆ 1975
2. Witch Water ◆ 1977
3. The Witch Herself ◆ 1978
4. The Witch's Eye ◆ 1990
5. Witch Weed ◆ 1992
6. The Witch Returns ◆ 1992

WITCH, GOBLIN, AND GHOST

Alexander, Sue
PANTHEON BOOKS
GRADES K–2
FANTASY

Here are heartwarming stories for beginning readers about a young witch, goblin, and ghost who are friends. They tell tall tales, get scared, and play games together.

1. Witch, Goblin, and Sometimes Ghost ◆ 1976
2. More Witch Goblin and Ghost Stories ◆ 1978

3. Witch, Goblin, and Ghost in the Haunted Woods ◆ 1981
4. Witch, Goblin, and Ghost are Back ◆ 1985

WIZARD AND WART

Smith, Janice Lee
HARPERCOLLINS
GRADES K–2
FANTASY | HUMOR

These I Can Read books follow a blundering Wizard and his wisecracking dog, Wart. Everywhere they go, they try to solve their problems with magic and only end up making things worse.

1. Wizard and Wart ◆ 1994
2. Wizard and Wart at Sea ◆ 1995
3. Wizard and Wart in Trouble ◆ 1998

WIZARD OF OZ *see* Oz

WIZARDRY

Duane, Diane
HARCOURT
GRADES 4–8
ADVENTURE | FANTASY

Nita is a 13-year-old girl tormented by bullies because she chooses not to fight back. While hiding in the local library, she discovers a book of instructions in the ancient art of wizardry. She meets Kit, a boy who is also a beginning wizard, and together they go on their first quest: to find the book that holds the key to preserving the universe. In the companion books, Nita and Kit go on other adventures: becoming whales to conquer the evil Lone Power in the deepest part of the Atlantic Ocean, cloning a computer and helping Nita's sister travel through several worlds in outer space, and becoming entangled in a magic battle in Ireland.

1. So You Want to Be a Wizard ◆ 1983
2. Deep Wizardry ◆ 1985
3. High Wizardry ◆ 1989
4. A Wizard Abroad ◆ 1993

WOLFBAY WINGS

Brooks, Bruce
HARPERCOLLINS
GRADES 4–8
REAL LIFE | RECREATION

The Wolfbay Wings are a Squirt A ice hockey team that has become very successful. Unfortunately, they have a new coach and a bunch of new players, so the upcoming season is uncertain. Each book in this series features a different player. For example, Dixon "Woodsie" Woods is 11 years old and is worried about the future of the team. William Fowler, "Billy," is only ten, and he is bothered by his overbearing father who bullies Billy, his teammates, and Coach Cooper. There are statistics about the featured player on the back of each book, and a tear-out sports card is included at the front of each book. With lots of details about hockey and ample action, this should be a good choice for sports fans.

1. Woodsie ◆ 1997
2. Zip ◆ 1997
3. Cody ◆ 1997
4. Boot ◆ 1998
5. Prince ◆ 1998
6. Shark ◆ 1998
7. Billy ◆ 1998
8. Dooby ◆ 1998
9. Reed ◆ 1998

WOLVES CHRONICLES

Aiken, Joan
DELACORTE; BANTAM
GRADES 4–8
ADVENTURE | FANTASY

High melodrama and an "unhistorical" setting mark this loosely connected series. In the England of this alternate world, King James III rules, Hanoverians are constantly plotting to put Prince George on the throne, and packs of vicious wolves menace the countryside. The Wolves Chronicles begin with the story of two little girls who are left in the care of an evil woman who schemes to take their inheritance. They are rescued by the mysterious orphan boy Simon, who later in the series is revealed to be a duke. Simon befriends a Cockney girl, Dido, whose parents are evil Hanoverians, and the rest of the series is about their adventures, by themselves and with other friends, as they defend the true king.

1. The Wolves of Willoughby Chase ◆ 1963
2. Black Hearts in Battersea ◆ 1964
3. Nightbirds on Nantucket ◆ 1966
4. The Whispering Mountain ◆ 1968
5. The Cuckoo Tree ◆ 1971
6. The Stolen Lake ◆ 1981
7. Dido and Pa ◆ 1986
8. Is Underground ◆ 1993
9. Cold Shoulder Road ◆ 1996

WORLD FAMOUS MURIEL

Alexander, Sue
HARPERCOLLINS
GRADES K–2
FANTASY | HUMOR | MYSTERY

World Famous Muriel is the world's best tightrope walker. She also solves mysteries. She lives in a cartoonish sort of Middle Ages kingdom where the King and Queen invite her to perform and do detective work. All of their little problems are solved, and the royalty is always delighted with Muriel. Minimal text and funny pictures of Muriel on every page make this series accessible to preschoolers and beginning readers.

1. World Famous Muriel ◆ 1984
2. World Famous Muriel and the Scary Dragon ◆ 1985
3. World Famous Muriel and the Magic Mystery ◆ 1990

WORLD OF ADVENTURE

Paulsen, Gary
BANTAM DOUBLEDAY DELL
GRADES 3–6
ADVENTURE | FANTASY

This series features a variety of characters in locations around the world and in different time periods. *Time Benders* features two boys, Zack Griffin and Jeff Brown, who sneak into the laboratory of an eccentric scientist and end up in ancient Egypt. In *The Creature of Black Water Lake*, Ryan Swanner, 13, meets up with an ancient monster. The characters have exciting adventures and often find themselves in unusual or implausible situations. Warren Trumbull, 11, works for an agency that rescues people from monsters (*The Gorgon Slayer*); and Jesse Rodriguez, 13, works at a skydiving school in Seattle (*Skydive!*). Short chapters and action-filled plots will interest reluctant readers.

1. The Legend of Red Horse Cavern ◆ 1994
2. Rodomonte's Revenge ◆ 1994
3. Escape from Fire Mountain ◆ 1995
4. The Rock Jockeys ◆ 1995
5. Hook 'Em Snotty! ◆ 1995
6. Danger on Midnight River ◆ 1995
7. The Gorgon Slayer ◆ 1995
8. Captive! ◆ 1995
9. Project: A Perfect World ◆ 1996
10. The Treasure of *El Patrón* ◆ 1996
11. Skydive! ◆ 1996
12. The Seventh Crystal ◆ 1996
13. The Creature of Black Water Lake ◆ 1997
14. Time Benders ◆ 1997
15. Grizzly ◆ 1997
16. Thunder Valley ◆ 1998
17. Curse of the Ruins ◆ 1998
18. Flight of the Hawk ◆ 1998

WORST PERSON

Stevenson, James
GREENWILLOW
GRADES K–3
HUMOR

"The worst person in the world" lives in a dirty house surrounded by poison ivy and signs saying "Keep Out." Then he meets the kind and cheerful Ugly, who decides to have a party at the Worst's house. Ugly cleans everything up, buys food, and sends out invitations. The Worst angrily orders them all away, but later he changes his mind. The series continues with the further encounters of the Worst with various funny, nice people who bring him out of his shell. When he goes on vacation, he meets an accordion-playing duo who, it turns out, are his neighbors at home. They all end up eating dry crackers and drinking prune juice on the Worst's front porch. Stevenson's expressive, cartoonish illustrations carry the fun along.

1. The Worst Person in the World ◆ 1978
2. The Worst Person in the World at Crab Beach ◆ 1988
3. The Worst Person's Christmas ◆ 1991
4. Worse than the Worst ◆ 1994
5. The Worst Goes South ◆ 1995

WORST WITCH

Murphy, Jill
CANDLEWICK
GRADES 2–4
FANTASY | HUMOR

Miss Cackle's Academy for Witches is a grim and forbidding place that looks more like a prison. Mildred is the worst pupil in the school. She can't cast spells or make her broom follow her orders. Even her cat is not a proper black cat. Her best friends, Maud and Enid, support her through thick and thin, but Ethel, the class "goody-goody," is out to get her. In a fit of temper, Mildred tries to turn Ethel into a frog, but turns her into a pig instead. Their humorless teacher, Miss Hardbroom, would like to get rid of Mildred altogether, but somehow Mildred always manages to save the day.

1. The Worst Witch ◆ 1974
2. The Worst Witch Strikes Again ◆ 1980
3. A Bad Spell for the Worst Witch ◆ 1982
4. The Worst Witch at Sea ◆ 1995

WOULD-BE-GOODS *see* Bastable Family

WREN

Smith, Sherwood
HARCOURT
GRADES 4–7
ADVENTURE | FANTASY

While living in an orphanage, Wren's friend Tess finds out that she is really Princess Teressa. This discovery changes the lives of both girls permanently. Along with their friends Tyron and Prince Connor, they battle the evil forces of King Andreus. The four friends learn to master the power of magic and use it only for the greater good.

1. Wren to the Rescue ◆ 1990
2. Wren's Quest ◆ 1993
3. Wren's War ◆ 1995

X FILES

Various authors

HARPERTROPHY

GRADES 5–8

FANTASY | HORROR

Terror in the forest, dying teenagers, a serial killer, a dead alligator man at the circus, and extraterrestrial entities—these are just a few of the problems investigated by Agents Mulder and Scully. Fans of the TV program will flock to this series, which is based on teleplays of specific episodes. Like the show, these books are gritty and grim, with enough twists in the plot to leave you wondering what really is true. There are many different X Files books, including ones for young adult and adult readers. Listed here are two X Files series that fit the guidelines of this book—one for a younger audience; one for a slightly older group.

X FILES (GRADES 5–8)

1. X Marks the Spot (Martin, Les) ◆ 1995
2. Darkness Falls (Martin, Les) ◆ 1995
3. Tiger, Tiger (Martin, Les) ◆ 1995
4. Squeeze (Steiber, Ellen) ◆ 1996
5. Humbug (Martin, Les) ◆ 1996
6. Shapes (Steiber, Ellen) ◆ 1996
7. Fear (Martin, Les) ◆ 1996
8. Voltage (Royce, Easton) ◆ 1996
9. E.B.E. (Martin, Les) ◆ 1996
10. Die Bug Die (Martin, Les) ◆ 1997
11. Ghost in the Machine (Martin, Les) ◆ 1997

X FILES (GRADES 7–8)

1. The Calusari (Nix, Garth) ◆ 1997
2. Eve (Steiber, Ellen) ◆ 1997
3. Bad Sign (Easton, Royce) ◆ 1997
4. Our Town (Elfman, Eric) ◆ 1997
5. Empathy (Steiber, Ellen) ◆ 1997
6. Fresh Bones (Martin, Les) ◆ 1997
7. Control (Owens, Everett) ◆ 1997
8. The Host (Martin, Les) ◆ 1997
9. Hungry Ghosts (Steiber, Ellen) ◆ 1998

X GAMES XTREME MYSTERIES

Hill, Laban

HYPERION

GRADES 4–8

MYSTERY | RECREATION

Fans of the *X Games* (on ESPN) will enjoy these fast-paced mysteries involving in-line skating, snowboarding, wakeboarding, snow mountain biking, and other extreme sports. In one mystery, Jamil and his friends are at a mystery party and investigate the theft of plans for a new wakeboard. In another book, Kevin is almost lost in a man-made avalanche. Other books feature Nat and Wall, who are also part of the Xtreme detectives. Merging sports action with mysteries could attract reluctant readers.

1. Crossed Tracks ◆ 1998
2. Deep Powder, Deep Trouble ◆ 1998
3. Rocked Out: A Summer X Games Special ◆ 1998
4. Half Pipe Rip-Off ◆ 1998
5. Lost Wake ◆ 1998
6. Out of Line ◆ 1998
7. Spiked Snow: A Winter X Games Special ◆ 1999
8. Totally Snowed ◆ 1999

YOUNG CAM JANSEN

Adler, David A.

VIKING

E Adl

GRADES 1–3

MYSTERY

Cam Jansen, the star of a mystery series for older readers, is in second grade in this series, and already sleuthing. Her friend Eric tells everyone about her amazing photographic memory, and she says "click" when she wants to remember something. When their friend is missing a cookie out of his lunch box, Cam remembers seeing crumbs and rightly concludes that it was his dog who stole the cookie. Young Cam Jansen is part of the Viking Easy to Read series featuring short sentences and easy vocabulary but not much word repetition. After reading these books, many children will go on to the Cam Jansen series.

1. Young Cam Jansen and the Dinosaur Game ◆ 1996
2. Young Cam Jansen and the Missing Cookie ◆ 1996
3. Young Cam Jansen and the Lost Tooth ◆ 1997
4. Young Cam Jansen and the Ice Skate Mystery ◆ 1998
5. Young Cam Jansen and the Baseball Mystery ◆ 1999

YOUNG INDIANA JONES

Various authors
RANDOM HOUSE
GRADES 4–6
ADVENTURE I FANTASY

The popularity of the Indiana Jones movies has led to several spin-offs, including a TV program and paperback books. Two series of books are listed here. The books are very similar in that they follow Indiana's adventures as a youngster, including time travel and encounters with fantastic creatures. These early experiences helped develop his spirit of adventure and willingness to take risks. Ghosts, dragons, mummies, and pirates should appeal to those readers who like books with monsters; while trips to the *Titanic*, the underworld, Stonehenge, and gold mines will attract those who like exotic locations. The two series of books differ in that one group parallels the episodes of the TV series.

1. Young Indiana Jones and the Plantation Treasure (McCay, William) ◆ 1990
2. Young Indiana Jones and the Tomb of Terror (Martin, Les) ◆ 1990
3. Young Indiana Jones and the Circle of Death (McCay, William) ◆ 1990
4. Young Indiana Jones and the Secret City (Martin, Les) ◆ 1990
5. Young Indiana Jones and the Princess of Peril (Martin, Les) ◆ 1991
6. Young Indiana Jones and the Gypsy Revenge (Martin, Les) ◆ 1991
7. Young Indiana Jones and the Ghostly Riders (McCay, William) ◆ 1991
8. Young Indiana Jones and the Curse of the Ruby Cross (McCay, William) ◆ 1991
9. Young Indiana Jones and the Titanic Adventure (Martin, Les) ◆ 1993
10. Young Indiana Jones and the Lost Gold of Durango (Stine, Megan, and H. William Stine) ◆ 1993
11. Young Indiana Jones and the Face of the Dragon (McCay, William) ◆ 1994
12. Young Indiana Jones and the Journey to the Underworld (Stine, Megan, and H. William Stine) ◆ 1994
13. Young Indiana Jones and the Mountain of Fire (McCay, William) ◆ 1994

14. Young Indiana Jones and the Pirates' Loot (Fox, J. N.) ◆ 1994
15. Young Indiana Jones and the Eye of the Tiger (McCay, William) ◆ 1994

TV TIE-INS

1. The Mummy's Curse (Stine, Megan, and H. William Stine) ◆ 1992
2. Field of Death (Martin, Les) ◆ 1992
3. Safari Sleuth (Singer, A. L.) ◆ 1992
4. The Secret Peace (McCay, William) ◆ 1992
5. Trek of Doom (Martin, Les) ◆ 1992
6. Revolution! (Scott, Gavin) ◆ 1992
7. Race to Danger (Calmenson, Stephanie) ◆ 1993
8. Prisoner of War (Martin, Les) ◆ 1993

YOUNG INDIANA JONES CHRONICLES: CHOOSE YOUR OWN ADVENTURE

Brightfield, Richard
BANTAM
GRADES 5–8
ADVENTURE | FANTASY

This series uses the popular Choose Your Own Adventure format in which readers turn to different pages based on what they want to happen. For example, if you decide to go to the party, turn to page 45; if you want to stay in the dorm, turn to page 51. These books feature the popular character of Indiana Jones when he is a young man and place him at the center of events around the world. The popularity of the character and the format should attract reluctant readers.

1. The Valley of the Kings ◆ 1992
2. South of the Border ◆ 1992
3. Revolution in Russia ◆ 1992
4. Masters of the Louvre ◆ 1993
5. African Safari ◆ 1993
6. Behind the Great Wall ◆ 1993
7. The Roaring Twenties ◆ 1993
8. The Irish Rebellion ◆ 1993

YOUNG JEDI KNIGHTS *see* Star Wars Young Jedi Knights

YOUNG MERLIN TRILOGY

Yolen, Jane

HARCOURT

GRADES 4–6

FANTASY | HISTORICAL

When he was eight years old, a boy was abandoned in the woods. Surviving in the wild as a wild thing, he was taken in by Master Robin, who tamed him and found his name, Merlin. This trilogy follows the adventures of Young Merlin (who uses the names of Hawk and Hobby), including his time with traveling performers and coming to understand and accept the importance of his dreams. In the third book, Merlin befriends a boy, Cub, who is later named Artus and will become King Arthur.

1. Passager ◆ 1996
2. Hobby ◆ 1996
3. Merlin ◆ 1997

Z.A.P. AND ZOE

Lord, Athena V.

MACMILLAN

GRADES 3–6

HUMOR | REAL LIFE

Zach (Zachary Athanasius Poulos) and Zoe are the children of Greek immigrants who run a lunch counter in upstate New York during the Great Depression. Zach is a lover of books and Greek myths and is something of a leader in his neighborhood. His parents hold him responsible for watching little Zoe and helping out in the restaurant. Every chapter in the series is a sketch of life in a lower-middle-class neighborhood in the late 1930s and early 1940s. Zach and Zoe have adventures and quarrels with the other kids, befriend an African American man, and generally get in and out of trouble.

1. Today's Special: Z.A.P. and Zoe ◆ 1984
2. The Luck of Z.A.P. and Zoe ◆ 1987
3. Z.A.P., Zoe, and the Musketeers ◆ 1992

THE ZACK FILES

Greenburg, Dan
GROSSET & DUNLAP
GRADES 3–5
FANTASY | HUMOR

Zack is a ten-year-old boy who becomes involved in weird situations. In one book, a ghost named Wanda bothers him and his dad. Wanda haunts their apartment because she is lonely. When another ghost named Cecil appears, Zack helps them communicate and arranges for them to haunt the Haunted House at the Adventureland Amusement Park. Another book features Zack looking in on a parallel universe, where he meets his double, Zeke. Then there is Zack when he can read minds and Zack doing body-traveling. With clones, ghosts, reincarnated grandpa, and Dr. Jekyll the Orthodontist, these are fast, funny books. Zack has a smart aleck attitude that will appeal to many middle grade readers.

1. Great-Grandpa's in the Litter Box ◆ 1996
2. Through the Medicine Cabinet ◆ 1996
3. A Ghost Named Wanda ◆ 1996
4. Zap! I'm a Mind Reader ◆ 1996
5. Dr. Jekyll, Orthodontist ◆ 1997
6. I'm Out of My Body . . . Please Leave a Message ◆ 1997
7. Never Trust a Cat Who Wears Earrings ◆ 1997
8. My Son, the Time Traveler ◆ 1997
9. The Volcano Goddess Will See You Now ◆ 1997
10. Bozo the Clone ◆ 1997
11. How to Speak Dolphin in Three Easy Lessons ◆ 1997
12. Now You See Me . . . Now You Don't ◆ 1998
13. The Misfortune Cookie ◆ 1998
14. Elvis, the Turnip . . . And Me ◆ 1998

ZELDA

Hall, Lynn
HARCOURT
GRADES 2–4
HUMOR | REAL LIFE

Zelda lives with her single mom in a trailer park, and she doesn't mean to cause trouble. When her Mom worries about how she will behave at a funeral, Zelda decides to go to a nearby funeral home for practice. The mourners there believe her story about being a long-lost relative of the deceased, and she ends up leading the funeral procession. Her crabby baby-sitter needs a boyfriend, so Zelda decides to try to find one for her, with more funny results. The short, self-contained chapters each tell about one of Zelda's crazy schemes, which are usually based on her misunderstanding of the adult world.

1. In Trouble Again, Zelda Hammersmith? ◆ 1987
2. Zelda Strikes Again! ◆ 1988
3. Here Comes Zelda Claus, and Other Holiday Disasters ◆ 1989

INDEXES
AND
APPENDIXES

Author Index

Authors are listed with the series to which they contributed. Series are listed in alphabetical order in the main section of this book.

A

Abbott, Donald. **Oz**
Abbott, Tony. **Danger Guys**
   Time Surfers
   The Weird Zone
Abrashkin, Raymond. **Danny Dunn**
Adler, David A. **Cam Jansen**
   Fourth Floor Twins
   Houdini Club Magic Mystery
   Jeffrey's Ghost
   My Dog
   Young Cam Jansen
Ahlberg, Allan. **Funnybones**
Aiken, Joan. **Arabel and Mortimer**
   Wolves Chronicles
Alexander, Brandon. **Full House: Club Stephanie**
Alexander, Lloyd. **Prydain Chronicles**
   Vesper Holly
   Westmark
Alexander, Martha. **Blackboard Bear**
Alexander, Nina. **The Adventures of Mary-Kate and Ashley**
   Full House: Michelle
   Magic Attic Club
Alexander, Sue. **Witch, Goblin, and Ghost**
   World Famous Muriel
Allard, Harry. **The Stupids**
Anastasio, Dina. **Ghostwriter**
   Space Above and Beyond
Anderson, C. W. **Blaze**
Anderson, Kevin J. **Star Wars Young Jedi Knights**
Anderson, Margaret J. **Time Trilogy**
Antilles, Kem. **Star Trek: Deep Space Nine**
Antle, Nancy. **Once Upon America**
Applegate, K. A. **Animorphs**
Appleton, Victor. **Tom Swift**

Archer, Chris. **Mindwarp**
Arden, William. **Three Investigators**
Armstrong, Jennifer. **Children of America**
Armstrong, Robb. **Patrick's Pals**
Arthur, Robert. **Three Investigators**
Asch, Frank. **Bear**
   Moonbear
Asimov, Isaac. **Norby**
Asimov, Janet. **Norby**
Averill, Esther. **Jenny and the Cat Club**

B

Bader, Bonnie. **The Adventures of Mary-Kate and Ashley**
   Carmen Sandiego Mysteries
Bagdon, Paul. **Scrapper John**
Baglio, Ben. **Animal Ark**
   Choose Your Own Adventure
Bailey, Linda. **Stevie Diamond Mysteries**
Baker, Alan. **Benjamin**
Baker, Barbara. **Digby and Kate**
Baker, Carin Greenberg. **Ghostwriter**
Baker, Jennifer. **Clueless**
Balan, Bruce. **Cyber.kdz**
Bale, Karen A. **Survival!**
Balian, Lorna. **Humbug**
Ball, Duncan. **Emily Eyefinger**
Banks, Jacqueline Turner. **Judge and Jury**
Banks, Lynne Reid. **Indian in the Cupboard**
Barkan, Joanne. **Wishbone Adventures**
Barklem, Jill. **Brambly Hedge**
Barnes, Johnny Ray, Jr. **Strange Matter**
Barnes-Svarney, Patricia. **The Secret World of Alex Mack**
   Star Trek: The Next Generation: Starfleet Academy

Star Trek: Voyager: Starfleet Academy
Barron, T. A. **Kate Gordon**
   Merlin
Barry, Miranda. **Ghostwriter**
Baum, Lyman Frank. **Oz**
Baum, Roger S. **Oz**
Beckett, Jim. **Choose Your Own Adventure**
   Passport
Bellairs, John. **Anthony Monday**
   Johnny Dixon
   Lewis Barnavelt
Belton, Sandra. **Ernestine and Amanda**
Bemelmans, Ludwig. **Madeline**
Benary-Isbert, Margot. **Lechow Family**
Benson, Lauren. **Magic Attic Club**
Bentley, Karen. **Full House: Stephanie**
   Thoroughbred
Berenstain, Jan. **Berenstain Bears**
   Berenstain Bears: Bear Scouts
   Berenstain Bears: Big Chapter Books
Berenstain, Stan. **Berenstain Bears**
   Berenstain Bears: Bear Scouts
   Berenstain Bears: Big Chapter Books
Best, Herbert. **Desmond**
Betancourt, Jeanne. **Pony Pals**
Bethancourt, T. Ernesto. **Doris Fein**
Beyers, Richard Lee. **Are You Afraid of the Dark?**
Bibee, John. **The Home School Detectives**
   Spirit Flyer
Billam, Rosemary. **Fuzzy Rabbit**
Blume, Judy. **Fudge**
Blundell, Judy. **Ghostwriter**
Blyton, Enid. **The Famous Five**
   The Secret Seven
Boegehold, Betty. **Pippa Mouse**

Bond, Michael. **Olga da Polga**
  Paddington
Bonham, Frank. **Dogtown Ghetto**
Bonsall, Crosby. **Private Eyes Club**
Bos, Burny. **Molesons**
Boston, L. M. **Green Knowe**
Bourgeois, Paulette. **Franklin**
Brandel, Marc. **Three Investigators**
Brandenberg, Franz. **Aunt Nina**
  Leo and Emily
Branscum, Robbie. **Johnny May**
Bray, Marian. **Lassie**
Bridwell, Norman. **Clifford**
  Witch
Bright, Robert. **Georgie**
Brightfield, Richard. **Choose Your**
  Own Adventure
  Choose Your Own Nightmare
  Young Indiana Jones
    Chronicles: Choose Your
    Own Adventure
Brisson, Pat. **Kate**
Brittain, Bill. **Coven Tree**
Brooks, Bruce. **Wolfbay Wings**
Brooks, Walter R. **Freddy**
Brouwer, Sigmund. **Winds of Light**
Brown, Jeff. **Stanley**
Brown, Laurie Krasny. **Rex and**
  Lilly
Brown, Marc. **Arthur**
  D.W.
Browne, Anthony. **Willy**
Bryant, Bonnie. **Pony Tails**
  The Saddle Club
Buchanan, Heather S. **George and**
  Matilda Mouse
Burke, Martin R. **Star Trek:**
  Voyager: Starfleet Academy
Butcher, Nancy. **Ghostwriter**
  Wishbone Adventures
  Wishbone Mysteries
Byars, Betsy. **Bingo Brown**
  The Blossom Family
  Golly Sisters
  Herculeah Jones

C

Calhoun, Mary. **Henry the Cat**
  Katie John
Calhoun, T. B. **NASCAR Pole**
  Position Adventures
Calmenson, Stephanie. **Gator Girls**
  Young Indiana Jones
Cameron, Ann. **Julian and Huey**
Cameron, Eleanor. **Julia Redfern**
  Tyco Bass

Campbell, Bill. **Oz**
Campbell, Joanna. **Thoroughbred**
Capeci, Anne. **Wishbone Mysteries**
Capucilli, Alyssa Satin. **Biscuit**
Carey, Diane L. **Star Trek: Starfleet**
  Academy
Carey, M.V. **Three Investigators**
Carlson, Karyl. **Oz**
Carlson, Nancy. **Arnie**
  Harriet
  Louanne Pig
  Loudmouth George
Carlson, Natalie Savage. **Orphelines**
  Spooky the Cat
Carlstrom, Nancy White. **Jesse Bear**
Carrick, Carol. **Christopher**
Carroll, Jacqueline. **Full House:**
  Michelle
  Full House: Stephanie
Cascone, A. G. **Deadtime Stories**
Caseley, Judith. **Kane Family**
Cates, Emily. **Haunting with Louisa**
Chaikin, Miriam. **Molly**
Charbonnet, Gabrielle. **Disney Girls**
Charles, Donald. **Calico Cat**
  Shaggy Dog
Chetwin, Grace. **Tales of Gom in**
  the Legends of Ulm
Chevat, Richie. **Ghostwriter**
Choi, Sook Nyul. **Sookan Bak**
Chorao, Kay. **Kate**
Christelow, Eileen. **Five Monkeys**
Christian, Mary Blount.
  Determined Detectives
  Penrod
  Sebastian (Super Sleuth)
Christopher, John. **Fireball**
  Sword of the Spirits
  Tripods
Christopher, Matt. **Mike and Harry**
  Peach Street Mudders
Ciencin, Scott. **Dinotopia**
Cleary, Beverly. **Henry Huggins**
  Jimmy and Janet
  Ralph S. Mouse
  Ramona Quimby
Cleaver, Bill. **Ellen Grae**
Cleaver, Vera. **Ellen Grae**
Clifford, Eth. **Flatfoot Fox**
  Harvey
  Mary Rose
Clifton, Lucille. **Everett Anderson**
Coffin, M. T. **Spinetinglers**
Cohen, Alice E. **Are You Afraid of**
  the Dark?
Cohen, Miriam. **First Grade**

Cole, Joanna. **Gator Girls**
  Magic School Bus
Coleman, Michael. **Internet**
  Detectives
Collier, Christopher. **The Arabus**
  Family Saga
Collier, James Lincoln. **The Arabus**
  Family Saga
Compton, Sara. **Choose Your Own**
  Adventure
Cone, Molly. **Mishmash**
Conford, Ellen. **Jenny Archer**
  Possum Family
Conly, Jane Leslie. **The Rats of**
  NIMH
Connor, Catherine. **Magic Attic**
  Club
Coombs, Patricia. **Dorrie**
Cooney, Caroline B. **Vampire**
  Promise
Cooper, Ilene. **Frances in the**
  Fourth Grade
  Holiday Five
Cooper, Susan. **Dark Is Rising**
Corbett, Scott. **Dr. Merlin**
  The Great McGoniggle
  Trick Books
Coren, Alan. **Arthur the Kid**
Cosby, Bill. **Little Bill**
Cosgrove, Rachel. **Oz**
Costello, Emily. **Full House:**
  Stephanie
  Soccer Stars
Cousins, Lucy. **Maisy the Mouse**
Cover, Arthur Byron. **Buffy, the**
  Vampire Slayer
Coville, Bruce. **Alien Adventures**
  Camp Haunted Hills
  Ghost Stories
  Magic Shop
  My Teacher
  Space Brat
Craig, Janet. **Nice Mice**
Cray, Jordan. **Danger.com**
Cresswell, Helen. **Bagthorpe Saga**
  Posy Bates
Crider, Bill. **Wishbone Adventures**
Cruise, Beth. **Saved by the Bell**
Curry, Jane Louise. **Abaloc (Apple**
  Lock)
Cushman, Doug. **Aunt Eater**
  Mouse and Mole
Cusick, Richie Tankersley. **Buffy,**
  the Vampire Slayer

Hurwitz, Johanna. **Aldo Sossi**
Ali Baba Bernstein
Edison-Armstrong School
Elisa
Nora and Teddy
Russell
Seasonal Adventures
Hutchens, Paul. **Sugar Creek Gang**
Hutchins, Pat. **Titch**
Very Worst Monster
Hyman, Fracaswell. **Ghostwriter**

I

Ichikawa, Satomi. **Nora**
Iwamura, Kazuo. **The Fourteen Forest Mice**

J

Jablonski, Carla. **Wishbone Adventures**
Jacks, Marie. **Clue**
Jackson, Dave. **Trailblazers**
Jackson, Neta. **Trailblazers**
Jacques, Brian. **Redwall**
Jakab, E. A. M. **Choose Your Own Nightmare**
James, Robert. **Eerie Indiana**
Jansson, Tove. **Moomintroll**
Jenkins, Jerry B. **Dallas O'Neil and the Baker Street Sports Club**
Dallas O'Neil Mysteries
Johnson, Crockett. **Harold and the Purple Crayon**
Johnson, Ken. **McGee and Me!**
Johnson, Lissa Halls. **China Tate**
Johnson, Seddon. **Choose Your Own Adventure**
Johnston, Norma. **Sterling Family**
Johnston, Tony. **Mole and Troll**
Jones, Marcia Thornton. **The Adventures of the Bailey School Kids**
Bailey City Monsters
Triplet Trouble
Jones, Rebecca C. **Germy**
Jones, Veda Boyd. **The American Adventure**
Jorvik, Irwin. **My Teddy Bear**

K

Kalman, Maira. **Max the Dog**
Katschke, Judy. **The Adventures of Mary-Kate and Ashley**
Kaye, Marilyn. **Camp Sunnyside Sisters**

Keats, Ezra Jack. **Louie**
Peter
Keene, Carolyn. **Dana Girls**
Nancy Drew
Nancy Drew Files
Nancy Drew Notebooks
Keep, Linda Lowery. **Hannah and the Angels**
Kehret, Peg. **Frightmares**
Keller, Beverly. **Desdemona**
Keller, Holly. **Geraldine**
Kellogg, Steven. **Pinkerton**
Kerr, Judith. **Anna**
Kessler, Leonard. **Old Turtle**
Keyishian, Amy. **Ghostwriter**
Kimball, Katie. **Full House: Stephanie**
Kincaid, Beth. **Silver Creek Riders**
King-Smith, Dick. **Sophie**
Kirk, David. **Miss Spider**
Kirwan, Anna. **Girlhood Journeys: Juliet**
Kjelgaard, Jim. **Red**
Klein, Leah. **B.Y. Times**
B.Y. Times Kid Sisters
Kleinbaum, N. H. **Ghostwriter**
Kline, Suzy. **Herbie Jones**
Horrible Harry
Mary Marony
Orp
Song Lee
Koller, Jackie French. **The Dragonling**
Koltz, Tony. **Choose Your Own Adventure**
Komaiko, Leah. **Annie Bananie**
Koontz, Robin Michal. **Chicago and the Cat**
Korman, Gordon. **Bruno and Boots**
Korman, Justine. **Grumpy Bunny**
Korman, Susan. **Ghostwriter**
Magic Attic Club
Krailing, Tessa. **Petsitters Club**
Kraus, Robert. **Little Mouse Spider**
Krensky, Stephen. **Arthur Chapter Books**
Lionel
Kroll, Steven. **The Hit and Run Gang**
Krulik, Nancy E. **The Adventures of Mary-Kate and Ashley**
Kudlinski, Kathleen V. **Girlhood Journeys: Marie**
Girlhood Journeys: Shannon
Once Upon America

Kushner, Ellen. **Choose Your Own Adventure**
Kwitz, Mary DeBall. **Little Chick**

L

Lahey, Vince. **Choose Your Own Adventure**
Landesman, Peter. **Full House: Stephanie**
Landon, Lucinda. **Meg Mackintosh: A Solve-It-Yourself Mystery**
Lasky, Kathryn. **Dear America**
Starbuck Family Adventures
Lawlor, Laurie. **Addie**
Heartland
Lazewnik, Libby. **Baker's Dozen**
Leavitt, Caroline. **Wishbone Adventures**
Wishbone Mysteries
Lebrun, Claude. **Little Brown Bear**
Leeden, Ivy D. **Ghostwriter**
LeGuin, Ursula K. **Catwings**
Earthsea
Leibold, Jay. **Choose Your Own Adventure**
Leitch, Patricia. **Horseshoes**
LeMieux, Anne. **Super Snoop Sam Snout**
L'Engle, Madeleine. **Time Fantasy Series**
Vicky Austin
Leonard, Marcia. **Here Come the Brownies**
Kids on Bus 5
Leppard, Lois Gladys. **Mandie**
Lerangis, Peter. **Three Investigators**
Leroe, Ellen W. **Fiendly Corners**
Lester, Alison. **Australian Children**
Lester, Helen. **Tacky the Penguin**
Levene, Nancy Simpson. **Alex**
Leverich, Kathleen. **Best Enemies**
Brigid Thrush books
Flower Girls
Levy, Elizabeth. **Brian and Pea Brain**
Gymnasts
Invisible Inc.
Magic Mystery
Sam and Robert
Something Queer
Lewin, Hugh. **Jafta**
Lewis, C. S. **Chronicles of Narnia**
Lewis, Zoe. **Magic Attic Club**
Lindgren, Astrid. **Pippi Longstocking**
Lindgren, Barbo. **The Wild Baby**

Lindquist, Jennie Dorothea. **Nancy Bruce**

Lipman, Ken. **The Secret World of Alex Mack**

Lipsyte, Robert. **Contender**

Lisle, Janet Taylor. **Investigators of the Unknown**

Litowinsky, Olga. **Wishbone Adventures**

Lloyd, Alan. **House of Horrors**

Lobel, Arnold. **Frog and Toad**

Locke, Joseph. **Sabrina the Teenage Witch**

The Secret World of Alex Mack

Lofting, Hugh. **Doctor Dolittle**

London, Jonathan. **Froggy**

Lord, Athena V. **Z.A.P. and Zoe**

Lough, Loree. **The American Adventure**

Lovelace, Maud Hart. **Betsy-Tacy**

Lowe, Kris. **Girls R.U.L.E.**

Lowell, Melissa. **Silver Blades**

Lowry, Lois. **Anastasia Krupnik**

Sam Krupnik

Lutz, Norma Jean. **The American Adventure**

M

McArthur, Nancy. **The Plant That Ate Dirty Socks**

MacBride, Roger Lea. **Little House: The Rose Years**

McCay, William. **Three Investigators**

Young Indiana Jones

McCully, Emily Arnold. **Grandma**

McDaniel, Becky Bring. **Katie**

MacDonald, Betty. **Mrs. Piggle-Wiggle**

McDonald, Megan. **Beezy**

McGowen, Tom. **Age of Magic Trilogy**

Magician Trilogy

McGraw, Eloise Jervis. **Oz**

MacGregor, Ellen. **Miss Pickerell**

Machale, D. J. **Are You Afraid of the Dark?**

McInerney, Judith Whitelock. **Judge Benjamin**

McKay, Hilary. **Exiles**

McKee, David. **Elmer**

McKenna, Colleen O'Shaughnessy. **Murphy Family**

McKinley, Robin. **Damar Chronicles**

McKissack, Fredrick. **Messy Bessey**

McKissack, Patricia. **Dear America**

Messy Bessey

McMahon, Maggie. **Full House: Michelle**

McMullan, Kate. **Lila Fenwick**

McMurtry, Ken. **Choose Your Own Nightmare**

Passport

McNaughton, Colin. **Preston**

McPhail, David. **Emma**

Pig Pig

Maestro, Betty. **Harriet**

Maestro, Giulio. **Harriet**

Magraw, Trisha. **Magic Attic Club**

Mahy, Margaret. **Cousins Quartet**

Maifair, Linda Lee. **Darcy J. Doyle, Daring Detective**

Makris, Kathryn. **Eco Kids**

Malcolm, Jahnna N. **Bad News Ballet**

Clue

Jewel Kingdom

Manes, Stephen. **Oscar J. Noodleman**

Marano, Lydia C. **The Mystery Files of Shelby Woo**

Mariana. **Miss Flora McFlimsey**

Markham, Marion M. **Dixon Twins**

Marney, Dean. **What Ate Who**

Marshall, Catherine. **Christy**

Marshall, Edward *see* Marshall, James

Marshall, James. **The Cut-Ups**

Fox

George and Martha

Miss Nelson

Martin, Ann M. **Baby-sitters Club**

Baby-sitters Club Mysteries

Baby-sitters Club Super Specials

Baby-sitters Little Sister

Baby-sitters Little Sister Super Specials

California Diaries

Kids in Ms. Coleman's Class

Martin, Jacqueline Briggs. **Bizzy Bones**

Martin, Les. **X Files**

Young Indiana Jones

Marzollo, Jean. **39 Kids on the Block**

Massie, Elizabeth. **Daughters of Liberty**

Matthews, Liz. **Teeny Witch**

Mayer, Mercer. **Frog**

Meddaugh, Susan. **Martha**

Meyers, Susan. **Always Friends**

Miami, Rita. **Full House: Stephanie**

Miller, Edna. **Mousekin**

Miller, Susan Martins. **The American Adventure**

Mills, Claudia. **Dinah**

Gus and Grandpa

Minarik, Else Holmelund. **Little Bear**

Mitchell, Mark. **Are You Afraid of the Dark?**

Mitchell, V. E. **Are You Afraid of the Dark?**

The Secret World of Alex Mack

Star Trek: The Next Generation: Starfleet Academy

Moesta, Rebecca. **Star Wars Junior Jedi Knights**

Star Wars Young Jedi Knights

Montgomery, Anson. **Choose Your Own Adventure**

Montgomery, Lucy Maud. **Avonlea**

Montgomery, R. A. **Choose Your Own Adventure**

Choose Your Own Nightmare

Montgomery, Ramsey. **Choose Your Own Adventure**

Montgomery, Raymond. **Choose Your Own Adventure**

Moore, Elaine. **Seasons with Grandma**

Moore, Leslie. **House of Horrors**

Moore, Lilian. **Cucumbers Trilogy**

Mooser, Stephen. **All-Star Meatballs**

Morganstern, Steve. **Clue Jr.**

Morris, Gilbert. **Bonnets and Bugles**

Moss, Marissa. **Amelia**

Mountain, Robert. **Choose Your Own Adventure**

Mueller, Kate. **Choose Your Own Adventure**

Passport

Murphy, Elspeth Campbell. **Ten Commandments Mysteries**

Three Cousins Detective Club

Murphy, Jill. **Worst Witch**

Murphy, Jim. **Dear America**

My Name Is America

Myers, Bill. **McGee and Me!**

N

Nabb, Magdalen. **Josie Smith**

Nash, Mary. **Mrs. Coverlet**

Naylor, Phyllis Reynolds. **Alice**

Bessledorf Hotel

Hatford Boys

Shiloh

Witch

Roddy, Lee. **American Adventure**
   D.J. Dillon Adventures
   Ladd Family
Rodriguez, K. S. **Are You Afraid of the Dark?**
Rogers, Mary. **Annabel Andrews**
Roos, Stephen. **New Eden**
   Pet Lovers Club
Rose, Miriam. **Baker's Dozen**
Ross, Pat. **M and M**
   Once Upon America
Rounds, Glenn. **Mr. Yowder**
Rowland, Della. **Clue Jr.**
Roy, Ron. **A to Z Mysteries**
Royce, Easton. **Space Above and Beyond**
   X Files
Rubin, Jim. **Doug Chronicles**
Ryder, Joanne. **First Grade Is the Best**
Rylant, Cynthia. **Henry and Mudge**
   Mr. Putter and Tabby
   Poppleton

S

Sachar, Louis. **Marvin Redpost**
   Wayside School
Sachs, Marilyn. **Amy and Laura**
Sadler, Marilyn. **Alistair**
   P.J. Funnybunny
St. Antoine, Sara. **Ghostwriter**
Salat, Cristina. **Ghostwriter**
Salmon, Michael. **Piganeers**
Samuels, Barbara. **Duncan and Dolores**
Sansevere, J. R. **Mercer Mayer's Critters of the Night**
Sathre, Vivian. **Wishbone Adventures**
Saunders, Susan. **Bad News Bunny**
   Black Cat Club
   Neptune Adventures
   Oz
   Sleepover Friends
   Stars
Scheffler, Ursel. **Rinaldo**
Schulte, Elaine L. **Twelve Candles Club**
Schwartz, Ellen. **Starshine!**
Scieszka, Jon. **Time Warp Trio**
Scollon, E. W. **Goners**
Scott, Gavin. **Young Indiana Jones**
Scott, Stefanie. **Moesha**
Seidman, David L. **Are You Afraid of the Dark?**

Selden, George. **Chester Cricket**
Shahan, Sherry. **Eerie Indiana**
Shanower, Eric. **Oz**
Sharmat, Marjorie. **Genghis Khan**
   Maggie Marmelstein
   Nate the Great
Sharp, Margery. **The Rescuers**
Shaw, Janet B. **American Girls: Kirsten**
Shaw, Murray. **Match Wits with Sherlock Holmes**
Shaw, Nancy. **Sheep**
Sheldon, Dyan. **Harry and Chicken**
Shreve, Susan. **Joshua T. Bates**
Siegel, Malky. **Baker's Dozen**
Siegman, Meryl. **Choose Your Own Adventure**
Simner, Janni Lee. **Phantom Rider**
Simon, Lisa. **Full House: Stephanie**
Simon, Seymour. **Einstein Anderson**
Simons, Jamie. **Goners**
Singer, A. L. **Young Indiana Jones**
Singer, Marilyn. **Sam and Dave Mysteries**
Singleton, Linda Joy. **Cheer Squad**
Sinykin, Sheri Cooper. **Magic Attic Club**
Slater, Teddy. **Junior Gymnasts**
Slobodkin, Louis. **Space Ship Under the Apple Tree**
Slote, Alfred. **Jack and Danny One**
Smith, Dona. **Clue**
Smith, Janice Lee. **The Adam Joshua Capers**
   Wizard and Wart
Smith, Sherwood. **Wren**
Smith, Susan. **Best Friends**
Snow, Jack. **Oz**
Snyder, Carol. **Ike and Mama**
Snyder, Midori. **Dinotopia**
Snyder, Zilpha Keatley. **Castle Court Kids**
Sobol, Donald J. **Encyclopedia Brown**
Speregen, Devra Newberger. **Full House: Stephanie**
Spinelli, Eileen. **Lizzie Logan**
Spinner, Stephanie. **Aliens**
   The Weebie Zone
Sprague, Gilbert M. **Oz**
Stadler, John. **Snail**
Stahl, Hilda. **Best Friends**
Standiford, Natalie. **Space Dog**
Stanley, George Edward. **Scaredy Cats**
Stanton, Mary. **Magical Mystery**

Steele, Alexander. **Wishbone Adventures**
   Wishbone Mysteries
Steele, Anthony. **Wishbone Mysteries**
Steiber, Ellen. **Full House: Stephanie**
   X Files
Stein, Aidel. **Baker's Dozen**
Steinberg, Ruth. **Baker's Dozen**
Stevenson, James. **Emma**
   Grandpa
   James Stevenson's Autobiographical Stories
   Mud Flat
   Worst Person
Stine, H. William. **Camp Zombie**
   Three Investigators
   Young Indiana Jones
Stine, Megan. **Camp Zombie**
   Full House: Michelle
   House of Horrors
   Three Investigators
   Young Indiana Jones
Stine, R. L. **Babysitter**
   Ghosts of Fear Street
   Goosebumps
   Goosebumps: Give Yourself Goosebumps
   Goosebumps Presents
   Goosebumps Series 2000
Stoeke, Janet Morgan. **Minerva Louise**
Stolz, Mary. **Barkham Street**
   Thomas and Grandfather
Stone, Bonnie D. **The Secret World of Alex Mack**
Stone, G. H. **Three Investigators**
Stone, Tom B. **Graveyard School**
Strasser, Todd. **Help, I'm Trapped**
Strickland, Barbara. **The Mystery Files of Shelby Woo**
   Star Trek: Starfleet Academy
   Star Trek: The Next Generation: Starfleet Academy
Strickland, Brad. **Are You Afraid of the Dark?**
   Johnny Dixon
   Lewis Barnavelt
   The Mystery Files of Shelby Woo
   Star Trek: Deep Space Nine
   Star Trek: Starfleet Academy
   Star Trek: The Next Generation: Starfleet Academy

TITLE INDEX

The series in which the title appears is shown in parentheses following the title. Series are listed in alphabetical order in the main section of this book.

A

Abandoned on the Wild Frontier (Trailblazers)

Abby and the Best Kid Ever (Baby-sitters Club)

Abby and the Mystery Baby (Baby-sitters Club Mysteries)

Abby and the Notorious Neighbor (Baby-sitters Club Mysteries)

Abby and the Secret Society (Baby-sitters Club Mysteries)

Abby in Wonderland (Baby-sitters Club)

Abby the Bad Sport (Baby-sitters Club)

Abby's Lucky Thirteen (Baby-sitters Club)

Abby's Twin (Baby-sitters Club)

The Abominable Snow Monster (Graveyard School)

Abominable Snowman (Choose Your Own Adventure)

The Abominable Snowman of Pasadena (Goosebumps)

Above the Rim (Super Hoops)

The Abracadabra Case (Hardy Boys: Frank and Joe Hardy: The Clues Brothers)

The Absent Author (A to Z Mysteries)

Absolute Zero (Bagthorpe Saga)

Absolute Zero (Hardy Boys Casefiles)

Absolutely Positively Alexander (Alexander)

The Accident (Christopher)

Achieving Personal Perfection (Clueless)

Achingly Alice (Alice)

Across the Wide and Lonesome Prairie (Dear America)

Acting Up (Hardy Boys Casefiles)

Adam Mouse's Book of Poems (Cucumbers Trilogy)

Addie Across the Prairie (Addie)

Addie and the King of Hearts (Addie)

Addie Meets Max (Addie)

Addie Runs Away (Addie)

Addie's Bad Day (Addie)

Addie's Dakota Winter (Addie)

Addie's Forever Friend (Addie)

Addie's Long Summer (Addie)

Addy Learns a Lesson (American Girls: Addy)

Addy Saves the Day (American Girls: Addy)

Addy's Surprise (American Girls: Addy)

Adios, Anna (Friends and Amigos)

Adrian Mole (Adrian Mole)

Adventure at Green Knowe (Green Knowe)

Adventure in an Indian Cemetery (Sugar Creek Gang)

Adventure in the Wilderness (The American Adventure)

Adventure in Walt Disney World (Disney Girls)

The Adventure of Black Peter; The Gloria Scott (Match Wits with Sherlock Holmes)

The Adventure of the Abbey Grange; The Boscombe Valley Mystery (Match Wits with Sherlock Holmes)

The Adventure of the Cardboard Box; A Scandal in Bohemia (Match Wits with Sherlock Holmes)

The Adventure of the Copper Beeches; The Redheaded League (Match Wits with Sherlock Holmes)

The Adventure of the Dancing Men; The Three Garridebs (Match Wits with Sherlock Holmes)

The Adventure of the Six Napoleons; The Blue Carbuncle (Match Wits with Sherlock Holmes)

The Adventure of the Speckled Band; The Sussex Vampire (Match Wits with Sherlock Holmes)

The Adventures of Ali Baba Bernstein (Ali Baba Bernstein)

The Adventures of Jack Ninepins (Jenny and the Cat Club)

The Adventures of Johnny May (Johnny May)

The Adventures of Laura and Jack (Little House Chapter Books)

The Adventures of Mole and Troll (Mole and Troll)

The Adventures of Obadiah (Obadiah Starbuck)

The Adventures of Paddy Pork (Paddy Pork)

The Adventures of Robin Hood (Wishbone Classics)

The Adventures of Snail at School (Snail)

The Adventures of Tom Sawyer (Wishbone Classics)

African Safari (Young Indiana Jones Chronicles: Choose Your Own Adventure)

After the Dinosaurs (Berenstain Bears)

Afternoon on the Amazon (Magic Tree House)

Aftershock (Mindwarp)

Aftershock (Star Trek: Starfleet Academy)

Against All Odds (Hardy Boys Casefiles)

The Against Taffy Sinclair Club (Taffy Sinclair)

Against the Odds (Sweet Valley High)

Against the Rules (Nancy Drew Files)

Against the Rules (Soccer Stars)

Against the Rules (Sweet Valley Twins)

Aggie's Home (Orphan Train Children)

Agnes May Gleason, Walsenburg, Colorado, 1932 (American Diaries)

The Agony of Alice (Alice)

Ahoy There, Little Polar Bear (Little Polar Bear)

Aimer Gate (Stone Book Quartet)

The Alaskan Adventure (Hardy Boys)

Albert and the Dragonettes (Albert the Dragon)

Albert the Dragon (Albert the Dragon)

Albert the Dragon and the Centaur (Albert the Dragon)

Albert's Alphabet (Albert)

Albert's Ballgame (Albert)

Albert's Christmas (Albert)

Albert's Field Trip (Albert)

Albert's Halloween (Albert)

Albert's Play (Albert)

Albert's Thanksgiving (Albert)

Albert's World Tour (Albert the Dragon)

Alcott Library Is Falling Down (Peanut Butter and Jelly)

Aldo Applesauce (Aldo Sossi)

Aldo Ice Cream (Aldo Sossi)

Aldo Peanut Butter (Aldo Sossi)

Alex and the Cat (Alex and the Cat)

Alex Remembers (Alex and the Cat)

Alex, You're Glowing! (The Secret World of Alex Mack)

Alexander and the Terrible, Horrible, No Good, Very Bad Day (Alexander)

Alexander, Who Used to Be Rich Last Sunday (Alexander)

Alexander, Who's Not (Do You Hear Me? I Mean It!) Going to Move (Alexander)

Alexandra the Great (Al)

Alexia Ellery Finsdale, San Francisco, 1905 (American Diaries)

Alfie and the Birthday Surprise (Alfie Rose)

Alfie Gets in First (Alfie Rose)

Alfie Gives a Hand (Alfie Rose)

Alfie's ABC (Alfie Rose)

Alfie's Feet (Alfie Rose)

Ali Baba Bernstein, Lost and Found (Ali Baba Bernstein)

Alias Diamond Jones (Ghostwriter)

Alice in April (Alice)

Alice In-Between (Alice)

Alice in Lace (Alice)

Alice in Rapture, Sort of (Alice)

Alice the Brave (Alice)

The Alien (Animorphs)

Alien Alert (Ghostwriter)

Alien Blood (Mindwarp)

Alien, Go Home! (Choose Your Own Adventure)

Alien in the Classroom (Nancy Drew Notebooks)

Alien Scream (Mindwarp)

Alien Terror (Mindwarp)

The Aliens Approach (Space Above and Beyond)

Aliens Ate My Homework (Alien Adventures)

Aliens Don't Wear Braces (The Adventures of the Bailey School Kids)

Aliens for Breakfast (Aliens)

Aliens for Dinner (Aliens)

Aliens for Lunch (Aliens)

Aliens in the Sky (Spooksville)

Aliens Stole My Body (Alien Adventures)

Alison Goes for the Gold (Magic Attic Club)

Alison of Arabia (Magic Attic Club)

Alison on the Trail (Magic Attic Club)

Alison Rides the Rapids (Magic Attic Club)

Alison Saves the Wedding (Magic Attic Club)

Alison Walks the Wire (Magic Attic Club)

Alistair and the Alien Invasion (Alistair)

Alistair in Outer Space (Alistair)

Alistair Underwater (Alistair)

Alistair's Elephant (Alistair)

Alistair's Time Machine (Alistair)

All About Sam (Sam Krupnik)

All About Stacy (New Kids at the Polk Street School)

All But Alice (Alice)

All Dads on Deck (Pee Wee Scouts)

All Hands on Deck (Goners)

The All-New Mallory Pike (Baby-sitters Club)

All Night Long (Sweet Valley High)

All-of-a-Kind Family (All-of-a-Kind Family)

All-of-a-Kind Family Downtown (All-of-a-Kind Family)

All-of-a-Kind Family Uptown (All-of-a-Kind Family)

All Rapped Up (Sister Sister)

All-Star Fever (Peach Street Mudders)

All That Glitters (Sabrina the Teenage Witch)

All Together Now (Angel Park All Stars)

All You Need Is a Love Spell (Sabrina the Teenage Witch)

The Almost Awful Play (Ronald Morgan)

Almost Married (Sweet Valley High)

Almost Ten and a Half (Kobie Roberts)

Aloha, Baby-Sitters! (Baby-sitters Club Super Specials)

Aloha, Salty! (Salty)

Alone in Snakebite Canyon (Goosebumps: Give Yourself Goosebumps)

Alone in the Crowd (Sweet Valley High)

Along Came a Spider (Deadtime Stories)

Al's Blind Date (Al)

Amalia (California Diaries)

Amalia, Diary Two (California Diaries)

Amanda Pig and Her Best Friend Lollipop (Oliver and Amanda Pig)

Amanda Pig and Her Big Brother Oliver (Oliver and Amanda Pig)

Amanda Pig on Her Own (Oliver and Amanda Pig)

Amanda Pig, School Girl (Oliver and Amanda Pig)

Amanda's Perfect Ten (Junior Gymnasts)

Amanda's Unlucky Day (Junior Gymnasts)

Amazement Park Adventure (Ghostwriter)

Amazing Anthony Ant (Anthony Ant)

Amazing Jessica (Sweet Valley Kids)

Amazing Stories (All-Star Meatballs)

The Amazon Stranger (Reel Kids Adventures)

Amber Brown Goes Fourth (Amber Brown)

Amber Brown Is Feeling Blue (Amber Brown)

Amber Brown Is Not a Crayon (Amber Brown)

Amber Brown Sees Red (Amber Brown)

Amber Brown Wants Extra Credit (Amber Brown)

Ambush at Amboseli (Anika Scott)

Amelia Bedelia (Amelia Bedelia)

Amelia Bedelia and the Baby (Amelia Bedelia)

Amelia Bedelia and the Surprise Shower (Amelia Bedelia)

Amelia Bedelia Goes Camping (Amelia Bedelia)

Amelia Bedelia Helps Out (Amelia Bedelia)

Amelia Bedelia's Family Album (Amelia Bedelia)

Amelia Hits the Road (Amelia)

Amelia Takes Command (Amelia)

Amelia Writes Again (Amelia)

Amelia's Notebook (With Help from Amelia) (Amelia)

An American Betty in Paris (Clueless)

The American Revolution (The American Adventure)

The American Victory (The American Adventure)

The Amethyst Ring (Julian Escobár)

Amos and the Alien (Culpepper Adventures)

Amos and the Chameleon Caper (Culpepper Adventures)

Amos and the Vampire (Culpepper Adventures)

Amos Binder, Secret Agent (Culpepper Adventures)

Amos Gets Famous (Culpepper Adventures)

Amos Gets Married (Culpepper Adventures)

Arthur Accused! (Arthur Chapter Books)

Arthur and the Crunch Cereal Contest (Arthur Chapter Books)

Arthur and the Great Detective (Arthur the Kid)

Arthur and the Lost Diary (Arthur Chapter Books)

Arthur and the Popularity Test (Arthur Chapter Books)

Arthur and the Purple Panic (Arthur the Kid)

Arthur and the Scare-Your-Pants-Off Club (Arthur Chapter Books)

Arthur Babysits (Arthur)

Arthur Goes to Camp (Arthur)

Arthur Lost and Found (Arthur)

Arthur Makes the Team (Arthur Chapter Books)

Arthur Meets the President (Arthur)

Arthur Rocks with BINKY (Arthur Chapter Books)

Arthur the Kid (Arthur the Kid)

Arthur Tricks the Tooth Fairy (Arthur)

Arthur Writes a Story (Arthur)

Arthur's April Fool (Arthur)

Arthur's Baby (Arthur)

Arthur's Back to School Days (Arthur the Monkey)

Arthur's Birthday (Arthur)

Arthur's Birthday Party (Arthur the Monkey)

Arthur's Camp Out (Arthur the Monkey)

Arthur's Chicken Pox (Arthur)

Arthur's Christmas (Arthur)

Arthur's Christmas Cookies (Arthur the Monkey)

Arthur's Computer Disaster (Arthur)

Arthur's Eyes (Arthur)

Arthur's First Sleepover (Arthur)

Arthur's Funny Money (Arthur the Monkey)

Arthur's Great Big Valentine (Arthur the Monkey)

Arthur's Halloween (Arthur)

Arthur's Halloween Costume (Arthur the Monkey)

Arthur's Honey Bear (Arthur the Monkey)

Arthur's Last Stand (Arthur the Kid)

Arthur's Loose Tooth (Arthur the Monkey)

Arthur's Mystery Envelope (Arthur Chapter Books)

Arthur's New Puppy (Arthur)

Arthur's Nose (Arthur)

Arthur's Pen Pal (Arthur the Monkey)

Arthur's Pet Business (Arthur)

Arthur's Prize Reader (Arthur the Monkey)

Arthur's Reading Race (Arthur)

Arthur's Teacher Trouble (Arthur)

Arthur's Thanksgiving (Arthur)

Arthur's Tooth (Arthur)

Arthur's TV Trouble (Arthur)

Arthur's Valentine (Arthur)

As Ever Gordy (Gordy Smith)

Ashleigh's Christmas Miracle (Thoroughbred)

Ashleigh's Diary (Thoroughbred)

Ashleigh's Dream (Thoroughbred)

Ashleigh's Farewell (Thoroughbred)

Ashleigh's Hope (Thoroughbred)

Ashley's Lost Angel (Forever Angels)

Ashley's Love Angel (Forever Angels)

Assassins in the Cathedral (Trailblazers)

At Home in North Branch (Grandma's Attic)

Atlantis Station (Star Trek: The Next Generation: Starfleet Academy)

Attaboy, Sam! (Sam Krupnik)

Attack in the Rye Grass (Trailblazers)

Attack of the Alien Mole Invaders! (The Weird Zone)

The Attack of the Aqua Apes (Ghosts of Fear Street)

Attack of the Beast (Disney Girls)

Attack of the Beastly Baby-Sitter (Goosebumps: Give Yourself Goosebumps)

Attack of the Graveyard Ghouls (Goosebumps Series 2000)

Attack of the Jack-O'-Lanterns (Goosebumps)

Attack of the Jack-O'-Lanterns (Goosebumps Presents)

Attack of the Killer Ants (Bone Chillers)

Attack of the Killer Crabs (Spooksville)

Attack of the Living Mask (Choose Your Own Nightmare)

Attack of the Mutant (Goosebumps)

Attack of the Mutant (Goosebumps Presents)

Attack of the Slime Monster (Ghostwriter)

Attack of the Two-Ton Tomatoes (Eerie Indiana)

Attack of the Vampire Worms (Ghosts of Fear Street)

Attack of the Video Villains (Hardy Boys)

Attila the Pun (Magic Moscow)

Aunt Eater Loves a Mystery (Aunt Eater)

Aunt Eater's Mystery Christmas (Aunt Eater)

Aunt Eater's Mystery Halloween (Aunt Eater)

Aunt Eater's Mystery Vacation (Aunt Eater)

Aunt Nina and Her Nephews and Nieces (Aunt Nina)

Aunt Nina, Good Night! (Aunt Nina)

Aunt Nina's Visit (Aunt Nina)

Aunt Weird (House of Horrors)

Aunt Zinnia and the Ogre (Beechwood Bunny Tales)

Author Day (Kids in Ms. Coleman's Class)

Autocrats of Oz (Oz)

Autumn Story (Brambly Hedge)

Autumn Trail (The Saddle Club)

B

B Is for Betsy (Betsy)

Babar and Father Christmas (Babar)

Babar and His Children (Babar)

Babar and the Ghost (Babar)

Babar and the Professor (Babar)

Babar and the Wully-Wully (Babar)

Babar and Zephir (Babar)

Babar Comes to America (Babar)

Babar Learns to Cook (Babar)

Babar Loses His Crown (Babar)

Babar Saves the Day (Babar)

Babar the King (Babar)

Babar Visits Another Planet (Babar)

Babar's ABC (Babar)

Babar's Battle (Babar)

Babar's Birthday Surprise (Babar)

Babar's Book of Color (Babar)

Babar's Castle (Babar)

Babar's Cousin, That Rascal Arthur (Babar)

Babar's Fair Will Be Opened Next Sunday (Babar)

Babar's French Lessons (Babar)

Babar's Little Circus Star (Babar)

Babar's Little Girl (Babar)

Babar's Mystery (Babar)

Babar's Picnic (Babar)

Babar's Spanish Lessons (Babar)

Babe Ruth and the Home Run Derby (All-Star Meatballs)

Babes in Boyland (Clueless)

The Baby Angel (Forever Angels)

Baby Animal Zoo (Kids in Ms. Coleman's Class)

The Baby Blues (The Adam Joshua Capers)

Baby Duck and the Bad Eyeglasses (Baby Duck)

The Baby Pony (Pony Pals)

A Baby Sister for Frances (Frances)

The Babysitter (Babysitter)

The Babysitter II (Babysitter)

The Babysitter III (Babysitter)

The Beggar Queen (Westmark)

The Beginners (Gymnasts)

Behind Closed Doors (Sweet Valley University)

Behind the Great Wall (Young Indiana Jones Chronicles: Choose Your Own Adventure)

Behind the Wheel (Choose Your Own Adventure)

The Bell, the Book, and the Spellbinder (Johnny Dixon)

The Bellmaker (Redwall)

Ben and the Porcupine (Christopher)

Ben There, Done That (Sabrina the Teenage Witch)

Beneath the Hill (Abaloc)

Benjamin and the Box (Benjamin)

Benjamin Bounces Back (Benjamin)

Benjamin's Balloon (Benjamin)

Benjamin's Book (Benjamin)

Benjamin's Dreadful Dream (Benjamin)

Benjamin's Portrait (Benjamin)

Benjy and the Power of Zingies (Benjy)

Benjy in Business (Benjy)

Benjy the Football Hero (Benjy)

Benny Goes Into Business (Boxcar Children: Adventures of Benny and Watch)

Benny Uncovers a Mystery (Boxcar Children)

Benny's New Friend (Boxcar Children: Adventures of Benny and Watch)

The Berenstain Bear Scouts and the Coughing Catfish (Berenstain Bears: Bear Scouts)

The Berenstain Bear Scouts and the Humongous Pumpkin (Berenstain Bears: Bear Scouts)

The Berenstain Bear Scouts and the Ice Monster (Berenstain Bears: Bear Scouts)

The Berenstain Bear Scouts and the Magic Crystal Caper (Berenstain Bears: Bear Scouts)

The Berenstain Bear Scouts and the Missing Merit Badge (Berenstain Bears: Bear Scouts)

The Berenstain Bear Scouts and the Really Big Disaster (Berenstain Bears: Bear Scouts)

The Berenstain Bear Scouts and the Run-Amuck Robot (Berenstain Bears: Bear Scouts)

The Berenstain Bear Scouts and the Sci-Fi Pizza (Berenstain Bears: Bear Scouts)

The Berenstain Bear Scouts and the Search for Naughty Ned (Berenstain Bears: Bear Scouts)

The Berenstain Bear Scouts and the Sinister Smoke Ring (Berenstain Bears: Bear Scouts)

The Berenstain Bear Scouts and the Terrible Talking Termite (Berenstain Bears: Bear Scouts)

The Berenstain Bear Scouts Ghost Versus Ghost (Berenstain Bears: Bear Scouts)

The Berenstain Bear Scouts in Giant Bat Cave (Berenstain Bears: Bear Scouts)

The Berenstain Bear Scouts Meet Bigpaw (Berenstain Bears: Bear Scouts)

The Berenstain Bear Scouts Save That Backscratcher (Berenstain Bears: Bear Scouts)

The Berenstain Bear Scouts Scream Their Heads Off (Berenstain Bears: Bear Scouts)

The Berenstain Bears: No Girls Allowed (Berenstain Bears)

The Berenstain Bears Accept No Substitutes (Berenstain Bears: Big Chapter Books)

The Berenstain Bears and Mama's New Job (Berenstain Bears)

The Berenstain Bears and Queenie's Crazy Crush (Berenstain Bears: Big Chapter Books)

The Berenstain Bears and the Bad Dream (Berenstain Bears)

The Berenstain Bears and the Bad Habit (Berenstain Bears)

The Berenstain Bears and the Bermuda Triangle (Berenstain Bears: Big Chapter Books)

The Berenstain Bears and the Big Date (Berenstain Bears: Big Chapter Books)

The Berenstain Bears and the Big Road Race (Berenstain Bears)

The Berenstain Bears and the Blame Game (Berenstain Bears)

The Berenstain Bears and the Bully (Berenstain Bears)

The Berenstain Bears and the Double Dare (Berenstain Bears)

The Berenstain Bears and the Dress Code (Berenstain Bears: Big Chapter Books)

The Berenstain Bears and the Drug Free Zone (Berenstain Bears: Big Chapter Books)

The Berenstain Bears and the Female Fullback (Berenstain Bears: Big Chapter Books)

The Berenstain Bears and the Galloping Ghost (Berenstain Bears: Big Chapter Books)

The Berenstain Bears and the Ghost of the Auto Graveyard (Berenstain Bears: Big Chapter Books)

The Berenstain Bears and the Ghost of the Forest (Berenstain Bears)

The Berenstain Bears and the Giddy Grandma (Berenstain Bears: Big Chapter Books)

The Berenstain Bears and the Green-Eyed Monster (Berenstain Bears)

The Berenstain Bears and the Haunted Hayride (Berenstain Bears: Big Chapter Books)

The Berenstain Bears and the Homework Hassle (Berenstain Bears)

The Berenstain Bears and the In-Crowd (Berenstain Bears)

The Berenstain Bears and the Love Match (Berenstain Bears: Big Chapter Books)

The Berenstain Bears and the Messy Room (Berenstain Bears)

The Berenstain Bears and the Missing Dinosaur Bones (Berenstain Bears)

The Berenstain Bears and the Missing Honey (Berenstain Bears)

The Berenstain Bears and the Nerdy Nephew (Berenstain Bears: Big Chapter Books)

The Berenstain Bears and the New Girl in Town (Berenstain Bears: Big Chapter Books)

The Berenstain Bears and the Perfect Crime (Almost) (Berenstain Bears: Big Chapter Books)

The Berenstain Bears and the Prize Pumpkin (Berenstain Bears)

The Berenstain Bears and the Red-Handed Thief (Berenstain Bears: Big Chapter Books)

The Berenstain Bears and the School Scandal Sheet (Berenstain Bears: Big Chapter Books)

The Berenstain Bears and the Showdown at Chainsaw Gap (Berenstain Bears: Big Chapter Books)

The Berenstain Bears and the Sitter (Berenstain Bears)

The Berenstain Bears and the Slumber Party (Berenstain Bears)

The Berenstain Bears and the Spooky Old Tree (Berenstain Bears)

The Berenstain Bears and the Trouble with Friends (Berenstain Bears)

The Berenstain Bears and the Trouble with Grownups (Berenstain Bears)

The Berenstain Bears and the Truth (Berenstain Bears)

The Berenstain Bears and the Week at Grandma's (Berenstain Bears)

The Berenstain Bears and the Wheelchair Commando (Berenstain Bears: Big Chapter Books)

The Berenstain Bears and Too Much Birthday (Berenstain Bears)

Beware the Wolfman (Sweet Valley High)

Beware the Wolfman (Sweet Valley High [Super Thrillers])

Beyond Escape! (Choose Your Own Adventure)

Beyond the Burning Lands (Sword of the Spirits)

Beyond the Great Wall (Choose Your Own Adventure)

Beyond the Law (Hardy Boys Casefiles)

Bicycle Hills (Spirit Flyer)

Bicycle Mystery (Boxcar Children)

Bicycle to Treachery (Miss Mallard)

The Big Audition (Silver Blades)

Big Bad Bugs (Ghosts of Fear Street)

Big Base Hit (Angel Park All Stars)

Big Boar's Mom Comes to Stay (Piganeers)

Big Brother's in Love Again (Sweet Valley Twins)

The Big Camp Secret (Sweet Valley Twins Super Edition)

The Big Concrete Lorry (Tales of Trotter Street)

· *A Big Decision* (Girlhood Journeys: Kai)

The Big Fix-up Mix-up (Full House: Stephanie)

Big Foot, Big Trouble (Strange Matter)

The Big Honey Hunt (Berenstain Bears)

The Big Lie (McGee and Me!)

Big Match (David and Goliath)

The Big Night (Sweet Valley High)

Big Party Weekend (Sweet Valley Twins)

The Big Pig Puzzle (Bobbsey Twins: The New Bobbsey Twins)

Big Race (Sweet Valley Kids)

Big Red (Red)

Big Sister Blues (Camp Sunnyside)

The Big Six (Swallows and Amazons)

The Big Stink & Five Other Mysteries (Ghostwriter)

Big Trouble for Roxie (Best Friends)

The Big Turkey Escape (Full House: Michelle)

Bigfoot Doesn't Square Dance (The Adventures of the Bailey School Kids)

The Bike Lesson (Berenstain Bears)

The Biker (Nightmare Hall)

Bill and Pete (Bill and Pete)

Bill and Pete Go Down the Nile (Bill and Pete)

Bill and Pete to the Rescue (Bill and Pete)

Billie's Secret (Sweet Valley University)

The Billion Dollar Ransom (Hardy Boys)

A Billion for Boris (Annabel Andrews)

Billy (Wolfbay Wings)

Billy Baker's Dog Won't Stay Buried (Spinetinglers)

Billy and Blaze (Blaze)

Bingo Brown and the Language of Love (Bingo Brown)

Bingo Brown, Gypsy Lover (Bingo Brown)

Bingo Brown's Guide to Romance (Bingo Brown)

The Bird Is the Word (The Weebie Zone)

Birdstones (Abaloc)

A Birthday Bike for Brimhall (Brimhall)

A Birthday for Frances (Frances)

The Birthday Party Mystery (Dixon Twins)

Biscuit (Biscuit)

Biscuit Finds a Friend (Biscuit)

Biscuit's Picnic (Biscuit)

The Bite of the Gold Bug (Once Upon America)

Biting for Blood (Choose Your Own Nightmare)

Bitter Rivals (Sweet Valley High)

The Bizarre Hockey Tournament (Dallas O'Neil and the Baker Street Sports Club)

Bizzy Bones and Mouse Mouse (Bizzy Bones)

Bizzy Bones and the Lost Quilt (Bizzy Bones)

Bizzy Bones and Uncle Ezra (Bizzy Bones)

The Black Cat (Funnybones)

The Black Cauldron (Prydain Chronicles)

The Black Dragon (Tom Swift)

Black Hearts in Battersea (Wolves Chronicles)

The Black Mask Trick (Trick Books)

The Black Pearl Mystery (Boxcar Children)

The Black Stallion (Black Stallion)

The Black Stallion and Flame (Black Stallion)

The Black Stallion and Satan (Black Stallion)

The Black Stallion and the Girl (Black Stallion)

The Black Stallion Challenged (Black Stallion)

The Black Stallion Legend (Black Stallion)

The Black Stallion Mystery (Black Stallion)

The Black Stallion Returns (Black Stallion)

The Black Stallion Revolts (Black Stallion)

The Black Stallion's Courage (Black Stallion)

The Black Stallion's Filly (Black Stallion)

The Black Stallion's Ghost (Black Stallion)

The Black Stallion's Shadow (Black Stallion)

The Black Stallion's Sulky Colt (Black Stallion)

Black Tuesday (The American Adventure)

The Black Widow (Nancy Drew Files)

Blackboard Bear (Blackboard Bear)

Blackmailed by Taffy Sinclair (Taffy Sinclair)

Blackout! (Ghostwriter)

Blackout in the Amazon (Cyber.kdz)

The Blackwing Puzzle (Hardy Boys)

Blast (Med Center)

A Blast with the Past (Ghostwriter)

Blaze and the Forest Fire (Blaze)

Blaze and the Gray Spotted Pony (Blaze)

Blaze and the Gypsies (Blaze)

Blaze and the Indian Cave (Blaze)

Blaze and the Lost Quarry (Blaze)

Blaze and the Mountain Lion (Blaze)

Blaze and Thunderbolt (Blaze)

Blaze Finds Forgotten Roads (Blaze)

Blaze Finds the Trail (Blaze)

Blaze Shows the Way (Blaze)

The Blind Pony (Pony Pals)

Blizzard (Med Center)

Blizzard (Survival!)

The Blob That Ate Everyone (Goosebumps)

Blockade Runner (Bonnets and Bugles)

The Blood Bay Colt (Black Stallion)

Blood Money (Hardy Boys Casefiles)

Blood on the Handle (Choose Your Own Adventure)

Blood Red Eightball (Spinetinglers)

Blood Relations (Hardy Boys Casefiles)

Blood Sport (Hardy Boys Casefiles)

Blooded (Buffy, the Vampire Slayer)

Blork's Evil Twin (Space Brat)

The Blossom Angel (Forever Angels)

Blossom Culp and the Sleep of Death (Blossom Culp)

A Blossom Promise (The Blossom Family)

The Blossoms and the Green Phantom (The Blossom Family)

The Blossoms Meet the Vulture Lady (The Blossom Family)

Blown Away (Hardy Boys Casefiles)

Bobbsey Twins Treasure Hunting (Bobbsey Twins)

Bobbsey Twins' Wonderful Secret (Bobbsey Twins)

The Bodies in the Bessledorf Hotel (Bessledorf Hotel)

Body Lines (Heart Beats)

Body Switchers from Outer Space (Ghosts of Fear Street)

The Bogeyman Caper (Eagle-Eye Ernie)

Bogeymen Don't Play Football (The Adventures of the Bailey School Kids)

The Bomb in the Bessledorf Bus Depot (Bessledorf Hotel)

Bombay Boomerang (Hardy Boys)

Bon Voyage, Unicorns! (Unicorn Club)

Bone Breath and the Vandals (Frightmares)

Bonjour, Alex! (The Secret World of Alex Mack)

Boo! (Preston)

Boo Who? (Bad News Ballet)

Boo Year's Eve (Graveyard School)

Booby-Trapped! (Clue)

Boogey's Back for Blood (Spinetinglers)

The Book Chase (Ghostwriter)

Book of Earth (Diadem)

Book of Horrors (Nightmare Hall)

Book of Magic (Diadem)

The Book of Merlyn (The Once and Future King)

Book of Names (Diadem)

Book of Nightmares (Diadem)

Book of Signs (Diadem)

The Book of Three (Prydain Chronicles)

Book of Thunder (Diadem)

Bookworm Buddies (Pee Wee Scouts)

Booster Boycott (Sweet Valley Twins)

Boot (Wolfbay Wings)

The Bootlegger Menace (The American Adventure)

The Borderline Case (Hardy Boys Casefiles)

The Borgia Dagger (Hardy Boys Casefiles)

Born to Be Wild (The Weebie Zone)

The Borrowers (The Borrowers)

The Borrowers Afield (The Borrowers)

The Borrowers Afloat (The Borrowers)

The Borrowers Aloft (The Borrowers)

The Borrowers Avenged (The Borrowers)

Bossy Anna (Silver Blades Figure Eights)

Bossy Steven (Sweet Valley Kids)

The Boston Massacre (The American Adventure)

Boston Revolts! (The American Adventure)

Bounce, Tigger, Bounce (Winnie the Pooh First Readers)

The Box and the Bone (Castle Court Kids)

Box Turtle at Long Pond (Long Pond)

The Boxcar Children (Boxcar Children)

A Boy, a Dog, a Frog, and a Friend (Frog)

A Boy, a Dog, and a Frog (Frog)

Boy-Crazy Stacey (Baby-sitters Club)

A Boy in the Doghouse (Lucky)

The Boy-Oh-Boy Next Door (Full House: Stephanie)

Boy Trouble (Sitting Pretty)

Boy Trouble (Sweet Valley High)

The Boy Who Ate Fear Street (Ghosts of Fear Street)

The Boyfriend Dilemma (Fabulous Five)

The Boyfriend Game (Sweet Valley Twins)

The Boyfriend Mess (Sweet Valley Twins)

Boyfriend War (Sweet Valley High)

Boyfriends for Everyone (Unicorn Club)

Boys Against Girls (Sweet Valley Twins)

Boys Against the Girls (Hatford Boys)

Boys Are Bad News (Cheer Squad)

Boys Are Even Worse than I Thought (Cousins Club)

Boys in the Gym (Gymnasts)

The Boys of Summer (Sweet Valley University)

Boys Only Club (Fabulous Five)

The Boys Start the War (Hatford Boys)

Bozo the Clone (The Zack Files)

Brace Yourself (Andie and the Boys)

The Bragging War (Fabulous Five)

Brain Juice (Goosebumps Series 2000)

The Brain Spiders (Star Wars Galaxy of Fear)

Brain Stealers (Visitors)

The Brain That Wouldn't Obey! (The Weird Zone)

The Brave (Contender)

Bravo, Amelia Bedelia! (Amelia Bedelia)

Bravo, Ernest and Celestine! (Ernest and Celestine)

Bravo, Tanya! (Tanya)

Bread and Honey (Bear)

Bread and Jam for Frances (Frances)

Breakaway (Star Trek: The Next Generation: Starfleet Academy)

Breakdown in Axeblade (Hardy Boys)

Breakfast of Enemies (Sweet Valley Twins)

Breakfast Time, Ernest and Celestine (Ernest and Celestine)

Breaking Away (Sweet Valley University)

Breaking the Ice (Silver Blades)

Breaking the Rules (Saved by the Bell)

Breaking Up (Fabulous Five)

Brian's Return (Brian Robeson)

Brian's Winter (Brian Robeson)

Bride of the Living Dummy (Goosebumps Series 2000)

Bridesmaid Blues for Becky (Twelve Candles Club)

The Bridge to Cutter Gap (Christy)

Bridle Path (The Saddle Club)

Bright Lights, Little Gerbil (The Weebie Zone)

A Bright Star Falls (Beany Malone)

Brigid Beware (Brigid Thrush books)

Brigid Bewitched (Brigid Thrush books)

Brigid the Bad (Brigid Thrush books)

Brilliant Doctor Wogan (Choose Your Own Adventure)

Brimhall Comes to Stay (Brimhall)

Brimhall Turns Detective (Brimhall)

Brimhall Turns to Magic (Brimhall)

Bring Me a Dream (Eerie Indiana)

Bring the Boys Home (Bonnets and Bugles)

Brittany's New Friend (Always Friends)

The Broken Anchor (Nancy Drew)

Broken-Hearted (Sweet Valley High)

Broken Horse (The Saddle Club)

Broken Promises, Shattered Dreams (Sweet Valley University)

Brooke and Her Rock Star Mom (Sweet Valley Twins)

Brother Against Brother (Hardy Boys Casefiles)

A Brother for the Orphelines (Orphelines)

Brotherly Love (Christy)

Brown Box Mystery at Sugar Creek (Sugar Creek Gang)

Brrr! (Grandpa)

Bruce's Story (Sweet Valley High)

BSC in the USA (Baby-sitters Club Super Specials)

Budgie and the Blizzard (Budgie)

Budgie at Bendick's Point (Budgie)

Budgie Goes to Sea (Budgie)

Budgie the Little Helicopter (Budgie)

Buffalo Arthur (Arthur the Kid)

Bugged Out! (Choose Your Own Nightmare)

The Case of Capital Intrigue (Nancy Drew)

The Case of the Absent Author (McGurk)

The Case of the Angry Actress (Darcy J. Doyle, Daring Detective)

The Case of the Artful Crime (Nancy Drew)

The Case of the Ballet Bandit (The Adventures of Mary-Kate and Ashley)

The Case of the Barking Dog (Clue Jr.)

The Case of the Bashed-Up Bicycle (Darcy J. Doyle, Daring Detective)

The Case of the Bashful Bank Robber (McGurk)

The Case of the Bashful Bully (Darcy J. Doyle, Daring Detective)

The Case of the Basketball Video (Sports Mysteries)

The Case of the Birthday Bracelet (Nicki Holland)

The Case of the Black-Hooded Hangman (Hank the Cowdog)

The Case of the Blackmail Boys (Baker Street Irregulars)

The Case of the Blue Ribbon Horse (The Adventures of Mary-Kate and Ashley)

The Case of the Cackling Car (Sam and Dave Mysteries)

The Case of the Car-Barkaholic Dog (Hank the Cowdog)

The Case of the Cat's Meow (Private Eyes Club)

The Case of the Chocolate Fingerprints (Clue Jr.)

The Case of the Choosey Cheater (Darcy J. Doyle, Daring Detective)

The Case of the Christmas Caper (The Adventures of Mary-Kate and Ashley)

The Case of the Cinema Swindle (Baker Street Irregulars)

The Case of the Close Encounter (Bobbsey Twins: The New Bobbsey Twins)

The Case of the Clubhouse Thief (Clue Jr.)

The Case of the Comic Crooks (Baker Street Irregulars)

The Case of the Condemned Cat (McGurk)

The Case of the Cool-Itch Kid (Polka Dot Private Eye)

The Case of the Cop Catchers (Baker Street Irregulars)

Case of the Cosmic Kidnapping (Hardy Boys)

The Case of the Counterfeit Cash (Nicki Holland)

Case of the Counterfeit Criminals (Hardy Boys)

The Case of the Crazy Collections (Bobbsey Twins: The New Bobbsey Twins)

The Case of the Creepy Campout (Darcy J. Doyle, Daring Detective)

The Case of the Criminal Computer (Baker Street Irregulars)

The Case of the Crooked Contest (Bobbsey Twins: The New Bobbsey Twins)

The Case of the Crying Clown (Bobbsey Twins: The New Bobbsey Twins)

Case of the Dangerous Cruise (Ladd Family)

The Case of the Dangerous Solution (Nancy Drew)

The Case of the Desperate Drummer (McGurk)

The Case of the Dirty Bird (Culpepper Adventures)

The Case of the Disappearing Deejay (Nancy Drew)

The Case of the Disappearing Diamonds (Nancy Drew)

The Case of the Disappearing Diplomat (Baker Street Irregulars)

The Case of the Double Bumblebee Sting (Hank the Cowdog)

The Case of the Double Cross (Private Eyes Club)

The Case of the Dragon in Distress (McGurk)

The Case of the Dumb Bells (Private Eyes Club)

The Case of the Dummy with Cold Eyes (Magic Mystery)

The Case of the Eyeball Surprise (Black Cat Club)

The Case of the Fagin File (Baker Street Irregulars)

The Case of the Fantastic Footprints (McGurk)

The Case of the Felon's Fiddle (McGurk)

The Case of the Fiddle-Playing Fox (Hank the Cowdog)

The Case of the Fixed Election (Sam and Dave Mysteries)

The Case of the Floating Crime (Nancy Drew)

The Case of the Four Flying Fingers (McGurk)

The Case of the Fun House Mystery (The Adventures of Mary-Kate and Ashley)

The Case of the Ghost Grabbers (Baker Street Irregulars)

The Case of the Giggling Ghost (Darcy J. Doyle, Daring Detective)

The Case of the Gobbling Squash (Magic Mystery)

The Case of the Goofy Game Show (Bobbsey Twins: The New Bobbsey Twins)

The Case of the Halloween Ghost (Hank the Cowdog)

The Case of the Haunted Camp (The Adventures of Mary-Kate and Ashley)

The Case of the Haunted Holiday (Baker Street Irregulars)

The Case of the Haunting of Lowell Lanes (Nicki Holland)

The Case of the Haystack Kitties (Hank the Cowdog)

The Case of the Hooking Bull (Hank the Cowdog)

The Case of the Hotel Who-Done-It (The Adventures of Mary-Kate and Ashley)

The Case of the Hungry Stranger (Private Eyes Club)

The Case of the Invisible Cat (Clue)

The Case of the Invisible Dog (McGurk)

The Case of the Karate Chop (Clue Jr.)

The Case of the Kidnapped Collie (Hank the Cowdog)

The Case of the Measled Cowboy (Hank the Cowdog)

The Case of the Midnight Rustler (Hank the Cowdog)

The Case of the Mind-Reading Mommies (Magic Mystery)

The Case of the Missing Cat (Hank the Cowdog)

The Case of the Missing Dinosaur (Bobbsey Twins: The New Bobbsey Twins)

The Case of the Missing Formula (Our Secret Gang)

The Case of the Missing Marble (Super Snoop Sam Snout)

The Case of the Missing Masterpiece (Baker Street Irregulars)

The Case of the Missing Max (Darcy J. Doyle, Daring Detective)

The Case of the Missing Movie (Clue Jr.)

The Case of the Missing Pitcher (Sports Mysteries)

The Case of the Mixed-Up Monsters (Darcy J. Doyle, Daring Detective)

The Case of the Muttering Mummy (McGurk)

The Case of the Mystery Cruise (The Adventures of Mary-Kate and Ashley)

The Case of the Mystery Ghost (Clue Jr.)

The Case of the Mystery Mark (Nicki Holland)

The Change (Animorphs)

The Change-Child (Abaloc)

Changes for Addy (American Girls: Addy)

Changes for Felicity (American Girls: Felicity)

Changes for Josefina (American Girls: Josefina)

Changes for Kirsten (American Girls: Kirsten)

Changes for Molly (American Girls: Molly)

Changes for Samantha (American Girls: Samantha)

Changing Places (B.Y. Times Kid Sisters)

Changing Times (The American Adventure)

Changing Times (B.Y. Times)

Channel X (Sweet Valley University Thriller Editions)

Charlotte Cheetham: Master of Disaster (Charlotte Cheetham)

Charlotte Shakespeare and Annie the Great (Charlotte Cheetham)

Charlotte the Starlet (Charlotte Cheetham)

Charm School Mystery (Sweet Valley Twins)

The Chase for the Mystery Twister (Hardy Boys)

The Cheating Heart (Nancy Drew Files)

Cheating to Win (Sweet Valley High)

Check in to Danger (Casebusters)

Check It Out—and Die! (Spinetinglers)

Checking In (Sitting Pretty)

Checkout Time at the Dead-End Hotel (Goosebumps: Give Yourself Goosebumps)

The Cheerleader (Vampire Promise)

Chelsea and the Alien Invasion (Best Friends)

Chelsea and the Outrageous Phone Bill (Best Friends)

Chelsea's Special Touch (Best Friends)

Cher and Cher Alike (Clueless)

Cher Goes Enviro-mental (Clueless)

Cher Negotiates New York (Clueless)

Cherry Cola Champions (Alex)

Cher's Frantically Romantic Assignment (Clueless)

Cher's Furiously Fit Workout (Clueless)

Cher's Guide to . . . Whatever (Clueless)

The Chessmen of Doom (Johnny Dixon)

Chester Cricket's New Home (Chester Cricket)

Chester Cricket's Pigeon Ride (Chester Cricket)

Chester's Way (Lilly)

Cheyenne Rose (Magic Attic Club)

Chicago and the Cat (Chicago and the Cat)

Chicago and the Cat: The Camping Trip (Chicago and the Cat)

Chicago and the Cat: The Family Reunion (Chicago and the Cat)

Chicago and the Cat: The Halloween Party (Chicago and the Cat)

Chicago and the Cat at the Country Fair (Chicago and the Cat)

Chicago World's Fair (The American Adventure)

Chicken Chicken (Goosebumps)

Chicken Pox Strikes Again (39 Kids on the Block)

Chicken Trek (Oscar J. Noodleman)

The Chief (Contender)

Child of the Hunt (Buffy, the Vampire Slayer)

Child Star (Once Upon America)

The Children of Green Knowe (Green Knowe)

Children of the Wolf (Werewolf Chronicles)

The Chilling Tale of Crescent Pond (Black Cat Club)

The Chimney Sweep's Ransom (Trailblazers)

A Chinatown Adventure (Girlhood Journeys: Shannon)

Chinese Dragons (Choose Your Own Adventure)

Chloe in the Know (Kane Family)

The Chocolate Bar Bust (Ghostwriter)

Chocolate Chips and Trumpet Tricks (Alex)

The Chocolate-Covered Clue (Bobbsey Twins: The New Bobbsey Twins)

Chocolate Horse (The Saddle Club)

The Chocolate Sundae Mystery (Boxcar Children)

The Choice (The Outer Limits)

Choke Hold (Hardy Boys Casefiles)

Chomp Chomp (Mercer Mayer's Critters of the Night)

Choosing Sides (Nancy Drew Files)

Choosing Sides (Sweet Valley Twins)

Christie & Company (Christie & Company)

Christie & Company Down East (Christie & Company)

Christie & Company in the Year of the Dragon (Christie & Company)

Christina Katerina and Fats and the Great Neighborhood War (Christina Katerina)

Christina Katerina and the Box (Christina Katerina)

Christina Katerina and the First Annual Grand Ballet (Christina Katerina)

Christina Katerina and the Great Bear Train (Christina Katerina)

Christina Katerina and the Time She Quit the Family (Christina Katerina)

Christina's Courage (Thoroughbred)

Christina's Dancing Angel (Forever Angels)

Christmas at Long Pond (Long Pond)

Christmas Break (Camp Sunnyside)

The Christmas Countdown (Fabulous Five)

The Christmas Dolls (Miss Know It All)

Christmas Dreams: Four Stories (Portraits of Little Women)

The Christmas Ghost (The Adam Joshua Capers)

Christmas Gift for Brimhall (Brimhall)

Christmas in Oz (Oz)

Christmas in the Big Woods (Little House: My First Little House Books)

Christmas Magic (Holiday Friends)

The Christmas Present Mystery (Dixon Twins)

Christmas Stories from Grandma's Attic (Grandma's Attic)

Christmas Treasure (The Saddle Club)

The Christmas Tree That Ate My Mother (What Ate Who)

Christmas with Morris and Boris (Morris and Boris)

Christy's Choice (Christy)

Christy's Magic Glove (Never Sink Nine)

Chronically Crushed (Clueless)

Chronicles of Avonlea (Avonlea)

Ciao, Sweet Valley (Sweet Valley Twins)

Cincinnati Epidemic (The American Adventure)

Cinderella's Castle (Disney Girls)

Cindy's Glory (Thoroughbred)

Cindy's Heartbreak (Thoroughbred)

Cindy's Honor (Thoroughbred)

Cindy's Runaway Colt (Thoroughbred)

Circle of Evil (Nancy Drew Files)

Circle of Footprints (Dana Girls)

Circle of Love (Orphan Train Adventures)

Circus F.R.E.A.K.S. (Spinetinglers)

Circus Pony (Pony Pals)

The City Bear's Adventure (D.J. Dillon Adventures)

A City of Dreams (Winds of Light)

The City of Gold and Lead (Tripods)

City of the Dead (Star Wars Galaxy of Fear)

Clues in the Woods (Liza, Bill, and Jed)

Clueless (Clueless)

Coach Amos (Culpepper Adventures)

Cobra Connection (Choose Your Own Adventure)

Coco Grimes (Thomas and Grandfather)

The Cocoa Commotion (Carmen Sandiego Mysteries)

Cody (Wolfbay Wings)

Cody's Secret Admirer (Cody)

The Coffin (Nightmare Hall)

The Cold and Hot Winter (Seasonal Adventures)

Cold as Ice (Nancy Drew Files)

The Cold Cash Caper (Hardy Boys)

The Cold People (Spooksville)

Cold Shoulder Road (Wolves Chronicles)

Cold Sweat (Hardy Boys Casefiles)

College Cruise (Sweet Valley University)

College Girls (Sweet Valley University)

College Weekend (Sweet Valley High)

Collision Course (Hardy Boys Casefiles)

Color Me Criminal (Carmen Sandiego Mysteries)

Color War! (Camp Sunnyside)

Come a Stranger (Tillerman Cycle)

Come Away with Me (Heartland)

Come Back, Amelia Bedelia (Amelia Bedelia)

Come Back, Wherever You Are (Beany Malone)

Come Out and Play, Little Mouse (Little Mouse)

Come to School, Dear Dragon (Dear Dragon)

Comedy of Errors (China Tate)

Comet Crash (Choose Your Own Adventure)

Comet in Moominland (Moomintroll)

Comic Book Criminal (The Mystery Files of Shelby Woo)

Coming Home (The American Adventure)

Commander Toad and the Big Black Hole (Commander Toad)

Commander Toad and the Dis-asteroid (Commander Toad)

Commander Toad and the Intergalactic Spy (Commander Toad)

Commander Toad and the Planet of the Grapes (Commander Toad)

Commander Toad and the Space Pirates (Commander Toad)

Commander Toad and the Voyage Home (Commander Toad)

Commander Toad in Space (Commander Toad)

The Competition (Silver Blades)

Competitive Edge (Hardy Boys Casefiles)

Computer Clues (Pee Wee Scouts)

Computer Confusion (Saved by the Bell)

Computer Crunch! (The Secret World of Alex Mack)

The Computer Takeover (Choose Your Own Adventure)

The Contender (Contender)

Control (X Files)

The Cookie Caper (Lunchroom)

Cookies and Crutches (Pee Wee Scouts)

Cool in School (Sister Sister)

Coot Club (Swallows and Amazons)

Copper Frame (The Mystery Files of Shelby Woo)

Corduroy (Corduroy)

Corduroy's Birthday (Corduroy)

Corduroy's Christmas (Corduroy)

Corduroy's Halloween (Corduroy)

Corey and the Spooky Pony (Pony Tails)

Corey in the Saddle (Pony Tails)

Corey's Christmas Wish (Pony Tails)

Corey's Pony Is Missing (Pony Tails)

Corey's Secret Friend (Pony Tails)

Corrie's Secret Pal (Here Come the Brownies)

Cosmic Boy Versus Mezmo Head (The Weird Zone)

A Costume for Noah (Noah)

The Cottontail Caper (Pet Lovers Club)

Could Be Worse! (Grandpa)

Count on Calico Cat (Calico Cat)

Count on Clifford (Clifford)

Count Your Money with the Polk Street School (Kids of the Polk Street School)

Countdown to Terror (Hardy Boys Casefiles)

Counterfeit Christmas (Nancy Drew Files)

Countess Veronica (Veronica)

County Fair (Little House: My First Little House Books)

Courting Danger and Other Stories (Ghostwriter)

Cousin Kelly's Family Secret (Sweet Valley Kids)

Cousin War (Sweet Valley Twins)

Cover Girls (Sweet Valley High)

The Cowardly Lion of Oz (Oz)

Cowgirl Megan (Magic Attic Club)

Cowpokes and Desperadoes (Culpepper Adventures)

Coyote Moon (Buffy, the Vampire Slayer)

Cranberry Autumn (Cranberryport)

Cranberry Birthday (Cranberryport)

Cranberry Christmas (Cranberryport)

Cranberry Easter (Cranberryport)

Cranberry First Day of School (Cranberryport)

Cranberry Halloween (Cranberryport)

Cranberry Mystery (Cranberryport)

Cranberry Summer (Cranberryport)

Cranberry Thanksgiving (Cranberryport)

Cranberry Valentine (Cranberryport)

Crash Landing! (Sweet Valley High)

Crashing the Boards (Super Hoops)

The Craziest Horse Show Ever (Riding Academy)

Crazy About the Future (Full House: Stephanie)

Crazy Campout (Stars)

Crazy for Cartwheels (Cheer Squad)

The Crazy Key Clue (Nancy Drew Notebooks)

The Creature Double Feature (Black Cat Club)

Creature Features (Strange Matter)

The Creature from Club Lagoona (Ghosts of Fear Street)

The Creature in the Teacher (Spooksville)

The Creature of Black Water Lake (World of Adventure)

Creature Teacher (Goosebumps Series 2000)

Creature Teacher (Graveyard School)

The Creepy Camp-Out (Black Cat Club)

The Creepy Computer Mystery (Invisible Inc.)

The Creepy Creations of Professor Shock (Goosebumps: Give Yourself Goosebumps)

The Creepy Creature (Spooksville)

Creepy Sleepaway (Ghostwriter)

Cricket Goes to the Dogs (Always Friends)

The Cricket in Times Square (Chester Cricket)

Cricket's Pet Project (Always Friends)

Crime at the Ch@t Café (Nancy Drew Files)

Crime in the Kennel (Hardy Boys)

Crime in the Queen's Court (Nancy Drew)

A Crime of Two Cities (Ghostwriter)

The Crimson Flame (Hardy Boys)

Crisis at Crystal Reef (Star Wars Young Jedi Knights)

Dagmar Schultz and the Powers of Darkness (Dagmar Schultz)

Daisy (Flower Girls)

Dana's Best Friend (Junior Gymnasts)

Dana's Competition (Junior Gymnasts)

Dance at Grandpa's (Little House: My First Little House Books)

Dance of Darkness (Winds of Light)

Dance of Death (Sweet Valley High)

Dance, Spider, Dance! (Spider)

Dance, Tanya (Tanya)

Dance Till You Die (Nancy Drew Files)

Dance with Rosie (Ballet Slippers)

Dandelion's Vanishing Vegetable Garden (Beechwood Bunny Tales)

Danger: Twins at Work! (Sweet Valley Kids)

Danger After Dark (Clue)

Danger at Anchor Mine (Choose Your Own Adventure)

Danger at Echo Cliffs (Lassie)

Danger for Hire (Nancy Drew Files)

Danger Guys (Danger Guys)

Danger Guys and the Golden Lizard (Danger Guys)

Danger Guys Blast Off (Danger Guys)

Danger Guys Hit the Beach (Danger Guys)

Danger Guys: Hollywood Halloween (Danger Guys)

Danger Guys on Ice (Danger Guys)

Danger in Disguise (Nancy Drew Files)

Danger in the Extreme (Hardy Boys)

Danger in the Fourth Dimension (Hardy Boys)

Danger in the Harbor (The American Adventure)

Danger in Tibet (Miss Mallard)

Danger on Crab Island (Neptune Adventures)

Danger on Midnight River (World of Adventure)

Danger on Parade (Nancy Drew Files)

Danger on the Air (Hardy Boys)

Danger on the Diamond (Hardy Boys)

Danger on the Flying Trapeze (Trailblazers)

Danger on the Railroad (The American Adventure)

Danger on Thunder Mountain (American Adventure)

Danger on Vampire Trail (Hardy Boys)

Danger Unlimited (Hardy Boys Casefiles)

Danger Zone (Hardy Boys Casefiles)

The Danger Zone (Reel Kids Adventures)

The Dangerous Canoe Race (Ladd Family)

The Dangerous Diamond (Clue)

Dangerous Love (Sweet Valley High)

Dangerous Loves (Nancy Drew Files)

A Dangerous Promise (Orphan Train Adventures)

The Dangerous Quest (Spooksville)

Dangerous Relations (Nancy Drew Files)

The Dangerous Voyage (Reel Kids Adventures)

Dangerous Waters (Strange Matter)

Danny and the Dinosaur (Danny and the Dinosaur)

Danny and the Dinosaur Go to Camp (Danny and the Dinosaur)

Danny Dunn and the Anti-Gravity Paint (Danny Dunn)

Danny Dunn and the Automatic House (Danny Dunn)

Danny Dunn and the Fossil Cave (Danny Dunn)

Danny Dunn and the Heat Ray (Danny Dunn)

Danny Dunn and the Homework Machine (Danny Dunn)

Danny Dunn and the Smallifying Machine (Danny Dunn)

Danny Dunn and the Swamp Monster (Danny Dunn)

Danny Dunn and the Universal Glue (Danny Dunn)

Danny Dunn and the Voice from Space (Danny Dunn)

Danny Dunn and the Weather Machine (Danny Dunn)

Danny Dunn, Invisible Boy (Danny Dunn)

Danny Dunn on a Desert Island (Danny Dunn)

Danny Dunn on the Ocean Floor (Danny Dunn)

Danny Dunn, Scientific Detective (Danny Dunn)

Danny Dunn, Time Traveller (Danny Dunn)

Danny Means Trouble (Sweet Valley Twins)

Daphne (Sisters)

Darci and the Dance Contest (Darci Daniels)

Darci in Cabin Thirteen (Darci Daniels)

Dare at the Fair (Nancy Drew Notebooks)

Daredevil Park (Choose Your Own Adventure)

Dark and Full of Secrets (Christopher)

The Dark Corner (Spooksville)

The Dark Is Rising (Dark Is Rising)

Dark Moon (Nightmare Hall)

The Dark Secret of Weatherend (Anthony Monday)

Dark Side of the Sun (Space Above and Beyond)

The Dark Stairs (Herculeah Jones)

The Darkangel (Aeriel Trilogy)

Darkest Knight (Star Wars Young Jedi Knights)

Darkness Falls (Hardy Boys Casefiles)

Darkness Falls (X Files)

The Dastardly Murder of Dirty Pete (Mary Rose)

Date with a Werewolf (Sweet Valley High)

A Date with Deception (Nancy Drew Files)

Dating Game (Sweet Valley High)

David and Goliath on Their Own (David and Goliath)

David's Search (Orphan Train Children)

Dawn (California Diaries)

Dawn and the Big Sleepover (Baby-sitters Club)

Dawn and the Disappearing Dogs (Baby-sitters Club Mysteries)

Dawn and the Halloween Mystery (Baby-sitters Club Mysteries)

Dawn and the Impossible Three (Baby-sitters Club)

Dawn and the Older Boy (Baby-sitters Club)

Dawn and the School Spirit War (Baby-sitters Club)

Dawn and the Surfer Ghost (Baby-sitters Club Mysteries)

Dawn and the We Love Kids Club (Baby-sitters Club)

Dawn and Too Many Baby-Sitters (Baby-sitters Club)

Dawn and Whitney, Friends Forever (Baby-sitters Club)

Dawn, Diary Two (California Diaries)

Dawn on the Coast (Baby-sitters Club)

Dawn Saves the Planet (Baby-sitters Club)

Dawn Schafer, Undercover Babysitter (Baby-sitters Club Mysteries)

Dawn Selby, Super Sleuth (Best Friends)

Dawn's Big Date (Baby-sitters Club)

Dawn's Big Move (Baby-sitters Club)

Dawn's Family Feud (Baby-sitters Club)

Dawn's Wicked Stepsister (Baby-sitters Club)

The Day It Rained Forever (Once Upon America)

The Day Jimmy's Boa Ate the Wash (Jimmy's Boa)

Day of Honor (Star Trek: Deep Space Nine)

Disappearing Act (Ghostwriter)

Disappearing Acts (Herculeah Jones)

The Disappearing Dinosaurs (Wishbone Mysteries)

The Disappearing Dog Trick (Trick Books)

The Disappearing Floor (Hardy Boys)

The Disappearing Friend Mystery (Boxcar Children)

Disaster at Parson's Point (Neptune Adventures)

Disaster for Hire (Hardy Boys Casefiles)

Disaster on Wheels (Ghostwriter)

The Discovery (Animorphs)

Disoriented Express (Wishbone Mysteries)

Diversity Alliance (Star Wars Young Jedi Knights)

The DNA Disaster (Tom Swift)

The Do-Gooders (Baker's Dozen)

Do Not Disturb (Baker's Dozen)

Do the Bright Thing (McGee and Me!)

Doctor Dolittle and the Green Canary (Doctor Dolittle)

Doctor Dolittle and the Secret Lake (Doctor Dolittle)

Doctor Dolittle in the Moon (Doctor Dolittle)

Doctor Dolittle's Caravan (Doctor Dolittle)

Doctor Dolittle's Circus (Doctor Dolittle)

Doctor Dolittle's Garden (Doctor Dolittle)

Doctor Dolittle's Post Office (Doctor Dolittle)

Doctor Dolittle's Puddleby Adventures (Doctor Dolittle)

Doctor Dolittle's Return (Doctor Dolittle)

Doctor Dolittle's Zoo (Doctor Dolittle)

A Dog at the Round Table (Wishbone Adventures)

The Dog Ate My Homework (Bone Chillers)

A Dog Named Toe Shoe (Bad News Ballet)

A Dog on Barkham Street (Barkham Street)

Dog Overboard! (Wishbone Adventures)

Dog Sled to Dread (Miss Mallard)

The Dog That Called the Pitch (Mike and Harry)

The Dog That Called the Signals (Mike and Harry)

The Dog That Pitched a No-Hitter (Mike and Harry)

The Dog That Stole Football Plays (Mike and Harry)

The Dog That Stole Home (Mike and Harry)

The Doggone Detectives (Hardy Boys: Frank and Joe Hardy: The Clues Brothers)

A Dog's Life (Sabrina the Teenage Witch)

Dollars and Cents for Harriet (Harriet)

Dollars and Sense (B.Y. Times)

The Dollhouse that Time Forgot (Eerie Indiana)

Dolls in Danger (Deadline for McGurk) (McGurk)

The Dolphin Trap (Neptune Adventures)

Dolphins at Daybreak (Magic Tree House)

Don Quixote (Wishbone Classics)

Donkey Rescue (Petsitters Club)

Don't Answer the Phone (Sweet Valley University Thriller Editions)

Don't Bake That Snake (Spencer's Adventures)

Don't Be Afraid, Amanda (Cucumbers Trilogy)

Don't Eat the Mystery Meat (Graveyard School)

Don't Eat Too Much Turkey! (First Grade)

Don't Ever Get Sick at Granny's (Ghosts of Fear Street)

Don't Give Up, Mallory (Baby-sitters Club)

Don't Go Home with John (Sweet Valley High)

Don't Go in the Basement (Sweet Valley Twins)

Don't Go Near Mrs. Tallie (Frightmares)

Don't Go to Sleep! (Goosebumps)

Don't Go to the Principal's Office (Spinetinglers)

Don't Hurt My Pony (Pony Pals)

Don't Look a Ghost Horse in the Mouth (Scaredy Cats)

Don't Look Twice (Nancy Drew Files)

Don't Talk to Brian (Sweet Valley Twins)

Don't Tell a Soul (Saved by the Bell)

Don't Tell Mummy (Graveyard School)

Don't Wake Up Mama! (Five Monkeys)

Don't You Know There's a War On? (James Stevenson's Autobiographical Stories)

Don't You Wish (Sierra Jensen)

Dooby (Wolfbay Wings)

Dooger, the Grasshopper Hound (D.J. Dillon Adventures)

Dooley Mackenzie Is Totally Weird (Andie and the Boys)

The Doom of the Haunted Opera (Lewis Barnavelt)

Doom Star (Time Surfers)

The Doomsday Ship (Star Wars Galaxy of Fear)

The Door in the Dragon's Throat (Cooper Kids)

The Door-to-Door Deception (Nancy Drew)

Doorway to Doom (Strange Matter)

Doris Fein: Quartz Boyar (Doris Fein)

Doris Fein: Phantom of the Casino (Doris Fein)

Doris Fein: The Mad Samurai (Doris Fein)

Doris Fein: Murder Is No Joke (Doris Fein)

Doris Fein: Superspy (Doris Fein)

Doris Fein: Dead Heat at Long Beach (Doris Fein)

Doris Fein: Deadly Aphrodite (Doris Fein)

Doris Fein: Legacy of Terror (Doris Fein)

Dorothy and the Magic Belt (Oz)

Dorothy and the Wizard of Oz (Oz)

Dorothy of Oz (Oz)

Dorothy's Darkest Days (Kane Family)

Dorrie and the Amazing Magic Elixir (Dorrie)

Dorrie and the Birthday Eggs (Dorrie)

Dorrie and the Blue Witch (Dorrie)

Dorrie and the Dreamyard Monsters (Dorrie)

Dorrie and the Fortune Teller (Dorrie)

Dorrie and the Goblin (Dorrie)

Dorrie and the Halloween Plot (Dorrie)

Dorrie and the Haunted House (Dorrie)

Dorrie and the Haunted Schoolhouse (Dorrie)

Dorrie and the Museum Case (Dorrie)

Dorrie and the Pin Witch (Dorrie)

Dorrie and the Screebit Ghost (Dorrie)

Dorrie and the Weather Box (Dorrie)

Dorrie and the Witch Doctor (Dorrie)

Dorrie and the Witch's Camp (Dorrie)

Dorrie and the Witch's Imp (Dorrie)

Dorrie and the Witchville Fair (Dorrie)

Dorrie and the Wizard's Spell (Dorrie)

Dorrie's Magic (Dorrie)

Dorrie's Play (Dorrie)

Double-Crossed (Sweet Valley High)

Double-Crossed in Gator Country (Eric Sterling, Secret Agent)

Double Dare (Silver Blades)

Double Dog Dare (Hobie Hanson)

Eddie's Friend Boodles (Eddie Wilson)

Eddie's Green Thumb (Eddie Wilson)

Eddie's Happenings (Eddie Wilson)

Eddie's Menagerie (Eddie Wilson)

Eddie's Pay Dirt (Eddie Wilson)

Eddie's Valuable Property (Eddie Wilson)

Edge of Destruction (Hardy Boys Casefiles)

The Edge of the Cloud (Flambards)

Edith and Little Bear Lend a Hand (The Lonely Doll)

Edith and Midnight (The Lonely Doll)

Edith and Mr. Bear (The Lonely Doll)

Edith and the Duckling (The Lonely Doll)

Edward in Deep Water (Edward the Unready)

Edward Unready for School (Edward the Unready)

Edward's Overwhelming Overnight (Edward the Unready)

Eenie, Meenie, Murphy, No (Murphy Family)

Eerie in the Mirror (Eerie Indiana)

The Eerie Triangle (Eerie Indiana)

Egg-Drop Blues (Judge and Jury)

Egg-Drop Day (Mr. Rose's Class)

Egg Monsters from Mars (Goosebumps)

Eggs, Thoughts, and Other Frances Songs (Frances)

Eggs With Legs (Pee Wee Scouts)

Eighteen and on Her Own (Grandma's Attic)

Einstein Anderson Goes to Bat (Einstein Anderson)

Einstein Anderson Lights Up the Sky (Einstein Anderson)

Einstein Anderson Makes Up for Lost Time (Einstein Anderson)

Einstein Anderson, Science Sleuth (Einstein Anderson)

Einstein Anderson Sees Through the Invisible Man (Einstein Anderson)

Einstein Anderson Shocks His Friends (Einstein Anderson)

Einstein Anderson Tells a Comet's Tale (Einstein Anderson)

The El Dorado Adventure (Vesper Holly)

Elisa in the Middle (Elisa)

Elizabeth and Jessica Run Away (Sweet Valley Kids)

Elizabeth and the Orphans (Sweet Valley Twins)

Elizabeth and Todd Forever (Sweet Valley University)

Elizabeth Betrayed (Sweet Valley High)

Elizabeth Is Mine (Sweet Valley High)

Elizabeth ♥ New York (Sweet Valley University)

Elizabeth Meets Her Hero (Sweet Valley Kids)

Elizabeth Solves It All (Sweet Valley Twins)

Elizabeth the Hero (Sweet Valley Twins)

Elizabeth the Impossible (Sweet Valley Twins)

Elizabeth the Seventh Grader (Sweet Valley Twins)

Elizabeth the Spy (Sweet Valley Twins)

Elizabeth the Tattletale (Sweet Valley Kids)

Elizabeth's Broken Arm (Sweet Valley Kids)

Elizabeth's First Kiss (Sweet Valley Twins)

Elizabeth's Heartbreak (Sweet Valley University)

Elizabeth's Horseback Adventure (Sweet Valley Kids)

Elizabeth's New Hero (Sweet Valley Twins)

Elizabeth's Piano Lessons (Sweet Valley Kids)

Elizabeth's Rival (Sweet Valley High)

Elizabeth's Secret Diary (Sweet Valley High)

Elizabeth's Secret Diary Volume II (Sweet Valley High)

Elizabeth's Secret Diary Volume III (Sweet Valley High)

Elizabeth's Summer Love (Sweet Valley University)

Elizabeth's Super-Selling Lemonade (Sweet Valley Kids)

Elizabeth's Valentine (Sweet Valley Kids)

Elizabeth's Video Fever (Sweet Valley Kids)

Ella of All-of-a-Kind Family (All-of-a-Kind Family)

Ellen Elizabeth Hawkins, Texas, 1886 (American Diaries)

Ellen Grae (Ellen Grae)

Ellen Is Home Alone (Sweet Valley Kids)

Ellen's Family Secret (Unicorn Club)

Elmer (Elmer)

Elmer Again (Elmer)

Elmer and the Dragon (Dragon)

Elmer and Wilbur (Elmer)

Elmer in the Snow (Elmer)

Elmer Takes Off (Elmer)

The Elusive Heiress (Nancy Drew)

Elves Don't Wear Hard Hats (The Adventures of the Bailey School Kids)

Elvis, the Turnip . . . And Me (The Zack Files)

The Emerald City of Oz (Oz)

The Emerald-Eyed Cat (Nancy Drew)

The Emerald Princess Finds a Fairy (Jewel Kingdom)

The Emerald Princess Plays a Trick (Jewel Kingdom)

Emily Arrow Promises to Do Better This Year (Kids of the Polk Street School)

Emily Eyefinger (Emily Eyefinger)

Emily Eyefinger and the Lost Treasure (Emily Eyefinger)

Emily Eyefinger, Secret Agent (Emily Eyefinger)

Emily Mouse Saves the Day (George and Matilda Mouse)

Emily Mouse's Beach House (George and Matilda Mouse)

Emily Mouse's First Adventure (George and Matilda Mouse)

Emily Mouse's Garden (George and Matilda Mouse)

Emma (Emma)

Emma at the Beach (Emma)

Emma Eileen Grove, Mississippi, 1865 (American Diaries)

Emma's Pet (Emma)

Emma's Vacation (Emma)

Empathy (X Files)

The Emperor's Plague (Star Wars Young Jedi Knights)

The Emperor's Shield (Hardy Boys Casefiles)

The Empty Envelope (A to Z Mysteries)

The Enchanted Apples of Oz (Oz)

Enchanted Island of Oz (Oz)

Enchanted Kingdom (Choose Your Own Adventure)

The Encounter (Animorphs)

Encounter at Cold Harbor (Bonnets and Bugles)

Encyclopedia Brown and the Case of Pablo's Nose (Encyclopedia Brown)

Encyclopedia Brown and the Case of the Dead Eagles (Encyclopedia Brown)

Encyclopedia Brown and the Case of the Disgusting Sneakers (Encyclopedia Brown)

Encyclopedia Brown and the Case of the Midnight Visitor (Encyclopedia Brown)

Encyclopedia Brown and the Case of the Mysterious Handprints (Encyclopedia Brown)

Encyclopedia Brown and the Case of the Secret Pitch (Encyclopedia Brown)

Family Secrets (Christy)

Family Secrets (Sweet Valley High)

Fancy Feet (New Kids at the Polk Street School)

Fang the Dentist (Funny Firsts)

Farewell, Dawn (Baby-sitters Club)

The Farmer and the Witch (Old Witch)

Farmer Boy (Little House)

A Farmer Boy Birthday (Little House: My First Little House Books)

Farmer Boy Days (Little House Chapter Books)

The Farthest Shore (Earthsea)

Fashion Victim (Sweet Valley High)

Fast Break (Hardy Boys Casefiles)

Fat Chance, Claude (Claude)

Fat, Fat Calico Cat (Calico Cat)

Fat Glenda Turns 14 (Fat Glenda)

Fat Glenda's Summer Romance (Fat Glenda)

Fatal Attraction (Nancy Drew Files)

Fatal Error (Three Investigators)

Fatal Ransom (Nancy Drew Files)

The Fate of the Yellow Woodbee (Trailblazers)

Father Bear Comes Home (Little Bear)

Father-Daughter Disaster! (The Secret World of Alex Mack)

Father Goose in Oz (Oz)

Fathom (Strange Matter)

Faye and Dolores (Duncan and Dolores)

Fear (X Files)

Fear of Falling (Gymnasts)

Fear on Wheels (Hardy Boys)

Fear Stalks Grizzly Hill (Casebusters)

Fearless Elizabeth (Sweet Valley Kids)

The Feathered Serpent (Julian Escobár)

Feel Better, Ernest! (Ernest and Celestine)

Felicity Learns a Lesson (American Girls: Felicity)

Felicity Saves the Day (American Girls: Felicity)

Felicity's Surprise (American Girls: Felicity)

The Fellowship of the Ring (The Lord of the Rings)

Field of Death (Young Indiana Jones)

Field of Screams (Ghosts of Fear Street)

Field Trip (Star Trek: Deep Space Nine)

Fifteen at Last (Kobie Roberts)

Fifth Grade, Here Comes Trouble (Murphy Family)

Fight Fire with Fire (Sweet Valley High)

Fight for Freedom (The American Adventure)

Fight for Freedom (Choose Your Own Adventure)

Figure in Hiding (Hardy Boys)

The Figure in the Shadows (Lewis Barnavelt)

Final Cut (Hardy Boys Casefiles)

Final Gambit (Hardy Boys Casefiles)

Final Notes (Nancy Drew Files)

The Final Scene (Nancy Drew Files)

Find Your Coat, Ned (Ned)

Finders Keepers (Kids on Bus 5)

Finders, Keepers (Saved by the Bell)

Finders Keepers for Franklin (Franklin)

Finders Weepers (Molly)

Finger-Lickin' Strange (Eerie Indiana)

Finn Family Moomintroll (Moomintroll)

Fire (Med Center)

Fire! (Once Upon America)

Fire (Survival!)

Fire Biker (Tom Swift)

Fire by Night (The American Adventure)

The Fire Cat (Jenny and the Cat Club)

Fire in the Sky (Hardy Boys Casefiles)

Fire on Ice (Choose Your Own Adventure)

Fire over Atlanta (Bonnets and Bugles)

Fireball (Fireball)

Firebird Rocket (Hardy Boys)

The Firehouse Mystery (Boxcar Children)

The Fires of Merlin (Merlin)

Fireside Manners (Saved by the Bell)

Firestorm (Danger.com)

Firestorm (Dinotopia)

Fireworks and Flamingoes (Full House: Club Stephanie)

First Date (Gymnasts)

First Day, Worst Day (Hardy Boys: Frank and Joe Hardy: The Clues Brothers)

First Farm in the Valley (Wisconsin Farm)

The First Four Years (Little House)

First Grade Elves (First Grade Is the Best)

First Grade Ladybugs (First Grade Is the Best)

First Grade Takes a Test (First Grade)

First Grade Valentines (First Grade Is the Best)

First Meet (Gymnasts)

First Olympics (Choose Your Own Adventure)

First Place (Sweet Valley Twins)

First Tomato (Voyage to the Bunny Planet)

Fish Face (Kids of the Polk Street School)

A Fish Out of Water (Disney Girls)

Fishing at Long Pond (Long Pond)

Fishy Wishes (Pee Wee Scouts)

Five Are Together Again (The Famous Five)

The Five Cat Club (Eco Kids)

Five Children and It (Five Children)

Five Fall Into Adventure (The Famous Five)

Five Get Into a Fix (The Famous Five)

Five Get Into Trouble (The Famous Five)

Five Girls and a Baby (Unicorn Club)

Five Go Adventuring Again (The Famous Five)

Five Go Down to the Sea (The Famous Five)

Five Go Off in a Caravan (The Famous Five)

Five Go Off to Camp (The Famous Five)

Five Go to Billycock Hill (The Famous Five)

Five Go to Demon's Rocks (The Famous Five)

Five Go to Mystery Moor (The Famous Five)

Five Go to Smuggler's Top (The Famous Five)

Five Have a Mystery to Solve (The Famous Five)

Five Have a Wonderful Time (The Famous Five)

Five Have Plenty of Fun (The Famous Five)

Five Little Monkeys Jumping on the Bed (Five Monkeys)

Five Little Monkeys Sitting in a Tree (Five Monkeys)

Five Little Monkeys with Nothing to Do (Five Monkeys)

Five on a Hike Together (The Famous Five)

Five on a Secret Trail (The Famous Five)

Five on a Treasure Island (The Famous Five)

Five on Finniston Farm (The Famous Five)

Five on Kirrin Island Again (The Famous Five)

Five Run Away Together (The Famous Five)

Fix It! (Emma)

Flambards (Flambards)

Flambards Divided (Flambards)

Flambards in Summer (Flambards)

Franklin Fibs (Franklin)

Franklin Goes to Day Care (Franklin)

Franklin Goes to School (Franklin)

Franklin Has a Sleepover (Franklin)

Franklin in the Dark (Franklin)

Franklin Is Bossy (Franklin)

Franklin Is Lost (Franklin)

Franklin Is Messy (Franklin)

Franklin Plays the Game (Franklin)

Franklin Rides a Bike (Franklin)

Franklin Wants a Pet (Franklin)

Franklin's Bad Day (Franklin)

Franklin's Blanket (Franklin)

Franklin's Christmas Gift (Franklin)

Franklin's Halloween (Franklin)

Franklin's New Friend (Franklin)

Franklin's School Play (Franklin)

Franklin's Secret Club (Franklin)

Freaky Friday (Annabel Andrews)

Freddy and Mister Camphor (Freddy)

Freddy and Simon the Dictator (Freddy)

Freddy and the Baseball Team from Mars (Freddy)

Freddy and the Bean Home News (Freddy)

Freddy and the Dragon (Freddy)

Freddy and the Flying Saucer Plans (Freddy)

Freddy and the Ignoramus (Freddy)

Freddy and the Men from Mars (Freddy)

Freddy and the Perilous Adventure (Freddy)

Freddy and the Popinjay (Freddy)

Freddy and the Space Ship (Freddy)

Freddy Goes Camping (Freddy)

Freddy Plays Football (Freddy)

Freddy Rides Again (Freddy)

Freddy the Cowboy (Freddy)

Freddy the Detective (Freddy)

Freddy the Magician (Freddy)

Freddy the Pied Piper (Freddy)

Freddy the Pilot (Freddy)

Freddy the Politician (Freddy)

Freddy's Cousin Weedly (Freddy)

The French Fry Aliens (Lunchroom)

French Fry Forgiveness (Alex)

Fresh Bones (X Files)

Friday Flight (Juli Scott Super Sleuth)

Fried Feathers for Thanksgiving (Emma)

Friend Against Friend (Sweet Valley High)

A Friend for Dear Dragon (Dear Dragon)

A Friend for Dragon (Dragon)

A Friend for Minerva Louise (Minerva Louise)

A Friend Like Phoebe (Sisters)

Friend or Faux (Clueless)

Friend or Flamingo? (Full House: Club Stephanie)

Friends Forever (Molly)

Friends to the Finish (Short Stirrup Club)

The Friendship Test (Peanut Butter and Jelly)

The Fright Before Christmas (Graveyard School)

Fright Camp (Goosebumps Series 2000)

Fright Christmas (Ghosts of Fear Street)

Fright Knight (Ghosts of Fear Street)

Fright Night (Choose Your Own Adventure)

Fright Wave (Hardy Boys Casefiles)

Frog and the Birdsong (Frog)

Frog and the Stranger (Frog)

Frog and Toad All Year (Frog and Toad)

Frog and Toad Are Friends (Frog and Toad)

Frog and Toad Together (Frog and Toad)

Frog, Duck, and Rabbit (Duck)

Frog Goes to Dinner (Frog)

Frog in Love (Frog)

Frog in the Middle (Duck)

Frog in Winter (Frog)

Frog Is a Hero (Frog)

Frog Is Frightened (Frog)

Frog on His Own (Frog)

Frog Punch (Lunchroom)

Frog, Where Are You? (Frog)

Froggy Gets Dressed (Froggy)

Froggy Goes to School (Froggy)

Froggy Learns to Swim (Froggy)

Froggy Plays Soccer (Froggy)

Froggy's First Kiss (Froggy)

From the Ashes (Strange Matter)

Frozen Dinners (Strange Matter)

Frozen Stiff! (The Secret World of Alex Mack)

Fudge-a-mania (Fudge)

Fugitive (Choose Your Own Adventure)

Fun for the Secret Seven (The Secret Seven)

Fun Gus & Polly Pus (Slimeballs)

Fun Gus Slimes the Bus (Slimeballs)

Fun/No Fun (James Stevenson's Autobiographical Stories)

Fun, Sun, and Flamingoes (Full House: Club Stephanie)

The Funnie Haunted House (Doug Chronicles)

Funny Business (Three Investigators)

The Funny Face Fight (Nancy Drew Notebooks)

Funny, Funny Lyle (Lyle)

Funnybones (Funnybones)

Further Adventures of Albert the Dragon (Albert the Dragon)

Further Adventures of Hank the Cowdog (Hank the Cowdog)

Further Adventures of the Sugar Creek Gang (Sugar Creek Gang)

Further Chronicles of Avonlea (Avonlea)

Fuzzy Rabbit (Fuzzy Rabbit)

Fuzzy Rabbit and the Little Brother Problem (Fuzzy Rabbit)

Fuzzy Rabbit in the Park (Fuzzy Rabbit)

Fuzzy Rabbit Saves Christmas (Fuzzy Rabbit)

G

Gaal the Conquerer (Archives of Anthropos)

The Gallant Boys of Gettysburg (Bonnets and Bugles)

Game Plan for Disaster (Hardy Boys)

Garbage Juice for Breakfast (Polka Dot Private Eye)

The Garbage Monster from Outer Space (Hank the Cowdog)

Garbage Snooper Surprise (Spencer's Adventures)

Gargoyles Don't Drive School Buses (The Adventures of the Bailey School Kids)

Garth Pig and the Ice Cream Lady (Mr. and Mrs. Pig)

Garth Pig Steals the Show (Mr. and Mrs. Pig)

The Gathering (Justice Trilogy)

Gathering of Pearls (Sookan Bak)

A Gathering of the Gargoyles (Aeriel Trilogy)

The Gator Ate Her (Graveyard School)

The Gator Girls (Gator Girls)

Gemini 7 (Danger.com)

Genghis Khan: A Dog-Gone Hollywood (Genghis Khan)

Genghis Khan: A Dog Star Is Born (Genghis Khan)

Genies Don't Ride Bicycles (The Adventures of the Bailey School Kids)

The Genius Thieves (Hardy Boys Casefiles)

George and Martha (George and Martha)

George and Martha Back in Town (George and Martha)

A Girl Called Al (Al)

The Girl They Both Loved (Sweet Valley High)

The Girl Who Couldn't Remember (Nancy Drew)

The Girl Who Cried Monster (Goosebumps)

The Girl Who Cried Monster (Goosebumps Presents)

The Girl Who Hated Ponies (Pony Pals)

The Girl Who Knew It All (Casey, Tracey and Company)

The Girls Get Even (Hatford Boys)

Girls' Night Out (Saved by the Bell)

Girls R.U.L.E. (Girls R.U.L.E.)

The Girls' Revenge (Hatford Boys)

Give Me Back My Pony (Pony Pals)

Give the Dog a Bone (Funnybones)

Give Us a Great Big Smile, Rosy Cole (Rosy Cole)

The Glass Cat of Oz (Oz)

Glass Slipper for Rosie (Ballet Slippers)

Glinda of Oz (Oz)

Glory in Danger (Thoroughbred)

Glory in the Flower (Sterling Family)

The Glory of Love (Cassie Perkins)

Glory's Rival (Thoroughbred)

Glory's Triumph (Thoroughbred)

The Gnome King of Oz (Oz)

Go Ahead, Secret Seven (The Secret Seven)

Go Eat Worms! (Goosebumps)

Go Eat Worms! (Goosebumps Presents)

Go Fetch! (Sabrina the Teenage Witch)

Go Fish (Thomas and Grandfather)

Go for It, Patti! (Paxton Cheerleaders)

Go for the Gold (Gymnasts)

Go for the Gold! (The Secret World of Alex Mack)

Go to Sleep, Dear Dragon (Dear Dragon)

Go to the Hoop! (Angel Park Hoop Stars)

Go to Your Tomb—Right Now! (Ghosts of Fear Street)

Goat in the Garden (Animal Ark)

The Goblin's Birthday Party (Mercer Mayer's Critters of the Night)

Goggles (Peter)

Going for the Gold (Silver Blades)

Going, Going, Gone! (Saved by the Bell)

Going on Twelve (Kobie Roberts)

Going to Town (Little House: My First Little House Books)

Going West (Little House: My First Little House Books)

The Gold Dust Letters (Investigators of the Unknown)

Gold Medal Horse (The Saddle Club)

Gold Medal Mystery (Short Stirrup Club)

Gold Medal Rider (The Saddle Club)

The Gold Medal Secret (Choose Your Own Adventure)

The Gold Miner's Rescue (Trailblazers)

Gold Rush Fever! (The Secret World of Alex Mack)

The Gold Train Bandits (American Adventure)

The Golden Angel (Forever Angels)

Golden Bees of Tulami (Dogtown Ghetto)

The Golden Globe (Star Wars Junior Jedi Knights)

The Golden Name Day (Nancy Bruce)

Goliath and the Burglar (David and Goliath)

Goliath and the Buried Treasure (David and Goliath)

Goliath and the Cub Scouts (David and Goliath)

Goliath and the Dognappers (David and Goliath)

Goliath and the School Bully (David and Goliath)

Goliath at Sports Day (David and Goliath)

Goliath at the Dog Show (David and Goliath)

Goliath at the Seaside (David and Goliath)

Goliath Gets a Job (David and Goliath)

Goliath Goes to Summer School (David and Goliath)

Goliath in the Snow (David and Goliath)

Goliath on Vacation (David and Goliath)

Goliath's Birthday (David and Goliath)

Goliath's Christmas (David and Goliath)

Goliath's Easter Parade (David and Goliath)

The Golly Sisters Go West (Golly Sisters)

The Golly Sisters Ride Again (Golly Sisters)

Gom on Windy Mountain (Tales of Gom in the Legends of Ulm)

Gondola to Danger (Miss Mallard)

Good-Bye, Elizabeth (Sweet Valley University)

Good-Bye, Eva? (Sweet Valley Kids)

Good-Bye, Mrs. Otis (Sweet Valley Kids)

Good-bye Pony (Pony Pals)

Good-bye Stacey, Good-bye (Baby-sitters Club)

Good-Bye to Love (Sweet Valley University)

Good Charlotte (Miss Know It All)

The Good Day Mice (Miss Know It All)

Good Dog, Bonita (Friends and Amigos)

Good Dog, Carl (Carl)

Good Driving, Amelia Bedelia (Amelia Bedelia)

The Good Fortunes Gang (Cousins Quartet)

Good Luck, Ronald Morgan (Ronald Morgan)

Good Old Secret Seven (The Secret Seven)

Good Switch, Bad Switch (Sabrina the Teenage Witch)

The Good, the Bad and the Goofy (Time Warp Trio)

Good Work, Amelia Bedelia (Amelia Bedelia)

Good Work, Secret Seven (The Secret Seven)

Goodbye, Arnold! (Webster and Arnold)

Goodbye House (Moonbear)

Goodbye, Middle School (Sweet Valley Twins Super Edition)

Goodbye, Sweet Prince (Christy)

The Goofy Gamble (Stars)

The Gorgon Slayer (World of Adventure)

Gorgonzola Zombies in the Park (Sam and Robert)

Gossip War (Sweet Valley Twins)

Got Game? (Patrick's Pals)

Grampa in Oz (Oz)

Grand Canyon Odyssey (Choose Your Own Adventure)

Grandaddy and Janetta (Grandaddy)

Grandaddy's Place (Grandaddy)

Grandaddy's Stars (Grandaddy)

The Grandma Mix-Up (Grandma)

Grandmas at Bat (Grandma)

Grandmas at the Lake (Grandma)

The Grandma's Attic Story Book (Grandma's Attic)

Grandma's Garden (Seasons with Grandma)

Grandma's House (Seasons with Grandma)

Grandma's Promise (Seasons with Grandma)

Grandma's Smile (Seasons with Grandma)

Halloween Parade (Kids in Ms. Coleman's Class)

The Halloween Party (Choose Your Own Nightmare)

Halloween Rain (Buffy, the Vampire Slayer)

Halloween War (Sweet Valley Kids)

Halloween with Morris and Boris (Morris and Boris)

Halloweird (Eerie Indiana)

The Hand of the Necromancer (Johnny Dixon)

Handy Mandy in Oz (Oz)

Hang On, Hopper! (Hopper)

Hang Time (Super Hoops)

The Hangman's Ghost Trick (Trick Books)

Hank the Cowdog (Hank the Cowdog)

Hannah and the Daring Escape (Best Friends)

Hannah and the Snowy Hideaway (Best Friends)

Hannah and the Special Fourth of July (Best Friends)

Hannah's Fancy Notions (Once Upon America)

Hannah's Secret (Nancy Drew Notebooks)

The Happiest Ending (Rinko)

Happily Ever After (Camp Sunnyside)

Happily Ever After (Sweet Valley High)

Happy Birthday Addy! (American Girls: Addy)

Happy Birthday Anna, Sorpresa! (Friends and Amigos)

Happy Birthday, Danny and the Dinosaur! (Danny and the Dinosaur)

Happy Birthday, Dear Beany (Beany Malone)

Happy Birthday, Dear Dragon (Dear Dragon)

Happy Birthday, Dolores (Duncan and Dolores)

Happy Birthday, Eeyore! (Winnie the Pooh First Readers)

Happy Birthday, Felicity! (American Girls: Felicity)

Happy Birthday, Henrietta (Henrietta)

Happy Birthday, Jesse Bear (Jesse Bear)

Happy Birthday, Josefina! (American Girls: Josefina)

Happy Birthday, Kirsten! (American Girls: Kirsten)

Happy Birthday, Maisy (Maisy the Mouse)

Happy Birthday, Mole and Troll (Mole and Troll)

Happy Birthday, Molly! (American Girls: Molly)

Happy Birthday, Moon (Moonbear)

Happy Birthday, Ronald Morgan (Ronald Morgan)

Happy Birthday, Rotten Ralph (Rotten Ralph)

Happy Birthday, Samantha! (American Girls: Samantha)

Happy Easter, Dear Dragon (Dear Dragon)

Happy Hauntings (Ghosts of Fear Street)

Happy Holidays, Jessi (Baby-sitters Club)

Happy Mother's Day, Lila (Sweet Valley Twins)

The Happy Orpheline (Orphelines)

Happy Valentine's Day, Emma! (Emma)

Hard Choices (Sweet Valley High)

Hard Times (Once Upon America)

Hard Times on the Prairie (Little House Chapter Books)

Harold and Chester in Creepy-Crawly Birthday (Bunnicula)

Harold and Chester in Hot Fudge (Bunnicula)

Harold and Chester in Rabbit-Cadabra (Bunnicula)

Harold and Chester in Scared Silly (Bunnicula)

Harold and Chester in the Fright Before Christmas (Bunnicula)

Harold and the Purple Crayon (Harold and the Purple Crayon)

Harold's ABC (Harold and the Purple Crayon)

Harold's Circus (Harold and the Purple Crayon)

Harold's Fairy Tale (Harold and the Purple Crayon)

Harold's Trip to the Sky (Harold and the Purple Crayon)

Harriet and the Crocodiles (Harriet the Troublemaker)

Harriet and the Garden (Harriet)

Harriet and the Haunted School (Harriet the Troublemaker)

Harriet and the Robot (Harriet the Troublemaker)

Harriet and the Roller Coaster (Harriet)

Harriet and Walt (Harriet)

Harriet at Home (Harriet)

Harriet at Play (Harriet)

Harriet at School (Harriet)

Harriet at Work (Harriet)

Harriet Goes to the Circus (Harriet)

Harriet Reads Signs and More Signs (Harriet)

Harriet the Spy (Harriet M. Welsh)

Harriet's Halloween Candy (Harriet)

Harriet's Recital (Harriet)

Harry and Arney (Kane Family)

Harry and Chicken (Harry and Chicken)

Harry and the Lady Next Door (Harry the Dirty Dog)

Harry by the Sea (Harry the Dirty Dog)

Harry Cat's Pet Puppy (Chester Cricket)

Harry Dresses Himself (Harry the Hippo)

Harry Gets an Uncle (Harry)

Harry in Trouble (Harry)

Harry Kitten and Tucker Mouse (Chester Cricket)

Harry on Vacation (Harry and Chicken)

Harry the Dirty Dog (Harry the Dirty Dog)

Harry the Explorer (Harry and Chicken)

Harry's Birthday (Harry)

Harry's Dog (Harry)

Harry's Mealtime Mess (Harry the Hippo)

Harry's Mom (Harry)

Harry's Pony (Harry)

Harry's Sandbox Surprise (Harry the Hippo)

Harry's Visit (Harry)

The Harvest (Buffy, the Vampire Slayer)

Harvest Moon (Sabrina the Teenage Witch)

Harvey's Horrible Snake Disaster (Harvey)

Harvey's Marvelous Monkey Mystery (Harvey)

Harvey's Mystifying Raccoon Mix-Up (Harvey)

Harvey's Wacky Parrot Adventure (Harvey)

Hasta La Vista, Blarney (Carmen Sandiego Mysteries)

A Hat for Minerva Louise (Minerva Louise)

Hatchet (Brian Robeson)

Hatchling (Dinotopia)

The Hateful Plateful Trick (Trick Books)

Hattie Be Quiet, Hattie Be Good (Hattie Rabbit)

Hattie Rabbit (Hattie Rabbit)

Hattie, Tom, and the Chicken Witch (Hattie Rabbit)

The Haunted Baby (Choose Your Own Nightmare)

The Haunted Bridge (Nancy Drew)

The Haunted Cabin Mystery (Boxcar Children)

Her Honor, Katie Shannon (Fabulous Five)

Herbie Jones (Herbie Jones)

Herbie Jones and Hamburger Head (Herbie Jones)

Herbie Jones and the Birthday Showdown (Herbie Jones)

Herbie Jones and the Class Gift (Herbie Jones)

Herbie Jones and the Dark Attic (Herbie Jones)

Herbie Jones and the Monster Ball (Herbie Jones)

Hercules Doesn't Pull Teeth (The Adventures of the Bailey School Kids)

Here Come the Bridesmaids (Baby-sitters Club Super Specials)

Here Comes Santa Claws (Graveyard School)

Here Comes the Brand-New Me (Full House: Stephanie)

Here Comes the Bride (Sweet Valley University)

Here Comes Zelda Claus, and Other Holiday Disasters (Zelda)

Here We Go Again (B.Y. Times)

Here's Hermione (Rosy Cole)

Here's Penny (Penny)

Here's Pippa Again! (Pippa Mouse)

Here's Spot (Spot)

Hermit Dan (Liza, Bill, and Jed)

The Hero and the Crown (Damar Chronicles)

Hero Over Here (Once Upon America)

He's All That (Sister Sister)

He's Watching You (Sweet Valley University Thriller Editions)

Hey, New Kid! (Cody)

Hey, Remember Fat Glenda? (Fat Glenda)

Hey Waiter! (Baker's Dozen)

Hi, Cat! (Peter)

The Hidden Beast (Spooksville)

The Hidden Harbor Mystery (Hardy Boys)

The Hidden Inheritance (Nancy Drew)

The Hidden Jewel (Trailblazers)

Hidden Meanings (Nancy Drew Files)

The Hidden Staircase (Nancy Drew)

The Hidden Treasures (Nancy Drew Notebooks)

Hidden Valley of Oz (Oz)

The Hidden Window Mystery (Nancy Drew)

Hide-and-Seek Elmer (Elmer)

Hide and Seek with Anthony Ant (Anthony Ant)

Hide and Shriek (Ghosts of Fear Street)

Hide and Shriek II (Ghosts of Fear Street)

High Country Ambush (American Adventure)

High Flyer! (The Secret World of Alex Mack)

The High Hills (Brambly Hedge)

High Horse (The Saddle Club)

The High King (Prydain Chronicles)

High Marks for Malice (Nancy Drew Files)

High Risk (Nancy Drew Files)

The High School War (Sweet Valley High)

High-Speed Showdown (Hardy Boys)

High-Wire Act (Hardy Boys Casefiles)

High-Wire Henry (Henry the Cat)

High Wizardry (Wizardry)

Higher on the Door (James Stevenson's Autobiographical Stories)

Highest Score (Star Trek: Deep Space Nine)

Highway Robbery (Carmen Sandiego Mysteries)

Highway Robbery (Hardy Boys Casefiles)

Hijacked! (Choose Your Own Adventure)

Hip Hop Till You Drop (Full House: Stephanie)

His Secret Past (Sweet Valley University)

Hit and Run (Fabulous Five)

Hit and Run Holiday (Nancy Drew Files)

The Hit-Away Kid (Peach Street Mudders)

Ho, Ho Benjamin, Feliz Navidád (Friends and Amigos)

The Hoax on You (Sam and Dave Mysteries)

Hobby (Young Merlin Trilogy)

Hobbyhorse (The Saddle Club)

Hobie Hanson, Greatest Hero of the Mall (Hobie Hanson)

Hobie Hanson, You're Weird (Hobie Hanson)

The Hockey Trick (Trick Books)

Hocus Pocus! (The Secret World of Alex Mack)

Hola, California! (¡Chana!)

Hold on Tight (Sierra Jensen)

Holiday for Edith and the Bears (The Lonely Doll)

A Holiday for Noah (Noah)

Holiday Horse (The Saddle Club)

Holiday Mischief (Sweet Valley Twins Super Edition)

Holiday Time (Kids in Ms. Coleman's Class)

The Holly Hudnut Admiration Society (Stars)

Hollywood Hook-Up (Moesha)

Home for Christmas (Sweet Valley University)

A Home for Melanie (Thoroughbred)

The Home Front (The American Adventure)

The Home Run Trick (Trick Books)

Homecoming (Tillerman Cycle)

Homegirl on the Range (Sister Sister)

Homer Sweet Homer (Wishbone Adventures)

Honestly, Katie John (Katie John)

Honey Bunny Funnybunny (P.J. Funnybunny)

The Hooded Hawk Mystery (Hardy Boys)

Hoof Beat (The Saddle Club)

Hook 'Em Snotty! (World of Adventure)

Hooray for Snail (Snail)

Hooray for the Golly Sisters! (Golly Sisters)

Hopper (Hopper)

Hopper Hunts for Spring (Hopper)

Hopper's Easter Surprise (Hopper)

Hopper's Treetop Adventure (Hopper)

Hoppin' Halloween (¡Chana!)

Hoppy Easter (Holiday Friends)

Horrible Harry and the Ant Invasion (Horrible Harry)

Horrible Harry and the Christmas Surprise (Horrible Harry)

Horrible Harry and the Drop of Doom (Horrible Harry)

Horrible Harry and the Dungeon (Horrible Harry)

Horrible Harry and the Green Slime (Horrible Harry)

Horrible Harry and the Kickball Wedding (Horrible Harry)

Horrible Harry and the Purple People (Horrible Harry)

Horrible Harry in Room 2B (Horrible Harry)

Horrible Harry Moves Up to Third Grade (Horrible Harry)

Horrible Harry's Secret (Horrible Harry)

The Horror at Camp Jellyjam (Goosebumps)

Horror Hotel (Ghosts of Fear Street)

Horror House (Choose Your Own Adventure)

Horror of High Ridge (Choose Your Own Adventure)

I

I Left My Sneakers in Dimension X (Alien Adventures)

I Live in Your Basement! (Goosebumps)

I Love You, Dear Dragon (Dear Dragon)

I Love You, Grumpy Bunny (Grumpy Bunny)

I Meant to Tell You (James Stevenson's Autobiographical Stories)

I Need You, Dear Dragon (Dear Dragon)

I Should Worry, I Should Care (Molly)

I Spy! (The Secret World of Alex Mack)

I Sure Am Glad to See You, Blackboard Bear (Blackboard Bear)

I Survived on Bus Five (Kids on Bus 5)

I Thought My Soul Would Rise and Fly (Dear America)

I Want a Pony (Pony Pals)

I Was a Sixth-Grade Zombie (Ghosts of Fear Street)

The Ice-Cold Case (Hardy Boys)

The Ice Cream Scoop (Nancy Drew Notebooks)

Ice Dreams (Silver Blades Figure Eights)

Ice Magic (Silver Blades)

The Ice Princess (Silver Blades)

The Ice Queen (China Tate)

If I Die Before I Wake (Sweet Valley Twins)

If Looks Could Kill (Nancy Drew Files)

If Looks Could Kill (Sweet Valley Twins)

If You Dream a Dragon (Mercer Mayer's Critters of the Night)

If You Only Knew (The Friendship Ring)

If You Say So, Claude (Claude)

Ike and Mama and the Block Wedding (Ike and Mama)

Ike and Mama and the Once-a-Year Suit (Ike and Mama)

Ike and Mama and the Once-in-a-Lifetime Movie (Ike and Mama)

Ike and Mama and the Trouble at School (Ike and Mama)

I'll Fix Anthony (Alexander)

The Ill-Made Knight (The Once and Future King)

I'll Meet You at the Cucumbers (Cucumbers Trilogy)

I'll Pulverize You, William (Cousins Club)

Illegal Procedure (Hardy Boys Casefiles)

Illusions of Evil (Nancy Drew Files)

The Illyrian Adventure (Vesper Holly)

I'm Dracula, Who Are You? (Funny Firsts)

I'm Out of My Body . . . Please Leave a Message (The Zack Files)

Ima Come Home (Baker's Dozen)

Impeach Screech! (Saved by the Bell)

The Impossible Lisa Barnes (Anika Scott)

Impossible, Possum (Possum Family)

Imprisoned in the Golden City (Trailblazers)

In Grandma's Attic (Grandma's Attic)

In Hot Pursuit! (The Secret World of Alex Mack)

In Love Again (Sweet Valley High)

In Love with a Prince (Sweet Valley High)

In Love with Mandy (Unicorn Club)

In Love with the Enemy (Sweet Valley High)

In Pursuit of Picasso (Cyber.kdz)

In Search of Scum (Cyber.kdz)

In Search of the Black Rose (Nancy Drew)

In Self-Defense (Hardy Boys Casefiles)

In the Circle of Time (Time Trilogy)

In the Dinosaur's Paw (Kids of the Polk Street School)

In the Face of Danger (Orphan Train Adventures)

In the Groove (NASCAR Pole Position Adventures)

In the Keep of Time (Time Trilogy)

In the Land of the Big Red Apple (Little House: The Rose Years)

In the Nick of Time (McGee and Me!)

In the Rain with Baby Duck (Baby Duck)

In the Shadow of the Tower (Dana Girls)

In the Spotlight (Heart Beats)

In the Spotlight (Silver Blades)

In the Zone (Super Hoops)

In Trouble Again, Zelda Hammersmith? (Zelda)

In Your Dreams (Sierra Jensen)

In Your Face! (Patrick's Pals)

In Your Face! (Super Hoops)

Inca Gold (Choose Your Own Adventure)

Incognito Mosquito Flies Again (Incognito Mosquito)

Incognito Mosquito Makes History (Incognito Mosquito)

Incognito Mosquito, Private Insective (Incognito Mosquito)

Incognito Mosquito Takes to the Air (Incognito Mosquito)

Incredible Madame Jessica (Sweet Valley Twins)

The Incredible Shrinking Kid! (The Weird Zone)

The Incredible Shrinking Stanley (Eerie Indiana)

The Indian in the Cupboard (Indian in the Cupboard)

Inferno of Fear (Hardy Boys Casefiles)

The Infinity Clue (Hardy Boys)

The Initiation (Nightmare Hall)

The Innocent (The Outer Limits)

Inside Outside Upside Down (Berenstain Bears)

The Inside Story (Baker's Dozen)

Inside UFO 54-40 (Choose Your Own Adventure)

An Instinct for Trouble (Nancy Drew Files)

The Internet Escapade (Casebusters)

Into the Jaws of Doom (Goosebumps: Give Yourself Goosebumps)

Into the Zonk Zone! (Time Surfers)

Into Thin Air (Nancy Drew Files)

The Invaders (The Outer Limits)

Invaders from the Big Screen (Goosebumps: Give Yourself Goosebumps)

Invaders from Within (Choose Your Own Adventure)

Invaders of Planet Earth (Choose Your Own Adventure)

The Invasion (Animorphs)

Invasion of the Appleheads (Deadtime Stories)

Invasion of the Body Squeezers, Part 1 (Goosebumps Series 2000)

Invasion of the Body Squeezers, Part 2 (Goosebumps Series 2000)

Invasion of the Fast Food (Lunchroom)

Invasion of the No-Ones (Spooksville)

The Invisible Intruder (Nancy Drew)

The Invisible Man and Other Cases (Einstein Anderson)

Invisible Stanley (Stanley)

An Invitation to Dance (Girlhood Journeys: Marie)

The Irish Rebellion (Young Indiana Jones Chronicles: Choose Your Own Adventure)

Irish Red, Son of Big Red (Red)

The Iron Sceptre (Archives of Anthropos)

Is That Really You, Amy? (Here Come the Brownies)

Is Underground (Wolves Chronicles)

Isabelle and Little Orphan Frannie (Isabelle)

Isabelle Shows Her Stuff (Isabelle)

Isabelle the Itch (Isabelle)

Island Dreamer (Christy Miller)

The Island Light (Voyage to the Bunny Planet)

Island of Doom (Choose Your Own Nightmare)

Island of Secrets (Nancy Drew Files)

Island of the Grass King (Anatole)

Island of Time (Choose Your Own Adventure)

Island Rose (Magic Attic Club)

The Island Stallion (Island Stallion)

The Island Stallion Races (Island Stallion)

The Island Stallion's Courage (Island Stallion)

It Came from Beneath the Sink! (Goosebumps)

It Came from the Deep (Deadtime Stories)

It Can't Happen Here (Sweet Valley Twins)

It Happened at Camp Pine Tree (Choose Your Own Nightmare)

It's a Dog's Life (Hank the Cowdog)

It's a Fiesta, Ben (Friends and Amigos)

It's About Time, Jesse Bear and Other Rhymes (Jesse Bear)

It's Circus Time, Dear Dragon (Dear Dragon)

It's George! (First Grade)

It's Halloween Time, Dear Dragon (Dear Dragon)

It's Not Easy Being a Bunny (P.J. Funnybunny)

It's Not Easy Being George (The Adam Joshua Capers)

It's Only a Nightmare (Goosebumps: Give Yourself Goosebumps)

It's Only Goodbye (Once Upon America)

It's the Thought That Counts (Saved by the Bell)

Ivanhoe (Wishbone Classics)

I've Got a Secret (Full House: Michelle)

J

Jack and the Beanstalker (Graveyard School)

The Jack-o'-Lantern That Ate My Brother (What Ate Who)

Jack Pumpkinhead of Oz (Oz)

Jafta (Jafta)

Jafta and the Wedding (Jafta)

Jafta: The Homecoming (Jafta)

Jafta: The Journey (Jafta)

Jafta: The Town (Jafta)

Jafta's Father (Jafta)

Jafta's Mother (Jafta)

Jamaica and Brianna (Jamaica)

Jamaica Tag-Along (Jamaica)

Jamaica's Blue Marker (Jamaica)

Jamaica's Find (Jamaica)

Jamie (The Elliott Cousins)

Jana to the Rescue (Fabulous Five)

Janet's Thingamajigs (Jimmy and Janet)

A Jar of Dreams (Rinko)

Jasmine and the Jumping Pony (Pony Tails)

Jasmine Helps a Foal (Pony Tails)

Jasmine Trots Ahead (Pony Tails)

Jasmine's Christmas Ride (Pony Tails)

Jasmine's First Horse Show (Pony Tails)

Jealous Lies (Sweet Valley High)

The Jedera Adventure (Vesper Holly)

Jedi Bounty (Star Wars Young Jedi Knights)

Jedi Under Siege (Star Wars Young Jedi Knights)

Jeepers Creepers (House of Horrors)

Jeffrey's Ghost and the Fifth Grade Dragon (Jeffrey's Ghost)

Jeffrey's Ghost and the Leftover Baseball Team (Jeffrey's Ghost)

Jeffrey's Ghost and the Ziffel Fair Mystery (Jeffrey's Ghost)

Jen Starts Over (B.Y. Times)

Jennifer Murdley's Toad (Magic Shop)

Jenny and the Cat Club; a Collection of Favorite Stories About Jenny Linsky (Jenny and the Cat Club)

Jenny Archer, Author (Jenny Archer)

Jenny Archer to the Rescue (Jenny Archer)

Jenny Goes to Sea (Jenny and the Cat Club)

Jenny's Adopted Brothers (Jenny and the Cat Club)

Jenny's Bedside Book (Jenny and the Cat Club)

Jenny's Birthday Book (Jenny and the Cat Club)

Jenny's First Party (Jenny and the Cat Club)

Jenny's Moonlight Adventure (Jenny and the Cat Club)

Jeremy Thatcher, Dragon Hatcher (Magic Shop)

Jess and the Fireplug Caper (Twelve Candles Club)

Jesse Bear, What Will You Wear? (Jesse Bear)

Jessi and the Awful Secret (Baby-sitters Club)

Jessi and the Bad Baby-Sitter (Baby-sitters Club)

Jessi and the Dance School Phantom (Baby-sitters Club)

Jessi and the Jewel Thieves (Baby-sitters Club Mysteries)

Jessi and the Superbrat (Baby-sitters Club)

Jessi and the Troublemaker (Baby-sitters Club)

Jessi Ramsey, Pet-Sitter (Baby-sitters Club)

Jessica Against Bruce (Sweet Valley High)

Jessica and Elizabeth Show (Sweet Valley Kids)

Jessica and the Brat Attack (Sweet Valley Twins)

Jessica and the Earthquake (Sweet Valley Twins)

Jessica and the Jumbo Fish (Sweet Valley Kids)

Jessica and the Money Mix-Up (Sweet Valley Twins)

Jessica and the Secret Star (Sweet Valley Twins)

Jessica and the Spelling Bee Surprise (Sweet Valley Kids)

Jessica Gets Spooked (Sweet Valley Kids)

Jessica on Stage (Sweet Valley Twins)

Jessica Plays Cupid (Sweet Valley Kids)

Jessica Plus Jessica Equals Trouble (Sweet Valley Kids)

Jessica Quits the Squad (Sweet Valley High)

Jessica Saves the Trees (Sweet Valley Twins)

Jessica Takes Charge (Sweet Valley Twins)

Jessica Takes Manhattan (Sweet Valley High)

Jessica the Babysitter (Sweet Valley Kids)

Jessica the Genius (Sweet Valley High)

Jessica the Nerd (Sweet Valley Twins)

Jessica the Rock Star (Sweet Valley Twins)

Jessica the Thief (Sweet Valley Twins)

Jessica the TV Star (Sweet Valley Kids)

Jessica's Animal Instincts (Sweet Valley Twins Super Edition)

Jessica's Bad Idea (Sweet Valley Twins)

Jessica's Big Mistake (Sweet Valley Kids)

Jessica's Blind Date (Sweet Valley Twins)

Jessica's Cat Trick (Sweet Valley Kids)

Jessica's Cookie Disaster (Sweet Valley Twins)

Jessica's Dream Date (Unicorn Club)

Jessica's First Kiss (Sweet Valley Twins Super Edition)

Jessica's Lucky Millions (Sweet Valley Twins)

Jessica's Mermaid (Sweet Valley Kids)

Jessica's Monster Nightmare (Sweet Valley Kids)

Jessica's New Look (Sweet Valley Twins)

Jessica's No Angel (Sweet Valley Twins Super Edition)

Jessica's Older Guy (Sweet Valley High)

Jessica's Secret (Sweet Valley Twins)

Jessica's Secret Diary (Sweet Valley High)

Jessica's Secret Diary Volume II (Sweet Valley High)

Jessica's Secret Diary Volume III (Sweet Valley High)

Jessica's Secret Friend (Sweet Valley Kids)

Jessica's Secret Love (Sweet Valley High)

Jessica's Snobby Club (Sweet Valley Kids)

Jessica's Unburied Treasure (Sweet Valley Kids)

Jessica's Zoo Adventure (Sweet Valley Kids)

Jessi's Baby-Sitter (Baby-sitters Club)

Jessi's Big Break (Baby-sitters Club)

Jessi's Gold Medal (Baby-sitters Club)

Jessi's Horrible Prank (Baby-sitters Club)

Jessi's Secret Language (Baby-sitters Club)

Jessi's Wish (Baby-sitters Club)

Jester in the Back Court (Alden All Stars)

The Jester's Quest (Winds of Light)

The Jewel Princess and the Missing Crown (Jewel Kingdom)

Jilly the Kid (Petsitters Club)

Jim Meets the Thing (First Grade)

Jimmy's Boa and the Big Splash Birthday Bash (Jimmy's Boa)

Jimmy's Boa Bounces Back (Jimmy's Boa)

Jim's Dog Muffins (First Grade)

Jina Rides to Win (Riding Academy)

Jina's Pain-in-the-Neck Pony (Riding Academy)

The Jingle Bell Jam (Lincoln Lions Band)

Jo Makes a Friend (Portraits of Little Women)

Joan of Arc (Wishbone Classics)

JoAnn and the Surprise Party (Here Come the Brownies)

A Job for Jenny Archer (Jenny Archer)

Johnny Lion's Bad Day (Johnny Lion)

Johnny Lion's Book (Johnny Lion)

Johnny Lion's Rubber Boots (Johnny Lion)

Johnny May (Johnny May)

Johnny May Grows Up (Johnny May)

The Joker's Revenge (Nancy Drew)

Jo's Story (Portraits of Little Women)

Jo's Troubled Heart (Little Women Journals)

Josefina Learns a Lesson (American Girls: Josefina)

Josefina Saves the Day (American Girls: Josefina)

Josefina's Surprise (American Girls: Josefina)

Joshua T. Bates in Trouble Again (Joshua T. Bates)

Joshua T. Bates Takes Charge (Joshua T. Bates)

Josie Smith (Josie Smith)

Josie Smith and Eileen (Josie Smith)

Josie Smith at School (Josie Smith)

Josie Smith at the Market (Josie Smith)

Josie Smith at the Seashore (Josie Smith)

Josie Smith in Hospital (Josie Smith)

Josie Smith's Christmas (Josie Smith)

The Journal of James Edmond Pease (My Name Is America)

The Journal of William Thomas Emerson (My Name Is America)

The Journey of Wishes (Spirit Flyer)

Journey to Stonehenge (Choose Your Own Adventure)

A Journey to the Center of the Earth (Wishbone Classics)

A Journey to the New World (Dear America)

Journey Under the Sea (Choose Your Own Adventure)

Judge Benjamin: Superdog (Judge Benjamin)

Judge Benjamin: The Superdog Gift (Judge Benjamin)

Judge Benjamin: The Superdog Rescue (Judge Benjamin)

Judge Benjamin: The Superdog Secret (Judge Benjamin)

Judge Benjamin: The Superdog Surprise (Judge Benjamin)

Julia and the Hand of God (Julia Redfern)

Julian, Dream Doctor (Julian and Huey)

Julian, Secret Agent (Julian and Huey)

Julian's Glorious Summer (Julian and Huey)

Julia's Magic (Julia Redfern)

Julie the Karate Kid (Sweet Valley Kids)

Julius, the Baby of the World (Lilly)

July (James Stevenson's Autobiographical Stories)

Jump Ship to Freedom (The Arabus Family Saga)

Jump Shot Detectives (Hardy Boys: Frank and Joe Hardy: The Clues Brothers)

Jumping Lessons (Horseshoes)

Jumping to Conclusions (Sweet Valley Twins)

The Jungle Pyramid (Hardy Boys)

Junie B. Jones and a Little Monkey Business (Junie B. Jones)

Junie B. Jones and Her Big Fat Mouth (Junie B. Jones)

Junie B. Jones and Some Sneaky Peeky Spying (Junie B. Jones)

Junie B. Jones and That Meanie Jim's Birthday (Junie B. Jones)

Junie B. Jones and the Stupid Smelly Bus (Junie B. Jones)

Junie B. Jones and the Yucky Blucky Fruitcake (Junie B. Jones)

Junie B. Jones Has a Monster Under Her Bed (Junie B. Jones)

Junie B. Jones Is a Beauty Shop Guy (Junie B. Jones)

Junie B. Jones Is a Party Animal (Junie B. Jones)

Junie B. Jones Is Not a Crook (Junie B. Jones)

Junie B. Jones Loves Handsome Warren (Junie B. Jones)

Junie B. Jones Smells Something Fishy (Junie B. Jones)

Junkyard Jitters! (The Secret World of Alex Mack)

Just Friends (Clearwater Crossing)

Just in Time (Ghostwriter)

Just Plain Al (Al)

Just Tell Me When We're Dead (Mary Rose)

Just the Thing for Geraldine (Possum Family)

Justice and Her Brothers (Justice Trilogy)

K

Kabumpo in Oz (Oz)

The Kachina Doll Mystery (Nancy Drew)

The Karate Class Mystery (Invisible Inc.)

The Karate Clue (Hardy Boys: Frank and Joe Hardy: The Clues Brothers)

Karen, Hannie, and Nancy (Baby-sitters Little Sister Super Specials)

Karen's Accident (Baby-sitters Little Sister)

Karen's Angel (Baby-sitters Little Sister)

Karen's Baby (Baby-sitters Little Sister Super Specials)

Karen's Telephone Trouble (Baby-sitters Little Sister)

Karen's Toothache (Baby-sitters Little Sister)

Karen's Toys (Baby-sitters Little Sister)

Karen's Treasure (Baby-sitters Little Sister)

Karen's Tuba (Baby-sitters Little Sister)

Karen's Turkey Day (Baby-sitters Little Sister)

Karen's Twin (Baby-sitters Little Sister)

Karen's Two Families (Baby-sitters Little Sister)

Karen's Unicorn (Baby-sitters Little Sister)

Karen's Wedding (Baby-sitters Little Sister)

Karen's Wish (Baby-sitters Little Sister Super Specials)

Karen's Witch (Baby-sitters Little Sister)

Karen's Worst Day (Baby-sitters Little Sister)

Kate Be Late (Miss Know It All)

Kate Heads West (Kate)

Kate on the Coast (Kate)

Kate the Boss (Sleepover Friends)

Kate the Winner! (Sleepover Friends)

Kate's Box (Kate)

Kate's Camp-Out (Sleepover Friends)

Kate's Car (Kate)

Kate's Crush (Sleepover Friends)

Kate's Quilt (Kate)

Kate's Sleepover Disaster (Sleepover Friends)

Kate's Snowman (Kate)

Kate's Surprise (Sleepover Friends)

Kate's Surprise Visitor (Sleepover Friends)

Kathy and the Babysitting Hassle (Best Friends)

Kathy's New Brother (Best Friends)

Katie Can (Katie)

Katie Couldn't (Katie)

Katie Did It (Katie)

Katie John (Katie John)

Katie John and Heathcliff (Katie John)

Katie Kicks Off (Never Sink Nine)

Katie Morag and the Big Boy Cousins (Katie Morag)

Katie Morag and the Grand Concert (Katie Morag)

Katie Morag and the New Pier (Katie Morag)

Katie Morag and the Tiresome Ted (Katie Morag)

Katie Morag and the Two Grandmothers (Katie Morag)

Katie Morag and the Wedding (Katie Morag)

Katie Morag Delivers the Mail (Katie Morag)

Katie Steals the Show (Camp Sunnyside)

Katie's Angel (Forever Angels)

Katie's Big Move (Junior Gymnasts)

Katie's Dating Tips (Fabulous Five)

Katie's Gold Medal (Junior Gymnasts)

Keep Out, Claudia! (Baby-sitters Club)

Keep Out, Pony! (Pony Pals)

Keep the Faith (Clearwater Crossing)

The Keeping Days (Sterling Family)

Keeping It Real (Moesha)

Keeping Secrets (Orphan Train Adventures)

Keeping Secrets (Sweet Valley Twins)

Keisha Discovers Harlem (Magic Attic Club)

Keisha Leads the Way (Magic Attic Club)

Keisha the Fairy Snow Queen (Magic Attic Club)

Keisha to the Rescue (Magic Attic Club)

Keisha's Maze Mystery (Magic Attic Club)

Kelly's Hero (Saved by the Bell)

Kenobi's Blade (Star Wars Junior Jedi Knights)

The Kestrel (Westmark)

Key to the Golden Dog (Wishbone Mysteries)

The Key to the Indian (Indian in the Cupboard)

Key to the Treasure (Liza, Bill, and Jed)

Kickoff Time (Angel Park Soccer Stars)

The Kid Next Door (The Adam Joshua Capers)

The Kid Next Door, and Other Headaches (The Adam Joshua Capers)

Kidnapped! (Choose Your Own Adventure)

Kidnapped (Nightmare Hall)

Kidnapped! (Sweet Valley High)

Kidnapped by a Cult (Sweet Valley High)

Kidnapped by River Rats (Trailblazers)

Killer at Sea (Sweet Valley University Thriller Editions)

Killer Clown of Kings County (Bone Chillers)

Killer Computer (Spinetinglers)

A Killer on Board (Sweet Valley High)

Killer Virus (Choose Your Own Adventure)

A Killing in the Market (Hardy Boys Casefiles)

Kimberly Rides Again (Unicorn Club)

The King and Us (Bad News Ballet)

King Arthur (King Arthur)

King Arthur and the Round Table (King Arthur)

Kirsten Learns a Lesson (American Girls: Kirsten)

Kirsten Saves the Day (American Girls: Kirsten)

Kirsten's Surprise (American Girls: Kirsten)

Kiss and Tell (Nancy Drew Files)

A Kiss Before Dying (Sweet Valley High)

A Kiss for Little Bear (Little Bear)

Kiss of a Killer (Sweet Valley High)

Kiss of the Mermaid (Mercer Mayer's Critters of the Night)

Kiss of the Vampire (Sweet Valley University Thriller Editions)

The Kissing Disaster (Fabulous Five)

Kittens in the Kitchen (Animal Ark)

Kitty from the Start (Kitty)

Kitty in High School (Kitty)

Kitty in the Middle (Kitty)

Kitty in the Summer (Kitty)

Klondike Arthur (Arthur the Kid)

The Knight at Dawn (Magic Tree House)

The Knight in Screaming Armor (Goosebumps: Give Yourself Goosebumps)

Knightmare (Strange Matter)

Knights Don't Teach Piano (The Adventures of the Bailey School Kids)

Knights of the Kitchen Table (Time Warp Trio)

Knights of the Round Table (Choose Your Own Adventure)

Knock, Knock . . . You're Dead (House of Horrors)

A Knot in the Grain and Other Stories (Damar Chronicles)

Krissy and the Big Snow (Here Come the Brownies)

Kristy and Mr. Mom (Baby-sitters Club)

Kristy and the Baby Parade (Baby-sitters Club)

Kristy and the Cat Burglar (Baby-sitters Club Mysteries)

Kristy and the Copycat (Baby-sitters Club)

Kristy and the Dirty Diapers (Baby-sitters Club)

Kristy and the Haunted Mansion (Baby-sitters Club Mysteries)

Kristy and the Middle School Vandal (Baby-sitters Club Mysteries)

Kristy and the Missing Child (Baby-sitters Club Mysteries)

Lights Out, Sarah! (Here Come the Brownies)

Lightsabers (Star Wars Young Jedi Knights)

Lila on the Loose (Unicorn Club)

Lila's April Fool (Sweet Valley Kids)

Lila's Birthday Bash (Sweet Valley Kids)

Lila's Christmas Angel (Sweet Valley Kids)

Lila's Haunted House Party (Sweet Valley Kids)

Lila's Little Sister (Unicorn Club)

Lila's Music Video (Sweet Valley Twins)

Lila's New Flame (Sweet Valley High)

Lila's Secret (Sweet Valley Kids)

Lila's Secret Valentine (Sweet Valley Twins Super Edition)

Lila's Story (Sweet Valley High)

Lili the Brave (Children of America)

Lilly's Purple Plastic Purse (Lilly)

Lily Vanessa and the Pet Panic (Twelve Candles Club)

The Limerick Trick (Trick Books)

Linda and the Little White Lies (Best Friends)

Line Drive (Angel Park All Stars)

A Line in the Sand (Dear America)

Line of Fire (Hardy Boys Casefiles)

Line of Fire (Star Trek: The Next Generation: Starfleet Academy)

The Lion, the Witch, and the Wardrobe (Chronicles of Narnia)

Lionel and His Friends (Lionel)

Lionel and Louise (Lionel)

Lionel at Large (Lionel)

Lionel in the Fall (Lionel)

Lionel in the Spring (Lionel)

Lionel in the Summer (Lionel)

Lionel in Winter (Lionel)

Lions at Lunchtime (Magic Tree House)

Listen to the Whippoorwill (Trailblazers)

Little Bear (Little Bear)

Little Bear Lost (Old Bear Stories)

Little Bear's Friend (Little Bear)

Little Bear's Trousers (Old Bear Stories)

Little Bear's Visit (Little Bear)

Little Brown Bear Can Cook! (Little Brown Bear)

Little Brown Bear Gets Dressed (Little Brown Bear)

Little Brown Bear Is Big! (Little Brown Bear)

Little Brown Bear Is Cross (Little Brown Bear)

Little Brown Bear Is Ill (Little Brown Bear)

Little Brown Bear Says No (Little Brown Bear)

Little Brown Bear Takes a Bath (Little Brown Bear)

Little Brown Bear Wakes Up (Little Brown Bear)

Little Brown Bear Wants a Kiss (Little Brown Bear)

Little Brown Bear Won't Eat! (Little Brown Bear)

Little Brown Bear's Bad Days (Little Brown Bear)

Little Brown Bear's Breakfast Egg (Little Brown Bear)

Little Brown Bear's Cold (Little Brown Bear)

Little Brown Bear's Playtime (Little Brown Bear)

Little Brown Bear's Snowball (Little Brown Bear)

Little Brown Bear's Story (Little Brown Bear)

Little Brown Bear's Tricycle (Little Brown Bear)

Little Brown Bear's Walk (Little Brown Bear)

Little Chick's Big Day (Little Chick)

Little Chick's Breakfast (Little Chick)

Little Chick's Friend, Duckling (Little Chick)

Little Chick's Story (Little Chick)

Little Clearing in the Woods (Little House: The Caroline Years)

Little Comic Shop of Horrors (Goosebumps: Give Yourself Goosebumps)

Little Drummer Girls (Sweet Valley Kids)

Little Eddie (Eddie Wilson)

Little Farm in the Ozarks (Little House: The Rose Years)

A Little House Birthday (Little House: My First Little House Books)

Little House Farm Days (Little House Chapter Books)

Little House in Brookfield (Little House: The Caroline Years)

Little House in the Big Woods (Little House)

Little House on Rocky Ridge (Little House: The Rose Years)

Little House on the Prairie (Little House)

Little Magic Shop of Horrors (Deadtime Stories)

Little Miss Stoneybrook . . . and Dawn (Baby-sitters Club)

Little Old Mrs. Pepperpot, and Other Stories (Mrs. Pepperpot)

The Little People (Spooksville)

Little People of the Lost Coast (Eric Sterling, Secret Agent)

Little Pet Shop of Horrors (Bone Chillers)

Little Pet Werewolf (Graveyard School)

Little Polar Bear (Little Polar Bear)

Little Polar Bear and the Brave Little Hare (Little Polar Bear)

Little Polar Bear Finds a Friend (Little Polar Bear)

Little Polar Bear, Take Me Home! (Little Polar Bear)

A Little Prairie House (Little House: My First Little House Books)

Little School of Horrors (Graveyard School)

The Little Silver House (Nancy Bruce)

Little Soup's Birthday (Little Soup)

Little Soup's Bunny (Little Soup)

Little Soup's Hayride (Little Soup)

Little Soup's Turkey (Little Soup)

Little Toot (Little Toot)

Little Toot & the Loch Ness Monster (Little Toot)

Little Toot on the Grand Canal (Little Toot)

Little Toot on the Mississippi (Little Toot)

Little Toot on the Thames (Little Toot)

Little Toot Through the Golden Gate (Little Toot)

Little Town at the Crossroads (Little House: The Caroline Years)

Little Town in the Ozarks (Little House: The Rose Years)

Little Town on the Prairie (Little House)

The Littles (The Littles)

The Littles and the Big Storm (The Littles)

The Littles and the Lost Children (The Littles)

The Littles and the Terrible Tiny Kid (The Littles)

The Littles and the Trash Tinies (The Littles)

The Littles and Their Friends (The Littles)

The Littles Give a Party (The Littles)

The Littles Go Exploring (The Littles)

The Littles Go to School (The Littles)

The Littles Have a Wedding (The Littles)

The Littles Take a Trip (The Littles)

The Littles to the Rescue (The Littles)

Live from Cedar Hills! (¡Chana!)

The Living Dead (Spooksville)

Lizard People (Spinetinglers)

Liza's Lucky Break (Sitting Pretty)

M

McBroom and the Beanstalk (McBroom)

McBroom and the Big Wind (McBroom)

McBroom and the Great Race (McBroom)

McBroom Tells a Lie (McBroom)

McBroom Tells the Truth (McBroom)

McBroom the Rainmaker (McBroom)

McBroom's Almanac (McBroom)

McBroom's Ear (McBroom)

McBroom's Ghost (McBroom)

McBroom's Wonderful One-Acre Farm (McBroom)

McBroom's Zoo (McBroom)

McDuff and the Baby (McDuff)

McDuff Comes Home (McDuff)

McDuff Moves In (McDuff)

McDuff's New Friend (McDuff)

McGurk Gets Good and Mad (McGurk)

Mad Dog of Lobo Mountain (D.J. Dillon Adventures)

The Mad Gasser of Bessledorf Street (Bessledorf Hotel)

A Made-Over Chelsea (Best Friends)

Madeline (Madeline)

Madeline and the Bad Hat (Madeline)

Madeline and the Gypsies (Madeline)

Madeline in London (Madeline)

Madeline's Christmas (Madeline)

Madeline's Rescue (Madeline)

Mademoiselle Jessica (Sweet Valley Twins)

Maggie (California Diaries)

Maggie, Diary Two (California Diaries)

Maggie Marmelstein for President (Maggie Marmelstein)

Maggie's Choice (The American Adventure)

The Magic Bicycle (Spirit Flyer)

The Magic Chest of Oz (Oz)

The Magic Dishpan of Oz (Oz)

Magic Master (Choose Your Own Adventure)

Magic Money (Houdini Club Magic Mystery)

Magic Moscow (Magic Moscow)

The Magic of Oz (Oz)

Magic of the Unicorn (Choose Your Own Adventure)

Magic Puppets (Sweet Valley Kids)

The Magic School Bus All Dried Up (Magic School Bus)

The Magic School Bus and the Electric Field Trip (Magic School Bus)

The Magic School Bus at the Waterworks (Magic School Bus)

The Magic School Bus Blows Its Top (Magic School Bus)

The Magic School Bus Butterfly and the Bog Beast (Magic School Bus)

The Magic School Bus Gets Ants in Its Pants (Magic School Bus)

The Magic School Bus Gets Baked in a Cake (Magic School Bus)

The Magic School Bus Gets Cold Feet (Magic School Bus)

The Magic School Bus Gets Eaten (Magic School Bus)

The Magic School Bus Gets Planted (Magic School Bus)

The Magic School Bus Goes Upstream (Magic School Bus)

The Magic School Bus Going Batty (Magic School Bus)

The Magic School Bus Hops Home (Magic School Bus)

The Magic School Bus in a Pickle (Magic School Bus)

The Magic School Bus in the Arctic (Magic School Bus)

The Magic School Bus in the Haunted Museum (Magic School Bus)

The Magic School Bus in the Rainforest (Magic School Bus)

The Magic School Bus in the Time of the Dinosaurs (Magic School Bus)

The Magic School Bus Inside a Beehive (Magic School Bus)

The Magic School Bus Inside a Hurricane (Magic School Bus)

The Magic School Bus Inside Ralphie (Magic School Bus)

The Magic School Bus Inside the Earth (Magic School Bus)

The Magic School Bus Inside the Human Body (Magic School Bus)

The Magic School Bus Lost in the Solar System (Magic School Bus)

The Magic School Bus Makes a Rainbow (Magic School Bus)

The Magic School Bus Meets the Rot Squad (Magic School Bus)

The Magic School Bus on the Ocean Floor (Magic School Bus)

The Magic School Bus Out of This World (Magic School Bus)

The Magic School Bus Plants Seeds (Magic School Bus)

The Magic School Bus Plays Ball (Magic School Bus)

The Magic School Bus Shows and Tells (Magic School Bus)

The Magic School Bus Spins a Web (Magic School Bus)

The Magic School Bus Takes a Dive (Magic School Bus)

The Magic School Bus Takes Flight (Magic School Bus)

The Magic School Bus Ups and Downs (Magic School Bus)

The Magic School Bus Wet All Over (Magic School Bus)

The Magic Show Mystery (Boxcar Children: Adventures of Benny and Watch)

The Magical Fellowship (Age of Magic Trilogy)

The Magical Mimics in Oz (Oz)

The Magician's Apprentice (Magician Trilogy)

The Magician's Challenge (Magician Trilogy)

The Magician's Company (Magician Trilogy)

The Magician's Nephew (Chronicles of Narnia)

Maid Mary Anne (Baby-sitters Club)

Mail-Order Brother (Full House: Stephanie)

The Mailbox Trick (Trick Books)

Maisy at the Farm (Maisy the Mouse)

Maisy Goes Swimming (Maisy the Mouse)

Maisy Goes to Bed (Maisy the Mouse)

Maisy Goes to School (Maisy the Mouse)

Maisy Goes to the Playground (Maisy the Mouse)

Maisy's ABC (Maisy the Mouse)

Maizon at Blue Hill (Maizon)

Major-League Melissa (Never Sink Nine)

Major League Trouble (Full House: Michelle)

Make a Wish for Me (Beany Malone)

Make Like a Tree and Leave (Matthew Martin)

Make No Mistake (Nancy Drew Files)

Make Room for Elisa (Elisa)

Make Up Your Mind, Marsha! (Here Come the Brownies)

Make Way for Dumb Bunnies (Dumb Bunnies)

Making the Team (Angel Park All Stars)

Making Waves (Nancy Drew Files)

Malibu Summer (Sweet Valley High)

Mall Mania (Fabulous Five)

Mallory and the Dream Horse (Baby-sitters Club)

Mallory and the Ghost Cat (Baby-sitters Club Mysteries)

Mallory and the Secret Diary (Baby-sitters Club)

Mallory and the Trouble with the Twins (Baby-sitters Club)

Mallory Hates Boys (and Gym) (Baby-sitters Club)

Mask of the Wolf Boy (Trailblazers)

The Masked Monkey (Hardy Boys)

Masquerade in Oz (Oz)

Master of Aikido (Choose Your Own Adventure)

Master of Judo (Choose Your Own Adventure)

Master of Karate (Choose Your Own Adventure)

Master of Kendo (Choose Your Own Adventure)

Master of Kung Fu (Choose Your Own Adventure)

Master of Martial Arts (Choose Your Own Adventure)

Master of Tae Kwon Do (Choose Your Own Adventure)

Masters of the Louvre (Young Indiana Jones Chronicles: Choose Your Own Adventure)

A Match of Wills (Ghostwriter)

Mattimeo (Redwall)

Max and Maggie in Autumn (Nice Mice)

Max and Maggie in Spring (Nice Mice)

Max and Maggie in Summer (Nice Mice)

Max and Maggie in Winter (Nice Mice)

Max and Ruby's First Greek Myth (Max and Ruby)

Max and Ruby's Midas (Max and Ruby)

Max in Hollywood, Baby (Max the Dog)

Max Makes a Million (Max the Dog)

Max Malone and the Great Cereal Rip-Off (Max Malone)

Max Malone Makes a Million (Max Malone)

Max Malone, Superstar (Max Malone)

Max Malone the Magnificent (Max Malone)

Maximum Challenge (Hardy Boys)

Max's Chocolate Chicken (Max and Ruby)

Max's Christmas (Max and Ruby)

Max's Dragon Shirt (Max and Ruby)

May Goes to England (Pony Tails)

May Rides a New Pony (Pony Tails)

May Takes the Lead (Pony Tails)

May the Best Team Win (Saved by the Bell)

Mayday! (Choose Your Own Adventure)

The Mayflower Adventure (The American Adventure)

The Mayflower Secret (Trailblazers)

Mayhem in Motion (Hardy Boys Casefiles)

May's Riding Lesson (Pony Tails)

May's Runaway Ride (Pony Tails)

The Maze (Dinotopia)

Me and Fat Glenda (Fat Glenda)

Me and My Little Brain (The Great Brain)

The Meanest Thing to Say (Little Bill)

Meet Addy (American Girls: Addy)

Meet Babar and His Family (Babar)

Meet Felicity (American Girls: Felicity)

Meet Josefina (American Girls: Josefina)

Meet Kirsten (American Girls: Kirsten)

Meet M and M (M and M)

Meet Me at Midnight (Sweet Valley High)

Meet Molly (American Girls: Molly)

Meet Posy Bates (Posy Bates)

Meet Samantha (American Girls: Samantha)

Meet the Austins (Vicky Austin)

Meet the Boxcar Children (Boxcar Children: Adventures of Benny and Watch)

Meet the Lincoln Lions Band (Lincoln Lions Band)

Meet the Malones (Beany Malone)

Meet the Molesons (Molesons)

Meg & the Secret Scrapbook (Always Friends)

Meg Mackintosh and the Case of the Curious Whale Watch (Meg Mackintosh: A Solve-It-Yourself Mystery)

Meg Mackintosh and the Case of the Missing Babe Ruth Baseball (Meg Mackintosh: A Solve-It-Yourself Mystery)

Meg Mackintosh and the Mystery at Camp Creepy (Meg Mackintosh: A Solve-It-Yourself Mystery)

Meg Mackintosh and the Mystery at the Medieval Castle (Meg Mackintosh: A Solve-It-Yourself Mystery)

Meg Mackintosh and the Mystery at the Soccer Match (Meg Mackintosh: A Solve-It-Yourself Mystery)

Meg Mackintosh and the Mystery in the Locked Library (Meg Mackintosh: A Solve-It-Yourself Mystery)

Meg Makes a Friend (Portraits of Little Women)

Megan in Ancient Greece (Magic Attic Club)

Megan's Balancing Act (Magic Attic Club)

Megan's Ghost (Camp Sunnyside)

Megan's Masquerade (Magic Attic Club)

Meg's Dearest Wish (Little Women Journals)

Meg's Story (Portraits of Little Women)

Melanie and the Cruise Caper (Twelve Candles Club)

Melanie and the Modeling Mess (Twelve Candles Club)

Melanie Edwards, Super Kisser (Fabulous Five)

Melanie's Identity Crisis (Fabulous Five)

Melanie's Last Ride (Thoroughbred)

Melanie's Treasure (Thoroughbred)

Melanie's Valentine (Fabulous Five)

Meltdown (Mindwarp)

The Melted Coins (Hardy Boys)

Memories (Sweet Valley High)

Memory in a House (Green Knowe)

The Mennyms (Mennyms)

Mennyms Alive (Mennyms)

Mennyms Alone (Mennyms)

Mennyms in the Wilderness (Mennyms)

Mennyms Under Siege (Mennyms)

Meredith (The Elliott Cousins)

Merger on the Orient Expressway (Determined Detectives)

Merlin (Young Merlin Trilogy)

The Merlin Effect (Kate Gordon)

Merlin's Destiny (Winds of Light)

Mermaids Don't Run Track (The Adventures of the Bailey School Kids)

Merry Christmas, Amelia Bedelia (Amelia Bedelia)

Merry Christmas, Davy! (Davy)

Merry Christmas, Dear Dragon (Dear Dragon)

Merry Christmas, Ernest and Celestine! (Ernest and Celestine)

Merry Christmas from Betsy (Betsy)

Merry Christmas from Eddie (Eddie Wilson)

Merry Christmas, Geraldine (Geraldine)

Merry Christmas, Henrietta (Henrietta)

Merry Christmas, World! (Full House: Michelle)

Merry Go Round in Oz (Oz)

The Message (Animorphs)

A Message from the Match Girl (Investigators of the Unknown)

The Message in the Haunted Mansion (Nancy Drew)

The Message in the Hollow Oak (Nancy Drew)

Messy Bessey (Messy Bessey)

Messy Bessey's Closet (Messy Bessey)

Moment of Truth (Hardy Boys Casefiles)

Mona Lisa Is Missing (Choose Your Own Adventure)

Mondo Meltdown (Time Surfers)

The Money Hunt (Hardy Boys)

Money Troubles (Little Bill)

Monkey Business (Hank the Cowdog)

Monster (Nightmare Hall)

Monster Blood (Goosebumps)

Monster Blood (Goosebumps Presents)

Monster Blood II (Goosebumps)

Monster Blood III (Goosebumps)

Monster Blood IV (Goosebumps)

The Monster Channel (Spinetinglers)

Monster Dog (Ghosts of Fear Street)

The Monster in the Third Dresser Drawer (The Adam Joshua Capers)

The Monster in the Third Dresser Drawer, and Other Stories About Adam Joshua (The Adam Joshua Capers)

Monster Jam (Super Hoops)

Monster Machine (Tom Swift)

The Monster Mouse Mystery (Bobbsey Twins: The New Bobbsey Twins)

Monster Rabbit Runs Amuck! (Kids of the Polk Street School)

Monster Vision (Fiendly Corners)

Monsters Don't Scuba Dive (The Adventures of the Bailey School Kids)

The Monsters Next Door (Bailey City Monsters)

Moominland Midwinter (Moomintroll)

Moominpappa at Sea (Moomintroll)

Moominpappa's Memoirs (Moomintroll)

Moominsummer Madness (Moomintroll)

Moon Bear (Moonbear)

The Moon by Night (Vicky Austin)

The Moon of the Alligators (The Thirteen Moons)

The Moon of the Bears (The Thirteen Moons)

The Moon of the Chickarees (The Thirteen Moons)

The Moon of the Deer (The Thirteen Moons)

The Moon of the Fox Pups (The Thirteen Moons)

The Moon of the Gray Wolves (The Thirteen Moons)

The Moon of the Moles (The Thirteen Moons)

The Moon of the Monarch Butterflies (The Thirteen Moons)

The Moon of the Mountain Lions (The Thirteen Moons)

The Moon of the Owls (The Thirteen Moons)

The Moon of the Salamanders (The Thirteen Moons)

The Moon of the Wild Pigs (The Thirteen Moons)

The Moon of the Winter Bird (The Thirteen Moons)

Moon Quest (Choose Your Own Adventure)

Moonbear's Pet (Moonbear)

Mooncake (Moonbear)

Moondance (Moonbear)

Moongame (Moonbear)

Moonlight Madness (Hank the Cowdog)

Moonstalker (Tom Swift)

The Moonstone Castle Mystery (Nancy Drew)

The Moosepire (Blue Moose)

The Mopwater Flies (Hank the Cowdog)

More About Paddington (Paddington)

More Adventures of the Great Brain (The Great Brain)

More Adventures of the Plant That Ate Dirty Socks (The Plant That Ate Dirty Socks)

More Alex and the Cat (Alex and the Cat)

More All-of-a-Kind Family (All-of-a-Kind Family)

More Bunny Trouble (Bunny Trouble)

More from the Molesons (Molesons)

More Sideways Arithmetic from Wayside School (Wayside School)

More Stories from Grandma's Attic (Grandma's Attic)

More Stories Huey Tells (Julian and Huey)

More Stories Julian Tells (Julian and Huey)

More Tales of Amanda Pig (Oliver and Amanda Pig)

More Tales of Oliver Pig (Oliver and Amanda Pig)

More Than Friends (Silver Blades)

The More the Merrier (Beany Malone)

More To and Again (Freddy)

More Witch Goblin and Ghost Stories (Witch, Goblin, and Ghost)

The Morning After (Sweet Valley High)

Morris and Boris (Morris and Boris)

Morris and Boris at the Circus (Morris and Boris)

Morris Goes to School (Morris and Boris)

Morris Has a Birthday Party (Morris and Boris)

Morris Has a Cold (Morris and Boris)

Morris Is a Cowboy, a Policeman, and a Baby Sitter (Morris and Boris)

Morris Tells Boris Mother Moose Stories and Rhymes (Morris and Boris)

Morris the Moose (Morris and Boris)

Mortimer Says Nothing, and Other Stories (Arabel and Mortimer)

Mortimer's Cross (Arabel and Mortimer)

Moss Pillows (Voyage to the Bunny Planet)

Mossflower (Redwall)

The Most Beautiful Girl in the World (Unicorn Club)

Most Likely to Die (Nancy Drew Files)

Most Wanted (Danger.com)

Mother-Daughter Switch (Sweet Valley Twins)

Mother Murphy (Murphy Family)

Mother Rabbit's Son Tom (Hattie Rabbit)

Motocross Mania (Choose Your Own Adventure)

Mountain Biker (Choose Your Own Adventure)

Mountain Light (Foxfire)

Mountain Madness (Christy)

Mountain-Peak Mystery (Dana Girls)

Mountain Survival (Choose Your Own Adventure)

Mountain Top Mystery (Boxcar Children)

Mouse & Mole and the All-Weather Train Ride (Mouse and Mole)

Mouse & Mole and the Christmas Walk (Mouse and Mole)

Mouse & Mole and the Year-Round Garden (Mouse and Mole)

The Mouse and the Motorcycle (Ralph S. Mouse)

Mousekin Finds a Friend (Mousekin)

Mousekin Takes a Trip (Mousekin)

Mousekin's ABC (Mousekin)

Mousekin's Birth (Mousekin)

Mousekin's Christmas Eve (Mousekin)

Mousekin's Close Call (Mousekin)

Mousekin's Easter Basket (Mousekin)

Mousekin's Fables (Mousekin)

Mousekin's Family (Mousekin)

Mousekin's Frosty Friend (Mousekin)

Mousekin's Golden House (Mousekin)

Mousekin's Lost Woodland (Mousekin)

Mousekin's Mystery (Mousekin)

Mousekin's Thanksgiving (Mousekin)

Mousekin's Woodland Birthday (Mousekin)

Mousekin's Woodland Sleepers (Mousekin)

The Movie Star Angel (Forever Angels)

My Robot Buddy (Jack and Danny One)

My Secret Admirer (New Eden)

My Secret Secret Admirer (Full House: Stephanie)

My Secret Valentine (Holiday Friends)

My Sister the Blabbermouth (39 Kids on the Block)

My Son, the Time Traveler (The Zack Files)

My Stars, It's Mrs. Gaddy (Mrs. Gaddy)

My Teacher Flunked the Planet (My Teacher)

My Teacher Fried My Brains (My Teacher)

My Teacher Glows in the Dark (My Teacher)

My Teacher Is an Alien (My Teacher)

My Teacher's a Bug (Spinetinglers)

My Teddy Bear at Home (My Teddy Bear)

My Teddy Bear at Play (My Teddy Bear)

My Teddy Bear at Work (My Teddy Bear)

My Teddy Bear on Vacation (My Teddy Bear)

My Three Weeks as a Spy (Full House: Stephanie)

My Trip to Alpha 1 (Jack and Danny One)

My Two Best Friends (Full House: Michelle)

My Worst Friend, Woody (Silver Blades Figure Eights)

Myself and I (Sterling Family)

The Mysterious Caravan (Hardy Boys)

The Mysterious Case (Reel Kids Adventures)

The Mysterious Case Case (Determined Detectives)

Mysterious Doctor Q (Sweet Valley Twins)

Mysterious Fireplace (Dana Girls)

The Mysterious Football Team (Dallas O'Neil and the Baker Street Sports Club)

The Mysterious Image (Nancy Drew)

The Mysterious Lights and Other Cases (Einstein Anderson)

The Mysterious Mannequin (Nancy Drew)

Mysterious Monday (Juli Scott Super Sleuth)

Mysteriously Yours, Maggie Marmelstein (Maggie Marmelstein)

Mystery at Bellwood Estate (Best Friends)

The Mystery at Claudia's House (Baby-sitters Club Mysteries)

Mystery at Devil's Paw (Hardy Boys)

The Mystery at Lilac Inn (Nancy Drew)

The Mystery at Magnolia Mansion (Nancy Drew)

The Mystery at Peacock Hall (Boxcar Children)

Mystery at Smokey Mountain (Reel Kids Adventures)

The Mystery at Snowflake Inn (Boxcar Children)

Mystery at Sugar Creek (Sugar Creek Gang)

The Mystery at the Alamo (Boxcar Children)

The Mystery at the Ballpark (Boxcar Children)

The Mystery at the Broken Bridge (The Home School Detectives)

Mystery at the Crossroads (Dana Girls)

The Mystery at the Crystal Palace (Nancy Drew)

The Mystery at the Dog Pound (Boxcar Children)

The Mystery at the Fair (Boxcar Children)

Mystery at the Masked Ball (Clue)

Mystery at the Meet (Gymnasts)

Mystery at the Paris Ballet (Girlhood Journeys: Marie)

The Mystery at the Ski Jump (Nancy Drew)

Mystery Behind the Wall (Boxcar Children)

The Mystery Bookstore (Boxcar Children)

The Mystery Cruise (Boxcar Children)

Mystery Day (Mr. Rose's Class)

A Mystery for Mr. Bass (Tyco Bass)

The Mystery Girl (Boxcar Children)

The Mystery Horse (Boxcar Children)

Mystery Horse (Horseshoes)

The Mystery in Lost Canyon (The Home School Detectives)

The Mystery in San Francisco (Boxcar Children)

The Mystery in the Cave (Boxcar Children)

Mystery in the Moonlight (Clue)

The Mystery in the Old Attic (Boxcar Children)

The Mystery in the Old Mine (Hardy Boys)

Mystery in the Sand (Boxcar Children)

The Mystery in the Snow (Boxcar Children)

The Mystery in Washington, D.C. (Boxcar Children)

Mystery of Cabin Island (Hardy Boys)

Mystery of Chimney Rock (Choose Your Own Adventure)

Mystery of Crocodile Island (Nancy Drew)

The Mystery of Death Trap Mine (Three Investigators)

Mystery of Echo Lodge (Choose Your Own Adventure)

The Mystery of Misty Canyon (Nancy Drew)

The Mystery of Misty Island Inn (Haunting with Louisa)

The Mystery of Monster Mountain (Three Investigators)

Mystery of Smuggler's Cove (Hardy Boys)

The Mystery of the African Gray (Three Cousins Detective Club)

Mystery of the Aztec Warrior (Hardy Boys)

Mystery of the Bamboo Bird (Dana Girls)

The Mystery of the Birthday Party (Three Cousins Detective Club)

The Mystery of the Black Hole Mine (D.J. Dillon Adventures)

The Mystery of the Blazing Cliffs (Three Investigators)

The Mystery of the Blue Ring (Polka Dot Private Eye)

The Mystery of the Brass-Bound Trunk (Nancy Drew)

The Mystery of the Campus Crook (The Home School Detectives)

The Mystery of the Carousel Horse (Ten Commandments Mysteries)

Mystery of the Chinese Junk (Hardy Boys)

The Mystery of the Copycat Clown (Three Cousins Detective Club)

The Mystery of the Coughing Dragon (Three Investigators)

The Mystery of the Cranky Collector (Three Investigators)

The Mystery of the Creep-Show Crooks (Three Investigators)

The Mystery of the Cupboard (Indian in the Cupboard)

The Mystery of the Dancing Angels (Three Cousins Detective Club)

The Mystery of the Dancing Devil (Three Investigators)

The Mystery of the Dead Man's Riddle (Three Investigators)

The Mystery of the Deadly Double (Three Investigators)

Mystery of the Desert Giant (Hardy Boys)

The Mystery of the Dolphin Detective (Three Cousins Detective Club)

The Mystery of the Double Trouble (Ten Commandments Mysteries)

The Mystery of the Eagle Feather (Three Cousins Detective Club)

Mystery of the Fat Cat (Dogtown Ghetto)

The Mystery of the Fiery Eye (Three Investigators)

The Mystery of the Fire Dragon (Nancy Drew)

The Mystery of the Flaming Footprints (Three Investigators)

Mystery of the Flying Express (Hardy Boys)

The Mystery of the Gingerbread House (Three Cousins Detective Club)

The Mystery of the Glowing Eye (Nancy Drew)

Mystery of the Golden Palomino (Dallas O'Neil Mysteries)

The Mystery of the Goldfish Pond (Three Cousins Detective Club)

The Mystery of the Gravestone Riddle (Ten Commandments Mysteries)

The Mystery of the Green Ghost (Three Investigators)

The Mystery of the Haunted Lighthouse (Three Cousins Detective Club)

The Mystery of the Headless Horse (Three Investigators)

The Mystery of the Hidden Beach (Boxcar Children)

The Mystery of the Hidden Painting (Boxcar Children)

Mystery of the Highland Crest (Choose Your Own Adventure)

The Mystery of the Hobo's Message (Three Cousins Detective Club)

The Mystery of the Homeless Treasure (The Home School Detectives)

The Mystery of the Honeybees' Secret (Three Cousins Detective Club)

The Mystery of the Hot Air Balloon (Boxcar Children)

The Mystery of the Invisible Dog (Three Investigators)

The Mystery of the Island Jungle (Ladd Family)

The Mystery of the Ivory Charm (Nancy Drew)

The Mystery of the Jade Tiger (Nancy Drew)

Mystery of the Kidnapped Kid (Dallas O'Neil Mysteries)

The Mystery of the Kidnapped Whale (Three Investigators)

The Mystery of the Lake Monster (Boxcar Children)

The Mystery of the Laughing Cat (Ten Commandments Mysteries)

The Mystery of the Laughing Shadow (Three Investigators)

Mystery of the Locked Room (Dana Girls)

The Mystery of the Lost Island (Three Cousins Detective Club)

The Mystery of the Lost Mine (Boxcar Children)

The Mystery of the Lost Village (Boxcar Children)

The Mystery of the Magic Circle (Three Investigators)

The Mystery of the Magi's Treasure (Three Cousins Detective Club)

The Mystery of the Masked Rider (Nancy Drew)

Mystery of the Maya (Choose Your Own Adventure)

The Mystery of the Messed-Up Wedding (Ten Commandments Mysteries)

The Mystery of the Mexican Graveyard (The Home School Detectives)

The Mystery of the Missing Cat (Boxcar Children)

Mystery of the Missing Crew (Star Trek: The Next Generation: Starfleet Academy)

The Mystery of the Missing Dog (Invisible Inc.)

The Mystery of the Missing Mascot (Nancy Drew)

The Mystery of the Missing Mermaid (Three Investigators)

The Mystery of the Missing Microchips (The Home School Detectives)

The Mystery of the Missing Millionaires (Nancy Drew)

The Mystery of the Missing Mummy (Bobbsey Twins: The New Bobbsey Twins)

Mystery of the Missing Sister (Dallas O'Neil Mysteries)

Mystery of the Mixed-Up Mail (Bobbsey Twins: The New Bobbsey Twins)

Mystery of the Mixed Up Teacher (Dallas O'Neil Mysteries)

The Mystery of the Mixed-Up Zoo (Boxcar Children)

The Mystery of the Moaning Cave (Three Investigators)

The Mystery of the Moss-Covered Mansion (Nancy Drew)

The Mystery of the Nervous Lion (Three Investigators)

The Mystery of the 99 Steps (Nancy Drew)

Mystery of the Phantom Gold (American Adventure)

Mystery of the Phony Murder (Dallas O'Neil Mysteries)

The Mystery of the Plant That Ate Dirty Socks (The Plant That Ate Dirty Socks)

The Mystery of the Purple Pirate (Three Investigators)

The Mystery of the Purple Pool (Boxcar Children)

The Mystery of the Queen's Jewels (Boxcar Children)

The Mystery of the Rogues' Reunion (Three Investigators)

Mystery of the Sacred Stones (Choose Your Own Adventure)

The Mystery of the Samurai Sword (Hardy Boys)

The Mystery of the Sand Castle (Three Cousins Detective Club)

The Mystery of the Scar-Faced Beggar (Three Investigators)

Mystery of the Scorpion Threat (Dallas O'Neil Mysteries)

The Mystery of the Screaming Clock (Three Investigators)

The Mystery of the Second Map (Ten Commandments Mysteries)

The Mystery of the Secret Message (Boxcar Children)

Mystery of the Secret Room (Choose Your Own Adventure)

The Mystery of the Shrinking House (Three Investigators)

The Mystery of the Silent Idol (Ten Commandments Mysteries)

The Mystery of the Silent Nightingale (Three Cousins Detective Club)

The Mystery of the Silly Goose (Three Cousins Detective Club)

The Mystery of the Silver Dolphin (Ten Commandments Mysteries)

The Mystery of the Silver Spider (Three Investigators)

The Mystery of the Silver Star (Hardy Boys)

The Mystery of the Singing Ghost (Boxcar Children)

The Mystery of the Singing Serpent (Three Investigators)

The Mystery of the Sinister Scarecrow (Three Investigators)

Mystery of the Skinny Sophomore (Dallas O'Neil Mysteries)

The Mystery of the Smashing Glass (Three Investigators)

The Mystery of the Sock Monkeys (Three Cousins Detective Club)

Mystery of the Spiral Bridge (Hardy Boys)

The Mystery of the Stolen Bike (Arthur Chapter Books)

The Mystery of the Stolen Boxcar (Boxcar Children)

The Mystery of the Stolen Football (Sports Mysteries)

The Mystery of the Stolen Music (Boxcar Children)

The Mystery of the Stolen Sword (Boxcar Children)

Mystery of the Stone Tiger (Dana Girls)

The Mystery of the Stuttering Parrot (Three Investigators)

The Mystery of the Talking Skull (Three Investigators)

The Mystery of the Tattletale Parrot (Ten Commandments Mysteries)

The Mystery of the Tolling Bell (Nancy Drew)

The Mystery of the Trail of Terror (Three Investigators)

The Mystery of the Traveling Button (Three Cousins Detective Club)

The Mystery of the Two-Toed Pigeon (Three Investigators)

The Mystery of the Vanishing Cave (The Home School Detectives)

The Mystery of the Vanishing Present (Ten Commandments Mysteries)

The Mystery of the Vanishing Treasure (Three Investigators)

The Mystery of the Wandering Caveman (Three Investigators)

Mystery of the Wax Queen (Dana Girls)

The Mystery of the Wedding Cake (Three Cousins Detective Club)

Mystery of the Whale Tattoo (Hardy Boys)

The Mystery of the Whispering Mummy (Three Investigators)

The Mystery of the White Elephant (Three Cousins Detective Club)

The Mystery of the Widow's Watch (The Home School Detectives)

The Mystery of the Wild Surfer (Ladd Family)

Mystery of the Winged Lion (Nancy Drew)

The Mystery of the Wrong Dog (Three Cousins Detective Club)

The Mystery of the Zoo Camp (Three Cousins Detective Club)

Mystery of Ura Senke (Choose Your Own Adventure)

The Mystery of Wreckers' Rock (Three Investigators)

Mystery on Makatunk Island (Hardy Boys)

Mystery on Maui (Nancy Drew)

The Mystery on Stage (Boxcar Children)

The Mystery on the Ice (Boxcar Children)

Mystery on the Menu (Nancy Drew)

Mystery on the Midway (Dallas O'Neil Mysteries)

Mystery on the Mississippi (Bobbsey Twins: The New Bobbsey Twins)

The Mystery on the Train (Boxcar Children)

Mystery on the Trans-Siberian Express (Passport)

Mystery Ranch (Boxcar Children)

Mystery Ride (The Saddle Club)

Mystery Tour (Funnybones)

Mystery with a Dangerous Beat (Hardy Boys)

N

Nancy's Mysterious Letter (Nancy Drew)

Nannies for Hire (Casey, Jenny, and Kate)

Narrow Escape (Bad News Bunny)

Nasty Competition (Gymnasts)

Nasty the Snowman (Fiendly Corners)

Natalia Comes to America (Silver Blades)

Nate the Great (Nate the Great)

Nate the Great and the Boring Beach Bag (Nate the Great)

Nate the Great and Me (Nate the Great)

Nate the Great and the Crunchy Christmas (Nate the Great)

Nate the Great and the Fishy Prize (Nate the Great)

Nate the Great and the Halloween Hunt (Nate the Great)

Nate the Great and the Lost List (Nate the Great)

Nate the Great and the Missing Key (Nate the Great)

Nate the Great and the Mushy Valentine (Nate the Great)

Nate the Great and the Musical Note (Nate the Great)

Nate the Great and the Phony Clue (Nate the Great)

Nate the Great and the Pillowcase (Nate the Great)

Nate the Great and the Snowy Trail (Nate the Great)

Nate the Great and the Sticky Case (Nate the Great)

Nate the Great and the Stolen Base (Nate the Great)

Nate the Great and the Tardy Tortoise (Nate the Great)

Nate the Great Goes Down in the Dumps (Nate the Great)

Nate the Great Goes Undercover (Nate the Great)

Nate the Great Saves the King of Sweden (Nate the Great)

Nate the Great Stalks Stupidweed (Nate the Great)

Natural Enemies (Nancy Drew Files)

Nechama on Strike (B.Y. Times)

The Negative Zone (Tom Swift)

Nelson in Love (The Adam Joshua Capers)

Nelson in Love: An Adam Joshua Valentine's Day Story (The Adam Joshua Capers)

Net Bandits (Internet Detectives)

The Never-Ending Day (China Tate)

Never Hit a Ghost with a Baseball Bat (Mary Rose)

Never Say Die (Nancy Drew Files)

Never Trust a Cat Who Wears Earrings (The Zack Files)

Never Trust a Flamingo (Full House: Stephanie)

The New and Improved Sarah (Camp Sunnyside)

The New Citizen (The American Adventure)

The New Coach (Gymnasts)

New Dawn on Rocky Ridge (Little House: The Rose Years)

New Elizabeth (Sweet Valley High)

New Faces New Friends (Grandma's Attic)

New Found Land (Fireball)

New Friends (Peanut Butter and Jelly)

New Girl (Sweet Valley Twins)

New Girl in Cabin Six (Camp Sunnyside)

The New Jessica (Sweet Valley High)

The New Kate (Sleepover Friends)

The New Kid in School Is a Vampire Bat (Scaredy Cats)

New Kid in Town (The Hit and Run Gang)

The New Kids (B.Y. Times)

A New Move (Silver Blades)

New Neighbors for Nora (Nora and Teddy)

The New One (Judge and Jury)

The New Stephanie (Sleepover Friends)

New Sugar Creek Gang Mystery (Sugar Creek Gang)

The New Teacher (First Grade)

New Treasure Seekers (Bastable Family)

The New Wizard of Oz (Oz)

New Year's Revolution! (The Secret World of Alex Mack)

New York, New York! (Baby-sitters Club Super Specials)

New York Nightmare! (The Secret World of Alex Mack)

Nutty and the Case of the Ski-Slope Spy (Nutty Nutsell)

Nutty Can't Miss (Nutty Nutsell)

Nutty for President (Nutty Nutsell)

Nutty Knows All (Nutty Nutsell)

Nutty, the Movie Star (Nutty Nutsell)

Nutty's Ghost (Nutty Nutsell)

O

Obadiah the Bold (Obadiah Starbuck)

Odysseus and the Cyclops (Tales from the Odyssey)

Odysseus and the Giants (Tales from the Odyssey)

Odysseus and the Great Challenge (Tales from the Odyssey)

Odysseus and the Magic of Circe (Tales from the Odyssey)

The Odyssey (Wishbone Classics)

The Odyssey of Ben O'Neal (Outer Banks Trilogy)

Off-Worlder (Strange Matter)

Oh Boy, Boston! (Kids of the Polk Street School)

Oh Honestly, Angela! (Angela)

Oink (Pigs)

Oink Oink (Pigs)

Ojo in Oz (Oz)

Old Bear (Old Bear Stories)

Old Bear Tales (Old Bear Stories)

Old Hat, New Hat (Berenstain Bears)

The Old Meadow (Chester Cricket)

The Old Motel Mystery (Boxcar Children)

Old Stranger's Secret at Sugar Creek (Sugar Creek Gang)

Old Turtle's Baseball Stories (Old Turtle)

Old Turtle's Soccer Team (Old Turtle)

Old Turtle's Winter Games (Old Turtle)

The Old Witch and Her Magic Basket (Old Witch)

The Old Witch and the Crows (Old Witch)

The Old Witch and the Dragon (Old Witch)

The Old Witch and the Ghost Parade (Old Witch)

The Old Witch and the Snores (Old Witch)

The Old Witch and the Wizard (Old Witch)

The Old Witch Finds a New House (Old Witch)

The Old Witch Gets a Surprise (Old Witch)

The Old Witch Goes to the Ball (Old Witch)

The Old Witch's Party (Old Witch)

Older Boy (Sweet Valley Twins)

Olga Carries On (Olga da Polga)

Olga Meets Her Match (Olga da Polga)

Olga Takes Charge (Olga da Polga)

Oliver, Amanda, and Grandmother Pig (Oliver and Amanda Pig)

Oliver and Amanda and the Big Snow (Oliver and Amanda Pig)

Oliver and Amanda's Christmas (Oliver and Amanda Pig)

Oliver and Amanda's Halloween (Oliver and Amanda Pig)

Oliver Pig at School (Oliver and Amanda Pig)

Oliver Twist (Wishbone Classics)

Olivia's Story (Sweet Valley High)

Olympics Otis (Never Sink Nine)

Omega Station (Jack and Danny One)

The On-Line Spaceman and Other Cases (Einstein Anderson)

On Our Own (Baker's Dozen)

On the Banks of Plum Creek (Little House)

On the Banks of the Bayou (Little House: The Rose Years)

On the Edge (Silver Blades)

On the Edge (Sweet Valley High)

On the Line (Angel Park Hoop Stars)

On the Other Side of the Hill (Little House: The Rose Years)

On the Run (Sweet Valley High)

On the Sidelines (Soccer Stars)

On Tour (Passport)

Once Upon a Time (Sweet Valley High)

One Crazy Christmas (Sister Sister)

One Day at Horrorland (Goosebumps)

One Frog Too Many (Frog)

One Hundred Thousand Dollar Dawn (Best Friends)

The 123 Zoo Mystery (Eagle-Eye Ernie)

One Last Kiss (Sweet Valley University)

One of the Gang (Sweet Valley Twins)

One of Us (Disney Girls)

One on One (Super Hoops)

One Pet Too Many (Disney Girls)

One Stormy Day at Sugar Creek (Sugar Creek Gang)

One T. Rex Over Easy (Carmen Sandiego Mysteries)

The One Way to Win (Silver Blades)

One Wild Weekend (Saved by the Bell)

Onion Sundaes (Houdini Club Magic Mystery)

The Only Game in Town (Spirit Flyer)

Only You—Sierra (Sierra Jensen)

Ooey Gooey (Mercer Mayer's Critters of the Night)

Ooh La La (Max the Dog)

Oops! (Preston)

The Ooze (Ghosts of Fear Street)

Open Season (Hardy Boys Casefiles)

Open Your Heart (Sierra Jensen)

Operation (Saved by the Bell)

Operation Love Match (Sweet Valley High)

Orange Knight of Oz (Oz)

Orbit Wipeout! (Time Surfers)

Ordinary Jack (Bagthorpe Saga)

Orp (Orp)

Orp and the Chop Suey Burgers (Orp)

Orp and the FBI (Orp)

Orp Goes to the Hoop (Orp)

The Orphelines in the Enchanted Castle (Orphelines)

Oscar J. Noodleman Television Network (Oscar J. Noodleman)

Oswald Bastable and Others (Bastable Family)

The Other Way Round (Anna)

The Other Woman (Sweet Valley University)

Otto and the Magic Potatoes (Otto)

Otto at Sea (Otto)

Otto in Africa (Otto)

Otto in Texas (Otto)

Our Town (X Files)

Our Veronica Goes to Petunia's Farm (Petunia)

Out and About with Anthony Ant (Anthony Ant)

Out of Bounds (Nancy Drew Files)

Out of Bounds! (Super Hoops)

Out of Control (Gymnasts)

Out of Control (Sweet Valley High)

Out of Line (X Games Xtreme Mysteries)

Out of Place (Sweet Valley Twins)

Out of Reach (Sweet Valley High)

Out of the Picture (Sweet Valley University)

Out of Time (Mindwarp)

Outcast (Sweet Valley High)

Outcast of Redwall (Redwall)

The Outer Space Mystery (Boxcar Children)

Outlaw Gulch (Choose Your Own Adventure)

Outlaw Red, Son of Big Red (Red)

Outlaws of Sherwood Forest (Choose Your Own Adventure)

The Outlaw's Silver (Hardy Boys)

Outrageously Alice (Alice)

Over Sea, Under Stone (Dark Is Rising)

The Phoenix Equation (Hardy Boys Casefiles)

Phone Call from a Flamingo (Full House: Stephanie)

Photo Finish (The Saddle Club)

Piano Lessons Can Be Murder (Goosebumps)

Pick a New Dream (Beany Malone)

Pickle Puss (Kids of the Polk Street School)

Picnic with Piggins (Piggins)

The Picts and the Martyrs (Swallows and Amazons)

A Picture for Harold's Room (Harold and the Purple Crayon)

A Picture for Patti (Doug Chronicles)

Picture Me Famous (Full House: Stephanie)

A Picture of Freedom (Dear America)

The Picture of Guilt (Nancy Drew Files)

Picture Perfect (Saved by the Bell)

The Picture-Perfect Crime (Clue)

The Picture-Perfect Mystery (Nancy Drew)

A Picture-Perfect Prom (Sweet Valley High)

Pictures of the Night (Egerton Hall Novels)

A Picture's Worth (Cyber.kdz)

Pig Pig and the Magic Photo Album (Pig Pig)

Pig Pig Gets a Job (Pig Pig)

Pig Pig Goes to Camp (Pig Pig)

Pig Pig Grows Up (Pig Pig)

Pig Pig Rides (Pig Pig)

Pig William (Pigs)

Pigeon Post (Swallows and Amazons)

The Piggest Show on Earth (Pigs)

Piggins (Piggins)

Piggins and the Royal Wedding (Piggins)

Pigs at Christmas (Pigs)

Pigs from A to Z (Pigs)

Pigs from 1 to 10 (Pigs)

Pigs in Hiding (Pigs)

Piles of Pets (Pee Wee Scouts)

The Pilgrim Village Mystery (Boxcar Children)

Pinheads, Unite! (Never Sink Nine)

Pinkerton, Behave! (Pinkerton)

Pinky and Rex (Pinky and Rex)

Pinky and Rex and the Bully (Pinky and Rex)

Pinky and Rex and the Double-Dad Weekend (Pinky and Rex)

Pinky and Rex and the Mean Old Witch (Pinky and Rex)

Pinky and Rex and the New Baby (Pinky and Rex)

Pinky and Rex and the New Neighbors (Pinky and Rex)

Pinky and Rex and the Perfect Pumpkin (Pinky and Rex)

Pinky and Rex and the School Play (Pinky and Rex)

Pinky and Rex and the Spelling Bee (Pinky and Rex)

Pinky and Rex Get Married (Pinky and Rex)

Pinky and Rex Go to Camp (Pinky and Rex)

Pioneer Sisters (Little House Chapter Books)

Pippa Mouse (Pippa Mouse)

Pippa Pops Out! (Pippa Mouse)

Pippa's Mouse House (Pippa Mouse)

Pippi Goes on Board (Pippi Longstocking)

Pippi in the South Seas (Pippi Longstocking)

Pippi Longstocking (Pippi Longstocking)

Pippo Gets Lost (Tom and Pippo)

Pirate Island Adventure (Liza, Bill, and Jed)

Pirate Soup (Mercer Mayer's Critters of the Night)

Pirates Don't Wear Pink Sunglasses (The Adventures of the Bailey School Kids)

The Pirates in Oz (Oz)

Pirates on the Internet (Cybersurfers)

Pirates Past Noon (Magic Tree House)

The Pitcher Who Went Out of His Mind (Tales from the Sandlot)

Pitching Trouble (The Hit and Run Gang)

The Pizza Mystery (Boxcar Children)

Pizza Zombies (Fiendly Corners)

A Place of My Own (Jenna V.)

A Place to Belong (Orphan Train Adventures)

A Place to Hide (Strange Matter)

The Planet of the Dips (Space Brat)

Planet of the Dragons (Choose Your Own Adventure)

Planet Pee Wee (Pee Wee Scouts)

Planet Plague (Star Wars Galaxy of Fear)

The Plant People (Strange Matter)

The Plant That Ate Dirty Socks (The Plant That Ate Dirty Socks)

The Plant That Ate Dirty Socks Gets a Girlfriend (The Plant That Ate Dirty Socks)

The Plant That Ate Dirty Socks Goes Hollywood (The Plant That Ate Dirty Socks)

The Plant That Ate Dirty Socks Goes Up in Space (The Plant That Ate Dirty Socks)

Play Ball, Amelia Bedelia (Amelia Bedelia)

Play-Off (Angel Park All Stars)

Playing Favorites (The Hit and Run Gang)

Playing for Keeps (Short Stirrup Club)

Playing for Keeps (Sweet Valley High)

Playing Hooky (Sweet Valley Twins)

Playing the Part (Fabulous Five)

Playing with Fire (Nancy Drew Files)

Playing with Fire (Sweet Valley High)

Playoff Champion (Choose Your Own Adventure)

Pleasant Fieldmouse (Pleasant Fieldmouse)

The Pleasant Fieldmouse Storybook (Pleasant Fieldmouse)

Pleasant Fieldmouse's Halloween Party (Pleasant Fieldmouse)

Pleasant Fieldmouse's Valentine Trick (Pleasant Fieldmouse)

Please Don't Feed the Vampire! (Goosebumps: Give Yourself Goosebumps)

Please Forgive Me (Sweet Valley High)

Please, Please, Please (The Friendship Ring)

Pleasure Horse (The Saddle Club)

Plymouth Pioneers (The American Adventure)

A Pocket for Corduroy (Corduroy)

A Pocket in My Heart (Jenna V.)

Point Guard (Angel Park Hoop Stars)

Poison (Med Center)

Poison in Paradise! (The Secret World of Alex Mack)

Poison Pen (Nancy Drew Files)

Poisoned Paradise (Hardy Boys Casefiles)

Polar Bears Past Bedtime (Magic Tree House)

The Pom-Pom Wars (Sweet Valley High)

Pony Club Rider (Horseshoes)

Pony Crazy (Pony Tails)

Pony Express (Short Stirrup Club)

A Pony for Keeps (Pony Pals)

A Pony in Trouble (Pony Pals)

Pony on the Porch (Animal Ark)

Pony-Sitters (Pony Pals)

Pony to the Rescue (Pony Pals)

Pooh Gets Stuck (Winnie the Pooh First Readers)

Pooh's Honey Tree (Winnie the Pooh First Readers)

Pooh's Pumpkin (Winnie the Pooh First Readers)

The Pool of Fire (Tripods)

Pool Party Panic! (The Secret World of Alex Mack)

Pooped Troop (Pee Wee Scouts)

Poopsie Pomerantz, Pick Up Your Feet (Casey, Tracey and Company)

Poor Lila (Sweet Valley Twins)

Poor Mallory! (Baby-sitters Club)

Poor Roger (Doug Chronicles)

Poor Stainless (The Borrowers)

Popcorn (Bear)

Poppleton (Poppleton)

Poppleton and Friends (Poppleton)

Poppleton Everyday (Poppleton)

Poppleton Forever (Poppleton)

Poppy's Babies (Brambly Hedge)

Poppy's Dance (Beechwood Bunny Tales)

The Popularity Trap (Fabulous Five)

Porkchop to the Rescue (Doug Chronicles)

Portrait in Crime (Nancy Drew Files)

Portrait in the Sand (Dana Girls)

Possessed! (Choose Your Own Adventure)

The Postcard Pest (Kids of the Polk Street School)

Posy Bates, Again! (Posy Bates)

Posy Bates and the Bag Lady (Posy Bates)

The Powder Puff Puzzle (Polka Dot Private Eye)

Power of Suggestion (Nancy Drew Files)

Power Play (Goosebumps: Give Yourself Goosebumps)

Power Play (Hardy Boys Casefiles)

Power Play (Sweet Valley High)

Power Trip (Doug Chronicles)

Prairie Day (Little House: My First Little House Books)

The Predator (Animorphs)

Prehistoric Pinkerton (Pinkerton)

Prelude to War (The American Adventure)

A Present for Grandfather (Boxcar Children: Adventures of Benny and Watch)

Pressure Play (Angel Park All Stars)

Preston's Goal! (Preston)

The Pretender (Animorphs)

Pretenses (Sweet Valley High)

Pretty Please (Nightmare Hall)

The Price of Love (Sweet Valley University)

Pride of the Rockets (The Hit and Run Gang)

Pride's Challenge (Thoroughbred)

Pride's Last Race (Thoroughbred)

The Prime-Time Crime (Hardy Boys)

Primeval (Strange Matter)

Prince (Wolfbay Wings)

Prince Amos (Culpepper Adventures)

The Prince and the Pooch (Wishbone Adventures)

Prince Caspian (Chronicles of Narnia)

The Prince in Waiting (Sword of the Spirits)

The Princess Club (Christy)

Princess Elizabeth (Sweet Valley Twins)

Princess Megan (Magic Attic Club)

Princess on Parade (Nancy Drew Notebooks)

The Principal from the Black Lagoon (Black Lagoon)

Prisoner of Cabin 13 (Sabrina the Teenage Witch)

Prisoner of the Ant People (Choose Your Own Adventure)

Prisoner of War (Young Indiana Jones)

Prisoners of Peace (Star Trek: Deep Space Nine)

Private Jessica (Sweet Valley University)

The Private Worlds of Julia Redfern (Julia Redfern)

Prize-Winning Private Eyes (Lottery Luck)

Probe (Strange Matter)

The Problem with Parents (Camp Sunnyside)

The Problem with Pen Pals (Full House: Michelle)

Professor Popkin's Prodigious Polish (Coven Tree)

Program for Destruction (Hardy Boys)

Project: A Perfect World (World of Adventure)

Project Black Bear (China Tate)

Project UFO (Choose Your Own Adventure)

Project Wheels (Judge and Jury)

A Promise Is Forever (Christy Miller)

Promises (Star Wars Junior Jedi Knights)

Promises (Sweet Valley High)

Promises, Promises (Clearwater Crossing)

The Proposal (Christy)

Psyched! (Angel Park Soccer Stars)

Psychic Sisters (Sweet Valley Twins)

Pumpkin Fever (Sweet Valley Twins)

Puppies in the Pantry (Animal Ark)

Puppy Fat (Keith Shipley)

Puppy Love (Pet Patrol)

The Puppy Problem (Nancy Drew Notebooks)

Pure Evil (Hardy Boys Casefiles)

Pure Poison (Nancy Drew Files)

Purebred (The Saddle Club)

Purple Climbing Days (Kids of the Polk Street School)

Purple Pickle Juice (Mercer Mayer's Critters of the Night)

Purple Prince of Oz (Oz)

The Puzzle at Pineview School (Nancy Drew)

Puzzle for the Secret Seven (The Secret Seven)

Q

Quarantine (Star Trek: Voyager: Starfleet Academy)

Quarter Horse (The Saddle Club)

Queen Ann in Oz (Oz)

Queen Anne's War (The American Adventure)

The Queen of Air and Darkness (The Once and Future King)

The Queen of the Gargoyles (Bone Chillers)

The Queen's Smuggler (Trailblazers)

Quest for the King (Archives of Anthropos)

Quest for the Lost Prince (Trailblazers)

The Quest of the Missing Map (Nancy Drew)

A Question of Magic (Age of Magic Trilogy)

Quick Moves (Angel Park Soccer Stars)

R

"R" for Revenge (Sweet Valley High)

R-T, Margaret and the Rats of NIMH (The Rats of NIMH)

Rabbit Gets Lost (Winnie the Pooh First Readers)

Rabbit Rambles On (Duck)

Rabid Transit (Goners)

Race Against Time (Nancy Drew)

Race Forever (Choose Your Own Adventure)

Race Ready (NASCAR Pole Position Adventures)

Race to Danger (Young Indiana Jones)

Race to Disaster (Frightmares)

Racehorse (The Saddle Club)

Rachel and Obadiah (Obadiah Starbuck)

Rachel's In, Lila's Out (Unicorn Club)

Racing Hearts (Sweet Valley High)

Racing to Disaster (Hardy Boys)

Racso and the Rats of NIMH (The Rats of NIMH)

Radical Moves (Hardy Boys)

Rags to Riches (Sweet Valley High)

Railroad Arthur (Arthur the Kid)

The Rainbow Fish (Rainbow Fish)

Rainbow Fish and the Big Blue Whale (Rainbow Fish)

Rainbow Fish to the Rescue! (Rainbow Fish)

Rainbow Valley (Avonlea)

Ralph S. Mouse (Ralph S. Mouse)

Ramona and Her Father (Ramona Quimby)

Ramona and Her Mother (Ramona Quimby)

Ramona, Forever (Ramona Quimby)

Ramona Quimby, Age 8 (Ramona Quimby)

Ramona the Brave (Ramona Quimby)

Ramona the Pest (Ramona Quimby)

Ranch Hands (The Saddle Club)

Randi's Missing Skates (Silver Blades Figure Eights)

Randi's Pet Surprise (Silver Blades Figure Eights)

Rat Teeth (Casey, Tracey and Company)

Re-elect Nutty! (Nutty Nutsell)

The Reaction (Animorphs)

The Real Hole (Jimmy and Janet)

Real Horror (Hardy Boys Casefiles)

The Real-Skin Rubber Monster Mask (First Grade)

Reality Check (Clearwater Crossing)

The Reality Machine (Choose Your Own Adventure)

The Rebel Spy (The American Adventure)

Rebound! (Super Hoops)

Recipe for Murder (Nancy Drew Files)

The Red Badge of Courage (Wishbone Classics)

Red Means Good Fortune (Once Upon America)

Red Tide Alert (Neptune Adventures)

The Red, White, & Blue Valentine (Lincoln Lions Band)

Redwall (Redwall)

Reed (Wolfbay Wings)

Reel Thrills (Hardy Boys)

Reel Trouble (Three Investigators)

Regina's Legacy (Sweet Valley High)

Rehearsing for Romance (Nancy Drew Files)

Relativity, As Explained by Professor Xargle (Professor Xargle)

Reluctantly Alice (Alice)

Rendezvous at Skull Mountain (Scrapper John)

Rendezvous in Rome (Nancy Drew Files)

Rent-a-Star (Stars)

Rescue at Marlehead Manor (Girlhood Journeys: Juliet)

The Rescue of Babar (Babar)

The Rescuers (The Rescuers)

Rest in Pieces (House of Horrors)

The Return of Odysseus (Tales from the Odyssey)

The Return of Rinaldo, the Sly Fox (Rinaldo)

Return of the Evil Twin (Sweet Valley High)

The Return of the Great Brain (The Great Brain)

The Return of the Indian (Indian in the Cupboard)

The Return of the King (The Lord of the Rings)

Return of the Moose (Blue Moose)

Return of the Mummy (Goosebumps)

Return of the Mummy (Goosebumps Presents)

Return of the Ninja (Choose Your Own Adventure)

The Return of the Plant That Ate Dirty Socks (The Plant That Ate Dirty Socks)

The Return of the Vampire (Vampire Promise)

Return to Atlantis (Choose Your Own Adventure)

Return to Foreverware (Eerie Indiana)

Return to Howliday Inn (Bunnicula)

Return to Ord Mantell (Star Wars Young Jedi Knights)

Return to Oz (Oz)

Return to Terror Tower (Goosebumps: Give Yourself Goosebumps)

Return to the Carnival of Horrors (Goosebumps: Give Yourself Goosebumps)

Return to the Cave of Time (Choose Your Own Adventure)

Revenge (Nightmare Hall)

Revenge of the Desert Phantom (Hardy Boys)

Revenge of the Dinosaurs (Graveyard School)

Revenge of the Goblins (Deadtime Stories)

Revenge of the Hairy Horror (Fiendly Corners)

Revenge of the Lawn Gnomes (Goosebumps)

Revenge of the Lawn Gnomes (Goosebumps Presents)

Revenge of the Mummy (Clue)

The Revenge of the Pirate Ghost (Black Cat Club)

Revenge of the Russian Ghost (Choose Your Own Adventure)

The Revenge of the Shadow People (Ghosts of Fear Street)

Revenge of the Tiki Men! (The Weird Zone)

The Revenge of the Wizard's Ghost (Johnny Dixon)

Revenge R Us (Goosebumps Series 2000)

Revolution! (Young Indiana Jones)

Revolution in Russia (Young Indiana Jones Chronicles: Choose Your Own Adventure)

Rewolf of Oz (Oz)

Rex and Lilly Family Time (Rex and Lilly)

Rex and Lilly Play Time (Rex and Lilly)

Rex and Lilly Schooltime (Rex and Lilly)

Rhymes for Annie Rose (Alfie Rose)

Ribsy (Henry Huggins)

Rich and Dangerous (Nancy Drew Files)

Rickshaw to Horror (Miss Mallard)

The Riddle and the Rune (Tales of Gom in the Legends of Ulm)

The Riddle in the Rare Book (Nancy Drew)

The Riddle of Baby Rosalind (Nicki Holland)

Riddle of the Frozen Mountain (Dana Girls)

The Riddle of the Red Purse (Polka Dot Private Eye)

The Riddle of the Ruby Gazelle (Nancy Drew)

The Riddle of the Wayward Books (Wishbone Mysteries)

Riding Camp (The Saddle Club)

Riding Class (The Saddle Club)

Riding Lesson (The Saddle Club)

Rigged for Revenge (Hardy Boys Casefiles)

Rilla of Ingleside (Avonlea)

Rilo Buro's Summer Vacation (Strange Matter)

Rinaldo on the Run (Rinaldo)

Rinaldo, the Sly Fox (Rinaldo)

A Ring of Endless Light (Vicky Austin)

The Ringmaster's Secret (Nancy Drew)

Rinkitink in Oz (Oz)

Riot in the Night (The American Adventure)

Rip-Roaring Russell (Elisa)

Rip-Roaring Russell (Russell)

Risk Your Life Arcade (Choose Your Own Nightmare)

Rival Roommates (Silver Blades)

Rivals in the Ring (Riding Academy)

The River (Brian Robeson)

The St. Patrick's Day Shamrock Mystery (Dixon Twins)

Salamandastron (Redwall)

Salem on Trial (Sabrina the Teenage Witch)

Salty Dog (Salty)

Salty Dog (Wishbone Adventures)

Salty Sails North (Salty)

Salty Scarecrow Solution (Alex)

Salty Takes Off (Salty)

Samantha Learns a Lesson (American Girls: Samantha)

Samantha Saves the Day (American Girls: Samantha)

Samantha's Journey (Thoroughbred)

Samantha's Pride (Thoroughbred)

Samantha's Surprise (American Girls: Samantha)

The San Francisco Earthquake (The American Adventure)

The Sanctuary Tree (Sterling Family)

Sandcake (Bear)

Santa Claus Doesn't Mop Floors (The Adventures of the Bailey School Kids)

Santa's Little Helper (Sabrina the Teenage Witch)

The Sapphire Princess Hunts for Treasure (Jewel Kingdom)

The Sapphire Princess Meets the Monster (Jewel Kingdom)

Sarah Anne Hartford, Massachusetts, 1651 (American Diaries)

Sarah's Dad and Sophia's Mom (Sweet Valley Twins)

Sarah's Incredible Idea (Here Come the Brownies)

Sarah's Room (B.Y. Times Kid Sisters)

Saturday Scare (Juli Scott Super Sleuth)

The Saturdays (Melendy Family)

Save D.A.D.! (Bad News Ballet)

Save the Unicorns! (Unicorn Club)

Saving Shiloh (Shiloh)

Say "Cheese" (Kids of the Polk Street School)

Say Cheese and Die! (Goosebumps)

Say Cheese and Die—Again! (Goosebumps)

Say Goodbye (Sweet Valley High)

Say Hola, Sarah (Friends and Amigos)

The Scalawagons of Oz (Oz)

The Scapegoat (Fabulous Five)

Scare Bear (Bone Chillers)

The Scarecrow of Oz (Oz)

The Scarecrow Walks at Midnight (Goosebumps)

Scared Silly (Mary Rose)

Scaredy-Cat Elizabeth (Sweet Valley Kids)

The Scarlet Slipper Mystery (Nancy Drew)

The Scary Baseball Player (Dallas O'Neil and the Baker Street Sports Club)

Scary Scraped-Up Skaters (All-Star Meatballs)

Scene of the Crime (Choose Your Own Adventure)

Scene of the Crime (Hardy Boys Casefiles)

Scene One, Take Two (Saved by the Bell)

Scent of Danger (Nancy Drew Files)

The Schmo Must Go On (Funny Firsts)

School Days (Little House Chapter Books)

The School for Cats (Jenny and the Cat Club)

The School Nurse from the Black Lagoon (Black Lagoon)

A School of Her Own (Grandma's Attic)

School Spirit (Edison-Armstrong School)

School Spirit Sabotage (Brian and Pea Brain)

Schoolhouse Mystery (Boxcar Children)

Schoolin' (Patrick's Pals)

Schooling Horse (The Saddle Club)

The Schoolmarm Mysteries (Girlhood Journeys: Shannon)

School's Out (Edison-Armstrong School)

The Schoolyard Mystery (Invisible Inc.)

Science Fair (Kids in Ms. Coleman's Class)

Science-lab Sabotage (Our Secret Gang)

Scream Around the Campfire (Graveyard School)

Scream of the Evil Genie (Goosebumps: Give Yourself Goosebumps)

The Scream Team (Ghosts of Fear Street)

Scream, Team! (Graveyard School)

The Scream Team (Nightmare Hall)

Screamers (Hardy Boys Casefiles)

Screaming Eagles (Frightmares)

The Screaming Skeleton (Clue)

Screech in Love (Saved by the Bell)

Scruncher Goes Wandering (Petsitters Club)

Sea City, Here We Come! (Baby-sitters Club Super Specials)

Sea Horse (The Saddle Club)

Sea of Suspicion (Nancy Drew Files)

Sea Star, Orphan of Chincoteague (Chincoteague)

The Sea Story (Brambly Hedge)

Seal Island Scam (Girls R.U.L.E.)

Search for Aladdin's Lamp (Choose Your Own Adventure)

The Search for Cindy Austin (Nancy Drew)

The Search for Snout (Alien Adventures)

Search for the Mountain Gorillas (Choose Your Own Adventure)

The Search for the Silver Persian (Nancy Drew)

The Search for the Snow Leopard (Hardy Boys)

Search the Amazon! (Choose Your Own Adventure)

Searching for Dragons (Enchanted Forest Chronicles)

Searching for Lulu (Hannah and the Angels)

Seaside Mystery (Choose Your Own Adventure)

Sebastian (Super Sleuth) (Sebastian)

Sebastian (Super Sleuth) and the Baffling Bigfoot (Sebastian)

Sebastian (Super Sleuth) and the Bone to Pick Mystery (Sebastian)

Sebastian (Super Sleuth) and the Clumsy Cowboy (Sebastian)

Sebastian (Super Sleuth) and the Copycat Crime (Sebastian)

Sebastian (Super Sleuth) and the Crummy Yummies Caper (Sebastian)

Sebastian (Super Sleuth) and the Egyptian Connection (Sebastian)

Sebastian (Super Sleuth) and the Flying Elephant (Sebastian)

Sebastian (Super Sleuth) and the Hair of the Dog Mystery (Sebastian)

Sebastian (Super Sleuth) and the Impossible Crime (Sebastian)

Sebastian (Super Sleuth) and the Mystery Patient (Sebastian)

Sebastian (Super Sleuth) and the Purloined Sirloin (Sebastian)

Sebastian (Super Sleuth) and the Santa Claus Caper (Sebastian)

Sebastian (Super Sleuth) and the Secret of the Skewered Skier (Sebastian)

Sebastian (Super Sleuth) and the Stars-in-His-Eyes Mystery (Sebastian)

Sebastian (Super Sleuth) and the Time Capsule Caper (Sebastian)

Second Best (Sweet Valley Twins)

Second Chance (The Hit and Run Gang)

Second Chance (Sweet Valley High)

Second Grade Baby (Kids in Ms. Coleman's Class)

Second Sight (Mindwarp)

Second Sighting (Strange Matter)

See You Tomorrow, Charles (First Grade)

The Seer (Antrian)

A Sending of Dragons (Pit Dragon Trilogy)

Serious Science (The Adam Joshua Capers)

Serious Science: An Adam Joshua Story (The Adam Joshua Capers)

The Serpent's Children (Foxfire)

The Serpent's Tooth Mystery (Hardy Boys)

The Seven Songs of Merlin (Merlin)

Seventeen Against the Dealer (Tillerman Cycle)

Seventeen and In-Between (Elsie Edwards)

Seventeen Wishes (Christy Miller)

The Seventh Crystal (World of Adventure)

Seventh-Grade Menace (Fabulous Five)

Seventh Grade Rumors (Fabulous Five)

Shadow Academy (Star Wars Young Jedi Knights)

Shadow Chaser (Strange Matter)

Shadow Dancers (Abaloc)

The Shadow Killers (Hardy Boys)

Shadow Man (Danger.com)

Shadow of a Doubt (Nancy Drew Files)

Shadow of the Swastika (Choose Your Own Adventure)

Shadow Over Second (Peach Street Mudders)

Shadows in the Water (Starbuck Family Adventures)

Shaggy Dog's Animal Alphabet (Shaggy Dog)

Shaggy Dog's Birthday (Shaggy Dog)

Shaggy Dog's Halloween (Shaggy Dog)

Shaggy Dog's Tall Tale (Shaggy Dog)

The Shaggy Man of Oz (Oz)

Shake Up (Angel Park Soccer Stars)

Shanghaied to China (Trailblazers)

Shani's Scoop (B.Y. Times)

Shape-Shifter (Mindwarp)

Shapes (X Files)

Shards of Alderaan (Star Wars Young Jedi Knights)

Shark (Wolfbay Wings)

The Shattered Helmet (Hardy Boys)

She Grows and Graduates (Rosy Cole)

She Walks in Beauty (Rosy Cole)

Sheep in a Jeep (Sheep)

Sheep in a Shop (Sheep)

Sheep on a Ship (Sheep)

Sheep Out to Eat (Sheep)

Sheep Take a Hike (Sheep)

Sheep Trick or Treat (Sheep)

Sheepdog in the Snow (Animal Ark)

Sheer Terror (Hardy Boys Casefiles)

Shenanigans at Sugar Creek (Sugar Creek Gang)

Sherlock Chick and the Case of the Night Noises (Sherlock Chick)

Sherlock Chick and the Giant Egg Mystery (Sherlock Chick)

Sherlock Chick and the Peekaboo Mystery (Sherlock Chick)

Sherlock Chick's First Case (Sherlock Chick)

She's Not What She Seems (Sweet Valley High)

Shield of Fear (Hardy Boys)

Shiloh (Shiloh)

Shiloh Season (Shiloh)

Shining's Orphan (Thoroughbred)

Ship Ahoy (Lottery Luck)

Shipboard Wedding (Sweet Valley University)

Shipwreck Saturday (Little Bill)

Shiver (Danger.com)

Shock for the Secret Seven (The Secret Seven)

Shock Jock (Hardy Boys Casefiles)

Shock Wave (Time Surfers)

A Shocker on Shock Street (Goosebumps)

Shoelaces and Brussels Sprouts (Alex)

Shoot the Works (Three Investigators)

Shop 'Till You Drop . . . Dead! (Goosebumps: Give Yourself Goosebumps)

The Shore Road Mystery (Hardy Boys)

Short-Wave Mystery (Hardy Boys)

The Shortstop Who Knew Too Much (Tales from the Sandlot)

Shot from Midfield (Alden All Stars)

Show and Tell Mystery (Bobbsey Twins: The New Bobbsey Twins)

The Show-and-Tell War (The Adam Joshua Capers)

The Show-and-Tell War, and Other Stories About Adam Joshua (The Adam Joshua Capers)

Show Horse (The Saddle Club)

Show Jumper Wanted (Horseshoes)

Show Time! (Super Hoops)

Showdown (Choose Your Own Adventure)

Showdown (Sweet Valley High)

Showdown at Burnt Rock (Scrapper John)

Showdown at the Mall (Sabrina the Teenage Witch)

The Shrinking of Treehorn (Treehorn)

Sibling Rivalry (Fabulous Five)

Sidetracked to Danger (Hardy Boys)

Sideways Arithmetic from Wayside School (Wayside School)

Sideways Stories from Wayside School (Wayside School)

Sierra Gold Mystery (Dana Girls)

Sierra's Steeplechase (Thoroughbred)

The Sign of the Crooked Arrow (Hardy Boys)

Sign of the Dove (Dragon Chronicles)

The Sign of the Falcon (Nancy Drew)

The Sign of the Twisted Candles (Nancy Drew)

The Silent Scream (Nightmare Hall)

Silent Superstitions (Christy)

The Silent Suspect (Nancy Drew)

The Silent Track Star (Dallas O'Neil and the Baker Street Sports Club)

Silly Billy (Very Worst Monster)

Silly Tilly and the Easter Bunny (Silly Tilly)

Silly Tilly's Thanksgiving Dinner (Silly Tilly)

Silly Tilly's Valentine (Silly Tilly)

The SillyOZbul of Oz and the Magic Merry-Go-Round (Oz)

The SillyOZbul of Oz & Toto (Oz)

SillyOZbuls of Oz (Oz)

The Silver Chair (Chronicles of Narnia)

The Silver Cobweb (Nancy Drew)

Silver on the Tree (Dark Is Rising)

The Silver Princess in Oz (Oz)

Silver Spurs (Saved by the Bell)

Silver Stirrups (The Saddle Club)

Silver Wings (Choose Your Own Adventure)

Simon and His Boxes (Simon)

Simon and Marshall's Excellent Adventure (Eerie Indiana)

Simon and the Snowflakes (Simon)

Simon and the Wind (Simon)

Simon at the Circus (Simon)

Simon Finds a Feather (Simon)

Simon Finds a Treasure (Simon)

Simon in Summer (Simon)

Simon in the Moonlight (Simon)

Simon Makes Music (Simon)

Simon Says, "Croak!" (Spinetinglers)

Simon Welcomes Spring (Simon)

Sing, Elvis, Sing (The Weebie Zone)

The Sinister Omen (Nancy Drew)

Sinister Parade (Nancy Drew Files)

Sinister Signpost (Hardy Boys)

Sink or Swim! (The Secret World of Alex Mack)

Sisters at War (Sweet Valley Twins)

Sisters in Crime (Nancy Drew Files)

Soup Ahoy (Soup)

Soup and Me (Soup)

Soup for President (Soup)

Soup in Love (Soup)

Soup in the Saddle (Soup)

Soup on Fire (Soup)

Soup on Ice (Soup)

Soup on Wheels (Soup)

Soup 1776 (Soup)

Soup's Drum (Soup)

Soup's Goat (Soup)

Soup's Hoop (Soup)

Soup's Uncle (Soup)

South of the Border (Young Indiana Jones Chronicles: Choose Your Own Adventure)

South Pole Sabotage (Choose Your Own Adventure)

Space and Beyond (Choose Your Own Adventure)

Space Bingo (Time Surfers)

Space Brat (Space Brat)

Space Camp (Star Trek: Deep Space Nine)

Space Dog and Roy (Space Dog)

Space Dog and the Pet Show (Space Dog)

Space Dog in Trouble (Space Dog)

Space Dog, the Hero (Space Dog)

Space Food (Lunchroom)

Space Patrol (Choose Your Own Adventure)

The Space Ship in the Park (Space Ship Under the Apple Tree)

The Space Ship Returns to the Apple Tree (Space Ship Under the Apple Tree)

The Space Ship Under the Apple Tree (Space Ship Under the Apple Tree)

Space Vampire (Choose Your Own Adventure)

Spark of Suspicion (Hardy Boys)

Special Christmas (Sweet Valley High)

Special Delivery Mess (Silver Blades Figure Eights)

The Speckled Rose of Oz (Oz)

Spectacular Stone Soup (New Kids at the Polk Street School)

The Specter from the Magician's Museum (Lewis Barnavelt)

Speed Demon (NASCAR Pole Position Adventures)

Speed Surf (Internet Detectives)

Speedy in Oz (Oz)

Spell of the Screaming Jokers (Ghosts of Fear Street)

The Spell of the Sorcerer's Skull (Johnny Dixon)

Spelling Bee (Kids in Ms. Coleman's Class)

The Spider Beside Her (Graveyard School)

The Spider Sapphire Mystery (Nancy Drew)

Spider's Baby-Sitting Job (Spider)

Spider's First Day at School (Spider)

Spiderweb for Two (Melendy Family)

Spiked! (Hardy Boys Casefiles)

Spiked Snow (X Games Xtreme Mysteries)

Spilling the Beans (Saved by the Bell)

Spirit Song (Cheer Squad)

Spitting Image (Goners)

Splash Crash! (Time Surfers)

Splitting Image (Strange Matter)

Spooky and the Bad Luck Raven (Spooky the Cat)

Spooky and the Ghost Cat (Spooky the Cat)

Spooky and the Witch's Goat (Spooky the Cat)

Spooky and the Wizard's Bats (Spooky the Cat)

Spooky Night (Spooky the Cat)

The Spooky Sleepover (Eagle-Eye Ernie)

Spore (Star Wars Galaxy of Fear)

Sport (Harriet M. Welsh)

Spot and Friends Dress Up (Spot)

Spot and Friends Play (Spot)

Spot at Home (Spot)

Spot at Play (Spot)

Spot at the Fair (Spot)

Spot Bakes a Cake (Spot)

Spot Counts from One to Ten (Spot)

Spot Goes Splash! (Spot)

Spot Goes to a Party (Spot)

Spot Goes to School (Spot)

Spot Goes to the Beach (Spot)

Spot Goes to the Circus (Spot)

Spot Goes to the Farm (Spot)

Spot Goes to the Park (Spot)

Spot in the Garden (Spot)

Spot Joins the Parade (Spot)

Spot Learns to Count (Spot)

Spot Looks at Colors (Spot)

Spot Looks at Opposites (Spot)

Spot Looks at Shapes (Spot)

Spot Looks at the Weather (Spot)

Spot on the Farm (Spot)

Spot Sleeps Over (Spot)

Spot Tells the Time (Spot)

Spot Visits His Grandparents (Spot)

Spot Visits the Hospital (Spot)

Spotlight on Cody (Cody)

Spot's Alphabet (Spot)

Spot's Baby Sister (Spot)

Spot's Big Book of Colors, Shapes, and Numbers (Spot)

Spot's Big Book of Words (Spot)

Spot's Birthday Party (Spot)

Spot's Busy Year (Spot)

Spot's Doghouse (Spot)

Spot's Favorite Baby Animals (Spot)

Spot's Favorite Colors (Spot)

Spot's Favorite Numbers (Spot)

Spot's Favorite Words (Spot)

Spot's First Christmas (Spot)

Spot's First Easter (Spot)

Spot's First Picnic (Spot)

Spot's First Walk (Spot)

Spot's First Words (Spot)

Spot's Friends (Spot)

Spot's Magical Christmas (Spot)

Spot's Touch and Feel Day (Spot)

Spot's Toy Box (Spot)

Spot's Toys (Spot)

Spot's Walk in the Woods (Spot)

Spreading the Word (Saved by the Bell)

Spring Break (Silver Blades)

Spring Break (Sweet Valley High)

Spring Fever (B.Y. Times)

Spring Fever (Sweet Valley High)

Spring Sprouts (Pee Wee Scouts)

Spring Story (Brambly Hedge)

Spring to Stardom (Cheer Squad)

The Spy Code Caper (Eagle-Eye Ernie)

Spy for George Washington (Choose Your Own Adventure)

Spy for the Night Riders (Trailblazers)

Spy Girl (Sweet Valley University)

The Spy on Third Base (Peach Street Mudders)

Spying Eyes (Sabrina the Teenage Witch)

Squeeze (X Files)

Squeeze Play (Nancy Drew Files)

SS Heartbreak (Sweet Valley University)

Stable Farewell (The Saddle Club)

Stable Groom (The Saddle Club)

Stable Hearts (The Saddle Club)

Stable Manners (The Saddle Club)

Stable Witch (The Saddle Club)

Stacey and the Bad Girl (Baby-sitters Club)

Stacey and the Cheerleaders (Baby-sitters Club)

Stacey and the Fashion Victim (Baby-sitters Club Mysteries)

Stacey and the Haunted Masquerade (Baby-sitters Club Mysteries)

Stacey and the Missing Ring (Baby-sitters Club Mysteries)

Stowaway to the Mushroom Planet (Tyco Bass)

Stowaways (Star Trek: Deep Space Nine)

Stranded (Survival!)

Stranded on Terror Island (Ladd Family)

Stranding on Cedar Point (Neptune Adventures)

Strange Brew (Bone Chillers)

The Strange Case of Dr. Jekyll and Mr. Hyde (Wishbone Classics)

Strange Invaders (Visitors)

Strange Memories (Nancy Drew Files)

Strange Message in the Parchment (Nancy Drew)

The Strange Swimming Coach (Dallas O'Neil and the Baker Street Sports Club)

The Stranger (Animorphs)

A Stranger at Green Knowe (Green Knowe)

Stranger in Right Field (Peach Street Mudders)

A Stranger in the House (Sweet Valley High)

The Stranger in the Shadows (Nancy Drew)

Strategic Moves (Hardy Boys Casefiles)

The Streak (The Hit and Run Gang)

Street Spies (Hardy Boys Casefiles)

Streetcar Riots (The American Adventure)

Stress Point (Hardy Boys Casefiles)

Stretching the Truth (Sweet Valley Twins)

Stroke of Luck (Angel Park All Stars)

Student Body (Nightmare Hall)

Student Exchange (Spinetinglers)

Stuffin' It (Patrick's Pals)

Stupid Cupid (Holiday Five)

Stupid Cupids (Bad News Ballet)

The Stupids Die (The Stupids)

The Stupids Have a Ball (The Stupids)

The Stupids Step Out (The Stupids)

The Stupids Take Off (The Stupids)

The Substitute Creature (Spinetinglers)

The Substitute Teacher (Full House: Michelle)

Suddenly! (Preston)

Sugar and Spice Advice (Full House: Stephanie)

Sugar Creek Gang (Sugar Creek Gang)

Sugar Creek Gang at Snow Goose Lodge (Sugar Creek Gang)

Sugar Creek Gang Digs for Treasure (Sugar Creek Gang)

Sugar Creek Gang Flies to Cuba (Sugar Creek Gang)

Sugar Creek Gang Goes North (Sugar Creek Gang)

Sugar Creek Gang Goes Western (Sugar Creek Gang)

Sugar Creek Gang in School (Sugar Creek Gang)

Sugar Creek Gang on the Mexican Border (Sugar Creek Gang)

Sugar Creek Goes Camping (Sugar Creek Gang)

Sugar Creek in Chicago (Sugar Creek Gang)

Sugar Snow (Little House: My First Little House Books)

Sugarcane Island (Choose Your Own Adventure)

Summer Daze (B.Y. Times)

Summer Daze (Sister Sister)

Summer Horse (The Saddle Club)

Summer in the Country (Girlhood Journeys: Marie)

Summer Jobs (Baker's Dozen)

Summer MacCleary, Virginia, 1720 (American Diaries)

Summer Promise (Christy Miller)

Summer Reading Is Killing Me (Time Warp Trio)

Summer Rider (The Saddle Club)

Summer School (Kids in Ms. Coleman's Class)

Summer Story (Brambly Hedge)

Summer Switch (Annabel Andrews)

A Summer Without Horses (The Saddle Club)

Summertime in the Big Woods (Little House: My First Little House Books)

Sunflower Girl (Jenna V.)

Sunny (California Diaries)

Sunny, Diary Two (California Diaries)

Sunny-Side Up (Kids of the Polk Street School)

Sunset of the Sabertooth (Magic Tree House)

Super Amos (Culpepper Adventures)

The Super-Duper Cookie Caper (Bobbsey Twins: The New Bobbsey Twins)

Super Duper Pee Wee! (Pee Wee Scouts)

The Super-Duper Sleepover Party (Full House: Michelle)

Super-Fine Valentine (Little Bill)

Superbike (Choose Your Own Adventure)

Supercomputer (Choose Your Own Adventure)

Superduper Teddy (Nora and Teddy)

Superfudge (Fudge)

Superkid! (The Adam Joshua Capers)

Superstar Team (Angel Park All Stars)

Surf Monkeys (Choose Your Own Adventure)

Surfboard to Peril (Miss Mallard)

Surf's Up (Saved by the Bell)

Surprise Endings (Christy Miller)

Surprise Island (Boxcar Children)

Surprise! Surprise! (Sweet Valley Kids)

A Surprise Twist (Silver Blades)

Survival (Star Trek: The Next Generation: Starfleet Academy)

Survival at Sea (Choose Your Own Adventure)

Survival of the Fittest (Hardy Boys Casefiles)

Survival Run (Hardy Boys Casefiles)

Susannah and the Blue House Mystery (Susannah)

Susannah and the Poison Green Halloween (Susannah)

Susannah and the Purple Mongoose Mystery (Susannah)

The Suspect in the Smoke (Nancy Drew)

The Suspect Next Door (Nancy Drew Files)

The Suspicion (Animorphs)

Swallowdale (Swallows and Amazons)

Swallows and Amazons (Swallows and Amazons)

Swami on Rye (Max the Dog)

The Swami's Ring (Nancy Drew)

The Swamp Monster (Hardy Boys)

The Swarm (Star Wars Galaxy of Fear)

Sweet Dreams (Christy Miller)

Sweet Dreams, Spot (Spot)

Sweet Kiss of Summer (Sweet Valley University)

Sweet Revenge (Nancy Drew Files)

Sweet Valley Blizzard! (Sweet Valley Kids)

The Sweet Valley Clean-Up Team (Sweet Valley Kids)

Sweet Valley Slumber Party (Sweet Valley Kids)

Sweet Valley Trick or Treat (Sweet Valley Kids)

A Swiftly Tilting Planet (Time Fantasy Series)

Swiss Secrets (Nancy Drew Files)

Switching Channels (Eerie Indiana)

The Sword and the Circle (Arthurian Knights)

The Sword Bearer (Archives of Anthropos)

The Sword in the Stone (The Once and Future King)

The Sword of the Spirits (Sword of the Spirits)

System Crash (Internet Detectives)

T

T-Bone Trouble (Alex)

Tacky in Trouble (Tacky the Penguin)

Tacky the Penguin (Tacky the Penguin)

Taffy Sinclair and the Melanie Makeover (Taffy Sinclair)

Taffy Sinclair and the Romance Machine Disaster (Taffy Sinclair)

Taffy Sinclair and the Secret Admirer Epidemic (Taffy Sinclair)

Taffy Sinclair, Baby Ashley, and Me (Taffy Sinclair)

Taffy Sinclair Goes to Hollywood (Taffy Sinclair)

Taffy Sinclair, Queen of the Soaps (Taffy Sinclair)

Taffy Sinclair Strikes Again (Taffy Sinclair)

Tagged for Terror (Hardy Boys Casefiles)

Take a Bow, Krissy! (Here Come the Brownies)

Take a Hike! (The Secret World of Alex Mack)

Take Back the Night (Sweet Valley University)

Take Me Out of the Ball Game (McGee and Me!)

Take the Mummy and Run (Carmen Sandiego Mysteries)

Take to the Sky (Heartland)

Takeout Stakeout (The Mystery Files of Shelby Woo)

Taking Charge (Sweet Valley Twins)

Taking Sides (Sweet Valley High)

The Tale of Cutter's Treasure (Are You Afraid of the Dark?)

The Tale of the Bad-Tempered Ghost (Are You Afraid of the Dark?)

The Tale of the Blue Monkey (Ghosts of Fear Street)

The Tale of the Campfire Vampires (Are You Afraid of the Dark?)

The Tale of the Curious Cat (Are You Afraid of the Dark?)

The Tale of the Deadly Diary (Are You Afraid of the Dark?)

The Tale of the Egyptian Mummies (Are You Afraid of the Dark?)

The Tale of the Ghost Cruise (Are You Afraid of the Dark?)

The Tale of the Ghost Riders (Are You Afraid of the Dark?)

The Tale of the Horrifying Hockey Team (Are You Afraid of the Dark?)

Tale of the Missing Mascot (Wishbone Mysteries)

The Tale of the Mogul Monster (Are You Afraid of the Dark?)

The Tale of the Nightly Neighbors (Are You Afraid of the Dark?)

The Tale of the Phantom School Bus (Are You Afraid of the Dark?)

Tale of the Pulsating Gate (Are You Afraid of the Dark?)

The Tale of the Restless House (Are You Afraid of the Dark?)

The Tale of the Secret Mirror (Are You Afraid of the Dark?)

The Tale of the Shimmering Shell (Are You Afraid of the Dark?)

The Tale of the Sinister Statues (Are You Afraid of the Dark?)

The Tale of the Souvenir Shop (Are You Afraid of the Dark?)

The Tale of the Stalking Shadow (Are You Afraid of the Dark?)

The Tale of the Terrible Toys (Are You Afraid of the Dark?)

The Tale of the Three Wishes (Are You Afraid of the Dark?)

The Tale of the Virtual Nightmare (Are You Afraid of the Dark?)

The Tale of the Zero Hour (Are You Afraid of the Dark?)

A Tale of Two Sitters (Wishbone Adventures)

A Talent for Murder (Nancy Drew Files)

Talent Night Aboard the Hogwash (Piganeers)

Tales from Moominvalley (Moomintroll)

Tales of a Fourth Grade Nothing (Fudge)

Tales of Amanda Pig (Oliver and Amanda Pig)

The Tales of Olga da Polga (Olga da Polga)

Tales of Oliver Pig (Oliver and Amanda Pig)

Tales Too Scary to Tell at Camp (Graveyard School)

Talking It Over (B.Y. Times)

Talking to Dragons (Enchanted Forest Chronicles)

Tall, Dark and Deadly (Nancy Drew Files)

Tall, Dark, and Deadly (Sweet Valley High)

Tallyho, Pinkerton (Pinkerton)

Tangled Fortunes (Cousins Quartet)

Tanya and Emily in a Dance for Two (Tanya)

Tanya and the Magic Wardrobe (Tanya)

Tanya Steps Out (Tanya)

The Tap Dance Mystery (Eagle-Eye Ernie)

Taran Wanderer (Prydain Chronicles)

Tarot Says Beware (Herculeah Jones)

Tarry Awhile (Beany Malone)

A Taste for Noah (Noah)

A Taste for Terror (Hardy Boys Casefiles)

Tattoo of Death (Choose Your Own Adventure)

Taxi to Intrigue (Miss Mallard)

Teach Us, Amelia Bedelia (Amelia Bedelia)

Teacher Creature (Bone Chillers)

Teacher Crush (Sweet Valley High)

The Teacher from the Black Lagoon (Black Lagoon)

Teacher's Pet (B.Y. Times Kid Sisters)

Teacher's Pet (David and Goliath)

Teacher's Pet (Edison-Armstrong School)

Teacher's Pet (Kids in Ms. Coleman's Class)

Teacher's Pet (Sweet Valley Twins)

Team Play (The Saddle Club)

Team Trouble (Gymnasts)

Teamwork (Sweet Valley Twins)

Teddy Bears ABC (Teddy Bears)

Teddy Bears at the Seaside (Teddy Bears)

Teddy Bears Cure a Cold (Teddy Bears)

Teddy Bears Go Shopping (Teddy Bears)

Teddy Bears' Moving Day (Teddy Bears)

Teddy Bears 1 to 10 (Teddy Bears)

Teddy Bears Stay Indoors (Teddy Bears)

Teddy Bears Take the Train (Teddy Bears)

The Teen Model Mystery (Nancy Drew)

Teen Taxi (Fabulous Five)

Teeny Weeny Zucchinis (Pee Wee Scouts)

Teeny Witch and Christmas Magic (Teeny Witch)

Teeny Witch and the Great Halloween Ride (Teeny Witch)

Teeny Witch and the Perfect Valentine (Teeny Witch)

Teeny Witch and the Terrible Twins (Teeny Witch)

Teeny Witch and the Tricky Easter Bunny (Teeny Witch)

Teeny Witch Goes on Vacation (Teeny Witch)

Teeny Witch Goes to School (Teeny Witch)

Teeny Witch Goes to the Library (Teeny Witch)

Teetoncey (Outer Banks Trilogy)

Teetoncey and Ben O'Neal (Outer Banks Trilogy)

Tehanu (Earthsea)

The Ten O'Clock Club (Miss Know It All)

Ten Thousand Minutes at Sugar Creek (Sugar Creek Gang)

Ten Ways to Wreck a Date (Full House: Stephanie)

The Tennis Trap (Camp Sunnyside)

Ten's a Crowd! (Lottery Luck)

Teresa (The Elliott Cousins)

A Terminal Case of the Uglies (Bone Chillers)

Terminal Shock (Hardy Boys)

Terri and the Shopping Mall Disaster (Best Friends)

Terri the Great (Best Friends)

The Terrible Terri Rumors (Best Friends)

The Terrible Tickler (All-Star Meatballs)

The Terrible Truth (New Eden)

The Terrible Tryouts (Bad News Ballet)

Terror at Forbidden Falls (Ladd Family)

Terror at High Tide (Hardy Boys)

Terror in Australia (Choose Your Own Adventure)

Terror in the Sky (American Adventure)

Terror in Tiny Town (Deadtime Stories)

Terror Island (Choose Your Own Adventure)

Terror on the Titanic (Choose Your Own Adventure)

Terror on Track (Hardy Boys Casefiles)

Terrorist Trap (Choose Your Own Adventure)

Tessa Snaps Snakes (Australian Children)

Texas Trail to Calamity (Miss Mallard)

Thank You, Amelia Bedelia (Amelia Bedelia)

The Thanksgiving Day Parade Mystery (Dixon Twins)

The Thanksgiving Surprise (Nancy Drew Notebooks)

The Thanksgiving Treasure (Addie)

That Dreadful Day (Grandpa)

That Fatal Night (Sweet Valley High)

That Game from Outer Space (Oscar J. Noodleman)

That Julia Redfern (Julia Redfern)

That Mushy Stuff (Pee Wee Scouts)

That Old Zack Magic (Saved by the Bell)

That Terrible Halloween Night (Grandpa)

That's Exactly the Way It Wasn't (Grandpa)

That's the Spirit, Claude (Claude)

Then There Were Five (Melendy Family)

There's a Body in the Brontosaurus Room! (Our Secret Gang)

There's a Ghost in the Boys' Bathroom (Graveyard School)

There's a Ghost in the Coatroom (The Adam Joshua Capers)

There's a Shark in the Swimming Pool (Scaredy Cats)

There's Nothing to Do! (Grandpa)

These Happy Golden Years (Little House)

They Say (Eerie Indiana)

Thick as Thieves (Hardy Boys Casefiles)

Thieves of Tyburn Square (Trailblazers)

The Thing in the Closet (Spooksville)

The Thing Under the Bed (Bone Chillers)

Things (Visitors)

Think, Corrie Think! (Here Come the Brownies)

Third Grade Detectives (Tales from Third Grade)

Third Grade Stars (Tales from Third Grade)

Third Planet from Altair (Choose Your Own Adventure)

Third-Prize Surprise (Bad News Bunny)

Thirteen (Kobie Roberts)

Thirteen Things Not to Tell a Parent (Cousins Club)

Thirteen Ways to Sink a Sub (Hobie Hanson)

The Thirteenth Pearl (Nancy Drew)

This Can't Be Happening at Macdonall Hall! (Bruno and Boots)

This Is the Bear (Fred Bear)

This Is the Bear and the Bad Little Girl (Fred Bear)

This Is the Bear and the Picnic Lunch (Fred Bear)

This Is the Bear and the Scary Night (Fred Bear)

This Side of Evil (Nancy Drew Files)

The Threat (Animorphs)

Three Cheers for Keisha (Magic Attic Club)

Three Cheers for Tacky (Tacky the Penguin)

Three Cheers for You, Cassie! (Paxton Cheerleaders)

Three Cheers, Secret Seven (The Secret Seven)

Three-Cornered Mystery (Dana Girls)

Three Evil Wishes (Ghosts of Fear Street)

Three-Ring Terror (Hardy Boys)

The Three-Seated Space Ship (Space Ship Under the Apple Tree)

Three-Star Billy (Very Worst Monster)

Three's a Crowd (Sweet Valley Twins)

Thrill on the Hill (Nancy Drew Notebooks)

Thriller Diller (Three Investigators)

Throne of Zeus (Choose Your Own Adventure)

Through the Black Hole (Choose Your Own Adventure)

Through the Medicine Cabinet (The Zack Files)

Through Thick and Thin (Baker's Dozen)

Throughout the Year with Harriet (Harriet)

Throw-Away Pets (Pet Patrol)

Thunder Falls (Dinotopia)

Thunder Valley (World of Adventure)

Thunderhead (Flicka)

Thursday Trials (Juli Scott Super Sleuth)

Thy Friend, Obadiah (Obadiah Starbuck)

Tianna the Terrible (Anika Scott)

Tic-Tac Terror (Hardy Boys)

Tick Tock, You're Dead! (Goosebumps: Give Yourself Goosebumps)

Tidy Titch (Titch)

Tiger, Tiger (X Files)

Tight Rein (The Saddle Club)

Tik-Tok of Oz (Oz)

Tiki Doll of Doom (Bone Chillers)

Till Death Do Us Part (Nancy Drew Files)

Time and Mr. Bass (Tyco Bass)

Time Benders (World of Adventure)

Time for Battle (The American Adventure)

Time for Bed, Ned (Ned)

The Time Machine and Other Cases (Einstein Anderson)

The Time Shifter (The Outer Limits)

Time Terror (Spooksville)

A Time to Cherish (Christy Miller)

Time to Rhyme with Calico Cat (Calico Cat)

Time Will Tell (Sierra Jensen)

The Tin Woodman of Oz (Oz)

Titanic (Survival!)

Titch (Titch)

Titch and Daisy (Titch)

To and Again (Freddy)

To Catch a Little Fish (Mercer Mayer's Critters of the Night)

To Catch a Thief (Sweet Valley High)

To Cheat or Not to Cheat (Full House: Stephanie)

Triplet Trouble and the Field Day Disaster (Triplet Trouble)

Triplet Trouble and the Pizza Party (Triplet Trouble)

Triplet Trouble and the Red Heart Race (Triplet Trouble)

Triplet Trouble and the Runaway Reindeer (Triplet Trouble)

Triplet Trouble and the Talent Show Mess (Triplet Trouble)

Trippin' Out (Moesha)

Trixie and the Cyber Pet (Petsitters Club)

The Trolley to Yesterday (Johnny Dixon)

Trouble Ahead (Saved by the Bell)

Trouble at Alcott School (Peanut Butter and Jelly)

Trouble at Bamboo Bay (Eric Sterling, Secret Agent)

Trouble at Camp Treehouse (Nancy Drew Notebooks)

Trouble at Coyote Canyon (Hardy Boys)

Trouble at Foxhall (Riding Academy)

Trouble at Home (Sweet Valley High)

Trouble at Lake Tahoe (Nancy Drew)

Trouble in Tahiti (Nancy Drew Files)

Trouble in the Gym (Gymnasts)

Trouble in the Pipeline (Hardy Boys Casefiles)

Trouble in Toyland (Bobbsey Twins: The New Bobbsey Twins)

Trouble on Cloud City (Star Wars Young Jedi Knights)

The Trouble on Janus (Jack and Danny One)

Trouble on Planet Earth (Choose Your Own Adventure)

Trouble on the Ohio River (The American Adventure)

Trouble on Tuesday (Juli Scott Super Sleuth)

Trouble Takes the Cake (Nancy Drew Notebooks)

The Trouble with Flirting (Fabulous Five)

The Trouble with Patti (Sleepover Friends)

The Trouble with Spider (Spider)

Troublemaker (Sweet Valley High)

Troubling a Star (Vicky Austin)

Truckers (Bromeliad)

True Blue (Sitting Pretty)

True Blue Hawaii (Clueless)

True Friends (Christy Miller)

True Romance (Silver Creek Riders)

True Thriller (Hardy Boys Casefiles)

Trumpet of Terror (Choose Your Own Adventure)

The Truth About Boys (Full House: Stephanie)

The Truth About Ryan (Sweet Valley University)

The Truth About Sixth Grade (Murphy Family)

The Truth About Stacey (Baby-sitters Club)

The Truth About Taffy Sinclair (Taffy Sinclair)

Truth or Die (Nightmare Hall)

Truth Trap! (The Secret World of Alex Mack)

Tub Time for Harry (Harry the Hippo)

Tucker's Countryside (Chester Cricket)

Tucket's Ride (The Tucket Adventures)

The Tuesday Cafe (Harper Winslow)

Tug of War (Sweet Valley Twins)

Tumbling Ghosts (Gymnasts)

Tune into Terror (Strange Matter)

The Turkey That Ate My Father (What Ate Who)

Turkey Trouble (The Adam Joshua Capers)

Turkey Trouble (Holiday Friends)

Turkey Trouble (Kids of the Polk Street School)

The Turkey's Side of It (The Adam Joshua Capers)

A Turn for Noah (Noah)

The Turnabout Trick (Trick Books)

The Turret (The Rescuers)

Tut Tut (Time Warp Trio)

'Twas the Fight Before Christmas (McGee and Me!)

The Twin Dilemma (Nancy Drew)

Twin Trouble (Kids in Ms. Coleman's Class)

Twin Trouble (Stars)

Twin Troubles (Full House: Stephanie)

The Twins and the Wild West (Sweet Valley Kids)

Twins Big Pow-Wow (Sweet Valley Kids)

Twins Get Caught (Sweet Valley Twins)

The Twins Go to College (Sweet Valley Twins Super Edition)

Twins Go to the Hospital (Sweet Valley Kids)

The Twins Hit Hollywood (Sweet Valley Twins)

Twins in Love (Sweet Valley Twins)

Twins in Trouble (B.Y. Times)

Twins' Little Sister (Sweet Valley Twins)

The Twins' Mystery Teacher (Sweet Valley Kids)

The Twins Take Paris (Sweet Valley Twins Super Edition)

The Twisted Claw (Hardy Boys)

The Twisted Tale of Tiki Island (Goosebumps: Give Yourself Goosebumps)

Twister and Shout (McGee and Me!)

Two-Boy Weekend (Sweet Valley High)

Two Dog Biscuits (Jimmy and Janet)

Two-For-One Christmas Fun (Full House: Stephanie)

Two Friends Too Many (Peanut Butter and Jelly)

Two in the Wilderness (Aiken Family)

Two Points for Murder (Nancy Drew Files)

2095 (Time Warp Trio)

The Two Towers (The Lord of the Rings)

Typhoon! (Choose Your Own Adventure)

Tyrone and the Swamp Gang (Tyrone)

Tyrone, the Double Dirty Rotten Cheater (Tyrone)

Tyrone, the Horrible (Tyrone)

U

The Ultimate Challenge (Goosebumps: Give Yourself Goosebumps)

U.N. Adventure (Choose Your Own Adventure)

Un-happy New Year, Emma! (Emma)

Uncivil War (Hardy Boys Casefiles)

Uncle Terrible (Anatole)

Under His Spell (Nancy Drew Files)

Under Loch and Key (Goners)

Under the Big Top (Lassie)

Under the Magician's Spell (Goosebumps: Give Yourself Goosebumps)

Under Wraps (Strange Matter)

Undercover Angels (Sweet Valley University)

The Underground (Animorphs)

Underground Kingdom (Choose Your Own Adventure)

The Underground Railroad (Choose Your Own Adventure)

The Unicorns at War (Unicorn Club)

Unicorns Don't Give Sleigh Rides (The Adventures of the Bailey School Kids)

The Unicorns Go Hawaiian (Sweet Valley Twins Super Edition)

Unicorns in Love (Unicorn Club)

The Unknown (Animorphs)

The Up and Down Spring (Seasonal Adventures)

Up to Bat (Angel Park All Stars)

Update on Crime (Nancy Drew Files)

The Weird Science Mystery (Bobbsey Twins: The New Bobbsey Twins)

The Weird Soccer Match (Dallas O'Neil and the Baker Street Sports Club)

Weird, Weird West (Strange Matter)

Welcome Back, Stacey! (Baby-sitters Club)

Welcome Stranger (Beany Malone)

Welcome to Alien Inn (Bone Chillers)

Welcome to BSC, Abby (Baby-sitters Club)

Welcome to Camp Nightmare (Goosebumps)

Welcome to Camp Nightmare (Goosebumps Presents)

Welcome to Dead House (Goosebumps)

Welcome to Horror Hospital (Choose Your Own Nightmare)

Welcome to My Zoo (Full House: Michelle)

Welcome to the Terror-Go-Round (Deadtime Stories)

Welcome to the Wicked Wax Museum (Goosebumps: Give Yourself Goosebumps)

The Well (Logan Family)

Well Done, Secret Seven (The Secret Seven)

We're in Big Trouble, Blackboard Bear (Blackboard Bear)

We're in This Together, Patti! (Paxton Cheerleaders)

We're Off to See the Lizard (The Weebie Zone)

The Wereing (Werewolf Chronicles)

A Werewolf Followed Me Home (Scaredy Cats)

The Werewolf of Fever Swamp (Goosebumps)

The Werewolf of Twisted Tree Lodge (Goosebumps: Give Yourself Goosebumps)

Werewolf Skin (Goosebumps)

Werewolves Don't Go to Summer Camp (The Adventures of the Bailey School Kids)

Werewolves for Lunch (Mercer Mayer's Critters of the Night)

West to a Land of Plenty (Dear America)

Western Star (The Saddle Club)

Westmark (Westmark)

What a Catch! (Angel Park All Stars)

What Does a Witch Need? (Old Witch)

What Eric Knew (Sebastian Barth)

What Happened at Midnight? (Hardy Boys)

What Have You Done, Davy? (Davy)

What Jessica Wants (Sweet Valley High)

What Winston Saw (Sweet Valley University Thriller Editions)

What Your Parents Don't Know (Sweet Valley University)

What's a Daring Detective Like Me Doing in the Doghouse? (Stevie Diamond Mysteries)

What's Claude Doing? (Claude the Dog)

What's Cooking, Jenny Archer? (Jenny Archer)

What's the Matter, Davy? (Davy)

What's the Matter with Herbie Jones? (Herbie Jones)

What's Under My Bed? (Grandpa)

What's Up, Brother (Moesha)

Wheels (Tales of Trotter Street)

When Frank Was Four (Australian Children)

When Hitler Stole Pink Rabbit (Anna)

When I Was Nine (James Stevenson's Autobiographical Stories)

When Jenny Lost Her Scarf (Jenny and the Cat Club)

When Love Dies (Sweet Valley High)

When the Chips Are Down (Cyber.kdz)

When the Tripods Came (Tripods)

When Will I Read? (First Grade)

When Will This Cruel War Be Over? (Dear America)

Where Are You, Ernest and Celestine? (Ernest and Celestine)

Where Are You Going, Little Mouse? (Little Mouse)

Where Have All the Parents Gone? (Spinetinglers)

Where Have You Gone, Davy? (Davy)

Where's Spot (Spot)

Where's the Baby? (Very Worst Monster)

While Mrs. Coverlet Was Away (Mrs. Coverlet)

While the Clock Ticked (Hardy Boys)

A Whisper and a Wish (Christy Miller)

The Whisperer (Nightmare Hall)

The Whispering Mountain (Wolves Chronicles)

The Whispering Statue (Nancy Drew)

Whistle for Willie (Peter)

White Boat Rescue at Sugar Creek (Sugar Creek Gang)

White Lies (Sweet Valley High)

White Magic (Magical Mystery)

The White Mountains (Tripods)

White Water Terror (Nancy Drew Files)

Who Are You? (Choose Your Own Adventure)

Who Framed Alice Prophet? (Eerie Indiana)

Who Framed Mary Bubnik? (Bad News Ballet)

Who Invited Aliens to My Slumber Party? (Scaredy Cats)

Who Is Carrie? (The Arabus Family Saga)

Who Killed Harlowe Thrombey? (Choose Your Own Adventure)

Who Killed Mr. Boddy? (Clue)

Who Needs Third Grade? (Tales from Third Grade)

Who Stole Captain Porker's Treasure? (Piganeers)

Who Took the Book? (Hardy Boys: Frank and Joe Hardy: The Clues Brothers)

Who Will Be Miss Unicorn Club? (Unicorn Club)

Who's at Home with Anthony Ant? (Anthony Ant)

Who's Been Sleeping in My Grave? (Ghosts of Fear Street)

Who's Got a Secret? (Bad News Bunny)

Who's Got Gertie and How Can We Get Her Back? (Stevie Diamond Mysteries)

Who's in Love with Arthur? (Arthur Chapter Books)

Who's Orp's Girlfriend? (Orp)

Who's Out to Get Linda (Best Friends)

Who's Reading Darci's Diary? (Darci Daniels)

Who's the Man? (Super Hoops)

Who's to Blame? (Sweet Valley High)

Who's Who (B.Y. Times)

Who's Who (Sweet Valley High)

Whose Mouse Are You? (Little Mouse)

Whose Pet Is Best? (Nancy Drew Notebooks)

Why Are Boys So Weird? (Tales from Third Grade)

Why I Quit the Baby-Sitter's Club (Bone Chillers)

Why I'm Afraid of Bees (Goosebumps)

Why I'm Not Afraid of Ghosts (Ghosts of Fear Street)

The Wicked Cat (Spooksville)

Wicked for the Weekend (Nancy Drew Files)

Wicked Ways (Nancy Drew Files)

Wiggins for President (Freddy)

The Wild Baby (The Wild Baby)

The Wild Baby Gets a Puppy (The Wild Baby)

The Wild Baby Goes to Sea (The Wild Baby)

The Wild Cat Crime (Nancy Drew)

The Wild Culpepper Cruise (Culpepper Adventures)

A Wrinkle in Time (Time Fantasy Series)

Write on, Rosy! (Rosy Cole)

Write Up a Storm with the Polk Street School (Kids of the Polk Street School)

The Wrong Chemistry (Nancy Drew Files)

The Wrong Kind of Girl (Sweet Valley High)

Wrong Side of the Law (Hardy Boys Casefiles)

The Wrong Track (Nancy Drew Files)

The Wrong Way (B.Y. Times Kid Sisters)

X

X Marks the Spot (X Files)

Y

Yankee Belles in Dixie (Bonnets and Bugles)

Yankee Doodle Drumsticks (Lincoln Lions Band)

Yankee in Oz (Oz)

Yankee Swap (The Saddle Club)

Yard Sale (Mud Flat)

Year of Impossible Goodbyes (Sookan Bak)

The Year Without Christmas (Sweet Valley Twins Super Edition)

The Yellow Feather Mystery (Hardy Boys)

The Yellow House Mystery (Boxcar Children)

The Yellow Knight of Oz (Oz)

You and Me, Little Bear (Little Bear Books)

You Are a Genius (Choose Your Own Adventure)

You Are a Millionaire (Choose Your Own Adventure)

You Are a Monster (Choose Your Own Adventure)

You Are a Shark (Choose Your Own Adventure)

You Are a Superstar (Choose Your Own Adventure)

You Are an Alien (Choose Your Own Adventure)

You Are Microscopic (Choose Your Own Adventure)

You Bet Your Britches, Claude (Claude)

You Can't Eat Your Chicken Pox, Amber Brown (Amber Brown)

You Can't Scare Me! (Goosebumps)

You Can't Scare Me! (Goosebumps Presents)

You Read My Mind (Sister Sister)

You'll Soon Grow into Them, Titch (Titch)

The Young Black Stallion (Black Stallion)

Young Cam Jansen and the Baseball Mystery (Young Cam Jansen)

Young Cam Jansen and the Dinosaur Game (Young Cam Jansen)

Young Cam Jansen and the Ice Skate Mystery (Young Cam Jansen)

Young Cam Jansen and the Lost Tooth (Young Cam Jansen)

Young Cam Jansen and the Missing Cookie (Young Cam Jansen)

Young Indiana Jones and the Circle of Death (Young Indiana Jones)

Young Indiana Jones and the Curse of the Ruby Cross (Young Indiana Jones)

Young Indiana Jones and the Eye of the Tiger (Young Indiana Jones)

Young Indiana Jones and the Face of the Dragon (Young Indiana Jones)

Young Indiana Jones and the Ghostly Riders (Young Indiana Jones)

Young Indiana Jones and the Gypsy Revenge (Young Indiana Jones)

Young Indiana Jones and the Journey to the Underworld (Young Indiana Jones)

Young Indiana Jones and the Lost Gold of Durango (Young Indiana Jones)

Young Indiana Jones and the Mountain of Fire (Young Indiana Jones)

Young Indiana Jones and the Pirates' Loot (Young Indiana Jones)

Young Indiana Jones and the Plantation Treasure (Young Indiana Jones)

Young Indiana Jones and the Princess of Peril (Young Indiana Jones)

Young Indiana Jones and the Secret City (Young Indiana Jones)

Young Indiana Jones and the Titanic Adventure (Young Indiana Jones)

Young Indiana Jones and the Tomb of Terror (Young Indiana Jones)

The Young Unicorns (Vicky Austin)

Your Best Friend, Kate (Kate)

Your Code Name Is Jonah (Choose Your Own Adventure)

Your Mother Was a Neanderthal (Time Warp Trio)

Your Old Pal, Al (Al)

Your Turn—to Scream! (Spinetinglers)

You're a Genius, Blackboard Bear (Blackboard Bear)

You're Out! (The Hit and Run Gang)

You're Plant Food! (Goosebumps: Give Yourself Goosebumps)

You're the Boss, Baby Duck (Baby Duck)

Yours for a Day (Sweet Valley Twins)

Yours Forever (Christy Miller)

Yuck! (Emma)

Z

Z.A.P., Zoe, and the Musketeers (Z.A.P. and Zoe)

Zachary in Camping Out (Just Me and My Dad)

Zachary in I'm Zachary (Just Me and My Dad)

Zachary in the Championship (Just Me and My Dad)

Zachary in the Present (Just Me and My Dad)

Zachary in the Wawabongbong (Just Me and My Dad)

Zachary in the Winner (Just Me and My Dad)

Zack in Action (Saved by the Bell)

Zack Strikes Back (Saved by the Bell)

Zack's Last Scam (Saved by the Bell)

The Zanti Misfits (The Outer Limits)

Zap! I'm a Mind Reader (The Zack Files)

Zapped in Space (Goosebumps: Give Yourself Goosebumps)

Zappy Holidays! (Super Edition) (The Secret World of Alex Mack)

Zelda Strikes Again! (Zelda)

Zero Hour (Time Surfers)

Zero's Slider (Peach Street Mudders)

Zip (Wolfbay Wings)

Zombie Surf Commandos from Mars! (The Weird Zone)

Zombies Don't Do Windows (Mercer Mayer's Critters of the Night)

Zombies Don't Play Soccer (The Adventures of the Bailey School Kids)

Zoom on My Broom (Mercer Mayer's Critters of the Night)

The Zucchini Warriors (Bruno and Boots)

GENRE/SUBJECT INDEX

This index gives access by genre (in bold capital letters) and by subject, enabling you to find series by genre and identify books that deal with specific topics, such as horseback riding or U.S. history.

Activities—Baby-sitting
Baby-sitters Club
Baby-sitters Club Mysteries
Baby-sitters Club Super Specials
Baby-sitters Little Sister
Baby-sitters Little Sister Super
  Specials

Activities—Dancing
Angelina Ballerina
Bad News Ballet
Ballet Slippers
Tanya

ADVENTURE
Aiken Family
The American Adventure
Anika Scott
Animorphs
Anthony Monday
Arthur the Kid
Arthurian Knights
Black Stallion
Brian Robeson
Buffy, the Vampire Slayer
Choose Your Own Adventure
Choose Your Own Nightmare
Choose Your Own Star Wars
  Adventures
Chronicles of Narnia
Cooper Kids
Cucumbers Trilogy
Culpepper Adventures
Cyber.kdz
Cybersurfers
D.J. Dillon Adventures
Damar Chronicles
Danger.com
Danger Guys
Danny Dunn
Darci Daniels
Dark Is Rising
Diadem
Dragon

Dragon Chronicles
The Dragonling
Emily Eyefinger
Eric Sterling, Secret Agent
The Famous Five
Frightmares
Girls R.U.L.E.
Goners
The Great McGoniggle
Hannah and the Angels
Henry the Cat
Henry the Explorer
Indian in the Cupboard
Internet Detectives
Island Stallion
Jack and Danny One
Ladd Family
Little Toot
Liza, Bill, and Jed
Magic Attic Club
Magic School Bus
Mandie
Mind Over Matter
Mindwarp
Miss Pickerell
My Teacher
Neptune Adventures
Nora
Norby
The Once and Future King
Outer Banks Trilogy
Passport
Pit Dragon Trilogy
Red
Redwall
Reel Kids Adventures
The Rescuers
Salty
Saved by the Bell
Scrapper John
The Secret Seven
The Secret World of Alex Mack
Soup
Star Trek: Deep Space Nine

Star Trek: Starfleet Academy
Star Trek: The Next Generation:
  Starfleet Academy
Star Trek: Voyager: Starfleet
  Academy
Star Wars Galaxy of Fear
Star Wars Junior Jedi Knights
Star Wars Young Jedi Knights
Sugar Creek Gang
Survival!
Swallows and Amazons
Sword of the Spirits
Three Investigators
Time Fantasy Series
Time Surfers
Tom Swift
The Tucket Adventures
Vesper Holly
Visitors
Westmark
Wishbone Adventures
Wishbone Classics
Wizardry
Wolves Chronicles
World of Adventure
Wren
Young Indiana Jones
Young Indiana Jones Chronicles:
  Choose Your Own Adventure

African Americans
American Girls: Addy
The Arabus Family Saga
Contender
Dogtown Ghetto
Ernestine and Amanda
Everett Anderson
Jamaica
Judge and Jury
Julian and Huey
Justice Trilogy
Little Bill
Logan Family
Ludell
Maizon

African Americans (cont.)

Messy Bessey
Moesha
Patrick's Pals
Peter
Sister Sister
Susannah
Thomas and Grandfather

Aliens

Alien Adventures
Aliens
Space Above and Beyond
Space Ship Under the Apple Tree
Tripods

Angels

Forever Angels

ANIMAL FANTASY

Albert
Alex and the Cat
Anatole
Angelina Ballerina
Anthony Ant
Arnie
Arthur
Arthur Chapter Books
Arthur the Monkey
Aunt Eater
Babar
Baby Duck
Bad News Bunny
Basil of Baker Street
Bear
Beechwood Bunny Tales
Benjamin
Berenstain Bears
Berenstain Bears: Bear Scouts
Berenstain Bears: Big Chapter
   Books
Bernard
Bill and Pete
Bizzy Bones
Blackboard Bear
Blue Moose
Brambly Hedge
Brimhall
Bullfrog Books
Bunnicula
Bunny Trouble
Carl
Catwings
Chester Cricket
Chicago and the Cat
Claude the Dog
Clifford

Commander Toad
Cucumbers Trilogy
Curious George
D.W.
Danny and the Dinosaur
Davy
Detective Mole
Digby and Kate
Dinosaurs
Doctor Dolittle
Duck
Dumb Bunnies
Edward the Unready
Elmer
Emma
Ernest and Celestine
Five Monkeys
Flatfoot Fox
The Fourteen Forest Mice
Fox
Foxwood
Frances
Frank and Ernest
Franklin
Freddy
Frog
Frog and Toad
Froggy
Gator Girls
George and Martha
George and Matilda Mouse
Geraldine
Grumpy Bunny
Hank the Cowdog
Harriet
Harry the Hippo
Hattie Rabbit
Henrietta
Henry the Cat
Hopper
Hugh Pine
Jenny and the Cat Club
Jesse Bear
Johnny Lion
Judge Benjamin
Kate
Lilly
Little Bear
Little Bear Books
Little Brown Bear
Little Chick
Little Mouse
Little Polar Bear
Louanne Pig
Loudmouth George
Lyle
Maisy the Mouse

Martha
Marvin the Magnificent
Max and Ruby
Max the Dog
Mike and Harry
Minerva Louise
Miss Mallard
Miss Spider
Mole and Troll
Molesons
Moonbear
Morris and Boris
Mouse and Mole
Mr. and Mrs. Pig
Mud Flat
Nice Mice
Old Turtle
Olga da Polga
Oliver and Amanda Pig
P.J. Funnybunny
Paddington
Paddy Pork
Penguin Pete
Penrod
Petunia
Pig Pig
Piganeers
Piggins
Pigs
Pippa Mouse
Pleasant Fieldmouse
Poppleton
Possum Family
Preston
Rainbow Fish
Ralph S. Mouse
The Rats of NIMH
Redwall
The Rescuers
Rex and Lilly
Rinaldo
Rotten Ralph
Sebastian (Super Sleuth)
Shaggy Dog
Sheep
Sherlock Chick
Silly Tilly
Snail
Spider
Spooky the Cat
Spot
Tacky the Penguin
Voyage to the Bunny Planet
Warton and Morton
Webster and Arnold
Willy
Winnie the Pooh First Readers

Animals—Moles (cont.)
Molesons
Mouse and Mole
Silly Tilly

Animals—Monkeys
Arthur the Monkey
Curious George
Five Monkeys

Animals—Moose
Blue Moose
Morris and Boris

Animals—Pigs
Freddy
Geraldine
Louanne Pig
Mr. and Mrs. Pig
Oliver and Amanda Pig
Paddy Pork
Pig Pig
Piganeers
Piggins
Pigs
Poppleton
Preston

Animals—Polar bears
Little Polar Bear

Animals—Porcupines
Hugh Pine
Penrod

Animals—Possums
Possum Family

Animals—Rabbits
Bad News Bunny
Beechwood Bunny Tales
Bunny Trouble
Chicago and the Cat
Davy
Dumb Bunnies
Grumpy Bunny
Hattie Rabbit
Hopper
Loudmouth George
Max and Ruby
P.J. Funnybunny
Voyage to the Bunny Planet

Animals—Rats
The Rats of NIMH

Animals—Sheep
Sheep

Animals—Snails
Snail

Arthurian legends
Arthurian Knights
Kate Gordon
King Arthur
Merlin
The Once and Future King
Young Merlin Trilogy

Asian Americans
The Mystery Files of Shelby Woo
Rinko
Song Lee

Australia
Keith Shipley

Autobiography
James Stevenson's Autobiographical
   Stories

Babies
Carl
The Wild Baby

Birds
Bill and Pete

Birds—Chickens
Henrietta
Little Chick
Minerva Louise
Sherlock Chick

Birds—Ducks
Albert
Baby Duck
Bear
Miss Mallard

Birds—Geese
Petunia

Birds—Penguins
Penguin Pete
Tacky the Penguin

Birds—Ravens
Arabel and Mortimer

Boats, ships
Little Toot

Camps, camping
Camp Haunted Hills
Camp Sunnyside
Camp Zombie
China Tate

Canada
Avonlea
Harper Winslow
Starshine!

Careers
Frank and Ernest

Cars
NASCAR Pole Position Adventures

China
Foxfire

Christian life
Alex
The American Adventure
American Adventure
Anika Scott
Best Friends
Bonnets and Bugles
Cassie Perkins
China Tate
Christy Miller
Clearwater Crossing
Cooper Kids
D.J. Dillon Adventures
Dallas O'Neil and the Baker Street
   Sports Club
Dallas O'Neil Mysteries
The Home School Detectives
Jenna V.
Juli Scott Super Sleuth
Ladd Family
Lassie
McGee and Me!
Reel Kids Adventures
Sugar Creek Gang
Ten Commandments Mysteries
Three Cousins Detective Club
Trailblazers
Twelve Candles Club
Winds of Light

Clubs
All-Star Meatballs
Always Friends
Baby-sitters Club
Baby-sitters Club Mysteries
Baby-sitters Club Super Specials
Baby-sitters Little Sister
Baby-sitters Little Sister Super
   Specials
Baker Street Irregulars
Black Cat Club
Clue Jr.
Dallas O'Neil and the Baker Street
   Sports Club

FAMILY LIFE (cont.)

Little House: The Caroline Years
Little House: The Rose Years
Little House Chapter Books
Little Women Journals
Lizzie Logan
Lottery Luck
Louanne Pig
Louie
Lucky
Ludell
Lyle
McGee and Me!
Maizon
Marvin Redpost
Matthew Martin
Melendy Family
Mennyms
Mishmash
Mitzi
The Moffats
Molesons
Molly
Moonbear
Mr. and Mrs. Pig
Mrs. Coverlet
Murphy Family
Nancy Bruce
Ned
New Eden
Noah
Nora and Teddy
Obadiah Starbuck
Oliver and Amanda Pig
Orphan Train Adventures
Orphelines
Penny
Pinkerton
Portraits of Little Women
Posy Bates
Ramona Quimby
Rex and Lilly
Rinko
Roommates
Rosa Trilogy
Rosy Cole
Russell
Sam Krupnik
Seasons with Grandma
Sierra Jensen
Sister Sister
Sisters
Sookan Bak
Sophie
Stanley

Starshine!
Sterling Family
Stone Book Quartet
The Stupids
Tales of Trotter Street
Thomas and Grandfather
Tillerman Cycle
Titch
Tom and Pippo
Very Worst Monster
Vicky Austin
Wisconsin Farm

Family life—Cousins
Cousins Club
Cousins Quartet
The Elliott Cousins
Harvey
Ten Commandments Mysteries
Three Cousins Detective Club

Family life—Grandparents
Baby Duck
Grandaddy
Grandma
Grandma's Attic
Grandpa
Gus and Grandpa
Katie Morag
Nancy Bruce

Family life—Siblings
Amy and Laura
Andie and the Boys
Angela
Arthur the Monkey
Boxcar Children
Brian and Pea Brain
Elisa
Exiles
Fudge
The Great Brain
Hatford Boys
Julian and Huey
Kane Family
Katie
Little Women Journals
Liza, Bill, and Jed
Mary Rose
Max and Ruby
Melendy Family
Murphy Family
Nora and Teddy
Oliver and Amanda Pig
Pigs
Portraits of Little Women

Ramona Quimby
Rex and Lilly
Roommates
Russell
Sam and Robert
Sisters

Family life—Triplets
Triplet Trouble

Family life—Twins
The Adventures of Mary-Kate and Ashley
Bobbsey Twins
Bobbsey Twins: The New Bobbsey Twins
Dixon Twins
Fourth Floor Twins
Jimmy and Janet
Judge and Jury
Sam and Dave Mysteries
Short Stirrup Club
Sister Sister
Sweet Valley High
Sweet Valley Twins
Sweet Valley Twins Super Edition
Sweet Valley University
Sweet Valley University Thriller Editions

FANTASY
Abaloc (Apple Lock)
The Adventures of the Bailey School Kids
Aeriel Trilogy
Age of Magic Trilogy
Albert the Dragon
Alistair
Anatole
Annabel Andrews
Archives of Anthropos
Bailey City Monsters
Blossom Culp
The Borrowers
Brigid Thrush books
Bromeliad
Budgie
Camp Haunted Hills
Chronicles of Narnia
Corduroy
Coven Tree
Damar Chronicles
Dark Is Rising
Dear Dragon
Diadem
Dinotopia
Dorrie

Dr. Merlin
Dragon
Dragon Chronicles
Dragon of the Lost Sea Fantasies
The Dragonling
Earthsea
Emily Eyefinger
Emma
Enchanted Forest Chronicles
Fireball
Five Children
Forever Angels
Fred Bear
Funnybones
Fuzzy Rabbit
Georgie
Ghost Squad
Green Knowe
Hannah and the Angels
Harold and the Purple Crayon
Harry and Chicken
Help, I'm Trapped
Indian in the Cupboard
Investigators of the Unknown
Jewel Kingdom
Johnny Dixon
Justice Trilogy
Kate Gordon
King Arthur
Lewis Barnavelt
Little Toot
The Littles
The Lonely Doll
The Lord of the Rings
McBroom
Magic Attic Club
Magic Moscow
Magic School Bus
Magic Shop
Magic Tree House
Magical Mystery
Mary Poppins
Mennyms
Mercer Mayer's Critters of the Night
Merlin
Mindwarp
Miss Flora McFlimsey
Miss Know It All
Moomintroll
Mrs. Pepperpot
Mrs. Piggle-Wiggle
My Teddy Bear
Nora
Old Bear Stories
Old Witch

Otto
The Outer Limits
Oz
Phantom Rider
Pit Dragon Trilogy
Prydain Chronicles
Sabrina the Teenage Witch
The Secret World of Alex Mack
Simon
Spirit Flyer
Tales from the Odyssey
Tales from the Sandlot
Tales of Gom in the Legends of Ulm
Teddy Bears
Teeny Witch
Time Fantasy Series
Time Surfers
Time Trilogy
Tom Swift
Treehorn
Very Worst Monster
Visitors
Wayside School
The Weebie Zone
Westmark
What Ate Who
The Wild Baby
Winds of Light
Witch
Witch, Goblin, and Ghost
Wizard and Wart
Wizardry
Wolves Chronicles
World Famous Muriel
World of Adventure
Worst Witch
Wren
X Files
Young Indiana Jones
Young Indiana Jones Chronicles: Choose Your Own Adventure
Young Merlin Trilogy
The Zack Files

Farms
Sophie
Wisconsin Farm

Fish
Rainbow Fish

France
Girlhood Journeys: Marie

Friendship
Addie
Al (Alexandra)

Alden All Stars
All-Star Meatballs
Always Friends
Amber Brown
Angel Park All Stars
Angel Park Hoop Stars
Angel Park Soccer Stars
Annie Bananie
Australian Children
B.Y. Times
B.Y. Times Kid Sisters
Baby-sitters Club
Baby-sitters Club Super Specials
Baby-sitters Little Sister
Baby-sitters Little Sister Super Specials
Bad News Ballet
Ballet Slippers
Beezy
Best Enemies
Best Friends
Betsy-Tacy
Bill and Pete
Black Cat Club
Bruno and Boots
California Diaries
Camp Sunnyside
Casey, Jenny, and Kate
Casey, Tracey and Company
Castle Court Kids
Charlotte Cheetham
Cheer Squad
Chester Cricket
Christy Miller
Clearwater Crossing
Cody
Culpepper Adventures
Danger Guys
Darci Daniels
Digby and Kate
Disney Girls
Duck
Eco Kids
Eddie Wilson
Edison-Armstrong School
Egerton Hall Novels
The Elliott Cousins
Elsie Edwards
Ernestine and Amanda
Fabulous Five
First Grade
First Grade Is the Best
Friends and Amigos
The Friendship Ring
Frog and Toad
Full House: Club Stephanie

Friendship (cont.)
Full House: Michelle
Full House: Stephanie
Gator Girls
George and Martha
Girls R.U.L.E.
Gymnasts
Harriet M. Welsh
Harry and Chicken
Henry Huggins
Herbie Jones
Here Come the Brownies
The Hit and Run Gang
Hobie Hanson
Holiday Five
Holiday Friends
Horrible Harry
Investigators of the Unknown
Invisible Inc.
Jamaica
Julian and Huey
Junie B. Jones
Junior Gymnasts
Kate
Kids in Ms. Coleman's Class
Kids on Bus 5
Leo and Emily
Lila Fenwick
Lincoln Lions Band
Little Bill
Little Soup
Lizzie Logan
Lottery Luck
Maggie Marmelstein
Magic Attic Club
Maizon
Mandie
Max Malone
Moesha
Mole and Troll
Molly
Never Sink Nine
New Eden
New Kids at the Polk Street School
Nutty Nutsell
Orp
Paxton Cheerleaders
Peanut Butter and Jelly
Pee Wee Scouts
Pet Lovers Club
Pet Patrol
Peter
Petsitters Club
Pinky and Rex
Pippi Longstocking
Pony Pals

Pony Tails
Poppleton
Reel Kids Adventures
Riding Academy
The Saddle Club
Seasonal Adventures
The Secret World of Alex Mack
Short Stirrup Club
Silver Blades Figure Eights
Silver Creek Riders
Sisters
Sitting Pretty
Sleepover Friends
Soccer Stars
Soup
Space Ship Under the Apple Tree
Stars
Starshine!
Susannah
Swallows and Amazons
Sweet Valley High
Sweet Valley Kids
Sweet Valley Twins
Sweet Valley Twins Super Edition
Sweet Valley University
Sweet Valley University Thriller
  Editions
Tales from Third Grade
39 Kids on the Block
Thoroughbred
Twelve Candles Club
Unicorn Club
Witch, Goblin, and Ghost
Wolfbay Wings

Frogs and toads
Bullfrog Books
Commander Toad
Frog
Frog and Toad
Froggy
Warton and Morton

Frontier and pioneer life
Addie
Aiken Family
American Girls: Kirsten
Golly Sisters
Little House
Little House: My First Little House
  Books
Little House: The Caroline Years
Little House: The Rose Years
Little House Chapter Books
The Tucket Adventures
Wisconsin Farm

Geography
Carmen Sandiego Mysteries

Germany
Lechow Family

Ghosts
Blossom Culp
Georgie
Ghost Squad
Ghost Stories
Ghostwriter
Green Knowe
Haunting with Louisa
Jeffrey's Ghost
Phantom Rider

Greenland
Tobias

Helicopters
Budgie

Hispanic Americans
American Girls: Josefina
¡Chana!
Dogtown Ghetto
Friends and Amigos
Rosa Trilogy

HISTORICAL
Addie
Aiken Family
All-of-a-Kind Family
American Adventure
The American Adventure
American Diaries
American Girls: Addy
American Girls: Felicity
American Girls: Josefina
American Girls: Kirsten
American Girls: Molly
American Girls: Samantha
Anna
The Arabus Family Saga
Arthur the Kid
Arthurian Knights
Avonlea
Bastable Family
Betsy-Tacy
Bonnets and Bugles
Children of America
Christy
Daughters of Liberty
Dear America
Ellis Island
Flambards

Foxfire
Girlhood Journeys: Juliet
Girlhood Journeys: Kai
Girlhood Journeys: Marie
Girlhood Journeys: Shannon
Golly Sisters
Gordy Smith
The Great Brain
Heartland
Ike and Mama
Johnny May
Julian Escobár
Kitty
Lechow Family
Little House
Little House: My First Little House
  Books
Little House: The Caroline Years
Little House: The Rose Years
Little House Chapter Books
Little Women Journals
Logan Family
Ludell
Mandie
Molly
Mr. Yowder
My Name Is America
Obadiah Starbuck
The Once and Future King
Once Upon America
Orphan Train Adventures
Orphan Train Children
Outer Banks Trilogy
Portraits of Little Women
Rinko
Scrapper John
Sookan Bak
Sterling Family
Stone Book Quartet
Survival!
Trailblazers
The Tucket Adventures
Winds of Light
Wisconsin Farm
Young Merlin Trilogy

Holidays
Addie
Cranberryport
Dear Dragon
Dragon
Emma
Grumpy Bunny
Henrietta
Holiday Five
Holiday Friends

Humbug
Lincoln Lions Band
Miss Flora McFlimsey
Noah
Rotten Ralph
Silly Tilly
Spider
Teeny Witch
What Ate Who

HORROR
Are You Afraid of the Dark?
Babysitter
Bone Chillers
Buffy, the Vampire Slayer
Camp Zombie
Choose Your Own Nightmare
Deadtime Stories
Eerie Indiana
Fiendly Corners
Ghosts of Fear Street
Goosebumps
Goosebumps: Give Yourself
  Goosebumps
Goosebumps Presents
Goosebumps Series 2000
Graveyard School
House of Horrors
Mindwarp
My Babysitter
Nightmare Hall
The Outer Limits
Spinetinglers
Spooksville
Strange Matter
Sweet Valley University Thriller
  Editions
Vampire Promise
Werewolf Chronicles
Witch
X Files

Hospitals
Med Center

HUMOR
Addie
Adrian Mole
The Adventures of the Bailey
  School Kids
Aldo Sossi
Alex and the Cat
Alexander
Ali Baba Bernstein
Alice
Alien Adventures

Aliens
Alistair
All-Star Meatballs
Amber Brown
Amelia Bedelia
Anastasia Krupnik
Angel
Angela
Annabel Andrews
Arabel and Mortimer
Arthur the Kid
Aunt Nina
Bad News Bunny
Bagthorpe Saga
Bailey City Monsters
Beany Malone
Bear
Beezy
Benjamin
Berenstain Bears
Berenstain Bears: Bear Scouts
Berenstain Bears: Big Chapter
  Books
Best Enemies
Betsy
Bingo Brown
Black Cat Club
Black Lagoon
The Blossom Family
Blue Moose
Bone Chillers
Brian and Pea Brain
Brimhall
Bruno and Boots
Bullfrog Books
Bunnicula
Bunny Trouble
Calico Cat
Camp Haunted Hills
Carl
Charlotte Cheetham
Chester Cricket
Claude
Clifford
Commander Toad
Curious George
The Cut-Ups
D.W.
Dagmar Schultz
Darci Daniels
Desdemona
Dinah
Doug Chronicles
Dr. Merlin
Dragon
Dumb Bunnies

HUMOR (cont.)

Duncan and Dolores
Edward the Unready
Elisa
Elmer
Emily Eyefinger
Emma
Exiles
Five Monkeys
Flatfoot Fox
Fox
Frances
Frank and Ernest
Fred Bear
Frog
Frog and Toad
Froggy
Fudge
Funny Firsts
Funnybones
Gator Girls
Genghis Khan
George and Martha
Georgie
Geraldine
Germy
Golly Sisters
Grandpa
Granny
The Great Brain
The Great Skinner
Grumpy Bunny
Hank the Cowdog
Harriet the Troublemaker
Harry
Harry and Chicken
Harry the Dirty Dog
Harvey
Hatford Boys
Hattie Rabbit
Help, I'm Trapped
Henry and Mudge
Henry Huggins
Henry Reed
Henry the Explorer
Herculeah Jones
Hobie Hanson
Hugh Pine
Humbug
Incognito Mosquito
Invisible Inc.
Isabelle
Jeffrey's Ghost
Jenny Archer
Jimmy and Janet
Jimmy's Boa

Johnny Lion
Josie Smith
Judge Benjamin
Julia Redfern
Junie B. Jones
Kids of the Polk Street School
Leo and Emily
Lila Fenwick
Lilly
Lincoln Lions Band
Little Soup
Loudmouth George
Lucky
Lunchroom
M and M
McBroom
McGurk
Madeline
Maggie Marmelstein
Magic Moscow
Magic School Bus
Martha
Marvin Redpost
Mary Rose
Matthew Martin
Max and Ruby
Max Malone
Mercer Mayer's Critters of the
    Night
Messy Bessey
Mike and Harry
Minerva Louise
Mishmash
Miss Mallard
Miss Nelson
Morris and Boris
Mr. and Mrs. Pig
Mr. Putter and Tabby
Mr. Yowder
Mrs. Coverlet
Mrs. Gaddy
Mrs. Pepperpot
Mrs. Piggle-Wiggle
Mrs. Toggle
Mud Flat
Murphy Family
Nate the Great
New Eden
Nice Mice
Nutty Nutsell
Old Turtle
Old Witch
Olga da Polga
Orp
Oscar J. Noodleman
P.J. Funnybunny

Paddington
Petunia
Pig Pig
Piganeers
Pigs
Pinkerton
Pippi Longstocking
The Plant That Ate Dirty Socks
Poppleton
Possum Family
Posy Bates
Preston
Professor Xargle
Ralph S. Mouse
Ramona Quimby
Rinaldo
Ronald Morgan
Rosy Cole
Rotten Ralph
Russell
Sabrina the Teenage Witch
Sam and Robert
Sam Krupnik
Scaredy Cats
Seasonal Adventures
Sheep
Slimeballs
Song Lee
Sophie
Soup
Space Brat
Space Dog
Spencer's Adventures
Stanley
The Stupids
Tales from the Sandlot
Tales from Third Grade
Time Warp Trio
Treehorn
Trick Books
Trig
Tyrone
Veronica
Very Worst Monster
Vesper Holly
Wayside School
The Weebie Zone
The Weird Zone
What Ate Who
The Wild Baby
Winnie the Pooh First Readers
Witch
Wizard and Wart
World Famous Muriel
Worst Person
Worst Witch

MYSTERY (cont.)

The Adventures of Mary-Kate and Ashley
Ali Baba Bernstein
Anthony Monday
Aunt Eater
Baby-sitters Club Mysteries
Baker Street Irregulars
Basil of Baker Street
Bessledorf Hotel
Blossom Culp
Bobbsey Twins: The New Bobbsey Twins
Boxcar Children
Brian and Pea Brain
Bunnicula
Cam Jansen
Carmen Sandiego Mysteries
Casebusters
Choose Your Own Adventure
Christie & Company
Clue
Clue Jr.
Cranberryport
Culpepper Adventures
Cyber.kdz
Dallas O'Neil and the Baker Street Sports Club
Dallas O'Neil Mysteries
Dana Girls
Danger.com
Danger Guys
Darcy J. Doyle, Daring Detective
Desmond
Detective Mole
Determined Detectives
Dixon Twins
Doris Fein
Eagle-Eye Ernie
Eerie Indiana
Einstein Anderson
Encyclopedia Brown
The Famous Five
Flatfoot Fox
Fourth Floor Twins
Foxwood
Frightmares
Ghost Squad
Ghost Stories
Ghostwriter
The Great McGoniggle
Hardy Boys
Hardy Boys: Frank and Joe Hardy: The Clues Brothers
Hardy Boys Casefiles
Harvey

Haunting with Louisa
Herculeah Jones
The Home School Detectives
Houdini Club Magic Mystery
Incognito Mosquito
Internet Detectives
Invisible Inc.
Jeffrey's Ghost
Johnny Dixon
Juli Scott Super Sleuth
Liza, Bill, and Jed
M and M
McGurk
Magic Mystery
Magic Tree House
Magical Mystery
Mandie
Match Wits with Sherlock Holmes
Meg Mackintosh: A Solve-It-Yourself Mystery
Mind Over Matter
Miss Mallard
My Dog
The Mystery Files of Shelby Woo
Nancy Drew
Nancy Drew Files
Nancy Drew Notebooks
Nate the Great
Nicki Holland
Nightmare Hall
Our Secret Gang
Piggins
Polka Dot Private Eye
Private Eyes Club
Sam and Dave Mysteries
Sam and Robert
Sebastian Barth
Sebastian (Super Sleuth)
The Secret Seven
Sherlock Chick
Something Queer
Sports Mysteries
Starbuck Family Adventures
Stevie Diamond Mysteries
Super Snoop Sam Snout
Susannah
Ten Commandments Mysteries
Three Cousins Detective Club
Three Investigators
Vicky Austin
Wishbone Mysteries
World Famous Muriel
X Games Xtreme Mysteries
Young Cam Jansen

Native Americans
Indian in the Cupboard

Nature
Long Pond
Neptune Adventures

Nigeria
Girlhood Journeys: Kai

Orphans
Miss Know It All
Orphan Train Adventures
Orphan Train Children
Orphelines
Penny
Winds of Light

Pets
Alex and the Cat
Animal Ark
Christopher
David and Goliath
Desmond
Duncan and Dolores
Frightmares
Jimmy's Boa
Lucky
Olga da Polga
Pet Lovers Club
Pet Patrol
Petsitters Club

Pirates
Piganeers

Polish Americans
Wisconsin Farm

REAL LIFE
The Adam Joshua Capers
Addie
Adrian Mole
Al (Alexandra)
Alden All Stars
Aldo Sossi
Alex
Alfie Rose
Ali Baba Bernstein
Always Friends
Amelia
American Diaries
American Girls: Addy
American Girls: Felicity
American Girls: Josefina
American Girls: Kirsten
American Girls: Molly

REAL LIFE (cont.)

Ronald Morgan
The Saddle Club
Salty
Seasonal Adventures
Shiloh
Short Stirrup Club
Silver Blades
Silver Blades Figure Eights
Silver Creek Riders
Sister Sister
Sisters
Sitting Pretty
Sleepover Friends
Soccer Stars
Song Lee
Stars
Super Hoops
Susannah
Sweet Valley High
Sweet Valley Kids
Sweet Valley Twins
Sweet Valley Twins Super Edition
Sweet Valley University
Sweet Valley University Thriller
  Editions
Taffy Sinclair
Tales from Third Grade
Tanya
The Thirteen Moons
39 Kids on the Block
Thoroughbred
Tobias
Trig
Triplet Trouble
Twelve Candles Club
Unicorn Club
Vicky Austin
Wolfbay Wings
Z.A.P. and Zoe
Zelda

RECREATION

Alden All Stars
All-Star Meatballs
Angel Park All Stars
Angel Park Hoop Stars
Angel Park Soccer Stars
Bunny Trouble
Cheer Squad
Gymnasts
The Hit and Run Gang
Horseshoes
Junior Gymnasts
NASCAR Pole Position Adventures
Never Sink Nine

Patrick's Pals
Paxton Cheerleaders
Peach Street Mudders
Pony Pals
Pony Tails
Riding Academy
The Saddle Club
Short Stirrup Club
Silver Blades
Silver Blades Figure Eights
Silver Creek Riders
Soccer Stars
Super Hoops
Tales from the Sandlot
Thoroughbred
Wolfbay Wings
X Games Xtreme Mysteries

Reptiles—Alligators, crocodiles

Bill and Pete
Gator Girls
Lyle

Reptiles—Snakes

Jimmy's Boa

Reptiles—Turtles

Franklin
Old Turtle

Robots

Jack and Danny One
Norby
Sonic the Hedgehog

Romance

Christy
Christy Miller
Clearwater Crossing
Egerton Hall
The Elliott Cousins
Flambards
Heart Beats
Saved by the Bell
Sweet Valley High
Sweet Valley University

Royalty

Jewel Kingdom

Scary stories

Bailey City Monsters
Black Cat Club
Black Lagoon
Camp Haunted Hills
Mercer Mayer's Critters of the
  Night
Scaredy Cats

The Weird Zone

School stories

The Adam Joshua Capers
The Adventures of the Bailey
  School Kids
Alistair
Arthur
Arthur Chapter Books
B.Y. Times
B.Y. Times Kid Sisters
Best Enemies
Best Friends
Bingo Brown
Black Lagoon
Bruno and Boots
Charlotte Cheetham
Cheer Squad
Christie & Company
Christy
Cody
Dana Girls
Darci Daniels
Dinah
Eagle-Eye Ernie
Edison-Armstrong School
Egerton Hall Novels
Fabulous Five
First Grade
First Grade Is the Best
Friends and Amigos
Full House: Club Stephanie
Germy
Harper Winslow
Harriet the Troublemaker
Help, I'm Trapped
Herbie Jones
Hobie Hanson
Horrible Harry
Joshua T. Bates
Judge and Jury
Junie B. Jones
Kane Family
Kids in Ms. Coleman's Class
Kids of the Polk Street School
Lunchroom
Madeline
Maggie Marmelstein
Magic School Bus
Marvin Redpost
Mary Marony
Miss Nelson
Mr. Rose's Class
Mrs. Toggle
My Teacher
New Kids at the Polk Street School
Peanut Butter and Jelly

Ronald Morgan
Rosy Cole
Saved by the Bell
Sister Sister
Sleepover Friends
Slimeballs
Song Lee
Stars
Sweet Valley High
Sweet Valley Kids
Sweet Valley Twins
Sweet Valley Twins Super Edition
Sweet Valley University
Sweet Valley University Thriller
  Editions
Tales from Third Grade
Wayside School

Science
Danny Dunn
Einstein Anderson
Magic School Bus
Mr. Rose's Class
The Thirteen Moons

SCIENCE FICTION
Alien Adventures
Aliens
Animorphs
Antrian
Choose Your Own Star Wars
  Adventures
Commander Toad
Danny Dunn
Ghostwriter
Goners
Jack and Danny One
Justice Trilogy
Magician Trilogy
My Teacher
Norby
Oscar J. Noodleman
The Plant That Ate Dirty Socks
Professor Xargle
Sonic the Hedgehog
Space Above and Beyond
Space Brat
Space Dog
Space Ship Under the Apple Tree
Star Trek: Deep Space Nine
Star Trek: Starfleet Academy
Star Trek: The Next Generation:
  Starfleet Academy
Star Trek: Voyager: Starfleet Academy
Star Wars Galaxy of Fear
Star Wars Junior Jedi Knights
Star Wars Young Jedi Knights

Sword of the Spirits
Time Warp Trio
Tripods
Tyco Bass

Scotland
Horseshoes
Katie Morag
Sophie

Seasons
Amy
Brambly Hedge
The Fourteen Forest Mice
Lionel
Long Pond
Nice Mice
Seasonal Adventures
Seasons with Grandma
Simon

Slavery
American Girls: Addy
The Arabus Family Saga

South Africa
Jafta

Space and space ships
Alien Adventures
Aliens
Choose Your Own Star Wars
  Adventures
Commander Toad
Diadem
Goners
Jack and Danny One
My Teacher
Norby
Space Above and Beyond
Space Brat
Space Ship Under the Apple Tree
Star Trek: Deep Space Nine
Star Trek: Starfleet Academy
Star Trek: The Next Generation:
  Starfleet Academy
Star Trek: Voyager: Starfleet Academy
Star Wars Galaxy of Fear
Star Wars Junior Jedi Knights
Star Wars Young Jedi Knights
Tyco Bass
Visitors

Spiders
Miss Spider
Spider

Sports
Alden All Stars

All-Star Meatballs
Dallas O'Neil and the Baker Street
  Sports Club
Mud Flat
Sports Mysteries
X Games Xtreme Mysteries

Sports—Baseball
Angel Park All Stars
The Hit and Run Gang
Never Sink Nine
Peach Street Mudders

Sports—Basketball
Angel Park Hoop Stars
Patrick's Pals
Super Hoops
Tales from the Sandlot

Sports—Cheerleading
Cheer Squad
Paxton Cheerleaders

Sports—Gymnastics
Gymnasts
Junior Gymnasts

Sports—Hockey
Wolfbay Wings

Sports—Horseback riding
Beware
Blaze
Horseshoes
Pony Pals
Pony Tails
Riding Academy
The Saddle Club
Short Stirrup Club
Silver Creek Riders
Thoroughbred

Sports—Ice skating
Silver Blades
Silver Blades Figure Eights

Sports—Racing
NASCAR Pole Position Adventures

Sports—Soccer
Angel Park Soccer Stars
Bunny Trouble
Soccer Stars

Supernatural
Antrian
Blossom Culp
Dark Is Rising
Eerie Indiana
Mike and Harry

Supernatural (cont.)
The Outer Limits
Starbuck Family Adventures
Tales from the Sandlot
Time Fantasy Series
Visitors

Survival stories
Aiken Family
Brian Robeson
Survival!
The Tucket Adventures

Swedish Americans
American Girls: Kirsten
Nancy Bruce

Tall tales
McBroom

Teaching
Christy

Time travel
Blossom Culp
Cooper Kids
Diadem
Fireball
Goners
Green Knowe
Justice Trilogy
Kate Gordon
Magic Attic Club
Magic Tree House
Star Trek: Deep Space Nine
Time Fantasy Series
Time Surfers
Time Trilogy
Time Warp Trio
World of Adventure

Toys
Old Bear Stories
Tom and Pippo

Toys—Dolls
The Lonely Doll
Miss Flora McFlimsey

Toys—Rabbits
Fuzzy Rabbit

Toys—Teddy bears
Bear
Corduroy
Fred Bear
My Teddy Bear
Teddy Bears

U.S. history
The American Adventure
American Girls: Josefina
Children of America
Ellis Island
Heartland
My Name Is America
Once Upon America
Orphan Train Adventures
Orphan Train Children
Portraits of Little Women
Rinko
Survival!

U.S. history—Civil War
American Girls: Addy
Bonnets and Bugles

U.S. history—Colonial period
American Girls: Felicity

U.S. history—Great Depression
American Adventure

U.S. history—Industrial Revolution
American Girls: Samantha

U.S. history— Revolutionary War
The Arabus Family Saga
Daughters of Liberty

Urban life
Dogtown Ghetto
Louie
Peter

VALUES
Alex
American Adventure
The American Adventure
Anika Scott
Best Friends
Cassie Perkins
China Tate
Christy
Christy Miller
Clearwater Crossing
Cooper Kids
D.J. Dillon Adventures
Dallas O'Neil and the Baker Street Sports Club
Dallas O'Neil Mysteries
Frog

Grandma's Attic
The Home School Detectives
Jenna V.
Juli Scott Super Sleuth
Ladd Family
Lassie
Little Toot
McGee and Me!
Reel Kids Adventures
Sierra Jensen
Sugar Creek Gang
Ten Commandments Mysteries
Three Cousins Detective Club
Trailblazers
Twelve Candles Club
Winds of Light

Weather
Amy

Weddings
Flower Girls

Weight control
Fat Glenda

Witches and wizards
Aeriel Trilogy
Age of Magic Trilogy
Dorrie
Dr. Merlin
Earthsea
Emma
Enchanted Forest Chronicles
Lewis Barnavelt
Magical Mystery
Merlin
Old Witch
The Once and Future King
Prydain Chronicles
Sabrina the Teenage Witch
Spooky the Cat
Tales of Gom in the Legends of Ulm
Teeny Witch
Witch
Witch, Goblin, and Ghost
Wizard and Wart
Wizardry
Worst Witch
Young Merlin Trilogy

World War II
American Girls: Molly
Anna
Gordy Smith

BOOKS FOR BOYS

These books were selected for their appeal to boys.

Adam Joshua
Alden All Stars
Aldo Sossi
Ali Baba Bernstein
Alien Adventures
Angel Park All Stars
Angel Park Hoop Stars
Angel Park Soccer Stars
Animorphs
Anthony Monday
Benjy
Bingo Brown
Brian Robeson
Bruno and Boots
Casebusters
Cody
Culpepper Adventures
Dallas O'Neil and the Baker
  Street Sports Club
Dallas O'Neil Mysteries
Dinotopia
Einstein Anderson

Eric Sterling, Secret Agent
The Goners
The Great Brain
Hardy Boys
Hardy Boys: Frank and Joe Hardy:
  The Clues Brothers
Harper Winslow
Harry (Porte)
Help, I'm Trapped
Herbie Jones
Hobie Hanson
Horrible Harry
Jeffrey's Ghost
Johnny Dixon
Joshua T. Bates
Judge and Jury
Lewis Barnevalt
Marvin Redpost
Matthew Martin
Max Malone
Mike and Harry
My Name Is America

My Teacher
NASCAR Pole Position
  Adventures
Nate the Great
The Outer Limits
Patrick's Pals
Peach Street Mudders
Russell
Slimeballs
Soup
Spencer's Adventures
Sports Mysteries
Super Hoops
Tales from the Sandlot
Three Investigators
Time Surfers
Tom Swift
Tucket Adventures
Wolfbay Wings
World of Adventure
The Zack Files

BOOKS FOR GIRLS

These books were selected for their appeal to girls.

Addie (Lawlor)
Addie (Rock)
The Adventures of Mary-Kate and Ashley
Al (Alexandra)
Alex
Alice
Always Friends
American Diaries
American Girls: Addy
American Girls: Felicity
American Girls: Josefina
American Girls: Kirsten
American Girls: Molly
American Girls: Samantha
Anastasia Krupnik
Angel
Angelina Ballerina
Annie Bananie
Avonlea
B.Y. Times
B.Y. Times Kid Sisters
Baby-Sitters Club
Baby-Sitters Club Mysteries
Baby-Sitters Club Super Specials
Baby-Sitters Little Sister
Baby-Sitters Little Sister Super Specials
Baker's Dozen
Ballet Slippers
Best Enemies
Best Friends (Smith)
Best Friends (Stahl)
Betsy
Betsy-Tacy
Beware
Brigid Thrush
Bromeliad
California Diaries
Camp Sunnyside
Casey, Jenny, and Kate
!Chana!
Cheer Squad
Christie & Company
Christy
Christy Miller
Clearwater Crossing
Clueless

Damar Chronicles
Daughters of Liberty
Dear America
Disney Girls
Elisa
The Elliott Cousins
Ellis Island
Elsie Edwards
Ernestine and Amanda
Fabulous Five
Flambards
Flower Girls
Forever Angels
Frances in the Fourth Grade
Friends and Amigos
The Friendship Ring
Full House: Club Stephanie
Full House: Michelle
Full House: Stephanie
Girlhood Journeys: Juliet
Girlhood Journeys: Kai
Girlhood Journeys: Marie
Girlhood Journeys: Shannon
Girls R.U.L.E.
Gymnasts
Hannah and the Angels
Heart Beats
Heartland
Here Come the Brownies
Holiday Five
Holiday Friends
Horseshoes
Isabelle
Jenna V.
Jenny Archer
Jewel Kingdom
Juli Scott Super Sleuth
Junior Gymnasts
Kate (Brisson)
Kitty
Lila Fenwick
Little House
Little House: My First Little House Books
Little House Chapter Books
Little House: The Caroline Years
Little House: The Rose Years
Little Women Journals

Lizzie Logan
Madeline
Magic Attic Club
Maizon
Mandie
Mary Marony
Med Center
Moesha
Molly (Chaikin)
Murphy Family
Nancy Drew
Nancy Drew Files
Nancy Drew Notebooks
Once Upon America
Paxton Cheerleaders
Peanut Butter and Jelly
Pee Wee Scouts
Phantom Rider
Polka Dot Private Eye
Pony Pals
Pony Tails
Portraits of Little Women
Riding Academy
Roommates
Rosy Cole
Sabrina the Teenage Witch
The Saddle Club
Short Stirrup Club
Silver Blades
Silver Blades Figure Eights
Silver Blades Gold Medal Dreams
Silver Creek Riders
Sister Sister
Sisters
Sitting Pretty
Sleepover Friends
Song Lee
Starshine
Sweet Valley High
Sweet Valley Kids
Sweet Valley Twins
Sweet Valley Twins Super Editions
Sweet Valley University
Sweet Valley University Thriller Editions
Thoroughbred
Twelve Candles Club
Unicorn Club

BOOKS FOR RELUCTANT READERS/ESL STUDENTS

These series were selected as those that would have the most appeal to reluctant readers. Series that are suitable for use with students of English as a second language are indicated with an asterisk.

A to Z Mysteries
The Adam Joshua Capers
Addie (Robins)★
The Adventures of Mary-Kate and Ashley
The Adventures of the Bailey School Kids
Aldo Sossi★
Alien Adventures
Aliens
All-Star Meatballs
Amber Brown
American Diaries
American Girls: Addy
American Girls: Felicity
American Girls: Josefina
American Girls: Kirsten
American Girls: Molly
American Girls: Samantha
Animorphs
Are You Afraid of the Dark?
Arthur (Brown)★
Arthur Chapter Books★
Baby-sitters Club
Baby-sitters Club Mysteries
Baby-sitters Club Super Specials
Baby-sitters Little Sister
Baby-sitters Little Sister Super Specials
Bailey City Monsters
Ballet Slippers★
Bear (Asch)★
Beezy★
Berenstain Bears★
Berenstain Bears: Bear Scouts★
Berenstain Bears: Big Chapter Books★
Beware★
Biscuit★
Black Cat Club
Bone Chillers
Boxcar Children: Adventures of Benny and Watch★
Brian Robeson★

Buffy, the Vampire Slayer
Bunnicula
Calico Cat★
California Diaries
Cam Jansen
Camp Haunted Hills
Camp Zombie
Casebusters
Choose Your Own Adventure
Choose Your Own Nightmare
Choose Your Own Star Wars Adventures
Clearwater Crossing
Clifford
Clueless
Culpepper Adventures
Cyber.kdz
Cybersurfers
D.W.★
Danger.com
Dear America
Dear Dragon★
Diadem
Digby and Kate★
Dinotopia
Disney Girls
Doug Chronicles
Dragon (Pilkey)★
Edison-Armstrong School★
Eerie Indiana
Einstein Anderson
Elisa★
The Elliott Cousins
Encyclopedia Brown
Fiendly Corners
Fourth Floor Twins
Franklin
Friends and Amigos★
Frightmares
Frog and Toad★
Full House: Club Stephanie
Full House: Michelle
Full House: Stephanie

Ghost Stories
Ghosts of Fear Street
Ghostwriter
Goners
Goosebumps
Goosebumps: Give Yourself Goosebumps
Goosebumps Presents
Goosebumps Series 2000
Graveyard School
Gymnasts
Hardy Boys: Frank and Joe Hardy: The Clues Brothers
Harper Winslow
Harry (Porte)★
Heart Beats
Help, I'm Trapped
Henry and Mudge★
Here Come the Brownies
Holiday Five
Holiday Friends
Horrible Harry
Houdini Club Magic Mystery
Internet Detectives
Invisible Inc.
Jack and Danny One
Jenny Archer
Jewel Kingdom
Julian and Huey
Junie B. Jones★
Junior Gymnasts
Katie★
Kids in Ms. Coleman's Class★
Kids of the Polk Street School★
Lincoln Lions Band
Lionel★
Little Bear (Minarik)★
Little Bill★
Little Chick
Little House Chapter Books★
The Littles
Liza, Bill, and Jed
Lucky

Magic Attic Club
Magic School Bus
Magic Tree House
Med Center
Meg Mackintosh: A Solve-It-
  Yourself Mystery
Messy Bessey★
Mind Over Matter
Mindwarp
Moesha
Moonbear★
Mr. Putter and Tabby★
My Babysitter
My Name Is America
My Teacher
The Mystery Files of Shelby Woo
Nancy Drew
Nancy Drew Files
Nancy Drew Notebooks
NASCAR Pole Position Adventures
Nate the Great
Neptune Adventures
New Kids at the Polk Street
  School★
Nora and Teddy★
Oliver and Amanda Pig★
Once Upon America
Orphan Train Adventures
Orphan Train Children
The Outer Limits
P.J. Funnybunny
Passport
Patrick's Pals

Peach Street Mudders★
Peanut Butter and Jelly
Pee Wee Scouts★
Pinky and Rex
The Plant That Ate Dirty Socks
Pony Pals
Pony Tails
Ralph S. Mouse
Ramona Quimby
Rex and Lilly★
Riding Academy
Ronald Morgan★
Russell★
Sabrina the Teenage Witch
The Saddle Club
Saved by the Bell
Scaredy Cats
Secret World of Alex Mack
Shaggy Dog★
Silver Blades
Silver Blades Figure Eights
Silver Blades Gold Medal Dreams
Silver Creek Riders
Sister Sister
Slimeballs
Snail★
Soccer Stars
Spencer's Adventures
Spinetinglers
Spooksville
Spot★
Star Trek: Deep Space Nine
Star Trek: Starfleet Academy

Star Trek: The Next Generation:
  Starfleet Academy
Star Trek: Voyager: Starfleet Academy
Star Wars Galaxy of Fear
Star Wars Junior Jedi Knights
Star Wars Young Jedi Knights
Super Hoops
Survival!
Thoroughbred
Three Investigators
Time Surfers
Time Warp Trio
Titch★
Tom and Pippo★
Tom Swift
Triplet Trouble★
Vampire Promise
Visitors
Wayside School
The Weebie Zone
The Weird Zone
Werewolf Chronicles
Winnie the Pooh First Readers★
Wishbone Adventures
Wishbone Classics
Wishbone Mysteries
Wolfbay Wings
World of Adventure
X Files
X Games Xtreme Mysteries
The Zack Files